W9-AIG-984

MARTIN HEIDEGGER

MARTIN HEIDEGGER

Between Good and Evil

RÜDIGER SAFRANSKI

Translated by Ewald Osers

HARVARD UNIVERSITY PRESS
Cambridge, Massachusetts
London, England
1998

C.1

Printed in the United States of America

Originally published as *Ein Meister aus Deutschland: Heidegger und seine Zeit,* copyright by Carl Hanser Verlag, München Wien 1994.

The publisher acknowledges the financial assistance of Inter Nationes e.V., Bonn.

Library of Congress Cataloging-in-Publication Data

Safranski, Rüdiger.
[Meister aus Deutschland. English]
Martin Heidegger : between good and evil / Rüdiger Safranski ; translated by Ewald Osers.
p. cm.
Includes bibliographical references and index.
ISBN 0-674-38709-0 (alk. paper)
1. Heidegger, Martin, 1889–1976. 2. Philosophers—Germany—Biography. I. Title.
B3279.H49S32413 1998
193—dc21
[B] 97-40754

FOR GISELA MARIA NICKLAUS

I owe a debt of gratitude to my friends who helped me
with their sympathy, their curiosity, and their own research:
Ulrich Boehm, Hans-Peter Hempel, Helmuth Lethen,
Cees Nooteboom, Peter Sloterdijk, Ulrich Wanner.

CONTENTS

PREFACE: A MASTER FROM GERMANY

Heidegger's story is a long one—whether the story of his life or of his philosophy. It covers the passions and disasters of a whole century.

In terms of philosophy, Heidegger came from a long way back. He treated Heraclitus, Plato, and Kant as if they were his contemporaries. He came so close to them he could hear and put into words what remained unuttered by them. In Heidegger we still find the whole wonderful metaphysics, albeit at the moment of its falling silent—or, to put it differently, at the moment when it opens out into something else.

Heidegger's passion was asking questions, not providing answers. That which he asked questions about and that which he was seeking, he called Being. Throughout a philosophical life he continually asked this one question about Being. The meaning of this question is nothing more and nothing less than giving back to life the mystery that threatened to disappear in the modern world.

Heidegger began as a Catholic philosopher. He accepted the challenge of the modern age. He developed the philosophy of a *Dasein* that finds itself thrown under an empty heaven and in the power of all-devouring time, endowed with the ability to design its own life. A philosophy that addresses the individual in his freedom and responsibility and takes death seriously. The question about Being in Heidegger's sense means to release "*Dasein* the way one weighs anchor to sail out, liberated, to the open sea." It is a sad irony of the history of philosophical effect that Heidegger's question about Being has very largely lost this liberating, lightening aspect, and that, if anything, it has tended to intimidate and cramp thinking. It would be important to relax this cramp. Then, perhaps, one might also be free enough to let the laughter of the Thracian maid—who laughed when her master, the philosopher Thales of Miletus, fell into a well while gazing at the stars—reply to many a miscarried profundity of this philosophical genius.

A good deal of uneasiness persists to this day about Heidegger's political involvement. On philosophical grounds he became, for a while, a National Socialist revolutionary, but his philosophy also helped him to free himself from the political scene. He learned a lesson from what he had done, and his thinking subsequently focused on the problem of the seducibility of the spirit by the will to power. Heidegger's philosophical way leads from resoluteness, via the metaphysics, to the great historical moment, to composure at the end, and to thinking that is a provident, stewardly intercourse with the world.

Martin Heidegger—a master from Germany.

He truly was a "master" from the school of the mystic Master Eckhart. More than anyone else, he kept open the horizon for religious experience in a nonreligious age. He found a way of thinking that remains close to things and avoids a crash into banality.

He really was very "German," as German as Thomas Mann's Adrian Leverkühn. The history of Heidegger's life and thought is, yet again, a Dr. Faustus story. What emerges is the lovable, the fascinating, and the abysmally profound element of a specifically German road in philosophy, one that was to become a European event. And finally, through his political activity he also had about him something of that "master from Germany" that Paul Celan's poem refers to.

Thus Martin Heidegger's name represents the most exciting chapter in the history of the German spirit in our century. It has to be told, the good and the evil, and beyond good and evil.

CHRONOLOGY

1889	September 26: birth of Martin Heidegger, son of Friedrich Heidegger (August 7, 1852–May 2, 1924), master cooper and sexton in Messkirch, and Johanna Heidegger, née Kempf (March 21, 1858–May 3, 1927).
1903–1906	Gymnasium in Constance on a scholarship. Accommodation in the Catholic boarding school, the Konradihaus. Preparation for a clerical career.
1906–1909	Gymnasium and archiepiscopal convent in Freiburg.
1909	Heidegger enters the novitiate with the Jesuits in Tisis near Feldkirch (Vorarlberg, Austria). Discharged on October 13 because of heart problems.
1909–1911	Study of theology and philosophy at Freiburg. Antimodernist articles in Catholic periodicals.
1911–1913	Clerical training discontinued. Study of philosophy, the humanities, and natural sciences at Freiburg. Scholarship for the study of Catholic philosophy. Friendship with Ernst Laslowski. Study of Edmund Husserl. Logic as a transcendent value of life.

1913	Doctorate, with a thesis on "The Doctrine of Judgment in Psychologism."
1915	Habilitation (title of *Dozent*), with a dissertation on "Duns Scotus's Doctrine of Categories and Meaning."
1915–1918	Enlisted for military service (limited fitness; postal censorship and meteorological service).
1917	Marries Elfride Petri.
1919	Birth of his son Jörg.
1919	Break with the "system of Catholicism."
1920	Birth of his son Hermann.
1918–1923	*Privatdozent* and assistant to Husserl in Freiburg. Friendship with Elisabeth Blochmann.
1920	Start of friendship with Karl Jaspers.
1922	Heidegger's interpretations of Aristotle excite much attention in Marburg.
1923	His ontology lectures establish his reputation as the "secret king of philosophy."
1923	Appointment to Marburg. Moves to his cabin at Todtnauberg. Friendship with Rudolf Bultmann.
1924	Beginning of love affair with Hannah Arendt.
1925	Arendt leaves Marburg.
1927	*Being and Time* published.
1928	Appointment to Freiburg as Husserl's successor.
1929	Inaugural lecture, "What Is Metaphysics?" March: lectures in the Davos university courses. Debate with Ernst Cassirer.
1929–30	Lectures on "The Fundamental Concepts of Metaphysics."
1930	First invitation to Berlin declined.
1931–32	New Year's Eve at the cabin: Heidegger supports National Socialism.
1933	Election to rectorate. May 1: joins the Nazi Party. May 27: rectorial address. Organization of the scholarship camp. Propaganda appearances in Leipzig, Heidelberg, Tübingen. Cooperation in Baden university reform (introduction of the führer principle). October: second invitation to Berlin declined. Summer: last visit to Jaspers.
1934	Faculty squabbles and differences with governmental and party

authorities result in his resignation from the rectorship in April. Summer: preparation of plans for a *Dozentenakademie* in Berlin.

1936 End of correspondence with Jaspers. Lecture in Zurich on "The Origin of the Work of Art." Lecture in Rome on "Hölderlin and the Essence of Poetry." Meeting with Karl Löwith.

1936–1940 In several Nietzsche lectures Heidegger critically discusses the power thinking of National Socialism. Under surveillance by the Gestapo.

1936–1938 Writes his "Beiträge zur Philosophie (Vom Ereignis)" (Contributions to Philosophy [On the Event]), intended for later publication.

1937 Heidegger declines participation in the International Philosophical Congress in Paris.

1944 Called up for the Volkssturm (People's Militia).

1945 January–February: in Messkirch to sort out and securely store his manuscripts.

1945 April–June: Philosophical faculty evacuated to Wildenstein Castle (near Beuron, Danube Valley). July: Heidegger before the denazification committee. Philosophically interested French occupation officers make contact with Heidegger. A planned meeting with Jean-Paul Sartre does not materialize. Correspondence with Sartre. Beginning of friendship with Jean Beaufret.

1946 Jaspers's expert opinion on Heidegger presented to denazification committee. Heidegger banned from teaching (until 1949). Beginning of friendship with Medard Boss. Letter to Beaufret: *On Humanism.*

1949 December: four lectures to the Club zu Bremen ("The Thing," "The Framework," "The Danger," "The Turn").

1950 Repeated lectures at the Bühlerhöhe spa and to the Bavarian Academy of Fine Arts.

1950 February: Arendt visits Heidegger. Their correspondence and friendship resume. Correspondence with Jaspers also resumes.

1951–52 Heidegger resumes his university lectures.

1952 Arendt's second visit.

1953 Bavarian Academy of Fine Arts lecture in Munich: "The Question of Technology." Beginning of Heidegger's postwar career. Friendship with Erhart Kästner.

1955	*"Gelassenheit"* (Composure) address at the Conradin Kreutzer celebration in Messkirch. March 21: lecture in Cérisy-la-Salle.
1957	Lecture in Aix-en-Provence. Acquaintance with René Char.
1959	Beginning of the Zollikon Seminars with Medard Boss.
1959	Appointed honorary citizen of Messkirch on September 27.
1962	First trip to Greece.
1964	Theodor Adorno's pamphlet against Heidegger, *Jargon of Authenticity,* published.
1966	First seminar at Le Thor; continued 1968, 1969, and 1973 in Zähringen.
1966	The *Spiegel* interview (published after Heidegger's death).
1967	Arendt visits Heidegger. From then on she visits him every year.
1975	The first volume of his *Collected Works* appears.
1976	Heidegger dies on May 26 and is interred in Messkirch on May 28.

ABBREVIATIONS

Following are the works by Heidegger cited in the text. The abbreviations shown have been used for citations from the German works and the published collections of correspondence. They follow the abbreviations used by the author in the German edition. A translation of each German title appears here in parenthesis; where a corresponding published English translation has been cited, that bibliographic information is also given.

GA 1 ff — *Gesamtausgabe: Ausgabe letzter Hand* (Collected Works: Author's Final Revision), series ed. Hermann Heidegger, Frankfurt.

INDIVIDUAL WORKS BY MARTIN HEIDEGGER

A — *Aufenthalte* (Sojourns). Frankfurt, 1989.

BZ — *Der Begriff der Zeit.* Tübingen, 1989. (*The Concept of Time,* trans. William McNeill, Cambridge, Mass., 1992.)

D — *Denkerfahrungen* (Thought Experiences). Frankfurt, 1983.

DJ — *Phänomenologische Interpretationen zu Aristoteles: Anzeige der hermeneutischen Situation* (Phenomenological Interpretations to Aristotle: Indication of the Hermeneutical Situation). In *Dilthey-Jahrbuch für*

Philosophie und Geschichte der Geisteswissenschaften, vol. 6. Göttingen, 1989.

EH — *Erläuterungen zu Hölderlins Dichtung* (Explications of Hölderlin's Poetry). Frankfurt, 1981.

EM — *Einführung in die Metaphysik.* Tübingen, 1987. (*An Introduction to Metaphysics.* Trans. R. Manheim. New Haven, Conn., 1987.)

FS — *Frühe Schriften* (Early Writings). Frankfurt, 1972.

G — *Gelassenheit.* Pfullingen, 1985. (*Discourse on Thinking: A Translation of* Gelassenheit. Trans. John M. Anderson and E. Hans Freund. New York, 1969.)

H — *Holzwege* (Wrong Paths). Frankfurt, 1950.

HK — "Die Herkunft der Kunst und die Bestimmung des Denkens" (The Origin of Art and the Mission of Thinking). In Petra Jaeger and Rudolf Lüthe, eds., *Distanz und Nähe: Reflexionen und Analysen zur Kunst der Gegenwart* (Distance and Proximity: Reflections and Analyses on Present-Day Art). Würzburg, 1983.

K — *Kant und das Problem der Metaphysik.* Frankfurt, 1991. (*Kant and the Problem of Metaphysics.* Trans. Richard Taft. Bloomington, Ind., 1990.)

L — *Logik* (Logic). Lectures, summer semester 1934, anonymous notes. Ed. Victor Farías. Madrid, 1931.

N I, N II — *Nietzsche,* 2 vols., Pfullingen, 1961. (*Nietzsche,* 4 vols. Trans. Joan Stambaugh, David Farrell Krell, and Frank A. Capuzzi. San Francisco, 1987.)

R — *Die Selbstbehauptung der deutschen Universität: Das Rektorat.* Frankfurt, 1983. ("The Self-Assertion of the German University." In Richard Wolin, ed., *The Heidegger Controversy: A Critical Reader.* New York, 1991.)

SuZ — *Sein und Zeit.* Tübingen, 1963. (*Being and Time.* Trans. John Macquarrie and Edward Robinson. San Francisco, 1962.)

TK — *Die Technik und die Kehre.* Pfullingen, 1962. ("The Question Concerning Technology." In David Farrell Krell, ed., *Martin Heidegger: Basic Writings,* rev. ed. San Francisco, 1993.)

ÜH — *Über den Humanismus.* Frankfurt, 1981. ("Letter on Humanism." In David Farrell Krell, ed., *Martin Heidegger: Basic Writings,* rev. ed. San Francisco, 1993.)

VA — *Vorträge und Aufsätze* (Lectures and Essays). Pfullingen, 1985.

VS — *Vier Seminare* (Four Seminars). Frankfurt, 1977.

W — *Wegmarken* (Track Markings). Frankfurt, 1978.

WHD — *Was heisst Denken?* Tübingen, 1984. (*What Is Called Thinking?* Trans. Fred D. Neick and J. Glenn Gray. New York, 1968.)

WM *Was ist Metaphysik?* Frankfurt, 1986. ("What Is Metaphysics?" In David Farrell Krell, ed., *Martin Heidegger: Basic Writings,* rev. ed. San Francisco, 1993.)

WW *Vom Wesen der Wahrheit.* Frankfurt, 1986. ("On the Essence of Truth." In David Farrell Krell, ed., *Martin Heidegger: Basic Writings,* rev. ed. San Francisco, 1993.)

Z *Zur Sache des Denkens* (On the Matter of Thinking). Tübingen, 1984. (*On Time and Being.* Trans. Joan Stambaugh. New York, 1972.)

ZS *Zollikoner Seminare* (Zollikon Seminars). Frankfurt, 1987.

CORRESPONDENCE AND OTHER DOCUMENTS BY HEIDEGGER

BwHB Martin Heidegger and Elisabeth Blochmann, *Briefwechsel* (Correspondence). Ed. Joachim W. Storck. Marbach, 1989.

BwHJ Martin Heidegger and Karl Jaspers, *Briefwechsel* (Correspondence). Ed. Walter Biemel and Hans Saner. Frankfurt and Munich, 1990.

BwHK Martin Heidegger and Erhart Kästner, *Briefwechsel* (Correspondence). Ed. Heinrich Wiegand Petzet. Frankfurt, 1986.

S Guido Schneeberger, *Nachlese zu Heidegger: Dokumente zu seinem Leben und Denken* (Late Gleanings on Heidegger: Documents on His Life and Thought). Berne, 1962.

OTHER CORRESPONDENCE

BwAJ Hannah Arendt and Karl Jaspers, *Briefwechsel* (Correspondence). Ed. Lotte Köhler and Hans Saner. Munich, 1985.

OTHER ENGLISH TRANSLATIONS OF WORKS BY HEIDEGGER

The Basic Problems of Phenomenology. Trans. Albert Hofstadter. Bloomington, Ind., 1982.

The Fundamental Concepts of Metaphysics: World, Finitude, Solitude. Trans. William McNeill and Nicholas Walker. Bloomington, Ind., 1995.

History of the Concept of Time, Prolegomena. Trans. Theodore Kisiel. Bloomington, Ind., 1985.

Schelling's Treatise on the Essence of Human Freedom. Trans. Joan Stambaugh. Athens, Ohio, 1995.

TRANSLATOR'S NOTE

The Heidegger literature in English, both primary and secondary, is still expanding, with hitherto untranslated works being translated, existing translations being revised and reissued, and new critical work being published both in America and in Britain. Therefore some of the more recent publications may not yet be listed in library catalogues or available to researchers. While I made every effort to verify the English texts of the numerous references in libraries on both sides of the Atlantic, as well as in online catalogues, it was sometimes, because of the fluidity of the situation, unavoidable that a quotation be attributed to an edition that is not the most recent.

In-text page citations are to the German editions of Heidegger's works and correspondence. When a published English translation is quoted, the reference appears in the notes; all other translations are my own.

The gale that blows through Heidegger's thinking—like that which still, after thousands of years, blows to us from Plato's work—is not of our century. It comes from the primordial, and what it leaves behind is something perfect which, like everything perfect, falls back to the primordial.

HANNAH ARENDT

A truth must be able to depart this world, as one used to put it; otherwise it remains worldless. The world has become so barren because so many manufactured ideas are drifting around in it, placeless and imageless.

ERHART KÄSTNER

Without man, Being would be mute; it would be there, but it would not be the True one.

ALEXANDER KOJÈVE

I

CHILDHOOD AND SCHOOL

In 1928 Martin Heidegger, by then famous, wrote to the former prefect of the clerical seminary in Constance where, for some years, he had been a student: "Perhaps philosophy shows most forcibly and persistently how much Man is a beginner. Philosophizing ultimately means nothing other than being a beginner."

Heidegger's commendation of beginning is open to many interpretations. He wishes to be a master of beginning. It was to the beginnings of philosophy in Greece that he looked for a past future, and it was in the present that he hoped to find the spot where, in the middle of life, philosophy is always born anew. This occurs in "mood." He criticizes any philosophy that professes to have its beginning in thought. In reality, Heidegger argues, it begins with a mood, with astonishment, fear, worry, curiosity, jubilation.

To Heidegger, mood is the link between life and thought, and there is some irony in the fact that in his own case he was much opposed to any investigation of the connection between the two. He once began a lecture on Aristotle with the lapidary sentence: "He was born, he worked, and he died." That is how Heidegger hoped that people would talk about him. This, no doubt, was his great dream—to live for philosophy and perhaps disappear within his own philosophy. That, too, is related to mood, which, perhaps all too quickly, discovers in the present that which is importunate and therefore searches for what is hidden. Life itself can be importunate. Heidegger's mood makes him state that "*Dasein* is thrown" and Being has "become manifest as a burden," for "Has *Dasein* as itself ever decided freely whether it wants to come into '*Dasein*' or not, and will it ever be able to make such a decision?" (SuZ, 228).[1]

Heidegger was fond of the grand gesture, and in consequence one can never be sure whether he is speaking of Western civilization or himself, whether Being as such is being discussed or merely his own Being. But if the principle is valid that philosophy springs not from thought but from mood, then ideas should be at home not only in skirmish with other ideas but also on the elevated plateau of tradition. Of course, Heidegger linked up with tradition, but for reasons which lead back to his own life. These evidently do not allow him to experience his own entry into the world as a gift or a promising arrival. It must have been a crash—that is what his mood demands.

But the world into which he felt "thrown" was not that of Messkirch at the end of the last century, where he was born on September 26, 1889, where he passed his childhood, and where he was always fond of returning. He felt "thrown" only when he was ejected from this domestic world that had shielded him from the presumptions of modernity. It should not be forgotten that coming into the world is not completed by being born. Several births are necessary during a human life, and it may well be that one never fully arrives in the world. But let us, for the moment, stay with his first birth.

Martin Heidegger's father, Friedrich Heidegger, was a master cooper and a sexton at St. Martin's Catholic church in Messkirch. He died in 1924. He was to see his son break with Catholicism, but he did not live long enough to see his philosophical breakthrough. His mother died in 1927, and on her deathbed Martin Heidegger placed his own copy of *Sein und Zeit (Being and Time).*

His mother came from the neighboring village of Göggingen. Whenever the cold winds sweep down from the plateaus of the Swabian Alb, the Messkirch people say: "It's blowing from Göggingen." Heidegger's maternal ancestors had lived there for generations on a fine farmstead, the Lochbauernhof. In 1662 an ancestor, Jakob Kemp, had received the farm in fief from the Cistercian monastery in Wald, near Pullendorf. In 1838 Heidegger's grandfather redeemed it for a price of 3,800 guilders. In spiritual matters, however, the family continued under the guardianship of the Church.

His paternal ancestors were small peasants and craftsmen. They had come from Austria in the eighteenth century. Local historians have established the existence of extensive relationships with the Mägerle and Kreutzer families. From one of these emerged the most famous preacher of the seventeenth century, Abraham a Sancta Clara, and from the other Konstantin Kreutzer, the composer. There was also a distant connection between the Heideggers and Conrad Gröber, Martin's spiritual mentor at the Constance seminary and a future archbishop of Freiburg.

Messkirch is a small town situated between Lake Constance, the Swabian Alb mountains, and the Upper Danube—a barren, previously poor region along the boundary between Alemannia and Swabia. The Alemannic character tends to be ponderous, melancholy, and brooding, while the Swabian character is more cheerful, more open, and also more dreamy. The former inclines toward sarcasm; the later toward emotionalism. Heidegger had something of each in him, and the figures he chose for his patrons were the Alemannic Johann Peter Hebel and the Swabian Friedrich Hölderlin. He saw both as molded by the region while towering in the great world. This was how he also saw himself: he wished to "open up to the vastness of the sky and at the same time be rooted in the dark of the earth" (D, 38).

In a 1942 lecture Heidegger interpreted Hölderlin's Danubian hymn "Der Ister." Attached to the lecture manuscript was a note that was not subsequently included in the printed text: "It was perhaps inevitable that the poet Hölderlin should become the determining influence on the critical thought of one whose grandfather was born at the very time when the 'Ister' hymn . . . [was] written—born, according to the records, *in ovili* (that is to say, in a sheepfold on a farm), which lies near the bank of the river in the valley of the Upper Danube, beneath the lofty crags."[2]

Self-mythicizing? Certainly an attempt to give himself a background he would have wished to have—the splendor of Hölderlin over the Donauhaus at the foot of Wildenstein Castle below Messkirch. There the Heideggers lived in the eighteenth century. The house still stands, and its occupants report that the professor with the Basque beret repeatedly visited the place.

Situated near the Donauhaus and Wildenstein Castle is Beuron with its famous Benedictine abbey, at one time an abbey of Augustine canons. This quiet monastic world, with its large library, its cowsheds and barns, attracted Martin Heidegger even after he had separated from the Church. In the 1920s, during breaks between semesters, he occasionally spent a few weeks there in a monastic cell. Between 1945 and 1949, when he was under a teaching ban, Beuron Abbey was the only place he appeared in public.

At the end of the nineteenth century Messkirch had some two thousand inhabitants, most of them engaged in agriculture and the crafts. There was also a little local industry—a brewery, a bobbin factory, and a dairy. In the town were the administrative offices of the district, commercial schools, a telegraph office, a railroad depot, a second-class post office, a district court, cooperative headquarters, and the administrations of the local castle and its estates. Messkirch was part of Baden, a circumstance of significance to its cultural atmosphere.

There had been a vigorous liberal tradition in Baden since the beginning of the nineteenth century. In 1815 it saw the enactment of a representative constitution, and in 1831 the abolition of press censorship. Baden was a bastion of revolution in 1848. In April of that year Hecker and Struve called for an armed rising from nearby Constance. The revolutionary contingents assembled at Donaueschingen. They were defeated, but a year later they briefly seized power. The grand duke fled to Alsace, and it was only with the help of Prussian troops that the old conditions were restored. The mood in Baden was not friendly toward Prussia, and after 1871—when Germany, under Prussia's leadership, was united as the German Reich—anything relating to the Reich retained an unpleasant Prussian taste. In the end, Badensian liberalism came to terms with the Reich, partly because it had found another adversary—the Catholic Church.

Ever since 1848 the Church, while otherwise fiercely opposed to it, had skillfully used the spirit of liberalism for its own ends. It demanded a free Church in the free state, abolition of state supervision of schools and universities, independent appointment to ecclesiastical benefits, and independent administration of Church assets. It held that obedience should be to God rather than to men. The conflict was exacerbated in 1845 when the Baden government ordered the arrest of the archbishop of Freiburg. Eventually the government yielded, realizing that the Church was evidently too firmly rooted in the customs and attitudes of the population, especially in the countryside and the smaller towns. This Catholic populism in southwest Germany was supportive of the Church and hostile to the state, hierarchical but demanding autonomy in relation to state power. It was anti-Prussian, more regionalist than nationalist, anticapitalist, agrarian, anti-Semitic, locally rooted, and particularly widespread among the lower social strata.

The conflicts between Church and state intensified once more when the Council of Rome in 1870 decreed the dogma of the infallibility of the pope. If, in the age of nationalism, it was impossible to restore the universal rule of the Church, then at least the Catholic world was to be effectively screened off against the state and secularized society.

Against this view there arose an opposition, the so-called Old Catholic movement, which had its social roots mainly in the national-liberal, Catholic, educated middle class of southern Germany. These circles did not wish to become too "Roman" and instead strove to combine Catholic and nationalist tendencies. Some Old Catholics went even further, hoping for an entire modernization of the Church—abolition of celibacy, limitation of the veneration of saints, self-determination of communities, election of priests.

This movement created its own ecclesiastical organization and elected a bishop but remained small numerically; at no time did it have more than 100,000 members, even though it enjoyed support from the governments, especially in Baden, where the Old Catholic movement developed vigorously. In the 1870s and 1880s Messkirch was one of its strongholds. At times almost half its population was Old Catholic.

Conrad Gröber, a committed champion of Roman Catholicism, has painted a gloomy picture of the Messkirch Kulturkampf period, which extended into Martin Heidegger's childhood:

> We know from our own bitter experience how much youthful happiness was destroyed in those years, when the wealthier Old Catholic children rejected the poorer Catholic children, applied nicknames to their clergy and to them, beat them up and immersed them in fountain-basins to rebaptize them. Unfortunately we also know from our own experience how even Old Catholic schoolmasters divided the sheep from the goats, pinned the nickname of "black sick" on Catholic students and, using their fists, made them realize that they could not tread Roman paths with impunity. Indeed, all but one defected and they were obliged to join the Old Catholics if they wished to get a definitive post in Messkirch. Even much later it was still clear that only by changing one's religion could one obtain a minor official post in the town on the Ablach.[3]

Among the steadfast was Heidegger's father. He remained with the "Romans," even though at first he derived only disadvantages as a result.

The government had granted the Old Catholics the right of codetermination in the town church of St. Martin. To the Romans this was a desecration of the building, and therefore they moved out. In 1875, with the active help of the Beuron monks, they converted an old fruit warehouse into an "emergency church" not far from the town church. There the cooper's workshop of Friedrich Heidegger, the sexton, was also accommodated, and there Martin was christened.

The clash between Romans and Old Catholics divided the town community into two camps. The Old Catholics were the "good families," the "liberals," the "modern" people. From their point of view the Romans were a drag on progress; they were blinkered, backward little people clinging to outdated ecclesiastical customs. When the Romans processed out into the fields for the spring and fall blessings of the crops, the Old Catholics remained at home, and their children threw rocks at the monstrances.

In these conflicts young Martin first experienced the clash between tradition and modernism, and he felt the hurtful aspect of that modernism. The Old Catholics belonged to "those at the top," and the Romans, though superior in numbers, were bound to feel vanquished. This made their community rally together all the more closely.

When, toward the end of the century, the number of Old Catholics declined drastically in Messkirch and the religious conflict abated, the Romans had the town church, with all its assets and lands, returned to them. The Heideggers moved back into the sexton's house on the church square. On December 1, 1895, a solemn divine service celebrated this victory over the "apostates." On this occasion little Martin unexpectedly found himself playing a leading part. The Old Catholic sexton found it embarrassing to hand over the church keys to his successor, and so he simply handed them to the sexton's small son, who happened to be playing in the square.

The world of Martin Heidegger's childhood was the sexton's small, cowering house on the church square, opposite the towering Church of St. Martin. The square opens toward the sixteenth-century Fürstenberg Castle. Through its great portals the children were able to penetrate to the inner courtyard and on into the castle park, as far as the garden gate at the distant end, where open country began with a farm track: "He runs from the princely garden gate to the Ehnried. The ancient lime trees of the castle park gaze after him over the wall, no matter whether at Easter time he shows up brightly among the sprouting crops and awakening meadows or at Christmas disappears under snowdrifts behind the next hill" (D, 37).

The "sexton's lads," Martin and his younger brother, Fritz, had to help with the church services. They were servers, they picked flowers to decorate the church, they ran errands for the priest, and they rang the bells. There were—as Heidegger recalls in *On the Secret of the Bell Tower (Vom Geheimnis des Glockenturms)*—seven bells in the tower, each with its own name, its own sound, and its own time. There was the "Four," to be rung at four in the afternoon; the "Alarm Bell," which roused the town's sleepers from their slumber; and the "Three," which was also the knell. The "Child" rang for sunday school and for rosary worship; the "Twelve" marked the end of morning lessons at the school; the "Klanei" was the bell struck by the hour hammer; and the one with the most beautiful ring was the "Big One"; it would ring on the eve and on the morning of high holidays. Between Maundy Thursday and Easter Saturday the bells were silent; instead there were rattles. A cranking handle set in motion a number of little hammers that struck against hard wood. A rattle stood in each of the four corners of the tower, and the boy bell ringers had to work the handles in turn to ensure that the harsh sound went out in all four directions of the compass. The most beautiful time was Christmas. Toward half past three in the morning, the boy ringers would come to the sexton's house, where mother Heidegger had laid the table with cakes and milky coffee. After this breakfast, lanterns were lit in the front-door passage, and everyone went out through the snow and the winter's night to the church opposite and up into the dark bell tower to the frozen ropes and ice-covered clappers. "The mysterious fugue," Martin Heidegger wrote, "in which the church feasts, the days of vigil, and the passage of the seasons and the morning, midday, and evening hours of each day fitted into each other, so that a continual ringing went through the young hearts, dreams, prayers, and games—it is this, probably, that conceals one of the most magical, most complete, and most lasting secrets of the tower" (D, 65 and 66).

Such was life under the Church's care in a small provincial town at the beginning of the century. In *Feldweg* Heidegger recalls sailing a little boat he had whittled in the school fountain: "The dreamlike quality of such voyages was enveloped in a splendor then hardly visible, which lay on all things. Their realm was encompassed by mother's eye and hand . . . Those voyages of our games knew nothing yet of wanderings during which all shores were left behind" (D, 38).

This splendor then hardly visible lies on all Heidegger's memories of his childhood in Messkirch. And this is probably not just the transfiguration of memory, because his brother, Fritz, experienced those years in a similar way. "Thus most of us, despite all rascally behavior, enjoyed the bliss of a permanent weightlessness not experienced since."[4] Fritz spent all his life in the place of his childhood; there he worked as an official of the local credit bank, and there he died.

To the Messkirch folk, Fritz Heidegger was a "card." He was so popular that even in later years the world-famous philosopher was invariably described as "Fritz's brother." Fritz Heidegger had a stammer, but only—according to Messkirch accounts—when he was "serious." Then Heidegger's term *Dasein* (existence) would come out as *"Da-da-dasein."* But he spoke without a stammer when he was clowning, as in his popular carnival speeches. On those occasions he knew no shyness. During the Hitler era he even picked a quarrel with well-known local Nazis; his popularity protected him. Fritz did not attend any university. The bank official sometimes called himself a "searchlight." For his brother he typed 30,000 pages of manuscript and kept them in his bank's strongroom during the war. In any case, he observed, they could be read with comprehension only in the twenty-first century, "when the Americans have long set up a huge supermarket on the moon."[5] He had, he said, helped with the collating and revising of the texts. He would not allow two ideas in one sentence. You've got to tear them apart, he told his brother. Through a narrow door things could pass only one at a time. In this case, therefore, Fritz favored clarity, though otherwise things could not be obscure enough. One of his favorite phrases was "Let people overlook me, but they are not to regard me as overseeable!" He appreciated the crazy aspects of philosophy and deplored philosophers' taking themselves too seriously. Anyone preserving his sense of the crazy can manage quite well with this *Da-da-dasein,* he used to say. "Within us, in the innermost corner of our hearts, there lives something that survives all hardship—joy, that last remnant of that original craziness that we scarcely surmise any longer."[6] Fritz Heidegger had a self-irony that his brother, Martin, lacked. His comment on his own birth, five years after Martin's, was "Life-pain begins for one person today and for another tomorrow. For the little earthworm in Schloss-Strasse it began on Ash

Wednesday—vomiting, tanning, terrible deviation. As is customary on Ash Wednesday."[7]

Martin Heidegger later dedicated a book in gratitude to his brother. "For my unique brother," he wrote with fine ambiguity.

Their parents were believers, but without fanaticism or rigid confessionalism, according to Fritz. Catholic life had so much become part of their flesh and blood that they had no need to defend their faith or assert it against others. They were all the more aghast when their son Martin turned away from the "right road," the one that was simply the most natural to them.

Their mother was a cheerful woman. "She would often say," Fritz Heidegger reports, "that life was so neatly arranged that there was always something to look forward to."[8] She was resolute, at times proud, and did not conceal the self-assurance of her well-to-do farming origins. She had a reputation for being hardworking, and she was almost never seen without an apron or a head scarf. The father was an introverted person, capable of being silent for days on end, inconspicuous, hardworking, honest. A man of whom the sons had little to say later.

The Heideggers were not affluent, but neither were they poor. Two thousand marks in immovable assets and a 960-mark income tax assessment (in 1903) put them in the lower middle class. This was enough for a family to live on, but not enough for the children to receive expensive higher education. At that point the Church lent a hand. It was the Church's usual practice to support gifted youngsters and at the same time recruit future priests, especially in rural regions.

The parish priest, Camillo Brandhuber, suggested to the parents that, after Martin's completion of the Messkirch *Bürgerschule* (a kind of junior high school)—there was also a gymnasium (senior high school) in the town then—they might wish to send their gifted elder son to the Catholic seminary in Constance, a residential institution for young priests. Brandhuber had given Martin Heidegger Latin lessons free of charge, thereby enabling him to go on to senior high school. The prefect of the Constance seminary was Conrad Gröber. Brandhuber and Gröber obtained a grant for Martin from a local foundation, and in 1903 he entered the Constance seminary and the local gymnasium. The Heideggers were proud that the Church was going to look after their son. For Martin, however, this was the beginning of a time of financial dependence on the Church. Now he owed it a debt of gratitude.

This dependence was to continue over a thirteen-year period, until 1916.

After his Weiss Grant for the Constance seminary (1903–1906), Martin received for his final high school years and the first four semesters he studied theology in Freiburg an Eliner Grant that was tied to training for the priesthood. His studies between 1913 and 1916 were financed by the Schätzler Donation, which imposed on recipients the obligation of preserving the philosophy and theology of St. Thomas Aquinas. Heidegger remained dependent on the Catholic world beyond the time when, in his mind, he had already begun to break clear of the Church. He had to adapt, and that made him ashamed; it was an affront for which he could not forgive what he called the "system of Catholicism." This institutional system, with its policy of interest in public life, became so distasteful to him that one of the reasons he later sympathized with the Nazi movement was its declared anticlericalism.

In 1903 Messkirch was still a closed world, even though echoes of the conflict with the Old Catholics lingered on. In Constance, however, only thirty miles away, the modern age was clearly perceptible.

Constance was a mix of religions. Its great history as a "free Reich city"—a city not subject to any local prince or ruler, but coming directly under the emperor—was still reflected in its architectural monuments. There was the old Merchant Hall, where in the sixteenth century the Council of Constance had sat, as well as the house where Jan Hus, the Czech reformer, had awaited his trial. The Dominican monastery where the "heretic" was imprisoned had meanwhile been turned into a hotel, the Insel-Hotel, or Island Hotel, whose assembly rooms were the center of the city's cultural life. It was the venue for concerts and lectures, which the students enjoyed attending. There homage was paid to the "modern spirit." There were discussions about Nietzsche, Ibsen, atheism, Hartmann's philosophy of the unconscious, Vaihinger's "as if philosophy," and even psychoanalysis and the interpretation of dreams. There had long been a progressive spirit in Constance; from the days of Hecker in 1848 the city had remained a bastion of Badensian liberalism. Günther Dehn, who attended the Constance gymnasium at the same time as Heidegger, recalled in his memoirs the thrill he and his classmates had experienced when they discovered that the attendant at the men's bathing establishment was a veteran of 1848 who had actually fought on the barricades. The local paper with the highest circulation, the *Abendzeitung,* was democratic, anticlerical, and cautiously anti-Prussian, despite (or perhaps just because of) a Prussian infantry regiment's being stationed in the city and the fact that officers came from all over Germany to enjoy their furloughs in the city on Lake Constance.

The seminary, Studienhaus St. Konrad, known simply as Konradihaus, had been closed during the years of the Kulturkampf and only reopened in 1888. The gymnasium, formerly a Jesuit college, was under state supervision. The seminarists, in consequence, attended a "temporal" school inspired by a moderately liberal, anticlerical, educational humanism. The modern languages teacher, for instance, Pacius, was a democrat, a freethinker, and a pacifist, much liked by the students for his forceful remarks. He annoyed the seminarists—who, as budding theologians, were supposed to revere Aristotle—with his assertion: "Aristotle—who was he, anyway, compared to Plato, that giant spirit?"[9] But Protestants, too, did not escape his sharp tongue. "Astrology," he was fond of saying, "according to my researches this superstition goes back to Melanchthon." As for the German and Greek master, Otto Kimmig, Lessing's *Nathan the Wise*—an eighteenth-century play preaching religious tolerance—was the only sacred text he accepted. The influence of these schoolmasters on their students, including Martin Heidegger, must have been considerable. "It was not until later that I realized the extent to which these two teachers led me, as it were unnoticed, out of the Christian world of ideas—which for them did not exist at all," concluded Günther Dehn.[10]

The seminarists in the Konradihaus were, as far as it was possible, immunized against the freethinking they encountered at school. They were equipped with apologetic polish; they were prepared for argument with the "secular." They were forever writing essays to show themselves well armed. There was, for instance, the question of whether man was really capable, by his own efforts, of attaining humanity and where the limits of tolerance lay; there was discussion of freedom and original sin; there was examination of the problem of whether Goethe's Iphigenie was a pagan Christian or a Christian German or only a pagan character. As a relief from such controversial topics there was local history: the history of Reichenau monastery, the customs and usages of the Hegau—the region north of Lake Constance—and the prehistoric pile-dwelling folk on the lakeshore. Now and again the seminarists behaved like other young people in Germany; on sunny days they would set out with guitars, singing as they marched, to the Mainau, to the Grafengarten in Bodman, or to the vineyards on the Lower Lake. They rehearsed dialectal plays, they made music; if their secular classmates boasted of their visits to the artistes of the theater, they could report about their latest nativity play. The seminarists certainly were no wimps. They elected—how else could they act in Baden?—their own representative body, which had a consultative vote in the running of their house, and they published a paper which at regular intervals recalled that Baden had been the first German state to abolish press censorship.

The seminarists lived under careful, but evidently not intolerant, supervision. Certainly Martin Heidegger looked back on his years in Constance without anger. To Matthäus Lang, then spiritual prefect of the younger students, he wrote in 1928: "I think back with pleasure and gratitude to the beginnings of my student career at the Konradihaus, and I become ever more aware of how closely all my efforts are bound up with my native soil. I can still remember clearly the trust I came to feel for you as the new prefect, a trust that has endured, and that made my time in the seminary one of joy."[11]

Less of a pleasure for the seminarists was their contact with their "free" fellow students at the gymnasium, especially when they came from better-off families. These sons of lawyers, officials, and merchants felt superior to the seminary "capons," as they called them. After all, the seminarists mostly came from rural areas and, like Martin Heidegger, from modest or even poor backgrounds. Dehn, the son of a chief postal director, recalled: "We always treated the 'capons' with some condescension. They were poorly dressed and, as we thought, also rather unwashed. We regarded ourselves as superior. But that did not prevent us from thoroughly exploiting them. They were made to execute their homework most meticulously. During break they then had to translate for us, which they always did willingly."[12]

The seminarists kept to themselves, so they could better assert themselves; they were a community rather smiled at by the others. They were barred from various pleasures of their "secular" classmates, either for lack of pocket money or because of outright prohibitions. They remained onlookers when for three days the carnival raged in the crooked little streets and taverns of the city, with the students representing their own crazy guild, and when summer vacationers poured into the city and the amusement boats with their colorful pennants sailed out to Meersburg, returning at nightfall with a reeling mass of humanity that streamed, singing and roaring, through the lanes of the Old City, the gymnasium students with their colored caps invariably among them. The day following such events, the boasting would begin: during the breaks between lessons there were accounts of experiences and conquests that made the seminarists' ears ring. At grape-picking time the slightly intoxicating *Sauser* was served everywhere. The gymnasium students were allowed to attend certain bars until ten o'clock. There they would meet their teachers over a jug of wine—a good opportunity for fraternizing, intimacy, and social advantage that was denied to the seminarists.

When all was said and done, the seminary students belonged to a different world and they were made to feel it. They had to fight against a sense of inferiority. Defiance was some help, however, for the outsiders could also see themselves as the elect.

It is possible that this tension between seminary and cheerful city life, between the Catholic world and the liberal civilian environment, gave rise even then in the student Martin Heidegger to a vision of two worlds—here the strict, persistent, slow world, and out there the fast-living, superficial one, indulging in momentary stimulations; here painful effort, and out there mere activity; here the striking of roots, and out there untrammeled behavior; the ones making things too hard for themselves, with the others seemingly taking the more comfortable path; the ones being profound, the others being frivolous; the ones remaining faithful to their own ego, while the others lose themselves in dissipation. This pattern would later become famous in Heidegger's philosophy under the concepts of "authentic being" and "inauthentic being."

In the autumn of 1906 Martin Heidegger switched from the Konradihaus in Constance to the archiepiscopal seminary of St. George in Freiburg, where he attended the renowned Bertold gymnasium. The grant from the Messkirch local foundation no longer covered the cost of the Constance institution. But Conrad Gröber and Camillo Brandhuber, those enterprising mentors of the sexton's son, had opened up another source of funds—the Eliner studentship. This grant had been established in the sixteenth century by Christoph Eliner, a theologian from Messkirch. Local candidates in theology were to be sponsored by it, the condition being that they attended the gymnasium and the university of Freiburg.

The move from Constance to Freiburg had the character of a promotion. Without rancor Martin left Constance, which he always held in fond memory. Even in later years he would attend the reunions of the Konradihaus alumni. He developed no similar feelings of attachment for the Freiburg seminary. As he was to spend nearly all his life in that city, he would have to create some distance between the seminary and himself. Here he would turn away from Catholicism, which in Freiburg cast a particularly massive shadow. The minster, completed in the High Gothic period, towers over the city. Like a mighty ship it lies at the foot of the ranges of the Black Forest, as though about to sail out into the bay of the Breisgau.

Until World War II Freiburg's Old City, clustering around the minster, remained almost completely intact. There were still numerous little streets radiating from the minster square, some of them hemmed by canals. The seminarists were accommodated near the fine residences of the clergy.

When young Martin Heidegger came to Freiburg, the city essentially still had the appearance that Sulpiz Boisseré had described to Goethe in a letter a century earlier: "About Freiburg I would have to write a whole book to you, this is a place of places, all that is old is so beautifully and lovingly maintained, a wonderful situation, in every street a crystal-clear stream, in every street an old fountain, . . . grapes growing all around; all the ramparts, formerly fortifications, are planted with vines."[13]

Martin was a keen student at the Bertold gymnasium. His intellectual ambition still sought an ecclesiastical field of activity. After graduation he intended to join the Jesuit order. His teachers supported this intention. The principal of the seminary wrote in his graduation report in 1909: "He is gifted, diligent, and of good moral character. He had already attained a certain maturity when he came to us, and he was used to studying on his own initiative; indeed his studies in German literature, an area in which he proved to be extremely well read, were sometimes pursued at the expense of his other subjects. Since he is quite sure he wishes to pursue a theological career and favors the life of a religious order, he will probably apply for entry to the Society of Jesus."[14]

Unlike some of his classmates, young Heidegger was not attracted to the "modern" intellectual trends of the age. The young authors of naturalism, symbolism, or art nouveau had not yet appeared on his personal reading list. About the stimuli he received at school, Heidegger had this to say in the curriculum vitae he composed for his habilitation in 1915:

> In my first year in Freiburg the emphasis in mathematics shifted from simple problem-solving towards a more theoretical approach, and my natural liking for this subject now became a really serious interest, which soon extended to physics as well. I also derived a lot of stimulation from my classes in religion, which prompted me to read widely on the biological theory of evolution. In my final year at school it was primarily

through the lectures on Plato . . . that I was introduced in a more conscious way to philosophical problems, albeit not yet with any theoretical rigor.[15]

Religious instruction, of all things, aroused his interest in the (then especially antireligious) theory of biological evolution. He was evidently attracted to intellectually dangerous spheres, where his Messkirch faith would have a difficult time. However, he was not afraid of intellectual adventure, for he still felt firm ground, the ground of faith, beneath his feet. Thus on September 30, 1909, he entered the Society of Jesus as a novice at Tisis near Feldkirch, in the province of Vorarlberg in western Austria. A mere two weeks later, however, on expiry of his probationary period, he was dismissed. Apparently, according to Hugo Ott, Heidegger had complained of heart trouble and had therefore been sent home for medical reasons. Two years later these pains would recur, causing him to discontinue his training as a priest. Perhaps his heart was rebelling against his head.

2

IDEALISM AND MATERIALISM: GERMAN PHILOSOPHY IN THE NINETEENTH CENTURY

Rejected by the Jesuits, Martin Heidegger applied for admission to the Freiburg Theological Seminary. For this he may well have had financial reasons. His parents could not pay for his studies, and the Eliner studentship, which he had been receiving since his time at the Freiburg gymnasium, was tied to the study of theology.

Heidegger embarked on his new course of study in the winter semester of 1909. In his *Lebenslauf* of 1915 he wrote: "The lectures in philosophy prescribed at the time failed to satisfy my needs, so I set out to study the scholastic textbooks on my own account. They gave me a certain formal training in logic, but in philosophical terms they failed to give me what I was looking for."[1]

Only one Freiburg theologian received special mention from him, and in later years, too, Heidegger would always refer to him as his *teacher*—Carl Braig. As a final-year high school student he had already studied Braig's compendium, *On Being: Outline of Ontology* (1896), and through it familiarized himself with some basic concepts of ontological tradition. It was also Braig who first encouraged him to examine Hegel and Schelling critically; on the walks on which Heidegger was allowed to accompany his teacher, he came to know Braig's "penetrating kind of thinking" (Z, 82). Braig, Heidegger recalled fifty years later, had the knack of turning ideas into a living present.

Carl Braig was a theologian of antimodernism. Ever since the papal encyclical *Pascendi domini gregis* of 1907, which had declared war on "modernism"—*De falsis doctrinis modernistarum*—"modernism" and "antimodernism" had become the banners of an intellectual battle not only within Catholicism. The antimodernists were not simply out to defend the Church's dogmas (such as that of immaculate conception) or the principles of clerical hierarchy (such as the pope's infallibility). That was how their opponents were fond of depicting them, regarding antimodernism as nothing but a dangerous or possibly ludicrous conspiracy of obscurantists against the scientific spirit of the age, against enlightenment, humanism, and progressive ideas of every kind.

Carl Braig was an illustration of the fact that one could be an antimodernist without becoming an obscurantist. His was a shrewd mind, discovering the unreflected prerequisites of faith in their numerous variants in the modern scientific attitude. That which believed itself to be without faith and without assumptions he wished to rouse from its "dogmatic slumber." The so-called agnostics, he argued, also had a faith, albeit a particularly primitive and homespun one: belief in progress, in science, in biological evolution that favors mankind, in economic and historical laws. Modernism, according to Braig, was "blinded to anything that is not its Self or serves its Self";[2] the autonomy of the subject had become a self-erected prison. Braig criticized modern civilization for its lack of respect for the inexhaustible secret of a reality of which we ourselves are a part and which surrounds us. If Man arrogantly places himself at its center, he is ultimately left only with a pragmatic relationship to truth: Truth, in that case, is what serves us and what brings us practical success. This is refuted by Braig: "Historical truth, like all truth—and the most brilliantly victorious is mathematical truth, the strictest form of eternal truth—comes before the subjective ego and exists without it . . . As soon as the ego of reason regards the reasonableness of things, they are not in truth . . . and no Kant . . . will change the law that commands man to act in accordance with things."[3]

Braig in fact wishes to go back beyond Kant, but with Hegel, who had remarked on the excessively cautious Kant that fear of error was itself error.

Braig encourages a crossing of the transcendental boundaries: Can we be certain that only we discover the world? Why should not the world discover us for itself? Do we perhaps recognize only because we have ourselves been recognized? We can think God—so why should we not be God's thoughts? Braig, often rather rudely, smashes the cabinet of mirrors in which he sees modern man to be imprisoned. Braig pleads openly for what may seem a premodern realism, spiritually and empirically. He justifies it by pointing out that, since we know about boundaries, we have already crossed them. By recognizing recognition and perceiving perception we are already moving in the sphere of the absolutely real. We must separate ourselves, Braig argues, from the absolutism of the subject in order to become free for the reality of the absolute.

It was in this arena of the modernist conflict that young Martin Heidegger made his first appearance. He had meanwhile become a member of the Gralbund (League of the Grail), a strictly antimodernist faction of the Catholic youth movement whose spiritual leader was the Viennese Richard von Kralik, a zealot for the restoration of a pure Catholic faith, as well as of the ancient Holy Roman Catholic Empire of the German nation. Its center was to be Habsburg, not Prussia. Clearly this was also a political concept for central Europe. The members of these circles dreamed of the romantic Middle Ages of Novalis and placed their trust in Stifter's "gentle law" of loyally preserved origins. The same circles, however, were also quite ready to defend such origins very robustly against modern presumptions and temptations. An occasion to do so arose for young Martin Heidegger in connection with the festive consecration of a monument to Abraham a Sancta Clara in August 1910 at Kreenhainstetten, a small village near Messkirch.

Messkirch local patriotism had always honored the memory of Abraham a Sancta Clara—who was born at Kreenhainstetten in 1644 and died in Vienna in 1709 a greatly revered court preacher—with articles in the local press and small ceremonies on round-figure anniversaries. Since the beginning of the century, however, a strident, polemically ideological aspect had entered this cozy local tradition. The antimodernists of southern Germany had chosen Abraham a Sancta Clara as their role model. They invoked him in their polemics against the liberal trend in Catholicism. In the writings of the famous Augustine monk it was easy to find strong words against pleasure-seeking and depraved urban life, against spiritual pride that no longer bowed to the revealed teachings of the Church, against the love of extravagance of the wealthy, but also against the so-called cupidity of "money-lending Jews." This preacher had taken the side of the small and poor people, and proudly admitted to his lowly origins. Not everyone born under a straw roof had his head full of straw, was one of his frequently quoted sayings. Abraham a Sancta Clara was Christian-Socialist, populist, crude, pious without being a bigot, rooted in his native soil, and also anti-Semitic—exactly the right mixture for the antimodernists.

The unveiling of his monument on August 16, 1910, was a great public event. Martin Heidegger had come over for it from Freiburg. The village had decorated itself with flowers. Streamers with sayings of the preacher were hanging from windows and were stretched across the village street. A procession set itself in motion, led by mounted heralds in historical costume of the time of Abraham a Sancta Clara, and including the monks from Beuron, ecclesiastical and civil dignitaries, schoolchildren with bright little flags, girls wearing flowers, the locals in regional costume. There was a band playing, speeches were made, poems and sayings of Abraham a Sancta Clara were recited by pupils of the Messkirch *Bürgerschule.*

These events were reported in the article Heidegger wrote for *Allgemeine Rundschau,* a Catholic conservative weekly published in Munich, a text that Heidegger thought worthy of inclusion in his *Collected Works.* "The natural, fresh, and healthy, at times coarse, accent lends the event its specific imprint. The undemanding village of Kreenhainstetten, with its tough, self-assured, reserved inhabitants, rests sleepily in a gentle valley. Even the church tower is an odd man out. Unlike its brethren, it does not look freely into the land, but with its awkward heaviness has to bury itself among the black and red roofs . . . Thus simply, clearly, and truthfully unrolled the unveiling ceremony" (D, 1).

It should not be forgotten that Martin Heidegger, when he wrote these sentences, had already sniffed city air—in Constance and, since 1906, in Freiburg. He knew what distinguished him from those who moved with assurance and skill in a bourgeois environment, fashionably dressed, versed in questions of the latest literature, art, and philosophy. He focuses on the difference between his own world, that of Messkirch and Kreenhainstetten, and the world outside—a hint already of the difference between autonomous and nonautonomous being. One may therefore read a kind of self-portrait of the author into his lines about the unveiling of the monument. The church tower is an "odd man out," just as Heidegger is. The others are "looking freely into the land," but he is forced by his "awkward heaviness" back into the ground from which he comes, "tough, self-assured, and reserved" as the locals. He would wish to be like those folk, but also like Abraham a Sancta Clara. The preacher had something of the "people's soundness in body and soul"; he had impressed by his "original Catholic force," his "loyal faith and love of God," but he had also shown himself well versed in the sophisticated intellectual culture of his day; he had mastered it without letting it master him. That was why, according to Heidegger, he could afford his "fearless striking at any mundanely overrated concept of life on this earth." Abraham a Sancta Clara knew what he was talking about. He was not one to bark at the grapes because they hung too high.

Young Heidegger argues against the "decadence" of his age. What does he accuse it of? Of a "stifling sultriness," of being a period of "outward culture," of "fast living," of an "all-overturning innovation mania," of "momentary excitements," and predominantly of "the mad leaping over the more profound spiritual content of life and art" (D, 3).

That is the usual conservative critique of culture. Such views are held and expressed not only in the League of the Grail; similar polemics against superficiality, the chase after cheap effects, fast living, and innovation mania are found also with Langbehn and Lagarde. It is striking, however, that anti-Semitism, normally notorious in such contexts, is absent in young Heidegger. This is the more remarkable as the financing of the Kreenhainstetten monument had been initiated by Karl Lueger, the mayor of Vienna, who owed his popularity to his anti-Semitism. Interesting, moreover, is the assurance with which Heidegger speaks of the "transcendental value of life," which he regards as betrayed in all these manifestations of his day. What should be understood by that term is explained in other articles (found by Victor Farías) written by Heidegger between 1910 and 1912 for the journal *Der Akademiker*, a monthly of the integralist Catholic University Students' Union.

In the journal's March 1910 issue he presented the autobiography of the Danish writer and essayist Johannes Jørgensen. *Life's Lie and Life's Truth* was the title of the book. It described the author's spiritual progress from Darwinism to Catholicism, depicted as a road from despair to security, from pride to humility, from unbridledness to living freedom. To the young Martin Heidegger this was an exemplary and therefore instructive road, because it traversed all the follies and temptations of modernity before finally coming to rest in the tranquility and salvation of religious faith, in the "transcendental value of life." Here a person frees himself of the great illusion of modernity, which hopes to bring the "*I* to unlimited development"; here someone at last demonstrates in his own person that he who places his faith in himself places it in nothing.

> In our day one speaks a great deal of "personality" . . . The artistic personality is coming into prominence. So now we hear of such interesting men: Oscar Wilde, the dandy, Verlaine, the "genial drunk," Gorky, the great vagabond, the Nietzschean superman. And if, when one of them were, in a moment of Christian grace, to become conscious of the Big Lie of his rootless life, the altars of the false gods would be shattered, they would then call it "insipid and disgusting."[4]

Later, in 1930, in his famous lecture "On the Essence of Truth," Martin Heidegger would say: "Freedom will make us true." In these youthful articles the exact opposite applies: Truth will make us free. And this truth is not something that man could arrive at on his own and from within himself, but something he receives from the living community of faith and its traditions. Only here does the "great happiness of possessing the truth" exist, one that no one can attain on his own. Young Heidegger represents the believing realism of his teacher Carl Braig. The Protestant-pietist piety of emotion is still too subjective for him. In a review of F. W. Foerster's *Authority and Freedom: Reflections on the Cultural Problem of the Church* he polemicizes against narcissistic indulgence in "experiences," against the impressionism of ideologies that reflect only "personal moods" but no objective content. Heidegger's standard argument against "ideologies" was that they adjusted to the requirements of life. But anyone striving for truth acts the other way around—he subjugates life to the command of his insights. To young Heidegger it is evidently a crucial criterion of truth that it is not to be had easily, that it can be attained only with the "art of self-grabbing and self-renunciation." Truth is recognized by the fact that it resists us, challenges us, and transforms us. Only he who can set himself aside, who "also attains his spiritual freedom toward the world of urges, will find the truth. It is an exaction of the spirit of unlimited autonomism." It illumines, but it is not spontaneously evident. Self-conceit must bow to "religious-moral authority. It is already an almost crushing fact that most people turn out to be for themselves, not interested in discovering the truth or attaining it; they would rather be nailed to the cross and remove every justification for an individualistic ethic."[5]

This argument is worth remembering, for Heidegger will be seen to adhere to it. Exaction and discomfort remain criteria of truth, even though later the supposed possession of truth under the tutelage of the faith becomes to him an easy way out and hence a betrayal of truth. The difficult and unpalatable element that one should demand of oneself is therefore the (previously suspect) freedom that faces up to its metaphysical homelessness and has no need of protection by the rigid truths of a believing realism.

Heidegger's invectives against the "cult of personality" are not free from resentment, as he cannot conceal the fact that he himself lacks that vilified personal polish. This Church-supported theological candidate makes a somewhat gauche impression in the middle-class environment of the gymnasium and the university. His movements in the nonphilosophical arena would always lack assurance. The "lower-class smell" clings to him. Even in the 1920s in Marburg, when he was by then the secret king of philosophy in Germany, many colleagues and students—unless they knew him personally—would take him for the heating engineer or the janitor. For the time being he totally lacked the "interesting element" against which he polemicized. Because he could not yet act the part that could be effectively produced, he avoided the social stage where instant effect was important. The impressive posing and stage management of the young Nietzsche followers, who would loll about in cafés, was contemptuously described by him as "Cesare Borgia enthusiasm." Whatever can be performed easily, whatever is carefree and spontaneous, is suspected by him of superficiality. This is the attitude of someone who has not yet found a suitable setting for his spontaneity and for whom what is his "own" becomes an inevitable burden out there among the others. If he surrounds "truth" with the halo of the difficult, the hard, and the recalcitrant, then this is a reflection of the opposition he himself feels out there from the "secular ones," an opposition against which he must assert himself. At home, by contrast, this truth of the faith loses all heaviness and burden. Thus his review of the Jørgensen book concludes with lyrical praise of the security of the Catholic homeland: "[Jørgensen] saw in the old German cities the shaded bay windows, the familiar images of the Madonna mounted on houses. He heard the murmuring of sleepy springs and eavesdropped on melancholy folk songs. The German June evening, in which one might be lost in dreamy silence, hovers over his beloved books. The convert's God-filled and fulfilling longings for home might well constitute the most powerful impetus for his art."[6]

In this world Catholic truth is still at home. It is a world that is the spitting image of the Messkirch world. Here faith is still part of the order of life, and one receives it without having to force oneself into "self-grabbing and self-renunciation." But when one moves out with one's faith into an alien environment, then discipline and logic must sustain it. In front of every faith there is an abyss opening. How can one cross it? Young Heidegger put his trust in tradition and discipline. Later it would be determination, decisiveness. Later still he would rely on imperturbability.

In about 1910 Heidegger still believes that the Church's "treasure of truth" is a gift, and not a savings account which one can dispose of freely. Nor is belief in that treasure of truth a mere emotion. To Braig and his disciple Martin Heidegger, purely emotional religion, in the manner of Schleiermacher, is a concession to modern subjectivism. Faith is not a sentimental comfort but a tough challenge. Small wonder that the enlightened world perceives it as an unacceptable demand—because faith, in effect, is just that. It demands, for instance, that, for the sake of "truth," the psycho-logic of "living it up" be renounced. Young Heidegger wrote: "And do you want a spiritual life? Do you want to gain your happiness? Then die, kill the base things in you, work with supernatural grace and you will be resurrected."[7]

This turning to God lacks all cozy mildness. It wishes to make life difficult for itself; it will not allow any mollycoddling by Schleiermacher-like emotion, nor does it wish to degenerate into an asylum of mere inwardness. Heidegger was seeking God's spirit elsewhere on earth. Braig's remark—"the most brilliantly victorious is mathematical truth, the strictest form of eternal truth"—had shown him the way. He therefore wrote in *Der Akademiker:* "A strong, ice-cold logic opposes the delicate modern soul. 'Thought' can no longer let itself be forced into the unchanging eternal bounds of logical principles. But, of course, we already have them. To the rigorously logical thinking, hermetically sealed against every affective influence of the spirit, to every genuine presuppositionless scientific work belongs a certain depth of ethical power, the power of self-control and self-renunciation."[8]

To Heidegger this is the same strength that is needed for the self-conquest of faith. The authoritarianism of faith and the objectivity of strict logic are one and the same to him. They are different ways of participating in the *eternal.* Yet even so this involves emotions, moreover very exalted ones. Only in the strict disciplines of faith and logic is there fulfillment of the craving for "complete and final answers to the questions of Being. It sometimes flashes so abruptly that on some days there is left only a weight of lead on the tortured, rudderless soul."[9]

When Heidegger, in his *Lebenslauf* of 1915, referred to his "training in formal logic," as though this had been propaedeutic, this was an understatement. To him, formal and mathematical logic was a kind of worship; he allowed logic to take him into the discipline of the eternal, and there he found stability on the swaying ground of life.

In 1907 Conrad Gröber had made a present to his pupil of Franz Brentano's dissertation, "On the Manifold Meaning of Being According to Aristotle." In it Heidegger found what he was to call "strict, icily cold logic," something for strong intellects that do not wish to live only by their opinions and emotions. It is significant that Gröber, a strictly observing churchman, should have chosen this particular book. Franz Brentano, born in 1838, the nephew of Clemens Brentano, the well-known writer of the romantic movement, was a philosopher who, as a Catholic priest, originally subjected philosophy to faith, but who, after the "Infallibility Council" of 1870, came into conflict with his superiors. Eventually he left the Church and married, and in consequence had to resign his professorship in Vienna. He taught at the university as a *Privatdozent*—an unsalaried assistant professor—until 1895, when, almost blind, he retired to Venice.

Brentano was Husserl's teacher and hence one of the founding fathers of phenomenology. The question that agitated Brentano was the nature of God's existence. If there is a God, what does "there is" mean? Is he an idea in our head? Is he outside in the world as its quintessence, as its highest being? In subtle analysis Brentano discovers that there is a third category, between the subjective idea and the "in-itself" of things—the "intentional objects." Ideas, according to Brentano, are not purely internal, but are always ideas "of something." They are the awareness of something that is, something that exists, or, more accurately, something that offers itself and presents itself to one. These intentional objects are something, in other words: they cannot be dissolved into the subjective actions through which we enter into relation with them. In this manner Brentano prepares an entire separate world of what is, a world occupying an intermediate position in the customary subject-object pattern. It is in this world of intentional objects that Brentano also places our relation to God. Here "there is" a God. The awareness of God cannot be verified by real objects of our experience, nor, on the other hand, is it based on abstract general concepts, such as the "supreme Good," the "supreme Being," and the like. Brentano undertakes the examination of Aristotle's concept of existence in order to show that the believed God is not the God whom we try to attain by way of abstraction from the fullness of what exists. With Aristotle Brentano demonstrates that, strictly speaking, there is no Whole. There are only discrete objects. There is no such thing as dimension in itself, there are only objects with dimension. There is no love, but only the many separate events of love. Brentano warns against falsely ascribing substance to conceptual things. Substance resides not in the general concepts but only in specific individual objects. These are of intensive infinity because they stand in infinitely numerous relations and can therefore be determined in an infinite number of respects. The world is inexhaustible but offers itself only in specificity and in the manifold gradations of the kinds of existence. To Brentano's way of thinking, God is in the detail.

Linking up with Aristotle, Brentano's work maps out the territory of the thinkable; in consequence, faith, which remains mandatory to him, is spared deceptive logification. It rests on a different basis from justification, even though—Brentano's dissertation suggests—it may one day be possible to describe precisely just what really occurs in the act of faith, in contrast, for instance, to judgment, imagination, or perception. These are the outlines of the phenomenological program for the next few years.

Reading Brentano was a tough task for Martin Heidegger. He records how, in the semester vacations in Messkirch, he struggled with the text. "When the riddles crowded upon one another and no way out was in sight, the *Feldweg* [path through the fields] helped." There, on a bench, matters once more seemed straightforward. "The vastness of all grown things around the *Feldweg* provides World. Only in what is unuttered in their language . . . is God" (D, 39).

By way of Franz Brentano, Heidegger came to Edmund Husserl. His *Logical Investigations*, published exactly at the turn of the century, became a personal cult book for Heidegger. After borrowing it from the university library, he kept the book in his room for two years. No one else seemed to ask for it, which gave him a sense of indulging in a solitary but also an exclusive passion. Even fifty years later, whenever he thought of the book, he raved about it: "I remained so fascinated by Husserl's work that I read in it again and again in the years to follow . . . The spell emanating from the work extended to the outer appearance of the sentence structure and the title-page" (Z, 81).[10]

In Husserl's work Heidegger found a vigorous defense of the assertion of logic against its psychological relativization. In an essay in 1912 he defined his position: "Fundamental for the realization of the absurdity and theoretical barrenness of psychologism is the distinction between the psychic act and its logical content, between real thought processes occurring in time and their ideal extratemporal identical meaning—in short, the distinction between what 'is' and what 'applies'" (GA 1, 22).

With this differentiation between "psychic act" and "logical content" Husserl at the beginning of the century had cut the Gordian knot of the psychologism argument—admittedly in such a subtle way that only few people, among them young Heidegger, realized what had happened. On the surface this looked like a problem for professional philosophers, but in fact these controversies reflected the opposing trends and tensions of the period.

Philosophy in about 1900 was in deep trouble. The natural sciences, in alliance with positivism, empiricism, and sensualism, were stifling it. The triumphalism of the sciences was based on an exact knowledge of nature and on a technical command of nature. Organized experience, experiment, formulation of a hypothesis, verification, the inductive process—these had become the components of the logic of scientific research. The ancient and venerable philosophical question of "what something is" was no longer being asked. It was known to lead into infinity, and because there was no longer any interest in the infinite, the question was dropped. To those modern scientists who began to see themselves as agents of a research process, the question of "how something functions" was much more promising. This might lead to something definite, along with the prospect that objects, and perhaps also people, might be made to work in accordance with these concepts.

Reason, of course, by which this entire process is set in motion, is itself part of nature. It should therefore be possible—this was the ambitious program—to explore it by the same methods as "external" nature. Toward the end of the nineteenth century, therefore, in conjunction with the disciplines of physiology and brain chemistry, there emerged a kind of "natural science" of the psychic—experimental psychology.

The principle of this research approach is to pretend ignorance and to act as if one knows nothing about the psyche, as if it could be observed from without, positivistically and empirically. Scientists want to explain, not to understand; they look for regularities, not for meaning, because comprehension would turn one into an accomplice of the subject under investigation. This, however, prevents one from having the psyche in front of one in neat isolation. The approach to experimental science, in psychology as elsewhere, calls for an aseptic object, as it is not the "meaning" but the "mechanism" of the psychic that is to be analyzed—the laws of the conversion of physiological stimuli into idea-images, the regular association structures in the idea complexes, and ultimately the laws of thought themselves: that is, logic.

From this perspective, logic appears to be a natural process in the psyche. And that is the "problem of psychologism." The naturalists of the psychic elevate this logic, this mechanism of thought, into a natural law of thought, meanwhile overlooking the fact that logic does not empirically describe how we think, but how we ought to think if we wish to arrive at judgments with a claim to truth—which, after all, is what science claims for itself. By analyzing thought as a natural psychic event, science entangles itself in a tricky contradiction. It examines thought as an event occurring according to laws; if, however, it studied itself more carefully, it would be bound to notice that thought is not a process evolving according to laws. Thought is not determined by laws but is merely tied to certain rules. In the wide field of the thinkable, logic appears not as a natural law but as something that applies if we allow it to apply.

The concept of law is, of course, ambiguous. It describes something that occurs regularly and inevitably in just the way it does occur, and it also describes a mechanism that claims to prescribe a certain course to an occurrence. In the former case these are laws of Being; in the latter they are laws of what should be. In one case they describe what is, in the other they prescribe.

Husserl's investigations aim at freeing logic from naturalism and bringing out once more its normative—that is, spiritual—character. Of course the logical work takes place within the psyche, but it is a normative product of the psyche and not a natural law of a psychic process.

This clarification, however, is immediately followed by the next problem—that of the relation between the psychic act and its product, between the genesis of thought and the validity of the thought content.

The calculating process of "twice two is four" is a psychic act, but "twice two is four" is valid also if the psychic act is not performed. The arithmetical result claims validity regardless of whichever head happens to be performing this calculation. Anyone calculating or performing any other logical operation arrives—this sounds very Platonic already—at a participation in a transsubjective realm of the spirit. The meaning and application spheres there accumulated are actualized and called upon whenever any actions of thought, which can be described as psychic events, are performed.

However, the formulation that logic is not the natural law of thinking but is part of an ideal sphere of validity can lead to misunderstanding, because it suggests that this may simply be a pragmatic agreement. In actual fact, we did not agree on the logic of syllogisms and then declare it to be "correct"; it *is* correct. All men are mortal—Socrates is a man—hence Socrates is mortal. This manner of concluding is evidently correct; it is valid. However, this does not necessarily mean that the judgments thus arrived at are empirically correct; that would depend on whether or not the premises ("All men are mortal . . .") are correct. We may use the correct manner of concluding and yet arrive at any number of false judgments (if all men were officials, Socrates would be one too). We cannot therefore state that we have become accustomed to concluding by syllogism because this has led us to successful cognition. Indeed it need not lead us to successful cognition in the empirical sense at all; far more often, it misleads us. These conclusions, therefore, are not confirmed by experience, but, like any logical operation, they are simply self-evident.

The more one immerses oneself in this evidence of logic, the more mysterious it becomes. From a simple analysis of the syllogism one suddenly finds oneself in the magic realm of a spirit that triumphs over all attempts to reduce it pragmatically, biologically, naturalistically, or sociologically.

Yet the epoch since the middle of the nineteenth century, under the impact of the practical successes of the empirical sciences, had developed a veritable passion for reduction, for driving the spirit out from the sphere of knowledge.

Nietzsche had described that century as "sincere" and "honest," though in a plebeian manner. It was "more subservient to reality of every kind, more true."[11] It had torn loose from the "domination of ideals" and instinctively looked for theories everywhere that could justify "subjection to the real." Nietzsche was referring to the philistine and fainthearted aspect of that realism. In fact, however, a realism had been triumphant since the middle of the century that subjected itself to reality only in order more completely to command and reshape it to its own liking. The "will to power," with which Nietzsche had credited the "free spirit," triumphed not in the elevated regions of "supermen," but in the busy, antlike activity of a civilization that had scientized its practical reason. This applied to the bourgeois world, but it also applied to the workers' movement, whose battle cry was, "Knowledge is power." Education was to lead to social advancement and provide resistance to deception of any kind. If someone knows something he cannot be fooled quite so easily; the most impressive aspect of knowledge is that one need not let oneself be impressed any longer. A gain of sovereignty is promised, and the need to bring things down to one's own, rather pitiful, level is being satisfied.

It is astonishing how, ever since the middle of the nineteenth century, after the idealistic flights of the absolute spirit, there has suddenly been a universal desire to make Man "small." That is when the thought pattern of "Man is nothing other than . . ." began its advance. To the romantics the world would burst into song if only one uttered the magic formula. The poetry and philosophy of the first half of the century was the breathtaking project of discovering and inventing ever-new magic formulas. The age called for exuberant meanings.

The matadors in this magical arena were "reflection athletes," but they did appear at the moment when the realists, their minds on facts, and armed with the formula "nothing other than . . . ," were standing in the door, like naive children who had romped about and thrown everything into a chaos; but now it was tidying-up time, now life began in earnest. The realists would see to it all. This realism of the second half of the nineteenth century would achieve the trick of thinking of Man as "little" but doing great things with him—provided one wishes to describe the scientized civilization, from which we are all benefiting, as "great."

The project of modernism begins with an attitude that rejects anything extravagant and fantastic. But even the most extravagant fantasy would have been unable, at that time, to imagine the monstrosities that the spirit of positivist disenchantment was yet to produce.

German idealism had been drained by a robust kind of materialism about the middle of the century. Breviaries of disenchantment suddenly became best-sellers. There was Karl Vogt with his *Physiological Letters* (1845) and his polemical tract *Simple Faith and Science* (1854); there was Jakob Moleschott's *Circulation of Life* (1852), Ludwig Büchner's *Force and Matter* (1855), and Heinrich Czolbe's *New Description of Sensualism* (1855). This ethos of a materialism of force and urge and glandular function was characterized by Czolbe: "It is indeed no proof of humility, but rather of arrogance and vanity, to improve upon the world we know by imagining a supersensuous world, and to wish to exalt man into a creature above nature by the addition of a suprasensuous part. Yes, certainly, dissatisfaction with the world of phenomena—the deepest root of supersensuous ideas—is not reason at all, but rather moral weakness."[12] Czolbe concludes with the advice: "Be content with the world as it is." But what, to such an approach, was the "world as it is"? The world of Becoming and Being—nothing other than a swirling of molecules and transformations of energy. What was holding sway was the world of the atomist Democritus. There was no need any longer for the nous of Anaxagoras or the ideas of Plato; there was no need for the God of the Christians, for the substance of Spinoza, for the cogito of Descartes, for the I of Fichte, for the spirit of Hegel. The spirit that lives in Man was nothing but a cerebral function. Ideas were to the brain as gall was to the liver or urine to the kidney. These ideas were "a little unfiltered," remarked Hermann Lotze, then one of the few survivors of the once numerous tribe of metaphysical philosophers. It was also Lotze who—unsuccessfully—pointed out to the materialists the folly of their *salto mortale.* He recalled Leibniz, who had long settled the whole materialist problem, especially the relation between awareness and body, in his discussion with Hobbes. If one thing is based on another, this does not mean that it is identical with it; for if it were, it would not be different from it, and it could not therefore be based on the other. Human life, Leibniz said, was based on breathing, but this did not mean that it was just air.

The victorious advance of materialism was not halted by clever objections, more especially because it had a metaphysical admixture: belief in progress. If we analyze objects and life down to their most elementary components, then—this belief in progress claims—we shall discover nature's secret of operation. Once we discover how everything is done, we shall be able to copy it. At work here is an awareness that is out to discover all secrets, including those of nature, which—by means of experiment—has to be caught red-handed. If one knows how it operates one can show it which way to continue.

This mental attitude also gave nourishment to Marxism in the second half of the nineteenth century. In laborious and painstaking work, Marx had dissected the body of society and separated its soul—capital. In the end it was no longer entirely clear whether the messianic mission of the proletariat—Marx's contribution to German idealism—would even stand a chance of prevailing against the unshakable law of capital—Marx's contribution to the post-1850 spirit of determinism. Marx, too, wishes to discover all secrets; this he does through a critique of ideology. For the ideology critics, ideas are not—as believed by the large crowd of philosophizing physiologists and zoologists—

sweated out by the brain, but by society. The ideology-critical sociologist similarly tries to strip the magic from the astonishing secretions of the mind. The campaigns of materialism are directed against validity.

In 1866 a striking critique of this attitude was published—F. A. Lange's classic *History of Materialism.* It did not exactly remain without effect. Nietzsche was greatly influenced by it, and even though his philosophy later detonated as a "life philosophy," blowing apart many particularly massive chunks of materialism, it was Lange who had lit the fuse. Neo-Kantianism, which will be discussed later because young Heidegger moved in its circles, was likewise set in motion by Lange.

Lange's fundamental idea is the restoration of that neat Kantian differentiation between a world of phenomena that we can analyze by laws, a world to which, as objects among objects, we ourselves belong with part of our being, and a world that reaches into us, which used to be called "spirit" and by Kant was called "freedom" with reference to the internal man, and the "thing in itself" with reference to the external world. Lange recalls Kant's definition of nature: nature is not where the laws which we call laws of nature apply, but the other way about. To the extent that we view something from the angle of such "laws," we ourselves constitute it as the appearance of "nature"; to the extent that we view it from the angle of spontaneity and freedom, we are dealing with "spirit." Both viewing angles are possible and necessary, and, most important, they are not convertible. We can analyze ourselves as a thing among things; we can, as Hobbes has deliberately done, view ourselves as a machine—but it is we who choose that perspective. We are free to make ourselves into machines. We are part of the world of phenomena—that is, nature according to the law, a thing among things—yet at the same time each person experiences within himself the spontaneity of freedom. Freedom is the secret of the world revealing itself to us, the back of the mirror of phenomena. The "thing in itself"—that is ourselves in our freedom; the core of all determination is the dimension in which we can determine ourselves.

This Kantian double perspective—Man is a thing among things and also freedom—is once more brought into play by F. A. Lange. Materialism as a research method in the natural sciences, Lange states, is entirely to be welcomed. Scientific experience must act as if there were only material reality. It must not, when it can make no further progress with its explanations, invoke the "spirit" as a stopgap. "Spirit" is not a link in a causal chain; instead it is the other side of the causal chain. It is possible to pursue the scientific physiology of the psychic, but it should not be forgotten that this will not touch upon the soul itself but only on its material equivalents. Lange criticized not only scientific methods but also the false awareness and poor philosophy that accompanied them—more particularly the idea that analysis could exhaust the *res extensa* of the human. If one thinks in spatial categories it is very easy to believe that everything that exists must be shown up at a particular point in space or in a spatially representable structure.

It was Lange's great achievement to have demonstrated that, just as there is a boiling point of idealism, where all spirit evaporates, so there is a freezing point of materialism, where nothing moves anymore—unless, of course, one cheats by introducing the spirit incognito, for instance in the form of the "vital force," which no one can define. Against idealist evaporation and the materialist freezing point, Lange pleads for a compromise of both spirit and matter.

Lange champions a cut-price metaphysics. To him it is a poetical creation of concepts, an inspiring mixture of poetry and knowledge. The same is true of religion. If it claims to possess knowledge of God, the soul, and immortality, then it lays itself open to scientific criticism and cannot prevail. A tactical retreat is necessary. The "standpoint of the ideal" cannot base its pride on recognizing truth, but only on creating values and thereby transforming reality. For empiricism there is truth, for the spirit there are values. Nietzsche would put an end to Lange's peaceful coexistence of truth and value by simply going one step further and offering the value of truth for discussion. Lange had wished to save the values from the assault of truths; with Nietzsche, conversely, the truths are swallowed up by the vitalism of values. At that point truth is only the illusion with which we are comfortable and which benefits us. Others, by contrast, will define values as mere states of affairs occurring within cultures—what Heinrich Rickert calls "state of value." They can be described from a cultural perspective, or one can talk about them in historical perspective. Validity is valid only when it has become a fact. Valid is only what has been valid. This will become the punch line of historicism.

Lange was seeking a compromise—materialism was to share power with the world of the spirit:

> Who will refute a Mass of Palestrina, or who will convict Raphael's Madonna of error? The "Gloria in Excelsis" remains a universal power, and will ring through the centuries so long as our nerves can quiver under

> the awe of the sublime. And those simple fundamental ideas of redemption of the individual man by the surrendering of his own will to the will that guides the whole; those images of death and resurrection which express the highest and most thrilling emotions that stir the human breast . . . those doctrines, finally, which bid us to share our bread with the hungry and to announce the glad tidings to the poor—these will not forever disappear in order to make way for a society which has attained its goal when it owes a better police system to its understanding, and to its ingenuity the satisfaction of ever-fresh wants by ever-fresh inventions.[13]

This idealism is intended to restore an equilibrium to a civilization driven by science and technology. It is an idealism "as if," because the values here recommended have lost their old dignity and viability since the self-made element was discerned in them. The idea, in fact, is only an idol, it sparkles with the false brilliance of the artificial. Evidently the idealists can hold on to the good and beautiful only in an attitude of involuntary frivolity. They utter their dogma with the smile of augurs who make others believe rather than believing themselves. A philosophical best-seller at the end of the century, giving eloquent expression to this educated-middle-class frivolity, was Hans Vaihinger's *Philosophy of "As If."* In it the values are described as useful fictions. They are mere inventions, but if they help us with the theoretical and practical mastery of our life's tasks, then they acquire a significance that normally we call "objective."

This "as if" pervaded the entire Wilhelminian epoch. There was widespread delight in the nongenuine. Impressive was what looked impressive. Every material used tried to pretend more than it was. It was the era of fake materials. Marble was painted wood, gleaming alabaster was plaster of Paris; the new had to look old: Grecian columns on the stock exchange, a factory in the form of a medieval castle, a newly built ruin. Historical association was in fashion. Courthouses suggested the Doge's Palace; a bourgeois living room contained Luther-style chairs, pewter tankards, and Gutenberg Bibles that turned out to be sewing boxes. Kaiser Wilhelm himself was not quite genuine either; his will to power was more will than power. The "as if" called for stage sets—indeed it lived by them. No one realized this better than Richard Wagner, who pulled out all the stops of theatrical magic to redeem his age—a time-limited redemption, a redemption "as if." All this went alongside a very reality-oriented frame of mind. Just because this was so effective it had to be dressed up a little, adorned, draped, chiseled, and so on, to make sure the whole thing looked good and was valid. After all, official German policy also went all out for validity or standing—Germany's standing in the world. If one is seen to have standing, he saves himself the trouble of having to become something.

This mixture of efficiency in the real world and an "as if" attitude opened the door to Germany for the Anglo-Saxon pragmatism of a William James and Charles Peirce. Pragmatism, of course, pleads for disarmament in matters of truth. Truth is pulled up from its anchoring in the realm of ideas and downgraded to a social principle of self-regulation of processes. The criterion of truth is practical success—and the same applies to so-called values. Their reality is tested not in the ominous and never sufficiently demonstrable agreement with some ideal Being, but in its effect. The spirit is what it accomplishes. Pragmatism replaces the correspondence theory of truth with the theory of efficiency. One need no longer be afraid of error. For one thing, following the abandonment of the objective truth criterion, error loses its ontological sinfulness—truth can now be defined as a useful error. And for another, error is part of the trial procedure. If a dog with a long stick in its jaws wants to get through a door, he will twist and turn his head until he achieves his goal. That is the method of trial and error. Just as the dog gets through the door, so Man gets through the gate of truth, which by then, however, is no longer what it used to be—it has lost its venerable pathos. What matters now is practical interests, not the need for certainty—clearly an attitude that still contains, incognito, a good deal of the religious. Pragmatism replaces the *examen rigorosum* of metaphysics with a practical test on the spot. It loosens the Teutonic tension that always aims at the whole, and it encourages unconcern by its moral principle of "our errors are leading us upward." "Our errors," William James says, "are not such terribly important things in the end. In a world where, despite all care, we cannot avoid them, a certain measure of carefree frivolity seems healthier than exaggeratedly nervous fear." [14]

This carefree attitude was supported by another powerful tendency at the time: the biology of evolution based on Darwin's discoveries. This teaches that, like ourselves, nature, too, proceeds by the trial-and-error method. Mutations are faulty transfers of genetic information. Variants emerge in the chain of species, a variability through accident. Selection is based on successful adaptation. That which proves itself is preserved. In this way—through accidental mutation plus natural selection in the struggle for survival—nature hits its target without aiming. Therefore nature, too, is led upward by its errors. The law of mutation and selection thus seemed to have solved the Kantian problem of natural teleology without telos. Blind chance produces a nature whose results look as if it had pursued a goal. God does not throw dice—perhaps not, but nature was believed to have been caught out playing dice. Evolutionary biology, then, seemed a grand legitimation of the method of attaining order through anarchy and achieving success through error, lending almost insuperable evidential force to the axiom that truth is nothing other than practical success.

Toward the end of the century Werner von Siemens impressively presented what he called the spirit of the "scientific age" at the Circus Renz, Berlin's largest assembly hall. It was a gala performance for the festive assembly of scientists who had come to welcome the new century:

> Therefore, gentlemen, we will not be shaken in our belief that our research and inventive activity leads mankind to higher levels of culture, ennobling it and making it more accessible to ideal aspirations, that the impending scientific age will diminish its hardships and its sickness, enhance its enjoyment of life, and make it better, happier, and more content with its fate. And even though we may not always see the road ahead clearly, the road leading to these better conditions, we will nevertheless hold on to our conviction that the light of the truth we are exploring will not lead us astray, and that the wealth of power it brings to mankind cannot diminish it but is bound to elevate it to a higher level of existence.[15]

The prerequisites of success are spiritual abstention and curiosity about what lies close, the invisible not in the beyond but in this world—for the microscopic study of the cells and the macroscopic study of electromagnetic waves. In both cases research penetrates into the realm of the invisible, producing visible results, for instance in the struggle against pathogenic microbes or in earth-girdling wireless telegraphy. Many a dream of metaphysics—sovereignty gained with regard to the body, the overcoming of space and time—have become technological reality.

As physics learns to fly, so the superfliers of metaphysics crash and have to continue on the ground. What they are able to do there is modest enough, as the example of the neo-Kantians shows. One of them, Paul Natorp, in 1909 defined the task of philosophy thus: "It is nothing other than a methodical effort by science to achieve self-transparency. In philosophy, science realizes its own principles, procedures, and value orientations." Natorp calls this the "signposting of science . . . not from the outside, but through elucidation of the inner law of the path which science has always described and unremittingly continues to describe."[16] This binds philosophy to an objective that is the exact reversal of its beginnings:

> At first philosophy hid in her womb the germs of all sciences; but once she had given birth to them and given them motherly care during their infancy, and once they had, under her tutelage, become mature and great, she is not averse to watching them go out into the big world in order to conquer it. For a while she watches them with loving care, perhaps now and again with a soft warning word that neither can nor wishes to restrict their newly won independence; eventually, however, she quietly withdraws to her retirement corner, from where one day, scarcely noticed and scarcely missed, she will have vanished from the world.[17]

Wilhelm Windelband, Natorp, Rickert, and Hermann Cohen were called neo-Kantians because they advised the modern natural sciences to apply Kant's methodical reflection, and because on the question of the justification of ethical norms they also went back to Kant. They represented a massive philosophical current until World War I. Despite much acuity and polemical spirit in detail, the group as a whole was on the defensive against the superior strength of the scientific spirit of the day. It was a philosophy that hoped it would, after the end of philosophy, be able to live on in its "children," the sciences. However, as Natorp conceded, things were not yet looking "hopeful" with regard to "philosophy in the sciences." There was still a lot of ideological ballast and smuggled speculative stuff in the baggage of empirical and exact scientists who were claiming the prestige of science for the childish and simple faith they had preserved. The zoologist Ernst Haeckel was one such scientist. From Darwin's evolutionary biology he distilled a monistic view of the world and the universe, with which he claimed to have solved the "riddle of the universe"—the title of his best-seller in 1889.

The neo-Kantians wanted to be the conscience of science in a double sense—a methodological conscience and an ethical conscience, because that was their second specialty, the problem of value. The question was, How can that process be scientifically analyzed which—unlike in the natural sciences—is not a case of something becoming something, but of something being regarded as something? To the neo-Kantians, culture was the quintessence of the sphere of values. The material substance of a sculpture, for instance, can be analyzed physically, chemically, and so on, but one will not thereby have understood what that sculpture is, because it is what it signifies. This signification is valid and is realized by everybody who does not regard the sculpture as a heap of stones but as art. In all cultural processes, Rickert argues, there is "incorporated some value recognized by Man."[18] Nature and culture are not separate spheres, but nature becomes a cultural object to the extent it is linked to values. Sexuality, for instance, is a value-free biological occurrence; culturally appropriated it becomes a very valuable event: love. Human reality is interwoven with value-creating processes. There is nothing mysterious about this; the world of values does not float over our heads, but everything that Man handles receives a value accent in consequence. A state of affairs thus becomes a "state of values." States of affairs are susceptible to explanation; states of value can only be understood. Human society altogether resembles King Midas—everything it touches, everything it draws into its spell, receives value.

Value philosophy was an obsession with the neo-Kantians. Engrossed in the mysteries of validity, those academic philosophers overlooked what was more valid than anything else: money. It was an outsider, Georg Simmel, who, at the beginning of the century, presented the inspired masterpiece of all value philosophy—the *Philosophy of Money.*

Simmel describes the transition from robbery to barter as the crucial event of civilization. He therefore calls civilized Man "the exchanging animal."[19] Barter absorbs violence, and money universalizes barter and exchange. Money, originally a material object, becomes the real symbol of all goods for which it may be given in exchange. Once money exists, everything it comes into contact with gets bewitched. It can now be appraised according to its value, no matter whether it concerns a pearl necklace, a funeral oration, or the mutual use of the sexual organs. Money is the truly existent transcendental category of socialization. The equivalence relations provided by money ensure the inner cohesion of modern society. Money is the magic means that transforms the entire world into a "commodity" that can be taxed according to its value and hence also utilized.

But how does something become money? The simple answer, though of incalculable consequences, is by becoming something that has validity. This something that has validity can then be employed to pay someone else for something that one desires. The rate of exchange is always accurately calculable; what remains obscure is from where that rate actually derives. Some say from work, others from the marketplace, others yet from demand, and others still from scarcity. Certainly the validity of money does not reside in its material nature; more probably it is social spirit turned into material power. The circulation power of money has outstripped the spirit of which it used to be said that it bloweth where it listeth.

Simmel's spirit, however, like money, penetrates into the most remote corners of social life. Simmel manages to link everything to everything. If money creates a common value term for things as disparate as a Bible and a bottle of brandy, then Simmel discovers in it a link with Nikolaus von Kues's concept of God; to him God means the "coincidentia oppositorum," the point at which all opposites are united.

> In so far as money becomes the absolutely commensurate expression and equivalent of all values, it rises to abstract heights way above the whole broad diversity of objects; it becomes the center in which the most opposed, the most estranged and the most distant things find their common denominator and come into contact with one another. Thus, money actually provides an elevated position above the particular and a confidence in its omnipotence, just as we have confidence in the omnipotence of a highest principle.[20]

Analysis of the power of validity, also in the case of money, cannot, therefore—as Simmel's example shows—do without reference to the metaphysical stock of concepts.

Thus during the antimetaphysical period prior to 1914, the sphere of validity, even if it was that of money, was a refuge for the remnants of metaphysics. And the same—to return to our point of departure—applies to Husserl, who defends the psychology-free validity of logic like a Platonic realm of ideas against the moles of naturalist psychology.

The young Martin Heidegger finds himself in a similar defensive position. He, too, along with Husserl (and with Emil Lask), discovers his metaphysical remnants in the mystery of validity, in the sphere of pure logic that resists all temptations of relativization through biology or psychology. In that sphere the "transcendental value of life" remains intact for him. But there is still some lack of clarity about the connection between logic and the life of the soul. In his 1912 essay "Recent Investigations into Logic," Heidegger calls the psychic the "operational basis" of logic, but some "peculiar, perhaps never entirely explicable problems" remain.

By means of logic Heidegger is hoping to snatch a corner of superindividual validity; this means a lot to him, as he wishes to believe in the objective reality of the spirit. The spirit should not be just a product of our heads. But he also wants to concede independent reality to the external world. It should not evaporate into a chimera of the subjective spirit, because anything like that would be the cognition-theory version of the "boundless autonomism of the ego" that he had criticized. Heidegger wants to avoid both the crash into materialism and the false ascension of subjective idealism. His first tentative philosophical steps are guided by a "critical realism" that asserts that "only he who believes in the determinacy of a real nature will turn his efforts toward its cognition" (GA 1, 15). And he is guided by the possibility of an objective spirit.

Such spirit he finds in the evident "treasure of truth" of the Church, but this does not satisfy the philosopher. Hence his second place of discovery: logic and its objective validity.

During his first few years of study we observe Martin Heidegger seeking a philosophy with which he can assert himself in the arena of modernism and which, simultaneously, will permit him to remain under the sky of Messkirch.

3

CAREER PLANNING AND CAREER PROBLEMS

Heidegger's first philosophical essays, "The Relativity Problem in Modern Philosophy" and "Recent Investigations into Logic," do not betray the fact that they were written in what was for him a time of crisis and upheaval. He argues in favor of the principle of a reliably identifiable reality and a metaphysical durability of logic at a moment when the plans for his personal life begin to rock. The year was 1911.

After three semesters at the seminary, while studying theology, his heart began to act up again. Perhaps he had "overexerted himself," as he recorded in his 1915 *Lebenslauf,* or perhaps his body was rebelling against the wrong kind of work. At the suggestion of the seminary physician, Martin was released in February 1911 for a few weeks of "absolute rest" in Messkirch. His superiors had gained the impression that the physical constitution of the talented theology student was not sturdy enough for later employment in the service of the Church.

Heidegger spends the whole of the summer with his parents in Messkirch. He does not know what road to take. His mood is gloomy; he seeks relaxation in poetic attempts. In these his career doubts are dramatically magnified into "Gethsemane Hours"—the title of a poem published in *Allgemeine Rundschau* in April 1911:

> Gethsemane hours of my life,
> in the dim light
> of doubt and despair
> how oft have you seen me!
>
> My tearful cries were never in vain.
> My youthful being,
> weary of lamentation,
> trusted only in the angel of mercy.[1]

Hugo Ott discovered this poem, as well as the letters of Ernst Laslowski, a history student in Heinrich Finke's Catholic Studies department at the University of Freiburg. In Laslowski, who came from Upper Silesia and studied for a few semesters in Freiburg, Martin Heidegger had found a committed friend who admired him at an early age. Laslowski wrote: "If only your father could support you for the three to five semesters you will need to get your doctorate and prepare for your habilitation, I'm sure the money could be found from somewhere."[2] But his father was simply unable to pay. The son of humble parents would have to remain under the care of the Church or struggle through in some other way.

In his correspondence with Laslowski the alternatives are examined. Was Martin to stick with theology and therefore with the clerical profession? Laslowski advises in favor. Martin would be provided for; he would only have to overcome the doubts of his superiors that he was not up to much physically. He would be able, without interference, to take his doctorate and establish himself as an associate professor. In the meantime, perhaps, an intermezzo in a rural parish for "maturing." After that he would undoubtedly make a brilliant career as a theologian.

Such visions are flattering, but Heidegger already knows that what fascinates him about theology is not the theological but the philosophical aspect. The second possibility is that of concentrating entirely on philosophy while remaining in the Catholic environment. The "Church's treasure of truth" would remain entirely untouched. Indeed, philosophy might be employed to protect it. Even though faith does not need any philosophical grounding, it would be possible philosophically to refute the antimetaphysical presumptions of a falsely understood scientific attitude. Most of the time these scientists were not aware of the extent to which they borrowed from metaphysics when they assigned truth to their theorems. If one could prove that the "transcendental value of life" is contained even in pure logic, then the Church, with its treasure of truth, would stand on a less hopeless foundation. If he were to turn toward a thus understood Catholic philosophy and apologetics, it might perhaps be possible to win sponsors among institutions and publications of the Catholic world, such as the Albertus Magnus Association or the Görres Society for the Promotion of Learning. Laslowski recommends that he make contact with the Catholic philosopher Clemens Baeumker, who is teaching in Strasbourg. Baeumker is president of the Görres Society and publisher of the *Philosophisches Jahrbuch, der Görres-Gesellschaft,* the philosophical annual of the Görres Society, and devotes himself primarily to the promotion of young Catholic students of philosophy. The prospects for Catholic philosophers are not favorable. They are not taken quite seriously by the rest of the philosophical world, and there are few professorships in the subject.

There is a third, the most modest, option—to study a school subject, take the state examination, and become a teacher. Heidegger considers it seriously: the prospect of an assured livelihood is tempting. The only subjects he would consider are the natural sciences.

Heidegger makes his decision after this difficult summer in Messkirch. He breaks off his theological studies. For the winter semester of 1911–12 he enrolls in the science faculty of the University of Freiburg, choosing the subjects mathematics, physics, and chemistry, though continuing his philosophical studies with undiminished zeal. He enters into contact with Clemens Baeumker, who publishes his essay "The Relativity Problem in Modern Philosophy" in the *Philosophisches Jahrbuch* in 1912, and with Josef Sauer, professor for history of art and Christian archeology at the University of Freiburg and publisher of the Catholic *Literarische Rundschau* (Literary Review). In that journal Heidegger's "Recent Investigations into Logic" was published in several installments during the same year.

In a letter to Sauer of March 17, 1912, Heidegger sets out his own research program. Sauer must have read with some astonishment about the young student's intention of cooperating in the "religious and cultural development of our Church: If the whole undertaking is not to become a sterile exercise in fault-finding, a scholastic exposure of contradictions, then the problem of time and space must at least be brought close to a preliminary solution by applying to it the principles of mathematical physics."[3]

How the Church might be helped by an orientation toward the time problem of modern physics probably remained a bit of a mystery to the philosophically rather uninformed Josef Sauer; nevertheless he was pleased with Heidegger, whose articles on logic had aroused considerable attention in Catholic circles. Heidegger learned about this from Laslowski, who on January 20, 1913, wrote to him: "My dear fellow, I have the feeling that you are destined to become one of the truly great, and the universities will be falling over each other to get you. Anything less would be inadmissible." Of course, Laslowski pointed out, "Catholicism doesn't fit in at all with the whole modern philosophical system."[4] He should not allow himself to be pigeonholed and shoved into the Catholic category. He should publish also in nonconfessional journals.

The difficulties of this balancing act—keeping the favor of the Catholic environment without becoming labeled a Catholic philosopher—are discussed at length in the correspondence of the two friends. "I suppose you'll have to start out as a Catholic. But this really is a confoundedly vexed question," Laslowski wrote. It would be best to cover himself for the time being. This would, moreover, have a favorable side effect: "You surround yourself with an air of mystery for a time, to arouse people's curiosity. Things will be easier for you after that."[5]

The enterprising Laslowski, probably a little in love with Heidegger, kept his ears open for vacant chairs in Catholic philosophy. On a visit to the Campo Santo Teutonico in Rome, where he meets the *Privatdozent* Engelbert Krebs, a priest and theologian from Freiburg, he promotes his friend. Krebs, Heidegger's senior by eight years, cannot do much for him, as he still has to make a career for himself. But Heidegger immediately gets in touch with him when, in 1914, Krebs returns to Freiburg from his stay in Rome. This develops into an amicable relationship that ends only when Heidegger breaks with the "system of Catholicism."

Laslowski also helps Martin find money. In his Catholic student fraternity in Breslau there is an old alumnus from whom, with the assurance that Heidegger is the great philosophical hope of German Catholics, he extracts a private loan. With that money, plus a small grant administered by the University of Freiburg, plus the income from some private tutoring, Heidegger manages to cope during the year following the termination of his theological studies. In the summer of 1913 he receives his doctorate of philosophy with the thesis, "The Theory of Propositions in Psychologism."

In his thesis Heidegger proves himself to be a diligent and attentive disciple of Husserl, whose "Logical Investigations" have had a marked effect on him. With Husserl he argues against the representatives of psychologism—that is, against the attempt to explain logic through psychology. Highly esteemed philosophers, such as Theodor Lipps and Wilhelm Wundt, are critically examined by the self-assured young scholar. This discussion of psychologism compels him, for the first time, to reflect on the great problem that is later his main concern—time.

Thought as a psychic act occurs in time; it requires time. "The logical content of thought, however," Heidegger claims, "is valid regardless of time. The logical is a 'static' phenomenon, standing beyond any development and change, something that does not become, or arise, but is valid; something that can at most be 'grasped' by the judging subject, but is not altered by that grasping" (FS, 120). As yet, time for Heidegger has not become that force of Being that draws everything into its motion; as yet there is a "beyond it." But what, Heidegger asks, is the "meaning" of this logic? "Perhaps we stand here before something ultimate, irreducible, of which any further elucidation is impossible, and about which any further question inevitably reaches deadlock" (FS, 112).

Static logic is bound to get into a state of tension with a dynamic reality, one that unrolls in time. Heidegger examines this in the example of a problem that is significant for his later philosophy—the question of the "Nothing." He examines negation in the act of statement. We can say, "The rose is not yellow" or "The teacher is not here." This "not" therefore means only that a certain something that we expect or to which we refer is not present. Lacking is the yellow of the rose or the presence of the teacher. From this lack, this "not," we can then abstract a "nothing"—but only as a thought-thing. Such a "nothing" therefore exists only in the act of statement, but not in reality. What applies here is "If something does not exist, then I cannot say: it exists" (FS, 125).

In his 1929 lecture "What Is Metaphysics?" Heidegger will place the origin of all metaphysics, including his own, in the experience of the Nothing. "The *Nothing* is more primordial than the *No* and negation," it erupts in "deep boredom, in the abysses of existence" (WM, 29). He will describe this Nothing as a Something that places the whole world of the Being into a questionable, and also alarming, mysterious state.

Although young Heidegger undoubtedly knows this mood, he does not yet include it in his philosophy; he is still the young academic who hopes to become someone and who therefore remains on academic ground. As yet he holds to the principle that the Nothing is found only in statement but not in reality. He does so by using arguments that the logical positivist Rudolf Carnap will later use against him and his philosophy of the Nothing.

But as young Heidegger, unlike Carnap, is a logician for metaphysical reasons, the discovery that the Nothing is found only in our statements—that is, only in our mind—will not prevent the ontological career of the Nothing, because whatever is in our mind is, ipso facto, an aspect of the great Being. Through us negation, the Nothing, comes into the world. Thus the modest semantics of negation grow into the impressive ontology of Being and Nothing. And this Nothing is no longer the cool "Not" of statement; it is a Nothing of angst. However, this mood does not yet find expression in Heidegger's philosophical attempts of 1912. He still treats the alarming aspects of reality in a rather cavalier fashion, for instance in the discussion of "impersonal statement" inherent in subjectless sentences: "We say, 'It lightens.' Who lightens? Am I trying to formulate a quality, a momentary state, of some mysterious 'it,' or has the statement a different meaning altogether?" (FS, 126). Who or what is this *It* that lightens here? Before getting too profound, as later on such occasions, Heidegger chooses the example of "It thunders." He writes: "If, for instance, in an army exercise, I hasten with a friend behind a rapidly advancing battery, which has gone into firing position, and, at the moment when we hear the thunder of the guns, say, 'Hurry up, it's thundering already,' then it is entirely certain what is thundering; the meaning of the statement lies in the thundering, in what is now (already) happening" (FS, 127).

Heidegger examines the "impersonal statement" because he wishes to demonstrate that, in certain conditions, neither "psychological investigation" nor the "unambiguous determination and clarification of the meaning of the words" brings out the content of a statement, but that it is necessary to know and understand the context of the action situation. A few years later Heidegger will make this same pragmatism of everyday life the arena for his existential question. For the time being he comes up against it once—in the thundering. We are on the eve of war. For a brief moment, in the example of the military exercise, the so-called world of life bursts into the strictly hermetical analyses.

On July 23, 1913, Heidegger passes his doctoral exam before the philosophical faculty with the overall grade of summa cum laude. His supervisor is Professor Arthur Schneider, holder of the Chair of Catholic Philosophy, who that summer accepts a call to the Reich University of Strasbourg. In Professor Heinrich Finke, a Catholic historian with a great reputation and with influence in the department, Heidegger finds a patron who raises the twenty-four-year-old's hopes of Schneider's now-vacant chair. Meanwhile the theological *Privatdozent* Engelbert Krebs is holding the chair on an acting basis and similarly hopes to be appointed to it. Krebs and Heidegger, who have an amicable relationship, become rivals. On November 14, 1913, Krebs records in his diary: "This evening between five and six he [meaning Heidegger] came to see me and told me how Finke had urged him to do his thesis on some aspect of the history of philosophy, and that Finke had clearly given him to understand that as long as the chair remained vacant Heidegger should seek to qualify as a lecturer as soon as possible, thereby making himself available as a candidate. So it may be that in my present caretaker role I am simply keeping the chair warm for Heidegger."[6]

For the time being the rivalry does not impair their friendship. After his first visit to Heidegger Krebs records: "An acute mind, modest but assured in his demeanor."[7] He is so impressed by their conversations that he is prepared, without envy, to accept Heidegger as the worthier successor to Schneider's chair. "A pity," he notes in his diary toward the end of 1913, "he was not this far on two years ago. We could do with him now."[8]

Krebs and Heidegger help each other with their scholarly work. Krebs has to give lectures on logic, about which he knows little. Heidegger prepares his lessons with him. "He helps me more than perhaps he himself realizes,"[9] writes Krebs, who in turn helps Heidegger with his knowledge of the history of scholasticism.

Heidegger had chosen the subject of his habilitation thesis from this area. Originally he had hoped to continue his logical research and work on the "Nature of the Number Concept," but as he now has hopes of a Catholic chair he turns to scholasticism. Besides, a scholarship he successfully applied for in 1913 stipulates that he work on such subjects. This is a well-endowed grant from the Foundation in Honor of St. Thomas Aquinas, established by the Schätzler family of Augsburg industrialists.

On August 2, 1913, in applying for this grant to the Freiburg Cathedral Chapter, Heidegger had written: "The obedient undersigned makes bold to submit a humble request to the Reverend Cathedral Chapter . . . for the award of a grant. The obedient undersigned intends to devote himself to the study of Christian philosophy, and to embark on an academic career. Since the writer lives in very modest circumstances he would be deeply obliged to the Reverend Cathedral Chapter . . ."[10] And so on. Such humbling letters leave a sting in those who write them, or have to write them. It is hard to forgive those to whom one has had to come as a supplicant. Despite, or perhaps because of, the fact that the reverend gentlemen supported him, he will not speak of them kindly in future. The church of the common people in Messkirch was something different. That was home, there he felt he belonged all his life. Whenever he was in Messkirch he would attend divine services at St. Martin's Church up into his old age, seating himself in the choir stalls where he had sat as a boy bell ringer.

As Heidegger was then still regarded as a highly promising Catholic philosopher, the Cathedral Chapter granted him a scholarship of 1,000 reichsmarks per semester—an amount that a student could live on comfortably. In his letter of grant, the suffragan bishop Julius Knecht expressly recalled the purpose of the foundation: "Trusting that you will remain true to the spirit of Thomist philosophy, we are pleased to award you a grant."[11]

For three years, until the summer of 1916, Heidegger receives the grant; for three years he is tied to Thomism and scholasticism in a manner in which duty and inclination are not always easily distinguishable—not even to himself. In his third application for the grant in December 1915 Heidegger writes: "The obedient undersigned ventures to think that he can show something at least of his lasting gratitude for the valued trust placed in him by the Reverend Cathedral Chapter by dedicating his scholarly lifework to the task of harnessing the intellectual and spiritual potential of scholasticism to the future struggle for the Christian-Catholic ideal."[12]

Heidegger's philosophical ambitions are still surprisingly modest. In *Lebenslauf* he describes the interpretation of the medieval thinkers as his future "life's work." Admittedly he intends to use the ideas discovered there for topical argument, for the "struggle for the Christian-Catholic ideal." Nevertheless there is nothing in his philosophical essays that suggests that a world war has meanwhile begun or that hundreds of thousands have meanwhile died on the battlefields while the philosophy of life triumphs.

After the materialism and mechanism of the late nineteenth century, against which Husserl's and hence also Heidegger's early philosophy of logic had been aimed, one would expect *Lebensphilosophie* (life philosophy) in its many variants to have become the great challenge to Heidegger. But only the term "liquefaction" suggests that he has made contact with life-philosophy themes. Liquefaction was a life-philosophy obsession of the age.

A few years previously, life philosophy had still been something for "sensitive modern souls"—therefore not for Heidegger. In an article for *Der Akademiker* in 1911 he had written: "Philosophy, in truth a mirror of eternity, today only reflects subjective opinions, personal views and wishes. Anti-intellectualism allows philosophy to become no more than 'inner experience'; one has turned it into impressionism . . . Today, world views are cut out of 'life,' rather than the other way around."[13] This strong reservation against life philosophy did not, in Heidegger, stem only from his Catholic "transcendental value of life," but came also from the school of the neo-Kantian Heinrich Rickert, under whose supervision Heidegger intended to write his habilitation thesis. And Rickert, whom Heidegger followed in this respect, later summed up his judgment on life philosophy in these words: "As researchers we have to master and consolidate life in conceptual terms, and must therefore advance from mere live fidgeting to a systematic world order."[14]

Lebensphilosophie, though opposed at the time by academic philosophers and hence also by young Martin Heidegger, had become the dominant intellectual current outside the universities. "Life" had become a central concept, much as Being, nature, God, and ego had earlier on, a battle concept facing two fronts. On the one hand, it was directed against the new "as if" idealism cultivated not only by the neo-Kantians in the German universities but also by middle-class moral conventions. Life stood against the laboriously deduced, or perhaps just thoughtlessly handed-down, eternal values. On the other hand, the slogan of Life was directed against a soulless materialism, the legacy of the late nineteenth century. Admittedly, neo-Kantian idealism had been an answer to materialism and positivism, but—so *Lebensphilosophie* claimed—a feeble one. One renders a poor service to the spirit if one dualistically separates it from material life, for that way it cannot be defended. Instead, the spirit has to be carried into material life itself.

For the life philosophers, the life concept becomes so elastic that everything fits into it—soul, spirit, nature, Being, dynamism, creativity. Life philosophy replays the Sturm und Drang protest against the rationalism of the eighteenth century. Then "Nature" had been the battle cry. Now the life concept has the same function. Life is a wealth of shapes, a treasure-house of invention, and an ocean of possibilities, so infinite and adventurous we no longer need any "beyond." There is enough of it in this world. Life is departure for distant shores and, at the same time, something quite close, one's own shape-demanding vitality. Life becomes the slogan of the youth movement, of the neoromantic movement, and of pedagogical reform ideas.

Prior to 1900, bourgeois youth had wished to look old. Youth was a career handicap. Newspapers advertised means to accelerate beard growth; spectacles became a status symbol. Young men copied their fathers by wearing stiff wing collars, and boys of pubertal age were dressed in morning coats and taught to walk with dignity. Life used to be something sobering; young people were to use it to sow their wild oats. Now life has become something elemental and dynamic, as youth itself. Now youth is no longer a blemish to be concealed. On the contrary, old age must now justify itself; it is under suspicion of having died off and rigidified. A whole culture, the Wilhelminian culture, is summoned before the "judgment seat of life" (Wilhelm Dilthey) and confronted with the question: Is this life still alive?

Lebensphilosophie sees itself as a philosophy of life in the sense of a subjective genitive—it philosophizes not about life, but it is life itself that philosophizes. As a philosophy it seeks to be an organ of that life; it strives to enhance it, to open up new shapes and forms for it. It does not wish only to discover which values are valid; it is demanding enough to wish to create new values. Life philosophy is the vitalistic variant of pragmatism. It asks not about the usefulness of knowledge but about its creative potential. For *Lebensphilosophie,* life is richer than any theory; that's why it detests biological reductionism. There the spirit is brought down to the level of life, whereas with *Lebensphilosophie* the spirit is elevated toward life.

The great protagonists of *Lebensphilosophie* before 1914 were Friedrich Nietzsche, Wilhelm Dilthey, Henri Bergson, and Max Scheler. Nietzsche had equated life with creative potency and, in that sense, called it the "will to power." Life wants itself, it wants to create itself. Consciousness stands in an ambivalent relation to this principle of self-creation of what lives. It can act as a factor of inhibition or of enhancement. Consciousness can produce anxieties, moral scruples, and resignation—the élan vital can therefore snap when confronted with consciousness. However, consciousness may also put itself in the service of life—it can perform value definitions that encourage life to free development, to refinement, to sublimation. But whichever way consciousness works, it remains an organ of this life, and for that reason the destinies that consciousness prepares for life are at the same time destinies that life prepares for itself. One time it enhances itself—through consciousness—and another it destroys itself—through consciousness. Whether consciousness acts in the one direction or the other, that is decided not by some unconscious life process, but by conscious will, hence by the freedom of consciousness with regard to life. Nietzsche's life philosophy tears life out of the determinist straitjacket of the late nineteenth century and returns to it its peculiar freedom. It is the freedom of the artist toward his work. "I want to be the poet of my life," Nietzsche proclaims, and it is well known what consequences this had on the concept of truth. There is no truth in the objective sense. Truth is the art of illusion, which turns out to be useful to life. This is Nietzsche's pragmatism; unlike Anglo-Saxon pragmatism it is related to a Dionysian concept of life. Nietzsche detests the Darwinian dogma of adaptation and selection as a law of the evolution of life. To him these are projections of a utilitarian morality. That, to him, is how the philistine visualizes nature, where allegedly even adaptation is rewarded with a career. To Nietzsche, "nature" is Heraclitus's world child at play. Nature shapes its forms and breaks them, a continuous creative process in which the powerful vital element, not the adapted, triumphs. Survival is not yet triumph. Life triumphs only in superabundance, when it squanders itself, when it lets itself go.

Nietzsche's life philosophy is activist and obsessed with art. His *Will to Power* initially achieved its effect as not a political but an aesthetic vision. It once more invested art with powerful self-assurance—which it had lost under the pressure of the scientific ideal, when it had bowed to the dogma of imitation. Those who followed Nietzsche were able to state: If art and reality do not agree with each other—so much the worse for reality!

The major artistic currents at the beginning of the century—symbolism, art nouveau, expressionism—are all inspired by Nietzsche. The aesthetic "will to power" is given a variety of names. In Freud's Vienna, where the unconscious is highly rated, the nervous are the truly vital: "Only when the nervous element is totally unfettered and man, especially the artist, surrenders himself totally to his nerves, without rational or sensual considerations, only then will lost joy return to art" (Hermann Bahr, 1891). The expressionists demand the "rebirth of society from the unification of all artistic means and powers" (Hugo Ball); belief in the "rebirth" of state and society is held also in Stefan George's circle and among the symbolists. Franz Werfel proclaims an "enthronement of the heart." It was the great moment for fantasies of the omnipotence of art and artists. The spirit of *Lebensphilosophie* once more liberated the arts from service to the reality principle. Once more the arts had confidence in the visions by which they protest reality in the conviction that reality will, in consequence, be transformed. Vision, protest, transformation—this was the holy trinity of expressionism.

While Nietzsche's life philosophy was concerned with unbridled life, Dilthey's centered on experiencing life. Dilthey was not interested in biology. He hoped to discover what Man really was through the history of thought—but he found only individual works and formulations, a wealth of points of view in which spiritual life exhibited its riches. Dilthey's life was the universe of books, full of sentences making sense but failing to combine into comprehensive meaning. The life of the spirit produces a wealth of forms, which can assume the appearance of an ossuary unless one succeeds in reviving the spirit that has rigidified into solid shapes, into objective works of culture. This is done through understanding. Understanding is the way in which the spirit experiences the objectivization of another spirit, in which it "liquefies" what has become rigid. Dilthey uses this term and Heidegger takes it over from him when he refers to the "liquefaction" of scholasticism in the struggle for the Catholic ideal. Understanding brings back past life. Understanding is repeating. The possibility of repeating experience is a triumph over the transience of time. But the works that arise within time do not allow their content to be fixed objectively and obligatorily. Every act of understanding is itself tied to its point in time; thus we are continually seized by flowing time, which ceaselessly brings forth something that is always new and always unique—viewpoints, perspectives, visions, ideologies in unceasing sequence. "Where are the means," asks Dilthey, "to overcome the anarchy of convictions that threatens to burst upon us?"[15] Anarchy was something too uncanny for this sensitive German scholar in the period of rapid industrial expansion. That is why he wanted to believe that the life of the spirit also submits to some secret order; he could not tell exactly how, but he certainly hoped that in this garden of humanity he might be the gardener. "Life" to Dilthey had a cozy ring, not a demoniac one, as it had for Nietzsche. "Life is the fundamental fact that must be the starting point of philosophy. It is what is known from within, it is that behind which one cannot go back. Life cannot be brought before the judgment seat of reason."

Nietzsche wants to turn his life into philosophy; Dilthey wants to resuscitate the works of the spirit to new life. The former conducts *Lebensphilosophie* as an existential adventure, the latter as an educational experience.

Nietzsche and Dilthey were of the nineteenth century. The genius of *Lebensphilosophie* in the twentieth century, however, was Henri Bergson. He had embarked on an attempt to develop this life philosophy into a system. His main work, *Creative Evolution,* was published in 1907. It immediately had an unparalleled success among the public. In his *Attempt at a Philosophy of Life (Vom Umsturz der Werte),* Max Scheler wrote: "Bergson's name is ringing through the cultural world with such intrusive loudness that the possessors of more delicate ears may well wonder if such a philosophy should really be read." He should be read, Scheler argues, because Bergson's philosophy expresses an entirely new

> attitude of Man to the world and to the soul. This philosophy faces the world with the gesture of an open, upward-pointing hand, of an eye opening freely and wide. This is not the blinking critical glance that Descartes casts upon things, nor Kant's eye from which the beam of the spirit falls upon things, alienated and sovereignly as though from "another" world, piercing them . . . Instead it is washed, down to its spiritual root, by the stream of Being, as a self-evident . . . beneficial element, as the stream of Being itself.[16]

Bergson, similarly to Schopenhauer before him, discovers two sources of cognition of life. One is reason, the other is intuition (what Schopenhauer calls the "inner experience of the will"). Reason is the skill that Kant had analyzed with such precision, and Bergson links up with this. Space, time, causality, extension—these are categories of reason. But now Bergson shifts his perspective—reason is viewed in terms of biological evolution. Thus it appears as a product of that evolution, as an organ for orientation in the control of action in the real world. It has clearly proved its worth and reflects an "ever more flexible adaptation of the living creature to the given conditions of its existence."[17] Reason therefore is a system that filters the thrusting plenitude and variety of Being and Becoming from the viewpoint of practical survival (for Schopenhauer, analogously, reason is an instrument of the will).

Up to this point Bergson is a pragmatic biologist. But now he ventures out on his crucial step—with a simple consideration. Since we can analyze reason within its limits, it means that we have invariably gone beyond it; otherwise we could not discover it in its entirety. There must be an "outside of" its sphere. Bergson's punch line is: this "outside of" is something internal, it is intuition. In intuition, in this internal experience, Being is not an object that we can separate out, but we experience ourselves directly as part of this Being: "Matter and life, which fill this world, are equally within us. We feel within ourselves the forces that operate in all things." Reason serves life in the sense of survival, but intuition brings us closer to the secret of life. Viewing the entirety of the world, life seems an infinite wave that flows freely in intuitive consciousness: "Let us therefore descend into our own inside: we will touch a much deeper point, and a much stronger impulse will drive us back to the surface . . . !"[18]

The miracle of Proust's *Remembrance* is due to this pointing into our own inside, where life reveals itself more mysteriously than elsewhere, stimulating fantasy in the inner experience of time. Outward-directed reason constructs physical time, Newton's measurable and uniform time *(tempus quod aequaliter fluit).* Internal experience—that is, intuition—knows a different time. This is duration *(durée).* That life "lasts" means that our life is in a continuous flux with changing rhythms, compressions, holdups, vortices. Nothing is lost, it is a steady growth, each point is unique because at no point is the preceding past, which impels us forward, identical. This is so because the passing Now is added to the past and therefore changes it. Man moves in time as in a medium, but he also "produces" time by leading his life; that is, he has initiative and spontaneity. He is a beginner creature. The innermost of time experience, according to Bergson, conceals the experience of creative freedom, a freedom that is present in the whole universe as creative potency. The creative freedom of the cosmos finds its self-awareness in the experience of human freedom. Intuition takes us into the heart of the world. "We revolve, we live in the absolute."

In this grand, enchanting, and enchanted manner, with this flight of fancy and promise, did philosophy before 1914 intone the theme of "life." Young Heidegger, however, does not allow himself to be swept along by this wave. He concludes his dissertation of 1913 with a dry and stiff prospect of "pure logic," by means of which one can "approach the problems of cognition theory" and "subdivide the overall sphere of 'Being' into its diverse manners of reality" (FS, 128).

There is no sign yet in Heidegger of that sense of upheaval that Max Scheler expresses in his *Attempt at a Philosophy of Life,* written at about the same time. Before our eyes, Scheler asserts, a "transformation of weltanschauung" is taking place.

> It will be like the first step into a flowering garden by a man kept for years in a dark prison. This prison will be our human environment bounded by a reason directed solely at what can be measured or mechanized, and the civilization of such an environment. And the garden will be God's colorful world that—albeit at a distance—we long to salute and have open up to us. And the prisoner will be European Man of today and yesterday, who, sighing and groaning, strides under the burden of his own mechanisms and who, his eyes turned earthward and heaviness in his limbs, has forgotten his God and his world.[19]

That this atmosphere of life-philosophy upheaval has not yet entirely seized the young Martin Heidegger is the more surprising as many of his later themes and motives are already swirling about out there in the philosophical tumult of his day—a different experience of time, liquefaction of the rigidified spirit, dissolution of the abstract subject of cognition, and art as the locus of truth.

Heidegger's world of yesterday would first have to collapse in the world war. Heidegger would first have to find himself in metaphysical homelessness before, in his own way, he would discover "life," which he would then call "facticity" and "existence."

4

THE OUTBREAK OF WORLD WAR I: HABILITATION, WAR SERVICE, AND MARRIAGE

Having recently obtained his degree of doctor of philosophy, Heidegger works on his habilitation thesis on "Duns Scotus's Doctrine of Categories and Meaning." The Schätzler Grant, on which he can live comfortably for the time being, obliges him to conduct the philosophical defense of the "Church's treasure of truth" in the shape of Thomism. If he moves fast he may have a chance of getting the still-vacant chair of Christian philosophy. Things do not look bad. Then war breaks out.

The enthusiasm that swept Germany at the beginning of the First World War naturally also engulfs the University of Freiburg, where the young students are sent off to active service with festive choirs, flowers, and solemn speeches. Heidegger is enlisted on October 10, 1914, but because of his heart trouble is classified as of "limited fitness" and deferred. He returns to his writing desk, where he engrosses himself in the subtle nominalistic debates of the Middle Ages.

Heidegger probably belonged to that curious species of student that Ludwig Marcuse, who then also was studying philosophy in Freiburg, has described in his autobiography: "Toward the end of July I encountered one of my most respectable seminar colleagues, Helmuth Falkenfeld, on Goethestrasse. He said despairingly, 'Have you heard what's happened?' I said, full of contempt and resignedly, 'I know, Sarajevo.' He said, 'Not that, tomorrow Rickert's seminar is cancelled.' I said, alarmed, 'Is he sick?' He said, 'No, because of the threatening war.' I said, 'What's the seminar got to do with the war?' He shrugged sadly."[1]

This friend regretted the outbreak of the war because it robbed him of the opportunity to present his carefully prepared essay to Rickert. He was enlisted during the very first days of the war and sent to the front. From there he wrote:

> I continue to be all right, even though the battle in which I participated on October 30 nearly deafened my ears with the roar of twenty-four artillery batteries. Nevertheless . . . I still believe that the third Kantian antonomy is more important than this whole world war and that war is to philosophy as sensuality is to reason. I simply do not believe that the events of this material world can, even in the least degree, touch upon our transcendental components, and I will not believe it even if a French shell fragment were to tear into my empirical body. Long live transcendental philosophy.[2]

For the strictly observing neo-Kantians, the rigorously maintained transcendental viewpoint evidently had an anesthetizing effect. The passions that the war aroused and the destinies it prepared for the individual were assigned to the crudely empirical world. The apriority of cognition and of the moral person remained unaffected. This was not to say that the meaning or the justification of the war were questioned, but it did mean that philosophy as strict philosophy simply had nothing explicatory or justificatory to say on the subject. Private opinions and judgments could overbrim with enthusiasm, but philosophy was to preserve its noble countenance. It was to follow its sovereign course without being recruited by the spirit of the age, even if, at the beginning of the war, this spirit set a whole nation in motion. If philosophers, including the strict neo-Kantians, let themselves be swept along, then it was not on the basis of their philosophy but because, at the outbreak of war, they discovered that there could be something more important than this philosophy. Emil Lask, for instance, the young genius of neo-Kantianism—who was killed in action in the second year of the war and to whom Heidegger was to dedicate his habilitation thesis—had observed even before the war that the mills of reason grind the more brilliantly the less life-matter is being ground: in other words, that the philosophical idea can sparkle only where it keeps aloof from the ambiguous substance of life. Lask felt this to be a flaw and, therefore, a few months after the beginning of the war, wrote to his mother from active service: "Finally it's time to leave. I've been terribly impatient with everything in jeopardy, feeling that I was being inactive instead of using absolutely all my available strength when everything is at stake. It's unbearable not to be able to contribute, not even in the smallest way."[3]

Heidegger does not seem to have had any regrets over being excluded, for the time being, from taking part in the war. He did not have to risk his life; he was able to continue working on his habilitation thesis and hence on his personal career. Otherwise he probably shared the general enthusiasm for the war, because this flared up powerfully also in his circle of Catholic friends and his Catholic environment. His patron Heinrich Finke in 1915 founded a Committee for the Defense of German and Catholic Interests in the World War. Events were staged and pamphlets published that invested the war with a religious meaning and that adopted mainly moderate attitudes in the debate on war aims. In this connection, Heidegger's friend Engelbert Krebs published numerous pamphlets, brought out in book form in 1916 under the title *The Secret of Our Strength: Thoughts on the Great War.*

The outbreak of war released a flood of publications. It is thought that a million and a half poems were written then by German authors. Rilke was in good company with his "Hymn to War":

> For the first time I see you arising
> most distant, incredible God of War, known only from hearsay
> . . .
> At last a God. Because often we no longer seized the peaceable one
> the Battle-God suddenly seizes us . . .
> Hail to me that I see men seized.[4]

Those "seized" included the professors. The *Declaration of University Teachers of the German Reich* of October 16, 1914, with its 3,016 signatures, gave voice to the "sense of outrage that Germany's enemies, with England at their head, are trying, allegedly in our favor, to make a distinction between the spirit of German scholarship and what they call Prussian militarism."[5]

The professors will not let themselves be severed from "militarism," nor do they accept it as a *factum brutum;* they wish to make something significant out of it. An unparalleled fever of interpretation seized the "seized": "Indeed, it is precisely the deepest forces of our culture, of our spirit and of our history, which sustain this war and give it its soul (Marcks, 'Where do we stand?')."[6] Thomas Mann, in his *Reflections of a Nonpolitical Man,* speaks of the war as an event in which the individuality of the different nations, their eternal physiognomies,[7] emerge forcefully, so that they can be comprehended only by a "fresco psychology." It was a time of national-identity declarations of exceedingly robust character. Thomas Mann was not the only one to conceive such grand cultural-philosophical typologies for combative purposes. There were plenty of effective confrontations: profound culture against superficial civilization, organized community against mechanical society, heroes against merchants, sentiment against sentimentality, virtue against mercenary calculation.

The philosophers react in different ways. Some continue to pursue their sober academic activities, unperturbed. Ludwig Marcuse has ridiculed these. Others—more particularly the fashionable "life philosophers"—wish to make a specifically philosophical contribution to the war by reinterpreting it as a battle of spirits. For that they mobilize their metaphysical reserves. With overbrimming eloquence Max Scheler celebrates the *Genius of the War*—the title of his great essay of 1915. Scheler maps out an entire anthropology *sub specie belli.* War brings out what is hidden in Man. Scheler remains a gentleman—he does not condemn the enemy powers, he concedes them the right to struggle. He views war as the secret of the self-assertion of cultures, which, just as individuals, are bound to clash as soon as they have attained their own unmistakable forms. At that point they have to enter the fire, where their forms are tempered. War brings confrontation with death and therefore compels the nation and the individual to understand themselves as a whole, admittedly as a whole that can be broken. War is the great analyst—it separates the genuine from the false, it reveals the true substance. War is the *examen rigorosum* of the state, the test in which it has to prove whether it merely administers a society or actually expresses the common will: "The picture of whole, great, extensive Man, of whom peace allowed only a small grayish middle zone to be visible

. . . this picture now stands plastically before us. Only war measures the circumference, the span of human nature; Man becomes aware of his entire greatness, of his entire smallness."[8]

What spiritual substance does war reveal? Some say it is a victory of idealism. For a long while it was stifled by materialism and utilitarian thought; now it breaks through and men are once more prepared to sacrifice themselves for nonmaterial values, for nation, fatherland, honor. That is why Ernst Troeltsch calls the war enthusiasm a return of "faith in the spirit" as it triumphs over the "adoration of money, hesitant skepticism, pleasure seeking, and dull resignation to the laws of nature."[9]

Others regard war as the liberation of a creative force that was in danger of becoming petrified during the long period of peace. They hail the natural power of war; at long last, they say, contact is once more made with the elemental. War, as "the most powerful of all destroyers of culture, is at the same time the most powerful of all bringers of culture," observes Otto von Gierke.[10]

War transforms everything; it will also—Max Scheler hopes—transform philosophy itself. People will no longer be content with "purely formalistic hairsplitting"; there will be a growing hunger for an "independently original view of the world."[11]

In point of fact, however, philosophy does not gain any new "original view" during the war. It lives on its metaphysical assets, which it employs in investing the catastrophic events of the war with "depth" and "significance." The truly political minds, from Max Weber to Carl Schmitt, feel repelled. Max Weber castigates "the talking and writing of the literati,"[12] who mistake their attitudinal acrobatics for political thought. And to Carl Schmitt the metaphysical exaltation of political elements is plain "occasionalism,"[13] an attitude that uses reality only as an occasion for narcissistic production of ideas.

Heidegger keeps aloof from all this. His philosophical élan does not roam through the field of politics. His thinking at this time has the peculiar stamp of philosophy in spite of history.

He had intended, after his thesis, to work on the "Nature of the Number Concept." His patron Heinrich Finke advises him to discuss this set of problems within the area of scholastic philosophy. Heidegger finds a suitable text in which he can examine what fascinates him most about the number concept—the reality of ideality. The title of the text he chooses for examination is *De modis significandi sive Grammatica speculativa* (On the Manners of Signification, or Speculative Grammar). In Heidegger's day this text was attributed to John Duns Scotus (1266–1308). More recently, however, it is believed that the author was Thomas of Erfurt, a philosopher of Duns Scotus's school.

Duns Scotus was the medieval philosopher of the critique of reason. With exceptional acuteness—in the Middle Ages he was nicknamed *doctor subtilis*—he tried to restrict the range of reason in questions of metaphysics. With our reason, he taught, we will not be able to comprehend the true nature of God; and as the world is God's creation and therefore shares in God's impenetrability by reason, the things around us, no matter how excellently we describe and comprehend them in detail, will retain their mysterious nature. This reasoned critique of reason is, with Duns Scotus, in the service of faith. What Kant later said of himself, that with a reasoned critique of reason he had intended to make room for faith, applies also to this master of scholasticism from Scotland. In Kant as in Duns Scotus, this critique has a dual thrust. The presumptions of reason as also the false use of faith are rejected. True faith transcends cognition, but it does not replace it. In other words, we must concede both to faith and to cognition that which is theirs. We must not try to supplant one with the other. Duns Scotus was a moderate nominalist, to whom concepts initially were just names *(nomen)* and not the substance of the thing itself. The thing itself, to the medieval philosopher, is of course primarily God and the world. The nominalists, therefore, proceed from a dualism between thinking and being. They do, however, seek a bridge. This is true especially of the work from the school of Duns Scotus that Heidegger has chosen.

Duns Scotus's fundamental idea was this: thought proceeds in language. Language is a system of symbols. It points to the thing just as the wreath on the tavern sign indicates the wine that can be drunk inside—this is the actual example given by the evidently life-enjoying Duns Scotus (or Thomas of Erfurt). Between thought and thing lies an abyss of difference ("heterogeneity") but there is also common ground ("homogeneity"). The bridge between the two is called analogy. Between our thought and that which is there exists the same relation of analogy as between God and the world. That is the punch line of the whole idea. At this point the vault of great medieval metaphysics again finds solid support. All elements of Being, all the way up to the highest Being, are analogically related to each other. The analogy relation between God and the world means that God cannot simply be identical with the world, because in that case he would be its captive; neither can he be something entirely different, since the world, after all, is his creation. The world points to God as the tavern sign points to wine, and it is obvious that it is not the tavern sign that quenches one's thirst but only the wine itself. The tavern sign may be real, but God and the world are more real. In medieval thought, Heidegger points out in his comment, there is the idea of "degrees of reality" (FS, 202), of levels of intensity. This highly speculative argument then comes up with the question: And on what level of reality is thought itself? Duns Scotus believes that Man, with his thought, is not as close to God as the concept-realists believe—they would almost credit Man with being able to rethink God's thoughts from which the world sprang. Neither is he as far away as the radical nominalists believe; they would let any thought before God drown in the night of *Ignorantia.*

What, then, is Heidegger looking for and what does he find in this cathedral of medieval thought? He looks for the concealed modernity of this thought. He wants to *liquefy* it and straightaway discovers a few subtleties that anticipate Husserl's phenomenological procedure. Thus Duns Scotus already makes the phenomenological distinction between *prima intentio* and *secunda intentio.* The *prima intentio* is the natural attitude, the focusing on the objects of perception and thought. The *secunda intentio* is that peculiar viewing angle when thought looks at itself and its own contents. This is Husserl's distinction between *noesis* (the act of intention) and *noema* (the content of intention)—these will be referred to later.

Heidegger liquefies this medieval philosopher by recruiting him for Husserl. He presents to us a scholasticist who, like Husserl, explores the field of pure consciousness and then, from it, conjures up the structure of the entire world. The thought of thought, this thought watching itself at work, unfolds a universe that cannot be removed from the world simply by declaring that it does not belong to the world. Suffice it that it signifies something. Heidegger: "Duns Scotus teaches the existential freedom of the real of significance" (FS, 243).

Martin Heidegger wanted to philosophize about the nature of number. He can indulge this obsession in the tracks of Duns Scotus, because the "speculative grammar" of the Scotists has drawn an entire ontology from one-ness and the number one.

The text, as well as Heidegger's analysis, begins with the fundamental categories that contain any reality for us. These fundamental categories—Duns Scotus, incidentally, does not place them at the base but, in typically medieval fashion, at the top—are called "transcendentals." They are *ens* (anything that is, generally), *unum* (one), *verum* (what is true), *bonum* (what is good). That something that is—*ens*—exists, where everything begins, is evident. Less self-evident, but, after some reflection, obvious is that the Being can always only appear as *one* Being, as a definite something, as a "one." But this one is one only in contrast to something different *(diversum)*. "The One and the Other," Heidegger states, "is the true origin of thought as possession-taking of an object" (FS, 160). At this origin begins the hairline crack between thought and Being. Is it then, one may ask, a characteristic of the one that it is not the other? No, because everything that is is what it is, and not-being-the-other is not one of its characteristics. This "not" is brought to the things only by comparative thinking. The things, in a manner of speaking, are trapped within themselves, they cannot compare themselves among each other, and therefore they cannot actively differ from one another. They do not differ, but they can be differentiated by our thought. This is a discovery of far-reaching importance. It states, in Heidegger's formulation: "What really exists is individual" (FS, 194). Duns Scotus calls this kind of individuality *haecceitas*, literally translated the "this-now-here-ness" of things. What each time occurs is something unique at its point in space-time.

The discovery is far-reaching because it reveals on an elementary plane that our reason is able, in a reasonable way, to abstract from itself and to distinguish between what the things are by themselves and what our thought does to them. By themselves they are nothing but details between which our reason, comparing, connecting, ordering, moves to and fro. Following Duns Scotus, Heidegger formulates this as follows: we project that which is, consisting as it does of nothing but different details (heterogeneities), into a *homogeneous medium*, where we can compare, comprehend, and indeed also count that which is. The nature of this homogeneity emerges with particular clarity in the sequence of numbers. If I count five apples, then it is not a characteristic of the third apple to be the third, because nothing is changed in the apple itself if I take it out of the row. There exists, therefore, on the one hand, a heterogeneous multiplicity and, on the other, the homogeneous medium of countability. In the multiplicity of what is there is no such thing as number, but—and this is crucial for the analogy relation—it is only that which is, in its multiplicity, that permits counting. Thus the two spheres are interconnected. Between the multiplicity of the individual and its ordering in a string of numbers there simply exists the relation of analogy.

The mystery of analogy, within which one moves even with simple counting, directly leads to the supreme mystery—to God. He stands to the entity of all that is ("the being") in roughly the same relation as the infinite progression of numbers to the countable but (in the literal sense) countless details of the being. The things are as they are, but additionally they are such that they fulfill the ideal meaning-content of our concepts (in this case, the number concept) only by way of analogy. But this means they are infinitely more, and other, than what they represent in the homogeneous medium of strict concepts. From this Heidegger now draws the following conclusion, which is of major importance for his future philosophy. A style of scholarship that orients itself by the ideal of the "univocally" used concept—the concept used in the same meaning—cannot adequately correspond to this "basic structure of real reality" in which "homogeneity and heterogeneity interlace in a peculiar manner" (FS, 199); a more adequate correspondence will be that of "live speech" in the "peculiar mobility of its meaning" (FS, 278). This conclusion will remain crucial for Heidegger in the later developmental phases of his thought. Even though later he will no longer use the analogy concept of scholasticism, he will cling to the conviction that not univocal logic but the spoken language, in its historicity, manifold meaning, and also its poetic form, is the more adequate organ of philosophy.

In the spring of 1915 Heidegger completes his thesis and submits it to Rickert. This lion-maned gentleman was then much in demand in Freiburg, playing the role of a superprofessor, surrounded by a swarm of unpaid assistants. He gave his lectures in the library; the great hall of the university, which he could have easily filled, gave him agoraphobia. His seminars were held in his private villa; admitted was only a hand-picked audience of professors, education-hungry city notabilities, doctors, and *Privatdozenten.* Heidegger was occasionally among this crowd. Rickert loved presenting himself as the principal of a school—like a general staff officer, he tried to influence appointment policy to chairs of philosophy throughout Germany. The field was still small enough for one to have such an overview. To get on his bad side meant a hindrance to a young scholar's career. Of young Heidegger he took no particular notice. To him, Heidegger belonged to the Catholic corner. He accepted his dissertation but had no intention of bothering to read it. He requested Engelbert Krebs, of whose friendship with Heidegger he presumably was unaware, to write an assessment for him. The way this was produced is described by Krebs in his diary: "As I read it, however, I had Heidegger sitting right there beside me, and we discussed all the difficult or problematic passages as we went along."[14] On July 27, 1915, the habilitation procedure concluded with a trial lecture by Heidegger on "The Time Concept in Historical Scholarship." As an epigraph Heidegger chose a sentence by Meister Eckhart, the German mystic of the late thirteenth and early fourteenth century: "Time is that which changes and turns manifold; eternity stays simple."

Heidegger is now a *Privatdozent* and will remain one for several years. To his friend Laslowski he offers as a motto "for university lecturers and aspiring university lecturers" a quotation from Nietzsche's friend Rhode: "There is no morass more calculated to turn even the boldest of pike into a bloated, full-blown, healthy frog than the conceit of the university academic."[15]

Heidegger berates the academic environment because his own ambitions are being disappointed. He had thought he stood a chance of winning the vacant chair in Catholic philosophy. Finke had dropped hints to him along these lines and seen to it that the chair remained vacant up until Heidegger's habilitation. In this he had been supported by Rickert, who was interested in the vacancy so he could remain the local kingmaker.

Krebs had been holding the chair on an acting basis since the winter semester of 1913–14 and after eighteen months was anxious to know if he himself had any hope left—also in view of the then-impending habilitation of his friend Heidegger. In March 1915 he therefore approached the Baden Ministry of Culture in Karlsruhe. He recommended himself and a few other candidates, but not Martin Heidegger. This was not an intrigue; he had informed his colleagues in Freiburg about his action. Heidegger, however, felt hurt and betrayed. Gradually, he wrote to Laslowski, one developed a hard, cool view of all kinds of humanity. Krebs was soon eliminated as a possible candidate, as he was promised a professorship of dogmatics at the Theological Faculty and indeed received it some time later. After the beginning of 1916 an unfavorable situation began to develop for Heidegger. The advertisement to fill the position was so clearly tailored for a historian of medieval scholasticism that Heidegger, who in his Duns Scotus study had proceeded systematically rather than historically, saw his prospects dwindle. Laslowski warns his friend not to exaggerate the modernization of scholasticism: "I wouldn't be giving you such an avuncular piece of advice if you yourself hadn't already hinted, in your last-but-one letter, that certain gentlemen were pricking up their ears. And you know yourself how pathologically hypersensitive theologians are and how highly developed their 'sense of responsibility' when it comes to intriguing against someone they consider 'unsound.' Your critique will come quite early enough for the people concerned."[16] Evidently Heidegger is then, in letters and private conversations, developing a critique of Catholic philosophy that he does not risk uttering publicly.

In the spring of 1916 Heidegger writes a concluding chapter to the printed version of his Duns Scotus essay. It is marked by a new note: not so much critical distance from scholasticism as a new impatience, vehemence, emphasis, and, above all (an until then quite unusual) stress on "life."

We recall that at the end of the main part of his thesis Heidegger referred to "live speech" in the "peculiar mobility of its meaning." Within the few pages of the concluding chapter there are twenty-three references to "life, living spirit, living deed," and the like. He looks back on his investigation and cannot avoid an impression of "a certain deadly emptiness"; he now wants to let "the spiritual unrest, kept down until then" (FS, 341), emerge at last.

In the impatience of his final chapter Heidegger is unjust to himself. He acts as if he had not started on the task he now vehemently demands—to explain logic from "translogical connections." The spirit of medieval metaphysics provides that connection. In the new final chapter, however, this spirit is now vigorously put under the pressure of life philosophy. "For the living spirit," he says, "the theoretical attitude of the mind" is not everything; "a gathering up of the totality of the knowable" is not enough, because what matters is the "breakthrough into true reality and real truth" (FS, 348). Which way is the journey to lead, where is true life to be found? Certainly not in "an attitude to life that is evanescent in content" and "operating on the surface," but in an enhancement of intensity that was made possible in the Middle Ages by the transcendental relation. And by what is this enhancement of intensity to be achieved today?

Heidegger's reference in this connection to the "optics of metaphysics" does not come as a surprise; what is new is the justification of this metaphysics. It rests no longer solely on the "Church's treasure of truth" but stems from the "meaningful and meaning-realizing deed." By this, however, metaphysics is brought down from heaven to earth and becomes the inner logic of historical action. In the final chapter of his Duns Scotus essay Heidegger is in the process of discovering the historical spirit of life. In other words, he discovers Hegel, whom he credits with having developed the "majestic system of a historical weltanschauung" in which "all preceding fundamental philosophical problem-motives" (FS, 353) are resolved.

This forward look to Hegel's historicism at the end of the Duns Scotus essay conceals the fact that hidden in it there is yet another option for Heidegger's further pondering. Heidegger had followed Duns Scotus's way of overcoming the threatening dualism between human spirit and external reality—the miniature edition of the great disparity between God and the world—in the concept of "analogy." This concept combines in thought both the differences between spirit and reality and the unity between the two. Moreover, human spirit is assigned a higher degree of reality, because in the series of realities analogically descending from God, the human spirit is nearest to God. Why? Because the human spirit, an analog of God, itself masters the art of analogy comprehension—that is, it is, up to a point, initiated into the operational secret of creation. Human consciousness therefore still rests in God. In his final chapter Heidegger looks back on that enchantment of an experienced relation with transcendency as on a lost world. There remains historical remembrance. It would be quite something if, with Hegel, one could believe in God in history. This is what Heidegger attempts in his final chapter. But this is not, as suggested above, the only perspective. The other stems from reflection about the peculiar category of *haecceitas.* Heidegger had stayed long enough with this concept, which the nominalists had coined for the miracle of the singularity of the real. Heidegger seems to be mesmerized by this concept: "What really exists is an individual something . . . Everything that really exists is a 'this-now-here.' The form of individuality *(haecceitas)* is destined to provide a primordial determination of real reality" (FS, 195).

Heidegger presents this nominalist idea as an early attempt not only to transfer the numinous into the divine beyond but also to discover it quite close, in the immediate concrete reality. Everything that is is in itself something inexhaustible. We do not exhaust its richness if we think of it as an "object." To really think the "this-now-here" would mean to overcome objectivized thinking. Only then can that which is appear in its full plenitude. Heidegger will later say that "the being"—that which is—that is encountered in this manner, is "present. Presence bursts the confinement of objectness."

Thought that thus leads to the singularity of reality is an alternative to Hegel. For Hegel, "singleness" is a philosophical nothing that demands nothing of thought, something heterogeneous that acquires meaning only when it is transferred into the homogeneous environment of concepts, into general and generalizable contexts.

Heidegger seeks "free mobility" and criticizes scholasticism for its inability "to place itself, with a jerk, above its own work" (FS, 141). But one does not place oneself *above* one's own movement only by embedding oneself, like Hegel, in the historical spirit; one must also overcome any kind of universalism, including historical universalism, and free oneself for the singularity of the real, for *haeccitas.* This comes about when Heidegger, following Husserl's appointment to Freiburg in 1916, seeks an intensive connection with the work of the founder and master of phenomenology, and eventually finds it. In 1915, however, when he was writing the final chapter of his habilitation thesis, Hegel's "system of a historical weltanschauung" was still dominant.

In a letter of farewell written at the end of 1918 to his clerical friend, the theologian Krebs, Heidegger would describe the living historical spirit, which he had come to know in Hegel and then in Dilthey, as the force that had made the "system of Catholicism problematic and unacceptable for me."[17] It is an idea of historicity that is now being viewed in a phenomenological manner. The "transcendental value of life" now becomes settled in that kind of history. The metaphysical vertical begins to tilt toward a historical-phenomenological horizontal.

After his habilitation Heidegger is recruited again by the military authorities. Once more the symptoms of his heart trouble appear. In the autumn of 1915 he is transferred for four weeks to the army hospital in Mühlheim/Baden and then, as a home reserve serviceman, he is assigned to the postal supervision center in Freiburg. The task of that center was postal censorship. Suspect letters, especially correspondence with enemy or neutral countries, were opened. The staff consisted of women enlisted for service and men not fit for garrison duty. Heidegger had not volunteered for this work, but neither did it, in wartime, seem objectionable to him. It was a cushy posting. He kept the job until the beginning of 1918, and it left him enough time for his scholarly work.

On June 23, 1916, came the decision about the chair of Catholic philosophy that had been vacant for a couple of years. It came as a disappointment to Heidegger, who for the past two years had been widely regarded as a front-runner. The commission came down in favor of the Münster professor Joseph Geyser, with an explanation that was humiliating for Heidegger: "The shortage of suitable candidates of lay status (and only lay candidates may be considered) is so acute that after mature consideration the Faculty finds itself able to recommend only one name."[18] Heidegger's name does not even appear on the list; even as an "extraordinary professor," in the event of Geyser's declining the appointment, he is clearly not in the running. All that the university is prepared to offer him is a temporary teaching job.

His friend Laslowski in distant Silesia consoles him: "They're afraid of you. It's all based on purely personal motives. They're simply incapable of making an objective judgement."[19]

Even though Heidegger had been proposed as a "confessionally suitable candidate" at the meetings of the commission, the Catholic faction, which had a decisive say in such appointments, may well by then have regarded him as unreliable. No doubt Heidegger's age was also against him. He had taken his doctorate only three years previously. And surely one could not allow this young man to make such a rapid career at home at a time when his coevals were fighting at the front and many indeed had already lost their lives. The vote therefore went to experience and an age beyond active service—Geyser was Heidegger's senior by twenty years.

Heidegger's hopes of obtaining a professorship at the first attempt were dashed. He would have to wait another seven years.

In the autumn of 1915 Heidegger meets his wife-to-be, Elfride Petri, an economics student at the University of Freiburg. Six months had passed since the breaking off of his engagement to a Strasbourg girl, the daughter of a minor customs official, a young woman who was gravely consumptive. Whether or not this was the reason for the parting we do not know. To Laslowski, however, who was fond of seeing his friend as a Nietzschean superman, the separation was of sublime significance: "I watched you growing day by day, until you had far outgrown the sphere in which 'love' and 'happiness' are able to flourish. I have known for a long time that you will have to tread paths—have to tread them, if you ever want to reach your goals—where 'love' must freeze to death."[20]

Elfride is the daughter of a senior Saxon officer, Protestant, from the north, and emancipated. Economics was then an unusual subject for a woman. She is a follower of Gertrud Bäumer, who was a liberal champion of women's rights and was connected with the Youth Movement. Martin Heidegger and Elfride meet at the university. Along with some friends they spend their semester vacations, just a few days, on the island of Reichenau.

Heidegger's poem "Evening Walk on Reichenau" is a reminiscence of that summer:

Seaward flows a silver radiance
to distant dark shores,
and in the summer-weary evening-moist
gardens, like a subdued word of love,
descends the night.
And between moon-white gables
a last bird's cry is caught
from the ancient tower roof—
and what the bright summer's day brought me
lies heavy with fruit—
from eternities
an enraptured cargo—
in the gray desert
of a great simplicity. (D, 7)

By the time this poem is published, toward the end of 1916, Heidegger and Elfride Petri are engaged, and three months later, in March 1917, they are married.

His friend Laslowski would have preferred him not to come to such a quick decision. He would have liked to retain the image he had made for himself of Heidegger—a wanderer along the peaks of philosophy, penetrating into a sphere where love and happiness, as during Zarathustra's peak wanderings, must "freeze up." Heidegger was to climb out of the human lowlands where people marry and establish families, and Laslowski, who modestly feels that he belongs in the lowlands, would have liked at least to have witnessed Heidegger's conquest of the summits. The sublime and its observer—that was how Laslowski would have characterized his friendship with Heidegger. On January 28, 1917, he writes to him: "My dear Martin: if only I could be with you at this time! I don't know what it is, but I cannot feel entirely happy about what Fräulein Petri told me in her letter. It would be wonderful if I were proved wrong. But I beg you to be careful! Wait until we are together again. I'm really very worried for you, particularly in a matter of such enormous importance as this. You understand my meaning when I ask you not to make a hasty decision."[21]

Martin Heidegger is not disconcerted by his friend's misgivings. He overcomes other misgivings too. For his pious parents in Messkirch it must have been a heavy blow to see Martin break off his preparations for a career in the priesthood and as a theologian and, to top it all, enter into a mixed marriage. And the Petris no doubt will have turned up their noses at this man from humble circumstances, who might be talented but so far had not found a professional livelihood. Would he be able to support a family? In the manner expected in senior-officer circles?

There was no great wedding. The *Privatdozent* Martin Heidegger and the economics student Elfride Petri were married very quietly in the university chapel of the Minster. No parents were present. At Heidegger's request the ceremony was performed by Engelbert Krebs, who recorded: "Wartime marriage service without organ, bridal dress, wreaths or veils, coaches and horses, wedding breakfast or guests; conducted with the blessing of both sets of parents (conveyed by letter), but in their absence."[22]

Krebs had gained the impression, in conversations with Elfride, that she was considering conversion to the Catholic faith. But this does not happen. Eighteen months later, when their first son is born, Elfride and Martin declare that they will be unable to fulfill the obligation, undertaken at their marriage, to bring up their children in the Catholic faith.

Husserl at the time believed that Heidegger had become a Protestant. In a letter to Rudolf Otto at the beginning of 1919 he writes that he "had no influence whatsoever on the decision of Heidegger . . . to convert to Protestantism," even though he was "bound to welcome" Heidegger as a "free Christian" and an "undogmatic Protestant."[23] This is how Husserl characterized young Martin Heidegger, whom by then he regarded as his most gifted pupil and whom he was treating almost as an equal partner in the great philosophical project of phenomenology.

5

THE TRIUMPH OF PHENOMENOLOGY: HUSSERL AND HEIDEGGER, FATHER AND SON

When Edmund Husserl came to Freiburg in 1916, the fame of phenomenology had not yet spread beyond the confines of philosophers working in the field. Yet a few years later, during the first postwar years, this specialized subject turned into what was almost an ideological hope. Hans-Georg Gadamer reports that, at the beginning of the 1920s, when "slogans about the decline of the West [were] omnipresent,"[1] the subject of phenomenology was included, alongside the teachings of Max Weber, Karl Marx, and Kierkegaard, among the countless suggestions put forward at a "Discussion among World Improvers." Within a few years, therefore, phenomenology had become a rumor of promise, one that induced Gadamer, like so many others, to go to Freiburg to sit at the feet of the phenomenological master and his sorcerer's apprentice. Phenomenology had the aura of a new dawn, which made it popular at a time when moods fluctuated between the extremes of doomsday despair and the euphoria of a new beginning.

Prior to 1916 the bastions of phenomenology had been Göttingen, where Husserl had taught between 1901 and 1915, and Munich, where a center independent of the "Göttingen crowd" had formed around Max Scheler and Alexander Pfänder. Phenomenology aspired to be more than just a school; it therefore called itself a movement. It aimed not only at the restoration of strict scholarship in philosophy—this was the semi-official self-description of the phenomenologists—but also at a reform of life altogether under the aegis of intellectual honesty. False bombast, ideological self-deception, indiscipline in thinking and feeling—all of these were to be overcome. Hedwig Conrad-Martius, who was part of it from the start, formulated the spirit of the Göttingen phenomenologists' circle as follows: "It was the ethos of professional purity and probity . . . Naturally, this was bound to rub off on a person's attitude, character, and way of life."[2] What the Stefan George circle was to the world of the arts—Stefan George (1868–1933), the leading poet of his day, had a close circle of followers—that, in the world of philosophy, was the new phenomenological movement. Both circles called for severity, discipline, and purity.

"Toward the things!" was the motto of the phenomenologists. But what was "the thing"? It certainly was regarded as hidden and lost in the tangle of prejudices, grand words, and ideological constructs. It was a similar impulse to that which Hugo von Hofmannsthal at the beginning of the century expressed in his famous *Letter.* "I have," Hofmannsthal has his Lord Chandos write, "totally lost the ability to reflect or speak coherently about anything . . . the abstract words that the tongue must inevitably use in order to utter any statement, have crumbled in my mouth like moldy fungi."[3] What has deprived him of speech is the mute, inexhaustible, oppressive, but also intoxicating, evidence of the things that offer themselves as though for the first time. To open themselves thus to evidence, that was also what the phenomenologists wanted; their great ambition was to disregard anything that had until then been thought or said about consciousness or the world. They were on the lookout for a new way of letting the things approach them, without covering them up with what they already knew. Reality should be given an opportunity to "show" itself. That which showed itself, and the way it showed itself, was called "the phenomenon" by the phenomenologists.

The phenomenologists shared with Hofmannsthal the conviction that the real alphabet of perception had first to be relearned. To begin with, everything that had been said before had to be forgotten and the language of reality rediscovered. To the early phenomenologists, however, it was consciousness that had to be acquired first of all, and only through it also external truth.

The phenomenologists were moderate in an immoderate manner by accusing the philosophers around them of constructing their systems without foundations. Consciousness, they argued, had not yet been anything like adequately investigated; it was an unexplored continent. People were beginning to explore the unconscious, though they were not even yet familiar with the conscious.

Husserl was the initiator of the movement. He urged his disciples to be thorough: "One must not feel too superior to work on the foundations," he used to say.[4] The disciples should regard it as an honor to be laborers in the "vineyard of the Lord"—though it was not quite clear which lord was actually meant. If one considers the spirit of humility and ascesis, of probity and purity, sometimes called "chastity" by the phenomenologists, one will not think it accidental that some of the phenomenologists later turned very pious. The most prominent example is Edith Stein, since beatified. She "served"—her own term—phenomenology during the early Göttingen years prior to 1914; from 1916 to 1918 she was Husserl's private assistant in Freiburg; in the 1920s she converted to Catholicism; eventually she joined a convent, from whence the Nazis snatched her and, because she was Jewish, murdered her in Auschwitz.

Phenomenology, according to Adolf Reinach, one of Husserl's disciples, was a project "that requires the work of centuries for its completion."[5] When Husserl died in 1938, he left a collection of 40,000 unpublished manuscript pages. By comparison the work published in his lifetime seems almost modest in volume. Subsequent to his *Logical Investigations* of 1901, two books established his fame and made his philosophy victorious: *Philosophy as a Strict Science* (1910) and the first volume, the only one to appear in his lifetime, of *Ideas Pertaining to a Pure Phenomenology and to a Phenomenological Philosophy* (1913).

In his bold dreams, which he confided in his diary, Husserl had imagined that the future of philosophy would be an organic continuation of what he had begun. Time and again he described himself as a "beginner." He was also a perpetual beginner in regard to his own work. If he was to prepare a recently written manuscript for publication, he would start to rewrite the whole text, to the despair of his assistants, who had to help him with it. With his own thoughts, too, he would forever start afresh; he found it difficult to accept as valid what he had written earlier. Consciousness, especially his own, was to him a river into which, as is known, one cannot ever step twice at the same point. This attitude gave rise in him to a veritable publication phobia. Other philosophers who did not have this difficulty—such as Max Scheler, who evidently found it easy to prepare three books simultaneously for publication—were suspect to him. He occasionally spoke of Scheler with disrespect, even though he acknowledged his genius: "One's got to have ideas, but one mustn't publish them," Husserl was fond of saying.[6] Scheler, who had his best ideas in conversation and, if he had no paper handy, would jot them down on his starched cuffs, would not and could not keep anything to himself. Husserl, on the other hand, brooded over his work until it grew into that gigantic collection of manuscripts that a Franciscan monk, in an adventurous operation, saved from the Nazis in 1938 by smuggling it to Belgium, where it is kept to this day in a specially established research institute.

Husserl, born in Moravia in 1859, grew up in the settled circumstances of the Jewish middle class in the Austro-Hungarian monarchy at a time when a "feeling of security was the most eagerly sought-after possession . . . the common ideal of life" (Stefan Zweig).[7]

He had studied mathematics because that science seemed to him reliable and exact. He had then discovered that mathematics, too, required a foundation. The fundamental, the reliable, the basic—that was his passion. Thus he came to philosophy, but not, as he writes in his autobiography, to "traditional philosophy," in which he saw "lack of clarity everywhere, unripe vagueness, halfheartedness, if not indeed intellectual dishonesty—nothing that one can accept or acknowledge as a piece, as the beginning of serious science."[8]

Where was one to start if one wanted to explore consciousness? His principle of starting, which he continually impressed on his pupils, was this: all theories about consciousness, all preconceived ideas and explanations, have to be set aside, so that we may observe, with the greatest possible impartiality and immediacy, what is taking place in consciousness, in my consciousness here and now. We see the sun rising. No amount of science has succeeded in weaning us from referring to the "rising of the sun." Worse still: we see the sun rising every day, yet we know that this is not what in fact happens. It merely appears to do so. Reality is different. This appearance-reality pattern enables us to blow our whole familiar world sky-high—nothing is what it is, it merely appears to be so. What is a fine August day, for instance, in Vienna in 1913? Robert Musil, who was also touched by phenomenology, cunningly describes it as follows: "There was a depression over the Atlantic. It was traveling eastwards, towards an area of high pressure over Russia . . . The isotherms and isotheres were fulfilling their functions."[9]

No August day will ever present itself to experience in the way Musil, mocking science, describes it. Looking out into the air we have never seen nor ever will see anything like isotherms. What we get instead is the summer's day of our lyrical sensations. It is, as Husserl would put it, a "phenomenon" of our world. And it exists even if we know how it comes about meteorologically. Everything that is given to consciousness is a "phenomenon," and consciousness research in Husserl's sense observes, in strict introspection, the internal order of our consciousness phenomena. It does not interpret or explain but tries to describe what the phenomena are "in themselves" and what they reveal. This attention to the consciousness processes themselves at one stroke eliminates the dualism of "being" and "appearing," or, more accurately, we discover that to make such a distinction is simply part of the operation of that consciousness. Consciousness is aware, in a strange way, of what it misses in perception. And because phenomenon is everything that enters consciousness, this invisibility, too, is a phenomenon of consciousness. Essence is not something hidden "behind" the phenomenon; it is itself phenomenon to the extent that we think it or to the extent that we think that it evades us. Even the Kantian "thing in itself," this nonconcept of the nonappearing, is still a phenomenon because it is something that is thought.

Husserl had no intention of reviving the artificial solipsistic doubts of the reality of the external world. On the contrary—he wished to demonstrate that the entire external world is already present within us, that we are not an empty vessel into which the external world is poured, but that we are invariably "relating" to something. Consciousness is always consciousness of something. The fact that consciousness is not "inside" but "outside," alongside what it is conscious of—that is observed as soon as one finally begins to raise consciousness to the level of consciousness. That is what phenomenology is.

For the purpose of this self-elucidation, Husserl develops a certain technique—"phenomenological reduction." Phenomenological reduction is a manner of performing a perception, or generally a conscious process, in such a way that attention is focused not on what is being perceived but on the process of perception. For reasons of methodology, one "steps out" of a perception, but not entirely, only far enough to get the performance into one's field of vision. I see a tree. If I perceive my perceiving the tree, I notice that I furnish the perceived tree with the label "real." But if I only imagine a certain tree, or recall it—what do I see then? Do I see recollections, ideas? No, I see trees, but this time trees furnished with the label "imagination" or "recollection." Just as there are many trees, so there are many kinds of being. Trees seen here and now, trees remembered, trees imagined. The same tree that at one time I regard with pleasure because it gives me shade, and another time from the viewpoint of the economic advantage of cutting it down, is not the same tree in these perceptions. Its being has changed, and if I examine it in what is called an "objective" and purely factual manner, then this too is only one of many means of letting the tree "be." Phenomenological reduction therefore brackets out the question of what the tree is "in reality" and examines only the different ways in which, and as what, it presents itself to consciousness, or, more accurately, how consciousness stays with it.

The exercise of phenomenological reduction includes what is called "natural" perception and excludes "external" reality; a whole world is lost but only, as Husserl puts it in his *Cartesian Meditations,* in order to "regain it by universal self-examination."[10]

Phenomenological reduction is the all-decisive aspect of phenomenology. It represents definite attention to the processes in our consciousness, also termed "phenomenological seeing," an attention that helps us discover to what extent the life of consciousness has latitude or "play" with regard to so-called external reality. But is it not empty play that is left when only the natural relation to reality is bracketed in? This is what Husserl says:

> This universal invalidation . . . of all attitudes to the given objective world . . . does not therefore confront us with a Nothing. What we instead acquire, or, more clearly, what I, as a meditating person, acquire as a result is my pure life with all its experiences and all its pure meaning-units, the universe of phenomena in the meaning of phenomenology. The "epoche" [invalidation of the natural relation to reality] is—to put it another way—the radical and universal method by which I understand myself as a pure Ego, and with my own pure consciousness-life, in which and through which the entire objective world exists for me, and in the way that it does exist for me.[11]

It is tempting to picture "pure consciousness" as an empty consciousness—an empty mirror or an empty stomach. But this would be a mere "pre-assumption" about consciousness, one that could not stand up to the real self-experience of consciousness. Because one discovers at this point that consciousness is at no moment severed from Being. There is no empty consciousness confronting objects with which it would fill its emptiness. Consciousness is always consciousness of something. Consciousness methodically "purged" of external reality cannot cease imagining an external reality—the external world of the internal world. Consciousness has no "within"; it is the "outside" of itself. If one buries oneself deep enough in consciousness, one unexpectedly finds oneself back with the objects outside, one is hurled out to them, as Jean-Paul Sartre put it in the early 1930s, when Husserl's writings had become an experience of conversion for him. He felt liberated from the paralyzing tradition of "digestion philosophy," which regarded consciousness as the stomach of the world.

For Husserl, therefore, consciousness is always "directed toward something." This basic structure of consciousness he calls "intention."

The different kinds of consciousness processes are matched by different kinds of intentions. To want to grasp something in distancing intention is only one of the possible forms of intentional consciousness. Alongside this intention, which is often erroneously identified with the entire consciousness phenomenon, there are many other forms of intention, that is, forms of being directed toward something. And it is not the case that an object is first grasped, as it were, "neutrally," so as subsequently, by an additional action, to become "wanted," "feared," "loved," "desired," "assessed." Wanting, assessing, loving—each of these has its entirely own object relation; in each of these actions the "object" is present quite differently. The same object is a different one for consciousness according to whether I grasp it with curiosity, with hope, with fear, with a practical or a theoretical intent. Love—Husserl elucidates this idea—will "constitute" its object as a "nonobject."

It is the achievement of phenomenology to have shown how subtly and variedly our consciousness in fact works, and how primitive and crude are the concepts by which consciousness endeavors to "become conscious" of its own operation. As a rule, it is the scheme in which a subjective internal space is confronted with an objective outer space, and when it is asked how these artificially separated spheres can be brought together again, how the world gets into the subject and the subject gets to the world. Phenomenology shows that our perceptions and thoughts operate differently from what we commonly think. It shows that consciousness is a phenomenon of the "in between," as the French phenomenologist Maurice Merleau-Ponty has called it—neither subject nor object in the traditional sense. Thought and perception are, to begin with, processes in a stream of consciousness of nothing but self-oblivious actions. Only an elementary reflection, therefore, the consciousness of consciousness, separates and discovers—here an Ego, a subject, as the owner of his consciousness, and over there the objects. Another formulation would be that consciousness, initially, is entirely what it is consciousness of, the will disappears in the willed, thinking in thought, perception in the perceived.

Husserl has opened a door, and an immense field opens before him—the world of consciousness. It is of such diversity and spontaneity that a faithful phenomenological description is bound to conflict with Husserl's intentions, which are guided by a systematic approach and acknowledgment of natural laws. The incomplete and uncompletable gigantic work left by Husserl conveys the impression that, despite its scientific and systematizing intent, it has itself become a reflection of that stream of consciousness that it was designed to describe. The fragments of system carried along by that stream suggest an episode from Stanislaw Lem's philosophical science-fiction novel *Solaris.* In the novel, researchers have discovered a planet that consists entirely of brain. A single oceanic plasma mass. This solitary brain drifting in the universe is evidently working. On its surface it grows huge shapes, waves and fountains, it forms vortices and abysses, an unparalleled multitude of shapes. The researchers take these processes as symbols and attempt to read them. Vast libraries come into being, systematic descriptions, names, and concepts are invented, until eventually the researchers realize—a terrible realization for an orderly mind—that the events at any point in this cerebral ocean are unrepeatable and incomparable, and that it is pointless to give them names because they will never again happen in the same way and there will be no other opportunity to identify them. All categorization patterns of cognition are drawings in the sand, wiped out by the next wave.

Husserl was a man of the nineteenth century, a respect-commanding, professorially paternal type of scholar who sought the ultimate foundations and certainties, even certainty about God. He hoped, he said at the beginning of his philosophical career, "to find the way to God and to a truthful life through strict philosophical scholarship."[12]

However, the empirical sciences were not particularly interested in the fundamental studies of this "crazy watchmaker," as the Freiburg students called him, because during his probing monologues he would often turn the middle finger of his right hand to and fro in the hollowed palm of his left. He was so immersed in his own stream of consciousness that he did not even notice that his students were keeping silent; when one of them, the student—and future philosopher—Hans-Georg Gadamer, once voiced some objection, he subsequently told his assistant Martin Heidegger: "Now today we really had a stimulating discussion again."[13] What a person loves becomes the center of his paradise. Thus Husserl could not understand that his students were living in other worlds and were involved in other matters. He once, in all seriousness, said to his personal assistant Edith Stein that she should stay with him until she got married. She should choose a husband from among his students, who might then also become an assistant, and—who knows?—maybe the children would also become phenomenologists . . .

There is some irony in the fact that this "skilled worker on foundations," as he sometimes called himself, in attempting to find firm ground for cognition, should philosophically discover the stream of consciousness, and that he should then make the rather comical effort to transform this infinitely lively and moving element into the foundation, the pedestal, of ultimate certainty and security. His hope is to build a house on a shifting dune, a house that, as he imagines, will endure for generations. Phenomenological consciousness research is a project for a whole century. In his euphoria he says: "Accordingly, it is understandable that phenomenology is, so to speak, the secret nostalgia of all modern philosophy."[14]

But there are also moments of temptation when he questions the sense of the whole enterprise. Does one not always inevitably remain a beginner when one attempts to traverse the vast field of consciousness? Is it not like trying to reach an ever receding horizon?

If, therefore, consciousness cannot be exhaustively described and analyzed, then—Husserl's way out of the impasse—the sack has to be closed at the other end, at the beginning. The name for this mental short circuit is "transcendental ego." It is the quintessence of all performances and operations of consciousness, the headwaters region of the stream of consciousness.

If, as Husserl teaches, ego consciousness develops only secondarily in the perception of perception, how then does one bring a transcendental ego to the beginning of the entire consciousness process? Quite simply by declaring the phenomenological attitude, with which one observes the consciousness process, as the locus of the transcendental ego. "Each 'cogito' with all its component elements arises or vanishes in the flow of experience. But the pure subject does not arise or vanish, although, in its own way, it 'enters' and again 'exits.' It goes into action and it goes out of action again. What it is, and what it is in itself and does, that we grasp, or rather: it grasps us, in self-perception that itself is one of its actions, moreover one that confirms the absolute indubitability of the constitution of being."[15]

Now it is out in the open: Husserl, having performed the trick of describing the consciousness process "before" its splitting into ego and world, and hence as an "egoless" one, now, on the transcendental plane, falls back on the idea he had hoped to overcome, the idea of the ego as the owner of its consciousness contents. The ego, only just deconstructed, once more, as in the Cartesian tradition, becomes the highest authority on certainty. It is this turn toward a transcendental ego, the outlines of which had been noticeable since 1913, that will provoke Heidegger's criticism in future. Husserl understands the transcendental ego as a kind of substance in which the contents may change without it itself changing. The transcendental ego has a suspicious resemblance to the divine spirit, which tradition has always thought of as the unchanging foundation of all world contents. It is not surprising, therefore, that Husserl said about the discovery of the transcendental ego: "If I do so by myself, then I am not the human ego."[16]

Husserl thus again performs a turn toward an ego from which, as with Johann Gottlieb Fichte, a whole world issues. Consciousness ceases to be merely the magical something that occurs in the world and to which a whole world can then appear as a world. Something ontic, whose characteristic it is to be ontological—this is how Heidegger will define this mysterious phenomenon in order to throw it back into the world, from where, with Husserl, it has surreptitiously sneaked out. Husserl's transcendental ego has the world in its head, but this head is no longer properly in the world.

One thing emerges clearly: if one wishes to suspend the rich life of consciousness from a firm point, while avoiding the naturalist or psychologistic reduction, then thought is very easily faced with the temptation of assuming a God-like perspective.

However, a consciousness that wishes to make the rich life of consciousness transparent for itself and acquire it without destroying it need not necessarily soar up to the God of transcendental philosophy; it can also turn poet. Ever since Plato, this has been the secret or uncanny surmise of the philosophers. Nor was it unknown to Husserl. "Philosophy and poetry," he said in conversation with a Japanese colleague, "are related in their innermost origin and have a secret kinship of the soul."[17]

In no philosophy is this "secret kinship" with poetry as marked as in phenomenology. The description of the life of consciousness and hence the experience of the world, attention to the phenomena of internal and external space, of internal and external time—these have always been the themes of the poet, more especially of the one who, in the school of Bergson and in the soundproof premises on the Boulevard Haussmann, indulged in his phenomenological exercises—Marcel Proust. If phenomenology really was the "secret longing of all modern philosophy" (Husserl), then one would have to describe Proust as embodying the secret longing of phenomenological philosophy.

One has only to read the beginning of Proust's *Remembrance of Things Past,* in which the narrator describes his awakening—an unsurpassable phenomenological description of the ego's rebirth every morning, when it has to accomplish a journey through space and time before finding itself again at the intersection of Here and Now.

> But for me it was enough if, in my own bed, my sleep was so heavy as completely to relax my consciousness; for the I lost all sense of the place in which I had gone to sleep, and when I awoke at midnight, not knowing where I was, I could not be sure at first who I was; I had only the most rudimentary sense of existence, such as may lurk and flicker in the depths of an animal's consciousness; I was more destitute of human qualities than the cave-dweller; but then the memory, not yet of the place in which I was, but of various other places where I had lived, and might now very possibly be, would come like a rope let down from heaven to draw me up out of the abyss of not-being, from which I could never have escaped by myself: in a flash I would traverse and surmount centuries of civilization, and out of a half-visualized succession of oil-lamps, followed by shirts with turned-down collars, would put together by degrees the component parts of my ego.[18]

Phenomenological attention to the world of consciousness processes requires an attitude that conflicts with the demands and complications of everyday life, because there we pay attention to objects, people, and ourselves, rather than to how all these are "presented" in our consciousness. This breach with the normal attitude toward the world has always been emphasized by Husserl. And Proust, likewise, was able to unfold the phenomenological universe of his remembrances only in the safe haven of his bedroom, which for the last twelve years of his life became his study. However, Husserl and, to a greater degree, Proust compensate us for this retreat into worldlessness with the discovery of an entire multiple internal ontology. There exists in it an infinitely variously graduated realm of the Being. The objects of remembrance, fear, longing, hope, and thought are as many "realities" spilling over the neat subject-object separations.

To Martin Heidegger, at any rate, whose philosophical initiation experience had been Brentano's book on the "multiple signification of the Being," Husserl's phenomenology is a philosophy that unlocks the multiplicity of the Being.

In his famous Marburg lecture of the summer of 1925, on the subject of the history of the concept of time, Heidegger will in retrospect list the aspects of Husserl's phenomenology that brought him to his own road, and he will point to the boundaries he had to cross in order to advance further. What was crucial was the phenomenological manner of approaching "objects" in an entirely new way—the demand that we "set aside our prejudices, learn to see directly and simply and to abide by what we see without asking out of curiosity what we can do with it." This unbiased matter-of-factness of phenomenology was so difficult because man's "element of existence is the artificial, the mendacious, where he is already cajoled by others" (GA 20, 37).[19]

The intraphilosophically *artificial,* which phenomenology overcomes, includes for Heidegger the stubborn dogma of the two spheres—essence and appearance. Phenomenology, Heidegger argues, has rehabilitated the phenomena, the world of appearances; it has sharpened the mind for that which appears. Appearance as understood by phenomenology is not a lesser, or perhaps even deceptive, reality, behind which the essence, be it metaphysical or scientific, is to be sought. This essence, too, is something that appears—be it God or the "subject" of logic or the so-called laws of nature. Phenomenology to Heidegger is not a speculation, not a mental construct, but the work of "laying open and letting be seen" (GA 20, 118).[20] What was uncovered—and Heidegger calls this the most important discovery of phenomenology—was the intentional structure of consciousness. To Heidegger this means that the traditional cognition-theory subject-object dualism has been overcome, moreover from two sides—by the appearing world and by consciousness that has always been related to the world.

In his 1925 lecture, however, Heidegger also clearly mapped out Husserl's limitations. Husserl, he said, may have, by his rescue of the phenomena, once more sharpened a sense for the different types of encountering Being, but he had never asked the question in what sense Man, or rather intentional consciousness, was something being. Husserl had penetrated only as far as the negative determination that Man was a "counterthrow of Nature." As for Heidegger's answer to the question of what and who Man is, we will come to that later.

During the first years of his intensive collaboration with Husserl, Heidegger is already busy lifting Husserl's ideas out of their consciousness-immanent connections and hurling them into the world. He is helped in this by his study of Dilthey's philosophy of historical life. From Dilthey's perspective, any philosophy is suspect that gets caught up in the self-misunderstanding that it could assure itself of a safe place beyond history. Husserl's construct of a transcendental ego is such a helpless "beyond" of consciousness. Moreover, his study of Kierkegaard helps Heidegger against Husserl's immanence of consciousness.

Kierkegaard's attack on the illusory sovereignty of the spirit proceeds not, as with Dilthey, from historical life, but from the ineradicable difference between thought and existence. Amid the complexities of life, we find ourselves time and again in situations in which we must decide who we wish to be. We leave the sphere of the merely thinkable; we must take a stand, assume responsibility; we cannot avoid turning from a possibility person, who can consider everything, into a reality person, who from the thinkable selects that which binds him in internal and external action. According to the existentialist critique of Kierkegaard, the philosophy of consciousness is the only escape from the risks of life lived.

Historical circumstances themselves will see to it that this power of historical and existential life will remain more than just an idea for Heidegger.

Ever since Husserl had come to Freiburg, Heidegger had been seeking the proximity of the master. But Husserl at first was reserved; to him Heidegger was a Catholic philosopher, which made him less interesting. Heidegger's unsuccessful wooing continued for almost a year before he eventually succeeded in arranging a personal meeting with Husserl. On September 24, 1917, Husserl wrote to him: "I will be glad to assist you in your studies in so far as I am able."[21]

In the winter of 1917–18 Husserl at last "discovered" Heidegger. A short while previously Edith Stein had given up her work as Husserl's personal assistant. She could no longer bear a situation in which, responsible for preparing his manuscripts for the press, this eternal "beginner" would give her ever new drafts and notes that completely overturned what had just been finished. Besides, Husserl had made excessive demands on Stein's services without helping her to realize her wish to become a *Privatdozent.* As Husserl now had to look around for a new collaborator, he became more favorably inclined toward Heidegger's approaches.

Over the last weeks of 1917 there must have been some very intense philosophical conversations between the two men. When Martin Heidegger was enlisted in January 1918 as a home defense recruit and posted for military training to the army training center in Heuberg, near his native Messkirch, Husserl informed him in a personal letter informed him how sadly he was missing their joint philosophizing. Cheerfully, no doubt also flattered, Heidegger replied; he seemed at that moment to draw his self-assurance not so much from philosophy as from the circumstance that he was standing up so well to the tough military training. Husserl, a nationally minded man, approved of such nonphilosophical fitness. It was perhaps not a bad thing, he wrote on March 28, 1918, that Heidegger was obliged to put philosophy aside altogether for the moment. At a later date—"hopefully the war won't last too much longer after the splendid victories in the West"—he would be able to "return with renewed vigor to the difficult problems."[22]

In the meantime Heidegger remains in active service. He is assigned to the frontline meteorological service—just as Jean-Paul Sartre would be at the beginning of World War II twenty years later—and in July 1918 he is sent to a meteorological instruction course in Berlin. The lively correspondence with Husserl continues; its tone becomes even more cordial and confiding. In a letter of September 10, 1918, Husserl commends Heidegger's unspoiled youth, his "clarity of vision, clarity of heart and clear sense of purpose." The letter concludes with the solemn exclamation: "To be young like you! What a joy and a real tonic it is to share in your youth through your letters."[23]

This paternally exuberant note may have something to do with the fact that, having lost his youngest son in the war in the spring of 1916, Husserl in the autumn of 1918 was worried about his second son, who was then in a military hospital with a bullet wound to his brain. Husserl takes up Heidegger as a substitute son. At the time of these letters to Heidegger, Edith Stein is staying in the Husserl home as a nurse and general aide. Malwine and Edmund Husserl are laid low with severe influenza, the maid has handed in her notice, and bad news keeps arriving from the military hospital. In her own letters to Roman Ingarden, Stein describes the depressing domestic atmosphere, in the midst of which his link with Martin Heidegger evidently is a source of succor and encouragement to Husserl. His belief in victory, which he so eloquently professed in the spring, has vanished. Instead, the "system" of imperial Germany is being criticized in the Husserl household. Malwine Husserl, according to Stein, had even, to her husband's chagrin, gone over to the "camp of the 'Independent'"—meaning the Independent Socialist Party (the USPD). There had been terrible marital disputes.[24]

Heidegger meanwhile had been posted to the western front at the end of August, to the weather station near Sedan in the Ardennes. The meteorological service had been set up there to provide weather forecasts for the employment of poison gas in the Marne-Champagne battle. An idea of how Martin Heidegger experienced this situation is provided by his first few letters to Elisabeth Blochmann.

Elisabeth Blochmann was a fellow student of Elfride. During the war she had spent some time in Strasbourg studying philosophy under Simmel, as well as German literature and education; later she worked for a while in the social health service. She had been molded by the spirit of the Youth Movement, as expressed in the 1913 Hohen-Meissner formula: "Free German Youth intends to shape its life on its own responsibility, according to its own decision, and inner truthfulness." It was in these Youth Movement circles that Martin Heidegger had first met Elisabeth Blochmann and his future wife Elfride.

The first few letters clearly breathe the spirit of the Youth Movement that unites both of them. There is a lot of talk about "truthfulness" and "responsibility"; amorous emotions are merely to be surmised. Both of them practice the art of the indirect, the hinted-at. Elisabeth Blochmann, three years younger than Martin Heidegger, admires him, and he in turn feels flattered and enjoys talking to her in the tone of a philosophical mentor and spiritual guide: "It should be our duty to utter to congenial spirits that which in our innermost truth we experience as something alive and urgent" (October 2, 1918, BwHB, 9).

> Spiritual life must again become truly real with us—it must be endowed with a force born of personality, a force that "overturns" and compels genuine rising—and this force is revealed as a genuine one only in simplicity, not in the blasé, decadent, enforced . . . Spiritual life can only be demonstrated and shaped in such a way that those who are to share in it are directly gripped by it in their most personal existence . . . Where belief in the intrinsic value of self-identification is truly alive, there everything that is unworthy in accidental surroundings is overcome from within and forever. (June 15, 1918, BwHB, 7)

Martin Heidegger witnesses the German army's last desperate resistance to the victoriously advancing Allies, realizing with blinding clarity that the "spirit" that imbued the culture of the prewar years no longer has any reality. The war has burned up everything—except for a naked nucleus that Heidegger, with vague grandiloquence, calls the "force of personality or belief in the intrinsic value or belonging to the central ego." This forcible return to the personal core is to him a great opportunity: now what is "unworthy in accidental surroundings" can be overcome—but only if one is strong enough, if one relies on oneself, and if one strips off the false spirit of civilizational comfort. Only then, according to Heidegger, will there be a rebirth of the spirit, initially in the small circle of the "truthful"; later, radiating from it, there will perhaps be a renewal in the breadth and the depth of the nation. On November 7, 1918, still at the front, Heidegger writes to Blochmann:

> What shape life generally will assume after this end, which was bound to come and which now is our only salvation, is uncertain. Certain and unshakable is the challenge to all truly spiritual persons not to weaken at this particular moment but to grasp resolute leadership and to educate the nation toward truthfulness and a genuine valuation of the genuine assets of existence. To me it is indeed a pleasure to be alive—even though some outward deprivation and some renunciation lie ahead—only inwardly impoverished aesthetes and people who until now, as "spiritual" people, have merely played with the spirit the way others play with

> money and pleasure, will now collapse and despair helplessly—hardly any help or useful directives can be expected from them. (BwHB, 12)

It is "a pleasure to be alive," Heidegger writes. He is excited at the thought that a world that "merely played with the spirit" is now collapsing. His political visions remain vague. His letters from the front scarcely contain accounts of what he is experiencing there—"the journey to the front was wonderful" (October 2, 1918, BwHB, 9)—but there are numerous expressions of joyful expectation of a new beginning in philosophy. First of all, he hints, he would have to pull down what is outdated, untruthful, conventional, merely artificial. There is talk of "primordial experiences," including those of a religious nature, that are only buried by philosophy and theology because they are credited with a false continuity and availability.

The reservist soldier Heidegger has discovered a new intensity. It is not war itself, but that which remains when the catastrophe all round burns up everything else. It is not the bath of steel of victory but the great slag removal through defeat. This is his way of believing "in the spirit and its power—he who lives in it and for it never fights a losing battle" (November 6, 1918, BwHB, 10). And later on: "The new life that we desire, or that desires us, has dispensed with being universal, i.e. being false and two-dimensional (superficial)—its asset is originality—not the artificially constructed, but the evident content of total intuition" (May 1, 1919, BwHB, 15).

Great, promising words—but not empty phrases, as the young *Privatdozent,* promoted to corporal in the final weeks of the war, immediately upon his return to Freiburg in November 1918 turns all his energies toward the endeavor to pursue this "total intuition"—to comprehend what seizes him—and to help this intuition, this evidence of moments, to philosophical expression in words, and, above all, to fit it into the continuity of life. In this connection he notices the dynamics of time—it produces the intuition and the evidence of the moment, but it does not preserve them, it does not endow them with duration. It happens, it is nothing "made," but everything depends on what we make of it. In May 1919, in an extensive letter to Blochmann that perhaps most forcefully reveals the intimate philosophical obsessions not only of young Martin Heidegger, he writes:

> It is a rationalist misunderstanding of the nature of the personal flow of life to believe, and demand, that it should vibrate in those same broad

> and sonorous amplitudes which well up at inspired moments. Such demands arise from a lack of inner humility before the mystery and grace of all life. We should be able to wait for high-tension intensities of meaningful life—and we must live in continuity with those moments—not so much enjoying them as fitting them into our lives, taking them along in the passage of life, and including them in the rhythm of all future life.
>
> And at moments when we directly feel ourselves and the direction in which we, as we live, belong, we should not only state, or simply record, the clarification that has come to us—as though it were simply confronting us as an object—but the comprehending possession of one's self is genuine only if it is truly lived, i.e. if it is, at the same time, a Being. (BwHB, May 1, 1919)

In 1919, therefore, Martin Heidegger is "happily" busy developing his intentions. That which is happening around him he calls "the lunatic conditions" (January 14, 1919, BwHB, 12).

6

REVOLUTION IN GERMANY AND THE QUESTION OF BEING

At the beginning of 1919 Max Weber gave a lecture in Munich on the subject of "the inner calling to science." He was speaking in a city that, like all other major cities in Germany, was in a state of revolutionary upheaval. A few weeks later open civil war was to erupt in Bavaria; a Republic of Councils would be proclaimed in which well-meaning writers, such as Ernst Toller and Erich Mühsam, who had hoped to establish the "realm of light, beauty, and reason," would for some time set the tone. To Max Weber all of that was irresponsible emotional politics, pursued by adventurers who refused to accept that politics is overtaxed when it is expected to establish sense and happiness. Karl Löwith, who was sitting in the lecture room at the time, recalls how, in that year before his death, Max Weber "strode through the overcrowded hall to the lectern, looking pale and tired. [His] face, surrounded by an unkempt beard, reminded me of the somber glow of the prophetic figures of Bamberg Cathedral. The impact was stunning. He tore down all veils from desirable objects, yet everyone none the less sensed that the heart of this clear-thinking intellect was profoundly humane. After the innumerable revolutionary speeches by the liberal activists, Weber's words were like a salvation."[1]

This speech, which was immediately published and which triggered a violent and widespread public controversy, contains a sober diagnosis of Weber's times. On the surface it deals with the ethos of the sciences, but basically Weber addresses the question of how the yearning for a meaningful life can still be fulfilled within the steel capsule of modern "rationalized" civilization. His answer is that science, which has, with its technological consequences, fundamentally transformed our daily lives, and which during the war proved the power of destruction inherent in it—this science has become our destiny while at the same time leaving us with the unanswered question of its meaning:

> What is . . . the point of science as a calling when all our former illusions, such as "the path to true Being," "the path to true nature," "the path to the true God," "the path to true happiness," have gone? The simplest answer was given by Tolstoy, when he said: "It is pointless, because it gives no answer to the only question important to us—What are we to do? How should we live?" The fact that it does not supply this answer is simply indisputable. The only question that remains is in what sense does it gives us "no" answer, and whether it might not instead accomplish something for him who asks the right question.[2]

Science can test the appropriateness of its means by applying them to preset purposes that are themselves based on value judgments. It can also analyze inner contradictions to and compatibility with other value judgments. It can therefore make a contribution to self-awareness, but it cannot relieve us of the decision on how to live our lives. Such a release from personal value judgments could be regarded as liberation from any tutelage. Hence the fact that science cannot make any decisions on meaning or value should represent not a problem but an opportunity. But this is not the case, because, Max Weber argues, our civilization has so thoroughly and comprehensively moved into a belief in rationality that it undermines the individual's confidence in his own ability to make decisions. Even with value judgments we would like to have the same objective certainty and guarantee that we are accustomed to in the technological world. If we travel by streetcar we do not need to know how it functions; we can rely on everything's having been correctly "calculated." But if one is surrounded by a world that can be "calculated" in such an infinite number of respects, and if one is accustomed to not understanding everything oneself but knowing that others do understand—for how else could they have produced these technological miracles?—then one will demand certainty and guarantees also where one cannot properly expect them—in the sphere of decisions on meaning and values. Instead of seizing the freedom thereby provided, one calls for the objectivity of science in these spheres too. The result is a boom in ideologies wooing our trust by donning scientific garb. This is the business of what Max Weber calls the "academic prophets" *(Katheder-propheten)*. They react to the lost mystery of a world disenchanted by rationalism by wrongly rationalizing the last magic that is left to it—the individual's personality and its freedom. They do not wish to suffer the tension between rationality and personality, but instead conjure up, from "experience," an interpretation of the world with which one can travel just as reliably as with a streetcar. Instead of leaving mystery where it still exists—in the soul of the individual—the "academic prophets" submerge the disenchanted world into the twilight of deliberate re-enchantment. Against this, Max Weber pleads for unmixing. On the one hand the rational reaching for and seizure of the world, and on the other respect for the mystery of the personality, even if this is at times anxious to strip off the burden of freedom. Max Weber calls for honesty. Facts should be faced, even unpleasant ones—in a world that we can rationally penetrate and technologically manage, God has disappeared. If he still exists, then he does so only in the soul of the individual, who must be prepared "on his own account" to make the "sacrifice of the intellect" and believe in him. Weber was fascinated by living faith in the way one is fascinated by an artist or virtuoso. He called such people "religious virtuosi." Any faith that confuses itself with science or endeavors to compete with its ideas he calls a dangerous deception. Only a faith that makes no fraudulent borrowings from science possesses, in his eyes, dignity and truth in the "transcendental realm of mystical life or in the brotherhood of direct relations among individuals."[3] There could be a breath of "prophetic pneuma," but one should be careful not to let it blow into the political arena.

Max Weber's warnings had no effect. The "academic prophets" reacted angrily. One of them, who was yet to get a chair (and with whom Martin Heidegger would have to deal during the National Socialist revolution), the primary-school master Ernst Krieck, made himself the spokesman of the "right wing" opposition to Weber. He attacked the "pose of objectivity" and the freedom of values. That, he claimed, was a typical symptom of decadence, an expression of "deracinated intellectualism." This was now showing also in the sciences: the nation had lost its soul. Krieck therefore called for "the revolution of science." It should cooperate in the shaping of a "national religion" that would lead the nation to "moral unity"[4] and raise the state above the level of a purely utilitarian machine. Max Weber was barely able to defend himself against the criticism, accusations, and defamation. He died in 1920. In any case, he could not have dealt with all of the prophets, visions, doctrines of salvation, and ideologies that were then springing up.

During the first few years of the Weimar Republic a powerful freelance competition arose to the "academic prophets" denounced by Weber. This was the time of the "saints of inflation," who were eager to save Germany or the world in the streets, in the woods, in market squares, in circus tents, and in the smoke-filled back rooms of bars. Oswald Spengler's *Decline of the West,* which was then selling 600,000 copies, was the grand theoretical design that fragmented into a thousand small splinters, into interpretations of the world in the spirit of "last days" and radical new beginning. Nearly every major town had one or more such "saints." In Karlsruhe there was one who called himself "Primal Vortex" and promised his followers a share in cosmic energy; in Stuttgart a "Son of Man" invited his followers to a redeeming vegetarian Last Supper; in Düsseldorf a new Christ preached the imminent end of the world and called for withdrawal into the Eifel Mountains. In Berlin the great halls were filled by the "spiritual monarch" Ludwig Haeusser, who demanded the "most consistent Jesus ethics" in the sense of original communism, propagated free love, and offered himself as a "führer" as "the only hope of a higher development of the nation, the Reich, and mankind."[5] Nearly all of the numerous prophets and charismatics of those years preached the millennium and the apocalypse; they were aberrations of the revolutionary excitement at the end of the war, decisionists of the renewal of the world, raving metaphysicians, and profiteers in the vanity fair of ideologies and surrogate religions. Anyone anxious to be taken seriously distanced himself from this sleazy scene, but the boundaries were exceedingly fluid. This was true also of the political scene in the narrower sense, where messianism and redemption doctrines flourished on the left and on the right. During the days of the Munich Republic of Councils a manifesto composed by Toller and Mühsam announced the transformation of the world into "a meadow full of flowers," where "everyone" could "pick his share."[6] Exploitation, any kind of hierarchy, and juridical thought were declared abolished, and daily papers were instructed to print on their front pages, alongside the latest revolutionary decrees, poems by Hölderlin or Schiller.

The feverish spirit of those years, regardless of political camp, addressed the giving of meaning to the meaningless. One was not prepared to accept the disenchantment of the modern world either in politics or in science. The spirit of realism and realpolitik (the "Weimar coalition") no longer commanded a majority after 1920, and among the humanities and social sciences Max Weber's call for ideological restraint met with scant response. In 1921 Eduard Spranger summed up the protest against Weber's factualness and disclaimer of metaphysics in these words: "Full of faith . . . the young generation is awaiting an inner rebirth . . . Today, more than ever before, the young adult . . . lives through the fullness of his intellectual and spiritual faculties." There is a "drive toward wholeness" and "a religious yearning: a groping back from artificial and mechanical circumstances to the eternal spring of the metaphysical."[7] Martin Heidegger's first postwar lecture, given in the emergency semester at the beginning of 1919, bears the title "The Idea of Philosophy and the Worldview Problem." The young *Privatdozent* wishes to intervene in the dispute of his day. His preliminary reflections proceed from Max Weber. He stresses the scholarly character of philosophy, "in which—as in any science—the personal attitude of the philosopher should remain excluded" (GA 56/57, 10).

However, Heidegger does not intend to stop at Weber's unmixing of scientific discovery and value judgment; he wishes not only to draw boundary lines but also to address as his problem the very fact that we do make value judgments and form views of the world. Unlike most of Max Weber's critics, he does not propose to reconcile science, value judgment, and worldview, bringing them together in some ultimately metaphysical synthesis. Instead he sets himself the ambitious aim of uncovering an area that lies prior to these differentiations. He asks: How do we experience reality before we arrange it for ourselves in a scientific, or value-judging, or worldview approach? The science of science he calls not a theory of science but "the idea of philosophy as the original science." This sounds as if he intends to continue Husserl's project of phenomenological justification of science; that is, a description of consciousness structures from which stem both science and a natural view of the world. Yet even this first lecture makes it clear that Heidegger is thrusting beyond Husserl. He quotes Husserl's principle—"Anything that presents itself in 'intuition' is original . . . and should be accepted as what it presents itself as" (GA 56/57, 109)—only to point out that Husserl described the kinds of "being given" only for the theoretically oriented consciousness. In point of fact, we are only in exceptional cases theoretically oriented in our experience of the world around us. The "original attitude of experience" (GA 56/57, 110) is entirely otherwise, it has not yet even entered the field of view of philosophy, the young *Privatdozent,* then still regarded as Husserl's most promising disciple, announces with great self-assurance.

"Experience," or indeed the "original attitude of experience"—is that not a label for hidden secrets, for the black sack from which metaphysical treasures may, after all, be conjured up? This, as we know from Karl Löwith and Hans-Georg Gadamer, is what it sounded like to the students. But anyone expecting such a thing, anyone who, hungry for worldviews or eager for metaphysics, was seeking new or old sense-offerings in *experience,* was disappointed by Heidegger's cool yet passionate, laconic yet cumbersome formulations. For instead of acting as an "academic prophet," as a prophet at the lectern, he invited the students to bring into their consciousness the precise *experience* of the lectern at which he was standing and lecturing. Because his entire lecture hinges on this lectern experience, a lengthy passage from this impressive phenomenological description of the situation will be quoted here:

> You come to this lecture room as usual, at the usual hour, and go to your usual place. You hold on to this experience of your "seeing your place," or else you can likewise put yourself in my place: entering the lecture room I see the lectern . . . What do I see: brown surfaces intersecting at right angles? No, I see something different—a box, moreover a biggish box, with a smaller one built upon it. No, that's not it at all, I see the lectern at which I am to speak. You see the lectern from which you are spoken to, from which I have already spoken. There is no—as it is called—founding connection in the pure experience; it is not as if I first saw brown intersecting surfaces, which subsequently present themselves to me as a box, then as a speaker's desk, and next as an academic speaker's desk, a lectern, as if, in a manner of speaking, I were sticking the lectern element on the box like a label. All that is a bad, misinterpreting interpretation, a deviation from purely gazing into the experience. I see the lectern at a single stroke, as it were; I don't only see it in isolation, I see the lectern adjusted too high for me. I see a book lying on it, directly

> disturbing to me . . . I see the lectern in an orientation, in a lighting, against a background . . . In this experience of the lectern-seeing, something presents itself to me from an immediate environment. This environmental something . . . these are not things with a definite character of meaning, objects, moreover conceived as meaning this or that, but the significant aspect is the primary experience, which presents itself to me directly, without any mental detour via a grasping of things. Living in an environment, it means to me everywhere and always, it is all of this world, it is worlding. (GA 56/57, 71–72)

"It is worlding"—here we have the first of Heidegger's personal word creations, of which there will be so many in the future. One can observe how the term is arrived at to describe a process that at first appears to be obvious but on closer inspection reveals a complexity for which no name as yet exists. He therefore invents one to describe that which normally we do not recognize because it is too close to us. Because it is a fact that, as we reflect on the seeing of a lectern, we unexpectedly slide into a different order that is no longer the order of perceiving. We then think in line with this pattern: there is a perceiving ego, and this ego encounters something, an object, and in that object the ego gradually notices a number of properties. Heidegger now wants to draw our attention to the fact that things do not encounter us like that in reality. The way they meet us in reality can only be demonstrated, by contrast, if we put the situation to the test—for instance by the experience of the lectern in Lecture Hall 2 of the University of Freiburg on a gray February day in 1919. One should try not to talk "about" the acts of perception, one should not dredge up convenient theories, but instead one should perform the act and, simultaneously, follow it with attention. Attention should therefore be focused on attention. In that case it is possible to duplicate what matters to Heidegger in this context and what he keeps circling around, so much so that one gets the impression that he is not moving forward at all. What becomes duplicatable is that we first perceive a diffuse, albeit significant, world-context, arriving at a "neutral" object only by way of abstracting from the natural act of perception. If we view the process from a customary theoretical viewpoint, we reverse it—we let it begin at the seemingly "neutral" thing to which we then assign properties and which we then place in the appropriate segment of a context with the world.

The murmuring concept of "primal experience" acquires a more precise meaning—it describes perception the way it actually occurs, beyond theoretical ideas about it. The lectern "is worlding" therefore means: I am experiencing the significance of the lectern, its function, its location in the room, its lighting, and the little episodes that are associated with it (an hour ago someone else was standing here; my recollection of the road I had to cover to get here; my irritation at standing here at the lectern listening to this incomprehensible stuff, and so on). The lectern "is worlding" means it assembles a whole world, in terms of time and space. We can quite easily put this to the test. If at some later time we recall something like this lectern experience, we shall discover—and since Proust, we do so especially well—that at the same time we recall an entire life situation. We dredge up the lectern, and a whole world comes up with it. Proust dunks his madeleine in his tea—and the universe of Cambrai unfolds. The madeleine, that sweet shell-shaped cake, "is worlding."

We do not experience every Something as "worlding" so powerfully, but every Something "worlds" to some extent. Heidegger imagines a "Senegalese Negro" wandering into the lecture hall. He would notice that strange wooden structure in front; would he not, Heidegger asks, perceive something incomprehensibly neutral, a naked object, so to speak? Would it still be true in that case that one always first perceives significances? It would still be true, also in this case, because the African would experience that Something in the sense of: "I don't know what to make of it."

In the beginning is "meaning," in the beginning there is "worlding," one way or another.

But what is the point of engrossing ourselves in this "experience" and this "worlding"? First of all, we are to realize what is in fact happening when we find ourselves in the world, for instance in front of the lectern. This situation, which always is an experience, is to become transparent to ourselves. But Heidegger wants more—he hopes to turn the spotlight on what occurs when we place ourselves in a theoretical, or what is commonly called "scientific," attitude to the world. In the so-called objectivizing scientific attitude we make the primary significance, the *environmental*, the experience-aspect disappear; we strip the Something down to its naked objectiveness—which can be successfully done only by pulling out our experiencing ego and erecting an artificial, new, secondary ego, which is now termed the "subject" and which then, in appropriate neutrality, confronts a likewise neutral "object," now also officially termed the "object." At this moment it becomes clear what Heidegger is aiming at—that that which modern philosophy and, proceeding from it, modern science postulate as the primal situation, as the premise-free beginning of reflection and the ultimate certainty, namely the confrontation of "subject-object," is in fact no premise-free beginning. That is not how things start. They do start with our finding ourselves, in the "worlding" manner described, in the world with its lecterns, madeleines, and Senegalese.

If, meanwhile, we have got used to Heidegger's murmuring "primal" and find ourselves able to duplicate its precise meaning (of what is always a situational beginning), then we will also understand why Heidegger speaks of the "primal intention of lived life," which has to be uncovered beneath the artificial and pseudo-initial subject-object opposition. He wishes, he explains, to protest any "unjustified absolutization of the theoretical" (of which he also accuses Husserl). "The deeply ingrained obsession with the theoretical . . . is a major obstacle to gaining an overview . . . of the domain of environmental experience" (GA 56/57, 88). With aggressive undertones he refers to the process of "progressive destructive infection of the environment by theory" (GA 56/57, 89) and finds a new name for this as well—"de-experience" *(Entleben).* The theoretical attitude, useful though it is, and even though it forms part of the repertoire of our natural attitudes to the world, is "de-experiencing"; later Heidegger will use instead the term "objectification" *(Verdinglichen),* taken over from György Lukács. In his lecture he states, "The objectness circumscribes an entirely original sphere, distilled from the environmental. The fact that 'it is worlding' is already expunged in it. The object alone still exists as such, that is, it is real . . . The significant is designified down to this remainder—to recognize something real for what it is. The historical ego is dehistoricized down to a remainder of specific ego-ness as a correlate of objectness" (GA 56/57, 91).

With such a theoretical attitude mankind began long ago to transform life, both its own and that of nature, to a useful but also a dangerous degree. That was possible only by "de-experiencing" it, as Heidegger put it, or "disenchanting" it, as Max Weber put it.

As the only Beyond to this disenchanted world, Max Weber had left the rationality of the privatized area of personal, and not further rationalizable, "value judgments." From this private refuge now stem the worldviews to which there is nothing to object, provided they do not claim scientific prestige.

Heidegger's critique of the "irrational" is even more unforgiving. That which the sciences call the "irrational"—Heidegger states—is in fact the name for the experience-remainder in the blind spot of the theoretical attitude. "Theoretically I myself come from the experience . . . which people now do not know what to make of and for which the comfortable name of the irrational has now been invented" (GA 56/57, 117).

This irrational then becomes an object of which, just because it is so "obscure," one can make whatever one chooses—a basement for the do-it-yourselfers of ideology, a rock for the new prophets, an obscure object of metaphysical desires, an asylum for nocturnal strollers producing their ineffable theories from ineffable suffering. Such irrational psychic constructs can then, for instance, assume the appearance of a psycho-hydraulic machine; or that of an affluent middle-class house with basement (Id), main floor (Ego), and attic (Superego); or that of a seascape with oceanic vastnesses, dams, floods, swamps, drainages, and so on. In treating the irrational one can also pretend that one wishes to ride the tiger.

However, as Max Weber apparently believes, this irrational may also be viewed as the origin of value judgments. But is it really true, Heidegger asks elsewhere, that we are faced with naked objects—people, situations, objects—"which initially are present as naked realities . . . which are subsequently, in the course of experiencing, clothed in a value character, so they should not run about so naked"? (GA 61, 91).

Heidegger pours scorn on Rickert's philosophy of values—which also influences Max Weber—and on the claims of an allegedly value-free science. And with downright cold fury he speaks about the edifying ideological kind of metaphysics that, in peaceful coexistence with the rest of our knowledge, paints a sky above us from which the values hang down like fruit from a tree—a metaphysics, therefore, that consolingly compensates for all suffering on the disenchanted steel capsule of the rational world and, in doing so, refers to "higher" or "deeper" experience. Heidegger (in a lecture given two years later) calls this an "appeal to vagueness as a refuge, a foggy emanation of unclean yet bombastic and self-deceiving so-called 'world feelings'" (GA 61, 101).

Heidegger names no names, but it is a fact that the great bulk of ideological literature during those years had a metaphysical trend. This is hardly surprising. The easiest way of escaping from the malaise of the physics of life was just this "meta" of a speculative overall interpretation. Martin Heidegger shudders with disgust; he begins virtually every lecture of those early years with a diatribe against the cultural scene, and he keeps emphasizing that philosophy must, at long last, give up its covetous glances toward heaven. He demands a "cold gaze"; all the worldview questions could safely be put "in cold storage" (GA 61, 45); anyone unable to tolerate being "thrust into absolute dubiousness" (GA 61, 37) had better keep his hands off philosophy.

These anathemas are ambiguous. Here a professional philosopher defends his territory against freelance metaphysicians and philosophizing columnists. This has in itself something of the philistinism that he attacks. On the other hand Heidegger acts as a bogeyman, provoking the guardians of what is beautiful, good, and true. He is flailing around against the culture of hollow exaltation, false soulfulness, grand phrases, and sham profundity. It is, in a word, a dadaist episode in philosophy.

As early as during the war, the dadaists—in Berlin, Zurich, and elsewhere—had mocked the aestheticism of the Stefan George circle, the "O Man" bombast of the expressionists, the traditionalism of the educated philistines, and the metaphysical portraits of heaven, because all these ideas had once again been made to look rather foolish by the reality of the war. But the provocation of the dadaists consisted chiefly in that, when asked, "So what do you want to set against all that?" they would reply, "Nothing! We only want what is the case anyway." Dadaism, the *Dadaist Manifesto* declared, "rips to shreds all slogans of ethics, culture, and soulfulness." In other words, a tramway is a tramway, war is war, a professor is a professor, a latrine is a latrine. Anyone talking merely proves that from the laconic tautology of Being he has switched over to the garrulous one of consciousness. "With Dadaism a new reality claims its rights" *(Dadaist Manifesto)*. This new reality is one that has been abandoned by all good spirits and whose cultural comforts have been destroyed. "The word *Dada* symbolizes the most primitive relationship with our ambient reality" *(Manifesto)*. All that is left is this and this and this.

If in that whole investment of acuity and academic philosophy of Heidegger's first lecture we wish to trace the dadaistic impulse, then we have to remind ourselves that he began with a question, the rather pretentious question of the "primal science," the "primal intention of life," the "principle of principles," to guide his expectant students into the obscure secret of the experience of a lectern. That is a provocation very much in dadaist taste. The same applies to the subsequent transformation of the ordinary into the exceptional. Through such attention the everyday experience becomes something mysterious and adventurous. The dadaists, or at least some of them, were, like

Heidegger himself, despite or perhaps just because of their iconoclastic inclination, engaged in the quest for the miraculous. After an evening in Zurich's Club Voltaire, Hugo Ball wrote in his Dada diary, *Flight out of Time:* "There are probably other ways of achieving the miracle and other ways of opposition too."[8] They remained, as did Heidegger, secret and eerie metaphysicians.

The "little magician from Messkirch," as he would soon be called, could philosophize about the experience of a lectern in a manner that took his students' breath away, even though they were accustomed to far more strident experiences in the war. Here ballast was jettisoned; there was a gesture of angry dismissal of ancient grand words and sweeping systems, of academic subtleties built on air, to be replaced by a return to entirely elementary questions: What precisely is happening here and now as I experience the lectern? This switching of focus is akin to that cultivated in German literature during the "clean sweep" period after 1945—"Smash your songs / burn your verses / say nakedly / what you have to say" (Schnurre), or "This is my cap / this is my coat / here is my shaving tackle / in a canvas bag" (Eich).

Heidegger's return to marginal observations contains a polemical and provocative thrust against a widespread readiness for credit fraud also in philosophy and for the issuing of bills on a future that one cannot control. The underlying message of Heidegger's frugality runs as follows: There are no longer any generals' hills in philosophy, we have trouble enough appropriately comprehending what is happening here and now. Many years later Heidegger is to rephrase this idea more elegantly as a return "into that nearest, which we invariably rush past, which surprises us anew each time we get sight of it" (*Unterwegs Zur Sprache;* GA 12, 94).

It is astonishing how Heidegger manages to captivate us for this "environmental" experience. Admittedly, his students then will have felt much the same as we do today—that one is drawn into this thought until one arrives at the moment of rubbing one's eyes in astonishment and asking oneself: That was quite something, but what use is the lectern experience to me? Karl Jaspers strikingly formulated this experience with Heidegger's philosophizing in his notes on Heidegger, which he had accumulated after the 1920s and which, at his death, were still lying within reach on his desk. This is what Jaspers said about Heidegger: "Among contemporaries the most exciting thinker, masterful, compelling, mysterious—but then leaving you empty-handed."

This environmental experience, as Heidegger describes it in his lecture, does in fact harbor an empty mystery. Heidegger shows how, as a rule, we fail to open up for ourselves the riches of direct experience. But when it comes to determining and describing these riches, practically nothing is left—apart from, it seems, a few trivialities.

However, Heidegger is not out to explore the essence of a lectern but to use this example to demonstrate, in repeatable form, a certain attention that he claims, for one thing, should be fundamental to philosophizing and, for another, that it was usually "precipitated," that is, dealt with overhastily, by us and by our entire philosophical tradition. True philosophizing requires the ability to put oneself into such an attitude—regardless of "objects" and situations. It is a method, albeit a paradoxical one. It consists of the exclusion of all other methods of theoretical approach and of grasping a situation as it is "given," even before it is made the subject of investigation or reflection. Even the term "given" already contains too much theory, because in the situation we do not say to ourselves, this situation is "given" to me, but we are inside the situation, and when we are inside it, then there is no longer any "ego" to confront that situation. The ego-consciousness is already a breach. Perception and experience do not begin with the ego; the ego comes in only when the experience receives a crack. We lose direct contact with the situation; some gap opens up. Or to use another picture: we view the objects through a pane of glass, and we see only ourselves when the pane of glass is no longer completely transparent, but reflects. Heidegger calls for an attention that directly captures a surrender to a situation. This is something in between the full expression of a lived situation, on the one hand, and the self-distancing, objectifying, abstract talking about it on the other. This is a "self-transparency of life in its separate moments."

Why this self-transparency? To begin with, to bring to consciousness that which is lost to us in a theoretical attitude. To this point Heidegger's intention is clear. But in the probing intensity of his philosophizing there is a peculiar surplus—and that is what makes his thought so fascinating, even at this early point in time. The surplus is located in the question that he does not yet ask so explicitly, but that he will later repeat in a downright ritualistic manner—the question of Being. Heidegger immerses himself in "experiencing" in order to discover our "Being in situations," and although he is only beginning to find a language for that Being, he knows very well that in our scientific theorizing and in the large canvases of ideologies, we invariably miss it.

An excess intention is directed toward Being. But what is excessive about it? This intention is excessive because it aims not only at an appropriate cognition of an experience situation, but also at a "Being-appropriateness" that has less to do with pure cognition than with successful life. Heidegger aims at the self-transparency of an experienced moment as if it contained a promise, almost a divine promise. Although this is pushed aside by him into the indirect, the cooled, even the academic, it nevertheless flashes through often enough. On one occasion he calls the restored self-transparency of a life situation simply "life sympathy" (GA 56/57, 110), on another he describes the point at which one has to decide whether one chooses theory or transparency: "We stand at the methodological crossroads that decides on the life or death of philosophy altogether, at an abyss—either into nothingness, that is, that of absolute facticity, or we succeed in leaping into another world or, more accurately, into the world altogether" (GA 56/57, 63).

"Empty releasing," says Jaspers. There does indeed remain an unredeemed surplus of intention. Perhaps the exercise of an unaccustomed intensity, of a more lucid presence of mind, will succeed—but has one not perhaps expected rather more, and has one not received from Heidegger, subliminally, a promise of something more, and did he not also expect something more himself?

Let us recall the phrases written by Heidegger to Elisabeth Blochmann about the time of that lecture: "The new life that we desire, or that desires within us, has given up the intention of being universal, that is, false and two-dimensional (superficial)—its possession is originality—not what is artificially constructed but what is evident in total intuition" (BwHB, May 1, 1919). This letter also contains mention of the "mysterious and grace character of all life," and that "we must be able to wait" for "high-tension intensities of meaningful life."

That same year a book is published that, in striking agreement with Heidegger's intention, likewise attempts to discover the promising Being in the "darkness of the lived moment." This is a major work of the philosophy of our century—Ernst Bloch's *Spirit of Utopia.* This book, expressionist in style and inspired by clear gnosis, simultaneously hungry for images and in love with images, begins with the statements: "Too close . . . while we live we do not see, we flow along. What therefore occurred, what we really were while amidst it, refuses to coincide with what we can experience. It is not what one is, and even less so what one means." Bloch possesses in abundance what Heidegger lacks—a spiritual power of imagination for the "darkness of the lived moment." Moreover, the philosophical outsider Bloch has an unselfconsciousness not found with Heidegger, who, despite his unconventional behavior, is still rooted in the discipline of the phenomenological school. Bloch declares straight out: Illumination of the darkness of the lived moment requires a "philosophical lyricism of the ultimate degree."[9]

To quote a sample, Bloch describes the experience of a jug that is standing before him, that he places before us:

> It is difficult to fathom what it looks like in the dark, spacious belly of the jug. That, one would rather like to know. The child's perpetual, curious question is opened up again. Because the jug is closely akin to the childish . . . Anyone regarding the old jug long enough carries its color and shape around with him. I do not go gray with every puddle, nor am I bent around the corner with every bend of the rail. But I can very well be shaped into a jug, viewing myself as something brown, strangely grown, Nordically amphora-like, and not only by imitation, by simple empathy, but in such a way that as a result I become richer by my share, more present, more grown into myself with this shape in which I participate . . . Anything that was ever made as lovingly and as purposefully leads a life of its own, towers into a strange, new territory, and with us, in a manner we cannot be in our own lives, returns shaped, decorated with a certain, however faint, sign, a seal of our Self. Here, too, one feels that one is looking into a long sunlit corridor with a door at its end, as with a work of art.[10]

Why should one not be able to demonstrate, by the experience of a jug, what our Being is all about? In a later essay Heidegger, too, will try his hand at the jug. Meanwhile the lectern experience of his early lecture lacks that fullness of Being that he, just as young Bloch, is seeking.

Heidegger, however, is concerned not only with this fullness but much more so with the other mystery—the wonderment at the "naked" That. That anything exists there at all. The relation between direct experience and its objectification had been characterized by Heidegger as a process of de-experiencing—the unity of the situation is dissolved, and experiencing turns into the self-perception of a subject confronted with objects. One has dropped out of direct Being and now finds oneself as someone who has "objects," including oneself as an object, called the subject. These objects, as well as the subject, can then be examined for their further characteristics, connections, causations, and so on; they are analytically determined and eventually appraised. In this secondary process the neutralized "objects" are once more built into a world-connection, or, as Heidegger puts it, a dress is put on them so they do not have to stand about naked.

This theoretical world construct has an abstract vanishing point. What this means is demonstrated by Heidegger with his environmental experience of the lectern. From a theoretical attitude (he argues) one can analyze this lectern as follows: "It is brown; brown is a color; color is a genuine perception-datum; perception data are the result of physical or physiological processes; the physical ones are the primary cause; this cause, the objective element, is a particular number of oscillations of the ether; the ether nuclei disintegrate into simple elements, between which, as simple elements, there exist simple regularities; the elements are the ultimate; the elements are something altogether" (GA 56/57, 113).

In this way one arrives at a "something altogether" as a kind of nucleus or essence of things. This presumed nucleus of the Something makes the whole graduated sequence appear as mere gradations of phenomena. The brown lectern is not what it appears to be. Although it is not nothing, it is not the Something that it appears to be. This way of understanding makes Werner Heisenberg remark that the modern scientific picture of the world represents a revival of ancient natural philosophy, according to which the atoms (or even subatomic particles) are what "the real substance" is.[11]

Heidegger shows that in this analytical reduction the mystery that there is actually something there is microcosmically shifted to subatomic conditions—it could equally well be shifted macrocosmically to the entirety of the universe—but that one fact is missed in this process, namely that the mystery of the Something is preserved at every level of reduction. After all, the color already is "something," just as are the perception data or the ether oscillations or the nuclei. By way of distinction from the Something that science is left with at the end of its reductions, Heidegger describes this Something, which at each point of experience manifests its astonishing presence, as something "before-worldly" *(Vorweltlich)* (GA 56/57, 102). Heidegger evidently chose this term as a complementary one to Nietzsche's term "behind-world" *(Hinterwelt),* designed to characterize the curiosity that penetrates the presumed substanceless phenomena to arrive at the "essence" behind or underneath or above them. This astonishing Something that Heidegger has in mind and that he calls before-worldly is the realization of the miracle that something exists there at all. Astonishment at the Something can attach itself to any experience.

Using the term "before-worldly" for this astonishment is a happy choice by Heidegger, because it suggests an astonishment as if one had just been born into this world. Thus, at the end of the lecture, one is reminded again of its beginning, when Heidegger described his attempt at bringing an experience to phenomenological self-transparency as a "leap into another world, or, more accurately, a leap into the world altogether."

This primal experience of astonishment is, to Heidegger, the exact opposite of theoretical de-experiencing. It does not indicate "absolute disruption of reference to life, no relaxation of de-experiencing, no theoretical fixation or freezing of something capable of being experienced; instead it is the index of the supreme potential of life, a fundamental phenomenon [occurring] at moments of especially intensive experiencing" (GA 56/57, 115). But when it occurs, albeit rarely, it is invariably linked with the realization that it is always latently present but remains hidden because as a rule we lock ourselves into our life references, without distance, or else with the de-experienced distances of a theoretical attitude. There can be no doubt. We have here the phenomenological clarification of an experience that, in its simplicity, is at the same time mystical, provided one characterizes mystery by Wilhelm Wundt's memorable statement: "It is always a feature of mystery that it transforms a concept back into intuition."[12] Looking at the lectern, we can participate in the mystery that we are and that there exists a whole world that gives itself to us.

Astonishment at the mysterious "that something is there at all" contains a question that cannot be satisfied by any possible answer, because any answer that explains that "That" with a "why" finds itself in infinite regression—each why can be followed by another why. And because no answer is possible, it is not even possible to formulate what exactly is being asked when we ask about the mystery of the That. Ernst Bloch, working on a kindred problem, therefore called this astonishment the "shape of the nonconstruable question." And at the crucial moment, when that astonishment was to be duplicated and made susceptible to experience, he wisely left the word to the poet. In his *Traces* he quotes a wonderful passage from Knut Hamsun's *Pan:*

> "'What do you know? Sometimes I see the blue fly. Yes, all this sounds so thin, I don't know if you understand.'—'Oh yes, I understand.'—'Oh yes. And sometimes I watch the grass and the grass perhaps watches me; what do we know? I watch a single blade of grass, maybe it trembles a little and I think, now this is something; and I think to myself: now here stands this

blade of grass and it trembles! And if it is a spruce I'm watching, then perhaps it has a branch that gives me some food for thought. But now and again I also encounter people in the mountains, that happens sometimes . . .'—'Yes, yes,' she said, standing up. The first drops of rain were falling. 'It's raining,' I said. 'Yes, what do you know, it's raining,' she said too, already walking away."[13]

7

PARTING WITH CATHOLICISM AND STUDYING THE LAWS OF FREE FALL WHILE FALLING

It was about the time of his lecture on the "lectern experience" that Martin Heidegger parted with Catholicism. On January 9, 1919, he wrote to his friend Engelbert Krebs, by then professor of Catholic dogmatism in Freiburg:

> The past two years, in which I have sought to clarify my basic philosophical position . . . have led me to conclusions for which, had I been constrained by extraphilosophical allegiances, I could not have guaranteed the necessary independence of conviction and of doctrine. Epistemological insights, applied to the theory of historical knowledge, have made the *system* of Catholicism problematic and unacceptable to me—but not Christianity per se or metaphysics, the latter albeit in a new sense. I believe I have felt too keenly . . . what values are enshrined in medieval Catholicism . . . My phenomenological studies in religion, which will draw heavily on the Middle Ages, will . . . demonstrate that in modifying my fundamental position I have not allowed myself to sacrifice objectivity of judgment, or the high regard in which I hold the Catholic tradi-

> tion, to the peevish and intemperate diatribes of an apostate . . . It is hard to live the life of a philosopher; the inner truthfulness toward oneself and those for whom one is supposed to be a teacher demands sacrifices and struggles that the academic toiler can never know. I believe I have an inner calling for philosophy, and that by answering the call through research and teaching I am doing everything in my power to further the spiritual life of man and work in the sight of God.[1]

Two years earlier Engelbert Krebs had performed the church wedding of Martin and Elfride and had received the couple's promise that their children would be baptized into the Catholic church. The occasion for this letter was the fact that Elfride was now expecting a child, and the couple had agreed not to let it be christened a Catholic. To Heidegger, separation from the "system of Catholicism" is therefore also a separation from its institutions. He did not formally leave the Church (which indeed is not possible under Catholic canon law), but in Husserl's circle he was now being regarded as an "undogmatic Protestant"—as Husserl put it in his letter to Rudolf Otto of March 5, 1919.

How far he had inwardly distanced himself from the Catholic world also emerges from his emphatic rejection of the temptation of "wild apostasy"—just as if it were a real option. His esteem for the values of the Catholic Middle Ages was holding him back from that course, he writes. Cold comfort for Krebs, as the present-day Catholicism evidently does not command such esteem from Heidegger. He states that he owes his spiritual development to his freedom from "extraphilosophical ties." In retrospect, therefore, it seems a good thing to him to have abandoned his priesthood career in good time. So what religious convictions are left to him? He was holding on to "Christianity" and "metaphysics—though, admittedly in a new sense," he declared.

This is no longer the metaphysics that in medieval Catholic thinking fused God and the world into a unity. In that thinking Heidegger had originally found a spiritual home—until his subtle perception discovered the hairline cracks in it, the cracks that foreshadowed the later breaking apart of the whole.

The metaphysics to which he adheres is one *after* the breaking apart of the former unity. The old heaven has fallen, the world has detached itself into worldliness; it is from this fact that he will proceed. Philosophy has not yet sufficiently ventured out into that worldliness, he asserts in a lecture during the war emergency semester of 1919.

At first glance it seems as if Heidegger's emphatic invitation to take the "worlding" of the world seriously at last marks the replay of a movement from the late nineteenth century—the discovery of real reality. Then, the economy was discovered behind the spirit (Marx), mortal existence behind speculation (Kierkegaard), the will behind reason (Schopenhauer), instinctive drive behind culture (Nietzsche, Freud), and biology behind history (Darwin).

Heidegger is truly buoyed up by this movement of "discovery" of real reality, more so than he admits to himself. Though his thinking had not so long before been under a Catholic heaven, he now intends to surpass these "discoveries" in radicalism if at all possible. To him these critical forays are still only attempts to develop ideologies providing a sense of security; they do not yet penetrate to the "potential of life"—the true seat of production of all self-interpretations and worldviews of a scientific and less scientific nature. In his winter 1921–22 lecture he finds a name for this real reality—"factual life."

This factual life is no longer sustained by any metaphysics; it crashes into the void and strikes upon existence. Not only the world but also individual factual life are, in the literal sense, the "fall."

To anticipate: we will not find in Heidegger's so-called factual life anything that would justify us in attributing any kind of truth value to a religious faith or a metaphysical construct. The medieval principle of a gliding transition between the finite human and the truth of the infinite, this boundary-crossing traffic, has become an illusion to factual life. In consequence, the God administered as an ever available "treasure of truth" by a Church that is rich in traditions and solidly established as an institution is likewise an illusion.

At the beginning of the 1920s Heidegger lectured on the phenomenology of religion. The subjects were St. Paul, St. Augustine, and Luther, as well as Kierkegaard. Otto Pöggeler has been able to study the manuscripts, however, and in them has discovered the "Protestant" Heidegger.

Heidegger interprets a passage from St. Paul's First Epistle to the Thessalonians: "But it is not necessary to write to you, beloved brothers, about times and hours; for you yourselves certainly know that the day of the Lord will come like a thief in the night." God is as unavailable as time. In the writings of the profound religious thinkers, Heidegger argues, God becomes a name for the mystery of time. He also discusses at some length a passage in the Second Epistle to the Corinthians, where St. Paul reminds those who boast of a special mystical link with God of Christ's words: "Be content with my grace; for my strength is powerful in the weak." One need only—as young Luther and, later,

Kierkegaard—penetrate once more into this primordially Christian religiosity of the unavailable moment of grace, and the cathedrals of metaphysics and theology, which had tried to make faith resistant to time, collapse in a heap.

Such attempts at transforming the unavailable "temporal" God into a credit balance are motivated, Heidegger suggests along with St. Augustine, by the "unrest" of the human heart, which is seeking rest. Augustine had drawn a strict distinction between the tranquility that one takes for oneself and the tranquility that one receives from God. It overwhelms one, and to it applies equally what St. Paul says about the Lord—it comes "like a thief in the night" and it takes away all unrest. We cannot make peace unless peace is granted us.

Everyone who, in the Christian tradition of the West, ever drew attention to the gulf between God and Man, and to the unavailable moment of grace, hence the mystery of time, is now summoned by Heidegger as a compurgator for his own attempt to prove that factual life is severed from God and that metaphysical refuges are chimeras.

In the introduction, written in 1922, to his *Phenomenological Interpretations to Aristotle*—a work to be discussed later—Heidegger writes: "Any philosophy that understands itself in what it is must know, as the factual How of the interpretation of life—especially when it still has a 'surmise' of God—that the snatching back of life performed by it represents, religiously speaking, a raising of a hand against God. But only thus does it present itself honestly to God, that is, according to the possibilities available to it as such; in atheistic terms, keeping itself free from a tempting anxiety that merely pays lip service to religiosity" (DJ, 246).

Heidegger speaks of God as Husserl does of reality outside consciousness. Husserl brackets reality in; Heidegger brackets God in. Husserl intended, by this bracketing, to attain the field of pure consciousness and demonstrate that this, in itself and from itself, already contains the full plurality of reality. And Heidegger brackets God in so as to embrace the pure worldliness of the world, free from any tendency to create in it substitute gods. Husserl says: "I must first lose the world . . . in order to regain it by a universal self-examination."[2] Is Heidegger pinning his hopes on a similar inversion? Does he hope to lose God through the self-transparency of factual life in order then to regain him as an unavailable event breaking into factual life "like a thief in the night"?

We shall see.

Meanwhile, at any rate, Heidegger, with his philosophical "atheism," is adopting a position complementary to the dialectical theology that experienced its great breakthrough in 1922 with the publication of the second version of Karl Barth's *The Epistle to the Romans.*

There is a "raising of the hand against God" also in Karl Barth, who has described his theology as a theology of crisis. It is the God of culture who got into a crisis—in the war and through the war. To Barth, this God of culture is in the same position as, to Heidegger, the Church's "treasure of truth." What is simply unavailable is falsely turned into a cultural asset. Like Heidegger, Barth wants to "snatch life back," to cut off its escape routes into comforting metaphysical constructs. There is no sliding transition to God; God is the negation of the world. It is self-deception, Barth declares, to try to develop a concept of God out of worldliness. This also is Heidegger's critique of metaphysics and culture devotion. Heidegger was aware of a sense of kinship with the great Protestant theologian, which is why, at the beginning of the 1920s, he once remarked that the only spiritual life of the age was in Karl Barth. Heidegger's "bracketed-in" God probably resembled Karl Barth's God:

> God, the pure and absolute boundary and beginning of all that we are and have and do; God who is distinguished qualitatively from men and from everything human and must never be identified with anything which we name, or experience, or conceive, or worship, as God; God who confronts all human disturbance with an unconditional command "Halt," and all human rest with an equally unconditional command "Advance"; God, the "Yes" in our "No" and the "No" in our "Yes," the First and the Last, and, consequently, the Unknown, who is never a known thing in the midst of other known things . . . this is the Living God.[3]

Turning against the cultural monopolization of God, Barth writes, "There is therefore no occasion here for romantic experience, no opportunity for enthusiastic rhapsody, no case for psychological analysis. There is no sign here of 'germ-cells' or of 'emanations' of divinity. There is nothing here of that overflowing, bubbling life in which we think we can discover a continuity of existence between us and God."[4] Much of this theology was a counterpart to Spengler's sensational book *The Decline of the West.* The "earthquake atmosphere" of God's judgment on our culture, so articulately conjured up by Barth, is a fairly close reflection of the shaken cultural optimism voiced in Spengler's book. Barth's theology still contains echoes of the catastrophe of the war, for instance when he refers to the "shell craters" left behind when God breaks into our lives.

"Snatching life back" from a false Beyond—this is now the most important task for Heidegger and Barth. Martin Heidegger tears life loose from God; Karl Barth tears God loose from life. This "life," which has to be snatched back to oneself, is examined by Heidegger in his lecture on phenomenological interpretations to Aristotle in the winter semester of 1921–22. No doubt his students, having expected an introduction to Aristotle, experienced a surprise. Although Heidegger begins with a few reflections on the reception of Aristotle—that is, with the history of philosophy—he does so merely to point out that the pursuit of the history of philosophy as a rule had little to do with philosophy. "The real foundation of philosophy is radical existential intervention and the production of questionableness; placing oneself and life and the crucial implementations into questionableness is the basic concept of all, and the most radical, illumination" (GA 61, 35). In his lecture during the war emergency semester Heidegger had used the lectern experience to demonstrate how poorly we understood the simplest experiences. Now the "crucial implementations" of life are to be brought into focus.

After the first surprise for the students—that instead of learning about Aristotle they were being told about factual life—there immediately followed another. If anyone had expected the "radical existential capture" to lead into the personal existential sphere, they were in for a disappointment. True, Heidegger kept emphasizing that one should philosophize not "about" factual life but "from inside" it. And admittedly there was some talk about "risk" and about the fact that in the performance of such thinking one might also "drown," and that "courage" was needed because radical questionableness implied "risking one's entire inner and outer existence." The prelude, therefore, is dramatic, excited, but later the whole business is strangely cooled by a complicated apparatus of concepts that might have their origin in the arsenal of neofactual aloofness. Reference is made to "ruinance, prestruction, destruction, larvance, relucence." Heidegger, who at that time was beginning to appear in peasant smocks, speaks not in a primordial or earthy manner but factually, almost technically, in a chilled mode. A gesture of sparkling modernity—that is how it must have seemed at the time. Not a trace of a jargon of intrinsicness.

It is in this lecture that the typical Heidegger tone of the next few years is first heard, that unique tension between existentialist heat and aloof neutrality, between abstract conceptuality and emotional concreteness, between appellative importunity and descriptive distance.

We live from day to day, but we do not know ourselves. We are in our own blind spot. If we are to become transparent to ourselves, then this requires an effort that "strikes back at life," Heidegger says. Heidegger's philosophy of life is a philosophy against a spontaneous life tendency. That is why it can be biting cold and, at the same time, existentially alive with high tension.

Heidegger's lecture on Aristotle thus begins with the explication of the idea that anyone wishing to comprehend Aristotle, anyone wishing to place himself into a relation of tension, must first have comprehended himself; at the least he must have comprehended what he wishes to comprehend in and through Aristotle. Anyone hoping to comprehend himself must be clear about the situation in which he finds himself. This is a further-education situation at the university in the subject of philosophy in the year 1921. This situation embraces a whole world, questions upon questions. Why study philosophy, of all things, just now? What role can philosophy play altogether at this time—at the university, as a profession, or as a preparation for another profession? What does one expect of one's life when one has chosen philosophy? Heidegger raises these questions, or rather, he stage-manages them. He hopes to create a blizzard of blurred and questionable ideas to make it clear how unclear and foggy the situation in fact is when we try to make it transparent. In this context we can once again observe how Heidegger's original word creations come about during the gradual completion of his ideas. We cannot, Heidegger states, view the life that we are in from the outside; we are always in the midst of it, surrounded by its details. Where we are there exists only "this" and "this" and "this." Heidegger describes this life with its many "this heres," and suddenly he has the appropriate term—the characteristic aspect of life is "thisness" (GA 61, 88). This thisness is hard to bear. Philosophy's answer, as a rule, is that it erects values, traditions, systems, idea constructions in which one may find shelter so one does not have to stand about "so naked" and unprotected in one's own time. One barricades oneself behind educational assets and deals with philosophy as if it were life insurance or a mortgage. One invests labor and effort, asking oneself: what profit does this yield, what use is it to me, what can I do with it? However, Heidegger claims, one can do nothing with philosophy; at most one can, by philosophizing, gain clarity about what one "does" at all. Philosophy deals with the "fundamental," the fundamental in the most literal sense—that is, what is at the beginning. What matters is not the question of how the world began, nor any principles in the sense of supreme values or axioms. The "fundamental" is what is driving one and what, time and again, makes one the beginner of one's life.

Laboriously and meanderingly Heidegger tries to describe a movement, heightening the tension. Everyone is eager to hear an answer to the question of what the actual moving principle is. The lecture is almost half over and the listeners are still left in the dark with the statement: "If one understands that factual life is, in essence, always escaping from the on-principle, then one will not be surprised by the fact that the appropriating reversal to it is not present 'just as a matter of course'" (GA 61, 72).

Orpheus was not allowed to turn around as he tried to lead Eurydice out of the realm of the dead. He did turn, and Eurydice sank back to join the shades. Heidegger wishes to induce the moved life to turn; it is to "comprehend itself from its roots," meaning that it should become aware of the ground from which it comes and from which it wants to escape, by "living itself firmly into" its world. But is not this reversal so difficult because life surmises that in its own heart there is "nothing," a void, a horror vacui, which drives it outward toward a quest for something to fill it? Must we not, for the sake of our life efficiency, conceal from ourselves what is driving us out into a world in which we have always had to provide something? Heidegger encourages us to do so, to cast a glance upon what is our serious daily concern, a glance that no longer permits the truly concerned to remain serious in the same manner. The magic formula by which Heidegger lets the everyday and commonplace appear suddenly as though transformed is concern. "Life is concern, more particularly in the inclination toward making-things-easy-for-oneself, in escape" (GA 61, 109).

The concept of concern will be at the center of *Being and Time,* but it makes an impressive appearance even in this lecture. Concern is the quintessence of attitudes such as, "One concerns oneself about something, one is worried, one intends something, one makes sure things are all right, one wishes to discover something." Thus understood, "concern" *(Sorgen)* and "providing" *(Besorgen)* are almost identical with action altogether. Heidegger has chosen this concept to emphasize the time-related character of this life activity. By acting "providingly" we are "ahead" of ourselves. We have something "ahead of us," in the spatial and temporal sense, something that we are concerned with, that we wish to realize; or we have it "behind us" and therefore wish to preserve it or get rid of it. Providing has around it a spatial, and even more so a temporal, horizon. Every action is Janus-headed; one face looks to the future, the other toward the past. One provides for the future to make sure one will not have omitted anything in the past.

It would be easy to understand this entire analysis as a description of triviality decked out with an extravagant vocabulary—namely, the fact that people always act in some way or other. But to understand Heidegger in this way would be to misunderstand him. The punch line would be lost. It consists of the following reflection: in concern one is not only "ahead of" oneself but—Heidegger argues—one is also lost to oneself. The world of concern covers us. We are hidden from ourselves, we "live ourselves firmly into" the concerns involved. "In concern, life bars itself against itself, and in this barring-itself-off it does not get rid of itself. It keeps seeking itself in an ever new looking-away" (GA 61, 107).

For this process—life "living out of itself" and "living itself firmly into" a concern, and in doing so "escaping" itself—Heidegger coins the term "ruinance." The association with "ruin, ruinous" is entirely deliberate. In the narrower sense, ruinance means "fall."

Concern and providing had been understood by Heidegger as movement into the future or into the past, in any case as "horizontal." Now he tips this motion from the horizontal into the vertical and, naturally, endows it with massive acceleration—a fall, a crash. But the "factual life," living from day to day, does not even notice that it is falling. Only philosophy opens our eyes to a situation that is no situation but a fall. Life, Heidegger says, should be snatched back to itself, if only to discover that it can find no hold in itself, nor indeed anywhere else. Heidegger makes a major effort to remove the misunderstanding that self-transparency of life would mean putting life to rest. On the contrary: philosophy is heightened unrest. It is, as it were, methodically operated unrest. Heidegger's philosophy during these years is characterized by the dadaist motto: "Surely I won't lose my head to such an extent that, while falling, I wouldn't study the laws of free fall" (Hugo Ball).

Where are we falling? This question Heidegger cannot avoid at the end of his lecture. His answer is an oracle that no doubt lets many students fall into despair: "The Whither of the fall is not something alien to it, it is itself of the character of the factual life, more accurately: 'the Nothing of factual life'" (GA 61, 145).

What is the "Nothing of factual life"? Factual life itself cannot be "nothing," seeing that it is taking place. Factual life exists, or better: it is the case. Hence the "Nothing of factual life" must be something that belongs to that life without dissolving it into nothingness. Does this Nothing belonging to factual life possibly mean death? But there is no mention of death in the lecture. Instead, Heidegger defines this Nothing as follows: factual life becomes a Nothing insofar as it loses itself in "ruinant existence." As Heidegger puts it, the "nonpresence [of factual life] in ruinant existence" (GA 61, 148).

Heidegger, by now suspecting that he is about to produce a new turn in philosophy, varies his idea of the nonpresence of factual life in ruinant existence with the idea of alienation that had played an exceedingly important historical role with Hegel and Marx in the nineteenth century. The idea states that Man so creates his world that he cannot recognize himself in it. His self-realization is his self-atrophy.

In this lecture Heidegger does not yet succeed in clearly differentiating his own reflections from the tradition of ideas. But everything depends on this differentiation. The philosophy of alienation presupposes an image of the "true self," an "idea" of Man as he is and as he could and should be. But it is over just this idea that Heidegger places a big question mark. Where do we get this alleged knowledge of Man's real destination? Heidegger suspects that behind such "knowledge" there is smuggled theological stuff. One may hang on to it, he says, but in that case one should correctly declare such ideas, and proclaim that one has accepted them in good faith; one must not pretend that they are philosophically provable.

We observe Heidegger rejecting this idea of a true self while still being in its thrall. This tension will remain. It will be expressly and magnificently resolved in *Being and Time* under the heading of "authenticity" *(Eigentlichkeit).*

In the early 1920s, while Heidegger is on the road toward his philosophy of the self-transparency of life—probing, searching, defining his position—into just that period falls the beginning of his friendship with Karl Jaspers, who is likewise searching for a new beginning for philosophy. It is the beginning of a delicate friendship between two beginners.

They met in the spring of 1920 at a party at the Husserls. After eighteen months of cautious probing they eventually, in the summer of 1922, felt united in "the knowledge of a rare and original comradeship-in-arms" (Heidegger to Jaspers, June 27, 1922). Even their first meeting was marked by a common opposition to academic rituals. Jaspers in retrospect describes the evening at the Husserl home in his *Philosophical Autobiography:*

> In the spring of 1920 my wife and I spent a few days in Freiburg . . . Husserl's birthday was being celebrated. There was a fairly large circle around the coffee table. Frau Husserl referred to Heidegger as the "phenomenological child." I recounted how a girl student of mine, Afra Geiger, a top-rank personality, had come to Freiburg to study under Husserl. According to the acceptance regulations of his seminar, he had rejected her. Thus both he and she had, thanks to the rigidity of academic rules, lost a good opportunity, because he had omitted having a look at the person herself. Heidegger cut in, vigorously, confirming my point. It was a kind of solidarity of the two younger men against the authority of abstract orders . . . The atmosphere of that afternoon was not good. I seemed to perceive something petit bourgeois, something constraining, something lacking the free movement from person to person, the spiritual spark . . . Only Heidegger seemed different. I visited him, sat alone with him in his den, saw his work on Luther, saw the intensity of his labor, felt sympathy for his forceful, terse way of speaking.[5]

Karl Jaspers, Heidegger's senior by six years, was then regarded as an outsider by professional philosophers. He was a medical man, coming from psychiatry; in 1913 he had made a name for himself with *General Psychopathology,* a book that soon became a standard work in that field. Jaspers, however, began to detach himself from medicine. He began to realize, largely through clinical boundary cases, that the psychic element could not be adequately understood within the framework of a psychology inclining toward the natural sciences. He had, while still on the territory of that psychology, received incentives from Dilthey's method of understanding and from the phenomenological cautiousness in describing consciousness phenomena. But the decisive breakthrough came from Max Weber and Kierkegaard.

Jaspers was impressed by Max Weber's strict distinction between factual research and value judgment. Like Weber he was convinced that erroneous scientific pretensions had to be refuted, but—and here he went beyond him—he believed that the area of value judgments, that is, personal responsibility in life, both required and was capable of self-illumination, which, while it could not be "scientific," was certainly more than a matter of merely private reflection or religion. Jaspers intended to render transparent what Weber called the "life powers," which underlay all decisions. For this kind of philosophizing, which he would later call "existential illumination," Jaspers found his great model in Kierkegaard. Weber had taken philosophy out of the body of the exact sciences and thereby liberated it; Kierkegaard had restored to it its existential emotion. That is how Karl Jaspers saw it.

His *Psychology of Ideologies,* published in 1919, represented a transition from psychology to philosophy in the sense of "existential illumination"; it was a book with an impact far beyond the specialized world of scholarship. Using Weber's method of idea-type construction, Jaspers examined the "attitudes and world pictures" that arise from fundamental problems such as freedom, guilt, and death, and that impress their peculiar profile on the philosophical constructs of a period. Descriptively, as it were "from outside," Jaspers designs a typology of such world pictures and attitudes, though not with a historical or sociology-of-knowledge intent. Nor does he aim at anything like "consciousness altogether," which was supposed to underlie all such patterns—a question then popular with the neo-Kantians. Although Jaspers's book was sometimes understood in historical, sociology-of-knowledge, or neo-Kantian terms, this was not his intention. Jaspers was concerned with the question of in what forms self-being could realize itself, how it could fail, and on what it could suffer shipwreck. It is the movement of freedom that Jaspers tries to follow, and it is also fear of freedom, of the resultant readiness to shut oneself into a "capsule" of allegedly safe principles and declarations. He was interested mainly in the patterns of behavior and thought in "marginal situations" (death, suffering, chance, guilt, struggle) in which the venturesome character of a life undertaken in free self-responsibility emerges. "Everything," Jaspers writes about this book in his *Autobiography,* "was seized as if in a swift grip . . . The mood of the whole was more comprehensive than what I succeeded in saying."[6]

With this book a new note entered philosophy. The public resonance was so great that Jaspers, though not a doctor of philosophy, was appointed in 1921 to a philosophy professorship in Heidelberg. But his position remained ambiguous. The exact scientists regarded him as a renegade, as someone who had sold himself to what was inexact, to philosophy, and the philosophers regarded him as a psychologist with a strong inclination toward preaching. Jaspers did not mind. He felt he was "on the way into the open."

It was in this situation that Jaspers and Heidegger met. And Jaspers understands Heidegger only too well when, characterizing his own work in a letter to him on August 25, 1921, he writes: "Whether I too will find my way out into the open I don't know; it'll be something if I get myself to the point of at least going" (BwHJ, 25).

Since 1919 Heidegger had been working on a review of Jaspers's book. In June 1921 he sent it to Jaspers; it had grown into a voluminous treatise that, just because of its bulk, could not, as planned, appear in *Der Göttingische Gelehrte Anzeiger,* and it was not published until 1973.

Heidegger begins with a lot of praise for the book, but soon, though in cautious formulation, proceeds to criticize it. Jaspers, he claims, had not gone far enough. He had written "about" the implementation of existence, but he had not placed his own reflections "into" this implementation of existence. He endeavored to preserve his freedom vis-à-vis the capsules of ideology and to refer to the core of personal existence, but such references would themselves become ideologies if that creative freedom at the bottom of self-being was described as something present, that is, ultimately as a scientifically confirmable fact. "True self-contemplation," Heidegger writes at the end of his review, "can meaningfully be released only if it is present, and it is present only in a strict being-awakened, and it can be genuinely awakened only in such a way that the Other is, in a certain manner, ruthlessly driven into reflection . . . To drive into reflection, to arouse attention, is possible only if one leads a stretch of the way oneself" (W, 42). But one can only lead the way if one seizes the "business" of philosophy for oneself. The "business" of philosophy, however, was "the philosophizing person himself and (his) notorious wretchedness" (W, 42).

Jaspers had no reason to take the reference to wretchedness personally; the context made it clear that what was meant was a kind of anthropological wretchedness. Jaspers therefore was not annoyed about the review, but he found himself at a loss. What did Heidegger mean by his demand that one should philosophize not "about" the implementation of existence but "out of it"? Either Heidegger had misunderstood him and failed to realize that he was already on the road suggested by him, the road of philosophy as "self-affliction" *(Selbstbekümmerung)*—Heidegger's word—or else Heidegger meant something totally different by that road, in which case his suggestions were insufficient. Jaspers certainly did not see how Heidegger intended to make headway on his road. There remained nevertheless a sense that they were traveling the same road. On August 1, 1921, Jaspers writes to Heidegger: "In my opinion your review, of all those I have read, is the one that digs most deeply to the root of ideas. It therefore affected me profoundly. However, I still miss . . . the positive method. Reading it, I always felt the potential for advancing, but then I was disappointed and thought that I, too, had come that far" (BwHJ, 23).

In his reply Heidegger described his review as a "ridiculous and poor beginner's piece"; he said he certainly did not believe that he was "any further than [Jaspers], especially as I have made up my mind to take a few detours" (August 5, 1921, BwHJ, 25). The correspondence rests for a year. Then, in the summer of 1922, Jaspers invites Heidegger to Heidelberg for a few days: "Surely it would be nice if we could philosophize a few days at suitable hours, and test and consolidate our 'comradeship-in-arms.' As I imagine it, we would be living together—each in his own room, my wife is away—each doing what he likes, and that we—apart from our meals—would meet and talk as we felt inclined, especially in the evenings, or as it may come about otherwise, without any constraint" (September 6, 1922, BwHJ, 32).

Heidegger accepts the invitation, and neither man will ever forget those September days. They will live off these memories, for soon their friendship will not be supported by anything else. The philosophical intensity, the friendly relaxed atmosphere, the sudden sense of a joint departure and beginning—for Jaspers, as he writes in retrospect, these were "overwhelming." In an unforgettable way Heidegger had become "close" to him. And Heidegger, after these sacred conversations, writes to him: "Those eight days at your home are continually with me. The sudden, outwardly noneventfulness of those days . . . the unsentimental rough step with which friendship came upon us, the growing certainty of a comradeship-in-arms sure of itself on both 'sides'—all this to me is uncanny in the sense that the world and life are uncanny to the philosopher" (November 11, 1922, BwHJ, 33).

So inspiring was that friendship in its initial phase that Jaspers proposed the foundation of a journal for which only the two of them would write, a "torch" of philosophy. The time had come for a voice to be raised in the "philosophical wasteland of the age" against professorial philosophy: "We will not rant, but discussion will be ruthless" (November 24, 1922, BwHJ, 36). But then Professor Jaspers remembers that Heidegger does not yet have a chair; the project of the journal would therefore have to wait until Heidegger was appointed to one. The worries professors have.

There is one other obstacle to the project—the two men are not yet so completely certain of their own position as they would have to be to open a campaign. Jaspers: "We don't know ourselves yet what we want; i.e. we are both borne by a knowledge that does not yet exist explicitly" (November 24, 1922, BwHJ, 36). And Heidegger replies that a lot was being accomplished already if he himself were becoming "more secure in the right kind of concrete insecurity" (July 14, 1923, BwHJ, 41).

In point of fact, between the summer of 1922 and that of 1923 Heidegger succeeds in taking important steps of self-clarification. The outlines of *Being and Time* begin to emerge. They can be found in the collection of texts, *Phenomenological Interpretations to Aristotle: Notice of the Hermeneutical Situation* (a collection only rediscovered in 1989), which toward the end of 1922 he sends to Marburg to accompany his application for a post; and in the "Ontology" lectures of 1923, given during his last Freiburg semester before his assumption of the Marburg professorship.

The *Phenomenological Interpretations* made a tremendous impression in Marburg. Paul Natorp regarded it as a "concept of genius" and for Hans-Georg Gadamer, who was then a doctoral student under Natorp and was permitted to see the manuscript, it was a "true inspiration." The text had such a "weight of impact" that he decided to go to Freiburg for the next semester to hear Heidegger and then follow him back to Marburg.

The ontology lecture series in the summer of 1923 must have made a similarly powerful impression. Quite a number of men who were later to achieve name and standing in philosophy were then sitting at the feet of *Privatdozent* Heidegger, who was beginning to be regarded as the secret king of philosophy, a king in Swabian loden cloth. They included Gadamer, Max Horkheimer, Oskar Becker, Fritz Kaufmann, Herbert Marcuse, and Hans Jonas.

In his Aristotle manuscript Heidegger offers a terse definition of his philosophical intention: "The subject of the philosophical question is human existence, the question being about the character of its Being" (DJ, 238). Only at a first glance is this definition uncomplicated. What else was philosophical research to do, or what else has it ever done but to explore human existence?

Admittedly, over the course of its history, philosophy had examined matters other than human existence. That was just why Socrates' protest became necessary when he tried to bring philosophy back to man's concern with himself. And this tension between a philosophy that tried to fathom God and the world and a philosophy concentrating on human existence continues to persist in the history of philosophy. Thales of Miletus looking at the sky and in consequence falling into the well is probably the first personification of this conflict. In Heidegger's philosophy, existence is still in the process of falling.

At first glance, similarly, the term "character of Being" seems to present no difficulty. What else would one discover in examining an object than the nature of its being? The character of Being of a molecule—is this not the elements of which it is composed, the nature of chemical reactions, its function in the organism, and so on? The character of Being of an animal—does one not discover this in its anatomy, its behavior, its place in evolution?

Understood thus, the term "character of Being" pales; it then simply encompasses everything one can know of an object. Such knowledge inevitably is knowledge of differences—the way one molecule differs from another, the way an animal differs from another animal or from plants or also from Man. The summary concept of "character of Being" becomes a plurality of "characters of Being."

From this viewpoint there is, on the one hand, the attitude of wishing to know, which in itself remains unchanged, and on the other, the different possible objects of which one wishes to know something—that is, whose character of Being one wishes to fathom, no matter for what purpose in the individual case.

Of course the sciences have long realized, certainly since Kant, that different objects have to be approached with different methods. This applies in particular to the two "worlds" of nature and Man—insofar as Man is more than nature, a culture-producing and hence self-producing creature. It was the neo-Kantians who focused awareness on the methodological difference between the humanities and the natural sciences. According to Windelband, the natural sciences seek general laws, the humanities seek understanding of the individual. Put differently, in Rickert's words, natural science examines facts while the humanities examine values. However, this kind of awareness of the different characters of Being is not nearly radical enough for Heidegger. What he is himself aiming at he formulates in his Aristotle manuscript in a single, exceedingly concise and therefore very difficult sentence, which I will first quote and then, using the ontology lectures for elucidation, briefly comment on: "This fundamental direction of philosophical questioning is not put upon or screwed on from the outside on the object questioned, but should be understood as the explicit seizure of a fundamental liveliness of factual life, which is in such a way that in the concrete emergence of its Being it is concerned about its Being, and that even where it avoids itself" (DJ, 238).

Not "put upon from outside"—Heidegger wishes to apply the phenomenological principle that what is to be examined should be given an opportunity to "show itself," to the examination of existence altogether. The ontology lectures therefore deal very extensively with preliminary considerations of how one may appropriately speak about Man—but presently one discovers that with these preliminary considerations one already finds oneself at the core of the problem.

If, says Heidegger, we approach a "subject" in order to discover what it is; if we wish to comprehend its "Being-meaning" *(Seinssinn),* we must first get into the "implementation meaning" *(Vollzugssinn),* from which alone its Being-meaning can be derived. Anyone entering our economic life from a strange culture, and still unable to grasp its implementation meaning, will be unable to comprehend the Being-meaning of money, even though he may touch it or weigh it in his hand; or: music remains a noise unless we stand in the implementation meaning of music. This applies to the different areas of Being—art, literature, religion, calculation with imaginary numbers, or football. These considerations, moreover, also—by argument *e contrario*—reveal the blinkered aspect of the reductionist method. If we say: thinking is a function of brain physiology, or love is a function of glandular secretion, then we are making a statement about the Being of thinking and of love without having placed ourselves in their implementation. The meaning of their Being, however, is revealed only in this implementation. Viewed from a nonimplementation angle, all this is not present at all—the game, the music, the picture, religion.

These reflections are of a phenomenological character. They are to provide clarity on what attitude is needed for the "phenomena" to be able to show themselves as "they are in themselves." A "game" cannot show itself in a nongame attitude. Love only reveals itself to love, God only reveals himself to faith. And how, Heidegger asks, must we observe to ensure that what Man "is" can reveal itself at all?

The answer can only be that thought of Being, if it wishes to understand that Being, must place itself in its implementation meaning. That is what Heidegger means with the quoted formulation from his Aristotle manuscript: "the explicit seizure of a fundamental liveliness of factual life."

This "fundamental liveliness" Heidegger for the first time, emphatically, calls "existence." Something "exists"—by this phrase we usually mean that we presume the existence of something, and if we then discover that the presumed something exists, we say it really exists. Galileo, on the strength of calculations, assumed that there must be a moon of Jupiter, and with the aid of a telescope he subsequently found that this moon of Jupiter "exists." But this meaning of existing in the sense of being "really present" is what Heidegger wishes to exclude. He uses the term in a transitive sense: by existing we are not merely present, but we must exist ourselves; we not only live, but we must "lead" our life. Existence is a mode of Being, more precisely: the "Being accessible to itself" (DJ, 245). Existence is something that is, something that, other than stones, plants, or animals, stands in a self-relationship. It not only "is," it also becomes aware that it is "here." Only because there is this self-awareness can the entire horizon of concern and time open for us. Existing, therefore, is not a being-present but an implementation, a movement. How much this insight moved Heidegger himself emerges from a letter to Karl Löwith of 1921: "I do only what I must do and what I believe to be necessary, and I do it as my powers permit. I do not embellish my philosophical labors with cultural requirements suitable for a vague historical present . . . I work for my own 'I am' and my particular spiritual origins. From this facticity surges the fury of 'Existence.'"[7]

The implementation meaning of existence is the (above-described) existing in a transitive sense, or, meaning the same thing, it is factual life as a concerned, afflicted, self-outlining life in time. Human existence becomes comprehensible only from its implementation meaning, but not if we place it before ourselves as an object present. The philosophy of existence, as Heidegger has it in mind and as he adumbrated it in outline a few years before *Being and Time,* does not stand as an observer "above" existence but is an expression, an organ of this existence. Philosophy is concerned life in presence-of-mind action. This extreme possibility of philosophy—Heidegger says in his ontology lectures—is "existence's alert awareness of itself" (GA 63, 15), which means ambushing it "where it avoids itself" (DJ, 238). It means making transparent life's "inclination to decay," cutting off its escape routes to presumed stability, and having the courage to surrender to life's restlessness in the knowledge that anything presumed durable, firmly established, obligatory is nothing but something done up, a mask that existence puts on or that it allows to be put on itself by "public attitudes," by prevalent opinions and ideas of morality and interpretations.

“Alertness of existence to itself” is described by Heidegger as the supreme task of philosophy. But because this truth does not allow us to discover a true self, instead simply hurling us back into the heart of unrest from which we are trying to escape, there is such a thing as “fear of philosophy” (GA, 19). For Heidegger during these years philosophy causes unrest. The fear of philosophy is the fear of freedom. Instead of “freedom,” Heidegger still speaks of the “possibility” of factual life.

Philosophy in Heidegger’s sense is therefore a coimplementation of concerned and providing existence, but it is also free mobility and contemplation of the fact that having possibilities is part of the reality of Man. Philosophy, therefore, is nothing other than alert existence and thus just as problematic and just as mortal as this existence.

The best that one can say about philosophy, including Heidegger’s philosophy, is that it is an event that, like all existence, has its time.

8

MARBURG UNIVERSITY AND HANNAH ARENDT, THE GREAT PASSION

Heidegger first applied for a professorship at Marburg University in 1920. At that time he merely achieved an honorable mention in third place; although the young *Privatdozent* had seemed quite promising, it was thought that he had not yet published enough. When the question of a possible appointment to Marburg once more came up in the summer of 1922—the vacancy was for what is called an extraordinary professorship—Heidegger had still not published anything new. But his reputation, based solely on his teaching, had meanwhile grown to such an extent that Paul Natorp, the head of the neo-Kantian Marburg School of Philosophy, wrote to Husserl on September 22, 1922, that Marburg was going "to take a fresh look at Heidegger," not only in the light of Husserl's glowing testimonial "but also in the light of what I have been told about his latest work."[1] Natorp inquired if Heidegger was preparing some publication that one might have a look at. Husserl passed the inquiry on to Heidegger, who—as he wrote to Jaspers—sat down "for three weeks," summarized his own essay on Aristotle, added a brief introduction, and dispatched the sixty-page manuscript to Marburg. It was entitled "Phenomenological Interpretations of Aristotle (Demonstration of the Hermeneutical Situation)."

"In Marburg, too, the work has now struck home," Heidegger wrote to Jaspers on November 19, 1922. Natorp had indeed informed Husserl that he and Nicolai Hartmann, an influential man at Marburg, had "read Heidegger's summary with the greatest interest, and found in it . . . a remarkable originality, depth and intellectual rigor."[2] Natorp thought Heidegger's prospects were very good.

At the same time the University of Göttingen was showing interest in Heidegger. There, Georg Misch drafted an almost extravagantly positive assessment. Heidegger, he said, "displays an absolute originality that stems from his own development and his consciousness of the historicity of human life."[3]

In Göttingen, Dilthey's son-in-law Misch cut little ice with his praise, despite the supporting fire from Husserl, who was championing Heidegger for a professorship not only at Marburg but also at his own former university. His chances looked better in Marburg. But Heidegger, who on his meager salary of an assistant could no longer feed what had become a family of four (which is why Elfride had to take a job in education), remained skeptical. To Jaspers he wrote: "The endless dance they lead you, the half-prospects, the praise and flattery, etc.—you end up in a terrible state" (November 19, 1922, BwHJ, 34).[4] However, Heidegger was successful. On June 18, 1923, he was offered an "associate professorship with the status and rights of a full professor,"[5] as he proudly reported to Jaspers the following day.

A year earlier Jaspers and Heidegger had formed a "fighting alliance." They had intended to publish a philosophical journal that would deal "ruthlessly" with the philosophical spirit of the time; the project, however, had been put aside because Heidegger was not yet firmly enough in the saddle. Although this had now changed, the two men did not revive their plan for a journal. Even so, Heidegger became aggressive, and in a letter to Jaspers of July 14, 1923, this is not to be overlooked. With cheerful anger the newly appointed professor pounces on his guild. About his rival Richard Kroner, who was placed third on the recommendation list, he writes: "I have never encountered such a miserable human being—now he lets himself be pitied like an old woman—the only act of charity that one might still show him would be to deprive him of the *venia legendi* (his position of *Dozent*) this very day." Kroner, he said, had promised Nicolai Hartmann that if he was appointed, he would attend his lectures like a student. "I certainly shan't be doing that," Heidegger informed

Jaspers, "but I shall give him hell by the manner of my presence; a whole combat patrol of sixteen is coming along with me."[6]

In the same martial manner Heidegger again invokes his fighting alliance with Jaspers, the moment for whose realization (he says) had now come: "A lot of idol worship has to be eradicated—i.e., the various medicine men of present-day philosophy have to be exposed for their awful and miserable craft—while they are alive, so they shouldn't think the kingdom of God had arrived with them already."

Although publicly Heidegger still describes Husserl as his teacher, and although he still benefits from his support, he has already distanced himself from him so far that, in a letter to Jaspers, he includes him among the blasphemed medicine men:

> No doubt you know that Husserl has an invitation to Berlin; he behaves worse than a *Privatdozent* who confuses a professorship with eternal bliss . . . Husserl has totally gone to pieces—if indeed he ever was in one piece—which I have lately been increasingly questioning—he vacillates this way and that and utters trivialities such as would reduce one to tears. He lives by his mission of being "the founder of phenomenology," no one has any idea what that is—anyone who has been here for a semester realizes what's happening—he is beginning to suspect that the people are no longer following him . . . And such a person today hopes to save the world in Berlin.

In point of fact, Husserl did not accept the flattering invitation to Ernst Troeltsch's Berlin professorship. His need to go to Berlin to save the world evidently was not as great as Heidegger assumed. There are some indications that Heidegger was projecting his own ambitions onto his former teacher. This pugnacious letter to Jaspers shows the extent to which Heidegger was already enjoying the role of a Hercules about to clean up the Augean stables of philosophy. Is this not exactly the salvationist attitude that Heidegger attributes to Husserl? In this letter to Jaspers he certainly indulges in fantasies of a "fundamental reform of philosophy" and of "revolution." That summer Heidegger discovers that he is Heidegger.

The ontology lectures of the summer semester, his last in Freiburg, are marked by great self-assurance. Full of enthusiasm, he tells Jaspers: "I leave to the world its books and its literary ado and instead get the young people—'get' means seizing them fiercely—so that for the whole week they are 'under pressure'; some of them can't take it—the simplest way of selection—some need two or three semesters before they understand why I will not allow any laziness, any superficiality, any cheating, or any phrases—least of all 'phenomenological' ones . . . My greatest joy is that I can here accomplish a change by example and that I am now free" (July 14, 1923, BwHJ, 41).

In financial matters he did not yet feel the same confidence, however. What salary could he demand? Was he entitled to an apartment, to a removal subsidy? Jaspers tried to tone down his expectations: "With regard to your salary you'll hardly be able to make demands" (June 20, 1923, BwHJ, 39).

Some time before moving to Marburg, Heidegger purchased a small plot of land in Todtnauberg, where he had a very modest cabin built. He took no part in the operation himself. Elfride organized and supervised everything. From then on, Todtnauberg was his place of retreat from the world and, at the same time, the commanding height of his philosophizing. From there all roads led downhill.

Heidegger arrived in Marburg in the fall of 1923; he was to leave the town again in the late summer of 1928 to succeed Husserl in Freiburg. His assessment of those five years in Marburg varied. To Jaspers he wrote at the end of his time in Marburg: "I cannot list anything for you that would speak in favor of Marburg. I wasn't happy here for a single hour" (May 13, 1928, BwHJ, 96). From a greater distance, however, Heidegger in a private conversation described these years as "the most exciting, the most concentrated and the most eventful" period of his life, as well as the "happiest."[7]

Heidegger's negative assessment of his time in Marburg, in his letter to Jaspers, also had a tactical aspect. Jaspers was then considering leaving Heidelberg and was anxious to know whether Heidegger would advise him to move to Marburg. But this Heidegger was unable to do, since it had not only been the situation at that university but also his commuting between Marburg and Todtnauberg that had made these years so productive for him. There was, moreover, another factor, which Heidegger was unwilling to disclose to Jaspers. We shall come to that shortly.

Marburg is a mainly Protestant, small, provincial town with an ancient university. In 1927 it celebrated its four hundredth anniversary. On that occasion—so Hermann Mörchen reports—one could see Heidegger in an unfamiliar cutaway and with a grim face enter the Catholic church, normally not attended by him, while the anniversary service was held in the reformed church. During the vacations between semesters the little university town would empty and fall asleep, but at those times Heidegger was in his cabin in Todtnauberg anyway. Marburg was a transparent place: everybody knew everybody else. It was a good place for intrigues, small-town gossip, the emergence of cliques, and the narcissism of minute distinctions. A small world that, because it was dominated by "the educated," believed itself to be great. Heidegger wrote to Jaspers: "The university boring. The students respectable, without special motivation. And since I concern myself a lot with negativity, I have here the best opportunity to study the appearance of 'Nothingness'" (December 2, 1926, BwHJ, 69).

There was no social life in Marburg, but then Heidegger attached no importance to such things. Nevertheless, he made an occasional appearance in the house of Frau Geheimrat Hitzig, where all new arrivals to the academic world were ceremoniously introduced. Rumor had it that this lady was a blood relation of ninety-one living full professors in Germany. There was also a circle of Stefan George admirers centered on the economic historian Friedrich Wolters. Those with "modern," new-factual, or left-wing views met at the house of the art historian Richard Hamann. Rudolf Bultmann headed a group in which once a week, from eight to eleven in the evening, Greek texts were read aloud; at eleven began the cozy part, which likewise conformed to a strict timetable—one hour of superior academic gossip, followed by wine and cigars, when jokes were permitted. The best of these anecdotes were, as befitted conscientious scholars, recorded in a register, to enable future reference. Persons such as Ernst Robert Curtius, who was used to an *haute-bourgeois* lifestyle, suffered under these conditions and occasionally took the train to neighboring Giessen to enjoy a good meal at the railway restaurant there. Because a good meal, as he used to say, was impossible in Marburg.

In this limited university world Heidegger very soon became a mysterious star. He gave his lectures in the early hours of the morning, which evidently was not a sufficient deterrent, because after a mere two semesters there were 150 students in his classes. Gadamer, until Heidegger's arrival a disciple of Nicolai Hartmann, reports that the Hartmann followers switched over to Heidegger in droves.

Hartmann, a Baltic baron, was a night bird. He would rise at noon and did not really come alive until midnight. He had gathered around him a cheerful crowd who would debate into the small hours. Gadamer records: "When Heidegger came to Marburg and scheduled his lectures for seven o'clock in the morning, a conflict became unavoidable and we ceased to be worth much after midnight in Hartmann's circle."[8]

Hartmann, who until Heidegger's arrival had been the philosophical center of Marburg and now found himself displaced, accepted an invitation to Cologne two years later—with a sense of relief and liberation. Before that time, the newly graduated Dr. Gadamer had tried to bring his old and new teachers together: "When in 1924, at the time of our greatest poverty, I had to organize a small student procession, with a farm cart, I had a noble team drawing it—Hartmann and Heidegger on the same shaft. And they were pulling in the same direction! Heidegger on such occasions displayed a charming boyish sense of humor. When, on the return journey, the cart was empty, he suddenly let Hartmann do all the pulling on his own . . . jumped onto the cart and opened his umbrella."[9]

Heidegger cut a striking figure in Marburg in his personal appearance. On winter days he could be seen walking out of the town with his skis shouldered. Occasionally he would turn up for his lectures in his skiing outfit. In the summer Heidegger wore his famous loden suit and knickerbockers—these were his glorified scouting garb. The students called these clothes his "existential suit." It had been designed by the painter Otto Ubblohde, and to Gadamer suggested something "of the modest resplendence of a peasant in his Sunday best."[10]

Heidegger very soon made contact with the Akademische Vereinigung Marburg, the Marburg Academic Association, a group that was connected with the Bündische Jugend (the Youth Movement), opposed the fraternity system, rejected alumni philistinism, championed the principle of self-education and personal responsibility, and sought to realize the ideal of interdisciplinary studies. This circle was characterized by a mixture of the severity of the Stefan George followers and the romanticism of the hikers' movement. In social and political matters its members tended toward the left, or at least were antibourgeois. On one occasion, when a student declared that he hoped to "educate himself into a personality," Heidegger sarcastically remarked that he had better give up that idea. The intellectual atmosphere was not unlike that described by Thomas Mann in his *Doctor Faustus.* Mann has Adrian Leverkühn and his friends engage in great discussions about God and the world while spending their hiking nights in barns, using "a sort of learned lingo, quite unaware how pompous they sounded, flinging about the stilted and pretentious phrases with artless virtuosity and self-satisfaction. 'Natural relations of life,' 'theonomic sanctions,' such were their preciosities. With gusto they propounded the 'problem of being,' talked about 'the sphere of the divine,' or 'the academic sphere'; about the 'structural principle,' 'condition of dialectic tension,' 'existential correspondences,' and so on."[11]

Heidegger gave a few lectures to the Academic Association. He added even greater emphasis to the strictness practiced in the group by declaring that existential problems, more than any others, had to be treated with "the icy coldness of the concept." He even invited the students to his house, on one occasion for a St. Nicholas party. There was a sing-along, Frau Elfride had baked a cake, and a St. Nicholas put in an appearance. Hermann Mörchen, who recorded the event, received a copy of Hegel's *Phenomenology of the Mind.* Heidegger and the students also went hiking together, with tent and guitar. Students of this circle were allowed to visit Heidegger at his cabin in Todtnauberg. There, the secret king of philosophy held court in the Bündische Jugend manner. At the summer solstice, wheels of fire were sent rolling downhill. Heidegger called out strong words after them. Sometimes a pile of wood was lit in the meadow in front of the cabin and he made a speech. "To be awake by the fire at night . . . ," he began on one occasion, and with the next sentence was back with his beloved Greeks. Parmenides in Todtnauberg.

Arnold von Buggenhagen, who failed as a student under Heidegger, describes his lecturing as follows: "Heidegger spoke in a medium-loud voice, without notes, and into his speech flowed an exceptional intellect, but even more so a force of will that determined the direction his speech would take, especially when the subject became dangerous. In the role of a speaker on ontological matters he presented not so much the image of a professor as that of a captain-commodore on the bridge of an ocean giant in an age when drifting icebergs could still mean the sinking of even a Titanic craft."[12]

Buggenhagen describes the effect of this new tone of philosophizing, which was christened "existential philosophy" only after the publication of Jaspers's principal philosophical work in 1932. It was a relief from the demands of a seemingly shallow rational universalism and an encouragement to bring oneself into play "somehow." Its charm was in the very vagueness of this "somehow." It soon became obvious that Heidegger's philosophizing was not concerned with personal confessions, with expressionism, or with practical help for living. Any such expectations had been rejected by him very firmly. In his lectures he frequently quoted Schelling: "The fear of life drives man from the center." The "center" to Heidegger was the self-encounter expressed in the simple sentence: "I observe that I am." Buggenhagen reports how Heidegger masterfully stage-managed the disquiet that arises, or should arise, from this "naked that." Anyone who had learned from Kant that the foundation of cognition lies in reason might now have the impression that it lies in the unexchangeable and irreplaceable existence of the individual. Not, therefore, in the generalizable, but in the individual. This as it were fundamental idea was always under discussion, even though unuttered, but it refused to take on clear outlines. Buggenhagen reports that he and many of his fellow students asked themselves shamefacedly whether they actually possessed "enough existential mass" to be able to escape generalizing reason.[13]

Heidegger's students soon realized that his philosophy course could not simply be "crammed for" like traditional university subjects. Although his lectures were full of intimidating erudition, it was clear that this was of slight importance to him; he handled his extensive learning almost casually. To watch this philosopher in action was an astonishing spectacle for the students. To some he seemed "like an eagle soaring in the sky," to others like "a man in a frenzy." Buggenhagen relates that it suddenly occurred to him to wonder "whether this philosopher was not some Aristotle gone berserk, arousing attention because he was pitting the greatness of his thinking power against his thinking, and because in that thinking he claimed not to be thinking at all, but to be existence."[14] But this Heideggerian "existence" remained a mystery to many of his students, and the best they could do was to look around for their own mysteriousness. Buggenhagen admits that he did not succeed in this. Others were to be more successful.

Hermann Mörchen reports that Heidegger could also be impressively "silent." To Mörchen who, alongside philosophy and German literature, was also studying theology, the lecture on "existence" had religious significance. He questioned Heidegger, who remained silent—for Mörchen, proof "that nothing speaks more definitely and louder than essential silence. At the same time it is an illustration of the kind of freedom that Heidegger left to those who passed through his school."[15] In class Heidegger once said: "We honor theology by keeping silent about it."

This silence, however, was made more difficult for him in Marburg than in Freiburg, since Marburg was a bulwark of Protestant theology. There, in particular, Protestantism's "modern" forms were in evidence, such as attempts to find a new approach to Christian belief through the dispute between the scientific spirit and culture.

Shortly after his arrival in Marburg, Heidegger attended a lecture by Eduard Thurneysen, one of the "dialectical" theologians gathered around Karl Barth. To Gadamer, Heidegger's contribution to the discussion remained unforgettable, because what he said ran counter not so much to the spirit of the place as to what rumor in Marburg attributed to Heidegger—that he had turned away from Church and faith. Heidegger said that it was "the true task of theology, the task to which it had to find the way back, to seek the word that was capable of calling to faith and to preserve in faith."[16]

This formulation more or less accurately describes the effort of the great local theologian Rudolf Bultmann, who had come to Marburg two years ahead of Heidegger. There he would renew Protestant theology, for the second time, after Karl Barth. Even though this theology would not experience its great breakthrough until after 1945, under the name of "demythologization," it was mapped out by Bultmann during Heidegger's years in Marburg. And it is a theology born of the spirit of Heidegger's philosophy. Of this, Bultmann himself left no doubt. It is from Heidegger's analysis of existence that Bultmann takes over his description of the human situation, of "existence"—being "thrown," anxiety, temporality, death and escape into nonitselfness. Also important to him is Heidegger's critique of a metaphysics in which thought pretends unto itself a totally unreal detachment from time and availability of life. What for Heidegger is critique of metaphysics is demythologization for Bultmann. Bultmann the philosopher attempts, like Heidegger, to reveal the "existential structure" of human existence; Bultmann the theologian next tries to confront this "naked" existence with the Christian message, similarly stripped of religious dogmas and reduced to its existential basic meaning. It is the fact that Heidegger, as Bultmann understands him, describes not an ideal of existence but merely the existential structures that makes him so acceptable to Bultmann's theology. Bultmann states: "Existential philosophy, while it gives no answer to the question of my personal existence, makes personal existence my own personal responsibility, and by doing so it helps to make me open to the word of the Bible."[17]

Heidegger and Bultmann soon became friends and would remain friends for life. However, the intellectual relationship between them remained asymmetrical. Heidegger was not influenced by Bultmann to the same extent as the other way around. He accepted Bultmann's theology on the premise of faith, which, however, could not be the concern of philosophy. To that extent he did not follow Bultmann. Bultmann, on the other hand, continues a good part along the way of Heidegger's philosophy to find the point at which he might encounter the Christian message.

At Bultmann's invitation Heidegger, in the summer of 1924, lectured the Marburg theologians on "The Concept of Time"—a perfect example of Heidegger's mastery of eloquent philosophical silence on matters of theology. He did not wish to say anything on theological or divine matters, he assured his audience at the beginning; he would confine himself to the "human." But he then talked about the human in such a way that a theology of the type of Bultmann's fitted like a key into a lock.

At the time of this lecture Heidegger is already developing the ideas that would become his work *Being and Time.* In concise form he presents an outline of the principal "fundamental structures of existence," all of which are determined by the character of time. Using this pointed definition for the first time, he explains temporality as liability to death: "*Dasein* . . . knows of its death . . . It is *Dasein*'s running ahead to its past" (BZ, 12).[18] Even in every action and experience here and now we notice this "past." The passage of life is always a passing away of away. Time is experienced by us on ourselves in this passing away. Hence this *past* is not the event of death at the end of our life, but the manner of the execution of life, "the 'how' of my *Dasein* pure and simple" (BZ, 18).[19]

In what do these reflections differ from the great tradition of meditation on death, from Socrates' ideas of death, from the Christian memento mori, from Montaigne's dictum "Philosophizing means learning how to die"? They differ in that Heidegger reflects on death not to triumph over it with thought, but to make it clear that it is only the thinking of death, the ever-present "in-the-past," that opens access to temporality and thus to the unavailability of existence.

This lecture confines itself to hints that will subsequently be massively developed in the famous chapter on death in *Being and Time.* Yet these hints are sufficient to represent a clear rejection of a massive tradition of theology and metaphysics. This is the tradition that establishes God or the Supreme Being as a sphere outside time, in which we, in belief or in thought, may participate. Heidegger interprets this as an escape from one's own temporality. This assumed link to the eternal does not extend beyond time but merely recoils from it; it does not enlarge our options but lags behind them.

This tradition, from which Heidegger distances himself, is the same against which Bultmann develops his theology of demythologization, a theology that places the Cross and the dying of a god at the center of the Christian message. Bultmann's theology presupposes the experience of temporality in the way Heidegger develops it. According to Bultmann, one must have experienced "Being unto death," with all the terrors and anxieties, before one can even become receptive to the Christian message. The Cross and Resurrection represent the transformation taking place in the life of a believer. Man's rebirth is not a fantastic event in some future eternity but something that is occurring here and now as a transmutation of the inner person—rebirth out of the radically experienced temporality, that is, the fatality, of life. In life embraced by death and in death embraced by life. That is the paradoxical and spare message of the New Testament, in Bultmann's interpretation.

The extent to which Heidegger's philosophy provided inspiration for the religious thinkers of his day is demonstrated also by the example of Hans Jonas, who studied with Heidegger and Bultmann. Jonas's great investigation, *Gnosis and the Spirit of Late Antiquity,* deals with a different spiritual tradition, just as Bultmann deals with that of Christianity. (Gnosis was the most powerful spiritual movement of late antiquity and early Christianity.) Like Bultmann, Hans Jonas uses Heidegger's analysis of existence as his "lock," into which the spiritual message then fits as a "key." And in his case it fits remarkably well. For gnosis—at least in Jonas's interpretation—lives by the experience of "being thrown." Gnostic mysticism and theology tell of the "crash" of the spirit (Pneuma) into the temporal world, where it must always remain alien and homeless. It can only assimilate to the temporal world provided it betrays and forgets its origin, provided it dissipates itself and loses itself to the world. For the salvational concepts of gnosis, everything depends on whether this spirit, drifting about in the world, overcomes its oblivion of existence, gathers itself up from its dissipation, and remembers its forgotten origin. In brief: Hans Jonas describes gnosis as a historically fixable religious movement in search of an "intrinsicalness" understood in the Heideggerian sense.

During his time in Marburg Heidegger experienced the surprising opportunity—the local theologians would call it a *kairos,* the great chance—of a very specific kind of intrinsicalness. It was an encounter that, as he would later confess to his wife Elfride, became "the passion of his life." At the beginning of 1924 an eighteen-year-old Jewish student had come to Marburg to study under Bultmann and Heidegger. Her name was Hannah Arendt.

She came from an assimilated Jewish bourgeois family in Königsberg, in East Prussia, where she had grown up. At the age of fourteen she had developed a philosophical curiosity. She had read Kant's *Critique of Pure Reason* and had such a good command of Greek and Latin that, at the age of sixteen, she founded a circle for the reading of ancient literature. Even before graduating from school, which she did as an external student in Königsberg, she had attended Romano Guardini's lectures in Berlin and read Kierkegaard. Philosophy to her had become an adventure. In retrospect she wrote: "It is as the rumor has it—thinking has come alive again, the educational treasures of the past, long believed to be dead, have been made to speak again, and it was found that they brought forth very different things than one had suspiciously assumed. There is a teacher; perhaps thinking can be learned . . . the thinking that springs as a passion from the simple fact of being-born-into-the-world and which . . . can have no more ultimate purpose . . . than life itself."[20]

Hannah Arendt was a young woman whose short hair and modish clothes attracted all eyes in Marburg. "The most striking thing about her was the suggestive force that emanated from her eyes," wrote Benno von Wiese—who was for a short while in the twenties her boyfriend—in his memoirs. "One virtually drowned in them and feared never to come up again."[21] Because of an elegant green dress that she was fond of wearing, the students called her "the green one." Hermann Mörchen recounts how at the neighboring tables in the dining hall conversation would suddenly fall silent when she was talking. One simply had to listen to her. She behaved with a mixture of self-assurance and shyness. During her obligatory admission interview for Bultmann's class, she turned the tables on him and laid down her own conditions for her attendance. Without beating about the bush she informed Bultmann that "there must be no anti-Semitic remarks." Bultmann assured her in his calm and gentle manner that "we two together will handle the situation" should any anti-Semitic remarks be made.[22] Hans Jonas, who made her acquaintance in Bultmann's class and became a friend, records that the students regarded their young woman colleague as an exceptional phenomenon. They perceived in her "an intensity, a purposefulness, a feeling for quality, a quest for the essential, a profundity that lent her an aura of magic."

She lived in an attic near the university. There her friends, some of whom had followed her from Königsberg and Berlin, would meet for philosophical discussions. There also, at times, she would offer them the charming spectacle of calling her little roommate, a mouse, out of its hole in order to feed it.

And in that attic, from February 1924 for the next two semesters, she also met with her philosophical mentor Martin Heidegger, in absolute secrecy and unknown even to her closest friends.

Elżbieta Ettinger has reconstructed the story of this relationship from Hannah Arendt's papers. She quotes from Arendt's letters and paraphrases those of Heidegger (which have not been released for publication). According to Ettinger's research, upon which the following account is based, the affair started in February 1924. Heidegger had been aware of the student for a couple of months when, at the beginning of February, he invited her to his office for a talk. Her image stayed with him: "wearing a raincoat, a hat pulled low over her face, now and then uttering a barely audible 'yes' or 'no.'"[23]

Hannah Arendt must have instantly and irresistibly felt attracted to the man she admired. On February 10, Heidegger wrote his first letter to Hannah. He addressed her formally as "Dear Miss Arendt." "Keeping a courteous distance," according to Ettinger, "he declared his respect for her, praised the qualities of her mind and soul, and asked her only that she let him help her to remain faithful to herself."[24] It was a letter that was both businesslike and emotional—lyrical, "beautifully phrased," Ettinger comments.[25] Heidegger's first letter to Elisabeth Blochmann had been along the same lines—a mixture of subtle homage and self-staging as spiritual guide. Then, on June 15, 1918, he had written: "and if I had not gained the conviction that you are worthy of being seized by such a spirit in your destiny, I should not have ventured to write to you today or to remain in spiritual contact in future. Remain strong and happy" (BwHB, 7). Heidegger's first letter to Hannah is perhaps a little less wooden but just as psychagogic. She is overcome and confused. The great master has turned to her. Four days later Heidegger writes, "Dear Hannah." And two weeks later he writes a few lines that, according to Ettinger, suggest "the beginning of physical intimacy."[26]

It was during that month of February that, as Hermann Mörchen reports, Heidegger in Bultmann's class presented an interpretation of Luther's commentary on Genesis 3, the story of the fall.

Hannah accepted the rules of their love affair as laid down by Heidegger. The most important of these was strict secrecy. Not only should his wife not know, but also no one at the university and in the small town must be allowed to know anything. Heidegger sent her cryptic notes, "giving the place and the time, down to the exact minute, of their next rendezvous, and the elaborate signals of lights switched on and off."[27] Hannah submitted to these arrangements, she told him, "because of my love for you, to make nothing more difficult than it already was."[28] She dared not demand of Heidegger that he should decide to choose her.

During the summer vacation of 1924, while Heidegger is in Todtnauberg, Hannah returns to her family in Königsberg and there composes a lightly encoded self-portrait and sends it to Heidegger. She is tormented by a feeling of not being really present in this relationship. She must not show herself, but in her "Shadows"—the title of her text—she intends to reveal herself at last. She tries to find a language for the "extraordinary and magical"[29] that has just happened and that has split her life into a "Here-and-Now" and a "Then-and-There."[30] She calls her love an "unbending devotion to a single one."[31] In a shadowy manner, totally dissolved into moods, Hannah Arendt sketches her inner emotions, which are dominated by the pressure of a worldless, aloof inwardness. In a text broken up by reflections, and using the detachment of the third person singular, she tells of a love that has not yet properly come into the world. There is something entirely elemental missing, something that Arendt will later, in *The Human Condition,* call the "worldly interspace: Love, by reason of its passion, destroys the in-between which relates to us and separates us from others."[32] What separates the lovers from the world in which they live is that they are worldless, that the world between them has burnt away.

This "worldly interspace" is extinguished not only by passion but also by the external constraint of secrecy. Where love dares not show itself, where there are no witnesses to it, there the criterion of distinction between reality and imagination is lost. This is what depresses Hannah, and in her "Shadows" she speaks of being "homeless."[33] And in a poem of those days we read:

> Why do you give me your hand
> shyly, as if it were a secret?
> Are you from such a distant land
> that you do not know our wine?[34]

Heidegger was her senior by seventeen years, the father of two boys, married to an ambitious woman who guarded most carefully the family's reputation and who was suspiciously watching her husband as he enjoyed the adulation of his female students. Elfride was especially reserved toward Hannah Arendt, not only because Heidegger was obviously treating her preferentially but also because she was Jewish. Elfride's anti-Semitism was notorious even in the 1920s. Günther Stern (Anders), who was subsequently married to Hannah Arendt for a number of years, recalls how, on the occasion of a party at Todtnauberg, Elfride Heidegger asked him if he did not want to join the National Socialist youth group in Marburg, and how horrified she was when he informed her that he was a Jew.

The fact that Hannah Arendt did not then compel Heidegger to come to a decision about her does not, of course, mean that she did not expect him to arrive at one. The secrecy, after all, was his game. In her eyes, it was he who would have to raise their relationship to a more compact reality. But he did not wish to do so; for him, Arendt's devotion was a piece of luck that would not entail any responsibility for him. In his letters he kept assuring her that no one understood him so well as she did—even, and especially, in philosophical matters. In point of fact, Arendt will later demonstrate how well she understood Heidegger. She will understand him better than he understood himself. She will, in the manner of lovers, respond to and complement his philosophy, endowing it with that reality that it was still lacking. To his "running ahead into death" she will reply with a philosophy of being born; to his existential solipsism of *Jemeinigkeit* (each-one-ness) she will reply with a philosophy of plurality; to his critique of *Verfallenheit* (helpless addiction) to the world of *Man* (One / They) she will reply with her *amor mundi.* To Heidegger's *Lichtung* (clearing) she will respond by philosophically ennobling the "public." Only thus does Heidegger's philosophy become an entity—but he will not notice it. He will not read Arendt's books, or only very cursorily, and what he does read will offend him. More of all this later.

Heidegger loves Arendt, and he will love her for a long time yet. He takes her seriously as a woman who understands him; she becomes his muse for *Being and Time.* He will admit to her that without her he could not have written that work. But at no time will he realize that he might learn from her. When Arendt's great book *The Origins of Totalitarianism* appears in 1955 and she considers a visit to Heidegger, she drops the idea. In a letter to Heinrich Blücher she explains her reason: "The fact that my book must be out just now . . . creates the worst possible constellation . . . As you know, I am quite ready to behave toward Heidegger as though I have never written a word and will never write one. And this the unspoken *conditio sine qua non* of the whole affair."[35]

Back to Marburg. The longer the affair lasts the more difficult it becomes to maintain the secrecy. Moreover, it is gradually becoming uncanny for Hannah. Since Heidegger is interested in the precious moments of encounter rather than in having Hannah about him—this role is reserved for Elfride—he suggests to Hannah at the beginning of 1925 that she should move, ideally to Heidelberg to his friend Karl Jaspers. Not an end to the affair, only a geographical separation. Hannah meanwhile has also been toying with the idea of leaving Marburg. But her reasons are different. She had probably, as Ettinger suspects, hoped that Heidegger would try to keep her with him, and she is hurt that the suggestion that she should leave should have come from him. But, as Ettinger also points out, it was not just a matter of tactics on her part. Ten years later she would write to Heinrich Blücher, who would become everything to her—lover, friend, brother, father, colleague—"It still seems unbelievable to me that I can have both, the 'great love,' and retain my own identity. And only now I have the former since I also have the latter. Finally I know what happiness actually is."[36]

Only in her union with Blücher—a fellow exile; a former communist; later, as an autodidact, appointed to a professorship in America—only with this intellectually charismatic, sovereign, and warm-hearted man will she find that fusion of surrender and being herself. With Heidegger that was not possible. To save herself she tries to get away from Heidegger toward the end of 1924. But she cannot tear herself away. Although she keeps her new Heidelberg address secret from him, she hopes in her heart of hearts that he will look for her and find her.

Heidegger discovers her Heidelberg address from Hans Jonas, and letters once more go to and fro. Arrangements became even more elaborate. In the spring of 1926 Heidegger travels to Switzerland for a lecture. The arrangement, according to Ettinger,[37] was that Hannah would meet Heidegger at a small town en route. He would break his journey for a day. They would spend the night at an inn. He promises to look out for her at every small station where the train stops.

Hannah informs Heidegger of her affair with Benno von Wiese, and later also of her relationship with Günther Anders. She finds his reaction hurtful. He congratulates her and arranges further rendezvous. He lets it be understood that, with his grand passion, he is above her petty, ephemeral love affairs. More important, he clearly fails to realize that her affairs are inept attempts to get free from him. Or if he does realize it, then it seems to her his behavior indicates that he wants to wield his power over her. She withdraws, does not answer his letters, but then just a single invitation, a plea, a declaration of love will bring her to him. Ettinger describes such an instance: Hannah is on a journey to Nuremberg with a woman friend in the late twenties. She receives a letter from Heidegger, "summoning her to a rendezvous"[38] just as the official Klamm summons Frieda in Kafka's *Castle.* And Hannah reacts just like Frieda: she hears the summons and hastens to Heidegger.

Six years after leaving Marburg, Hannah Arendt wrote her book about Rahel Varnhagen. Her description of Rahel's broken love affair with Count Finckenstein suggests that her own experience and disappointments have entered into her writing. Rahel wanted the count to acknowledge her, not only in her salon but also before his family. She, the Jewess, wished to be pulled across into his *Junker* world, and if he lacked the courage to make her, as Arendt puts it, the present of "visibility" and of "being known," then at least he should decide to make a clean break. Rahel, according to Arendt, had been humiliated chiefly by the fact that the count allowed things to run their course, thereby making it possible for the inertia of circumstances to triumph over the adventure of love. "He was the victor, and had attained what he wished: namely, mastery over his own life and his own destiny, in spite of those claims of hers which to him appeared immoderate and mad, and he had achieved this mastery as he wished without committing himself to evil or good, without taking any stand at all."[39]

Was not Heidegger also such a "victor," who, by his indecision, assured that "destiny" would remain master over her "immoderate and mad claims"?

When "destiny" had done its work, separating the two for many years, and Arendt met Heidegger again in 1950, she wrote to Heinrich Blücher: "At bottom, I was happy at the confirmation that I was right never to have forgotten."[40] That new encounter would be the beginning of a new chapter of this lifelong story.

The inspiration for Heidegger's work continues, even after his muse's departure. In the vacations, he works in Todtnauberg on the manuscript that would be published in 1927 under the title *Being and Time.* He has rented a room from a peasant of the neighborhood; the hut is too confining and too noisy when his family is present. In his letters to Jaspers, to whom he does not reveal his relationship with Hannah Arendt, he demonstrates a grim and vigorous energy. On July 24 he writes: "On Aug. 1 I'm off to the cabin—and am looking forward a lot to the strong mountain air—this soft light stuff down here ruins one in the long run. Eight days lumbering—then again writing" (BwHJ). On September 23, 1925: "It's marvelous up here—I'd love to stay up here with my work until spring. I have no desire for the company of professors. The peasants are much more agreeable and even more interesting" (BwHJ). On April 24, 1926, comes the triumphant news from Todtnauberg: "On April 1 I started printing my essay 'Being and Time' . . . I am working full tilt and am annoyed only by the coming semester and the philistine air that surrounds one again . . . It's late night already—the storm is sweeping over the hill, the beams are creaking in the cabin, life lies pure, simple, and great before the soul . . . Sometimes I no longer understand that down there one can play such strange roles" (BwHJ).

The impetus for completing at least part of *Being and Time* had come from outside. In 1925 Nicolai Hartmann had accepted an appointment to Cologne, and the Marburg faculty was anxious to make the *Extraordinarius* (associate professor) Heidegger an *Ordinarius,* a full professor. The appointment commission therefore exerted some gentle pressure on Heidegger: it was time he submitted a new publication. They referred to a statement by Hartmann that "an absolutely outstanding work by Heidegger" was on the point of completion. This assurance was enough for the philosophical faculty to propose Heidegger on August 5, 1925, as a successor to Hartmann. From Berlin, however, came a rejection. On January 27, 1926, Minister of Culture Carl Heinrich Becker wrote: "With all due recognition of Professor Heidegger's successes as a teacher, it does not seem appropriate to me to entrust him with an established full professorship of the historical importance of the Chair of Philosophy at your university until major literary achievements have earned that special recognition from his colleagues in the field which such an appointment calls for" (quoted in BwHJ, 232). On June 18, 1926, the philosophical faculty once more wrote to the ministry, requesting the appointment of Professor Heidegger. He had meanwhile sent a major work to the printer. Printers' sheets were enclosed. On November 25 the sheets were returned. The ministry held to its decision. At the beginning of 1927 *Being and Time* was published as an offprint by the *Jahrbuch für Philosophie und Phänomenologische Forschung* (Annual for Philosophy and Phenomenological Research) edited by Husserl and Max Scheler. Now at last the ministry understood what kind of work it was that had just been published. On October 19, 1927, Heidegger was promoted from associate to full professor.

It had been an irritating business. On April 24, 1926, Heidegger wrote to Jaspers: "To me the whole affair is . . . a matter of total indifference"—but at least Heidegger had been compelled to publish his work, even though he himself may not have considered it quite finished. Jaspers was being sent the sheets as they came off the press, along with Heidegger's rather modest comment. On May 24, 1926, Heidegger wrote: "On the whole, this is an intermediate piece to me" (BwHJ). On December 21, 1926, he observed that he did not assess his work "excessively highly," though he had "on its basis learned to understand . . . what greater ones have aimed at" (BwHJ). And on December 26, 1926: "This work is not going to yield to me more than what I already possess of it—that I have worked myself free and can now, with some certainty and direction, pose questions" (BwHJ).

In the spring of 1927 Heidegger's mother was dying. Heidegger hints to Jaspers how it pains him to be regarded by his pious mother as a son who has lapsed from the faith. "That I am a great worry to her, making her dying more difficult, you will probably appreciate. The last hour I spent with my mother . . . was a piece of 'practical philosophy' that will remain with me. I believe that to most philosophers the question of theology and philosophy, or rather faith and philosophy, is a purely academic question" (March 1, 1927, BwHJ, 73).

On March 9, 1927, during the time that his mother was dying, Heidegger gives a lecture in Tübingen entitled "Phenomenology and Philosophy," which a year later he will repeat in Marburg in revised form. In it Heidegger states that faith, in its innermost core, as a specific option of existence, remains the mortal enemy of . . . the existential form that, in its nature, belongs to philosophy. This conflict, however, does not rule out "mutual respect and appreciation," but these are possible only if the difference is clearly observed and not fudged. Christian philosophy is "wooden iron." Philosophy must be able to rely on itself "as the free questioning of existence resting purely upon itself" (W, 66).

This is how he understands his philosophy. With *Being and Time* he believes he has arrived at it. That is why, as a farewell present, he places an author's copy of the newly published book on his mother's deathbed.

9

BEING AND TIME: WHAT BEING? WHAT MEANING?

Let me recapitulate. After a theological prelude, Martin Heidegger had begun as a Catholic philosopher. His thought had moved about the sphere of the question of God as the coping stone and guarantor of our cognition of the world and ourselves. Heidegger came from a tradition that could maintain itself only defensively against a modernist movement for which God had lost his meaning. Heidegger wanted to defend the heaven above Messkirch—even with the weapons of the modernist movement, such as Husserl's thesis of the transtemporal and transsubjective validity of logic, an idea he found preformed in the metaphysical philosophy of the Middle Ages. However, he also discovered there the nominalistic self-doubt of a reason that admits to itself that not only God but also *haecceitas,* the uniquely singular, remains incomprehensible to it. *Individuum est ineffabile.*

It was only the idea of historicity that unveiled for him the whole questionableness of metaphysics. Although metaphysical thought does not postulate the unchangeability of man, it does postulate the unchangeability of the ultimate conceptual references. Heidegger learned from Dilthey that truths, too, have their history. Toward the conclusion of his habilitation thesis he performed his decisive shift of perspective. He now viewed medieval thought, to which he had come so close, from a greater distance—and in that view it appeared as a charming but declining epoch of the spirit. Dilthey's discovery "that meaning and significance only originate in man and his history" became crucial for him. The radical idea of historicity destroys any universalist claim to validity. In man's self-understanding it possibly represents the greatest break in Occidental history. It also means the end of Heidegger's "Catholic philosophizing."

Real history, the collapse of yesterday's world in a world war, also persuaded Heidegger that the ground was shaking and that a new beginning had to be made.

To post-1918 Heidegger, historical life becomes the foundation of philosophizing. This realization, however—according to him—does not get one very far so long as the concept of "life" remains undefined. Phenomenology had taught him that there was a problem here. In the proper phenomenological manner he asked himself: What attitude must I choose in order that human life can *reveal* itself in its specificity? The answer to this question provided the basis for his own philosophy—the critique of *Vergegenständlichung,* of objectivization. Human life escapes us, he taught, if we try to capture it from a theoretical, objectivizing attitude. We notice this even in the attempt to bring the "lectern experiment" to our consciousness. In objectivizing thought, the wealth of life-worldly references disappears. The objective attitude "de-experiences" experience and "de-worlds" the world we encounter. Heidegger's philosophy turns toward the darkness of the lived moment. This is not a case of mysterious profundity, of any underworld of the subconscious or superworld of the spiritual, but of the "self-transparency" of life performances, including the common everyday ones. Philosophy to Heidegger becomes the art of the "growth of *Dasein* for itself." This turn toward the everyday world has a polemical accent, aimed against a philosophy that still believes that it knows man's calling. Heidegger enters the scene with the grand gesture of a new beginning. His early lectures betray a dadaist pleasure in destroying exalted cultural values and unmasking traditional meaning-attributions as mere ghostly spectacle. He was "raging" with his "facticity" and did not give a damn for the "cultural tasks for a universal today," he wrote to Löwith in 1921. Laboriously at first, but with a crescendo of triumphant success, he gradually lifts from the darkness of *Dasein*—as he now calls human life—those structures that are presented as "existentials" in *Being and Time*—"Being-in" *(In-Sein),* "state of mind" *(Befindlichkeit),* "deterioration" *(Verfallen),* "care" *(Sorge).* He finds the formula of a "*Dasein* that is concerned with its own potentiality-for-Being."

The years between 1923 and 1927, when *Being and Time* appeared, were a period of enormous productivity for Heidegger. In major lectures the themes of *Being and Time* were already being developed. Compared to this massif of ideas—in his *Collected Works* it accounts for fifteen hundred pages—*Being and Time* is little more than the tip of the iceberg. But in this work his ideas are presented with architectural refinement and terminological sophistication. Moreover, the scaffolding, the methodological provisions, were left standing, which was bound to lend the work an appearance of monstrous ponderousness. This did not lessen its effect in the academic world, however, which tends to treat anything simple with suspicion. Among the general public the obscurity of the book enhanced its aura. It was left open whether *Dasein* itself was so obscure or only its analysis. Certainly the whole thing seemed somehow mysterious.

In *Being and Time* Heidegger develops the philosophical proof that human existence, *Dasein,* has no other support than this *da,* this there-ness. In a sense he continues Nietzsche's work: to think the death of God and criticize the "last humans" (Nietzsche) who make do with pitiful substitute gods and do not even permit appalled horror over the disappearance of God. In *Being and Time* the formula for the capacity to experience horror is "Courage for anxiety."

Being and Time: a title that promises that here all is at stake. It had been known in the academic world that Heidegger was preparing a major work, but it had not been expected to signal such a massive claim. It should not be forgotten that Heidegger then was not yet regarded as a constructive philosopher but as the virtuoso interpreter of philosophical tradition, a man who knew how to present it like no one else, a man who dealt with Plato and Aristotle the way Rudolf Bultmann dealt with Christ—revitalizing them.

Hermann Mörchen recalls how, at the beginning of 1927, at an informal meeting with his Bündisch students, he "wordlessly, expectantly, like a child showing off his favorite toy, produced a galley-proof sheet straight from the printer—a title page: *Being and Time.*"[1]

The work, with assured dramatic effect, begins—in a sense like Goethe's *Faust*—with a "prologue in heaven." Plato enters. A sentence from his *So-*

phistes dialogue is quoted: "For manifestly you have long been aware of what you mean when you use the expression 'being.' We, however, who used to think we understood it, have now become perplexed."[2]

This "becoming perplexed," Heidegger states, is still there, but we do not admit it to ourselves. We still do not know what we mean when we say that something is "being." The prologue complains about a double forgetting of Being. We have forgotten what Being is, and we have even forgotten this forgetting. "So it is fitting that we should raise anew the question of the meaning of Being," but because we have forgotten our forgetting, "first of all we must reawaken an understanding for the meaning of this question."[3]

As befits a prologue, there is a hint at the very beginning of what this is all leading to—"the interpretation of time as the possible horizon of any understanding whatsoever of Being."[4] The meaning of Being is—Time. The punch line is disclosed, but to make it comprehensible Heidegger needs not only this whole book but also the rest of his life.

The question of Being. Strictly speaking, Heidegger asks two questions. The first is: What do we actually mean when we use the term "being"? The question is about the meaning of the term. From this question Heidegger proceeds to a totally different one as to the meaning of Being itself. As for this question with its double meaning, Heidegger asserts that there is a lack of understanding even for the meaning of the question. An odd assertion.

As to the question of the meaning of Being (not just of the term), it may be stated that this is the question that has continually occupied human reflection from the beginnings of history to the present day. It is the question as to the sense, the purpose, and the meaning of human life and of nature; the question about the values and signposts of life; the question of the why and wherefore of the world and the universe. Practical-moral life makes man ask this question. In earlier days, when physics, metaphysics, and theology still belonged together, scholarship had tried to answer the question as to meaning. However, since Kant discovered that as moral creatures we are bound to ask the *Sinnfrage,* the question as to the meaning, although we cannot as scholars answer it, strict scholarship has shown reserve with regard to this question. Yet practical moral life continues to pose it, every day, in advertisements, in poetry and moral reflection, and in religion. How can Heidegger claim that there is no longer any understanding for the question? He can do so only because he believes that all kinds of meaning endowments and their related questions about meaning actually miss the "meaning of Being." A bold assertion, which first of all places the philosopher himself in the right light. He emerges as someone who is rediscovering what had lain forgotten and hidden since Plato's days. Even in the "prologue in heaven" Heidegger stages himself as the protagonist of an epochal caesura. What he has to contribute in detail to the meaning of Being we shall see presently. Heidegger is a master at making approach roads long. We can only really rejoice in light if it appears at the end of the tunnel.

To begin with, Heidegger sets aside the question as to the meaning of Being—we shall call it here the "emphatic question." He starts with another question, the semantic question, which is: What do we mean when we use the term "being" *(seiend),* in what "sense" do we speak of Being *(Sein)?* This question certainly belongs to the context of the modern sciences. Every discipline—physics, chemistry, sociology, anthropology, and so on—deals with a certain area of what is being, or else it deals with the same area with different sets of questions and methods. Any methodical reflection on how one has to approach a certain subject implies a regional ontology, even if one no longer calls it so. Heidegger's assertion that one no longer realizes in what meaning one tackles Being in each separate subject area does not therefore at first seem to make sense. After all, neo-Kantianism had developed an extraordinary sense of awareness of method. There were Rickert's and Wildebrand's subtle distinctions between the natural and the cultural sciences, Dilthey's hermeneutics, Max Weber's understanding sociology, Husserl's phenomenological method, the psychoanalytical hermeneutics of the unconscious. None of these disciplines was methodologically naive; each possessed an ontological awareness of problems by reflecting on their place in the overall context of the exploration of reality. The same, therefore, applies to the semantic-methodological question as applies to the emphatic question with regard to the meaning of Being. On both occasions Heidegger claims that there is no understanding for the meaning of the questions—and yet they are being posed everywhere, the emphatic one in practical moral life, the methodological-semantic one in the sciences.

Heidegger must be after something special—but we do not yet know what. He skillfully builds up our suspense before he puts forward his thesis. In the exploration of Man in particular, he argues, it becomes obvious that the sciences are not clear about the sense in which they allow Man to be "being." They act as if it were possible to get Man as a whole into focus, as one can other objects in the world. In so doing they follow a spontaneous tendency of

"*Dasein* to understand its own Being . . . in terms of that entity towards which it comports itself proximally and in a way which is essentially constant—in terms of the 'world'" (SuZ, 15).[5] But this is a self-mystification of *Dasein*, which, so long as it lives, is never finished, entire, or completed, as an object might be, but always remains open for the future, full of possibilities. *Dasein* (being here) implies being possible *(Möglich-sein)*.

In contrast to the rest of what is, Man has a relationship with his own Being. This Heidegger calls "Existence." Existence—as I showed earlier in Heidegger's interpretation of Aristotle—has a transitive meaning. The intransitive aspect of *Dasein* is called "thrownness" *(Geworfenheit)* by Heidegger. "Has *Dasein* as itself ever decided freely whether it wants to come into '*Dasein*' or not?" (SuZ, 228).[6] But if—intransitively—we are here, then we cannot but live transitively that which we are intransitively. That which we have become intransitively, we can and must be transitively. Sartre would later find a formula for it: "Make something of what we were made into." We are a self-relationship and hence also a Being-relationship. "*Dasein* is ontically distinctive in that it is ontological" (SuZ, 12).[7]

The term "ontic" designates everything that exists. The term "ontological" designates the curious, astonished, alarmed thinking about the fact that I exist and that anything exists at all. Ontological, for instance, is the inimitable sentence by Grabbe: "Only once in the world, and of all things as a plumber in Detmold!" *Dasein* or existence therefore means we not only exist, but we perceive also that we exist. And we are never finished like something that exists, we cannot walk around ourselves; at each point we are open for a future. We must *lead* our lives. We are charged with ourselves. We are what we become.

At the very beginning—at the question, How can one speak appropriately of *Dasein*?—Heidegger focuses on time. Gazing ahead into time, we observe that many an uncertainty lies before us. But there is one certainty, the great "in-the-past," death. We are acquainted with it not only because others are dying but also because we can experience that in-the-past at any moment—the flow of time, a series of little departures, lots of little deaths. Temporality is the experience of the present, the future, and eventually the fatal in-the-past.

Both aspects of temporality—its concluding and its initializing aspect, Being-toward-death and being possible—are major challenges to *Dasein*. That is why—and here the circle closes and we stand once more at the beginning—*Dasein* is inclined to deal with itself as with something that exists, something that one believes one can cope with, even before one is finished. Man's scientific objectivization is to Heidegger an avoidance of the disturbing temporality of *Dasein.* Yet the sciences merely continue the stubborn tendency of everyday *Dasein* to understand itself "from the world"—that is, as a thing among things. Science is the cultured and methodical form of the everyday self-objectivization of *Dasein.* It is this stony heart that Heidegger intends to assail.

He links the two questions, the emphatic one as to the meaning of Being and the methodological-semantic one about the meaning of the term "Being," in the thesis: the tendency to throw *Dasein* among things persists also in the emphatic question as to the meaning of Being. The "meaning" is sought as something that exists in the world, or in some imaginary Beyond, as something present-at-hand, something that one can hold on to and orient oneself by—God, a universal law, the stone tablets of morality.

This manner of asking about the meaning of Being as though it were something present-at-hand is to Heidegger an escape of *Dasein* from its temporality and its potentiality-for-being. The question as to the meaning of Being had been asked and answered in the dimension of a metaphysics of existence—and therefore missed. That kind of nonsense was then rampant—"meaning" was being practiced; there were meaning research programs; there was talk of the shortage of sense-and-meaning resources, which therefore should be used economically. It was a particularly foolish metaphysics of existence.

This is not a theoretical "mis-attitude." The question as to the meaning of Being—as mentioned earlier—is no longer a question of the strict sciences, which have made brilliant progress just because they got out of the habit of asking it. The question as to the meaning is put instead by daily practical-moral awareness. But how is that attitude of awareness to be understood?

It is one of the theatrical refinements of *Being and Time* that Heidegger does not raise the real subject of the question as to the meaning of Being until halfway through the work. The subject, the "who" of this question, is a mood, the "basic state of mind of anxiety."[8] In a state of anxiety *Dasein* asks about the meaning of Being, the meaning of its being. The famous paragraph forty is devoted to the analysis of anxiety. There are no paragraphs in *Being and Time* devoted to rejoicing or love—moods from which the question as to the meaning of Being might just as well spring—despite Hannah Arendt. This has to do not only with the philosophically justifiable distinction of certain moods with regard to their philosophical yield capacity, but also with the author, with his real moods and with his predilection for certain moods.

Anxiety is the shadowy queen among moods. It has to be distinguished from fear.[9] Fear is directed toward something definite, it focuses on detail. Anxiety, on the other hand, is vague and as boundless as the world. The "of what" of anxiety is "the world as such." In the face of anxiety everything sinks to the ground, stripped of all significance. Anxiety is sovereign, it can grow powerful within us, triggered by nothing. And why not, seeing that its real counterpart is nothingness? If a person suffers from anxiety, then "the world has nothing more to offer him, nor has the *Dasein*-with of others." Anxiety tolerates no other gods beside it; it isolates in two respects. It breaks the bond to fellow beings and lets the individual drop out of his familiar relationships with the world. It confronts *Dasein* with the naked "That" of the world and of its own self. But what remains when *Dasein* has passed through the cold fire of anxiety is not nothing. That which anxiety consumes also lays bare the hot kernel of "*Dasein*—the Being—free for the freedom of choosing itself and taking hold of itself."[10]

It is in anxiety, therefore, that *Dasein* experiences the uncanniness of the world and its own freedom. Thus anxiety can be two things at a time—world anxiety and anxiety of freedom.

This analysis is inspired by Kierkegaard, with whom anxiety of freedom is anxiety of becoming guilty. Kierkegaard attempts to overcome this anxiety by the "leap" into faith, a leap across the chasm. He has lost the faith of his origins. For Heidegger it is the anxiety after the leap, when one is about to plunge downward.

Obviously Heidegger's philosophy of anxiety also stems from the general crisis mood of the 1920s. The malaise of culture—Freud's essay under this title appeared in 1929—was widespread. The worldview essays of the period were marked by an uneasy sense of a declining, perverted, or alienated world. The diagnoses were gloomy and the therapies offered numerous. A boom was enjoyed by attempts to cure the ailing whole from one point. Just as in Weimar politics the democratic center was being eroded by the extremism of totalitarian reformers, so the crisis philosophy of those years was dominated by a resort to extremist solutions. These bore various names—the proletariat, the unconscious, the soul, the sacred, the people's community, and so on. This fairground of crisis-management philosophies was examined at the time by

Carl Christian Bry in his book *Verkappte Religionen* (Masked Religions), a best-seller of the 1920s. When the book appeared, two years ahead of *Being and Time,* fanatical anti-Semitism and racial ideas were rampant, the Bolshevization of the German Communist Party was beginning, Hitler was writing *Mein Kampf* in Landsberg prison, millions were seeking salvation in sectarian movements—occultism, vegetarianism, nudism, theosophy and anthroposophy—there were countless promises of salvation and offers of a new road. The trauma of devaluation had made the businesses of the inflation saints flourish. Anything, Bry wrote, can become a "masked religion" if it becomes, "monomaniacally," the sole principle for the interpretation of meaning and salvation. Bry, himself a religious man, found a surprisingly simple criterion for distinguishing between religion and substitute religion. A genuine religion educates Man for reverence for the inexplicability of the world. In the light of faith, the world grows bigger, and also darker, because it retains its mystery, and Man sees himself as part of it. For the monomaniac of a "masked religion," on the other hand, the world shrinks. "In each and every thing he finds only the confirmation of his opinion," which he defends with the fervor of faith against the world and against his own doubts.[11]

Being and Time fitted into this general crisis mood, but it differed from the bulk of the genre by not offering a therapy. In 1929 Freud had introduced his diagnosis of the "discontents of civilization" with the words: "My courage fails, therefore, at the thought of rising up as a prophet before my fellow-men, and I bow to their reproach that I have no consolation to offer them, for at bottom this is what they all demand."[12] These words apply also to Heidegger's enterprise. He, too, thinks on the basis of his experience of malaise and refuses to stand up as a prophet "offering consolation."

True enough, Heidegger's emphatic question as to the meaning of Being might well arouse such expectations. And they were indeed aroused—but not fulfilled. For these expectations to be disappointed was part of the message of *Being and Time,* the message that states: there is nothing behind it. The meaning of Being is Time; but Time is not a cornucopia of gifts, it gives us no content and no orientation. The meaning is Time, but Time "gives" no meaning.

Anxiety in Heidegger's analysis of *Dasein* marks the point of peripeteia—man drops out of the relations in which he had "entered and settled." The analyses that precede the chapter on anxiety have as their theme a *Dasein* that has settled firmly in its world. It turns out that anxiety, because it lets the world slip away and in that respect is a distance phenomenon, is easier to describe than this strange, distanceless, firmly settled "Being-in-the-world" of daily existence. If one wants to make it transparent, one has, in a manner of speaking, to "share" in this distanceless movement of *Dasein* and not adopt a standpoint outside it. Here, more than elsewhere, the phenomenological principle applies: one must not speak about the phenomenon but instead choose an attitude that will allow the phenomenon to "show" itself.

In this respect philosophy has frequently sinned in the past. It either described how consciousness originates from the world (naturalism) or how the world is constructed from consciousness (idealism). Heidegger seeks a third way. His original but convincing approach is: one must start from the *In-Sein*, the Being-in, because "phenomenologically" one neither first experiences oneself and then the world nor, the other way about, first the world and then oneself, but in experience the two are simultaneously present in indissoluble union. This experience had been named "intentionality" by phenomenologists. For Heidegger this is the most important insight of phenomenology, though he understands it only as the world-reference of *Dasein* and not, as Husserl, as a structure of consciousness.

The analysis of Being-in leads to bizarre terminological convolutions. Any conceptual statement must avoid relapsing into the tempting separation of subject and object or into a choice between subjective (internal) and objective (external) standpoints. In consequence we see the emergence of those hyphenated verbal monstrosities designed to describe the structures in their indissoluble connections. A few examples: *In-der-Welt-sein* (Being-in-the-world) means *Dasein* does not confront the world but always already finds itself present in it; *Mit-sein-mit-anderen* (being-with others): *Dasein* always already finds itself in joint situation with others; *Sich-vorweg-sein* (Being-ahead-of-oneself): *Dasein* gazes from the present moment into the future not occasionally but continually, with concern. These expressions demonstrate the paradoxical character of the whole undertaking. Analysis means that something is taken apart. Heidegger, however, attempts, while analyzing the effects of his analysis, to reverse the splitting into parts and elements again. Heidegger reaches into *Dasein* as into a colony of algae. No matter where one grabs it, one will always have to pull it out as a whole. This endeavor to seize something individual while always taking along with it everything that is connected with it at times leads to involuntary self-parody. Thus *Sorge* (care) is defined as *Sich-vorweg-schon-sein in (einer Welt) als Sein-bei (innerweltlich begleitendem Seienden)* (ahead-of-itself-already-being-in [a world] as Being-alongside [entities encountered within-the-world]) (SuZ, 327).[13]

The complexity of the language is to be appropriate to the complexity of everyday *Dasein.* In his summer 1925 lecture "Prolegomena on the History of the Concept of Time," Heidegger says: "If we are forced here to introduce ponderous and perhaps inelegant expressions, it is not a matter of personal whim or a special fancy for my own terminology, but the compulsion of the phenomena themselves . . . If such formulations come up often, no offence should be taken. There is no such thing as the beautiful in the sciences, least of all perhaps in philosophy" (GA 20, 204).[14] The special terminology is also—analogously to Bertolt Brecht's practice—an alienation technique, because what is being examined here is "not a strange and unfamiliar matter, but on the contrary the nearest, which is perhaps precisely why it leads us astray into mistakes" (GA 20, 205).[15] To that extent this is a calculated language. It states the obvious in a way that even philosophers can grasp. And to the same extent the language also testifies to the difficulties of philosophy in exploring the everyday life that hitherto it has, as a rule, avoided. "That which is ontically closest and well known, is ontologically the farthest and not known at all; and its ontological signification is constantly overlooked" (SuZ, 43).[16]

The analysis of *Dasein* is called by Heidegger "existential analysis," and the fundamental determinants of *Dasein* are "existentials." This concept has given rise to numerous misunderstandings, but it was created simply in analogy to the traditional concept of category. Traditional philosophy customarily called the fundamental determinants of its "objects" categories, such as space, time, extension, and so on. As *Dasein* to Heidegger is not an object that is present but "existence," he calls his fundamental determinants not categories but existentials.

Heidegger therefore begins his analysis of *Dasein* with *In-Sein* (Being-in), because *Dasein* itself begins with it. Being-in means not only that one finds oneself somewhere, but also that one has always been dealing with something, been concerned with something.

To be radical is to get at the roots. To Marx, Man's roots were "working man." Heidegger's "dealing with something" as Man's fundamental determination is even more comprehensive. Labor was defined by Marx as "metabolism with nature." With Heidegger, "dealing with," while referring to the (objective, natural) world around him, refers equally to the "self-world" (the self-relationship) and to the "with-world" (society).

Heidegger's approach is pragmatic because action—and "dealing with" means just that—is seen as the fundamental structure of *Dasein.* Pragmatical also is his linking of action and cognition. In Heidegger's terminology, primary dealing-with always has its own *Umsicht* (circumspection). Cognition is a function of action. It would therefore be a mistake, he says, to try to understand recognizing awareness outside of itself. This statement is aimed against Husserl's phenomenological exploration of awareness. As cognition stems from practical dealing with the world, it needs to be explored through the practical activity of life.

Is this not a return to the well-known materialist principle of "Being determines consciousness"? Heidegger's objection is that if one allows consciousness to be determined by Being, one is pretending to know what Being is. But we do not know, Heidegger argues; we are asking about it. One can only attentively observe and phenomenologically describe how the "environment" *(Umwelt),* the "with-world" *(Mitwelt),* and the "self-world" *(Selbstwelt)* encounter *Dasein.*

He asks, first of all: How and as what does the objective environment encounter us? It does so as "equipment" *(Zeug)* which, in the radius of my activity, has a definite "involvement" *(Bewandtnis).*

An illustration. The door that I customarily open is not perceived by me as a painted wooden panel. When I am attuned to it, I do not perceive it at all. I open it to get into my study. It has its "location" in my living space, and also in my lifetime; it plays a certain part in the ritual of my daily life. Its creaking is part of it, as are traces of wear and tear, memories "attaching" to it, and so on. This door, in Heidegger's terminology, is "ready-to-hand" *(zuhanden).* If unexpectedly it were to be locked one day, and I knocked my head against it, then I would painfully perceive the door as the hard wooden panel that in reality it is. Then the ready-to-hand *(zuhanden)* door would have become a present-at-hand *(vorhanden)* door.

The references into which we have thus entered form the world of "readiness-to-hand" *(Zuhanden).* There is a connection of meaning to which I am adjusted even without recognizing it in detail. We "live" these meanings without expressly bringing them into our awareness. Only when a disturbance occurs, either from outside or from our consciousness, does this connection fall apart and the objects are seen as something merely present-at-hand. In this presentness-at-hand, however, the lived significances of the readiness-to-hand have disappeared or at least become invalid. Only by the transformation of readiness-to-hand into presentness-at-hand do things become objects in the strict sense, objects that can be explored from a theoretical attitude.

Heidegger's analysis attempts to save the world of readiness-to-hand for thought, because most of the time it is "overtaken" by philosophical recognition. We are all too ready to arrange objects (and people) in such a way that they are merely present-at-hand in an indifferent manner. Later Heidegger will call this transformation of the world into something merely present-at-hand "oblivion of Being" *(Seinsvergessenheit),* and the conscious preservation of ready-to-hand living space will become Being-closeness, understood as "closeness to" or "dwelling with the things." The corresponding attitude will be called "composure" *(Gelassenheit).* In *Being and Time,* meanwhile, a different existential ideal predominates—as will be seen presently.

The fundamental structure of this dealing with the world is called "anxiety," or "care," by Heidegger. To illustrate this point he quotes the late-antique *Cura* fable of Hyginus.

> Once when "Care" was crossing a river, she saw some clay; she thoughtfully took up a piece and began to shape it. While she was meditating on what she had made, Jupiter came by. "Care" asked him to give it spirit, and this he gladly granted. But when she wanted her name to be bestowed upon it, he forbade this and demanded that it be given his name instead. While "Care" and Jupiter were disputing, Earth arose and desired that her name be conferred on the creature, since she had furnished it with part of her body. They asked Saturn to be their arbiter, and he made the following decision, which seemed a just one: "Since you, Jupiter, have given its spirit, you shall receive that spirit at its death; and since you, Earth, have given its body, you shall receive its body. But since 'Care' first shaped this creature, she shall possess it as long as it lives." (SuZ, 198)[17]

"Care" does not mean that, now and again, one is worried about something. Care is a basic characteristic of the human condition. Heidegger uses the term in the meaning of providing, planning, looking after, calculating, foreseeing. The time reference is important here. Only a creature that sees before it an open and unavailable time horizon, into which it has to enter, can be caring. We are caring and providing creatures because we expressly experience a time horizon open ahead. Care is nothing other than lived temporality.

As we are, in caring, driven by time, we actively encounter a world that, from the perspective of dealing with it, can be present-at-hand or ready-to-hand. *Dasein* itself, however, is neither something present-at-hand nor ready-to-hand but "existence." To exist means having a self-relation, having to adopt an attitude to oneself and to one's Being. How does man become aware of his own Being? Heidegger's answer: in "mood." The possibilities of disclosure that belong to cognition reach far too short a way compared with the primordial belonging to moods, in which *Dasein* is brought before its Being as "there" (SuZ, 134).[18]

Heidegger emphatically fights against a persistent self-mystification of philosophy. Because philosophy is an effort of thought, it credits thought with the greatest capacity of disclosure. Emotions and moods are claimed to be subjective and hence not suitable to bearing objective cognition of the world. The so-called affects, of course, have always been the object of theoretical curiosity. They were allowed to be objects of cognition but were not, as a rule, admitted as organs of cognition. This had changed with Nietzsche and life philosophy—but not radically enough for Heidegger. Philosophizing out of moods, had, according to Heidegger, allowed itself to be "banished to the sanctuary of the irrational"—a bad place of residence for philosophy. "Irrationalism, as the counterplay of rationalism, talks about the things to which rationalism is blind, it does so only with a squint" (SuZ, 136).[19]

Heidegger takes a close look at moods, directly, without squinting. We are always in some mood or other. Mood is a "state of mind." Although we can drive ourselves into a mood, the essential characteristic of moods is that they arise, seep into us, creep up on us, pounce on us. We are not the master of them. In mood we experience the limits of our self-determination.

Heidegger explores not all possible moods but just those few that fit into his concept. As the basic everyday mood, he highlights "the pallid, evenly balanced lack of mood" *(Ungestimmtheit),* with traces of irritation and boredom. This, he claims, "discloses the burdensome character of *Dasein*" (SuZ, 134).[20] Everyday activity is an escape from that mood. *Dasein* pulls itself together, turns active, refuses to admit to itself what the mood notifies. "*Dasein* for the most part evades the Being which is disclosed in the mood" (SuZ, 135).[21]

Heidegger's fundamental ontology might be seen as an elaborate attempt to cut off *Dasein* from its routes of retreat. With the same elaborate and persistent intensity, Heidegger focuses on those moods in which "the burdensome character of *Dasein*" is revealed—pallid and everyday in irritation and boredom, lurid and dramatic in anxiety.

However, the assertion that the burdensome moods are the fundamental ones is by no means cogent. Max Scheler, who, similarly to Heidegger, ascribes fundamental character to the moods, arrives at different results. In his essay *Nature and Forms of Sympathy* (1912) he declares love and affection, "vibration in tune and going along with," to be the fundamental state of mood and, unlike Heidegger, he regards the gloomy and burdensome as a disturbance and a suspension of this sympathetic basic condition.

It would be easy to say that Heidegger had taken his own predominant basic mood and the mood of the crisis period of the Weimar Republic as his starting point. This would be justified in the sense that he himself invariably emphasizes the "mineness" *(Jemeinigkeit)* and the "historicity" *(Geschichtlichkeit)* of a mood. Yes, in spite of *Jemeinigkeit* and *Geschichtlichkeit* he tries to make statements that would be fundamentally ontologically justified—not only his *Dasein* and that of his period but *Dasein* altogether is to be seized in its basic moods.

With his analysis of *Dasein* Heidegger had intended to pose the question of Being, and he did not wish to see it understood merely as a contribution to philosophical anthropology. It is the more remarkable that leading philosophical anthropologists of the day, for example Helmuth Plessner and Arnold Gehlen, likewise proceed from the burdensome character of human existence, but they draw different conclusions from it. By way of contrast, Heidegger's approach becomes particularly clear. Plessner, in his principal anthropological work, *The Steps of the Organic and Man* (1928), defines man by reference to his "eccentric" position. He has no special organic environment into which he is wholly integrated. He is open to the world. He does not, like animals, live "from his middle into his middle," but must first seek and create his middle.[22] He is a creature of distance, heavily bearing the burden of himself and his eccentric position, for it involves him in delicate contradictions. He seeks a position for himself, he establishes connections, but he does not succeed in being totally absorbed in them. Time and again he cuts through these connections by experiencing himself, from within, as a reflexive creature. He acts into the world and reflects himself from it outward. Thus he is eccentric not only vis-à-vis the world but also vis-à-vis himself. "As the I, which enables the complete return of the living system to itself, Man no longer stands in the 'Here-Now,' but 'behind' it, behind himself, unlocalized, in nothingness . . . His existence is truly placed upon Nothing."[23]

Eccentricity means one must bear life more than one is borne by it, or, put positively, one must lead one's life. Human life stands under the law of "natural artificiality."

This finding is further developed in the 1930s by Arnold Gehlen. For him, too, Man is open to the world, not fitted by secure instinct into any specific environment. This nonadaptation would impair his biological chances of survival if these failings were not compensated in other ways. What he lacks through nature, Man must achieve by culture. He must himself create his own suitable environment. In doing so he proceeds on the principle of least effort. As he has to "do" such a lot, he endeavors to shape things and himself in ways that would call for the least input of spontaneity, motivational energy, and drive. Man therefore tries to eliminate his eccentricity and reflexivity by so arranging his world that it relieves him of what an entire philosophical tradition used to regard as the quintessence of human dignity—spontaneity, reflexivity, freedom.

Life becomes more burdensome the more inward Man becomes. Such inwardness, as a rule, is too weak to bear his own world, but it is strong enough to let him perceive the necessary objectivization and institutionalization of his social world as an imposition and an "untruth." Eventually Man, suffering from the "hiatus" of this inwardness, yields to the inevitable and permits civilization to relieve him of the burdens of *Dasein*—even though in doing so he feels that he is losing himself. Man goes into himself and loses the world, and he goes into the world and loses himself. From this Gehlen concludes: "Man can maintain a lasting relation with himself and others like himself only indirectly; he must, denying himself, find himself again by a detour, and that is where the institutions are. These are, of course, forms produced by people, in which the spiritual has been objectivized, woven into the march of things, and, by just that, placed upon duration. Thus at least people are burned and consumed by their own creations and not by raw nature, as are the animals."[24]

Gehlen and Plessner, just as Heidegger, proceed from the burdensome character of *Dasein* and next describe the cultural techniques of unburdening as an elementary requirement of survival. Although Heidegger speaks of the proximal and predominant "tendency to take things easily and make them easy" (SuZ, 127),[25] it is, for him, just this tendency that deprives Man of his "authentic potentiality-for-Being." The manner in which one deals with the burdensome character of *Dasein* decides on inauthenticity or authenticity. Unburdening, at any rate, is initially suspect to Heidegger as a maneuver of escape, evasion, or deteriorating—that is, of "inauthenticity." The "real hero" bears the weight of the world like Atlas and is, moreover, expected to accomplish the trick of having an upright gait and a bold plan of life.

Along with the famous chapter on death, it was the analysis of authenticity and inauthenticity that earned the work such huge publicity in the 1920s. Heidegger's description of the inauthentic world bears a clear critical reference to his own day, even though he has always denied this. Nevertheless, criticism of mass culture, urbanization, unstable public affairs, the vastly growing entertainment industry, hectic everyday life, the superficial character of intellectual life—all of these enter into his account of a *Dasein* that lives not from its own "ability-to-be" but from "They" *(Man):* "Everyone is the other, and no one is himself" (SuZ, 128).[26]

This world of They has been described by other authors of the 1920s, at times even more impressively and accurately than by Heidegger. Robert Musil, in his *Man without Qualities,* says:

> "One must value it if there's a man still left nowadays who is striving to be something integral," said Walter . . .
>
> "There's no longer any such thing," Ulrich countered. "You only have to look into a newspaper. You'll find it's filled with immeasurable opacity. So many things come under discussion that it would surpass the intellectual capacity of a Leibniz. But one doesn't even notice it. One has become different. There is no longer a whole man confronting a whole world, but a human something floating in a universal culture-medium."[27]

Walter Mehring, in his song "Hoppla, wir leben!" says:

> Here in our Earth Hotel
> the cream of society lodged.
> With an elegant carefree gesture
> they bore the burden of life.

And Vicky Baum, in her best-selling novel *Grand Hotel* (1931), writes: "When you leave another arrives and takes your bed. *Finito.* Sit for an hour or two in the Lounge and keep your eyes open. You'll see that the people there have no individuality. They're dummies, all of 'em. Dead, all the lot and don't know it."[28]

Heidegger's They is a similar dummy: "The 'they,' which supplies the answer to the question of the 'who' of everyday *Dasein,* is the 'nobody' to whom every *Dasein* has already surrendered itself in Being-among-one-another" (SuZ, 128).[29]

Heidegger's descriptions of the contemporary Weimar scene are impressive because of the setting in which he places them. In consequence, the trivial and unremarkable are given a great entrance on his fundamentally ontologically prepared stage. They play the leading part in the drama of our existence. That is why Heidegger does not wish to be understood as a critic of his period, because critique would be something ontic, whereas he is interested in the ontological.

These "nobodies" perform a spectral play on Heidegger's stage. They are masks, but there is nothing behind the masks. No self. What has happened to the self? Is inauthenticity a state of aversion, of apostasy, or of alienation from the authentic self? Is the true self waiting in the wings until, at long last, it is once more realized? No, says Heidegger. Inauthenticity is the "primordial" shape of our *Dasein,* not only in the sense of the (ontically) customary, but also ontologically, because inauthenticity is just as much an existential as Being-in. We always find ourselves in a situation in which we are actively absorbed. This was first illustrated by the example of the environment, but of course it applies equally to the with-world and the self-world. This means *Dasein* is "proximally and mostly" not alongside itself but out there alongside its business and alongside the others.

> Proximally it is not "I," in the sense of my own Self, that "am," but rather the Others, whose way is that of the "they" . . . Proximally *Dasein* is "they," and for the most part it remains so. If *Dasein* discovers the world in its own way [*eigens*] and brings it close, if it discloses to itself its own authentic Being, then this discovery of the "world" and this disclosure of *Dasein* are always accomplished as a clearing away of concealments and obscurities, as a breaking up of the disguises with which *Dasein* bars its own way. (SuZ, 129)[30]

We already know one moment when "disguises" break up and authentic Being discloses itself—the moment of anxiety. The world loses its significance, it appears as a naked "that" against the background of nothingness, and *Dasein* experiences itself as homeless, unguarded and unguided by any objective Being. The breakthrough to authentic Being thus takes place as a contingency shock, as the experience of "there is nothing behind it." Even more clearly than in *Being and Time,* Heidegger formulated this initiation experience for a philosophy of authenticity in his Freiburg inaugural lecture of 1929. Philosophy, he then said, only begins when we have the courage to "let nothingness encounter us." Eye to eye with nothing, we then observe not only that we are "something" real, but also that we are creative creatures, capable of letting something emerge from nothing. The decisive point is that man can experience himself as the place where nothing becomes something and something becomes nothing. Anxiety leads us to this turning point. It confronts us with the "being possible" that we are ourselves.

Heidegger's analysis of anxiety expressly does not have fear of death as its subject. It would be more correct to say that its subject is fear of life, of a life that one suddenly becomes aware of in its whole contingency. Anxiety reveals that everyday life is fleeing from its contingency. That is the meaning of all attempts to firmly root oneself in life.

One might assume that They are only Everyman, but they are also the philosophers. Because these, Heidegger remarks critically, firmly root themselves in their grand constructs, their worlds of values and metaphysical backworlds. Philosophy, too, is for the most part busy removing the contingency shock or, better still, not admitting it in the first place.

And now to authenticity itself. It is the negation of negation. It resists the tendency to escape, to evade. Authenticity has made nothingness its own affair. Authenticity means being born again. Authenticity discovers no new areas of *Dasein.* Everything can, and probably will, remain as it was; only our attitude to it changes.

If anxiety is the initiation experience of authenticity, then Heidegger's famous "anticipation of death" is part of the success of this authenticity. That is why the chapter on death in *Being and Time* has its place in the section on "Being-a-whole of *Dasein*"—another term for "authenticity."

In relation to death, too, Heidegger chooses for contrast the common understanding of death, which may be reduced to the formula "One of these days one will die too, in the end; but right now it has nothing to do with us" (SuZ, 253).[31] One's own death, while one is alive, "is proximally not yet present-at-hand for oneself, and is therefore no threat" (SuZ, 253).[32]

It would not be particularly original, from the philosophical point of view, if Heidegger were to enrich the thousand-year-old tradition of memento mori with a new sermon on penitence and reversal—even though he alludes to it by quoting from Johannes Tepl's late-medieval work *Der Ackermann aus Böhmen:* "As soon as Man comes to life, from that moment he is old enough to die."

Heidegger intends to describe phenomenologically the different ways in which we are met by death in our lives—not in emotional language, but with exalted, factually aloof terminology. Nevertheless we feel here an excitement indicating that we find ourselves in the hot zones of his philosophizing. Death, Heidegger says, is not the end of life but "Being to the end," it is not only impending as our final hour but it also stands "into" our life, since we all know about our death. Death is the "possibility" that is constantly before us, and as such it is the "possibility of the impossibility of our own existence." Although everyone is affected by death, we each have to die our own death. We are not helped by the thought of the universality of this fate. Death individualizes, even though dying takes place in huge numbers. The attempt to understand death as the absolute boundary must, at the same time, understand it as the boundary of understanding. Relation with death is the end of all relation. Thought of death is the end of all thought. In thinking about death, Heidegger hopes to get on the trail of the mystery of time. Death is not an event "in" time but the end of time. Death appears as an event "in" time when we experience the death of others. Then we are under the suggestion of spatialized time. The space of time is so large that, after the death of the other, we still find room in it. Such spatial images of time stem from inauthentic time-thinking. This fails to consider "own-time," the fact that the irreversible lapse of time, the great "in-the-past," passes through us. The inauthentic images of space take time as something present-at-hand.

Heidegger, it should be remembered, had distinguished between being as existence and the present-at-hand. In connection with his analysis of death, this distinction becomes particularly important. That which is present-at-hand is what is spatialized. Human *Dasein,* on the other hand, is surrendered, suffered, lived-to-the-end time. "Being-present-at-hand" is confronted by "Being-in-the-past." Things are "in" time, but *Dasein* has its own time, it "times itself" *(zeitigt sich),* and as this is an excessive expectation with regard to the need for security and durability, there is a powerful tendency toward the self-objectivization of life. One would like to rest in time, the way things do. These reassuring thoughts of immortality summon the strength of enduring space against passing time.

The question, posed at the beginning, as to the meaning of Being suddenly appears in a new light in connection with temporality. One realizes the sense in which the question about the meaning is usually asked—that is, as a question about an enduring meaning or about the meaning of endurance. It is against this endurance, against the secret and sinister suggestion of space, that Heidegger's thought is now turned. The meaning of Being is time. This means Being is nothing enduring, it is something transient, it is nothing present-at-hand but an event. He who really dares to think his own death will discover himself as a finite event of Being. This discovery is almost the maximum of self-transparency that *Dasein* can achieve for itself. If self-concealment is inauthenticity, then this self-transparency is an act of authenticity. As Heidegger's philosophy works on this self-transparency, it understands itself as such an act of authenticity.

Some interpreters of *Being and Time* endeavor to cleanse Heidegger's philosophy of authenticity, fundamentally and ontologically of all ethics, to forestall any suspicion that there might be a connection between this authenticity and Heidegger's later involvement with National Socialism. Such efforts are doing inadmissible violence to the formalism of that philosophy of authenticity. After all, he expressly declared that "a factical ideal of *Dasein* [underlies] our ontological interpretation of *Dasein*'s existence" (SuZ, 310).[33]

This ideal, to begin with, is negatively defined. *Dasein* is authentic when it has the courage to base itself on itself and not to rely on Hegel's so-called substantial morality of state, society, or public morals; when it can dispense with the unburdening offers on the part of the world of They; when it finds the strength to bring itself back from "being lost"; when it no longer toys with the thousand possibilities existing but instead seizes the possibility that one is oneself.

If Heidegger, the great interpreter of Aristotle, deploys his ethics of authenticity against public ethics, then he must abandon the Aristotelian tradition of a practical ethics of public life. Aristotle, in contrast to Plato, had brought the "philosophy of goodness" back to the plane of the social reality of his day. He had rehabilitated what was usual and what was customary. To him, what was morally good was to be gained not in opposition to what was socially valid but by proceeding from it.

For Aristotle and his tradition, and all the way to ethical pragmatism and the theory of communicative reason, the starting point and yardstick of successful and ethically responsible life is just that area that Heidegger describes as the world of the They.

If the Self retrieves itself from the They and returns to itself, where then does it arrive? Heidegger's answer: at the awareness of mortality and time, at the realization of the unreliability of all civilizational solicitude for *Dasein,* and, above all, at the awareness of its own potentiality-for-Being, hence at freedom in the sense of spontaneity, initiative, creativity. It is a point at which, by a different route, the German poet Gottfried Benn hopes to arrive. In his poem "Destille" he says:

> I let myself fall apart,
> I remain close to the end,
> then between fragments and piles
> a great hour will stand.

With Benn, *Dasein,* arriving at itself, must first "fall apart"; with Heidegger it must tear itself free, and it finds no ground beneath its feet but the abyss of freedom—yet also a "great hour." In the spectacular debate with Ernst Cassirer in Davos in 1929, Heidegger will declare that "Man exists at the peak of his own possibilities only at very few moments" (K, 290).

What matters in Heidegger's authenticity is not primarily good or ethically correct action but the opening up of opportunities for great moments, the intensification of *Dasein.* Insofar as ethical aspects are concerned at all, Heidegger's ideas in *Being and Time* can be summed up in one sentence: Do whatever you like, but make your own decision and do not let anyone relieve you of the decision and hence the responsibility. The Marburg students who, parodying Heidegger, said: "I am determined, but I don't know what for," had perfectly understood Heidegger's decisionism and yet misunderstood it. They had understood it in the sense that Heidegger really supported determination without reference to the content or values that one would have to decide about. They had misunderstood him in expecting from his philosophy such directives or signposts. Heidegger expressly wants to disappoint such expectations as belonging to the inauthentic way of philosophizing. Philosophy is not a moral inquiry office; it is, at least for Heidegger, the task of removing and deconstructing presumed ethical objectivities. What is left after this task is truly nothing—measured against the rich tradition of ethical thought.

In good moral-philosophy manner, Heidegger also investigates conscience, though only to demonstrate there as well this nothingness of concrete determinations. Conscience calls us to authenticity but fails to tell us what we have to do to become authentic. "What does the conscience call to him to whom it appeals? Taken strictly, nothing . . . 'Nothing' gets called to [*zu-gerufen*] this Self, but it has been summoned [*aufgerufen*] to itself—that is to its ownmost potentiality-for-Being" (SuZ, 273).[34]

Heidegger does not shrink from the charge of formalism. In his Marburg lecture on the concept of time, he points to the formalism of Kant's moral philosophy, which, after all, has similarly not yielded any other moral maxim than that in one's own actions the other person's reason, and that means his freedom, should be respected. In popular terms: Do not do unto others what you would not wish to be done unto yourself.

In analogy to Kant's postulate of mutual respect for reason and freedom, Heidegger develops his principle of mutual respect for the *Dasein* in another: "But these entities towards which *Dasein* as Being-with comports itself do not have the kind of Being which belongs to equipment ready-to-hand; they are themselves *Dasein.* These entities are not objects of concern, but rather of solicitude" (SuZ, 121).[35]

Heidegger chooses a descriptive formulation that in reality, however, contains a demand. The point is that this "solicitude" describes not the everyday, socially customary manner in which people comport themselves toward each other but the way in which they should "authentically" comport themselves toward each other. "This kind of solicitude pertains essentially to authentic care—that is, to the existence of the Other, not to a 'what' with which he is concerned; it helps the Other to become transparent to himself in his care and to become free for it" (SuZ, 122).[36]

In the gesture of description Heidegger here formulates his categorical imperative: it is part of authenticity not to make either oneself or the other into "equipment." And "*Dasein*'s resolution towards itself" is similarly, again hidden under a descriptive formulation, tied to a moral postulate. This resolution is to open up the possibility "to let the Others who are with it 'be' in their ownmost potentiality-for-Being . . . Only by authentically 'Being-their-selves' in resoluteness can people authentically be with one another" (SuZ, 298).[37]

However, what this "authentically being with one another" might be remains, for the moment, just as indefinite as the authentic Being-their-selves. The only information here is again negative. Being with one another, just as Being-their-selves, must find its way out of the "Being-lost into They." Is a collective breakout and departure from inauthenticity thinkable?

Heidegger's distinction between the inauthentic and the authentic being with one another has frequently been equated with the distinction between community and association, as made by Ferdinand Tönnies in his book, *Community and Society,* which was published in 1887 but initially produced no effect. In the 1920s, however, it became a sociological best-seller, providing conservative critics of the modern mass society with all their principal concepts. Accordingly, community has a higher value than association, or society. Community means a "living organism" and a "lasting and genuine" coexistence. Association is a "mechanical aggregate and artifact," providing only "transitory and superficial" coexistence. In community people are "united despite all division," while in association they are "divided despite all unity."[38]

In actual fact Heidegger's authentic Being-with-one-another is not coextensive with the concept of community. For surely the concept of community includes the individual's wish to rid himself of his burdens of distance, his loneliness, his individuality. Heidegger's authenticity, however, rejects any conformism. Since he encourages *Dasein* in its "unsubstitutable"—in other words, individual—potentiality-for-Being, a community of dense homogeneity is bound to seem to him rather suspect. However, Heidegger will draw other political conclusions from his ethics of authenticity. He will see the National Socialist revolution as a collective breakout from inauthenticity and therefore join it. But these conclusions do not inevitably follow from the worldview of *Being and Time.* Others have drawn different conclusions from it. Heidegger's fundamental ontology, including his philosophy of authenticity, are vague enough to allow for different options in political matters. The earliest Heideggerians, such as Herbert Marcuse, Jean-Paul Sartre, Günther Anders, Hannah Arendt, and Karl Löwith, are evidence of this.

Yet there can be no doubt that, despite his ontology of freedom in *Being and Time,* Heidegger reveals himself as an opponent of pluralist democracy. He has no sympathy for the principle of a democratic public. "Publicness proximally controls every way in which the world and *Dasein* get interpreted, and it is always right—not because . . . it avails itself of some transparency on the part of *Dasein* which it has explicitly appropriated, but because it is insensitive to every difference of level and of genuineness and thus never gets to the 'heart of the matter'" (SuZ, 127).[39]

What Heidegger here accuses the democratic public of is nothing other than its structural principle. It is indeed a feature of it that all opinions and ideas can exist in it, no matter whether they possess the "transparency of *Dasein*" or not. It is part of this type of publicness that in it everybody may arise in their full averageness and "level-less-ness" and speak out, whether authentically or not. Such publicness, at least in its idea, is a mirror image of life, no matter how trivial and undistinguished—inauthentic—it may be. And it is, moreover, part of it that the truths have to suffer being degraded to mere opinions in the market of opinions. The democratic public is truly a playground of the They.

It is well known that the academic mandarins, molded as they were by an unpolitical or antidemocratic tradition, only in the rarest cases warmed to the democracy of the Weimar Republic. They despised everything that went with democracy—the party system, the multiplicity of opinions and lifestyles, the mutual relativization of so-called truths, averageness and unheroic normality. In these circles the state, the people, the nation were regarded as values in which a vanished metaphysical substance continued to live—the state, above the political parties, effective as an ethical idea purifying the national body; leader figures charismatically representing the spirit of the nation. In the year that *Being and Time* appeared, the rector of Munich University railed against the antidemocratic sentiments of his colleagues: "Always in new disguises the old unreason—a metaphysical, speculative, romantic, fanatical, abstract and mystical politicizing . . . you can hear sighs about how filthy, how incurably dirty all political business is, how untruthful the press, how deceitful the cabinets, how common the parliaments, and so on. While they are lamenting in this way, they think themselves too exalted, too spiritual for politics."

The authentic Heidegger similarly places himself above the parties and looks down with contempt on the business of politics.

But how does Heidegger at that time envisage the overcoming of inauthenticity in the political sphere? To this question *Being and Time* does not provide a convincing answer. On the one hand, conversion to authenticity remains an act of radical individualization. Heidegger approvingly quotes Count Yorck von Wartenburg: "To dissolve elemental public opinion, and, as far as possible, to make possible the moulding of individuality in seeing and looking, would be a pedagogical task for the state. Then, instead of a so-called public conscience—instead of this radical externalization—individual consciences—that is to say, consciences—would again become powerful" (SuZ, 403).[40]

On the other hand, Being-in-the-world also includes the fact that Man is embedded in the history of his people, in his "destiny" and his "inheritance." And since authenticity does not represent a special area of action with specific objectives and values, but merely a changed position and attitude to every sphere of life, *Dasein* can place itself into this "destiny" of the people authentically or inauthentically. But what an authentic takeover and continuation of the destiny of a people might look like—that is not spelled out in *Being and Time.* There is only a hint: *Dasein,* including collective *Dasein,* finds its authenticity not through norms, constitutions, or institutions, but by lived example, by the fact that "*Dasein* may choose its hero" (SuZ, 385).[41]

In spite of these sombre hints about a collective road to authenticity, the individualist element remains predominant. At one point Heidegger even calls his starting point "existential solipsism" (SuZ, 188).[42] On the crucial questions of existence, everyone remains alone. No people and no collective destiny can relieve the individual of his decisions in the area of "authentic potential of Being." In the face of collective destiny it is important "to have a clear vision for the accidents of the Situation that has been disclosed" (SuZ, 384).[43] Heidegger emphatically rejects any long-term projects of historical action. What remains is historical occasionalism. The moment has to be exploited, the opportunity has to be seized. But for what?

Not for an objective in the remote historical future; if indeed there is such an objective, then it is the moment itself. This is about an intensification of the sense of *Dasein.* Authenticity is intensity, nothing else.

So far Heidegger has found his moments of intensity mainly in philosophy. Before long he will also find them in politics.

10

THE MOOD OF THE TIME: WAITING FOR THE GREAT DAY

Being and Time was a torso. It was planned in two parts, but not even the first part was quite finished, even though Heidegger, under pressure, eventually worked on it day and night. It was probably the only time in his life that he did not shave for days on end. However, all the subjects of the chapters announced but not included in *Being and Time* were dealt with by him in later works. A draft version of the lacking third section of part one became the subject of his summer 1927 class, "The Fundamental Problems of Phenomenology."

The extensive part two of *Being and Time*—the planned destruction of exemplary ontologies in Kant, Descartes, and Aristotle—was turned by Heidegger into separate essays or lectures over the next few years. *Kant and the Problem of Metaphysics* appeared in 1929; his lecture on "The World Picture," with its critique of Cartesianism, was given in 1938; his arguments against Aristotle were developed in his lectures in the 1930s.

In that sense *Being and Time* was being continued and completed. Even his so-called turning point—as the Heidegger school subsequently mystified it—

was foreshadowed within the framework of this project. It is first mentioned as a task in his "Logic" lecture of the summer semester of 1928: "The temporal analytics is, at the same time, the turning point" (GA 26, 201).

This turning point means: the analytics of *Dasein* first "discovers" time, but then turns about toward its own thinking—under the viewpoint of comprehended time. The thinking of Time thinks about the temporality of thinking—not, however, in the sense of an analysis of the historical circumstances. This is not, to Heidegger, the core of temporality. The temporality of *Dasein* proceeds, as we already know, in "care." Caring, *Dasein* lives into its open time horizon, making provision and taking precautions in the search for points of support and reliabilities in the flux of time. Such points of support can be work, rituals, institutions, organizations, values. Such points of support, however, are bound, for a philosophy that has turned toward the awareness of its own temporality, to lose all substantial dignity. By discovering the flux of time, philosophy cannot do anything other than comprehend itself as part of it. Deprived of its universalist, time-stripped pretensions, this "turned" philosophy discovers that, in the meaning of Being is Time, there can be no escape from Time into a reliable Being. The lines of escape are cut off. Philosophy no longer provides answers; it can only comprehend itself as caring questioning. Philosophy is nothing other than care in action, "self-caring" *(Selbstbekümmerung)*, as Heidegger calls it.

Because of its pretensions to wisdom, philosophy has a rather nontransparent way of deceiving itself. By philosophizing Heidegger hopes to discover the tricks of philosophy. What, in point of fact, can it achieve? Heidegger's answer: it can, by discovering Time as meaning, sharpen our sense for the throbbing heart of Time, for the "moment." The turning point: after the Being of Time we have now the Time of Being. But this teeters on the tip of the moment in question.

The "moment" has a strange pathos for Heidegger. What he means by it is not the commonplace that elapsing time always passes through a present, through a moment-point. To him, the moment is not simply "given" but has to be discovered, for the simple reason that our customary relation with time conceals momentariness under an empty or stable and-so-forth. Momentariness is not an occurrence but an achievement of *Dasein*, a virtue of authenticity. "The moment of vision is nothing other than the look of resolute disclosedness in which the full situation of an action opens itself and keeps itself open" (GA 29/30, 224).[1] To face up to the moment and hence to the compulsion to decision is what Heidegger calls a "fundamental possibility of *Dasein*'s existence proper" (GA 29/30, 224).[2]

Heidegger's discovery and distinction of the "moment of vision" is part of the feverish curiosity and joy in experimenting which characterized the 1920s. The philosophical concepts of the fracture of the period—from Ernst Bloch's "darkness of the lived moment" to Carl Schmitt's "moment of decision," from Ernst Jünger's "sudden fright" to Paul Tillich's *Kairos*—all refer, as does Heidegger, to the "moment," which began its career with Kierkegaard.

Kierkegaard's "moment" is the one when God bursts into life and the individual feels summoned to make the decision to risk his leap into faith. At such a moment the historical time that separates the individual from Christ loses its significance. Anyone addressed by Christ's message and work of salvation exists "simultaneously" with Christ. The entire cultural tradition, in which religion is dragged along as a cultural possession and conventional morality, is burned to nothing at that existentially heated moment. Ever since Kierkegaard, the "moment" has been the banner of antibourgeois religious virtuosi like Carl Schmitt, who, with his mystique of the moment, strays into politics and constitutional law, or Ernst Jünger, who finds himself among the warriors and surrealists. The flat and-so-forth of bourgeois stability is confronted by the blinding pleasure of intensive infinity—in the moment.

The moment thus understood promises a relation with the "entirely Other," it means a different experience of time and the experience of a different time. It promises sudden turns and transformations, perhaps even arrival and redemption, but at any rate it enforces decision. At such a moment horizontal time is intersected by a vertical one. The moment—in the definition of Rudolf Otto in his impressive book *The Saint,* 1917—is the subjective time equivalent of the encounter with the numinous. Indeed, the numinous in any shape was the objective of the intensity-seeking spiritual life of the 1920s. The metaphysical impulse is transformed into anxiety lest one should miss the crucial moment. "The central clock of an abstract epoch has exploded," Hugo Ball wrote in his *Flight out of Time,*[3] while at the Club Voltaire he staged a thousand small cultural revolutions in expectation of the great revolution. Dadaism is the only training program for the great moment that would make everything new. "To be a dadaist means letting oneself be thrown by things, opposing all sedimentation; to have for a moment sat on a chair means to have endangered life" *(Dadaist Manifesto).* In a spiritually and materially destabilized environment, presence of mind is the great ideal. Presence of mind is a sense of opportunity. This presence of mind is dealt with also in Kafka's novel *The Castle,* written in the early 1920s. In it, missed opportunity and lack of presence of mind become a metaphysical horror scenario. The geodetist Josef K., through being asleep, misses his appointment with the castle authority. Perhaps it could have saved him.

The New Realism, metaphysically greatly cooled, also attaches importance to presence of mind. It admits as standard only that which is "at the peak of its time." For Brecht, the boxer becomes a cult figure; he is the athlete of presence of mind. The good boxer has an instinct for the moments when to duck and when to punch. The mobility fantasies of the New Realism are dominated by the obsession that one can miss one's time the way one misses a train. A certain type of time analysis of the final years of the Weimar Republic seeks historical truth not in a time continuum, but in rupture and break. Bloch's *Spuren* (Traces), Benjamin's *Einbahnstrasse* (One-Way Street), and Ernst Jünger's *Abenteuerliches Herz* (Adventurous Heart) are examples. To all those attempts, Benjamin's statement that "the Now of recognizability is the moment of awakening" applies.[4]

History is a volcanic crater: it does not occur, it erupts. That is why one has to be swiftly and meaningfully present before one is buried. A person loving the moment must not be too worried about his safety. Dangerous moments call for adventurous hearts. Since "world history proceeds from catastrophe to catastrophe"—according to Oswald Spengler—one must be prepared for the decisive to take place "as abruptly as a flash of lightning or an earthquake. Here again we have to emancipate ourselves from the nineteenth-century idea . . . of an *evolutionary* process."[5]

Kierkegaard was one thinker of the nineteenth century who initiated the twentieth century into the mystery of the moment. The other was Nietzsche. Kierkegaard's moment meant the break-in of the wholly Other. Nietzsche's moment means breakout from the accustomed. At the moment of the "great liberation" there occurs, for Nietzsche, the birth of the free spirit:

> The great liberation comes . . . suddenly, like the shock of an earthquake: the youthful soul is all at once convulsed, torn loose, torn away—it itself does not know what is happening. A drive and impulse rules and masters it like a command; a will and desire awakens to go off, anywhere, at any cost; a vehement dangerous curiosity . . . flames and flickers in all its senses . . . A sudden terror and suspicion of what it loved, a lightning-

bolt of contempt for what is called "duty," a rebellious, arbitrary, volcanically erupting desire for travel.[6]

Nietzsche's moment is heightened intensity, attained not by contact with the absolute, as with Kierkegaard, but in independent transcending—"the great detachment." An endogenous heating up. There is no orientation by superior values, which have all disappeared—"God is dead!" The intensity of the moment stems from freedom, from absolute spontaneity. From nothingness. Of course such moments are exceptional states. But it is only this exception that illustrates what in regular life remains hidden. "The rule proves nothing, the exception proves everything . . . In the exception the power of real life breaks through the crust of a mechanism that has become torpid by repetition."[7]

These are sentences from Carl Schmitt's *Political Theology* (1922), vigorously pleading for decisions that, looked at normatively, emanate from nothingness.[8] The power of decision has no other foundation than the will to power; in lieu of legitimation, the intensity of a powerful original moment. This theory of decision stemming normatively from nothingness was called "political romanticism" by Paul Tillich in 1932—a romanticism containing within itself the demand "to create the mother from the son and to summon the father from nothingness."[9] To Carl Schmitt the state is a numinous state of exception placed on duration; the nationalized sacred moment is called by him sovereignty. Its sharp definition is: "Sovereign is he who decides on the exception."[10] Schmitt admits to the theological content of his concept of sovereignty. To jurisprudence the state of exception, or emergency, has a significance analogous to the miracle in theology. The sovereignty of God is revealed in the miracle, as the sovereignty of the state is revealed in a state of exception or emergency.

The admirers of great moments in the years of the Weimar Republic were nearly all adventists of nothingness, priests without glad tidings; one's attitude was the content.

Heidegger's moment, when *Dasein* returns to itself from dispersal, is also a state of exception in which "the crust of a mechanism that has become torpid through repetition" (Carl Schmitt) is broken through. It is a moment also in the sense of Nietzsche and Kierkegaard—something is breaking in and something is breaking out. What matters, Heidegger says in his lecture series on "The Fundamental Concepts of Metaphysics" (1929–30), is that the moment of "inner terror" should be admitted, the terror "that every mystery carries with it and that gives *Dasein* its greatness" (GA 29/30, 244).[11]

Meanwhile Heidegger had again returned to Freiburg. In 1928 he was appointed to Husserl's chair. Husserl himself had championed Heidegger as his successor. Heidegger's writings and lectures after 1929, his 1928 Freiburg inaugural lecture, "What Is Metaphysics?," his 1929 lectures on "The Essence of Reason," his 1930 lectures "On the Essence of Truth," and above all his great 1929–30 set of lectures, "The Fundamental Concepts of Metaphysics," all betray a new tone. The temperature is rising. Eventually New Realism comes to an end in Heidegger's work too. The cool, almost engineered, fundamental-ontological descriptions are now expressly put under an existential pressure. Heidegger begins to turn up the heat on his students.

During his work on the 1929–30 lectures he wrote to Elisabeth Blochmann: "My metaphysics lecture is giving me a lot of trouble; but the whole work is more free. Scholastic constraint and perverted scientific attitudes and whatever is connected with these, has dropped off me" (Dec. 18, 1929, BwHB, 34). What had happened?

As recently as in his 1928 lecture "Metaphysical Initial Foundations of Logic" Heidegger, in summing up the "results" of *Being and Time,* emphasized that existential analysis is pure description, that it speaks of existence, but not *to* it. "The analytics of *Dasein* therefore precedes all prophecy and ideological revelation; nor is it wisdom"—it is merely analytics (GA 26, 172).

Analysis of *Dasein* makes neither of the two claims that Aristotle stated to be the basic possibilities of ethical thought. It is neither *sophia* (wisdom), nor *phronesis* (practical sense, circumspection). It is not an ideological revelation counseling how one should behave in, and with regard to, time. Nor is it a kind of wisdom aiming at a standpoint beyond the turbulence of time. It is not concerned either with eternal truths or with time-limited cleverness. The analysis is merely designed to show the condition of *Dasein* altogether. And, without any fear of simplification, this is reduced in the 1928 lecture to a few concise theses.

First, *Dasein* is factually always initially *dispersed* in its world (the body, nature, society, culture).

Second, this dispersal would not even be perceived if it were not for the "original positivity and extent of *Dasein,*" which lose themselves in dispersal but can be snatched back from it. Without original massiveness there would not be anything to be dispersed. The dramatic fundamental happening of

Dasein unrolls between origin and dispersal, whereby, paradoxically, dispersal is more original than original massiveness, which one never possesses but can always only attain from dispersal.

Third, this snatching back from dispersal requires an impulse through evidence—of the moment of true sensation. For Heidegger this is the mood of anxiety, of boredom. In this mood the voice of the calling conscience, by which *Dasein* is summoned to itself, becomes audible.

Fourth, this fluctuation between dispersal and concentration, between the great moments and everyday cares, becomes visible only if *Dasein as a whole* is successfully brought into focus. The fluctuation between dispersal and origin is the whole; there is nothing more.

Fifth, this focusing on the whole is possible only "on the basis of the extreme existential engagement" of the philosophizing person himself (GA 26, 176). The fundamental ontologist can *existentially* analyze only what he has *existentially* lived through.

What can the philosophizing person stake? Answer: his own anxiety and boredom, his own listening to the call of conscience. Any philosophizing that does not take its beginning from the moments of true sensation is devoid of roots and relevance.

Whatever this "extreme existential engagement" may mean in detail, it is certain that Heidegger's analysis of *Dasein* can be understood only if the same engagement is brought into play by the listener or reader. Heidegger must manage somehow to challenge this "existential engagement." He cannot merely talk about "existence," he must awaken the "original positivity and massiveness" in the *Dasein* of the other. He who wants to hear, and, even more so, he who wants to understand, must feel. The philosopher cannot confine himself to "describing the consciousness of Man," he must master the skill of "invoking the *Dasein* in Man." This means that the perspectives of fundamental ontology reveal themselves "only in and from a transformation of the human *Dasein*." In short, existential analytics, to be understood at all, requires existential engagement. Heidegger therefore must find a way to conjure up in his students those moments of true sensation. He must, in a sense, stage-manage them. These efforts will then be initiations, exercises, and meditations free from "scholastic constraint and perverted scientific attitudes." The moments of true sensation—anxiety, boredom, call of conscience—have to be aroused in his students so that the "mystery of *Dasein*" that inhabits them may show itself. Heidegger's new style is "event philosophy." Philosophy must conjure up state of mind, which it then endeavors to interpret. For instance, it must give *Dasein* a fright, displace it into anxiety, drive it into boredom so that it may then make the discovery that it is a nothingness that drifts in those moods.

This new note of existential action philosophy had a tremendous effect on his students at the time. Heinrich Wiegand Petzet, who as a student attended the inaugural "What Is Metaphysics?" lecture, reports: "It was as if a gigantic flash of lightning was rending a darkness-clothed sky . . . in almost painful brightness the things of the world lay revealed . . . it was not a matter of a system, but of existence . . . It had me speechless when I left the Aula. I felt as though for a moment I had gazed at the foundations of the world."[12]

Indeed it is as if Heidegger wants to compel his audience to gaze for a moment at the foundations of the world. The foundations, the justification, all these statements about the sufficient reason, the scientific attitude, and the everyday feeling of life—wherever one looks there is a need to stand on firm ground. With a gently mocking note in his voice, Heidegger reviews the different variants of solidity and being settled. But what about nothingness? he asks in between. He who radically asks about foundations and reasons, must he not sometime discover that the ground is an abyss? That a Something can be perceived by us only against the background of Nothing?

For a while Heidegger assumes the part of the positivist scientists and logicians, for whom, as is well known, the Nothing does not exist. The scientist invariably deals only with a Something, and the logician points out that the Nothing is merely a linguistic artifice, the substantivization of a negative statement ("The flower is not yellow," or "He is not coming home"). These objections provide Heidegger with an opportunity for polemicizing against the inner "necrosis" and "rootlessness" of modern science. It shuts itself off, he claims, against elementary experiences. "The idea of 'logic' itself disintegrates in the turbulence of a more original questioning" (WM, 37).[13] Heidegger remains on the trail of the Nothing. However, he cannot demonstrate it by argument; he has to awaken an experience. This is the moment of anxiety, which we have already encountered. "Anxiety reveals the Nothing. We 'hover' in anxiety. More precisely, anxiety leaves us hanging because it induces the slipping away of beings as a whole" (WM, 9).[14]

This "slipping away" is cramping and draining at the same time. Draining because everything loses its meaning and becomes null and void. Confining because the void penetrates into the feeling of self. Anxiety drains and this void cramps: the heart contracts. The external world becomes objectivized, rigidifies into lifelessness, and the inner self loses its center of action, it depersonalizes itself. Anxiety is objectivization outside and depersonalization inside. "This implies that we ourselves—we men who are in being—in the midst of beings slip away from ourselves. At bottom therefore it is not as though 'you' or 'I' feel ill at ease; rather it is this way for some 'one'" (WM, 32).[15]

At this zero point of anxiety Heidegger performs a surprising turnabout. This momentary drowning in nothingness he calls "being beyond beings as a whole." It is an act of transcending, and it alone enables us to speak of being as a whole. Of course we can address the subject of the whole also in the abstract. Purely intellectually we create a superconcept or an overall concept—*totum,* the whole. But the whole thus understood has no experienced reality: it is a concept without content. Only when the worrying feeling arises that there is nothing special about this whole does it become experienced reality, a reality that does not approach us but slips away from us. The individual for whom reality slips away in anxiety thereby experiences the drama of distance. The worrying distance proves that we are not entirely of this world, that we are being driven beyond it, not into another world but into a void. In the midst of life we are encompassed by emptiness. In the transcendence of this empty field of play that opens up between us and the world, we experience the "being held out into the nothing" (WM, 38).[16] Every "why" question feeds on the ultimate question: Why is there Something and not rather Nothing? Whoever can think himself and the world away, whoever can say no, acts in the dimension of the nothing. He proves that there is such a thing—the Nothing. Man, Heidegger says, is "a placeholder of the nothing" (WM, 38).[17]

The transcendence of *Dasein,* therefore, is Nothing.

The religious among the philosophers of the moment allow the numinous to emerge in the moment (Rudolf Otto), or that "which unconditionally concerns us" (Paul Tillich), or "the kingdom of God" (Karl Barth), or the "encompassing" (Karl Jaspers). Heidegger's moment, too, leads to a transcendence, but to a transcendence of the void. The transcendence of Nothing. It proceeds from the peculiar movement between Nothing and Something that man can perform with his consciousness. That is his numinous playing field, which allows him to experience as a miracle the miracle that something exists at all. And not only that: equally astonishing against this background is man's creative potency. He can produce something; he discovers himself with the full contingency of his Being-thus, but he can shape himself and his world, he can allow Being to grow or he can destroy it. In the anxiety of emptiness, one loses a world, and yet one experiences a new world being always born again out of Nothing. Through anxiety one can come into the world anew.

Dasein means existing in this playing field in this open manner. The field for play is opened up by the experience of the Nothing. The wheel can turn because at its hub it has "play"—that is, freedom. This freedom implies not only that *Dasein* experiences the Nothing but also that it can create space for itself by negation under "unyielding antagonism" or "stinging rebuke," in "galling failure" and "merciless prohibition" (WM, 37).[18]

No and Nothing are to Heidegger the great mysteries of freedom. That area of play between Nothing and Something that has opened up in *Dasein* provides the freedom for separation *(Scheiden),* for distinguishing *(Unterscheiden),* and for decision *(Entscheiden).* "Without the original revelation of the nothing, no selfhood and no freedom" (WM, 37).[19]

The fundamental metaphysical event of *Dasein* is therefore this: by being able to transcend into the Nothing, *Dasein* is also able to experience being as something that steps out of the night of nothingness into the light of Being.

In the summer of 1929, a few weeks after the "What Is Metaphysics?" lecture, Elisabeth Blochmann visits Heidegger at Todtnauberg. There is a suppressed love affair between the two of them. Later that same summer, Hannah Arendt had confessed to Heidegger in a letter that he still represented "the continuity" of her life, and she had "boldly" reminded him of "the continuity of our—please let me say this—love."[20] And now here is Blochmann. Heidegger is between the two women. To Blochmann he speaks of "the limits of our friendship," which he had touched upon by "compelling her about something" that "was bound to be distasteful to her." Heidegger had hurt Blochmann, either by getting too close to her or by not getting close enough. The ambiguity of his letter of September 12, 1929, allows of both interpretations. The letter refers to an excursion the two of them had made to Beuron. They had visited the church of the Benedictine abbey there. Their conversation had centered on the subject of religion. Heidegger had explained to Blochmann his attitude toward the Catholic Church, and the letter recalls that conversation. The truth, he writes, "is not a simple thing." It requires "its day and its hour when we have the *Dasein* in its entirety." And further on: "God—or whatever they call it—calls everyone with a different voice." One must not arrogate to oneself a "power of attorney" over it. No institution and no dogma are capable of holding the truth in safekeeping. All that was "brittle pretense."

Then he refers to the situation that must have irritated Blochmann after this lengthy conversation. They had both jointly attended the nocturnal service, compline, in the abbey church, and Heidegger had been deeply moved, much to the surprise of Elisabeth, who was still under the impact of his fierce polemics against the Catholic Church. In this letter he therefore tries to explain his attitude. This experience in Beuron, he writes, would "unfold as a seed corn for something essential."

His attempt to describe this "essential" is almost a paraphrase of the central idea of the metaphysics lecture—or perhaps it would be more correct to say that the metaphysics lecture is a paraphrase of the experience of the nocturnal service in Beuron. Heidegger says: "That man each day walks out into the night is a banality for present-day man . . . Compline still contains the mythical and metaphysical primeval power of night, which we have to pierce continually in order truly to exist. Because the Good is only the Good of the Evil."

The compline, he writes, had become for him a symbol of "existence being held out into the night and of the inner necessity of daily readiness for it." And then he links this experience with his philosophy of the Nothing. "We believe that we are producing the essential, forgetting that it grows only if we live totally—and this means: in the face of the night and of the Evil—in accordance with our heart. The decisive thing is this primally powerful negative—to place nothing in the path of the profundity of *Dasein.* This is what, concretely, we have to learn and to teach."

In an important respect, however, the letter goes beyond the lecture, in that it refers to a dimension of night that is not revealed in the metaphysics lecture. In the lecture this Nothing is not yet explicitly linked to Evil—as it is in the letter. In the letter Heidegger says we should live "totally in the face of the night and of the Evil." The fact that Heidegger in, of all places, his letter to Elisabeth Blochmann addresses the aspect of evil in the Nothing—could this have something to do with an irresistible feeling that he is a seducer? At any rate his thinking on nothingness still contains echoes of the Christian gnostic metaphysics that for him represents a living tradition.

In that tradition, evil still belongs to the human condition. In that tradition, ranging from St. Paul via St. Augustine and Luther to Kant, it had not yet been forgotten that any reflection, whether aiming at comprehension of the entire Being, at morality, or at politics, had to work its way out of the all-underlying night, which was called chaos, or evil, or simply nothingness. And any brightness of thought and civilization was seen against that background. It had come out of the night and was doomed to sink back into night. One was aware that even in seemingly stable phases of civilization the abyss of temptation, destruction, and annihilation might open again at any moment. To early Christianity, still strongly molded by gnostic thinking, the question of evil in the world was almost identical with the question, What is the world? The definitions of the world and of evil were almost congruent. Then, with the birth of Christ, the most effective answer for some time had been found to the question of the existence of evil in the world, namely the belief that although we are in this world, we are not of this world. The plasticity and vividness of early images of the devil were merely popular versions of a mystery, unable to conceal the fact that evil was seen to be equally unfathomable as God himself. Perhaps even more unfathomable, because evil does not represent an order but is the negation of order. Here reason cannot penetrate, which is why initially no attempt was made to understand evil or to explain it away. It should simply be resisted, with trust in the mercy of the Lord. Admittedly there was the great problem of why God the Almighty should even permit evil to exist. This problem was so weighty that the entire philosophy and theology of the Middle Ages could not free itself from it. The theodicean problem of the justification of God in view of the evil in the world held all thinking in thrall all the way down to modern times, when it was secularized into the anthropodicean problem. The old metaphysics had tried to cope with the theodicy problem through intensified reflection on human freedom. God, it was claimed, as the creator of the world, had made man in his own image by giving him freedom. Through man's freedom, evil had come into the world, or, more precisely, that freedom was the "open point in creation" through which the evil, which underlies creation as nothingness or chaos, burst into the world. Even for that way of thinking, man, just because he was free and could also be creative, was a "placeholder of the Nothing."

Heidegger would return to this idea time and again, especially in his interpretations of Schelling's writing on freedom, which wholly proceeds from this tradition. Time and again Heidegger's reflections would betray his intimate acquaintance with the metaphysics of the Nothing, which simultaneously means temptation by evil.

The metaphysics lecture, unlike the letter to Blochmann, avoids the ethical significance of the discussion of nothingness and night. The letter, however—"the Good is only the good of the Evil"—positively directs attention to the moral problem of how the Good was to be wrested from the Evil, how one endures the night, and how one finds one's way back into the day. In his lecture Heidegger speaks of the tendency of *Dasein* to hide from the abyss of the Nothing and to indulge in a false sense of security and safety. Anxiety, he says, "sleeps." He therefore calls for a "daring *Dasein*" that would seize the dangerous area of freedom. One must have passed through anxiety in order to "break loose from the idols which everybody has and to which he is in the habit of sneaking away."

Translated into moral terms, the problem presented in the metaphysics lecture would be: It is not just a matter of resisting evil; first of all one has to notice that this evil, this night in ourselves and around ourselves, actually exists. The problem is the dreary one-dimensionality of our culture, which feels secure from the abysmal and the evil. Modern man, Heidegger says in his letter, turns night "into day, as he understands the day, as the continuation of a pursuit and a frenzy."

If in his metaphysics lecture Heidegger had really spoken of evil instead of the Nothing, his encouragement to face the Nothing and to pass through it would have acquired a scintillating double meaning. Fascination with the Nothing would have combined with the meaning that there are those who, hungry for intensity and oblivious of morality, allow themselves to experience evil like some strangely alluring wild experience—just as Ernst Jünger's revolutionary nihilism openly propagated at the time. "One of the best means of getting ready for a new, bolder life," Jünger wrote in his essay *Der Arbeiter* (The Worker) in 1932, "lies in the destruction of the values of a detached and lately autocratic intellect, in the destruction of the educational work performed on man by the bourgeois era . . . The best reply to the high treason of the spirit against life is the high treason of the spirit against the spirit; and it is one of the great and cruel joys of our age to be a participant in these destructive acts."[21]

Heidegger's encouragement for "daring *Dasein*" may aim in a similar direction, though it does not actually speak of courage to embrace evil or of the abysmal pleasure of militant, anarchical, adventurous amorality, but "merely" of courage to face the Nothing. "Man as a placeholder of the nothing" need not be Ernst Jünger's warrior type. But how else are we to imagine him?

Let us go to the icy altitudes of Davos, where in the spring of 1929, Heidegger, at the Davoser Hochschulwoche (Davos University Week), had his now legendary discussion with Ernst Cassirer. Both men gave a number of lectures before an invited international audience. The highlight of the week was a debate between the two. It was a major event. The world press had arrived on the scene. Anyone who claimed to have anything to do with philosophy was either present or at least read the reports—the age of radio transmission had not yet dawned. Martin Heidegger was on the first peak of his fame. Cassirer, too, was a star and enjoyed a great reputation. His principal work, *The Philosophy of Symbolic Forms,* had appeared in the 1920s, a monumental work of the philosophy of culture. Cassirer, coming from neo-Kantianism, had freed himself of the narrow problems of a theory of scientific cognition and arrived at a comprehensive philosophy of the creative spirit of mankind. For his studies he had been able to make use of the huge collections of the Aby Warburg Library in Hamburg. Cassirer was regarded as the great representative of a humanist tradition and a universally attuned cultural idealism. In 1929, shortly before the Davos summit, he had assumed the rectorship of Hamburg University—the first Jew to be elected rector of a German university. This was the more remarkable as, much to the annoyance of the reactionary majority among the professors, Cassirer had publicly championed the republic. At the invitation of the Hamburg city government he had, in Hamburg's City Hall, given the festive address on the anniversary of the Weimar Constitution. In defiance of the widespread prejudice in professorial circles that the republican parliamentary constitution was "un-German," he had demonstrated that republicanism was indeed foreshadowed in the philosophy of Leibniz and Wolf and had found its perfect expression in Kant's writings on peace. "It is a fact," Cassirer declared, "that the idea of a republican constitution as such is by no means a stranger in the history of German thought, much less a foreign intruder, but that, on the contrary, it grew from its own soil and was nurtured by its most genuinely own forces, by the forces of idealist philosophy."

The speech triggered protests and polemics in Hamburg. Cassirer, a conciliatory man, found himself between angry opposing fronts—which was why his election as rector was celebrated far beyond Hamburg as a triumph of the liberal spirit. Cassirer was a genuine constitutional democrat.

This grand seigneur of political humanism and idealist cultural philosophy had been invited by the Davos organizers to be the opponent of Martin Heidegger, who stood for what was new and revolutionary. Those present felt reminded of the legendary disputations of the Middle Ages, when the champions of the powerful movements of the day would clash. A metaphysical clash of arms on the sparkling snowy heights of Davos. And there was one more reminiscence—not in the depth of time, but in the space of imagination.

Up there in Davos Thomas Mann, in his *Magic Mountain* (published in 1924), had let the humanist Settembrini and the Jesuit Naphta conduct their great debate. They were archetypes of the spiritual battle of the period. On the one side Settembrini, an unrepentant child of enlightenment, a liberal, an anticlerical, a humanist of boundless eloquence. On the other Naphta, the apostle of irrationalism and the Inquisition, in love with the eros of death and violence. To Settembrini the spirit is a power of life, given to man to help him, while Naphta loves the spirit against life. Settembrini wants to elevate, comfort, and extend people; Naphta wants to scare them, to rouse them from the humanist "bed of idleness," to drive them out of their residences of learning and to break the neck of their conceit. Settembrini means to be kind to people, whereas Naphta is a metaphysical terrorist.

The participants in the Davos University Week indeed felt reminded of that imaginary event. Kurt Riezler, the curator of Frankfurt University and a companion of Heidegger on his ski tours in the mountains, in his report for *Neue Zürcher Zeitung* (March 30, 1929, morning edition) alludes to the *Magic Mountain* episode. Was there the ghost of Settembrini behind Cassirer and that of Naphta behind Heidegger? Heidegger certainly had read the *Magic Mountain* with Hannah in their amorous summer of 1924.

O. F. Bollnow, a student who had been invited by Heidegger to attend the event, describes the meeting as "breathtaking." Those present had the "exalting sense of being present at a historic hour, not unlike that characterized by Goethe in his campaign in France: 'From here and from today a new epoch is beginning in world history'—in this case in philosophical history—'and you can say you witnessed it.'"[22]

Heidegger disliked such exaggerated expectations. In a letter to Elisabeth Blochmann he speaks of the "danger" that "the whole thing might turn into a sensation"; he was, more than he really liked, being "pushed into the limelight." He had therefore decided to divert philosophical interest from himself by concentrating entirely on Kant. He did not object so much to the attention he caused in the elegant setting of the Grand Hotel with his unconventional appearance. He reports to Blochmann on how, with a friend (this was the above-mentioned Kurt Riezler), he had between the events climbed up into the mountains for "magnificent tours. With beautiful weariness, full of sun and mountain freedom, the whole élan of the long downhill runs still in our bodies, we would always in the evenings, still wearing our ski outfits, join the elegance of the evening clothes. Such immediate unity of professional research work and totally relaxed and joyful skiing was something unheard of for most of the university staff and students" (April 12, 1929, BwHB, 30).

That was how he wished to be seen—as an earnest worker in the quarries of philosophy, contemptuous of the elegant world, a sportsman and nature lover, a conqueror of peaks and a man of daring downhill runs. This, more or less, was how witnesses of this philosophical summit experienced him on the slopes of the Magic Mountain. Reports one of the participants:

> The debate between Heidegger and Cassirer also meant a great deal to us in human terms . . . on the one hand, this short dark-brown man, this fine skier and sportsman, with his energetic unflinching mien, this rough and distant, at times downright rude, person who, in impressive seclusion and with deep moral seriousness, lives for and serves the problems he has posed for himself on the one hand—and on the other hand that man with his white hair, not only outwardly but also inwardly an Olympian with wide spaces of thought and with comprehensive sets of problems, with his serene features, his kindly courtesy, his vitality and elasticity and, last but not least, his aristocratic elegance.[23]

Toni Cassirer, the wife of the philosopher, recalls in her memoirs, written in 1950, that she and her husband had been expressly warned of Heidegger's strange behavior by the philosophers present. "We knew about his rejection of all social conventions."[24] Their friends expected the worst; Heidegger, it was rumored, was out "if possible to annihilate" Ernst Cassirer's philosophy.

However, the personal hostility that Toni Cassirer later claimed to remember was not apparently being felt at the time. According to the above-quoted eye-witness, the debate took place in "a wonderful collegial spirit." Heidegger himself, in a letter to Elisabeth Blochmann, described the meeting with Cassirer as a personal gain, though he regretted that the polite atmosphere had prevented their opposition from emerging sharply enough. "Cassirer was exceedingly gentlemanlike and almost courteous in the discussion. Thus I met with insufficient opposition, and this prevented the problems from being given the necessary sharpness of formulation" (BwHB, 30).

The record of the debate, however, does not support this impression. The conflicts were as sharp as could be imagined.

Cassirer asks whether Heidegger is willing to "give up" the "entire objectivity" and "absoluteness" represented in culture by "withdrawing" to the "finite being" of man (K, 278). He aims at making comprehensible the symbol-creating and hence culture-creating force of the human spirit as a world of "forms." They may not represent infinity in the traditional metaphysical sense, but they are more than the mere self-preserving functions of a finite being. Culture to him is transcendence turned into form; it erects man's spacious dwelling, which is more easily destroyed than preserved, a fragile protection against the barbarism that, as a permanent possibility, threatens man's culture.

Heidegger accuses Cassirer of making matters too easy for himself in the dwellings of the spirit. While he is quite correct in seeing all culture, any action of the spirit, as an expression of freedom, this freedom could become rigidified in its forms. That was why freedom must always again become liberation; if it congealed into a state of culture it was already lost. "The only adequate reference of freedom in man is that freedom's freeing itself in man" (K, 285).

To Heidegger the problem is that man "freezes into" the culture he has himself created, in his search for an anchor and security, and that he thereby loses the awareness of his freedom. It is important that this awareness should be reawakened. This cannot be achieved by any philosophy of coziness in culture. It is necessary to bring *Dasein* face to face with its original nakedness and "thrownness." Cassirer, Heidegger argues, was turning his attention to the transcending achievements of culture—"from the chalice of this spirit realm flows infinity for him," Cassirer had quoted Hegel; he was saving man from the confrontation with his finiteness and nothingness, and was therefore mistaking the real task of philosophy, which consisted in "throwing man, in a manner of speaking, out of the lazy aspect of a man who merely uses the works of the spirit, back into the hardness of his fate" (K, 291).

At the peak of the debate Heidegger asks: "To what extent is it the task of philosophy to allow liberation from anxiety? Or is it not its task radically to deliver man to anxiety?" (K, 286). Heidegger has already given his own answer. Philosophy, he argues, should first of all give man a fright and force him back into that homelessness from which he then, always anew, embarks on his flight into culture.

Cassirer, however, in his answer proclaims his cultural idealism. The fact that man can create culture, he states, "is the seal of his infinity. I would wish the meaning, the actual objective, to be liberation in this sense: 'Cast out from yourselves the anxiety of the earthly!'" (K, 287). Cassirer is concerned with the art of living in culture, while Heidegger wants to turn "the ground into an abyss" (K, 288). He pleads for the task of creating meaning through culture, for the work that, with its inner necessity and endurance, triumphs over the contingency and evanescence of human existence.

All this Heidegger rejects with a grand gesture. What remains are a few moments of great intensity. One should no longer conceal from oneself the fact "that the highest form of existence of *Dasein* can be reduced to only a few rare moments in the duration of *Dasein* between life and death, that man exists at the peak of his own potentialities at only a very few moments" (K, 290).

One such moment for Heidegger was his attendance at the nocturnal mass at the abbey church of Beuron, when he became aware of "the mythical and metaphysical primeval power of night, which we have to pierce continually in order truly to exist."

Another such moment was a childhood scene that Heidegger sometimes related to friends: how, as a boy bell ringer, still in the small hours of the morning, his mother had lit his candle; how, shielding the flame in the hollow of his hand, he had crossed the square to the church and there stood at the altar; and how, with his fingertips, he had pushed up the wax trickling down the candle to make sure it burned longer. And although the candle had gone out eventually, he had awaited that moment by delaying it.

If *Dasein* has two acts—the night from which it is born and the day which overcomes night—then Cassirer focuses on the second act, on the day of culture. Heidegger, however, is concerned with the first act: he gazes into the night from which we all come. His thinking is fixed on that Nothing against which a Something is perceived. One of the two men looks at what has emerged, the other at its origin. The one is concerned with the dwelling of human creation, while the other, fascinated, tarries before the abysmal mystery of the *creatio ex nihilo,* a creation that continues to take place so long as man awakens to the awareness of his existence.

II

A SECRET PRINCIPAL WORK: THE METAPHYSICS LECTURES OF 1929–30

When in February 1928 Martin Heidegger was appointed to Husserl's chair at the University of Freiburg, he wrote to Karl Jaspers: "Freiburg for me will once more be a test of whether anything of philosophy is left there or whether it has all turned into learnedness" (November 24, 1928, BwHJ). Heidegger was to perform the test on himself. But there was not only the temptation of learnedness; there were also the problems of his new fame. "Less agreeable to me is the public existence in which I find myself," he wrote to Jaspers on June 25, 1929 (BwHJ). Heidegger's lectures became a public attraction. Siegfried Kracauer had this to report about Heidegger's lecture to the Kant Society in Frankfurt on January 25, 1929: "We end this report by saying that the personality of the speaker brought a great crowd of spectators, who were no doubt unversed in the problems of philosophy, but who put themselves at risk and entered the complex world of subtle definitions and distinctions."[1]

Yet, needless to say, Heidegger enjoyed his public appearances as well as his fame. He felt flattered when Jaspers informed him that "Heidegger" was now read and discussed in the Heidelberg seminar. But he does not wish to be seen merely as the author of *Being and Time.* In his letters to Jaspers he played the book down: "I no longer think of the fact that a short while ago I wrote a so-called book" (September 24, 1928, BwHJ).

During the first few years after the publication of *Being and Time,* he had to face the fact that the philosophical public expected from him a systematically rounded-off account of man in his world, an account embracing all spheres of his life. *Being and Time* was read as a contribution to philosophical anthropology, and it was hoped that the project would be continued.

In his 1929 book on Kant, Heidegger expressly rejected such expectations as a misunderstanding. It is impossible, he stated there, to develop any rounded-off philosophy *about* man or his fundamental aspects of life. Expectation of such a rounding off contradicts the basic character of *Dasein*—its finiteness and historicity. Whenever philosophizing awakens in man it always starts anew, and its end is not achieved from inside as a systematic rounding off; the real and sole end of philosophizing is its contingent cessation—by death. Philosophy, too, dies.

However, philosophy can "die" even before its definitive end—when living thought rigidifies in what has been thought before, when the past triumphs over the present and future, when what has already been thought captures thinking. In the early 1920s Heidegger had intended to "reliquefy" the ideas of philosophical tradition from Aristotle to Husserl; now he made it his task to dissolve his own fundamental ontology—meanwhile quotable as a system and applicable as a method—into the movement of thinking.

On September 12, 1929—referring to the fuss made about his person and his work—he wrote to Elisabeth Blochmann: "As an outcome of the prevailing hullabaloo and its successes and results we are fundamentally misguided in our search—we believe that the essential thing is to produce" (BwHB, 32).

He does not wish simply to continue, to build on his own ideas, his own system: "With my metaphysics lecture in the winter," he says in the same letter, "I shall achieve an entirely new beginning."

Reference has already been made to the great metaphysics lectures of 1929–30, advertised by Heidegger under the title "The Fundamental Concepts of Metaphysics: World—Finitude—Solitude." Here a new style is attempted, an "event philosophy." In these lectures Heidegger states that philosophy should arouse the "fundamental occurrence within human *Dasein*" (GA 29/30, 12).[2] What fundamental happening? The words "finitude" and "solitude" in the title already suggest that Heidegger intends to deepen the experience of the "not-at-home." Philosophy "is the opposite of all comfort and assurance. It is turbulence, the turbulence into which man is spun, so as in this way alone to comprehend *Dasein* without delusion" (GA 29/30, 29).[3]

In that case, however, the concepts of such philosophizing will have to have a different function and a different kind of *strictness* than the concepts of science. Philosophical concepts remain empty "unless we have first been gripped [*ergriffen*] by whatever they are supposed to comprehend" (GA 29/30, 9).[4] Heidegger regards the concepts of philosophy as an "attack" on any kind of self-assurance and world reliance. "Philosophy," he says, "constantly remains in the perilous neighborhood of supreme uncertainty." However, "elementary readiness for the perilousness of philosophy"[5] is rarely encountered, which is why there is no real philosophical argument—despite the meanwhile huge number of philosophical publications. "They all want to prove their own truths in the face of one another, and in so doing forget the single, actual, and most difficult task of driving one's own *Dasein* and that of others into a fruitful questionableness" (GA 29/30, 29).[6]

There is a lot of talk in these lectures about danger, uncanniness, and questionability. For this, undertaking to live philosophical life wildly and dangerously, Heidegger claims the title of metaphysics—though not metaphysics in the sense of the teaching of things suprasensory. He wants to give the aspect of transcending (meta) a different, and—as he claims—its original, meaning. This, he argues, is a transcending not in the sense of seeking another "place" or a world beyond, but a "peculiar turnaround in the face of everyday thinking and inquiry" (GA 29/30, 66).[7]

For this reversal, too, it is evidently useful for "*Dasein* to choose its hero" (SuZ, 385).[8] The reason is that there are people who have "the strange fate of being a spur for others, so that philosophizing awakens in them" (GA 29/30, 19).[9]

No doubt Heidegger counted himself among those people. He realizes that he is a charismatic figure in philosophy, that he has a mission. To Karl Jaspers, he wrote on December 3, 1928: "That is just what brings such a strange loneliness into *Dasein*—that dark standing before one's own otherness that one believes one has to bring to time" (BwHJ, 114). And Jaspers, still overcome by a visit from Heidegger, wrote back: "Since time immemorial I have not listened to anyone as I did to you today. I felt free as though in pure air in this ceaseless transcending" (December 5, 1929, BwHJ, 129).

Heidegger's analysis of anxiety had already shown where this transcending aims—at the Nothing from which the exceedingly surprising and alarming Something then emerges. For Heidegger's event philosophy, as it explores the enigma of time and the moment, it is therefore natural that it concerns itself with the other great event of emptiness—boredom. And his findings in this respect are among the most impressive ideas ever put forward by Heidegger. Only very rarely, in the entire tradition of philosophy, has a mood been described and interpreted as in this lecture. Here boredom really becomes an event.

Heidegger wants to make his audience plunge into the great emptiness—they are to hear the fundamental roar of existence; he wants to open up the moment when nothing matters any longer, when no world content offers itself to provide a handhold or something to fill oneself with. The moment of pure lapse of time. Pure time, its pure presence. Boredom—that is, the moment when one notices that time is passing because it will not just then pass, when one cannot drive it away, make it pass, or, as the saying goes, fill it meaningfully. With unassailable patience—in the printed text this passage runs to 150 pages—Heidegger sticks with this subject. He stages boredom as an initiation event of metaphysics. He demonstrates how in boredom the two poles of metaphysical experience—the world as a whole and individual experience—are paradoxically linked with each other. The individual is gripped by the whole of the world just because he is not gripped by it but left behind, empty. Heidegger wants to lead his audience to the point where they have to ask themselves: "Have things ultimately gone so far with us that a profound boredom draws us back and forth like a silent fog in the abysses of *Dasein?*" (GA 29/30, 119).[10]

In the face of the abysses of that boredom we are, as a rule, seized by the *horror vacui.* But this horror has to be endured because it makes us intimately acquainted with that Nothing that raises the old metaphysical question, Why is there Something and not, rather, Nothing? Heidegger expects his audience to accept the Nothing as an exercise in the art of remaining empty.

This does not—Heidegger points out—require a deliberate, artificial mood or any forced attitude but, on the contrary, "the releasement [*Gelassenheit*] of our free everyday perspective" (GA 29/30, 137).[11] In everyday life, Heidegger says, we often feel empty, but we cover up that emptiness in an equally everyday manner. He invites us to avoid this hasty covering up for a while. This avoidance, admittedly, is hard won in philosophical terms, because it runs counter to a spontaneous everyday effort that would rather fall back into the world and not, as in that maintained empty moment, fall out of it. But there is no alternative. Philosophy cannot be had without this falling out of, this being lost and being abandoned, without this emptiness. Heidegger proposes to demonstrate the birth of philosophy from the nothingness of boredom.

In the course of his reflections on the daily latency of boredom, Heidegger touches on the spiritual situation of the day. There was a widespread malaise in contemporary culture, a malaise formulated by authors such as Spengler, Klages, Scheler, and Leopold Ziegler. Heidegger dismisses their diagnoses and prognoses in very few words. All this may be interesting, he says, and clever, but, to be honest, it does not *touch* us. "On the contrary, the whole affair is something sensational, and this always means an unconceded yet once again illusory appeasement" (GA 29/30, 112).[12] Why? Because these reflections "release us from ourselves" and present us to ourselves "in a world-historical situation and role" (GA 29/30, 112).[13] Dramas, he says, are being performed with us strutting about in the boots of cultural subjects. Even alarming visions of doom flatter our sense of self-worth, or, more accurately, our need to represent ourselves and see ourselves represented. Heidegger concludes his critique of this kind of philosophical diagnosis of the age with the apodictic remark: "Such philosophy attains merely the setting-out [*Darstellung*] of man, but never his *Da-sein*" (GA 29/30, 113).[14] In the abyss of *Dasein,* however, lurks boredom, from which life tries to escape in forms of representation.

Heidegger's analysis turns into an exploration of the center of the desert. He maintains a sense of heightening dramatic effect. Suspense grows with the growing emptiness of the location to which thinking leads. He starts from being bored by *something.* Here we still have an identifiable object—a thing, a book, a festive event, a certain person—to which we can attribute that boredom. In a manner of speaking, it penetrates into us from outside, it has an external cause. But if that object can no longer be so unequivocally determined, if boredom both penetrates from outside and arises from within, then it is a case of "being bored amid something." One cannot say that a train that arrives late bores one, but the situation in which one finds oneself as a result of the delay can be boring. One is bored at, or on the occasion of, a certain event. The irritating aspect of that boredom is that, in the situations in question, one begins to be bored with oneself. One does not know what to do with oneself, and the result is that it is now the Nothing that does something with one. A boring evening conversation—Heidegger with obvious enjoyment describes one such in an academic setting—arouses not only irritation but even causes mild panic, for the simple reason that such situations turn oneself into a bore. The situation is genuinely complicated, because the thing that causes boredom is, as a rule, something that was designed to dispel boredom. Boredom lurks in the measures of diversion. Whatever is mobilized against it is invariably already infected by it. Those in danger of crashing must be diverted. But to where does time divert, or to where does diverting *Dasein* drift? Is there a kind of black hole of existence that attracts and swallows up?

The deepest boredom is the totally anonymous kind. It is not produced by anything specific. "It bores one" *(Es langweilt einen),* we say. Heidegger subjects this German phrase to a subtle analysis. There is here a double indeterminacy: *It*—that is, everything and nothing, certainly nothing definite. And *one*—that is, oneself, but as a creature of indeterminate personality. Just as if the boredom had also swallowed up the *I,* which could still have been ashamed of being a bore. This "It bores one" is taken by Heidegger as an expression of that total absence of any fulfilled or fulfilling time, for that moment when nothing any longer addresses one or occupies one. This "being left empty" he describes as "being delivered over to beings' telling refusal of themselves as a whole" (GA 29/30, 214).[15]

There exists a surprising comprehension of the whole, but of a whole that no longer concerns one. An empty Something is face to face with an empty Whole and in this absence of relationship, relates to it. Thus we have a threefold negativity—a nonself, a null whole, and an absence of relationship as a negative relationship. It emerges clearly that this is the high point or the low point to which Heidegger intended to lead his exciting analysis of boredom. We are at the heart of a metaphysics to Heidegger's taste. At this point he also reaches the goal of his intention to "press forward to the essence of time through our interpretation of the essence of boredom" (GA 29/30, 201).[16] How, Heidegger asks, is time experienced amid this total absence of anything fulfilling? It refuses to pass, it stands still, it holds one in inert immobility, it "thralls." This comprehensive paralysis reveals that time is not simply a medium in which we move, but that it is something that we produce out of ourselves. We evolve time, and when we are paralyzed by boredom, we have ceased to evolve it. But this cessation is never total. The process of time production that pauses or ceases for moments remains in relationship with the flow of time that we are ourselves—but in the mode of suspension, thrall, and paralysis.

This ambivalent experience of the stalling of the flow of time is the point of peripeteia in the drama of boredom staged and analyzed by Heidegger. From the threefold negativity—the nonself, the nullified whole, and the absence of relationship—there is only one way out. One has to tear oneself away. If nothing works anymore, one has to set out oneself. This is Heidegger's cumbersome formulation of his punch line: "But what the enthrallment as such, the time . . . gives to know and properly makes possible . . . is nothing less than the freedom of *Dasein* as such. For this freedom of *Dasein* only is *Dasein*'s freeing itself. The self-liberation of *Dasein*, however, only happens in each place if *Dasein* resolutely discloses itself to itself" (GA 29/30, 223).[17]

As, however, this Self has been thinned out into an insubstantial ghost, this resolution will not be able to fall back on a compact Self that is waiting to go into action. In a sense it is not found but invented—by resolving. This alone opens up that which was locked up. The "moment of resolution" stems from boredom and brings it to an end. Heidegger can therefore point out that "the time to which we are *ein thrall*" (in boredom) gives rise to *Dasein*'s "being impelled into the extremity of that which properly makes possible . . . *Dasein*'s existence proper" (GA 29/30, 224).[18] Put more popularly: in boredom you notice that nothing of any importance exists unless you do it yourself.

Dasein awakening to itself therefore must have crossed the zone of deep boredom, that "emptiness as a whole." At this point of his reflections Heidegger turns away from the more "private" and "intimate" moods of boredom and focuses, in cultural-philosophical terms, on the prevailing social-historical situation. He asks, Is this hardship of "emptiness as a whole" still experienced at all, or is it not overlaid or displaced by the necessary struggle with other, more immediate, hardships?

This was the winter of 1929–30. Large-scale unemployment and impoverishment as a result of the worldwide economic slump had already set in. Heidegger risks a quick glance at the contemporary scene: "Everywhere there are disruptions, crises, catastrophes, needs—the contemporary social misery, political confusion, the powerlessness of science, the erosion of art, the groundlessness of philosophy, the impotence of religion. Certainly, there are needs everywhere" (GA 29/30, 243).[19] Against these hardships there are programs, parties, measures on offer, there is busy activity of every kind. Yet, according to Heidegger, "this bustling self-defense against these needs precisely does not allow any need to emerge as a whole" (GA 29/30, 243).[20]

The "need as a whole," therefore, is not some individual hardship but the quintessence of *Dasein*'s burdened character altogether—a character experienced more particularly in the mood of boredom—the fact "that *Dasein* as such is demanded of man, that it is given to him—to be there" (GA 29/30, 246).[21] Anyone evading this "essential oppressiveness" *(Bedrängnis)* (GA 29/30, 244)[22] lacks that defiant "in defiance of" that to Heidegger makes up everyday heroism. He who has not experienced life as a "burden" in this sense knows nothing of the "enigma" of *Dasein.* In consequence, what is lacking is "the inner terror that every mystery carries with it and that gives *Dasein* its greatness" (GA 29/30, 244).[23]

Enigma and terror. Heidegger is alluding to Rudolf Otto's definition of the numinous. He had interpreted the experience of the saint as the terror of a power that we encounter as an enigma. Heidegger accepts the symptoms of the numinous, thus understood, but deletes the reference to the beyond. *Dasein* itself is the numinous, the mysterious cause of terror. This terror is the dramatically heightened astonishment that there is something and not nothing; the terrifying enigma is the Being in its naked That. It is this terror that Heidegger speaks of in the next few sentences—a fact that needs emphasizing, as these statements were later invested with a political meaning that they did not yet have at the time.

> If in spite of our neediness, the oppressiveness of our *Dasein* still remains absent today, and the mystery still lacking, then we must principally concern ourselves with preparing for man the very basis and dimension upon which and within which something like a mystery of his *Dasein* could once again be encountered. We should not at all be surprised if the contemporary man in the street feels disturbed or perhaps sometimes dazed and clutches all the more stubbornly at his idols when confronted with this challenge . . . It would be a mistake to expect anything else. We must first call for someone capable of instilling terror into our *Dasein* again. (GA 29/30, 255)[24]

Who can inject this terror? For the time being this is none other than the charismatic philosopher who bears "the strange fate of being a spur for others, so that philosophizing awakens in them" (GA 29/30, 19).[25] In other words, it is Heidegger himself who believes that to inject terror and cause philosophizing to awaken are, at the moment, still one and the same thing.

As though he suspected that this statement could be misunderstood politically as a call for the "strong man," Heidegger pointed out at the end of the passage quoted above that no political event, not even the World War, had been able to cause that awakening by itself. We are therefore still dealing not with a political but with a philosophical awakening. Hence also Heidegger's critique of all attempts to erect the "worldview" as an edifice[26] in the political field and of all calls to live in it (GA 29/30, 257). Once *Dasein* has become transparent to itself, it ceases to erect such edifices. "Invoking *Dasein*" in man means nothing other than to set it in motion, so that such edifices must collapse.

Heidegger has covered a great deal of ground—260 pages in the printed version of his lectures. The fundamental metaphysical questions posed by him at the beginning—What is the world? What is finitude? What is solitude?—had almost been forgotten. Now he takes them up once more, pointing out that the treatment of boredom hitherto had been a preparation, an attempt to awaken a mood, or stage it, in which the world, finitude, and solitude are encountered in a way that alone makes operation of the concept possible. Everything depends on the "how" of that encounter. That which is to be understood must first have happened, moreover here and now, on Thursday afternoons in the 1929–30 winter semester.

The "world as a whole"—why should a special mood be necessary for experiencing it? Surely the world is always there; it is everything in question. Surely we are always in the middle of it. Just so, but as we have seen by now, to Heidegger this everyday world is, at the same time, being in thrall to it. We have vanished in it. That is why he specially features the mood of boredom, because in it—just as in the mood of anxiety analyzed in *Being and Time*—the whole of the world appears removed to a distance that renders possible the metaphysical attitude of astonishment or terror, as the third act of an existential drama. In act one, one is daily absorbed in the world, and the world fills one. In act two, everything is removed to a distance, the event of the great emptiness, the threefold negation (nonself, null world, absence of relationship); in act three, finally that which had been removed, one's own self and the world, once more returns. The self and the things become, as it were, "more existent"; they acquire a new intensity. That is what everything comes to. Rarely has Heidegger formulated this so clearly and vulnerably: "At issue is nothing less than regaining this originary dimension of occurrence in our philosophizing *Dasein,* in order once again to 'see' all things more simply, more vividly and in a more sustained manner" (GA 29/30, 35).[27]

The "world as a whole" is too wide a subject for the searching gaze. That may be so. For just that reason Heidegger endeavors to show that this wide subject, even if too wide for research, is directly experienced every day in such moods as boredom—more precisely, in the slipping away of the world. From the end it becomes clear that the painstaking analysis of boredom is nothing other than an attempt at describing the manner in which we have the "world as a whole."

However, the perspective can also be turned around. That we "have world" is one thing; that the world "has" us is something different. Not only in the sense that we are absorbed into the world of They and in the "providing of being-ready-to-hand," as shown by Heidegger in *Being and Time,* but also in the sense that we belong to the realm of nature.

In the second part of his lecture series, Heidegger for the first time puts forward a kind of nature philosophy—an attempt unique for him and never to be repeated later. The importance he attaches to it emerges from the fact that he places these reflections on an equal basis with *Being and Time.*

The previous year, two major works of philosophical anthropology had appeared—Max Scheler's *Man's Place in Nature* and Helmuth Plessner's *The Steps of the Organic and Man.* Scheler and Plessner attempted, each in a different way, to combine the results of biological research and philosophical interpretation, thereby revealing the connection and the break between man and the rest of nature. In *Being and Time* Heidegger had so strongly emphasized the breach between *Dasein* and nonhuman nature that, as Karl Löwith later criticized, the impression was bound to arise that human existence was lifted out of its corporeal or natural preconditions. Scheler and Plessner, both inspired by Heidegger, returned man into a context with nature, though—and this was important to them—without naturalizing him.

Scheler's attempt in particular excited much attention at the time. It made Heidegger feel challenged to make his own excursion into the field of nature-philosophical anthropology.

Nature is part of the world. But has nonhuman nature any "world" at all? A stone, an animal—do they have a world, or do they only occur in it? In it—that means in a world horizon that exists only for man, the world-creating natural creature?

Heidegger had stated that the manner of Being of nature, the inorganic and the organic, or body-linked life, "can become accessible only if we consider it in a deconstructing fashion" (GA 29/30, 371).[28] That is not so easy: consciousness is expected to comprehend the unconscious, cognition the cognitionless.

Dasein is to comprehend an entity *(ein Seiendes)* for which this "there" does not even exist.

The nature-philosophical part of this lecture is a single meditation on this "there" and on how we can even comprehend nature, which does not know this "there." This is the darkness into which Heidegger intends to penetrate in order, from there, to cast one more glance on man—an alienating glance, for which the event that it becomes light within man, and hence light in nature generally, becomes something totally unusual. That is what he is after: coming from nature to discover that within man a *Da-sein,* a "being-there," has opened up—a clearing, as Heidegger would later call it—to which the things and the creatures which to themselves are hidden can appear. *Dasein* gives the stage over to nature. The only meaning of Heidegger's nature philosophy is the staging of this epiphany of that "there."

The things and creatures appear before us. But can we also put ourselves into them? Can we share their kind of existence? Do they present themselves to us, or do we present ourselves to them?

We share with them a world into which they have sunk and which, to us, is "there." To that extent we endow them with the "there" that they themselves lack. And we receive from them the magic of that tranquility and immersion into what they are. In this respect we may experience in ourselves a downright lack of Being.

Heidegger starts his reflections with the stones. A stone is "worldless." It occurs in the world without being able, of its own, to establish a relationship with the world. In describing the world relations of animals, Heidegger mainly follows the research of Jakob von Uexküll. He calls animals "world-poor." Their environment is a "surround ring" *(Umring)* by which the animals' urges are "benumbed." According to the stimuli coming from it, certain behavior patterns and aspirations are triggered and "unlocked" (GA 29/30, 347). World to the animal is environment. It cannot experience anything in separation from it. Heidegger quotes the Dutch biologist Buytendijk: "Thus it is clear that in the animal world as a whole the way in which the animal is bound to its environment is almost as intimate as the unity of the body itself" (GA 29/30, 375).[29] This environment as an extended body is called by Heidegger the "disinhibition ring." The animal reacts to whatever breaks through this ring; it reacts to something, but it does not perceive that something as a specific something. In other words, it does not perceive that it perceives anything. The animal has a certain openness toward the world, but the world cannot become "manifest" to it as the world. That happens only in man. Between man and his world, a free space opens. His world connection has loosened to such an extent that man can relate to the world, to himself, and to himself as something occurring in the world. Not only is man differentiated, but he can also, on his own, differentiate himself from others. And he can not only relate to different things but also differentiate between things. This "area of play"—as we already know—is called by Heidegger "freedom." The existing entity acquires a different character of reality within the horizon of freedom. It stands out as something real against the background of being possible. A creature that has possibilities cannot but view reality as the realization of possibilities. The latitude of the possible, that opens out for man, lends outline, sharpness, and detail to the real. It stands on a horizon of comparability, of genesis, and of history, and hence also of time. All this makes it possible for a something to be identified as a something, to be distinguished, to be questioned. From the state of "being benumbed," in which the world is lived but not experienced, not "lived through," it surfaces as an expressly perceived world. The possible includes the thought that something could also not be. As a result the world acquires a peculiar transparency. Although it is everything in question, it is, for this very reason, not everything. It is embedded in the even larger space of the possible and the null. It is only because we have a sense for the absent that we can experience presence as such—in gratitude, astonishment, terror, jubilation. Reality, as it is experienced by man, is snatched into the motion of arriving, of hiding, of temporalizing himself.

This familiarity with being-possible and with nothingness—which does not exist in an animal's world relationship—demonstrates the loosened world relationship that Heidegger calls "world creating."

Just as Max Scheler, in his anthropological study *Man's Place in Nature,* interpreted the spiritual personality of man by following up Schelling's idea of "God coming into being within man and through man," so Heidegger, at the end of his lectures, takes up another great idea of Schelling's: nature opens its eyes within man and notices that it exists.

Schelling's "look into the light" (GA 29/30, 529)[30] is called by Heidegger the "open dimension" that has opened up in man's locked-up existence. Without man, Being would be mute; it would be present-at-hand, but it would not be "there." It is in man that nature has erupted into self-visibility.

These lectures in the winter of 1929–30—probably the most important ever given by Heidegger and almost a second principal work—had begun with the analysis of boredom, that mood of pallid remoteness. They end with a turnabout into the totally different mood of enthusiasm. They contain one of the few passages in Heidegger's work that are inspired by a celebration of life: "Man is that inability to remain and is yet unable to leave his place . . . And only when there is the perilousness of being seized by terror do we find the bliss of astonishment—being torn away in that wakeful manner that is the breath of all philosophizing" (GA 29/30, 531).[31]

12

BALANCE SHEETS AT THE END OF THE REPUBLIC

In 1928, shortly before his death, Max Scheler said in a lecture: "In the roughly ten thousand years of history, ours is the first period when man has become completely and totally problematical to himself, when he no longer knows what he is, but at the same time knows that he knows nothing."[1] Scheler's diagnosis referred to two aspects of the historical situation at the end of the Weimar period. The first concerned fragmentation into a multitude of mutually hostile ideologies and worldviews, nearly all of which were attuned to collapse, upheaval, and departure, and which together merely created a sense of helplessness.

"It is as if the world had turned liquid and was running through our fingers"[2]—that was how Walther Rathenau, as early as 1912, described a development whose more advanced stage, at the end of the World War, Robert Musil could only comment on satirically:

> Whenever a new *ism* appears, one believes oneself to be a new person, and the end of every school year marks the beginning of a new epoch . . .

> Uncertainty, lassitude, a pessimistic hue characterize everything that today is the soul . . . Naturally enough, this is reflected in an unprecedented intellectual go-it-alone attitude. The political parties of the farmers and of the manual workers have different philosophies . . . The clergy has its network, but the Steiner followers have their millions, and the universities their prestige. I once actually read in a waiters' trade-union bulletin about the ideology of assistant innkeepers, which must always be held high. It is a Babylonian madhouse—from a thousand windows shout a thousand different voices.[3]

Weimar's output of ideologies was a reaction to the obvious overloading of traditional interpretation and orientation patterns by recent events and conditions. These new conditions include the pluralism of a liberal, open society that is defined by the very stipulation that it makes no ideology or human model mandatory. Mandatory now are not statements on issues but only the rules of the game, which are meant to be binding also on contrasting ideological models and to ensure peaceful coexistence. In the pluralist environment of intellectual variety, so-called truths are downgraded to mere opinions—a hurtful affront to anyone who believes to have found the word of salvation. Democracy as a pattern of life relativizes claims to absolute truth. Hans Kelsen, among lawyers one of the few champions of the republic, formulated it as follows: "A metaphysically absolute ideology entails an autocratic attitude, a critically relativist one entails a democratic attitude. Anyone who considers absolute truth and absolute values of human cognition to be barred to us, must at least regard an opposite opinion as being possible. That is why relativism is the ideology presupposed by the democratic idea."[4]

In the Weimar Republic everybody benefited from the liberal guarantees of freedom of opinion and speech, but very few were prepared to accept its consequences—this very relativism. A study of the intellectual attitude of German youth in 1932 established that, for the major part of all young people, liberalism was dead: "These young people have only unspeakable contempt for the 'liberal' world that intellectual absolutism disdainfully calls starry-eyed; they know that compromises in matters spiritual are the beginning of all vices and lies."[5]

A spokesman of that antiliberalism was the Russian philosopher Nikolay Berdyayev, much read in Germany at the time, who had lived in Berlin in the 1920s and come to know and despise the laboratory of "modernity." His essay

The New Middle Ages (1927) settles accounts with democracy, which he blames for allowing a "majority vote" to decide what truth is. "Democracy is freedom-loving, not from respect for the human spirit or the human personality, but from indifference towards truth."[6]

Berdyayev equates democracy with a lack of respect for the intellect. Max Scheler, too, speaks of a rampant contempt for the intellect. This, after helplessness, is the second aspect of his philosophical analysis of the present. Scheler, however, blames this contempt for the intellect not on democracy but on its opponents. To him, contempt of the intellect stems from all those movements that escape from the stresses of civilization into the allegedly natural and elemental, and that invoke blood and soil, instinct, intoxication, ethnic community, and destiny as primal forces. "All these things suggest a systematic rebellion of urges in the man of the new age."[7] It is, Scheler says, a revolt against the reason of compromise. Thomas Mann, influenced by Scheler, similarly described the predominant intellectual attitude of his day in his *German Address* (1930). He speaks of "schoolboys let loose," escaped from the "idealistic humanist school" and now performing a "St. Vitus' dance of fanaticism. The eccentric mood of mankind escaped from the idea is matched by Salvation Army pretensions, mass seizures, fairground bell-ringing, hallelujahs, and dervishlike repeating of monotonous slogans, until everyone is foaming at the mouth. Fanaticism becomes a principle of salvation, enthusiasm becomes epileptic ecstasy, politics becomes the Third Reich's opiate of the masses or of a proletarian eschatology, and Reason hides her face."[8] Mann commends the businesslike republican common sense of the Social-Democratic workers' movement. He backs the political forces of the left center and warns the intellectual against the erosion of basic humanist convictions. He advises mistrust of the exaltations of an adventurous heart that, hungry for intensity, desires revolt at any price and celebrates destruction as metaphysical ecstasy. Mann is aiming at the wild men of the kind of Ernst Jünger, who, in the mid-1920s, declared: "We shall not stand anywhere where the flamethrower has not performed the great purification through Nothingness."[9]

Thomas Mann's argument is explicitly political, while Scheler keeps to the philosophical plane. He pleads for a kind of self-control of the intellect that, self-critically, should realize that the days of great intellectual syntheses are gone. But this does not mean that it should abdicate or resign. It should seize its own questionability as an opportunity. Scheler finds an exalted significance in helplessness. His last work, *Man's Place in Nature*, concludes with the reflection that man's loss of certainties may well, at the same time, be a process through which a new God is born. A God no longer of "safety and protection," no longer an "omnipotent being, beyond man and the world" but a God of freedom.[10] A God whom we allow to grow through our own free actions, our spontaneity and initiative. This God offers no asylum for the footsore of modernity. "Absolute Being does not have to function to protect or to complement man's weaknesses and needs, which always want to make an 'object' out of this being."[11]

Scheler's God thus reveals himself in courage for freedom. The contemporary turbulence and disorientation have to be endured. From the force that withstands the fanatical onesidedness and dogmatism a new humanism will arise as the "idea of the eternal, objective Logos, . . . whose . . . secrets are not to be penetrated by a single nation, a single cultural sphere, but only by all of them jointly, including any future cultural subjects, irreplaceable in united . . . cooperation because they are individual."[12]

In his essay "Power and Human Nature" (1931), Helmuth Plessner quotes these reflections by Scheler as an example of a desire, not overcome even by free spirits, for formulas of compromise, for "overvaultings" in a situation of spiritual homelessness. "How can we, when everything is in a state of flux here, hope to achieve any lasting synthesis that will not be outdated in a few years? Nothing is to be expected from overvaultings, except that they collapse."[13]

Plessner's anthropological principle is: man is defined by not being definitively definable, because every ethical, scientific, or religious frame of reference for a possible definition is itself a historical product of man. "Man," in a definitional, substantively comprehended sense, always remains an invention of the culture he himself has created. No statements about man can ever view man as a complete, substantial entity. Every possible perspective stems from the "sphere of power of creative subjectivity." This should be taken in a radically historical sense. History, however, is not merely the "stage" on which, "in accordance with some context, the bearers of extratemporal values have their entrances and exits"; it should instead be understood as the "place of production and destruction of values" (ibid., 304). But even this idea of historicity is a historical idea. Even the idea of the self-relativization of values through history is not an absolute position. There were and still are civilizations that do not know this kind of self-thematization. What remains is the "disturbing" realization of man's "unfathomability." He is unfathomable because he still has his foundations before him. What man is invariably emerges only at the moment of decision. Man's determination is self-determination. Man is what he will have decided for. He outlines himself from a situation of uncertainty. "In this relation of uncertainty with regard to himself, man comprehends himself as a power and discovers himself for his life, in theory and practice, as an open question" (321).

From this Plessner concludes that it is not philosophy but practical action in necessarily opaque situations that decides what man is at any given moment in history. The essence of man cannot be found "in any neutral definition of a neutral situation" (319). In this context Plessner now refers to Heidegger. Heidegger's fundamental ontology, Plessner maintains, already contains a surfeit of neutral definitions of human *Dasein.* His existential concepts, he continues, are historically indifferent, and that is their weakness. Thus even the concept of historicity itself is not understood historically.

Max Scheler and Martin Heidegger, according to Plessner, were, each in their own way, staging their "perspectives of the absolute" (286). The one placed the absolute in the creative spirit, the other in the existential foundations.

For Heidegger this eventually leads to contempt for the entire political sphere, which he regards as a sphere of the "They" and of "inauthenticity," separated from a sphere of authentic self-being. But this is nothing but German "inwardness," says Plessner, the last metaphysical refuge from the violence of history.

Plessner, on the other hand, wants to expose philosophy to this violence from inside, even if, as a result, it suffers a mauling. Philosophy must accept the "bottomlessness of reality" (345), which means that it would become aware that, whether it liked it or not, it stood within the "original life relationships of friend and foe" (281). There was no comfortable Outside for it, no position above the contending parties. The age would permit no universalist relaxation; there was no time to draw breath. Any philosophy claiming a grasp of reality must enter into the elementary friend-foe patterns and try to understand them by understanding itself through them. Plessner here deliberately connects with Carl Schmitt's definition of the political.

Helmuth Plessner's essay was written at a time when civil war had already begun in Germany. The elections of September 1930 marked the breakthrough of the National Socialists. The SA brownshirts were marching through the streets and engaging in street battles with the Red Front fighters of the Communist Party and with the defenders of the republic. The political center, the world of reason and compromise, was ground to dust. The political scene was characterized by militant camps.

In this situation Plessner demands that philosophy should at last awaken from its dream that it might comprehend the "fundamentals" of man. Philosophy was no more clever than politics. Both shared the same field of view "that is opened into the unfathomable Whither from which philosophy and politics by daring outreach . . . shape the meaning of our lives" (362).

The concept of radically understood historicity leads Plessner to the realization that philosophy must step into the risky sphere of the political, not only in the sense of some outward obligation but also because of its inner logic. However, as soon as philosophy faces up to politics, it discovers that it is exceedingly difficult to match up to the demands of the age. Philosophical thought "is never as far as life and always further than life" (349). Presence of mind at the historical moment seems to be beyond philosophy's constitutional capacity. That is why, as a rule, it has confined itself to formulating principles or visions. It keeps either to the sphere of prerequisites or to that of expectations. It evades the confusion of the present, the moment of decision. Politics, on the other hand, "is the art of the right moment, of the favorable opportunity. It is the moment that matters" (349). Plessner thus demands a philosophy that opens up to this "moment."

What, then, does the moment demand of the philosopher in 1931? According to Plessner, he must grasp the significance of "ethnicity" *(Volkstum)*. "Ethnicity is an essential trait of man, just as being able to say I and you, like familiarity and strangeness" (361). To allow this "belonging" simply to disappear in some universal humanity is bad idealism. The specific "own" must assert itself, both in the individual and in a nation. Such self-assertion, however, does not mean hegemony or hierarchy. As all nations and cultures stem from the "sphere of power of creative subjectivity," Plessner concedes the "equality of all cultures in democratic value" (318) and hopes for the "gradual overcoming of the absolutization of one's own nationhood" (361). In plain political language, this means national self-assertion vis-à-vis the demands of the peace treaty of Versailles and Germany's reparation payments and yet, at the same time, rejection of any national, let alone racial, chauvinism. Nevertheless, a person's belonging to his own ethnicity remains an "aspect of absoluteness," because the individual cannot choose his nationality but invariably finds himself in it. "It is into his nation's field of vision that all the political problems of a person are locked, because he exists only within that field of vision, in the accidental fracture of these possibilities." This situation allows man "no pure realization, either in thought or in action . . . but only the one relative to one particular ethnicity to which, by blood and tradition, he has always belonged" (361).

Plessner concludes his essay with a second critique of Heidegger, accusing him of a lack of relationship to ethnicity. With his philosophy of authenticity, Plessner argues, he was widening the traditional German "rift between the private sphere of the soul's salvation" and the public sphere of violence. Heidegger favored "political indifferentism." This, according to Plessner, was a danger to "our state and our nation."

The reason Plessner has been treated so fully here is that his philosophy, which links up with Heidegger's, elaborately performs the politicization and nationalization that, in Heidegger, takes place in a more concealed manner. But since it has taken place, albeit in a concealed manner, Heidegger had no need to feel attacked by it when Plessner's critique appeared in 1931. In the meantime he had been busy seeking an express relationship with ethnicity and hence also with politics—in a manner not unlike Plessner's.

Let us recall the arguments on "historicity, fate, and people" in *Being and Time.* There the link to the national community had already played a part, although not a central one. Even though the existential ideal of *Being and Time* is tailored to the free self-relationship of the individual, Heidegger does not wish this to be understood as individualism. That is why he emphasizes the "factic" powers of *Dasein* in the community and the nation, which have to be taken over as aspects of the thrownness into one's own outline of *Dasein.* He who has arrived at accepting the "thrownness of his own *Dasein* in a way that is more free from Illusion" (SuZ, 391)[14] is bound to realize that he cannot choose the people to which he belongs, that he is also thrown into that people, born into its history, its tradition, and its culture. "Fate" is what Heidegger calls this entanglement of the individual *Dasein* with the "historizing of the community, of a people" (SuZ, 384).[15] This belonging, however—and indeed any other life performances—can be lived in various ways, "authentically" and "inauthentically." *Dasein* can consciously "take over" the national fate thus understood; it is prepared to share in the bearing of that fate and to be responsible for it; it makes the nation's cause its own cause, all the way to readiness to "sacrifice" its own life; it "chooses its hero" (SuZ, 385)[16] from that nation's stock of tradition. Yet despite all this, the individual does not surrender his self-responsibility. The authentic relationship with the nation remains a relationship with one's own self. Inauthentic, on the other hand, is the action of a person who seeks his people's community to escape from his own self; to him the "nation" is nothing other than the world of the They.

As therefore there exists an authentic and an inauthentic relationship with the nation, all talk about nation and national belonging must remain within that "ambiguity" that attaches to everything that is meant "authentically." "Everything looks as if it were genuinely understood, genuinely taken hold of, genuinely spoken, though at bottom it is not; or else it does not look so, and yet at bottom it is" (SuZ, 173).[17]

In *Being and Time* Heidegger does not get beyond this ambiguity. There is talk of nation and fate, but there is as yet no endeavor of thought to discover the command of the hour, the concrete demand of the moment of history. Heidegger has not yet chosen his hero. He has not yet left the terminologically well-barricaded area of the fundamental, of fundamental ontology. Specific history is suspected of inauthenticity and is formalized into "historicity," a hollow mold that can contain any historical matter or none. Thinking, on its own, calls for a historical-political opening (fate of the nation), but it does not execute it.

Contemporary criticism was certainly aware of this ambiguity, this fluctuating between unhistorical ontology and the postulate for historicity. Plessner's critique of Heidegger is evidence of this. Even earlier, Georg Misch, in an extensive review of *Being and Time,* had expressed the view that Heidegger the ontologist had triumphed over the hermeneutist of historical life.

Heidegger himself, while often complaining about what he regarded as uncomprehending reviews of *Being and Time,* felt much the same. Soon after the publication of his work, he began to continue his reflections along the lines indicated by Plessner and Misch, toward a more radical historicity, a relationship with the moment and political determination.

On September 18, 1932, he wrote to Elisabeth Blochmann that *Being and Time* had meanwhile become remote to him and that the road he had then chosen now looked to him all "overgrown" and no longer passable. From 1930 onward his letters to Blochmann and to Karl Jaspers would often contain references to the need for a "new beginning," but also some doubt as to whether he could accomplish such a new beginning. In a letter to Jaspers of December 20, 1931, he openly admitted that he "had ventured out too far, beyond [his] own existential strength and without clearly perceiving the narrowness of what [he] could actually ask questions about." In this letter he refers to the "Berlin episode," which had taken place a year earlier.

On March 28, 1930, Heidegger had received an invitation to Berlin, to the most important chair of philosophy in Germany. The appointment commission, initially under the chairmanship of Prussian minister of culture Carl Heinrich Becker, had favored Ernst Cassirer. Admittedly Heidegger was shortlisted, but opposition to him had prevailed. Victor Farías has researched what went on at the time. According to Farías, Eduard Spranger had been the principal opponent of Heidegger's appointment. He had asked whether Heidegger did not owe his popularity to his personality rather than his philosophy, which was hardly suitable for teaching or study. In the report of the commission, we read: "For some time there has been much talk about Martin Heidegger at Freiburg. Although there are questions about his publications, it is clear that he has his own notions and, especially, that his personal attraction is powerful. Yet even his partisans recognize that hardly any of the students who flock to him can in fact understand him. This is a time of crisis for Heidegger; it would be best to wait for its outcome. To have him come now to Berlin would be wrong."[18]

The rumor that Heidegger was going through a crisis was based, for one thing, on the fact that the second volume of *Being and Time* had not yet appeared, nor had it even been advertised. His book on Kant had met with an ambivalent echo, but certainly it was not received as part of the continuation of *Being and Time.* Heidegger's performance in Davos had contributed to the impression of a crisis. What was remembered was a brusque rejection of cultural philosophy and his announcements of a new beginning, which, however, remained vague.

In the spring of 1930 there was a change in the Prussian ministry of culture. Adolf Grimme succeeded Becker. Grimme, a philosophically trained politician, a disciple of Husserl, coming from the circle of religious socialists around Paul Tillich, rejected the list submitted by the faculty and, against their express wishes, issued an invitation to Martin Heidegger. Grimme wanted to appoint a prominent figure. Besides, Heidegger's antibourgeois and cultural-revolutionary demeanor did not scare off a man like Adolf Grimme, who himself was a product of the antibourgeois youth movement. The liberal papers in Berlin were outraged at the minister's high-handed action: "A socialist minister wanted to bring to Berlin a cultural reactionary."[19]

In April 1930 Heidegger went to Berlin for negotiations. He traveled via

Heidelberg, to consult with Jaspers. Jaspers had learned of the invitation from the papers and had written to him: "You will be stepping into the most visible post and in consequence will experience and process hitherto unknown impulses of your philosophizing. I believe that there is no better opportunity" (March 29, 1930, BwHJ, 130). As he had himself earlier had hopes of Berlin, he felt a "gentle pain . . . but it is the slightest possible now that you have this invitation."

Heidegger, who had been informed by the minister about the opposition from the faculty, nevertheless conducted serious negotiations. Thus he demanded measures to ensure that he could "live and work in peace, without the problems of urban life"; this was an indispensable "basis" of his philosophizing.[20]

Back in Freiburg, however, Heidegger decided to decline the offer. "The rejection was difficult for me only out of consideration for Grimme himself," he wrote to Elisabeth Blochmann on May 10, 1930. To Grimme he explained his decision as follows: "Today, when I have just arrived at the beginning of a secure work, I do not feel sufficiently equipped to fulfill the Berlin professorship in the manner I must expect of myself and everybody else. Truly enduring philosophy can only be one that is a true philosophy of its time, i.e. that is in control of its time."

This is a crucial statement. Heidegger openly admits that he does not yet feel "sufficiently equipped," that he has not yet arrived at a "true philosophy," which not only, in a Hegelian manner, expresses its time in ideas, but which is "in control" of it—that is, that would have to show the way to it. Or, as he would say a year later in his Plato lectures, would have to "overcome the present." While he did not feel up to this self-set demand as yet, he was—as he also wrote—on the way to it; a "beginning" had been made.

Although this first invitation to Berlin caused a lot of public attention, Heidegger did not, at that time, make any triumphant programmatic "declaration in favor of the province"; he merely stated modestly that he was not yet ready for it. Heidegger's letter to Grimme concluded with the request that he would show understanding for the limits which were set even on him.

True philosophy must be in control of its time, Heidegger had written. He had thereby confronted philosophy and himself with a big task—they must demonstrate time-diagnostic and prognostic force and, moreover, recommend certain definite decisions, and not merely decidedness. There must be philosophical insights of politicizable precision; alternative courses of action must become visible and, if possible, philosophically decidable. All this Heidegger expects of philosophy if it is to be "in control" of its time.

His demands are in line with the trend of Heidegger's day. This emerges with particular clarity from the great dispute about the sociology of knowledge, which then agitated the scholarly world. This debate was triggered by Karl Mannheim's spectacular presentation at the Sociologists' Congress in September 1928. One of the participants, young Norbert Elias, then spoke of a "spiritual revolution"[21] that had just taken place, and the sociologist Alfred Meusel described his "alarming sense of trying to sail a storm-churned ocean on an unseaworthy ship."[22] What had happened?

Karl Mannheim had spoken on the "Meaning of Rivalry in the Intellectual Sphere" and in doing so had offered something that, at first glance, seemed like the customary Marxist explanation of intellectual structures from social conditions. What was provocative for the Marxists was that Mannheim turned the ideological suspicion normally used by the Marxists against their opponents against the Marxists themselves. He challenged their universalist pretensions. However, this affront to the Marxists would not have been enough to cause such a general uproar in the scholarly world. The most provocative aspect was that Mannheim elevated the inclusion of the question of truth in the analysis of spiritual structures into a principle. For him there were only different "styles of thinking" in the intellectual field—Mannheim himself called his approach "relationist." These styles related directly to natural and civilizational reality and related to each other, which in turn resulted in an exceedingly complex process of tradition forming, consensus communities, rivalries, and hostilities, all of which produced a pattern almost indistinguishable from an unfettered market economy. This whole process, of course, had a "basis," but this was comprehensible only through a style of thinking. That which contains the roots of thinking must itself remain contentious in the clash of styles of thinking. Hence there can be no ready-made concept for this basis. Mannheim uses the term "Being," meaning the totality of everything to which thinking can relate or by which it is challenged. Thinking, according to Mannheim, is never concerned with naked reality or real reality but always moves within an interpreted, comprehended reality. Mannheim criticizes Heidegger's analysis of the They.

> The philosopher looks at this "They," this secretive Something, but he is not interested to find out how it arose, and it is just at this point, where the philosopher stops, that the work of the sociologist begins. Sociological analysis shows that this public interpretation of existence is not simply 'there,' nor, on the other hand, is it the result of a 'systematic thinking out,' it is the stake for which we fight. And the struggle is not guided by motives of pure contemplative thirst for knowledge. Different interpretations of the world for the most part correspond to the peculiar positions the various groups occupy in their struggle for power.[23]

Mannheim's relativism does not endorse any ideological party or any interpretational pattern. Like Ranke's historical epochs, all intellectual structures are equivalent, not perhaps before God but before their underlying Being. There are no privileged approaches. All thinking—each in its way—possesses "attachment to Being" *(Seinsgebundenheit).* Above all, it is in each case a specific Being in which the thinking of the individual or of groups is rooted. In the fundamentals there are the "paradigmatic primal experiences of certain spheres of life,"[24] which then take shape in the different intellectual structures and which therefore possess a core of "irreconcilablenesses of an existential kind."[25] For this reason there can be no complete settlement of the differences in the form of some common world picture or in any principles of action derived therefrom. However, according to Mannheim, it is the political task of the sociology of knowledge to reduce conflicts and tensions by remembering that the "parties" engaged in dispute and suppression rivalry are each conditioned by their own attachment to Being. This act of understanding is intended to drain the torn whole of some of its antagonistic energy. Once this step has been accomplished, different views of the world will confront each other in society, but none of them will be able to claim absoluteness. In the best scenario, their opposition and competition, disciplined by self-transparency, will drive historical development forward. A society that consists only of the relationships of its sections should have the sociology of knowledge assigned to it, much as a counselor-therapist is assigned to a quarrelling married couple. No privileged attachment to Being, no timelessly valid truth—only a "freely floating intelligence" can qualify the sociology of knowledge for its function of political arbitration and neutralization of opposites—as far as possible. It knows that it is neither possible nor desirable to achieve perfect homogeneity. The intellectual-policy program of the sociology of knowledge hopes to reduce conflicts by understanding the irreconcilably different portions of Being attached in the "deep layers of human world shaping."[26]

Mannheim's sociology of knowledge is an impressive scientific-political attempt to save liberalism at the end of the Weimar Republic by underpinning it with a kind of ontological pluralism. Thinking is called upon to differentiate between reconcilable and irreconcilable conflicts, to look for rational settlement wherever possible, and, where it is not, to allow the mystery of the "irreconcilabilities of an existential nature" to take their course. Karl Mannheim concludes with the words: "He who would wish to have the irrational where, de jure, the clarity and astringency of reason should still hold sway, is afraid of looking in the eyes of the mystery in its proper place."[27]

Heidegger takes note of this program of détente through the sociology of knowledge. But he cannot accept the attempt to save liberalism by reducing it to an ontological pluralism as a contribution to the mastery of pressing problems of the day. He simply disputes that the sociology of knowledge has come closer to the "mystery in its proper place" by even a single step.

In his 1931–32 winter semester lectures on Plato, which deal very extensively with the simile of the cave from *The Republic,* Heidegger places the sociologists of knowledge in the cave among the captives who can observe only the play of shadows on the wall, without being able to see the real objects, let alone the all-illuminating sun. Anyone liberated from the cave into the light of truth and then returning into the darkness to liberate his former fellow prisoners, would not be amicably received by them. "He would be told he was one-sided, he was, coming from somewhere, holding (in their view) a one-sided attitude; and presumably, nay certainly, they have down there a so-called 'sociology of knowledge,' with whose help he would be informed that he was operating with so-called ideological prerequisites, which of course gravely disturbed the community of collective opinion in the cave and therefore had to be rejected." The genuine philosopher, however, who had seen the light, would attach no importance to such "cave prattle" but would *try* to seize a few deserving ones, "touch them roughly and drag them out" and in a "long story lead them out of the cave" (GA 34, 86).

In 1930 Heidegger had claimed that philosophy must be in "control of its time." Over the next few years, however, we can observe him immersing himself more and more deeply into the history of Greek thought. Is he trying to escape from history? Almost furiously he rejects this suspicion in the Plato lectures referred to above: "In genuine retreat into history we gain that distance from the present which alone provides us with the space for the run-up that is needed if we wish to leap out beyond our own present, i.e. to take it for what every present deserves to be taken—for being overcome . . . In the end only our retreat into history brings us into that which is actually happening today" (GA 34, 10).

Heidegger, however, is in danger of getting stuck in the past, and whether his run-up will actually lead to a leap into the present seems to him, at times, doubtful. The impact he receives from Platonic philosophy is so overpowering that, time and again, he wonders if he has anything to add of his own. In a letter to Jaspers he describes himself as a kind of "attendant" in the museum of great philosophy, whose sole duty is to make sure "that the blinds over the windows are raised and lowered correctly, so that the few great works of tradition receive a more or less adequate illumination for the chance observer" (December 20, 1931, BwHJ, 144). How serious he is about this rather comical self-criticism emerges from a letter to Elisabeth Blochmann. "The more strongly I get into my own work, the more securely I am invariably forced back into the great beginnings among the Greeks. And frequently I hesitate over whether it would not be more essential to abandon all my own attempts and merely make sure that this world does not become only a pale tradition, but that it once more stands before our eyes in its exciting greatness and exemplariness" (December 19, 1932, BwHB, 55).

Heidegger had concerned himself with the Greek beginnings of philosophy ever since the early 1920s. But now they affect him with such force that he is in danger of losing his own philosophical self-assurance. He becomes humble—but only in the face of the Greeks, not before the philosophers of his own time.

Heidegger's intensive occupation with the Greeks is accompanied by mixed emotions. A vast horizon is opening up before him, one that inspires him and gives him a great sense of freedom of movement. But it is also a horizon before which he feels small and insignificant. There is a strong temptation simply to disappear in that past, but his understanding of radical historicity, which demands that philosophy should be "in control of" the historical moment, does not permit him to linger in the "origins." He has to reinterpret his enjoyable immersion in the past as a preparation for leaping into the present. However, he admits to himself without illusions that, as an academic philosopher, he is still stuck in the "strait" of the "factually questionable" and inhibited through "entanglement in [his] own work" (letter to Blochmann, May 10, 1930, BwHB, 35). In his depressed moments Heidegger knows that he is himself sitting in the cave. Strictly speaking, he still has nothing special, nothing original, to say on the pressing problems of the present, and this torments him. His mood fluctuates—at times he feels the strength for a new beginning, he feels himself the equal of Plato, and at other times he feels empty, without originality, without creative power. He is, on the one hand, swept along by his overreaching intentions and, on the other, depressed. To Jaspers he clothes this in the Platonizing formula: philosophy has the duty of a "knowing guide and guardian" among the "genuine public" (December 20, 1931, BwHJ, 144).

What does he find in Plato that is so powerful that "his own ideas" are blurred (letter to Jaspers, December 8, 1932, BwHJ, 149), and what are the insights that qualify one to be a "knowing guide"?

The first half of the Plato lectures of 1932 are, as we have mentioned, devoted to the simile of the cave from the *Politeia, The Republic.* In detail Heidegger describes and interprets the separate phases of what is happening. Act one: the dwellers in the cave watch the play of shadows on the opposite wall. Act two: one of them is unfettered and released. Act three: he can turn around, he sees the objects and the fire behind them; he is led out to the light of day. Blinded, he at first sees nothing, but then the objects gleam before him in the light, they become "more existent," and finally he sees the sun that not only illuminates everything but also makes everything grow and thrive. Act four: the released man returns to the cave to liberate his companions, but they offer resistance to being torn out of their accustomed existence. Their liberator seems to them crazy, ludicrous, presumptuous, and dangerous. They will kill him when they get hold of him.

This simile would seem to be as clear as day, the more so as Plato himself once more interprets it. The prisoners are fettered by their external senses, by their external sensations. Liberation frees the inner sense, thinking. Thinking is the contemplative capacity of the soul. Whereas the other two capacities of the soul entangle in the world of senses, thinking offers release from it and provides a view of the objects as they really are. The sun, to the viewing of which thinking raises itself, is the symbol of supreme truth. But what is this truth? Plato says it is the Good. But what is the Good? The Good is like the sun. This means two things. First, it lets the objects be visible, it makes it possible for them to be recognized and it thereby also makes possible our cognition. Second, it allows everything that is to originate, grow, and thrive.

The Good makes possible the triumph of visibility, a fact from which the cave dwellers benefit as well, since the fire, a descendant of the sun, makes them at least see the shadowy shapes; and the Good ensures that Something exists at all and that this Something keeps in Being. This comprehensive Being, which lives by the strength of the Good, is viewed by Plato as a justly regulated commonwealth—the ideal polis. The dialogue had started with the question as to the nature of justice, and Plato expressly declares that justice—that is, Being ordered by the Good—is difficult to recognize by way of the exploration of the soul, and that it is better to view it on a greater scale, the scale of the polis. Once one has recognized it in the *makroanthropos* of the polis, one will readily recognize it again in the soul of the individual. The fundamental principle of justice, as demonstrated by Plato in his ideal republic, is the realization of the right measure and of order. In a hierarchically graduated world of unequal human beings, each one is assigned the place where he can develop his peculiar abilities and apply them to the whole. The picture of the harmonically collaborating whole is enlarged by Plato beyond the polis to the even more comprehensive dimension of the Pythagorean harmony of the spheres. And so the circle closes. The soul is of cosmic origin, and the cosmos is soul-like. Soul and cosmos both vibrate in a sphere of tranquility and unchangeability. They are pure Being, in contrast to changeable time, to Becoming.

This kind of Platonism, however, is no use to Heidegger. Let us start at the last-named aspect, Being's ideal of everlastingness. To Heidegger the meaning of Being is Time: passing and happening. To him there is no Being's ideal of permanency; indeed he holds that the task of thinking is to make man sensitive to the passage of time. Thinking opens up the time horizon wherever the daily tendency toward objectivization makes relationships and situations freeze in a false timelessness. Thinking should "liquefy," it should hand over that-which-is, above all *Dasein,* to the flow of time; it dissolves the metaphysical world of the beyond, of eternal ideas. Nothing is to have endurance in the "turbulence of questions."

Heidegger has to read Plato against the grain if he is to gain anything from him. This applies to the Platonic Being at rest, in contrast to Heidegger's time. It also applies to the aspect of "truth."

In Plato there is truth that endures, which therefore has to wait to be discovered by us. The shadow images on the wall are copies of the originals, of the shadow-casting objects that are carried past, behind the watchers, in the light of the fire. A copy relates to an original, yet even the "original" objects are, in relation to the next higher step, the ideas, no more than inadequate copies. True cognition reaches through these copies and discovers the original, that which authentically *is.* Truth is correctness, the appropriateness of a cognition in relation to the recognized. The perceptions of the cave dwellers are untrue because they comprehend only the appearance while missing the Being appearing to them. For Plato there is the absolute truth of ideas. This can be comprehended in an upsurge of the soul, by thinking between mathematics and mystic ecstasy. For Heidegger, however, there can be no such truth; for him there is only a "truth happening" that takes place in man's self-relationship and world relationship. Man discovers no truth existing independently of him; he conceives an interpretative horizon—a different one in each epoch—in which the real is given a certain meaning. This concept of truth had been in outline by Heidegger in *Being and Time* and unfolded in his 1930 lecture, "On the Essence of Truth."

Truth, he points out, exists neither on the side of the subject, in the sense of a *truthful* statement, nor on the side of the object, in the sense of correct description, but it is a happening unfolding in a double movement—a movement from the world, which reveals itself, emerges, appears; and a movement from the individual, who takes possession of the world and opens it up. This double happening unrolls at the distance at which man is placed with regard to himself and to his world. He is aware of this distance and is therefore also aware of the existence of a world that reveals itself to him and evades him. He is aware of this because he experiences himself as a creature that can show itself and conceal itself. This "distanceness" is the open region of freedom. "The essence of truth is freedom" (WW, 15).[28] Freedom in this sense means having distance, open space. This distance, providing an open space, is also called "openedness" by Heidegger. Only in this openedness is there a play of concealment and unconcealment. If this openedness did not exist, man could not distinguish himself from what surrounds him. He could not even distinguish himself from himself, and thus would not even know that he is there. Only because this openedness exists can man conceive the idea of measuring his statements about reality by what of reality reveals itself to him. Man does not possess any unassailable truths, but he stands—unassailably—in a truth relationship that produces the play of concealment and disclosure, emergence and disappearance, Being-there and Being-away. Heidegger finds the shortest expression for this understanding of truth in the Greek term *aletheia,* literally unconcealment. Truth has been wrested from concealment, either as a result of the revealing or emergence of something that exists, or as a result of its being brought out, unveiled. In either case it is a kind of struggle being waged.

These reflections must lead to the conclusion that there cannot be any metahistorical criterion of truth. There is no longer that unending history of approximation to a truth, nor Plato's upsurge of the soul into the heaven of ideas; there is only a "truth happening," which means a history of designs of Being. This history, however, is identical with the history of the lead paradigms of cultural epochs and civilizational types. The modern age, for instance, is determined by its nature-based design of Being. "The decisive aspect is that a design was executed that, anticipating, circumscribed what was to be understood by nature and natural process—a space-time-defined motional connection of mass points" (GA 34, 61). This design of Being—which should not be viewed as the product of a single brain, but as a cultural synthesis, determines the modern age in all its aspects. Nature becomes an object of calculation, and man looks on himself as a thing among things. Attention is narrowed down to those aspects of the world that, in some way or other, seem controllable and manipulable. This instrumental basic attitude is the result of technological development. Our whole civilization, Heidegger maintains, is the expression of a definite design of Being, in whose sphere we move even during the "trivial happening of any journey through the city by the electrical tramway" (GA 34, 121). Our insights do not become "truer" because they lead to technical skills, but nature offers different answers according to how we question it. Under our attack it each time "unconceals" a different aspect. And since we ourselves are part of nature, we are ourselves transformed, too, through the manner of our attack. We too unconceal ourselves and allow other aspects of our essence to become effective.

There is no truth in the sense of some great unknown *X* that we approach in an infinite progression, to which we match our statements in an ever more appropriate and correct manner; there is only the active "discussion" with that-which-is, during which we also show ourselves differently. And all this is a creative process, since every design of Being produces, materially and spiritually, a world interpreted and organized in a definite way.

If therefore there is no absolute criterion of truth but only a dynamic happening of truth, Heidegger nevertheless finds a further-going criterion for the assessment of that happening of truth—the criterion of success. As a result of the manner in which we approach it or let it be, that-which-is *(das*

Seiende) can have the effect of "being more being" *(seiender)* or less being. The modern technological-rational understanding of nature is to Heidegger a design of Being that allows that-which-is to pale. "It is a separate question whether, through that science, that-which-is *(das Seiende)* has become more being *(seiender)* or whether something totally different has inserted itself between that-which-is and cognitive man, as a result of which his relationship with that-which-is has been eroded, his instinct for the essence of nature driven out of him—and his instinct for the essence of man choked" (GA 34, 62).

These formulations reveal that Heidegger, with the comparative criterion of the "more being," is concerned with an enhancement or a reduction of the living—whether that-which-is can show itself in the fullness of its potential, whether we "release" ourselves and the world, whether the manner of our attention permits that-which-is to emerge in its entire richness and to grow, just as we ourselves grow in the process. An "essential eye for the potential" is what Heidegger calls the attention that possesses its special organs—"original philosophy" and "great poetry." Both of these make that-which-is "more being" *(das Seiende seiender)* (GA 34, 64).

From 1933 onward Heidegger would tend to philosophize along the track of "great poetry"; at the beginning of the 1930s his emphasis is still on the "original philosophy" of a man like Plato. For Heidegger's understanding of truth as a truth happening, however, Plato, the metaphysician of an absolute truth par excellence is unlikely to provide any starting points. But who can tell?

Heidegger concedes—and it would be difficult to deny—that in Plato this fundamental experience of *aletheia,* understood as unconcealed truth happening (without *objective* truth) had already begun "to become ineffective" and to transform itself into the "ordinary concept of the essence of truth in the sense of the correctness of statements" (GA 34, 17).[29] If Heidegger wishes to make sure of the Great Beginning among the Greeks, he has to understand Plato better than Plato understood himself. That is why he eliminates Plato's point of reference for truth, the world of ideas—with the supreme idea of the Good, symbolized by the sun, at the top—and instead directs his attention almost exclusively to the process of liberation and the upward climb of the soul. According to Heidegger, it is irrelevant whether or not some "spiritual behind-world" is discovered. What happens during this liberation is a change in attitude and stance, which makes "that-which-is more being" *(das Seiende seiender).* Heidegger distinguishes Plato's upsurge from any kind of escape from reality. The opposite is true. Only he who frees himself from the cave of shadows (of opinions, habits, and everyday attitudes) is truly born into the world, into the real world. And what is the real world? We should know it by now—Heidegger has often enough described it. It is the world viewed from the perspective of authenticity, the arena of thrownness and design, of care, of sacrifice, of struggle, a world permeated by fate, threatened by the Nothing and the Null—a dangerous place, where only those resigned to homelessness, the truly free, can hold out without having to seek protection under the roof of pregiven truths. As Heidegger is concerned with this picture of the world, he does not dwell at any length on the real high point of the cave simile, the moment of redemption in the ecstatic sight of the sun, but hurriedly returns to the cave with the returning freed man. Only there does the simile reach its climax for Heidegger. The one liberated into the light now becomes the liberator. The liberator, however, has to be a man of "violent action" (GA 34, 81), because the prisoners have made their world comfortable for themselves and, not knowing anything else, do not wish to be liberated from their situation. Heidegger extensively exploits two aspects of this happening for his image of the heroic philosopher—he is called to be a guide and guardian, and he must be prepared to become a martyr in the attempt to free the prisoners, because they will resist and offer violence to anyone using violence against them. They may kill him in order to be left alone by him.

Thus we have the philosophical leader whose mission it is to set a new truth happening into motion for a whole community and to create a new truth relationship. And the philosopher as a martyr, who not only, as Socrates, dies the death of a philosopher, but must perhaps even suffer the death of philosophy. The "poisoning" of philosophy, Heidegger says, occurs because it submits to the customs and practical considerations of the cave dwellers. Heidegger sketches out a sarcastic picture of the philosophy business—philosophy as an atrophied form of religious edification, as a cognition-theory handmaiden of the positive sciences, as ideological chatter, as lightweight writing in the fairground of intellectual vanities. All this implies that philosophy would have to endure "its own essence to become null and powerless" (GA 34, 84). Authentic philosophy, which in Plato sees the sun of the Good and in Heidegger has eaten of the fruits of freedom, which in Plato possesses truth and in Heidegger triggers a truth happening, this authentic philosophy finds itself in a blind alley, because it cannot defend itself against poisoning by instrumentalization for the useful and the convenient, and it will, if it does not participate, be despised and marginalized. The ethos of being free, however, also forbids it to shirk danger. It must not withdraw from the cave, for "being free, being a liberator means participating in history" (GA 34, 85). Heidegger sums it up as follows: "authentic philosophizing is powerless within the sphere of prevailing matter-of-course-ness; only to the extent that this transforms itself can philosophy appeal" (GA 34, 84).

Again we encounter history. The "prevailing matter-of-course-ness" must transform itself before real philosophy can appeal. What else is left but waiting for the great historical moment? Admittedly there is still the other possibility, that one day a great philosopher may come who, as Heidegger put it in his metaphysics lecture series of 1929–30, possesses the charisma that will make him become a destiny for others, "a spur for others, so that philosophizing awakens in them" (GA 29/30, 19).[30] Heidegger, who in the museum of philosophy makes sure the great works are properly lit, already rehearses a new part—that of the precursor who, as he put it in his Plato lectures, "clears the road" for him who is to come (GA 34, 85). "Can one succeed," Heidegger at the same time asks in a sibylline letter to Jaspers, "to create a foundation and a space for philosophy for decades to come, will there be people who within them carry a distant mission?" (December 8, 1932, BwHJ, 149).

If there is to be such a great change in history, with the philosophers playing a part, if authentic philosophizing is to be seen as an act of liberation, then the reference to politics can no longer be avoided. After all, even the upsurge of the soul, as described by Plato in *The Republic,* leads into a political dimension. There Plato develops the idea that a commonwealth can be properly ordered only if the true philosophers in it become the kings. Plato himself had tried this idea on the tyrant Dionysus in Syracuse and, as is well known, fared rather badly. He was sold into slavery and only by a stroke of luck regained his freedom.

But this will not trouble Plato. The true philosopher is illuminated by the idea of the Good. As a result he creates order within himself; the potential of his soul—desires, courage, wisdom—are in a state of harmony. Applying this model of inner harmony, he will then be able to order the commonwealth. This commonwealth is structured in three levels, just like the well-ordered soul: the desires are matched by the working class, courage by the class of warriors and guardians, wisdom by the philosophical superiors. These are the three orders on which political thought in the Western world would remain fixed for a long time. In the Middle Ages they were formulated as the triad of peasants, knights, and priests, and these ideas will still haunt Heidegger's rectorship address when he invokes the trinity of "labor service, military service, and service to knowledge."

The philosopher who has looked at the sun and who returns to the cave as liberator carries with him some ethical maxims. Plato's *Republic* is undoubtedly a work of philosophical ethics. It is the more surprising that Heidegger, whose thoughts revolve around the problem of how philosophy might become powerful in its day, should assert that Plato's idea of the Good has "nothing at all to do with ethics or morality" and that one should "avoid any sentimental picture of that idea of the Good" (GA 34, 100).

Hence the question arises with increasing insistence: If Heidegger dismisses Plato's solid political ethics, what then is the admirable power that he detects in Plato's philosophy? In the simile of the cave, the man liberated into light need not necessarily return to the cave as liberator. He might content himself with having been saved for truth, with having attained the highest form of life, the *bios theoretikos.* Why does he again mix with the people, why does he wish to perform his act of liberation, why does *wisdom* return to the political marketplace? Plato poses these questions and in doing so differentiates between the virtuous ideal of political justice and the ideal of dissociation from all political entanglements. Practical philosophy is confronting the philosophy of redemption. The philosopher can choose:

> When the few members of his band have glimpsed the joy and happiness to be found in mastering philosophy and have also gained a clear enough impression of the madness of the masses; when they've realized that more or less every political action is pernicious . . . once he has grasped all this with his rational mind, he lies low and does only what he's meant to do. It's as if he's taken shelter under a wall during a storm, with the wind whipping up the dust and rain pelting down; lawlessness infects everyone else he sees, so he is content if he can find a way to live his life here on earth without becoming tainted by immoral or unjust deeds, and to depart from life confidently, and without anger and bitterness.[31]

This possibility of self-redemption through philosophy always remains a temptation to Plato, an alternative to political ethics.

If Heidegger brackets out Plato's political ethics, can his enthusiasm possibly relate to this temptation of self-redemption through philosophy? No. Heidegger explicitly declares it to be the philosopher's duty to "act as a participant in history" (GA 34, 85). If, therefore, it is neither the expressly formulated Platonic ethics nor the will to philosophical self-redemption, what inspires Heidegger to link up with Plato's philosophy?

It is quite simply the act of becoming free, of stepping out into an open expanse, a "primordial experience" for which anything that possesses a definite culture and civilization of customary practices, obligations, and value signposts loses its final obligation. This does not, of course, mean an adoption of nonobligation, but the experience that everything that obliges one is transformed into something that one has chosen oneself. The open expanse into which the man liberated from the cave steps allows him to see that-which-is "as a whole." "As a whole" means in the horizon of the Nothing from which that-which-is emerges and from which it stands out. The liberated cave dweller has embraced nothingness, he chooses his position "in the questionability of that-which-is as a whole" *(des Seienden im Ganzen)*; he therefore comports himself "to Being and to its boundary in the Nothing" (GA 34, 78). Heidegger's formula for this attitude reads: "empowerment" (GA 34, 106). What does this mean? Heidegger denies us an answer. "As for what it means, there is no need now to speak any more about it, we merely have to act" (GA 34, 78). With the experience of empowerment the "limit of philosophy" (GA 34, 106) has been reached.

Heidegger's thinking at this time revolves around the idea of empowerment. He seeks a way to cross the limits of philosophy—but with philosophical means and for philosophical reasons.

Heidegger, deeply engrossed in Plato, intoxicated by the gigantomania he discovers there, fluctuating between the light-headedness of the summit and a sense of discouragement, is about to find a role for himself. He intends to be the herald of a historical-political and, simultaneously, philosophical epiphany. There will come a time that is worthy of philosophy, and there will come a philosophy that is in control of its time. And in some way he will be one of the party, as a squire or as a knight. Now he has to be vigilant, lest he miss the moment when politics can and must become philosophical and philosophy political.

13

THE NATIONAL SOCIALIST REVOLUTION AND COLLECTIVE BREAKOUT FROM THE CAVE

Plato was drawn to politics. The reason was the political instinct of the polis citizen, philosophy's susceptibility to being seduced by power, and his longing for a social organization that would allow philosophy the undisturbed happiness of theory. Much though he tried to remove himself from ordinary life, Plato remained a citizen of his city, unable to sever himself from it. Even the academy subsequently established by him put itself under the protection and in the service of the polis.

Martin Heidegger, involved in Plato, is not yet drawn to politics, even though he hopes for a historical turning point that might give rise to a new understanding of Being. As yet he keeps the creative forces of history separate from so-called current politics, which he views as "wheeler-dealing," sterile excitement, bustle, and party-political squabbling. Authentic history, to him, occurs at depths of which politics is allegedly unaware.

Grand gestures of philosophy of history were fashionable during the years of the Weimar Republic. Political diagnosticians with philosophical ambitions regarded political events as if they were taking place on the wall of Plato's cave, trying to discover the real battle of giants behind the shadow play of everyday events. Behind everyday politics they endeavored to see grand polarities—primal myth against prophecy (Tillich); Faustian man against fellahdom (Spengler); the new Middle Ages against the demonism of the modern age (Berdyayev); total mobilization against bourgeois coziness (Jünger).

Heidegger, too, favors the style of the grand gesture. He hurries through the bustle of the day in order to reach "authentic" history. In his Plato class of 1931–32 he speaks of an "overturning of the entire human Being at the beginning of which we are standing" (GA 34, 324). But the outlines of this are still blurred. What is clear at this moment is only the departure and turning point in the solitary philosophical ecstasy of the cave simile. This ecstasy, formulated as "that-which-is becomes more being" *(das Seiende wird seiender),* is to be led out from the cave of mere inwardness and to be socialized. How is this to be done? Possibly by the ecstatic philosopher's turning into the "founder" of a new society. For the time being, Heidegger confines himself to awakening the spirit of philosophy in his seminar rooms and embarking on vast journeys into the immeasurable distances of philosophical tradition. But he knows that this does not yet imply that philosophy is "in control" of its time. And that is what is needed. Heidegger is still waiting. Probably it is necessary for history to present itself powerfully before the philosopher can feel empowered.

However, anyone waiting for history and grand politics must hold opinions on day-to-day politics. So far Heidegger had mostly kept these to himself, or else uttered them casually, almost offhandedly. After all, to him this was just "cave chatter."

At the turn of 1931–32, during the break in the Plato semester, Hermann Mörchen visited with Heidegger at his cabin in Todtnauberg. Mörchen recorded his impressions in his diary:

> One sleeps a lot up there; in the evening it is "lights out" at half past eight. Even so it is dark long enough in winter for some time to be left for a chin-wag. Admittedly the talk was not about philosophy, but mainly about National Socialism. The once so liberal follower of Gertrud Bäumer has become a National Socialist and her husband is following her. I would have never believed it, but it is not really surprising. He doesn't understand much about politics, and that is probably why his detestation of all mediocre halfness lets him expect great things of the party that promises to do something decisive and, above all, effectively to

oppose communism. Democratic idealism and Brüning's conscientiousness cannot, he believes, achieve anything any more, now that things have reached the present pass; that was why a dictatorship that does not shrink from draconian measures must be approved. Only by means of such a dictatorship could the worse communist dictatorship, which destroys all individual personal culture and hence all culture in the Western sense altogether, be avoided. He doesn't seem to concern himself with political details. If a man lives up here, he has different yardsticks for everything.[1]

Hermann Mörchen was taken aback by Heidegger's political sympathies. He could explain them only by the philosopher's ignorance of "political details." Another student of Heidegger, Max Müller, similarly recalls the surprise among Heidegger's students when he revealed himself as a follower of National Socialism: "Not one of his students ever thought of politics then. There was never a political word in his classes."[2]

At the time of Mörchen's visit in Todtnauberg and the Plato lectures of the winter of 1931–32, Heidegger's support for the Nazi Party was no more than a political opinion. He regarded the party as a force of order amid the hardships of the economic slump and the chaos of the collapsing Weimar Republic, and above all as a bulwark against the danger of a communist revolution. "Rudeness can only be answered with rudeness," he said to Mörchen. As yet his political sympathies for Nazism were not reflected in his philosophy, but a year later this would change fundamentally. Then the great moment of history would have arrived for Heidegger, that "overturning of the entire human Being" of which he had spoken in his Plato lectures. Then the National Socialist revolution would become for him a *Dasein*-controlling event, one that would penetrate his philosophy to its core, forcing the philosopher beyond the "boundaries of philosophy." In his Plato lectures he had broken off his analysis of philosophical ecstasy with the remark that "there is no need now to speak any more about it, we merely have to act" (GA 34, 78). In February 1933 the moment of action arrived for Heidegger. Ecstasy suddenly seemed to be possible also in politics.

In his Plato lectures Heidegger had stated that he wished to return to the Greek beginnings in order to gain distance for the leap into the present and beyond it. His leap was too short and did not land him in the present. But now history was coming to meet him; it overwhelmed him and swept him along.

He need no longer leap, he could let himself drift—were it not for his ambition to be one of the drivers himself. "One must involve oneself," Heidegger said to Jaspers in March 1933.

In a subsequent retrospective justification, Heidegger stressed the hardships of the period, which had called for resolute political action: unemployment, economic depression, the still-unresolved issue of reparations, civil war in the streets, the danger of a communist overthrow. The political system of the Weimar Republic was incapable of dealing with these problems, and its efforts only resulted in interparty squabbling, corruption, and lack of responsibility. He had wanted to join the forces that he sensed had a genuine will to make a new start. He had harbored the hope—he said in a letter to the student Hans-Peter Hempel on September 19, 1960—"that National Socialism would acknowledge and absorb within itself all constructive and productive forces."[3]

Hempel had written to Heidegger about the conflict he was finding himself in as a result of admiring his philosophy and detesting his politics. Heidegger took the trouble to reply to him at length. He wrote:

> Your conflict remains unresolvable so long as you read, for instance, "The Essence of Reason" one morning and the same evening see reports and documentary film clips from the later years of the Hitler regime, so long as you are viewing National Socialism solely in retrospect from today and judging it with regard to what gradually came to light after 1934. At the beginning of the 1930s the class differences in our nation had become intolerable for any German with a sense of social responsibility, as had also Germany's economic throttling by the Treaty of Versailles. In 1932 there were 7 million unemployed, who, with their families, saw before them nothing but hardship and poverty. The confusion stemming from these circumstances, which today's generation can no longer even imagine, also spread to the universities. (Letter to Hempel, September 19, 1960)

Heidegger lists rational motives, but makes no mention of his revolutionary enthusiasm. In retrospect, as Max Müller pointed out, he "no longer wishes to admit . . . the radicalism of his intentions."[4]

To Heidegger the National Socialist seizure of power was a revolution. It was far more than politics; it was a new act of the history of Being, the beginning of a new epoch. Hitler, to him, meant a new era. That is why, in his letter to Hempel, Heidegger exculpates himself by referring to Hölderlin and Hegel, who had similarly "slipped up": "Greater men have made such mistakes—Hegel saw Napoleon as the World Spirit, and Hölderlin saw him as the prince of the feast to which the gods and Christ had been invited."

Hitler's seizure of power triggered a revolutionary mood at the moment when it was realized, with terror but also with admiration and relief, that the Nazi Party was in fact getting down to smashing the Weimar system, which by then was supported only by a minority. The country was impressed by resoluteness and brutality. With the exception of the Social Democrats and the (by then arrested) Communists, all the political parties on March 24 voted in favor of the so-called Empowering Law. The fact that the Weimar parties dissolved was due not only to fear of reprisals but also to the fact that all were swept along by the Nazi revolution. Theodor Heuss, then a deputy for the German Democratic Party, noted approvingly on May 20, 1933: "Revolutions seize the opportunity of engaging 'public opinion.' This has always been so . . . Moreover, they raise the historical claim to refashioning the 'national spirit.'"[5]

There were overwhelming demonstrations of the new community spirit, mass oaths under floodlit cupolas, bonfires on the mountains, and the Führer's speeches on the radio—people would assemble, festively attired, in public places to listen to them, in the great halls of the universities and in taverns. There was choral singing in the churches in honor of the Nazi seizure of power. *Generalsuperintendant* Otto Dibelius, in his sermon in St. Nicholas's church on March 21, 1933, the Day of Potsdam, said: "Through north and south, through east and west there marches a new will to a German state, a yearning, to quote Trietschke, no longer 'to be deprived of one of the most noble sensations in a man's life,' that of the enthusiastic pride in his own state."[6] The atmosphere of those days is difficult to describe, writes Sebastian Haffner, who experienced it himself. It formed the real power base of the new führer state. "It was—there is no other way of putting it—a widespread feeling of deliverance, of liberation from democracy."[7] This sense of relief at the demise of democracy was shared not only by the enemies of the republic. Most of its supporters, too, no longer credited it with the strength to master the crisis. It was as if a paralyzing weight had been lifted. Something genuinely new seemed to be beginning—a people's rule without political parties, with a leader of whom it was hoped that he would unite Germany once more internally and make her self-assured externally. Even in distant observers of the events, the impression was created that Germany had once more returned to herself. Hitler's "peace speech" of May 17, 1933, when he declared that "boundless love and loyalty to one's own nation" included "respect" for the national rights of other nations, had its effect.[8] The London *Times* observed that Hitler had "indeed spoken for a united Germany."[9]

Even among the Jewish population—despite the boycott of Jewish businesses on April 1 and the dismissal of Jewish public employees after April 7—there was a good deal of enthusiastic support for the "national revolution." Georg Picht recalls that Eugen Rosenstock-Huessey, in a lecture in March 1933, declared that the National Socialist revolution was an attempt by the Germans to realize Hölderlin's dream. In Kiel, Felix Jacoby began his lecture on Horace in the summer of 1933 with the words: "As a Jew I find myself in a difficult position. But as a historian I have long learned not to view historical events from a private perspective. I have voted for Adolf Hitler since 1927 and I am happy that in the year of the National Rising I am allowed to lecture on Augustus. Because Augustus is the only figure in world history that may be compared to Adolf Hitler."[10]

The yearning for nonpolitical politics suddenly seemed to be fulfilled. For most people, politics had been a laborious business of preserving and asserting their interests, a matter of quarreling, selfishness, and conflict. The political stage had seemed to be peopled by groups and associations, by string pullers and conspirators, by gangs and cliques. Heidegger had himself voiced this resentment against politics when he assigned the whole sphere to the They and to "talk." "Politics" was seen as a betrayal of the values of "true" life, family happiness, spirit, loyalty, courage. "A political person is distasteful to me," Richard Wagner had said. The antipolitical mood would no longer reconcile itself to the fact of the plurality of human beings; instead it was looking for the great singular—the German, the *Volksgenosse,* the laborer of hand and head, the spirit.

Whatever was left of political wisdom lost all credibility overnight. What mattered now was enthusiasm. Gottfried Benn then apostrophized the literary émigrés: "Metropolis, industrialization, intellectualism, all the shadows that the age had cast over my thoughts, all the powers of the century that I confronted in my production, there are moments when this entire tormented life drops away and nothing is left but the plain, the expanse, the seasons, simple words—the people."[11]

These were also Heidegger's sentiments, about whose last visit in June 1933 Karl Jaspers provides the following account:

> Heidegger himself seemed to have changed. Straight away on his arrival there arose an atmosphere dividing us. National Socialism had become an intoxication of the population. I went to Heidegger's room to welcome him. "It's just like 1914 . . . ," I began, intending to continue: "again this deceptive mass intoxication," but when I saw Heidegger radiantly agreeing with my first words, the rest stuck in my throat . . . Face to face with Heidegger himself gripped by that intoxication I failed. I did not tell him that he was on the wrong road. I no longer trusted his transformed nature at all. I felt a threat to myself in view of the violence in which Heidegger now participated.[12]

For Heidegger himself it was a redeeming violence; the moment of truth had arrived. He who had so joyfully engaged in the business of thinking now called for judgment day on philosophy. In his last conversation with Jaspers he said, with anger and fury in his voice, that it was "nonsense that there should be so many professors of philosophy, only two or three need be kept in Germany."[13] When Jaspers asked which ones, Heidegger remained meaningfully silent.

It was a philosophical somersault into primitivity. In a lecture to the student body of Tübingen University on November 30, 1933, Heidegger explicitly confirmed this: "To be primitive means to stand, from an inner urge and drive, at the point where things begin to be primitive, to be driven by internal forces. Just because the new student is primitive, he has a calling to implement the new demand for knowledge."[14]

It was a case of trying to cut the Gordian knot of reality, of taking angry leave from the troublesome subtleties of one's own thinking on Being. A hunger for concreteness and compact reality suddenly erupted, and solitary philosophy sought immersion in the multitude. A bad time for differentiations. Heidegger even swept aside his most prominent difference, the one between Being *(Sein)* and that-which-is *(das Seiende),* by allowing it to be understood that Being had at last arrived: "We are under the orders of a new reality."[15]

What was happening in Germany would later be called by Hannah Arendt, in her great essay *The Origins of Totalitarianism,* the "alliance between the Mob and the Elite."[16] An intellectual elite, whose traditional values of the world of yesterday had vanished in the World War, was burning the bridges behind it at the moment the fascist movements got to power. It was "the mass into which the postwar elite wished to be immersed."[17]

In "the vortex of philosophical questions," Heidegger had said earlier, our matter-of-course relationships with reality are lost. Now it is the other way around—Heidegger's philosophy surrenders itself to the vortex of political reality. But he is able to do so only because, at that moment, he regards reality as a piece of philosophy become real.

> The German, at odds with himself, with deep divisions in his mind, likewise in his will and therefore impotent in action, becomes powerless to direct his own life. He dreams of justice in the stars and loses his footing on earth . . . In the end, then, only the inward road remained open for German men. As a nation of singers, poets and thinkers they dreamed of a world in which the others lived, and only when misery and wretchedness dealt them inhuman blows did there perhaps grow up out of art the longing for a new rising, for a new Reich, and therefore for a new life.[18]

The man who then appeared as the realization of the secret dreams of artists and thinkers was Adolf Hitler in his speech on the Day of Potsdam, March 21, 1933.

The Austrian satirist Karl Kraus once said that he could not think of anything else to say about Hitler. Heidegger had a lot of things to say about Hitler; he had, as he told the denazification commission of Freiburg University in 1945, "believed" in Hitler. This is how the record of the commission summed up his statements: "He believed that Hitler would grow beyond the party and its doctrine, and that the movement could spiritually be guided onto other tracks, so that everything would come together on the basis of a renewal and concentration for a Western responsibility."[19]

In retrospect Heidegger presented himself as a man who had acted on the grounds of sober political considerations and social responsibility. But in actual fact Heidegger, during that first year, was bewitched by Hitler.

"How can such an uneducated man as Hitler govern Germany?" Jaspers, quite aghast, asked Heidegger on his last visit in June 1933. Heidegger replied, "Education is quite irrelevant . . . just look at his wonderful hands!"[20]

It was not a tactical maneuver, not an adjustment to events, but a matter of the heart when Heidegger, on November 3, 1933, the occasion of the plebiscite that led Germany to leave the League of Nations, concluded his "Appeal to German Students" with the words: "Let not axioms or 'ideas' be the rules of your Being. The Führer himself and alone is the present and future German reality and its law."[21]

Later, in his letter to Hans-Peter Hempel, who had challenged him on this sentence, Heidegger gave the following explanation: "If I had intended only that which is understood on casual reading, then 'the Führer' would have to have been in spaced type. But the deliberately spaced 'is' . . . implies that 'foremost and at all times the leaders are also the led—led by fate and the law of history.'"[22] In this 1960 letter Heidegger therefore argues, by way of excuse, that when writing that ominous sentence he had been thinking of something quite special, something that was bound to escape the casual reader. This something special, however, is just what Hitler always asserted about himself—that he was the personification of destiny. And this was in fact how Heidegger experienced him.

What Heidegger omits to mention, though it lent real meaning and a special emphasis to his statements and actions during those few months, is the fact that the National Socialist revolution had electrified him philosophically; that he discovered a fundamental metaphysical happening, a metaphysical revolution, in the events of 1933, a "total overturning of our German *Dasein*" (Tübingen address, November 30, 1933).[23] An overturning, moreover, that not only affected the life of the German nation but opened a new chapter in Western history. This, he claimed, was the "great second clash of arms" after the "first beginning" with Greek philosophy, the origin of Western culture.[24] This second clash of arms had become necessary because the impulse of the first beginning had meanwhile spent itself. Greek philosophy had placed man's *Dasein* into the open expanse of indeterminacy, freedom, and questionability. Meanwhile, however, man had withdrawn again into the shell of his world images and values, his technological and cultural "wheeler-dealing." In the Greek beginnings there had been a moment of authenticity. Since then, however, world history had returned to the dim light of inauthenticity, to Plato's cave.

Heidegger interpreted the 1933 revolution as a collective breakout from the cave, as an advance into that open expanse that normally gives room only to solitary philosophical questions and thought. With the revolution of 1933 the historic moment of authenticity had arrived for him.

The events to which Heidegger reacted were political events, and his actions took place on the political stage—but it was the power of philosophical imagination that governed his reactions and actions. And this philosophical imagination transformed the political scene into a historical-philosophical stage on which a play from the repertoire of the history of Being was being enacted. Real history was scarcely recognizable in it—but that was irrelevant. Heidegger intended to stage his own historical-philosophical drama and to recruit fellow actors for it. Although in all his speeches during those few months he refers to the "power of command of the new German reality," it is his philosophy—and he leaves no doubt about this—that reveals the authentic meaning of the "commands." Philosophy so moves the people into the power sphere of those commands that they can be transformed from within. For this reason he organizes a "scholarship camp," speaks to an audience of the unemployed whom he brings to the university, issues countless addresses and appeals, all designed to "deepen" the political events of the day in a way that would make them appropriate for his imaginary metaphysical stage. This power is exerted by philosophy only when it does not speak "about" conditions and events, but "out of" them. Philosophy must itself become part of the "revolutionary reality" of which it speaks. This revolutionary reality "can be experienced only by he who has the right sense for experiencing it, not by the observer . . . because revolutionary reality is not something present-at-hand, but it is in its nature that it only unrolls . . . Such reality calls for an entirely different relationship than does a fact" (Tübingen address, November 30, 1933).

Heidegger had always maintained the principle that "mood" determines our Being-in-the-world. That is why he now takes the revolutionary mood of upheaval, rising, and the new community as his starting point. Reprisals by the state, rioting by the mob, and anti-Semitic actions are for him concomitant phenomena that have to be accepted.

We are therefore faced with a Heidegger who is woven into his own dream of a history of Being, and his movements on the political stage are those of a philosophical dreamer. In a later letter (April 8, 1950) he would concede to Jaspers that he had dreamed "politically" and had therefore been mistaken. But that he was politically mistaken because he had dreamed "philosophically"—that he would never admit, because as a philosopher who wished to discover the essence of historical time he was bound to defend—even before himself—his philosophical interpretative competence for what was happening in political history.

It would have been different if he had hurled himself into the political adventure without a philosophical justification, if he had acted without being instructed and guided by his own philosophizing, or if, during action, his philosophical fuses had blown. But he had a philosophical reason for Hitler, he introduced philosophical motives, and he constructed an entire imaginary philosophical stage for the historical happening. Philosophy had to be "in control" of its time, he had written in 1930. In order not to have to give up the control principle of philosophy, he blames his political inexperience, rather than his philosophical interpretation of events, for having "been mistaken" about the Nazi revolution. Later still, admittedly, he would turn this "being mistaken" into a philosophical story, assigning to himself a grand role—it had been Being itself that had been mistaken in him and through him. He had borne the cross of the "error of Being."

"One must involve oneself," Heidegger had said to Jaspers. His involvement began in March 1933, when he joined the Cultural-Political Working Community of German University Teachers, a kind of National Socialist group within the German Academics' Association, the official professional organization of university staff. The members of this "community" regarded themselves as the vanguard of the Nazi revolution in the universities. They advocated the early *Gleichschaltung* (political alignment with the Nazi Party) of the German Academics' Association, the introduction of the führer principle in the universities, and the ideological alignment of teaching—a point on which there were considerable differences.

The initiator and center of the group was Ernst Krieck, a man who had worked his way up from primary school teacher to titular professor of philosophy and education studies at the Pedagogical Academy in Frankfurt. Krieck's ambition was to become the leading philosopher of the Nazi movement, in competition with Alfred Rosenberg and Alfred Baeumler. The Working Community was to become his power base. Krieck had made propaganda for the Nazi Party at a time when this was not yet helpful to a person's career. In 1931 he had been disciplined for Nazi propaganda with a transfer to another post, and in 1932 he had been suspended. Hitler's seizure of power helped him to regain a professorship, first in Frankfurt and then in Heidelberg. Within the party he was regarded as a "philosopher of the new era." Krieck stood for a heroically populist realism that opposed cultural idealism: "Radical critique teaches us to realize that so-called culture has become totally irrelevant."[25] To this "culture swindle" Krieck opposed the new type of heroic man: "He lives not from the intellect, but from blood and soil. He lives not in erudition, but in action." The "heroism" demanded by Krieck resembles Heidegger's "boldness," in that "culture" is made contemptible as the refuge of the weak. One must learn, Krieck argues, to live without the so-called eternal values. The house of "erudition, culture, humanism, and the pure intellect" had collapsed, and the universalist ideas had become open self-deception.

In this situation of metaphysical homelessness Krieck, unlike Heidegger, mobilizes his new blood-and-soil values; instead of metaphysics from above, he goes for metaphysics from below. "The blood," he writes, "revolts against formal reason, race against rational purpose, ties against 'freedom,' which is another name for arbitrariness, organic wholeness against individualistic dissolution . . . nation against single individual and mass."[26]

In March 1933 Krieck tried to get the Working Community to adopt a cultural policy program along his own ideological lines. This was opposed by Heidegger, who did not accept the blood-and-soil ideology. Agreement was reached only on a critical attitude to the Academics' Association and its educational idealism, which was only superficially attuned to the new conditions. Although the association's chairman, the philosopher Eduard Spranger, had addressed a declaration of loyalty to the "fighting state," he had, at the same time, appealed for the "spirit" to be spared. Heidegger mocked this attempt at compromise as "a tightrope dancer's adjustment to the epoch." This is what he called it in a letter to Elisabeth Blochmann, written on March 30, 1933, after one of the first meetings of the Working Community in Frankfurt. His letter also contains a thumbnail portrait of Krieck. He was a man of "a subaltern mind," Heidegger wrote, who was prevented by "today's phraseology" from comprehending the "real greatness and weight of the task." It was altogether a characteristic of the present revolution that everything was taken only "politically"; this was "gluing oneself to the superficial." While this may be an awakening for "the multitude," a "second and more profound awakening" would have to follow. With this ominous "second awakening" Heidegger wishes to differentiate himself from an ideologist like Ernst Krieck. In his letter to Blochmann, who, being half Jewish, was to lose her position as assistant professor a month later, Heidegger gives only dark hints about what he means by that second awakening. There is talk of a "new ground" that would allow one to "expose oneself to Being itself in a new way and appropriation" (BwHB, 60). But certainly this "ground" does not mean "blood and race," as it does for Ernst Krieck.

Heidegger wanted to enlist Alfred Baeumler in the Working Community. Baeumler, at that time still on friendly terms with Heidegger, was, like Krieck, competing for the role of the leading philosopher of the Nazi movement.

Baeumler's political decisionism was closer to Heidegger's thinking. In a lecture to Nazi students in February 1933 Baeumler put forward the "political person" against the "theoretical person." The latter believed himself to be inhabiting a "superior spiritual world," while the former realized himself as a "primally acting creature." In this primal dimension of action—according to Baeumler—ideas and ideologies no longer played a decisive part. "To act does not mean to decide for something . . . , because that presupposes that one knows what one is deciding for; to act means to choose a direction, take sides on the strength of a fate-ordained mission, on the strength of one's 'own right' . . . A decision for something that I have recognized is only secondary."[27]

These are formulations that might also come from Heidegger. Decision as a "pure" act is the primary aspect, that jerk that man gives himself in order to jump out of his customary track. The "wherefore" of the decision is, by comparison, no more than the trigger releasing the emergence of the force of the upturn of the entire *Dasein.* For Heidegger it is the They that asks the concerned questions about the "wherefore," that is afraid of the decision and therefore tarries at the weighing of the "possibilities," reduces them by talk, and "has always stolen away whenever *Dasein* presses for a decision" (SuZ, 127).[28] This shying away from decision is, to Heidegger, "guilt," and this is also how Baeumler, who has learned from Heidegger, sees it. Baeumler, too, links this decisionism, which in Heidegger had remained strangely empty in the late 1920s, to the Nazi revolution. Baeumler makes propaganda for the "pure" movement; it is the existential substance, whereas ideology is just a pale accidental feature. Anyone keeping aloof from the movement makes himself guilty "through neutrality and tolerance."

Heidegger could not persuade Krieck to have Baeumler invited to join the Working Community. Krieck regarded Baeumler as a dangerous rival. But this did not block Baeumler's career, enjoying as he did the support of Rosenberg's department. The party appointed him "political educator" of the Berlin student body and set up for him an Institute for Political Pedagogics. Eduard Spranger, who held the professorship of philosophical pedagogics in Berlin, entered a protest—also because he regarded Baeumler as responsible for the denunciation campaign against liberal and Jewish scholars. On April 22 Spranger issued a declaration against "Lies, Moral Blackmail, and Nonintellectual Manners."[29] This provided Baeumler with an opportunity for a counterattack. In his speech on the occasion of the central book burning program in Berlin on May 10, he attacked Spranger by pillorying the "old spirit" of the university. "A university that, even in the year of the Revolution, speaks of leadership only through intellect and idea, and not of leadership by Adolf Hitler and Horst Wessel, is unpolitical."[30]

Heidegger is electrified by the Nazi rise to power and is anxious to act—but he is not yet clear about what he should do. We would be looking in vain for precise ideas. Naturally he focuses mainly on Heidelberg University, and subsequently, in his postwar justification, he would claim that he allowed himself to be pressured to accept the rector's post at Freiburg in order to "be able to contain the penetration of unsuitable persons and the threatening predominance of the Party apparatus and of Party doctrine" (R, 24).

A totally different picture, however, emerges from the materials compiled by Hugo Ott, Victor Farías, and Bernd Martin. According to them, a group of Nazi professors and assistant professors, headed by Wolfgang Schadewaldt and Wolfgang Aly, acting in agreement with Heidegger, had, ever since March 1933, been deliberately working for his appointment. The key document is a letter written by Wolfgang Aly, the senior party member on the Freiburg faculty and the party organization's indoctrination speaker, to the Ministry of Education on April 9, three weeks before the election of the rector. In it Aly records that "Professor Heidegger has already entered into negotiations with the Prussian Ministry of Education"[31] and that he enjoyed the "full confidence" of the party group in the university. The authorities might regard him as the university's "spokesman." At the next meeting of the Cultural-Political Working Community in Frankfurt, on April 25, Heidegger would already be able to act as "the spokesman for our university."[32]

At that moment in time, Heidegger's election to the post of rector was settled for the party circle. It is not impossible that Heidegger himself may still have hesitated, not because the Nazi Party support was disagreeable to him but because he may have doubted whether he would be able to meet the expectations placed in him by the "revolutionary forces." He wanted to act and to involve himself, but he was still looking for the "right point of attack" (letter to Jaspers, April 3, 1933, BwHJ).

In a letter to Elisabeth Blochmann of March 30, 1933, he confesses his perplexity but immediately dismisses his misgivings:

> Nobody knows what is going to happen about the universities . . . Unlike the bigwigs, who only a few weeks ago were describing Hitler's work as

> "utter nonsense" and are now jittery about their salaries and suchlike, sensible people must tell themselves that there is not much to be spoiled. After all, there's nothing left; the university has long ceased to be a truly concentrated, effective, or leading world. An enforced pause for reflection—even if mistakes occur—can only be beneficial. (BwHB, 61)

You can't make an omelette without breaking eggs. Anyone entering revolutionary new territory must undergo the risk of making mistakes and losing his way. Heidegger certainly will not be deflected by warning shouts of "scholarship in danger!" Besides, the matter was too important to be left only to the *Parteigenossen,* the party members, Heidegger wrote to Blochmann on April 12, 1933, three weeks before he himself publicly joined the party.

While preparations were going on behind the scenes for Heidegger's assumption of the rector's gown, Josef Sauer, a Catholic Church historian, held the office. The installation of Wilhelm von Möllendorf, the rector designate elected at the end of 1932, was scheduled for April 15. Möllendorf, professor of anatomy, was a Social Democrat.

According to the version told by Martin Heidegger and his wife, Elfride, it was Möllendorf himself who, following the Nazi seizure of power, was no longer prepared to assume the rectorship. Möllendorf was a friend of Heidegger and approached him directly to discuss his expected difficulties with the rectorship. Heidegger, who had a sabbatical semester in the winter of 1932–33, returned to Freiburg from Todtnauberg on January 7. According to Frau Heidegger's recollection, Möllendorf had expressed the "urgent wish" that Heidegger, "who had no kinds of party-political ties," should assume the office. "He repeated this wish many times during his visits, in the morning, at noon, and in the evening."

It is hardly surprising that the Social Democrat Möllendorf should have had misgivings about assuming the office of rector of the university. In Freiburg, as everywhere else, the persecution of Social Democrats had already begun, and under Reich Commissioner Robert Wagner it was especially vicious. There had been outrages against the trades union building and the offices of the Social Democratic Party as early as the beginning of March, as well as arrests and house searches. A serious incident occurred on March 17 at the home of the Social Democratic diet deputy Nussbaum. Nussbaum, who had recently spent some weeks under psychiatric treatment, resisted two policemen and fatally wounded them, whereupon the witch hunt against the Social Democrats in the city was intensified. In the cathedral square a demonstration was held against Marxism—it was to be exterminated "all the way to the roots," the agitators demanded. Already two concentration camps were being set up near the Heuberg. The local press carried photographs of the transportation of the arrested. The Nazi Party next attacked the mayor, Dr. Bender of the Center Party, alleging that he had reacted too feebly to the Nussbaum incident. Bender had referred to an "accident." He was now to be chased out of office. A citizens' delegation stood up for him, and one of its spokesmen was Möllendorf. Bender was given a leave of absence on April 11. His successor was the Nazi Party district leader Franz Kerber, who was also the editor of the Nazi paper *Der Alemanne.* In this paper Heidegger would publish an article. As a result of the Nussbaum-Bender affair, Möllendorf had become totally unacceptable to the Freiburg National Socialists. Möllendorf may have had misgivings about accepting the rector's office, but he was no coward and eventually declared himself prepared to assume it. He was installed, as planned, on April 15. The night before, Schadewaldt had called on the departing rector, Professor Sauer, on behalf of the party group. He voiced its doubts as to whether Möllendorf was the right person to perform the necessary nazification of the university and proposed Heidegger instead. Sauer, a man of the Catholic Church and an opponent of Heidegger's anticlericalism, showed reservations. In consequence Möllendorf was in office for five days. On April 18, the day on which Möllendorf presided over his first university senate meeting, *Der Alemanne* published a violent attack on the new rector. It concluded with the words: "We urge Professor von Möllendorf to seize the opportunity—and not stand in the way of the reorganization of our university system."[33] Now it became clear to Möllendorf that he could not maintain himself in office. He called a meeting of the senate for April 20, at which he and the entire senate announced their resignation and proposed Martin Heidegger as Möllendorf's successor. According to Elfride's account, Möllendorf had called at their house the previous evening and said: "Herr Heidegger, you've got to take on the office now!"[34]

Heidegger, for whom a powerful section of faculty members had been making propaganda for a month, claims to have been undecided up to the last moment: "Even on the morning of election day I still hesitated and wished to withdraw my candidacy" (R, 21). The plenary assembly elected Heidegger with virtual unanimity, but then thirteen of the ninety-three professors had already been excluded as Jews, and of the remaining eighty only fifty-six took part in the ballot. There was one vote against, and two abstained.

Considering his alleged hesitation before, Heidegger displayed a remarkable burst of activity immediately after his election.

On April 22 he wrote to Carl Schmitt, inviting him to join the movement. Schmitt had no need of such an invitation—he already belonged to it, although for a contrary reason. Heidegger wanted revolution, while Schmitt wanted order. The plenary meeting had elected moderate, mostly old-conservative senate members: Heidegger was to be "fenced in." But he foiled this plan by not convening the academic senate. In a speech on May 27 he proclaimed the führer principle and the *Gleichschaltung* of the university. Shortly after May 1, the "national holiday of the people's community," he demonstratively joined the Nazi Party, having previously discussed the tactical aspect of that date with the party authorities. His invitation to the students and teaching staff to attend the May Day festivities was drafted in the style of a military order: "The construction of a new intellectual and spiritual world for the German nation has now become the single most important task of the German universities. This is 'national labor' of the highest kind."[35] When Reich Commissioner Wagner—a notorious hardliner who was responsible for the transportation of opponents to the Heuberg concentration camp—was appointed *Reichsstatthalter* (governor) in early May, Heidegger congratulated him bombastically: "Delighted by your appointment as *Reichsstatthalter,* the Rector of the University of Freiburg im Breisgau greets the Führer of our native borderland with a *'Sieg Heil'* from a brother-in-arms. Heidegger."[36]

On May 20 he signed a telegram from a number of National Socialist rectors to Hitler. They were requesting a postponement of the reception of a delegation of the Academics' Association on the grounds that "only a new board elected on the basis of *Gleichschaltung* enjoys the confidence of the universities. Moreover, the present board has been the object of most severe mistrust by the German students."[37]

On May 26, one day before the rectorship ceremony, Heidegger made his first public speech at a memorial ceremony for Leo Schlageter, the Free Corps fighter who in 1923 had performed bombing outrages against the French occupying forces in the Ruhr and had therefore been court-martialed and executed. Among German nationalists he was regarded as a martyr for the national cause. Heidegger also felt close to him because Schlageter was a fellow alumnus of the Konradihaus in Constance. May 26 was the tenth anniversary of Schlageter's death; in Freiburg, as everywhere else, it was observed with much pomp.

In his memorial address Heidegger, for the first time before a big audience, attempts a political application of his authenticity philosophy. He depicts Schlageter as a figure who reveals what it means, in terms of concrete history and politics, to encounter the mystery of the Being of that-which-is *(das Mysterium des Seins des Seienden)*. Schlageter, Heidegger argues, suffered the "most difficult" death. Not in common combat, not carried and shielded by a community, but alone, wholly "thrown back" upon himself, in "failure" (S, 48). Schlageter realizes the existential ideal of *Being and Time,* he "accepts" death as "that possibility which is own's ownmost, which is non-relational, and which is not to be outstripped" (SuZ, 250).[38] The participants in the memorial ceremony should let the "hardness and clarity" of that death "stream into them." But where did Schlageter get his strength from? It came to him from the mountains, the forests, and the sky of his homeland. "The mountains are primal rock, granite . . . They have long fashioned the hardness of the will . . . The autumnal sun of the Black Forest . . . has long been nourishing the clarity of the heart" (S, 48). Only to the comfortable do the mountains and forests convey a sense of security; for the hard and determined they act as a call to the conscience. Conscience, Heidegger had explained in *Being and Time,* called not for a definite deed but for authenticity. What has to be done concretely is decided by the situation. In Schlageter's case, its decision was such that, at the hour of humiliation, he had to save Germany's honor. He "had to" go to the Baltic (to fight against the communists), he "had to" go to the Ruhr (to fight against the French). He followed the destiny he had chosen and that had chosen him. "Put up helpless to face the rifles, the hero's inner gaze soared up above the rifle muzzles, over to the day and to the mountains of his homeland, in order that, with his gaze on the Alemannic land, he might die for the German nation and its Reich" (S, 49). That was a moment of truth, because the essence of truth—as Heidegger had said in his eponymous lecture of 1930, though in divergence from the subsequently published text—is an event that takes place on "the soil of the Fatherland."[39] What matters is that one should open up to the powers of *Dasein.* Autochthony is a prerequisite for this. A day later came the rectorship address.

There had been a good deal of commotion in the days preceding the event. On May 23 Rector Heidegger had issued a memorandum on the order of events at his inauguration ceremony. The "Horst Wessel Song," the Nazi Party anthem, was to be sung, and *Sieg Heil* was to be shouted. The whole ceremony was to have the splendor of a national holiday. There was a certain degree of irritation among the professors. In a supplementary circular Heidegger explained that "the raising of the right hand" was intended to signify not allegiance to the party but attachment to national resurgence. He also signaled readiness for compromise: "After conferring with the leader of the student body I have decided to confine the raising of the hand to the fourth verse of the 'Horst Wessel Song.'"[40]

Heidegger was aware that the world of philosophy was watching him at that moment. Over the past few weeks he had not missed any opportunity to demonstrate his leadership—senior party figures, government ministers, rectors of other universities, and members of the press had called on him—more brownshirts than morning coats. Heidegger had ventured far forward. "Everything," he wrote to Jaspers on April 3, 1933, "depends on whether we prepare the right point of attack for philosophy and help it to speak out." He had now found the point of attack; would he also find the right philosophical word?

The theme of his inaugural address was "The Self-Assertion of the German University." He starts with the question: What is the "Self" of the university, what is its "essence"? The essence of the university is not to enable young people to receive their training for an occupation or to acquire the necessary knowledge for it. The essence of the university is learning. But what is the essence of learning?

With this question Heidegger finds himself instantly at his beloved "Greek beginnings of philosophy," the region to which he had gone back in order to gain distance for making the leap into the present. The essence of learning, he points out, emerged with the Greeks. At that time, "against the superior power of destiny," the will to knowledge arose in defiant rebellion. This "supreme defiance" seeks to know what is happening to it, what forces of *Dasein* control it, and what it means that this entirety actually exists. This knowledge cuts a clearing out of the thicket.

Heidegger dramatizes the happening of truth. Precisely what truths are involved here remains unclear. Instead the central metaphor pervading the whole text acquires an independent shape. It is the metaphor of struggle, or, more accurately, of a shock-troop engagement.

The essence of the Greek beginnings is therefore the conquest of a few visibilities amid the dark that-which-is in the whole *(des dunklen Seienden im Ganzen).* This is the heroic beginning of the history of truth, and therein—Heidegger says—lies also the true Self of learning and of the university.

What, then, threatens learning thus understood? The darkness of that-which-is, of course, but that is its pride. Facing it in battle is precisely what the essence of learning is about. More threatening is degeneration through "a calm, pleasurable activity, an activity free of danger, which promotes the mere advancement of knowledge" (R, 13).[41]

The threat comes from the noncombatant rear, from the familiar scholarship business, where careers are made, vanities satisfied, and money earned. The cozy life behind the lines is all the more scandalous as great and dangerous things have been happening out on the front of knowledge. The fact is that the position of *Dasein* vis-à-vis the darkness of that-which-is has changed. The event of truth has entered a critical phase. The Greeks still had an "admiring tarrying" in the face of the questionability of all that is. There was still security, faith in Being, trust in the world. But that faith in Being has meanwhile disappeared, for God is dead. Little of all this has been noticed behind the lines, however. There, a "moribund pseudo-civilization" would have been comfortably indulged in, had not the revolution come, that "glory and greatness of this new beginning" (R, 19).[42]

What is happening in this revolution? With it, Heidegger fantasizes, Nietzsche's finding that "God is dead" has at last been correctly understood, and a whole nation deliberately accepts the "abandonment of man today in the midst of Being" (R, 13).[43] It overcomes the degenerate phase of the "last men" of Nietzsche's *Zarathustra*,[44] who no longer have any "chaos" within themselves and are therefore unable to give birth to a "star," who in fact content themselves with having invented comfortable "happiness" and having "left the regions where it was hard to live," who are satisfied with their "little pleasures for the day and one's little pleasures for the night" and who "have a regard for health."

For Heidegger, therefore, the Nazi revolution is the attempt to "give birth to a star" in a godless world. That is why he pulls out all the stops of his metaphysical penny-dreadful romanticism to lend events an unsuspected profundity.

The students and party bosses at his feet, the professors, dignitaries, ministerial officials, and civil servants, along with their wives, are addressed by Heidegger as though they are part of that metaphysical shock-troop unit that is setting out for the area of "the most acute danger in the midst of overpowering Being."[45] And Heidegger himself is in command of the unit. Leaders, as is well known, venture out the farthest into the darkness, to where they are no longer covered by their own men; they are not afraid of "being completely exposed to and at the mercy of what is concealed and uncertain,"[46] and in this way they prove their "strength to go alone" (R, 14).[47]

There is no doubt that Heidegger is trying to upgrade himself and his audience. They are all part of the shock troops, of that bold handful of fighters. The speaker himself—their leader—is perhaps a little bolder still because he demonstrates, or at least claims, the "strength to go alone."

Everything hinges on danger—and sight is lost of the simple fact that in this particular situation it was more dangerous not to belong to the shock troops of the revolution. What danger is Heidegger focusing on? Is it the danger referred to by Kant when he invites man to "have the courage to use your own reason"? Independent thought calls for courage, because it dispenses with the protection and comfort of consensus-creating prejudices.

This is not a danger to which Heidegger exposes himself with his rectorship speech. Admittedly, at the dinner following the ceremony, people would say to him under their breath that he had just presented his own "personal National Socialism," but this did not change the fact that he continued to be "one of them." With this speech he had not yet put himself offside.

Is it the danger of cognition, as Schopenhauer so brilliantly formulated it when he compared the true philosopher with Oedipus, "who, seeking elucidation of his own terrible fate, continues to seek indefatigably even when he already surmises that the Terrible will be revealed to him in the answers"?[48] By this "Terrible" Schopenhauer meant the metaphysical abyss that opens before man when he asks about the meaning of life, and that abyss is also focused on by Heidegger; he calls it the "abandonment of present-day man amid that-which-is." But that abandonment can be lived through and thought through only by the individual as an individual, thrown out from collective meaning-relationships. How could there be any talk of "abandonment" when a whole nation is "on the march"?

In point of fact, Heidegger interprets the revolution as a collective breakout from the caves of false consolations and comfortable meaning-certainties. A nation becomes authentic, it arises and asks the disturbing question of Being: Why is there something and not, rather, nothing? It defiantly surrenders itself to the powers of "*Dasein*—nature, history, language; the *Volk* [people], custom, the state; poetry, thought, belief; sickness, madness, death; law, economy, technology" (R, 14)[49]—in the knowledge that they do not provide an ultimate support but lead out into darkness, uncertainty, adventure.

A person active in this manner does not conquer any separate world of the spirit that might bring him relief from the troubles of the day. For such escapism Heidegger has only contempt. He to whom that-which-is has become questionable does not retreat in the face of it but ventures forward, inspired by the spirit of attack. It is not a case of fathoming out anything transcendental but simply of being "engaged in the work." This is how Heidegger translates the Greek term *energeia.*

Heidegger wants to repeat the Greek beginning of philosophy, but without being seduced by the idea of the contemplative life, by Plato's sun. He sweeps it aside by claiming that he understands the Greeks better than they understood themselves. Theory, in the Greek sense, happens "only as a result of the passion to remain close to what is as such and to be beset by it" (R, 12).[50] Now this is not what Plato's simile of the cave means. There the theme is salvation, liberation from suffering in the cave. Heidegger aims at a paradoxical objective—he wants Plato's ecstasy without Plato's heaven of ideas. He wants the breakout from the cave, but without belief in a place beyond the cave. *Dasein* is to be gripped by infinite passion, but not by the passion for the infinite.

In 1930 Thomas Mann had warned against the dangers of "exploding antiquities." One such dangerous antiquity can be found in Heidegger's address, when he speaks of the three services, "labor service—military service—service to knowledge." This is a rehearsal of the venerable image that dominated the social imagination of the Middle Ages, the image of the "three orders": peasants, warriors, and priests. The medieval definition of that order was, "Threefold therefore is the house of God that we suppose to be one—here on earth some pray, others do battle, yet others labor. These three belong together and do not suffer being divided; in such a manner that upon the function of the one the work of the other two is based, with all lending their assistance to all when needed" (Adalbert of Laon).[51]

In the medieval picture of the three orders, the priests are the link between the social organism and heaven. They ensure that spiritual energies circulate within the temporal. For Heidegger the place of the priests is taken up by the philosophers, or, more accurately, those philosophers who are in control of their time. But where heaven used to be, there is now the darkness of the hidden that-which-is, the "world uncertainty," and the new priests have in fact become the "placeholders of the nothing," proving themselves, if possible, even more daring than the warriors. They no longer have any messages to direct from heaven to earth, yet they still radiate a dim reflection of that ancient priestly power that once was based on the monopoly of great invisible and rapturous things.

Heidegger, in the role of a priest, interferes in politics and takes the stage when the final blow is to be dealt to the Weimar Republic. Fifteen years earlier, at the beginning of that republic, Max Weber in his Munich speech on "The Calling of Learning" had urged intellectuals to bear the "disenchantment of the world." In this context Weber, too, had recalled the "wonderful image" of Plato's cave. But now it is only a melancholy reminiscence, because the Platonic unity of strict cognition and rapturous meaning is irrevocably lost. The great salvation, an exit from the cave, is not in sight, and Max Weber had warned against the murky business of deliberate reenchantment by the "academic prophets."

Heidegger does not favor the "academic prophets" either—but it is always the others who are those prophets. When he first referred to Plato's simile of the cave, in his lecture in the summer of 1927, Heidegger had described liberation from the cave as a process that unrolled "in all sobriety and in the complete disenchantment of purely objective inquiry" (GA 24, 404).[52]

But now Heidegger is standing there, erect, martially rattling words, the priest without a message, the metaphysical storm-troops leader, surrounded by flags and standards. He had dreamed himself into the figure of the liberator who unfetters the prisoners in the cave and leads them out of it. Now he observes that the cave dwellers are already all marching ahead. He merely needs to place himself at their head.

14

IS HEIDEGGER ANTI-SEMITIC?

"The rectorial address was spoken into the winds and by the following day the inaugural ceremony was forgotten . . . Life was proceeding along the path of faculty policy, trodden over the decades," Heidegger wrote in *Tatsachen und Gedanken,* his postwar justification, in 1945 (R, 34).

In reality his speech was not forgotten so quickly. It was published twice as an offprint during the Nazi period, and it was commended in the party press. The daily *Kieler Blätter,* for instance, in an article in 1938, reviewing the road covered by Nazi scholarship policy, said: "Like Baeumler, Martin Heidegger, in his Rector's Address, develops the essence of science out of the notion of an active heroic attitude in the sense of a 'questioning attitude,' standing firm and open amidst the uncertainties of being as a whole."[1]

Immediate reaction was still more enthusiastic. The local press, as well as papers of more than regional circulation, described the speech as a great pioneering event. The periodical of the Nazi student body warned against the opportunism of many scholars who were only superficially adjusting to the new conditions, pointing to Heidegger's rectorial address as a positive exception; it was a true expression of the spirit of a new beginning and revolution. Even the periodical *Volk im Werden* in 1934—when its editor, Ernst Krieck, was already a personal enemy of Heidegger—carried an article by a certain Heinrich Bornkamm, who declared: "Out of the voluminous literature dealing with the reform of our universities of our day, Heidegger's Rector's Address in Freiburg offers, as far as I can see, the most significant beginnings."[2]

Even the less official press reacted positively. Eugen Herrigel, the future Taoist (author of *The Art of Archery*), called the speech a "classical text," and *Berliner Börsenzeitung* observed: "There are probably few rectors' speeches that exercised such a bewitching and compelling effect."[3]

But there was also some perplexity. Karl Löwith, commenting on the immediate effect of the rectorial address, remarked that it was not quite clear whether one should now study the pre-Socratic philosophers or join the SA brownshirts. This is why contemporary commentators are fond of falling back on those passages that are readily attributable to Nazi doctrine, such as Heidegger's program of the "three services"—labor service, military service, and service to knowledge.

The predominant note in foreign comment was incredulous amazement; some papers were even horrified. *Neue Zürcher Zeitung* observed: "Heidegger's speech, after three or four readings, remains the expression of an abysmal and destructive nihilism, that cannot be canceled by its affirmation of the blood and earth of a nation."[4] Benedetto Croce, in a letter to Karl Vossler of September 9, 1933, said: "I have now at last read the whole of Heidegger's address, which is stupid and servile at the same time. I am not surprised at the success his philosophizing will have for some time—the vacuous and general is always successful. But it produces nothing. I too believe that he will have no effect on politics, but he dishonors philosophy, and that is a pity also for politics, especially future politics."[5]

Karl Jaspers's reaction is rather surprising. On August 21, 1933, he wrote to Heidegger:

> I want to thank you for your rectorial address . . . The great sweep of your starting point among the early Greeks again touched me as a new and, at the same time, obvious truth. In this you are in agreement with Nietzsche, but with the difference that one may hope that you will one day by philosophical interpretation realize what you are proclaiming. As a result your speech has a credible substance. I am not talking about style

> or density, which—as far as I can judge—make this speech the only document so far of a present-day academic will, a document that will endure. My trust in your philosophy . . . is not upset by those characteristics of your speech as are in line with our age, by something in it that strikes me as a little forced, or by sentences which seem to me to have rather a hollow ring. All in all I am happy that somebody can speak like that, that he touches on the genuine boundaries and origins. (BwHJ, 155)

Two months prior to this letter Heidegger had visited Jaspers for the last time. At the invitation of the Nazi students of Heidelberg he had given a lecture on "The University in the New Reich." The Nazi students hoped that his speech would strengthen their front against the conservative professors and, more particularly, the not yet nazified rector, Willy Andreas. In this Heidegger evidently succeeded. A participant at the event, the historian Gerd Tellenbach, notes in his memoirs: "One student was turned into a fanatic by the agitating speech and said to another that, after what had just been said, Andreas ought to be shot in the head."[6] In point of fact, Heidegger had been very militant. He had declared the "traditional university as dead," used strong words to "reject the humanizing Christian ideas," and called for "work for the state." He had talked of the risk of a thirst for knowledge and of the fact that "only a tough generation with no thought of itself" could survive the struggle. But, he'd said, he "who does not survive the struggle is left lying" (S, 75).

The professors had turned up in ceremonial robes, as the event had been much publicized in the press. Heidegger, however, appeared in youth-movement attire: in shorts and without a tie. Jaspers recorded in his memoirs: "I was sitting in front, to the side, with my legs stuck out, my hands in my pockets, and did not budge."[7] During their private conversation afterward, Heidegger had seemed to him like "a man intoxicated, with something threatening emanating from him."

And yet, two months later Jaspers praises the rectorial address. In his personal notes he later explained his behavior as an attempt to interpret the speech "in the best possible way" in order to stay on speaking terms with Heidegger. In actual fact, he said, he had felt revulsion at the "intolerably low and strange level" of Heidegger's words and actions.[8]

Jaspers's approval of the rectorial address did have the tactical purpose suggested by him in retrospect. There continued to be points of contact between the two men—surprisingly, even in the area of university reform along Nazi lines. In his letter of August 23, 1933, Jaspers described the new university statute, just issued by the Baden Ministry of Education, as an "extraordinary step," even though its core was the introduction of the führer principle and the stripping of collegial bodies of their powers. Jaspers thought the "new statute right." The "great era" of the university was long over and the time had come for a new start.

In the summer of 1933 Jaspers had himself drafted some theses on university reform. They were to be consulted by the Heidelberg faculty. Jaspers had told Heidegger about them when Heidegger last visited him, hoping that he might encourage the governmental authorities to get in touch with him, Jaspers. For this contingency Jaspers had drafted a cover letter to the effect that his ideas on reform did "not conflict" with any "principles that may have reached the government by now" but were "in agreement" with them.[9] In the end Jaspers abstained from going public with his theses. The reason for this, as he noted on a sheet attached to the folder containing them, was that, "Unasked I cannot do anything, as I shall only be told that, as a person not belonging to the party and the husband of a Jewish wife, I am merely tolerated and can enjoy no confidence" (BwHJ, 260).

In his theses, which he would in 1946 use as the basis of his paper on university reform, Jaspers drew a picture of a university in dissolution. His diagnosis agreed with Heidegger's. The obvious failings of the universities, according to him, were fragmentation into specialized disciplines; increasing school-type teaching and one-sided orientation toward occupational training; proliferation of administration; a decline in the overall level of teaching; and abuse of free access, "with its corollary, the exclusion of those who fail," being no longer applied.[10] At the time he wrote them—summer 1933—there was "an opportunity that might never come again" for overcoming all obstacles and ossifications "through the decisive rulings of a man with unlimited command over the university, who can base himself on young people conscious of the powerful impulse of the situation and the uncommon readiness of those who are otherwise lukewarm and indifferent." Unless decisive action were taken now, the universities would be facing "certain death."

In detail Jaspers's reform plans provided for deregulation of studies, abolition of study courses and formal evidence, and simplification of administration through enhancement of the responsibilities of the leading levels. Rector and deans were no longer to be dependent on majority decisions. Jaspers wanted the führer principle, but with the proviso that those responsible for decision making should answer for their decisions and, if necessary, be voted out. These would be safety devices against an abuse of the führer principle. Whether the new university statute of Baden would provide for them, only time would tell. In any event, he wished every success to the newly installed "aristocratic principle," Jaspers wrote to Heidegger in that letter of August 23, 1933 (BwHJ, 156).

Jaspers, therefore, in the summer of 1933, shared Heidegger's conviction that the National Socialist revolution could also vouchsafe a sensible renewal of the universities, provided those in power heeded scholars of stature. Jaspers, too, wished to "involve himself" in his own way. He even made concessions to the concept of labor service and military service. These were to him part of the "reality of the transcendent" that provides the link with the "foundations of *Dasein* and the people as a whole." However, Jaspers decidedly opposed the primacy of politics. "No other authority in the world" could set an objective to research and teaching "than the light produced by true knowledge itself."

Heidegger's stance so far had not been all that different. In his rectorial address he did not derive the spirit of learning from politics, but, on the contrary, justified political action by the attitude of correctly understood philosophical questioning. However, as far as the mood and the manner of inner participation in the political movement were concerned, there was a wide gulf between Jaspers and Heidegger. Jaspers defended the aristocracy of the spirit while Heidegger endeavored to crush it. It was absurd, Heidegger said in his last conversation with Jaspers, that there were so many philosophy professors; two or three would be quite enough.

For Heidegger, who as recently as April 1933 had written to Jaspers that everything depended on finding for philosophy "the right point of attack" in the "new reality" and helping it to "be heard," this "new reality" is now the National Socialist revolution.[11] Jaspers, by way of contrast, is anxious to preserve the word of philosophy unfalsified by politics. With amazement and horror he watches Heidegger upgrading the powers in whose thrall he finds himself into *Dasein* powers of the metaphysical type. But he also feels that underlying Heidegger's political doings there is still a philosophical furor. And this fascinates Jaspers. He wants to understand how this "new reality" could have gained such philosophical striking power and significance for Heidegger.

Hence his ominous remark on Heidegger's inaugural address "that it is to be hoped that one day you will implement philosophically what you are saying" (BwHJ, 155).

After his election to the rectorship, Heidegger de facto introduced the führer principle in Freiburg, even before it was officially established by the Baden university reform. For months on end he failed to call the academic senate and thereby brought about its emasculation. His memorandums and circulars to the faculty bodies and departments were drafted in a shrill tone of command. Heidegger, a man without front-line experience in the World War, was fascinated by the notion of introducing a military spirit to the teaching staff. He instructed Professor Stieler, a former naval commander, to draft a code of honor for the university staff, to be based on the relevant regulations for the officer corps. Heidegger, who had shown a good deal of skill in negotiating his own terms, now wished to put an end to all haggling for raises, funding of chairs, and the like; the spirit of the marketplace and economic competition was to be overcome. That was why the draft of the code of honor contained the sentence: "We seek to nurture and develop that spirit of true comradeship and genuine socialism among ourselves which does not view one's colleagues as rivals in the struggle for survival."[12]

This draft, approved by Heidegger, also stated: "We seek to cleanse our ranks of inferior elements and thwart the forces of degeneracy in the future."[13] It is possible that "inferior elements" in this context meant to Heidegger persons of inadequate professional and character qualifications, but for the Nazi revolution it meant primarily Jews and political opponents. Heidegger must have been aware of this.

As early as the beginning of March, the SA brownshirts in Freiburg had called for the boycott of Jewish stores and circulated lists of Jewish attorneys and doctors. The Nazi student body had begun to demand the boycott of Jewish professors. On April 7 the Law on the Reestablishment of a Permanent Civil Service was enacted; this provided for the dismissal from public employment of all "non-Aryans" engaged after 1918. In Freiburg, Reich Commissioner Robert Wagner had the previous day issued an even more severe decree, providing for the provisional suspension, with the aim of eventual dismissal, of all Jewish officials, even if they had been in public employment prior to 1918. It was on the basis of this decree that Husserl was given an enforced leave of absence on April 14, 1933. At that time Heidegger was not yet in office. When Wagner's decree was rescinded in favor of the Law on the

Reestablishment of a Permanent Civil Service, Husserl's mandatory leave had to be revoked. This was the task of the newly elected rector. Heidegger accompanied it with a personal gesture. He got Elfride to send flowers to Husserl. Husserl had felt his leave to be the "supreme affront" of his life.[14] He felt injured mainly in his national sentiment. In a letter he said: "I was not the meanest of Germans (of the old style and of the old school), and my house was a place of true national sentiment, as evidenced by all my children, who volunteered for service in the field or . . . in a military hospital during the war."[15]

Neither the bouquet of flowers nor the note with them could change Husserl's disenchantment with Heidegger. In a letter of May 4, 1933, to his pupil Dietrich Mahnke, he calls Heidegger's "very theatrical" entry into the Nazi Party "the perfect ending to this supposed bosom friendship between philosophers."[16] This had been accompanied over the few preceding years by Heidegger's increasingly patent anti-Semitism, including toward his group of enthusiastic Jewish pupils and faculty colleagues.

Was Heidegger anti-Semitic? Certainly not in the sense of the ideological lunacy of Nazism. It is significant that neither in his lectures and philosophical writings, nor in his political speeches and pamphlets are there any anti-Semitic or racist remarks. Thus, when Heidegger in his circular before the May Day celebrations described "the building of a new spiritual world for the German people" as the "command of the hour," he did not wish to exclude from this task anyone willing to cooperate.

Heidegger's Nazism was decisionist. What mattered to him was not origin but decision. In his terminology, man should be judged not by his "thrownness" but by his "design." To that extent he was even able to help hard-pressed Jewish colleagues. When Eduard Fraenkel, professor of classical philology, and Georg von Hevesy, professor of physical chemistry, were to be dismissed because they were Jews, Heidegger in a letter to the Ministry of Education tried to prevent this. He used the tactical argument that a dismissal of these two Jewish professors, "whose extraordinary scientific standing was beyond doubt,"[17] would be especially harmful to a "borderland university,"[18] on which foreign critical eyes were particularly focused. Besides, both men were "Jews of the better sort, men of exemplary character." He could vouch for the irreproachable conduct of both men, "insofar as it is humanly possible to predict these things."[19] Fraenkel was dismissed despite Heidegger's submission, while Hevesy was allowed to stay on for the time being.

Heidegger also engaged himself for his Jewish assistant Werner Brock. Although he could not keep him at the university, he arranged for a research fellowship for him in Cambridge, England.

After 1945 Heidegger pointed to his engagement for Jewish scientists at the time, as well as to the fact that within a few days of assuming office he had risked a conflict with the Nazi student body by forbidding the anti-Semitic poster "Against the Un-German Spirit" to be displayed within the university. These patterns of behavior show Heidegger's reserve toward a crude or ideological anti-Semitism.

At the beginning of 1933, shortly before her emigration, Hannah Arendt wrote to Heidegger. Certain reports had come to her ears. Was it true "that he excluded Jews from his seminars, didn't greet his Jewish colleagues on the campus, rejected his Jewish doctoral students, and behaved like an antisemite?"[20] In her account of their relationship, Elżbieta Ettinger paraphrases his reply. He answered in a furious tone, in what was his last letter to Arendt until 1950: "One by one he listed the favors he accorded to Jews—his accessibility to Jewish students, to whom he generously gave of his time, disruptive though it was to his own work, getting them stipends and discussing their dissertations with them. Who comes to him in an emergency? A Jew. Who insists on urgently discussing his doctoral degree? A Jew. Who sends him voluminous work for urgent critique? A Jew. Who asks him for help in obtaining grants? Jews."[21]

Quite regardless of the fact that what Heidegger here calls "favors" were part of his official duties, his justification makes it clear that he did draw "a distinct line between Germans and German Jews, between himself and the German Jews, his colleagues and students"[22] and moreover it hints that he finds the Jews at the university importunate. A letter discovered in 1989, written by Heidegger on October 20, 1929, to Victor Schwörer, the acting president of the Hardship Committee for German Science, an organization for the granting of scholarships, reveals that Heidegger shared the "competition anti-Semitism" (a term coined by Sebastian Haffner)[23] that was then widespread in academic circles. Heidegger: "There is a pressing need for us to remember that we are faced with the choice of either bringing genuine autochthonous forces and educators into our German spiritual life, or finally abandoning it to the growing Judaization in the wider and narrower sense."[24]

"Competition anti-Semitism" was basically a refusal to accept the assimilation of the Jews, instead continuing to identify them as a special group and objecting to the fact that they were occupying a dominant position in cultural life, beyond their proportional share of the overall population. In this context Max Müller reports that in a conversation prior to 1933 Heidegger had pointed out to him that "originally only two Jewish physicians had worked in the department of internal medicine, and that eventually only two non-Jews were to be found in that department. This certainly annoyed him somewhat."[25]

It is therefore hardly surprising that, in his engagement for his Jewish colleagues Hevesy and Fraenkel vis-à-vis the Ministry of Education, Heidegger expressly conceded the "need to enforce to the letter the Law on the Reestablishment of a Permanent Civil Service."[26]

In the cultural field, competition anti-Semitism generally includes the assumption of a specific "Jewish spirit." But this Jewish spirit that one should beware of does not exist for Heidegger. Indeed he always objected to this kind of "spiritual" anti-Semitism. In a lecture in the mid-1930s he defended Spinoza, declaring that if his philosophy was "Jewish," then all philosophy from Leibniz to Hegel was Jewish too. This rejection of "spiritual" anti-Semitism is all the more surprising as Heidegger is usually fond of emphasizing the *German* element in philosophy, contrasting it with the rationalism of the French, the utilitarianism of the English, and the obsession with technology of the Americans. But unlike his comrades-in-arms and rivals Krieck and Baeumler, Heidegger never used this "German element" in philosophy for differentiation from the "Jewish" one.

Karl Jaspers, asked in 1945 for an opinion on Heidegger's anti-Semitism, came to the conclusion that in the 1920s Heidegger had not been anti-Semitic. "With respect to this question he did not always exercise discretion. This doesn't rule out the possibility that, as I must assume, in other cases anti-Semitism went against his conscience and his taste."[27]

Certainly his kind of anti-Semitism had not been a reason for him to join the Nazi movement. Nor, on the other hand, did the (soon to be revealed) brutality of Nazi anti-Semitism deter him from the movement. He did not support its actions, but he accepted them. When Nazi students in the summer of 1933 stormed the building of a Jewish student fraternity and proceeded with such violence that the public prosecutor's office could not avoid initiating an investigation, and in this context requested information from Rector Heidegger, he brusquely refused to pursue any further inquiries on the grounds that those involved in the raid had not all been students.[28]

When Elisabeth Blochmann, dismissed from her post in accordance with the Law on the Reestablishment of a Permanent Civil Service because she was half Jewish, sent a letter to Heidegger asking for his help, Heidegger promised to intervene for her in Berlin—as it turned out, he was unsuccessful—but even in this personal relationship, where no tactical considerations were necessary, he expressed no words of outrage at these measures. He sympathized with Blochmann as if she had simply suffered a misfortune. It seems that it never occurred to him that his own actions, woven into the collective actions of the revolution, were aimed also against his woman friend, who wrote to him in desperation: "I have some very difficult days behind me, I had never imagined that I could ever be made such an outcast. Perhaps I have lived too naively in the security of a deep sense of belonging of spirit and emotion—thus at first I was totally helpless and in despair" (BwHB, 64). And Heidegger replied to her: "I am at all times entirely available for your wishes and needs" (October 16, 1933, BwHB, 77).

Hannah Arendt, Elisabeth Blochmann, Karl Löwith—people from Heidegger's closest circle—were forced to leave Germany, but this still did not impair his "community of will" with the National Socialists. He felt he belonged to the movement, even when the first concentration camps were being set up in his native region, Jewish students were being brutally attacked, and the first proscription lists were being circulated in the city. And when Heidegger did formulate his first cautious criticism of official policy, it was not because he was outraged by its anti-Semitic excesses but because he was outraged by its concessions to the old bourgeois forces.

What had come to Hannah Arendt's ears at the beginning of 1933—that Heidegger was withdrawing from his Jewish colleagues and his Jewish students—and what in his reply to her he denied, in fact occurred over the next few months. From the moment he became rector he put an end to personal contact with Jewish colleagues and no longer graduated any of his Jewish students. Instead he passed them on to faculty colleagues. "Heidegger wanted his Jewish students to receive their doctorates, but not from him," wrote Müller.[29] To Wilhelm Szilasi, a Jewish scholar who had been his friend, he said: "In the present situation we have to break off our contacts."[30]

Heidegger also broke off his contacts with Edmund Husserl. That he banned his old teacher and friend from entering the university and the library is an inaccurate rumor. But he took not a single step on his own initiative toward piercing Husserl's increasing isolation. It was Heidegger's colleague in the Catholic chair, Martin Honecker, who kept up the contact and, through the "go-between" Max Müller, regularly passed on to Edmund Husserl the "best regards from the philosophical seminar" as well as information on what was going on at the institute. Husserl, Max Müller recalls, "seemed to me like a 'sage,' because he was not interested in any everyday issue, even though the politics of the day were a constant threat to him as a Jew and to his Jewish wife. It was as though he was unaware of this threat or simply refused to take note of it."[31] Husserl showed little interest in institute matters but was always keen to hear about Heidegger. After his initial outrage at his "betrayal" in 1933 his judgment eventually turned milder: "He is no doubt the most talented of all those who ever belonged to my circle," he told Müller.[32]

When Edmund Husserl died in 1938, a lonely man, and was cremated on April 29, no one from the Department of Philosophy, with the exception of Gerhard Ritter, was present. Martin Heidegger did not attend either, but he was sick in bed. On the evening of that day the economist Karl Diehl gave a commemorative speech on Husserl before a small gathering of colleagues. Diehl used to call this circle "the faculty of decent people."[33]

At the beginning of the 1940s Heidegger, pressed by his publishers, was to withdraw the dedication to Husserl on the flyleaf of *Being and Time.* An acknowledgment hidden in the footnotes was to be retained.

But to return to 1933. In his rectorial address Heidegger had outlined the scenario of an epochal break, a second beginning of the history of mankind. Everyone was invited to become witnesses or actors in a decisive act of the gigantomachy of the history of Being. But in his case this did not yield much more than a struggle against the *Ordinarien-Universität,* the university where the full professors had a decisive say. Later, Heidegger would write to Jaspers: "I was 'dreaming' and basically only thought of the university that I had before my mind's eye" (April 4, 1950, BwHJ, 200).

This struggle for a new university has some similarity with the student revolt of 1967. Heidegger emphasizes his allegiance to the youth movement; he appears as the spearhead of the revolutionary students, who are "on the march." Heidegger appears in knee breeches and with an open-necked shirt, against the stodginess under the academic gowns. Heidegger plays the card of the Nazi student representatives against the professors, and he supports the independence of the assistants. This is the hour of the *Privatdozenten,* the unsalaried associate professors, whose hopes are being raised. Heidegger makes a point of involving all service personnel in consultations.

Heidegger was not so presumptuous as to think that he "could lead the Führer"—as Jaspers later asserted—but in the area of university politics he certainly aimed at a leading position in the struggle against the rule of the full professors. At the meeting of the Academics' Association in June 1933 the group of Nazi university teachers, in which Heidegger claimed a leading position, succeeded in getting the association's old board members to resign. At the rectors' conference that followed, Heidegger called for the dissolution of the association. Moreover, Freiburg was to be declared an "advance post" of the National Socialist transformation of the universities, and in that event Heidegger would truly become a kind of führer of the German universities. He had the necessary ambition. But he failed to prevail against the other rectors. The Nazi faction thereupon walked out in protest. As his activities on the national level did not yield the hoped-for success, Heidegger determined to create a role model at least at the regional level. Today there is no doubt that during the summer of 1933 he collaborated in the drafting of the Baden university reform which came into force on August 21, 1933. Baden thus became the first German *Land*, or province, where the alignment of the universities according to the führer principle was accomplished.

For Heidegger, stripping the professors of their former powers meant the continuation of his struggle against bourgeois idealism and the modern spirit of the positivist disciplines. This motive, too, would reemerge in the student revolt of 1967. The kinds of people whom Heidegger was then fighting were later called "idiot specialists" by the students of 1967. The critique of 1967 was that bourgeois society promoted an interest in the sciences as a disinterest in society. It is this responsibility of science for the societal whole that Heidegger speaks of, albeit in different words: "The construction of a new intellectual and spiritual world for the German nation has now become the single most important task of the German universities. This is 'national labor' of the highest kind."[34]

One of the goals of the 1967 student movement was the "abolition of the division between manual and brain work." That was also Heidegger's goal. At the enrollment ceremony on November 25, 1933, he made a programmatic speech on "The German Student as a Worker." With formulations echoing Ernst Jünger's essay *The Worker,* published in 1932, Heidegger polemicized against the arrogance of the educated. A student should not try to gather spiritual treasures for his own use or for his career, but should ask himself how he could best put his research and knowledge to the service of his people. "Such service provides the basic experience of the origin of true comradeship." A student should view his studies quite simply as "work" and should in fact actually lend a hand—helping with the harvest, with amelioration projects in the surroundings of Freiburg, with the "citizens' kitchen," and so on. "The National Socialist state is a workers' state," Heidegger declares, and students should, each in his own place, with their research and knowledge, regard themselves as "in service."

It is surprising that Heidegger, who until then had always wished to keep the spirit of true scholarship and philosophy free from any considerations of utility or practical orientation, is now calling for an instrumentalization of scholarship for national goals. He used to caricature the orientation of philosophy on "values" as the "moribund phase" of bourgeois idealism; now he is digging up the values of national self-assertion to demand, in its name and with philosophical authorization, "readiness to make the extreme sacrifice" and "comradeship to the end." All this is specifically placed in context in his speech at the Leipzig Demonstration of German Science for Adolf Hitler on November 11, 1933, with his philosophical axiom that the "primal demand" of all Being is "that it should retain and save its own essence" (S, 149).

To begin, he explains to the workers assembled before him what it means that they are assembled before him. By being there they are already helping to "build and edify within the new future of our people."[35] However, they were now unfortunately out of work—a good opportunity for Heidegger to cautiously introduce the first philosophical terms by describing their difficult situation as "not capable of *Dasein*." They would become "capable of *Dasein*" only when they could serve the state and the nation as a whole. The provision of work was therefore the first task of the national state. The second task was provision of knowledge. "Every worker of our German people must know why and to what end he is where he is."[36] Only thus would the individual become "rooted in the totality of the people and in the destiny of the people."[37] However, as Heidegger cannot leave the unemployed standing amid the questionability of Being-in-the-whole as a form of the knowledge the *Volksgenosse* needs, and as he does not wish to draw the attention of those thrown out of work to their own thrownness, he must offer and provide some specific help. This speech betrays the difficulties he has with this. He cannot think of the right words. So he speaks of what they should know, to wit, "how this people is come together . . . what is happening to help the German people in this National Socialist state . . . [they must know] the meaning of the future health [*Gesundung*] of the body of the people . . . and what state urbanization has brought German men."[38] With such knowledge the workless before him could become "German men, clear and resolute."[39] The knowledge providers from the university would help them with this, and they would be pleased to do so. Because the scientists knew that they, too, could become *Volksgenossen* if they took their knowledge to the working man. Unity of hand and head was the true reality. "This will to find work is a true acquisition of knowledge; this will ought to be for us the innermost certainty and never a wavering belief."[40] This faith, however, has its support in the "eminent will of our Führer."[41] Heidegger concluded his speech with *"Sieg Heil!"*

In an address to the Tübingen student body on November 30, 1933, Heidegger describes the process of "conquering the new reality" as though it were the creation of a work of art. It was high time to leave the space of the traditional university, which was now only "the empty island of an empty state." But he who was fighting was, as it were, inside a nascent work of art. He received the fullness of *Dasein* and became a "co-owner of the nation's truth in his state."[42]

Philosophical ecstasy has been replaced by the mystique of the people's community. Philosophy as lonely thinking and questioning is temporarily set aside. But it goes without saying that the whole business remains a philosophical matter, because Heidegger allows himself to be philosophically enchanted by the movement—and he succeeds in enchanting others. One of those then enchanted recalls: "When Heidegger spoke it was like scales falling from my eyes."

A project on which Heidegger was especially keen was the Wissenschaftslager, or Scholarship Camp. He first came out with this idea on June 10, 1933, at a training seminar of the Office of Science of the German Student Union in Berlin. This was intended to be a mixture of scout camp and Platonic academy. Live together, work together, think together—for a limited period in open nature. Science was once more to awaken to the "living reality of nature and of history"; the "sterile preoccupation with ideologies" of Christianity and "positivist fact-mongering" were to be overcome.[43] The participants would be able to open up to the new powers of *Dasein*. That was the project. It was realized from October 4 to 10, 1933, in a place below the Todtnauberg cabin. They departed from the university in closed marching order. For his first attempt Heidegger had selected a small circle of associate professors and students and drawn up the stage directions: "The company will proceed to the destination on foot . . . SA or SS service uniform will be worn; the uniform of the Stahlhelm (with armband) may also be worn."[44] The daily roster began with reveille at 06.00 hours and ended with the tattoo at 22.00 hours. "The real work of the camp will be to reflect on ways and means of fighting for the attainment of the university of the future for the German mind and spirit."[45] The themes for the working parties and classes, prescribed by Heidegger, were university affairs, organization of specialized groups, National Socialist university reform, the führer principle, and so on. The most important thing, however, according to Heidegger, was "to create the appropriate ambience and attitude" to the ongoing revolution.[46] Heidegger wants to bring a group of young people to his peaceful Todtnauberg to build campfires, share food, have conversation, sing along with guitar—but he announced the project as if it were a march into enemy country, where dangers had to be overcome: "The success of the camp depends on how much new courage we can muster, . . . on the strength and resolve of our will to loyalty, sacrifice and service."[47] The only danger of the enterprise was that Heidegger would make himself look foolish and that it would turn into nothing other than an ordinary camp with people who were really a little beyond Cub Scout age. Heinrich Buhr, one of the participants, reports how Heidegger spoke impressively at the campfire against the "devaluation of the world, contempt for the world and denial of the world" through Christianity, praising the "great noble awareness of the insecurity of 'existence.'" Buhr, who later became a Protestant pastor, felt reminded of Ernst Jünger's *Adventurous Heart.*[48] It was an edifying event, for some perhaps a moving one, but no courage was required to survive it. It was romantic, but it was not dangerous. A certain note of unpleasantness was provided by a cabal between Heidegger's faithful followers and a group of SA brownshirt students from Heidelberg, who confronted the Youth League tradition with their own military spirit and championed a militant anti-Semitism. In his self-justification for the denazification procedure in 1945 Heidegger inflated this into a political conflict. "The Heidelberg group had instructions to break up the camp," he wrote.

In the course of the disputes, *Privatdozent* Stadelmann, one of Heidegger's followers, left the camp on his orders. Hugo Ott has discovered the correspondence between Stadelmann and Heidegger about the incident. The impression one gains from it is as though something highly dramatic had occurred between a knight and his squire, involving loyalty unto death, sacrifice, betrayal, foul play, remorse, mortification. Heidegger wrote: "I don't suppose anyone actually passed the 'test' of the camp. But everyone came away with the great awareness that the revolution is not yet at an end. And that the goal of the university revolution is the SA student."[49] And Stadelmann, clearly offended by Heidegger's action in removing him from combat prematurely, wrote: "I realized more clearly than ever before that my place is in the camp of revolution . . . I shall maintain discipline—but I had hoped for more, I had believed in the possibility of true allegiance."[50] Heidegger replied: "I know that I must now set about winning back your allegiance, which remains as important to me as it ever was."[51]

The powers of *Dasein* that are evidently involved here are of a men's club and scout variety. Heidegger, however, manages to set up a stage on which conspiracy, intrigue, and intergroup tensions have the appearance of something "great," something that, as Heidegger put it in his rectorial address, "stands in the storm." Heidegger becomes a prisoner of the meanings that he himself has put into reality.

He retrieves the free mobility of his thinking when he no longer wants to be a participant in the overall "work of art" of the people's community, but instead turns again to the works of art and philosophy. These, after all, he was better able to read than the political reality. By *involving* himself in the real politics of the revolutionary movement he had made an excessive demand on himself. He was soon to retire again into the comparatively safe quarters of philosophical thought.

15

HEIDEGGER'S STRUGGLE FOR THE PURITY OF THE MOVEMENT

Philosophy, Heidegger had said, should be "in control" of its time. In his attempt to meet this demand, he tears his fundamental ontology out of its anchorage.

Let us recall that in *Being and Time* he had described man's *Dasein* on an elementary plane, below the historical differentiations and contradictions of individual outlines of life. The moods of boredom and anxiety, which he had analyzed in his lectures of the early 1930s, had likewise been related to Being-in-the-world generally, and not to individual *Dasein* locations in specific situations.

Even though Heidegger had occasionally made Being-with his subject, his thinking nevertheless was always focused on man in the singular—the man, the *Dasein.* And that which confronts man, or amid which he finds himself, is also aligned to the singular—the world, the that-which-is *(das Seiende),* the Being *(das Sein).*

Yet between *the* man and the great whole—Being, spirit, history—there is another realm, that in-between, where men exist in their plurality: the many who differ from one another, pursue diverse interests, encounter each other in action, and only then give rise to what may be called political reality. This whole sphere, whose ontological significance lies in the multiplicity and diversity of individuals, disappears in Heidegger's *Dasein* panorama. There are only two kinds of *Dasein,* the authentic and the inauthentic, the Self and the They. Of course, Heidegger would not deny that the *Dasein* patterns of individuals differ, but these differences are to him no positive challenge; he does not include them among the fundamental conditions of existence. That we have to live with the fact that we are surrounded by people who differ from us, whom we do not understand or whom we understand all too well, whom we love or hate, who are indifferent to us or who are enigmas to us, from whom we are separated by a gulf or by nothing at all—this whole universe of possible relationships is disregarded by Heidegger and is not included by him among his "existentials." Heidegger, the inventor of "ontological difference," never conceived the idea of developing an "ontology of difference." Ontological difference means the distinction of Being from that-which-is. An ontology of difference would mean accepting the philosophical challenge of the disparity of people and the difficulties or opportunities arising as a result.

In philosophical tradition there has long been this mystification that there is always talk only of man, even though men invariably occur in the plural. The actors on the philosophical stage are God and Man, I and the World, the *ego cogito* and the *res extensa;* now, in Heidegger, there are *Dasein* and Being. Heidegger's talk of *Dasein* also assumes, if only by the suggestion of the language, the identity of everything that is *Dasein. Dasein* is "exposed" to "that-which-is-in-the-whole," Heidegger states. To begin with, however, the individual *Dasein* is exposed to the world of the other humans in existence *(der anderen daseienden Menschen).*

Instead of considering the fundamental plurality of this world of humans, Heidegger escapes into the collective singular—the nation. And this national singular is placed under the existential ideal of Self-being, an ideal that had "authentically" evolved from the individual thrown back upon himself. "The primal demand of all *Dasein,* that it should retain and save its own essence" is expressly transferred by Heidegger, at the Demonstration of German Science for Adolf Hitler in Leipzig on November 11, 1933, to the nation that must "retain and save its own essence." And what is it threatened by? By the humiliation of the Treaty of Versailles, the severance of formerly German territories, and reparations. What organization sanctions this injustice? The League of

Nations. It was therefore correct that Adolf Hitler should have declared Germany's exit from the League of Nations and was now—by means of a plebiscite (linked to the election of the Reichstag with a unified single list)—obtaining retrospective approval of that step. This political maneuver received supreme consecration from Heidegger with his philosophy of authenticity shifted from the individual to the nation—the "primal demand of *Dasein.*"

Heidegger's speech of November 1933 was applied national fundamental ontology. In his "Logic" lectures of the summer of 1934—so far published only in a mutilated form recorded at the time—Heidegger expressly reflected on this transformation of "mineness" *(Je-meinigkeit)* into "ourness" *(Je-unsrigkeit).* "The Self," he argued, "is not a distinguishing determination of the 'I.'" What is important is the "we-ourselves." In his endeavors for the "I-myself," the individual loses the ground under his feet; he "stands in the lostness to the Self" because he seeks the Self in the wrong place, in the detached "I." It can be found only in the "We," even though not every assembly of persons—"a skittle club, a robber band"—necessarily represents such a We. The distinction between authenticity and inauthenticity exists also on the plane of the We. The inauthentic We is the They, the authentic We is the nation that asserts itself as one man. "A national whole, therefore, is a man on the large scale" (L, 26 ff.).

The pathos of authenticity in *Being and Time* was loneliness. If the nation becomes the collective singular of *Dasein,* then this loneliness disappears in the ominous unity of the nation. Yet Heidegger is reluctant to abandon the existential pathos and therefore chooses a stage on which an entire nation can be presented in resolute loneliness. The German nation is lonely amid the other nations. It has ventured too far forward with its revolution, into the uncertainty of "that-which-is-in-the-whole." This is familiar ground from his rectorial address: the nation has advanced under the empty heaven of Zarathustra, a community that has set out to venture the giving of meaning amid the meaningless, a nation organized in formations, retinues, alliances. The German nation, the metaphysical nation.

It was Hannah Arendt—as a reply to Heidegger—who was to develop what real political thinking is. It stems from the "Being-together and Being-alongside of the disparate"[1] and resists the temptation of gnostically deepening or overexalting the swarming of historical happening into an "authentic" history, which then possesses that automatism and logic that must always be lacking in the chaos of real history, consisting as it does of an infinity of intersecting histories. Instead of arriving at political thought, Heidegger merely arrived at such a gnosis of history. This would not have mattered so much had he only noticed that he lacked the political concepts. It was not the fact that he was an unpolitical person that made his political actions during those months so dangerous, but that he failed to realize it and therefore confused his gnosis of history with political thought. Had he, as a gnostic of history, developed his "authentic" histories without wanting to make "politics" out of them, he would have remained the artist of philosophy that he was. However, swept along by the revolution, he tried to become the politician of philosophy. Thus he stands at the solstice bonfire, calling out to those who, deeply moved, listen to him: "The days are passing, they are getting shorter again. But our courage to break through the impending darkness is increasing. Never must we go blind in the struggle. Flame, teach us and light us, show us the road from which there is no way back! Flame, ignite; hearts, burn!"

Most of the professors in Freiburg regarded their rector as a radical visionary gone wild. At times he was also regarded as comical. The story was told of how a few students, led by the philosophy *Dozent* and former lieutenant-commander Stieler, were drilling with wooden dummy rifles in the clay pit of a brickwork when Heidegger drove up in a car and jumped out. Stieler, who was over six feet five inches tall, stood to attention before the stocky Heidegger and made a correct military report, and like a commanding officer, Heidegger, whose war service had been confined to postal censorship and a meteorological observatory, formally received his report and saluted. Such was the nature of Heidegger's battle scenes.

In September 1933 Heidegger was offered a chair at the University of Berlin, and in October he was offered one at the University of Munich. Victor Farías has researched the background of these invitations, and according to Farías, both invitations were made against the opposition of the faculties concerned. In Berlin, Alfred Baeumler had very strongly championed Heidegger, describing him, in his expert opinion, as a "philosophical genius."[2] During his simultaneous negotiations with Munich, Heidegger pointed out that Berlin had promised him a professorship "with a special political task"; would he, he inquired, be similarly called upon in Munich for the "reshaping of the university system"? He would make his choice dependent on where and how he could "best serve the work of Adolf Hitler."[3] Opposition to Heidegger came from two quarters—the conservative professors could not see any "positive" teaching in Heidegger's philosophy, and the hard-line Nazi ideologists like Ernst Krieck and Erich Jaensch could not see any avowal in favor of the National Socialist worldview.

In the background of Heidegger's candidacy for the Berlin and Munich posts, there circulated an expert opinion by the psychologist Jaensch, a colleague from Heidegger's time in Marburg. This described Heidegger as a "dangerous schizophrenic"[4] whose writings were just "psychopathological documents." Heidegger's thinking was essentially Jewish in character, "talmudist-rabbinic," and therefore admired by his Jewish followers. Heidegger had skillfully remolded his "existential philosophy" to the "tendencies of National Socialism." A year later, when Heidegger's name was considered for the directorship of the National Socialist *Dozentenakademie,* Jaensch drew up a second expert opinion. This warned of Heidegger's "schizophrenic babblings, banalities with an appearance of depth."[5] Jaensch wrote that Heidegger simply had "an innate penchant for revolution," and one had to expect that on "the day that revolution with us would cease" he would probably "no longer be on our side but would be a turncoat."[6] Ernst Krieck, the pretender to the role of "official" philosopher of the movement, characterized Heidegger's position as "metaphysical nihilism." Unlike Jaensch, Krieck went public in 1934 with his critique in the periodical *Volk im Werden,* of which he was the editor:

> The fundamental ideological tone of Heidegger's teaching is determined by the concept of concern and anxiety, both of which aim at nothingness. The meaning of this philosophy is downright atheism and metaphysical nihilism of the kind that used to be represented in our country mainly by Jewish literati—in other words, an enzyme of decomposition and dissolution for the German people. In *Being and Time* Heidegger consciously and deliberately philosophizes around "everydayness"—there is nothing in it about nation and state, about race, or any of the values of our National Socialist ideology. If his rectorial address suddenly strikes a heroic note, then this was an adjustment to the year 1933, one that is in total contradiction to the basic attitude of *Being and Time* (1927) and *What Is Metaphysics?* (1931), with their teaching of concern, of anxiety, and of the Nothing.[7]

The polycentrism of the Nazi power apparatus also had its effect on the science policy and ideological sectors. The ministries of education in Bavaria and Berlin were both anxious to acquire Heidegger because of his international reputation. They needed a prominent figurehead, and they were unperturbed by the fact that Heidegger's "personal National Socialism" would remain incomprehensible to most party members or indeed even seem suspect. Krieck actually voiced the suspicion that Heidegger was linking the revolution with nihilism and anxiety in order eventually to drive the German nation into "the saving arms of the Church."[8] In no case, he argued, was Heidegger suitable for the task of "creating a spiritual and ethical nucleus for the movement."[9]

Walter Gross, the head of the Nazi Party's Racial Policy Office, also had Heidegger's version of National Socialism in mind when, in a memorandum of 1936, he came to the conclusion that the "traditional human common sense of professionally competent and racially and politically unobjectionable scientists contained virtually no elements useful for National Socialism." Any "political alignment" of the universities was therefore pointless; it would be more to the point to enhance the economic and technical effectiveness of the sciences. Gross recommended a "depoliticization" of the universities to put an end to the "embarrassing efforts" of the full professors "to play at National Socialism." The development and propagation of the National Socialist ideology would be better left to the relevant party authorities, whose task it would be to ensure the succession, within roughly a decade, of an "ideologically impeccable" generation of scientists.

In the ideological power centers of Nazism, Heidegger was therefore regarded as someone "playing at National Socialism." It was Gross who urgently warned the Nazi ideologist Alfred Rosenberg's department against Heidegger, when, in the late summer of 1934, his name was being considered within the party for the directorship of a Nazi *Dozentenakademie* to be established for the ideological schooling of young scientists. Gross referred to the expert opinions of Jaensch and Krieck, as well as to unfavorable internal reports on Heidegger's "activities" in Freiburg.

Despite all this opposition Heidegger had nevertheless been offered professorships at both Munich and Berlin. In the end he declined the offers. Officially and for domestic purposes, he justified his refusal with the argument that he was still needed for the university reform in Freiburg and that there was no suitable successor for the rector's office. "If I retire," he wrote to Elisabeth Blochmann on September 19, 1933, "everything in Freiburg will collapse" (BwHB, 73).

Matters were viewed differently at Freiburg University. Most of the professors there would have liked to see Heidegger give up his office sooner rather than later. There was no love lost for the military tone of his circulars, appeals, and memorandums. Although most on the teaching staff were ready enough to come to terms with the new political conditions, they did not wish to see research or teaching affected by them. What irritated the professors most was the loss of seminar or lecture time to paramilitary exercises and labor service engagements organized by the SA brownshirt students. Heidegger, on the other hand, put great store by these; to him they were a manifestation of the new spirit of the National Socialist revolution. Erik Wolf, whom Heidegger had installed as dean of the faculty of law, was particularly eager to reshape the law school along Heidegger's lines to provide time for paramilitary exercises and labor service. In these efforts he encountered the vigorous resistance of the conservatively minded law professors. Frustrated, Wolf wished to give up his office on December 7, 1933, offering Heidegger his resignation. He was suffering mental torment, he said; he doubted if he was the right person for the post, but he would leave it, as he respectfully informed Heidegger, "to the judgment of Your Magnificence, which discerns the deeper reasons that others cannot see, to determine whether the failure of my efforts to execute the functions of my office with success is due to the inadequacy of my abilities . . . or to the fact that the tasks entrusted to me met with a degree of opposition that could not be overcome."[10] Heidegger did not accept his resignation: "The whole point of the new constitution and the struggle we are presently engaged in is that you enjoy *my* confidence first and foremost, and not so much that of the Faculty."[11] Heidegger considered it his duty to side with his loyal, though somewhat shaken, supporter and therefore sent the recalcitrant academic staff into the Christmas vacation with the following reminder:

> Since my first days in office the determining purpose and ultimate goal—which can only be attained by gradual degrees—has been the radical transformation of scientific education in line with the dynamics and dictates of the National Socialist state.[12] A merely formal overhaul of the university system, for instance by selecting and redistributing the lecture subjects to the "present conditions," is not only not enough but deceives the students and university teachers about the real task. The time that becomes free for the teaching staff, as a result of the canceling of lectures, must at all costs be put to the service of reflection on the inner recon-

struction of lectures and workshops . . . Conflicts and clashes arising from a truly shared will to transform the universities are more essential to me than any all-round satisfaction of colleagues, when nothing is done and past practices are merely covered up. I shall be grateful for any assistance, however small, that will advance the cause of the universities as a whole. However, I shall judge the work of the faculty and of individual university teachers only according to the degree to which their collaboration in the attainment of the future becomes visible and effective. What is clear is that only the unbending will to tackle the tasks that lie ahead can give meaning and substance to our present endeavors. The individual, whatever his place, counts for nothing. The destiny of our nation within the state counts for everything.[13]

Heidegger was threatening that he would appropriately *judge* the unwilling. This could mean a lot of things—reprimands, denunciation to superior authorities, even dismissal from office or arrest. As far as paramilitary exercises and labor service were concerned, however, Heidegger was in a weak position, since the party authorities responsible were by then once more tending toward restoring normal practices in university teaching.

In his postwar justification Heidegger claimed that the ministry in Karlsruhe had demanded the dismissal of the deans Erik Wolf and Wilhelm von Möllendorf on political grounds, and that he had been unable to accept this, especially in the case of the Social Democrat Möllendorf, and had therefore resigned from his office. This version does not stand up in light of research by Hugo Ott and Victor Farías. Heidegger did not resign out of solidarity with a Social Democrat but because party policy, to his mind, was not revolutionary enough. Heidegger was concerned not, as he later claimed, with the defense of the university's Western spirit, the *universitas,* but with the defense of the revolution against academic conservatism and bourgeois realpolitik, which was interested solely in the economic and technological usefulness of the universities. That was why, in his Tübingen lecture on November 30, 1933, he was able to declare: "The revolution in the German universities is not at an end; it has not even begun yet."[14] And that was why on April 23, 1934, he resigned, having been advised by the Ministry of Education on April 12 to recall Erik Wolf from the dean's post for reasons of "not entirely unfounded misgivings." No mention was made of Möllendorf. This was a hint by the ministry that it regarded the revolutionariness of the "overturn of the entire German *Dasein*" (Heidegger) at the University of Freiburg as excessive. Heidegger's resignation from the rectorship was therefore related to his campaign for the purity of the revolutionary movement, as he saw it: renewal of the Western spirit after the "death of God."

He also defended this purity of the revolutionary movement against the clerical tendencies that were then especially powerful in Freiburg. When the Catholic student fraternity Ripuaria was suspended by the local party authorities in 1934, with Heidegger's approval, but subsequently, following the conclusion of the Concordat between Germany and the Vatican, had to be readmitted, Heidegger wrote angrily to Oskar Stäbel, the leader of the German Student Association: "We must in no way allow this clear Catholic victory to continue, especially in this region. A greater damage to the work already done could not be imagined . . . I have been aware of the local situation and the forces at work here in their smallest details . . . We misconstrue the tactics of the Catholic Church. Some day this error will be costly for us."[15]

For Heidegger, who had severed himself painfully enough from his Catholic origins, the Catholic Church's vast organizational and spiritual influence in Freiburg constituted a considerable obstacle to the "overturn of the entire German *Dasein.*" That was why, in his Scholarship Camp, his main attack had been directed against Christianity as represented in the churches. There, he had argued, real godlessness reigned, because their God had been molded for the comfortable and the cowardly, as a kind of life insurance. His metaphysical revolution, on the other hand, was something for the strong, the bold, and the resolute. Heidegger's radical critique of Catholicism was not accepted by the Nazi Party authorities, who, for the time being, were anxious to come to terms with the traditional powers.

It was also his campaign for the purity of the revolutionary movement that induced Heidegger in two instances to denounce political undesirables. Eduard Baumgarten, a nephew of Max Weber, had begun his scholarly career in the United States, where in his philosophy he moved close to American pragmatism. In Freiburg in the 1920s he became a friend of Heidegger, who was actually the godfather of one of Baumgarten's daughters. They had philosophical differences, but these were initially discussed in an amicable manner. Baumgarten then moved to Göttingen, where he obtained a teaching assignment for American studies. As he proved highly successful with his lectures, he was to be given an appointment as *Dozent,* or associate professor, with the right to examine candidates. He was prepared to adapt himself politically and applied for membership in the SA brownshirts and in the National Socialist

Dozentenschaft. It was at this point that Heidegger intervened. On December 16, 1933, he wrote to the NS-Dozentenschaft:

> By family and spiritual attitudes, Dr. Baumgarten comes from that liberal-democratic circle of intellectuals gathered around Max Weber. During his time here he was everything but a National Socialist . . . After disappointing me, he became closely tied to the Jew Fränkel who had been active at Göttingen and was later expelled. I suppose Baumgarten found some protection [in Göttingen] by this shift in affiliation. I deem it impossible to bring Baumgarten into the SA as well as to bring him into the teaching body. Baumgarten is a gifted speaker. In his philosophy, however, I think he is pompous and without solid and true knowledge.[16]

In his public speeches Heidegger had always warned against those who adapted to the new conditions only superficially. To that extent his statement against Baumgarten was entirely in line with his consistent revolutionism. This opinion, however, supplied by Heidegger, struck the head of the Göttingen Dozentenschaft as "charged with hate" and was shelved as "useless." Baumgarten continued with his career—with the aid of the party. He subsequently became director of the Philosophical Seminar in Königsberg and an honorary block leader of his local organization, and Rosenberg's department invited him to its conferences.

Karl Jaspers learned of Heidegger's assessment via Marianne Weber in 1935. He never got over it; it was "one of the most hurtful experiences" of his life.[17] A swipe at the "liberal-democratic circle of intellectuals gathered around Max Weber" was bound to hit him too. What pained him even more was that Heidegger, whom until then he had not known as an anti-Semite, was ready to use anti-Semitic insinuations to blacken a scholar he disliked. Jaspers was horrified, but by then he also feared Heidegger and therefore dared not mention the matter to him directly. Not until the end of 1945, when—on Heidegger's suggestion—the denazification commission requested Jaspers's expert opinion on Heidegger, did he make the Baumgarten episode public.

Another incident concerned Hermann Staudinger, a professor of chemistry and subsequently, in 1953, a Nobel Prize laureate. Hugo Ott discovered the relevant documents and reconstructed the case. On the occasion of a visit to Freiburg on September 29, 1933, by Eugen Fehrle, the Baden government official responsible for university affairs, in connection with Heidegger's appointment as *Führer-Rektor* under the new university statute, Heidegger informed Fehrle that Staudinger was under suspicion of political unreliability. Fehrle immediately initiated investigations, because under the Law on the Reestablishment of a Permanent Civil Service, the time for such proceedings expired on September 30. Heidegger had begun gathering information on Staudinger during the summer. The charges against him related to the period of the World War. From 1912 Staudinger had been a professor at the Technological University in Zurich, but he had kept his German nationality. For health reasons he was not at first enlisted for military service. During the war he published pacifist articles, calling for political rethinking in view of the development of war technology that was becoming a threat to mankind as a whole. In 1917 he applied for Swiss citizenship. At that time files were kept on Staudinger by the Germans, who suspected him of having given war-related information in the field of chemistry to the enemy powers. Although this suspicion was later dropped, a note was added to his file in 1919 to the effect that during the war Staudinger had adopted an attitude apt "to do grave damage to Germany's cause in the eyes of the international community."[18] When Staudinger came to Freiburg in 1925 the matter was raised again, but even the national-conservative professors no longer voiced any objection, since Staudinger had meanwhile become an internationally famous figure.

Now, however, Heidegger's concern gave rise to investigations designed to drive Staudinger from his post. The Gestapo compiled a dossier and on February 6, 1934, submitted it to Heidegger for comment. Heidegger itemized the charges against Staudinger: "in the hour of the fatherland's greatest need" he had applied for Swiss citizenship; he had been granted Swiss citizenship "without the written approval of the German authorities"; he had publicly declared "that he would never support his country by taking up arms or performing any other kind of service." These facts were sufficiently incriminating. "I would have thought this was a case for outright dismissal rather than early retirement," Heidegger wrote. It was imperative "that action be taken, especially as Staudinger now claims to stand 100 per cent behind the present national awakening."[19]

As in the Baumgarten case, Heidegger's principal aim was again the discovery of so-called opportunists. What further stimulated his zeal was his mistrust of the pragmatic alliance between the state and the specialized sciences. "The overturn of the entire German *Dasein*" would, in his view, fail if the "deracinated" specialized disciplines were, through their political usefulness, once more to move to the fore. Hence the campaign against Staudinger, who for his part now made an all-out effort to demonstrate the importance of his research to the national awakening. During the week when he was subjected to ruthless interrogation, Staudinger published an article that emphasized the importance of chemistry to the new Germany in its quest for economic self-sufficiency and also stated "that he had greeted the outbreak of the national revolution with great joy."[20] As senior party officials intervened in Staudinger's favor, Heidegger retreated, and on March 5, 1934, he recommended early retirement instead of dismissal, "given his international standing within his professional field."[21] But Heidegger failed even with this proposal. After a complicated arrangement, Staudinger was permitted to continue in his post.

There was a follow-up to this story. When Heidegger in 1938 gave his lecture "The Justification of the Modern View of the World through Metaphysics," in which he criticized the technicalization of the modern sciences, the Nazi Party journal *Der Alemanne* carried an article in which Heidegger was confronted, as an illustration of uselessness (a philosopher "who owes his celebrity solely to the fact that nobody can understand him, and who teaches the doctrine of Nothing"), with the "vital work of professional scientists."[22] The implication of this attack emerges from the fact that just below it appeared an announcement of a lecture by Professor Staudinger on "The Four-Year Plan and Chemistry."

Heidegger mentioned this incident in his defense when he was questioned by the denazification commission on December 15, 1945. But he concealed the fact that prior to it he had denounced Staudinger. It is likely that Heidegger kept quiet about his denunciation not only because he did not wish to incriminate himself, but also because he may not even have viewed his action as a denunciation. He felt he was a part of the revolutionary movement, and it was his intention to keep opportunists away from the revolutionary awakening. They were not to be allowed to sneak into the movement and use it to their advantage. For Heidegger, Staudinger was one of those scientists who would serve any objective provided it brought them personal advantage, who sought nothing more than "the tranquil comfort of an occupation without danger."

By the irony of history, it was not the philosophers, like Heidegger, who served the regime best, but the "unpolitical" specialized scientists. It was they who lent practical striking power to the system that Heidegger wished to serve in his own revolutionary-visionary manner.

16

DEPARTURE FROM THE POLITICAL SCENE

Where are we actually when we think?

Xenophon relates an amusing story about Socrates. He had taken part, as a gallant soldier, in the Peloponnesian War. On one occasion, however—when the troops were on the march—he had suddenly stopped, lost in thought, and there he had stood for a whole day, oblivious of himself, oblivious of his surroundings, oblivious of the situation. Something had occurred to him, or something had struck him that made him think, and so he had dropped out of his reality. He had come under the power of his thinking, which transported him to some Nowhere where he seemed, in a strange way, to feel at home. This Nowhere of thinking is the great interruption in the events of the ordinary day, and it is an alluring Elsewhere. Judging by everything we know of Socrates, the experience of this Elsewhere of the spirit was a prerequisite to his triumph over fear of death. Socrates, seized by thinking, had become untouchable. They would be able to kill his body, but his spirit would live. He was released from struggle for *Dasein.* It was Socrates, standing there motionless and lost in thought while things were taking their course around him, that

Aristotle had in mind when he praised philosophy for its talent for the Everywhere and the Nowhere, because it needed "neither implements nor special places for its trade, wherever on earth somebody devotes himself to thinking, he will attain the truth everywhere as though it were present."[1]

Socrates, however, was also a philosopher of the polis, of the Athens marketplace. There he wanted to be present with his Elsewhere, with his philosophical absences. Philosophy is at once placeless and place-bound.

Heidegger was a particularly place-bound philosopher, and during the time of his political engagement he campaigned mightily against what he called "powerless and bottomless" thinking. But now, after resigning as rector, he observed that the ground of the new revolutionary reality, on which he had hoped to set foot, was rocking. While he was negotiating about a professorship in Berlin he wrote to Elisabeth Blochmann: "The whole affair would have been bottomless. I felt relieved when I left Berlin again" (September 19, 1933, BwHB, 74).

In this letter Heidegger describes being pulled one way and another: "I believe . . . I know only one thing—that we must prepare ourselves for great spiritual transformations and participate in bringing them about." On the other hand: "I am at the moment away from my own work, even though I feel every day that the everyday action . . . is driving toward it."

Where does it drive him? The places of his thinking can be quite accurately determined: an imaginary and a real place—ancient Greece of his philosophy and his province, more accurately, Todtnauberg.

As for the dream of Greece, which Heidegger hoped to realize with the National Socialist revolution, all that was necessary had been said by Nietzsche half a century earlier:

> German philosophy as a whole . . . is the most fundamental form of romanticism and homesickness that has ever been . . . One is no longer at home anywhere; at last one longs back for that place in which alone one can be at home, because it is the only place in which one would want to be at home: the Greek world! But it is in precisely that direction that all bridges are broken—except the rainbow bridges of concepts! . . . concepts! . . . To be sure, one must be very subtle, very light, very thin to step across these bridges! But what happiness there is already in this will to spirituality, to ghostliness almost! . . . One wants to go back, through the Church Fathers to the Greeks . . . German philosophy . . . is at least will

> to Renaissance . . . the digging up of ancient philosophy, above all of the pre-Socratics—the most deeply buried of all Greek temples! . . . We are growing more Greek by the day; at first, as is only fair, in concepts and evaluations, as Hellenizing ghosts, as it were; but one day, let us hope, also in our bodies![2]

Heidegger, as has been shown, wished for a return of the Greek world in the social life of the revolution as the restoration of the original "power" of the "awakening of Greek philosophy" (his rectorial address).

The other place was the province, Todtnauberg. On his hill in the Black Forest, Heidegger had felt close to his Greek dream; from there he had descended into the political lowlands, where he might gain something because it was in an uproar—for "everything great stands in the storm."

Over the months of his political engagement Heidegger has to make the painful discovery that he cannot bring the two worlds—the one he lives in and the one he is thinking in—together in the way he had hoped. There has been much condemnation of his broadcast lecture of March 1934—"Creative Landscape: Why Do We Stay in the Province?"—which contained his official rejection of the Berlin offer. Many have seen in it nothing more than ideologized rustic and native-soil romanticism. Yet in it, in his own way, Heidegger revealed something of a simple, to him essential, experience: "My entire work . . . is borne and guided by the world of these mountains and peasants. At times my work up there is now interrupted for lengthy periods by negotiations, lecture tours, talks, and my teaching work down here. But as soon as I get up there again the whole world of earlier questions again presses in on me during the very first hours of my cabin existence, moreover entirely in the form in which I had left it. I am quite simply placed into the specific oscillation of work and I am basically unable to control its hidden law" (D, 11).

Heidegger realizes, and admits to himself, that the world of his life and that of his thinking are in harmony in his Todtnauberg cabin, and only there. Only in his "cabin existence" does "the whole world of earlier questions," that rehearsing of the Greek beginnings, become living reality; only there does it acquire essence. That is why he feels relieved to be able to return to the "location" of his thinking after the failure of his rectorship. "Back from Syracuse?" Wolfgang Schadewaldt is reported to have asked mockingly at a chance meeting in the street. It was in Syracuse that Plato had intended to realize his political utopia and had only just escaped slavery.

By resigning from the rectorship on April 23, 1934, Heidegger gave up a politically exposed position, but for the time being he held on to his intention of providing the "right point of attack" for philosophy (letter to Jaspers, March 10, 1933, BwHJ, 150) in the new revolutionary reality. However, as he did not wish to leave the rediscovered "locality" of his thinking ever again, he had no other choice than to try to transplant that "locality," to carry it with him like the snail's house of his philosophy. He had declined the offer of a professorship in Berlin because things there were "bottomless," yet during the summer of 1934 he developed his ideas for the creation of a *Dozentenakademie* in Berlin, signaling his readiness to go there, provided he was given the chance to realize his ideas. His plans were for the establishment of a kind of monastery of philosophers, a Todtnauberg refuge, in the middle of Berlin.

Heidegger had been negotiating with Berlin on this issue since the fall of 1933. The project of the *Dozentenakademie* had been launched by party circles in Berlin and by the Ministry for Science and Education. It was conceived as a further training institution in politics that all young scholars hoping to become professors would have to pass through. The objective, naturally, was their ideological alignment with nationalist ideas. The granting of the *venia legendi,* the license to teach at a university, was to be made dependent on graduation from the *Dozentenakademie* and thus to be taken away from the universities. The party authorities had arrived at the regrettable fact that the "traditional human common sense of professionally competent and racially and politically unobjectionable scientists" contained "virtually no elements useful for National Socialism"; the new institution was to ensure that, in something like a decade, an "ideologically impeccable" generation of scientists was raised. Heidegger was being mentioned as a possible director. He made detailed proposals and sent them to Berlin on August 28, 1934. In his view it was to become not an academy, not a club of dignitaries nor a political education center, but an "educational community." He saw it rather like an order of chivalry, having its "own spirit" and creating its own "tradition," one that would impose an "enduring obligation." The "unspoken effect of its atmosphere" would be the decisive factor. That was why the teaching staff would have to "be effective mainly through what and who they are, and not through what or about what they 'speak.'" Teachers and students were to live together in the daily routine of a "natural alternation of scientific work, relaxation, contemplation, war games, physical work, marches, sport, and festivities."

There would also have to be occasion for "genuine solitude and contemplation," because that which served the community could not solely "stem from the community." This alternation between solitude and community would have to be encouraged by the external facilities—lecture room, dining hall with a lectern, rooms for festivities and artistic pursuits, communal dormitories. There would also be "monastic cells" where individuals might retire for mental work and contemplation. The library should be sparsely equipped, containing only what was essential—"it belongs to a school as a plough belongs to a peasant." The students should be involved in the selection of the books in order to learn "what genuine and thorough judgment of literature means." In conclusion, Heidegger sums up the central idea of this monastery of learning: "To reduce, and later to eliminate, the excessive importance of an 'Americanized' sort of scientific activity, the sciences must be organized so that they can be developed according to their own needs. This has never taken place and never will do so without the decisive influence of individuals."[3]

The *Dozentenakademie* as envisaged by Heidegger did not materialize. There had been intrigues and cabals. Rosenberg's department had been warned by other party authorities. On February 14, 1934, Krieck had written to Jaensch: "I have confirmed rumors that say that Heidegger may receive the post of director of the Academy of Professors, which would put him in control of a whole generation of Prussian professors. This would be a great concern. I beg you for a report on this man, on his behavior, his philosophy, his use of the German language."[4] Jaensch, who had already intervened against Heidegger's hiring during the Munich and Berlin negotiations, provided such an expert opinion. In it he said:

> If you require such an opinion from me, I would like to preface it with Adolf Hitler's dictum that he always acknowledges above him the laws of sound common sense. Conflict with reason in crucial steps of the life of a state inevitably and irretrievably leads to disaster . . . It would be in conflict with sound common sense if what is possibly the most important post for the intellectual life of the immediate future were to be filled by one of the greatest muddle-heads and eccentric recluses that we have in our university life . . . To appoint to the post of supreme educator of our young academic generation a man whose eccentric, vague, schizoform, and in part already schizophrenic, thinking would obviously have a devastating effect among the students, as we can clearly discern here in Marburg.[5]

Although the ministry rejected this opinion, it favored the appointment of an ideological official. Heidegger was therefore eliminated from the list of candidates. However, he was still considered of some use to the party's ideological apparatus, which is why in May 1934 he was appointed to the Board for Philosophy of Law of the Academy for German Law. The chairman of the board, Hans Frank, the Reich commissioner for justice, in his opening speech defined the character and the duties of the board. New foundations were to be laid for a German legal system based on the values of "race, state, Führer, blood, authority, faith, land, and idealism"; to this extent it must be "understood as a fighting committee of National Socialism."[6] Heidegger was a member of this board, which until 1936 met at the Nietzsche Archive in Weimar. Nothing is known of his input to it. In 1935 Julius Streicher was admitted to that institution. This caused such an uproar that Karl Löwith drew Heidegger's attention to it in Rome in 1936. After some hesitation, Löwith later wrote, Heidegger replied: "One need not waste words over Streicher, *Der Stürmer* was nothing more than pornography. He couldn't understand why Hitler didn't get rid of this guy—he must be afraid of him."[7]

Heidegger's faith in Hitler and in the need for revolution was unbroken, but he nevertheless gradually loosened his ties with politics. His philosophy had sought a hero, and it had been a political hero. But now he was once more separating the spheres. Philosophy was placed "deeper," it again became the basic event of the spirit, an event that necessitated politics but did not get absorbed in politics. At the beginning of the Schelling lecture in 1936 he was to say: "The profound untruth of those words that Napoleon had spoken to Goethe in Erfurt was soon to come to light: Politics is fate. No, Spirit is fate and fate is Spirit. The essence of Spirit, however, is freedom" (GA 42, 3).[8]

The turning away from politics and back to the spirit was first foreshadowed in Heidegger's lecture series of the summer semester of 1934. This was entitled "The State and Science." The first lecture was attended by everybody who was anybody—party officials, civic dignitaries, colleagues. The students were in a minority. Everyone was anxious to hear what Heidegger would have to say after his resignation from the rectorship. The lecture was a social event. Heidegger pushed his way through the overcrowded auditorium, where the brownshirts predominated, mounted the podium, and announced that he had changed his subject. "I shall speak about logic. Logic comes from 'logos.' Heraclitus said . . ." At that moment it became obvious that Heidegger was about to delve into his depths and that, while he would not speak against politics, he would yet keep his former distance from it. With his very first sentences he rejected "undisciplined ideological talk" and, equally, the "formula rubbish" that bourgeois scholarship usually offers under the heading of "logic." "Logic, to us, is the questioning search of the reasons of Being, of the location of questionability" (L, 2). By the time the second lecture came around, his audience was reduced to only those interested in philosophy.

It had been a difficult beginning, Heidegger wrote to Jaspers a year later, looking back to the first semesters after his rectorship. "For me it is a . . . laborious probing; it was only a few months ago that I again found a contact with the work I completed . . . in the winter of 1932–33, but it is a thin babbling, and then there are also two posts—the argument with the faith of my origins and the failure of my rectorship—quite enough of what really should be overcome" (July 1, 1935, BwHJ, 157).

In this task of understanding his own religious and political impulses Heidegger is helped by another "hero"—Hölderlin. He gives his first Hölderlin lecture in the winter semester of 1934–35. Henceforth Hölderlin will remain a permanent point of reference of Heidegger's thinking. From Hölderlin he will find out what the divine is that we are lacking, and what "politics" above the business of the day means. Hölderlin, Heidegger states, is a "power in the history of our nation," but one that has not yet truly emerged. This will have to change if the German nation wishes to find itself. To help with this endeavor is for Heidegger "'politics' in the highest and most authentic sense, so much so that whoever achieves anything here has no need to speak of 'politics'" (GA 39, 214).

There was a Hölderlin renaissance when Heidegger turned his attention to this poet. Hölderlin was no longer, as he had been at the beginning of the century, merely a lyrical poet of interest to literary historians, a poet who had also written a strange novel in letter form, *Hyperion,* and who was one of the admirers of ancient Greece of whom German classicism abounded. Neither Dilthey nor Nietzsche, both of whom had urgently drawn attention to him, had succeeded in bringing him to the consciousness of the German public. This was achieved only on the eve of World War I by the Stefan George circle, more especially its member Norbert von Hellingrath, who discovered and commented on Hölderlin's late writings and embarked on editing his collected works. The George circle viewed Hölderlin as the inspired precursor of "symbolism"—not of an artistically playful symbolism but of an existentially urgent one. "It is as though a curtain had been raised from the holiest of holies and the unutterable offered itself to the gaze."[9] This was the note to which Hölderlin enthusiasm in the 1920s and 1930s was attuned. Max Kommerell included Hölderlin among the "poets as leaders"; with him one was in touch with a "German current of force."[10] Among the youth movement, Hölderlin was considered a genius of the heart. Time and again these sentences from *Hyperion* were quoted: "It is a harsh word and yet I utter it, for it is the truth: I cannot think of a nation that is more torn than the Germans, you see workmen but no human beings, thinkers but no human beings, masters and servants, young people and sedate, but no human beings—is this not like a battlefield, where hands and arms and all limbs lie about each other mutilated while the shed lifeblood seeps into the sand?"[11]

With his longing for a new wholeness of life, Hölderlin became a significant role model for a broad spectrum of the educated, more particularly for those who were on the lookout for a new experience of the sacred—as Rilke put it in his poem "To Hölderlin":

> Oh, what the best aspire to, you, undesiring, laid
> brick upon brick; it stood up. But its very collapse
> left you composed.[12]

Hölderlin's subsequent madness merely gave his poetry an additional authenticity; had he not become deranged because he had ventured forward further than others into the dangerous and mysterious zones of life?

The poet of the Germans; the poet overcome by the power of poetry; the accoucheur of new gods, the frontier crosser and the magnificent failure—these were the roles in which Hölderlin was seen and from which Heidegger proceeded.

Heidegger's Hölderlin essay has three centers of gravity. First, it examines, after the failure of his own "power politics," the nature of power and the hierarchy of the *Dasein* powers. Poetry, thinking, and politics—in what relation were these to one another? Second, Heidegger hopes to find a language in Hölderlin for that which we lack. He quotes Hölderlin as the poetically articulate witness to our lack of Being ("Night of the Gods") and as a messenger of the possible overcoming of that lack. Third, he hopes, through Hölderlin, that "poet of poetry," to comprehend his own actions, the thinking of thinking. He reflects himself in Hölderlin, especially in his failure. He draws, indirectly, a picture of himself: how he sees himself and how he wishes to be seen.

In his lecture he discusses Hölderlin's two late hymns "Germania" and "The

Rhine." As the basis of his interpretation he quotes an aphorism of Hölderlin's: "Poets have mostly arisen at the beginning or at the end of a world period. With song the nations step out of the heaven of their childhood into active life, into the land of Culture. With song they return into original life" (GA 39, 20). It is through the word of the poet—Heidegger says—that at each period in a nation's history and culture "all that emerges into the open that we then discuss and treat in everyday language."

For a poet, this is a flattering vision of the power of the poetic word. Poets give a nation its identity. They give their nation its gods, as Homer and Hesiod did, and thereby establish "custom and usage." The poets are the real inventors of a nation's culture. Because Hölderlin in his poems made this power of poetry his own theme, Heidegger calls him the "poet of making poetry."

Heidegger next relates this culture-creating act of making poetry to the other great creative acts—the philosophical opening up of the world and the foundation of a state. "The fundamental mood, and this means the truth of a nation's *Dasein*, is originally donated by the poet. The thus revealed Being of that-which-is [*Seyn des Seienden*] is comprehended as Being [*Seyn*] . . . by the thinker, and the thus comprehended Being [*Seyn*] is . . . placed into determined historical truth through the fact that the nation is brought to itself as a nation. This is accomplished by the creation . . . of the state by the state-creator" (GA 39, 144).

Poetry, thinking, and politics have this in common: they can all be *works* of great power. "It may be that one day we shall have to move out of our everydayness and move into the power of poetry, that we shall never again return into everydayness as we left it" (GA 39, 22).

The poets, the thinkers, the statesmen become destiny for others because they are "creative," as a result of which something comes into the world that has a "halo" around it in which new *Dasein* relationships and visibilities exist. This creation of works which then stand about powerfully and magically in the landscape of the existent is also called "battle" by Heidegger. In his lecture series "Introduction to Metaphysics," given the following year, he describes that battle: "It is this conflict that first projects and develops what had hitherto been unheard of, unsaid and unthought. The battle is then sustained by the creators, poets, thinkers, statesmen. Against the overwhelming chaos they set the barrier of their work, and in their work they capture the world thus opened up" (EM, 47).[13]

Heidegger had already shown himself to be "fascinated" by the "creative" state-founding action of Hitler. Now he addresses the "sphere of power" of Hölderlin's poetry, to which the same applies as to the National Socialist revolution. In his Tübingen lecture "The University in the National Socialist State," given on November 30, 1933, he had warned against viewing the "revolutionary reality" as "something present-at-hand" or merely "factic," for then one would never discover what it is. One has to step into the magic circle of that reality and let oneself be transformed. The same applies to Hölderlin and to all great poetry. It demands a decision as to whether one wants to expose oneself to its "turbulence" or maintain a safe distance. Hölderlin's poetry reveals itself only to the resolute, for whom—just as politics or thinking—it can then become a revolutionary event, the "overturn of the entire *Dasein.*" But only a few wish to embark on this adventure. Heidegger investigates the tactics of the safe distance, all of which aim at simply not exposing oneself to the commanding word of poetry. There exists the understanding of poetry as an "expression" of experiences and fantasy, both entertaining and good for the extension of one's mental horizon. Or else there is poetry as an ideological superstructure, as a transfiguration or concealment of real conditions. And there is also the idea—and here Heidegger quotes Nazi ideology—of "poetry as a biologically necessary function of a people" (GA 39, 27). Digestion, too—Heidegger observes sarcastically—is a necessary function of the people. This attitude of not entering into the power sphere of a phenomenon is called by Heidegger the "liberalist" basic attitude. "If anything can and should be labeled by the much-abused title of 'liberalist,' then it is this mode of thinking. Because it, on principle and in advance, steps out of what it means and thinks, making it the mere object of its meaning" (GA 39, 28).

His is a rather idiosyncratic use of the term "liberalist." What Heidegger means by it is a thoughtless and unfeeling, or methodical, refusal to surrender to an object's own meaning; a wish to get "above, under, or behind" the things, and certainly a reluctance to being drawn *into* them. With this critique Heidegger has arrived at a state of mind that for Hölderlin is characteristic of the "night of the gods."

We "people of today," Hölderlin says, may be "greatly experienced" in the sense of scientific knowledge, but we have lost the ability to perceive things, nature, and human relationships in their plenitude and liveliness. We have lost the "divine," which means that the "spirit" has gone out of the world. We have subjected nature to our will; the telescope penetrates into the remotest distances of the universe, yet at the same time we "precipitate the festive ascent" of the appearing world. We have turned the "love bonds" between nature and man into "ropes," we have "mocked" the bounds of the human and the natural. We have become a "cunning generation" that, moreover, is proud of being just that. Thus one no longer *sees* the earth, no longer *hears* the cry of a bird, and language among men has "withered."[14] All this, for Hölderlin, is the "night of the gods." This means, therefore, the loss of the immanent significance and radiating power of worldly, human relationships. As Hölderlin sees it, it is up to the poet to raise this entire lost world to life again. If he can do no more than recall that which has been lost, then he is a "poet in a needy age."

To Hölderlin the divine is not some region in the beyond but a transformed reality within man, between man and his relation to nature. An enhanced, adventurous, intensive, wide-awake life, opened toward the world, in the particular as well as in the general. Jubilation at Being-in-the-world.

For this Hölderlinesque divine Heidegger had, in the 1920s, coined the term "authenticity." He now finds a new name for it: "relation to Being" *(Bezug zum Seyn). Dasein,* as Heidegger had explained in *Being and Time,* always stands in relation to Being *(Sein).* Evasion into inauthenticity also belongs to that relation. *Bezug zum Sein* becomes *Bezug zum Seyn* if it is explicitly grasped—in other words, "authentically" lived. Henceforth Heidegger will write *Seyn* with a *y* (a spelling in use a few hundred years earlier) whenever he means the "authentic" relation that deifies *Dasein* in this sense. And the opening toward the divine in *Dasein* means just that—to open up and venture forward all the way to one's own abysmalness and to the miracle of the world.

One might think that this opening out was entirely the achievement of the individual resolute *Dasein.* In the authenticity philosophy of *Being and Time,* this individual aspect does indeed predominate, and this individualism lives on in the image of the poet and thinker heroes who "endow" a whole nation with its gods and divinity. Now, however, Heidegger puts greater emphasis on the historical and collective aspect. There are periods of history that favor such a *Seyns-Bezug*—such a "relation to Being"—and others that render it more difficult or even impossible. The "night of the gods," or, as Heidegger calls it, the "darkening of the world," engulfs entire epochs. For Heidegger, Hölderlin is such a giant just because, at a time of the decline of an epoch, when the old gods had disappeared and the new ones had not yet arrived, he was both late born and prematurely born, suffering the pain of what had been lost and the violence of what was to come.

But, my friend! we have come too late. Though the gods are living,
Over our heads they live, up in a different world . . .
For not always a frail, a delicate vessel can hold them

Hölderlin says in a late poem,[15] which Heidegger connects with lines from the poem "As on a Holiday":

Yet fellow poets, us it behooves
Bare-headed beneath God's thunderstorms
To grasp the Father's ray with your own two hands
and, wrapping in song
The heavenly gift,
To offer it to the people. (quoted in GA 39, 30)[16]

This image of "God's thunderstorm" above the poet's head is interpreted by Heidegger as "exposure to the superior power of Being [*Seyn*]" (GA 39, 31). In this context he quotes Hölderlin's letters to his friend Böhlendorff. In one, written December 4, 1801, shortly before his departure for Bordeaux, Hölderlin says: "Now I can rejoice over a new truth, a better view of what is above us and around us, though I fear that things may eventually go with me as for ancient Tantalus, who received more from the gods than he could digest." And back from his journey, confused and worn, he wrote: "The vast element, the fire of the heavens, and the quietude of the people . . . constantly affected me, and, as is said of heroes, I might well say that Apollo has struck me" (November 1802).

Hölderlin, in Heidegger's interpretation, had ventured forward too far, "into the region where a new total threat to spiritual-historical *Dasein* takes effect" (GA 39, 113). While the nation around him remains in the "need of needlessness, unable to make use of a poet," the poet has to bear everything on his own, the pain and the overwhelming happiness. The "fundamental mood" in which Hölderlin lives and from which he writes his poetry does not yet find a resonance in the nation. The nation needs first to be "retuned." To "this struggle of retuning of persisting and persevering moods the firstborn have to be sacrificed. They are those poets who in their speech predict the future Being [*Seyn*] of a nation and, while they are doing so, are inevitably unheard" (GA 39, 146).

"They are those poets," Heidegger says, but what he means is also: "They are those thinkers." Here he has arrived at his self-portrait. For he believes that what happened to Hölderlin has also happened to him. He too has opened up to "God's thunderstorm," he too has been struck by the lightning of *Seyn,* he too must wrestle with the "need of needlessness" of the nation, he too has "donated" a work that has not yet been properly accepted. "But they cannot use me," he quotes ambiguously and, with reference to the present revolution, continues: "How much longer will the Germans fail to hear this terrible word? If the great turning point of their *Dasein* does not open their eyes, what then shall give them ears to hear?" (GA 39, 136).

Here it is again, the "great turning point," the metaphysical revolution of the Nazi awakening. Surely this should be the moment when Hölderlin, the "donor" of a new *Seyn,* would at last be heard. Surely Hölderlin has walked ahead of the nation in the adventure of "once more risking its luck with the gods, in order thus to create a historical world" (GA 39, 221).

Once again, therefore, Heidegger celebrates the great "awakening." If this is Hölderlin's historical hour, how should it not also be Heidegger's hour? However, after the failure of his rectorship he realizes that "organizing and administering" are not his kind of thing after all. His task is to serve the "awakening by a different metaphysics—that is, by a new basic experience of *Seyn*" (GA 39, 195).

Six months later, in his "Introduction to Metaphysics" lectures, Heidegger describes the large-scale trends that threaten that "new awakening" and might cut it short. He ventures on to the area of a topically philosophical diagnosis of his period. At the center of his reflections he places what he calls the "emasculation of the spirit" (EM, 34).[17]

The spirit is first reduced to instrumental reason, called by Heidegger "intelligence." This is concerned only with "calculation and examination of the given things and their transformation and reconstitution." This calculating intelligence is then placed in the service of an ideology, of an ideological doctrine. Heidegger in this context mentions Marxism, obsession with technology, and also ethnic racism. "Whether this use of intelligence relates to the regulation and domination of material conditions of production (as in Marxism) or in general to the intelligent ordering and explanation of everything that is present and already posited at any time (as in positivism), or whether it is applied to the organization and regulation of a nation's vital resources and race" (EM, 36)[18]—in any event the "powers of spiritual happening" must lose their free mobility and their purpose-oriented dignity. As a result they also lose their "openness" to the demands of "Being." This total mobilization, economically, technologically, and racially, result in the "darkening of the world, the flight of the gods, the destruction of the earth, the transformation of men into a mass, the hatred and suspicion of everything free and creative" (EM, 29).[19]

Into this gloomy panorama Heidegger also places the German reality of 1935. The spirit of the awakening of 1933 is under threat, externally, from America (technological mobilization) and Russia (economic mobilization).

> This Europe, in its ruinous blindness, for ever on the point of cutting its own throat, lies today in a great pincers, squeezed between Russia on one side and America on the other. From a metaphysical point of view, Russia and America are the same; the same dreary technological frenzy, the same unrestricted organization of the average man. At a time when the farthermost corner of the globe has been conquered by technology and opened to economic exploitation; when any incident whatever, regardless of where or when it occurs, can be communicated to the rest of the world at any desired speed . . . when time has ceased to be anything other than velocity, instantaneousness, and simultaneity, and time as history has vanished from the lives of all peoples; when a boxer is regarded as a nation's great man; when mass meetings attended by millions are looked on as a triumph—then, yes then, through all this turmoil, a question still haunts us like a specter: What for?—Whither?—And what then? (EM, 29)[20]

But the spirit of the awakening is under threat also from within—from racism ("organization and regulation of a nation's vital resources and race").[21]

Heidegger had viewed the Nazi revolution as a force resisting the disastrous development of the modern age. That, to him, was "the inner truth and greatness of this movement" (EM, 152). But in 1935 he was seeing a danger that the best of the impulses were being frittered away and falling victim to "the dreary technological frenzy, the same unrestricted organization of the average man" (EM, 28).[22] In this situation it was up to the philosopher to preserve and defend the original truth of the revolutionary new beginning. He must arm himself with patience. Philosophy was in its nature nontemporal, because it was one of the few things whose destiny it remained never to find, and never to be allowed to find, an echo of its Today.

Heidegger, however, makes no mention of the fact that, not so long before, he himself had succumbed to the temptation of producing an immediate echo. After philosophy's unsuccessful seizure of power, Heidegger once more returns to a solitary philosophy that, on Hölderlin's model, hopes to fend off the "darkening of the world" in single combat. His failed excursion into politics had at least taught him one thing—"the preparation of the true" is not achieved overnight. Even though the "revelation of Being" occasionally takes place in philosophy, in his philosophy, a great deal of time will have to elapse before this event radiates into society as a whole and transforms it from the foundations up. That is why it would remain a "needy age." In such a place of "metaphysical need," the spirits, whether Hölderlin or Heidegger, must hold out to keep awake the memory of what is still missing.

Heidegger therefore holds on to his philosophical fantasy, but he is beginning to detach it from its entanglement with National Socialist politics. National Socialism, as it really exists, increasingly becomes for him a system of the betrayed revolution, which to him had been a metaphysical revolution, a "revelation of Being" on the soil of a national community. Thus the authentic National Socialist, as which Heidegger continues to regard himself, becomes a thinker in a "needy age."

Heidegger puts the best possible face on the failure of his rectorship: he inscribes himself in the history of Being as a herald who arrived too early and is therefore in danger of being crushed and rejected by his time. A brother of Hölderlin.

17

THE AGE OF IDEOLOGY AND TOTAL MOBILIZATION: HEIDEGGER BEATS A RETREAT

In the last free elections of November 6, 1932, the National Socialists gained 33.5 percent of the votes. In the March 5, 1933, elections, after the Reichstag fire, after the elimination of the Communist Party and the massive intimidation of the rest of the opposition, the Nazis still did not have the majority of the people behind them. In the Reichstag elections of November 12, 1933, however, when there was only a one-party list and when the elections were linked to a plebiscite about leaving the League of Nations, the National Socialists eventually gained 92 percent of the votes. This figure probably did not reflect the public mood adequately; support for Hitler was not yet so massive at that time. During the late 1930s, however, it may be assumed that the overwhelming majority of the nation more or less supported Hitler's politics. Not only because terror, nazification, and intimidation had been so effective, but also because Hitler's policies then seemed to have proved successful in the eyes of the great majority. On April 28, 1939, Hitler reviewed these successes in a major speech:

> I overcame chaos in Germany, restored order, enormously raised production in all fields of our national economy . . . I succeeded in completely resettling in useful production those seven million unemployed who so touched all our hearts . . . I have not only politically united the German nation but also rearmed it militarily, and I have further tried to liquidate that Treaty sheet by sheet whose 448 Articles contain the vilest rape that nations and human beings have ever been expected to submit to. I have restored to the Reich the provinces grabbed from us in 1919; I have led millions of deeply unhappy Germans, who had been snatched away from us, back into the Fatherland; I have restored the thousand-year-old historical unity of German living space; and I have . . . attempted to accomplish all that without shedding blood and without inflicting the sufferings of war on my people or any other. I have accomplished all this . . . as one who 21 years ago was still an unknown worker and soldier of my people, by my own efforts.[1]

Heidegger would have fully agreed with this balance sheet of successes. He welcomed the internal political unity of the nation, which had been achieved by dictatorial methods. Having despised the Weimar democracy, he had no regrets about the elimination of the political opposition. Nor did he have any objections to the principle of the leader and the led. The Nazi regime had put large numbers of people back into jobs again and thereby made them "capable of *Dasein,*" as Heidegger put it in a lecture in February 1934. Germany's exit from the League of Nations and the unilateral renunciation of the Treaty of Versailles were seen by Heidegger as evidence of the nation's will to assert itself, as the fulfillment of that "primal demand of *Dasein* that it should preserve and save its own essence." He supported Hitler's policy of annexation, having always regarded it as a scandal that "18 million Germans belong to the People but are not part of the Reich because they live beyond its borders."[2] The regime's domestic and foreign policy were entirely in line with Heidegger's political ideas, which in any case had never been very clearly defined.

National Socialism, he said to Karl Löwith in Rome in the summer of 1936, was "the right course for Germany; one had only to 'hold out' long enough."[3] His approval, however, was by then reduced to a political statement of opinion. The metaphysical pathos had gone. It was simply Heidegger's belief that the Nazis were pursuing a reasonably sound policy—abolition of unemployment, social peace, revision of the Treaty of Versailles, and so on. He realized by then that his vision of the metaphysical revolution, which had lured him into the political arena, had not become reality. And as, with "laborious probing"—as he wrote to Jaspers on July 1, 1935—he was trying to pick up his "interrupted work" from the winter semester of 1932–33, he would not shut his eyes to the realization that the breakthrough to the new age was meanwhile confined to solitary thinking—a thinking that hopes to discover the overwhelming dynamic of the new age, and with it the deeper causes of the failure of his own political-philosophical ambitions. He had clearly underestimated that dynamic when he experienced the National Socialist revolution as a breakthrough into the depths of his time. The years from 1935 to 1938 were dedicated to the task of reinterpretation. As recently as 1935, in his metaphysics lectures, he had confirmed the "inner truth and greatness" of National Socialism, characterizing its resistance to the new age. Over the next few years, during which he explored the open dimension of the "modern age," his focus shifted until he regarded National Socialism no longer as a breakout from the modern age, but as its especially consistent expression. He discovered that National Socialism was itself the problem whose solution he had once thought it was. He saw the furor of the new age rampant in National Socialism: technological frenzy, government, and organization—in other words, inauthenticity as total mobilization.

Admittedly Heidegger did not shrink from smuggling these later insights into his earlier remarks about the movement. This was done, for instance, when the metaphysics lectures of 1935 were published in 1953. Then, after the war, he endeavored to explain his remark about the "inner truth and greatness" of the movement by adding, in brackets, that this meant the greatness of the terrible, the "encounter between a globally determined technology and modern man." As will be seen presently, this is an interpretation that Heidegger did not develop until after the metaphysics lectures—in his Nietzsche lectures; in his secret philosophical notes, the *Beiträge zur Philosophie,* his *Contributions to Philosophy;* and in his lecture "Justification of the Modern Picture of the World through Metaphysics," which was published after the war under the title *Die Zeit des Weltbildes* (The Age of Ideology)—one of the most powerful of Heidegger's writings.

Between 1935 and 1938 Heidegger therefore processed his disappointment that the metaphysical revolution did not take place as a political one. He tried to comprehend the overwhelming power of the new age—in other words, to comprehend that which had gripped him and also how one could escape from that grip.

What kind of Moloch was this new age that had frustrated Heidegger's political hopes and caused him to seek refuge in solitary thinking? In *The Age of Ideology* Heidegger describes the new age in terms of a total mobilization. In this he refers to Ernst Jünger without actually quoting him. Engineering technology, science, and research, he argues, had combined into a powerful system, a system of labor and needs. Technological thinking governed not only research and production in the narrow sense, but also the attitudes of people toward each other and to nature. Man interpreted himself in concepts generated by technology. This applied also to art, which, as "art production," remained locked into the productive universe of the new age. Culture altogether was viewed as a stock of "values" that could be managed, calculated, employed, and planned. Included in these cultural values were religious experiences and traditions that likewise declined into a means of securing the whole. With such an instrumentalization of the transcendent, a state of total "de-deification" (H, 74) had been reached. The new age, to Heidegger, was therefore engineering technology, instrumental science, the culture business, and de-deification. These, however, were only the most obvious and most pressing symptoms. Underlying them was a metaphysical "fundamental mood," a view of the existent *(das Seiende)* governing all areas of life and activities, a decision on what was to be regarded as existent and what mattered in all human actions. This fundamental attitude, according to Heidegger, was defined by man's transformation into a "subject" for whom the world became the quintessence of "objects"—that is, a multitude of real and possible objects that could be controlled, used, consumed, repulsed, or eliminated. Man was straightening up; he no longer experienced himself as incorporated in a world; but this world now became his vis-à-vis, which he perpetuated in his "world picture. Man becomes the center of reference of the existent [*des Seienden*] as such" (H, 86).

But has this not always been the case? No, says Heidegger, things used to be different. And on pain of final decline, they would have to become different again.

Things were different in ancient Greece. In his lecture Heidegger presents a brief imagined picture of the "original" manner of living in the world. For ancient Greece (and also for our own future, provided we want to have one) the following applies:

> The existent [*das Seiende*] is that which sprouts and opens itself up, that which, as being present, comes upon man as he is present; in other words, upon him who opens himself up to that which is present by perceiving it. The existent does not become existent as a result of man first looking upon it, let alone in the sense of imagining . . . Instead it is man who is looked upon by the existent, by that which opens itself up to that which is present and assembled around him. Looked upon by the existent, included in its openness, and contained there and borne by it, driven around by its contradictions and marked by its discrepancies—that is the essence of man in the great period of Greece. (H, 88)

This outline is not clear enough for one to dispense with a commentary here. To Greek thinking the world is a stage on which man moves among the others like him and among the things, in order to act there and to see, and to be acted on and be seen. Man's place is a place of visibility in a double sense: he shows himself (and only when he shows himself is he real; otherwise he is in the cave of the private, an "idiot"), and he is the being to whom the rest of the existent can show itself. "Appearance," to Greek thought, is not a deficient mode of Being. Rather, Being is appearance and nothing else. Only that which appears exists. That is why for Plato the highest Being was—as an idea—assigned to seeing. Man was understood as a being that shared with the rest of the world both seeing and the ability to be seen. Not only man but also nature generally is pressing to appear; it is not merely something viewed passively, the material for our vision and intervention. In Greek thought the world, as it were, looks back. Man most clearly reflects the fundamental cosmic move that urges everything to appear and is therefore the point of highest visibility, in the active and passive sense. That was why Greek man invented the theater, replicating the stage of the world. To him the universe as a whole had stage characteristics. Man is the open spot of Being.

It is Heidegger's belief that in these circumstances there exists a richer, more intensive Being, a wide-open expanse. In contrast to it, modern man is a prisoner of his projects, and anything that happens to him is experienced by him as a deviation, an incident, an accident. Thus the mystery is lost from the world, and so are the abyss, destiny, and grace. "Only where the existent [*das Seiende*] has become the object of imagining does the existent, in a certain sense, forfeit Being [*Sein*]" (H, 99).

Heidegger's history of Being thus breaks down as follows. The Greeks acted on an open stage, where man and the world appeared and, together, enacted their tragedies and comedies in the awareness of the superior power and superior plenitude of Being, which itself remained mysterious and hidden. In the Christian era, Being was secure in God, who was approached with reverence, even though simultaneously one was curiously looking out for similarities between the Creator and the *creatum,* the created, eventually becoming ambitious enough to repeat the creation oneself. The new age, finally, had fully gone over to the "attack" (H, 106). "In the worldwide imperialism of technologically organized man, man's subjectivism reaches its highest peak, whence it will descend into the lowlands of organized uniformity and there arrange itself. This uniformity becomes the surest instrument of complete, because technological, domination over the earth" (H, 109).

Taking up Max Weber's idea of the disenchanted modern world, Heidegger, reversing it, speaks of our "enchantment" by the world of technology. Contemporary history progresses under a spell. Is there a way out?

In 1933 Heidegger had believed that the collective breakout from the steel cage of the modern age had become a historical reality. Five years later he had to acknowledge that the chance of a fundamental turning point did not then exist, nor would it come about on the political plane for the time being. He now comprehended that revolution and all that stemmed from it was a process that was still entirely under the spell of contemporary total mobilization—but without reflecting self-critically on his own engagement.

This was his diagnosis. The new age was entering the stage of fiercest confrontation between rival world-control concepts—Americanism, communism, National Socialism. The basic positions of each of these were clearly differentiated and resolutely defended, but all of this was happening on the common soil of the technologically spellbound modern age. "For this battle . . . man is bringing into play the unrestricted power of calculation, planning, and cultivation of all things" (H, 92).

"Calculation" stands for Americanism, "planning" for communism, and "cultivation" for National Socialism.

From the global perspective of Heidegger, the critic of the new age, who also, in his Nietzsche lectures, called it the "age of consummate meaninglessness" (N II, 9),[4] all this represents a single "doom connection," as Adorno was to call it, in different jargon, later.

If one gazes into darkness for any length of time, one always sees something there. Heidegger endeavors to make out distinctions in the universal darkness. Although the new age generally is a "rebellion of the subject," it makes a difference whether "man wishes to be, and must be, the subject as an *I* let loose with limitation as to his own choice and arbitrariness, or as the *We* of society, whether as an individual or as a community, whether as a personality in the community or a mere member of the group, whether as a state and nation or as a people, or as the universal mankind of the new-age man that, as a new-age creature, he already is" (H, 90).

Heidegger's own preference is clear. He states it clearly enough when, a few sentences later, he refers to the "mischief of subjectivism in the sense of individualism." The *We,* the "personality in the community," and the "people"—these are the least demoralized forms of subject-Being in the new age. Thus he sanctions his political activities, not in the sense of his original understanding of a metaphysical revolution but at least as the preferable option among the general mischief of the new age. But, of course, this is not the right course, the one that would be necessary.

Heidegger has to avoid misunderstandings. This is not a "negation of the era." Thinking that insists on the "power claim of negation" remains tied to the negated and thereby loses its revealing power. Nor is it a case of "unhistorical" mysticism. The Being of the existent *(das Sein des Seienden),* to which thinking opens up, is not a worldless God. On the contrary. Such thinking hopes to regain a perspective in which the world once more becomes a space in which (as Heidegger put it in his metaphysics lectures of 1935) "each thing—a tree, a mountain, a house, the cry of a bird—loses all indifference and commonplaceness" (EM, 20).[5]

The extent to which such thinking belongs to the neighborhood of art is explained in Heidegger's lecture—first given in 1935—"The Origin of the Work of Art." Using the example of a painting by Van Gogh, representing the artist's own worn-out boots (which Heidegger mistakenly believes to be a peasant's boots), he describes how art makes things appear so that they lose their "indifference and commonplaceness." Art does not describe; it makes visible. What it raises into a work of art consolidates into a world of its own that remains transparent to the world generally, yet in such a way that the world-shaping act can be experienced as such. Thus the work at the same time represents itself as a meaning-providing force that "worldifies" *(weltet),* through which the existent becomes "more existent" *(das Seiende seiender).* Heidegger therefore can state that it is the essence of art "that in the midst of the existent it reveals an open place in the openness of which everything is different from usual" (H, 58).

The work of art is also something that has been produced. How then does Heidegger make a distinction between being produced by art and the technological production analyzed by him in the ideology article?

To define the difference, Heidegger introduces the concept of "earth." Earth is impenetrable, self-sufficient nature. "Earth is the essentially self-shutting-off element" (H, 33). Technologically scientific objectivization attempts to penetrate into nature, to snatch from it the secret of its functioning. By that route, however, we shall never understand what nature is. There is this "existing-in-itself" of nature, its way of eluding us. To experience this "eluding" means to open up to the fascinating closedness, to the "earthness" of nature. Art attempts nothing else. We can determine the weight of a stone, break up colored light into oscillations—yet these determinations do not comprise the heavy feel of the stone or the brilliance of the color. "Earth thus lets any penetration into it splinter against itself" (H, 32). Art, however, renders visible the "undiscoverable" (H, 32) of earth; it produces something that cannot otherwise be reached by any imagination; it opens up a space wherein the "self-shutting-off" of earth can reveal itself. It reveals a mystery without touching it. Art not only represents a world, but it also creates the astonishment, the horror, the jubilation, the indifference in the face of the world. Art encloses its own into a world of its own. Heidegger says it "creates" a world that can for a while resist the general "world loss and world disintegration." It is this world-creating aspect and hence the special potency of art that matters to him most. Take the example of a Greek temple. For us today it is only a monument of the history of art, yet at one time it was the center of reference around which the life of a community was organized, filling it with meaning and significance. "The temple work first assembles and simultaneously gathers together the unity of those routes and references in which birth and death, misfortune and blessing, victory and disgrace, perseverance and decay win for the human creature the shape of his destiny" (H, 27). As a result, the temple grants man the "prospect of himself" (H, 28). In this powerful constellation, the work of art provides the *God* of the community, its supreme authorization and its meaning-giving instance. For this reason

Heidegger also calls art the "setting-to-work of truth" (H, 48). From this angle he draws a parallel, as he did in his Hölderlin lecture, between art, thinking, and the "state-founding deed."

This is a solemn pragmatism that, first of all, established the historicity of endowed "truths." These are of limited durability. Second, these "truths" are nowhere else than in the works. "The establishment of truth in a work is the production of such an existent [*eines solchen Seienden*] as has not been before and will never be again" (H, 48).

Heidegger's description of the primal power of endowed truth reveals that his excitement of 1933, when he experienced the National Socialist revolution as the complete work of art of state-founding action, had not yet abated. "The putting-into-work of truth bursts open the uncanny and simultaneously overturns the canny and what one regards as it. The truth opening up in a work cannot be attested or derived from anything that was before. The Before in its exclusive reality is refuted by the work" (H, 61). These statements, seen from Heidegger's point of view, apply equally to the political work of art of the revolution and to a Greek temple, a tragedy by Sophocles, a fragment of Heraclitus, or a poem by Hölderlin. In each case it is a creative action that transfers man into a transformed relationship to reality; he gains a new scope, a different relation to Being. Yet every founding deed is subject to the law of aging and becoming ordinary. That which had revealed itself once more shuts itself off. This is what Heidegger experienced with the political revolution. "The beginning is the strangest and mightiest. What comes afterward is not development but the flattening that results from mere spreading out; it is inability to retain the beginning; the beginning is emasculated and exaggerated" (EM, 119).[6] The initial breakout from the modern world, however, has stalled, and it is up to thinking in alliance with poetry to keep open the "scope" (H, 110) for an entirely different relation to Being. What the precise nature of this "entirely different relation" is was formulated by Heidegger in his ideology article as the overcoming of "being-the-subject," or, more accurately, "that mankind's being-the-subject never was the only possibility of the incipient essence of historical man, nor ever will be" (H, 109).

But here Heidegger finds himself in serious trouble—the overcoming of being-the-subject is to be opened up by thought and poetry that spring from the will to the work. The work, however, is an expression of supremely activist attunement. After all, what is it that the poets and thinkers are doing? "Against the overwhelming chaos they set the barrier of their work, and in their work they capture the world thus opened up" (EM, 47).[7] Is not Heidegger's will to the work a particularly crass subjective empowerment? Is one not tempted to identify this will to the work with Nietzsche's will to power, which can also be understood as a subjective empowerment? Are not both of them subjective objections and claims to power against the rampant modern nihilism that both Heidegger and Nietzsche have diagnosed?

Heidegger, who in his rectorial address had explicitly appropriated Nietzsche's diagnosis "God is dead," is very much aware of his closeness to Nietzsche. In his ideology article he sees him as a thinker who had almost, but only almost, succeeded in overcoming the new age. There he summarizes a central idea of his Nietzsche lectures given after 1936—Nietzsche got stuck in his thinking on new-age values. The age he had hoped to overcome had eventually defeated him and spoiled his best ideas. Heidegger intends to understand Nietzsche better than he had understood himself. He hopes to overtake him on the way to a new thinking about Being. In this endeavor he cannot avoid discussing the appropriation of Nietzsche by Nazi ideologists such as Alfred Baeumler. Such an appropriation was by no means uncontroversial among the hard-line Nazi ideologists. Ernst Krieck, for instance, sarcastically warned against an adaptation of Nietzsche. "All in all, Nietzsche was an opponent of socialism, an opponent of nationalism, and an opponent of the idea of race. If one overlooks these three intellectual trends he might perhaps have made an outstanding Nazi."[8]

Arthur Drews, professor of philosophy in Karlsruhe, was absolutely outraged in 1934 about the Nietzsche renaissance. Nietzsche, he said, was an "enemy of everything German," he championed the development of a "good European," and in this process actually assigned to the Jews "a key role in the fusion of all nations." He was an out-and-out individualist, and nothing could be further from him "than the National Socialist principle that the common good comes before personal advantage. In view of all this it seems downright incredible that Nietzsche is now elevated to the role of philosopher of National Socialism, considering that he preaches . . . in virtually all things the opposite of National Socialism." The fact that such an elevation was nevertheless being practiced "probably . . . has its main reason in the fact . . . that most people today who make statements about Nietzsche are only picking the 'raisins' out of the cake of his 'philosophy' and, given his aphoristic way of writing, have no clear idea at all about the context of his thoughts."[9]

It was Alfred Baeumler who, in his impressive book *Nietzsche, the Philoso-*

pher and Politician (1931), skillfully succeeded both in picking out the "raisins" and yet keeping the "context of his thoughts" in sight. He exploited the philosophy of the will to power and Nietzsche's experimenting with the biologism of his day. Darwinism of vital forces, the idea of a master race and of the creative urge that uses human conglomerates as a moldable material, the invalidation of morality by vital decisionism—from these elements Baeumler mapped out his philosophy of Nietzsche, for which, admittedly, he could not use the teaching of the eternal return of the same. "In truth this idea, viewed from Nietzsche's system, is irrelevant," he wrote. With Nietzsche, Baeumler hoped to put an end to traditional metaphysics. There was no transcendent world of values and ideas, and of course no God; there was only a base of urges. Baeumler merely needed to radicalize Nietzsche's physiological interpretation until, eventually, it turned into "race" and "blood."

The mystique of blood and race is, in point of fact, a possible consequence of a physiologically understood will to power. This is realized also by Heidegger, even if, unlike Baeumler, he assesses that consequence negatively.

> For Nietzsche, subjectivity is absolute as the subjectivity of the body, that is, of drives and affects; that is to say, of will to power . . . The absolute essence of subjectivity necessarily develops as the *brutalitas* of *bestialitas*. At the end of metaphysics stands the statement: *Homo est brutum bestiale* [Man is a brutish beast]. Nietzsche's phrase about the "blond beast" is not a casual exaggeration, but the password and countersign for a context in which he consciously stood, without being able to peer through its essential historical connections (N II, 200).[10]

The glorification of the "blond beast," according to Heidegger, is the nihilistic consequence of the "rebellion of the subject." Heidegger himself had been accused of nihilism by the Nazi philosophers. Krieck, as quoted in an earlier chapter, wrote in 1934: "The meaning of this philosophy is downright atheism and metaphysical nihilism of the kind that used to be represented in our country mainly by Jewish literati, in other words, an enzyme of decomposition and dissolution for the German people."[11] In his Nietzsche lectures Heidegger turned the tables on the Nazi philosophers by trying to demonstrate that the will to power, to which they referred, was not the overcoming but the perfection of nihilism, even though the Nietzsche followers were unaware of this. Thus Heidegger's Nietzsche lectures represent a frontal attack on the traditional metaphysics of racism and biologism. Heidegger concedes that Nietzsche is partially usable for the reigning ideology, while distancing himself from it. At the same time, he endeavors to proceed from Nietzsche, but in such a way that he presents his own thinking as an overcoming of Nietzsche in Nietzsche's footsteps.

Nietzsche had wanted to overthrow traditional metaphysics by proceeding from a profoundly metaphysical thesis that, in Schelling's formulation, ran: "Volition is primal Being." Nietzsche understands the will differently from the tradition down to Schopenhauer. Will is not desire, a dull urge, but it is "ability to command," a force that can let Being grow. "Volition is the same as wanting-to-be-stronger, wanting to grow."

Will is the will to enhance the vital power. To Nietzsche, self-preservation is possible only in the logic of enhancement. Whatever has no more than the strength of self-preservation goes under. It is preserved only if it enhances itself, intensifies, expands. That which lives has no transcendental meaning, but it has an immanent sense of direction—it aims at intensification and success. It attempts to integrate the strange into its own power sphere and its own shape. That which lives functions by overpowering. It is an energetic process and as such "meaningless," because it does not relate to any superior goal. Is it therefore nihilistic? Nietzsche presents his teachings as the overcoming of nihilism through its perfection.

He wants to perfect nihilism by revealing the secret nihilism in the long history of metaphysical meaning giving. People, Nietzsche argued, had always viewed something as a "value" if it served the maintenance and enhancement of their own will to power or the repulse of superior powers. Behind every value definition and value statement there was, therefore, the will to power. This was true also of the "highest values"—God, ideas, the transcendental. Over a long time, however, this will to power had not been transparent to itself. It had embroidered something self-made with the aura of a superhuman origin. People thought they had discovered independent essences when in fact they had merely invented them—from the will to power. They had misread their own value-creating energy. They evidently preferred to be victims and receivers of gifts rather than agents and givers—possibly from fear of their own freedom. This fundamental devaluation of their own value-creating energy was further enhanced through the established transcendental values. Proceeding from the transcendental, they had devalued the body and finitude. Evidently they had lacked the courage for finitude. To that extent, therefore, those transcendental values, invented as a bulwark against the threat of nullity and finitude, have themselves become the force for the nihilistic devaluation of life. Under the heaven of ideas, Nietzsche said, humans never properly came into the world. This heaven of ideas he now hoped to bring crashing down—this was the perfection of nihilism—so that mankind could at last learn what it meant to "remain faithful to the earth." This was the overcoming of nihilism.

God is dead but the rigor of humility remains; this was Nietzsche's diagnosis, and the "monstrous" task he speaks of consisted in the removal of that rigor of humility, in the breakthrough toward an intoxicating, euphoric "Yes" to Dionysian life. Homage to earthly life is what matters to Nietzsche. In this he hopes to differ from the nihilism of mere sobering up. Modern nihilism loses the Beyond without gaining the Here. Nietzsche, however, wants to teach the art of winning if one loses. All the ecstasy, all the bliss, all the soaring of feeling, all the intensities that used to be associated with the Beyond are to be concentrated in this life. The forces of transcendence are to be preserved, but redirected into immanence. Transcending, but "remaining faithful to earth"—that is what Nietzsche expects of his superman, of the man of the future. Nietzsche's superman is free from religion, though not in the sense of having lost it; he has taken it back within himself. Thus his teaching of the eternal return of the same has no mark of resigned wistfulness. The whirligig of time will not empty events into pointlessness and futility, but the idea of return should intensify them. Nietzsche's imperative is: You should so live the moment that you can wish for it to return to you without horror. Once more from the beginning!

Now back to Heidegger. He goes along with Nietzsche in the critique of idealism and in his call to "remain faithful to the earth." But on just this point he criticizes Nietzsche, accusing him of not having remained faithful to the earth with his philosophy of the will to power. To Heidegger, "remaining faithful to the earth" means not to forget Being over one's involvement in the existent. Nietzsche, Heidegger argues, proceeding from the principle of the will to power, drew everything into the sphere of value-assessing man. The Being, with which man is concerned, and which he himself is, was viewed entirely as a "value." Being was, regrettably, lost, because it always had "value" for him. Nietzsche wanted man to encourage himself for himself, to straighten up. Heidegger argues that this straightening up had turned into uprising, into a rebellion of technology and of the masses, who, thanks to technological control, were now entirely becoming what Nietzsche had called the "last humans," who, "blinking their eyes," were settling back in their small happiness and defending themselves with extreme brutality against any impairment of their security or their possessions. "Man turns to rebellion," Heidegger says, also with an eye to the German present, "the world becomes an object . . . The earth itself can only show itself as the object of attack . . . Nature everywhere appears . . . as the object of technology." According to Heidegger all this is foreshadowed in Nietzsche because, with him, Being is viewed only from the point of view of aesthetic, theoretical, ethical, and practical values, and therefore is missed. For the will to power, the world is reduced to the quintessence of "preservation and enhancement conditions."

But, asks Heidegger, "Can Being be estimated higher than being specifically elevated to a 'value'?" He answers: "Even by being appreciated as a 'value,' Being is already reduced to a condition set by the will to power itself," and as a result "the road to the experience of Being itself is expunged."

"Experience of Being"—as has been shown—does not mean experience of a higher world but experience of the inexhaustibility of reality and astonishment over the fact that in its midst an "open place" has revealed itself, where nature opens its eyes and notices that it is there. In the experience of Being, man discovers himself and his play space. He is not captured or trapped in the existent *(im Seienden)*. Amid the things he has free "play," just as a wheel must have "play" at its hub in order to move. The problem of Being, Heidegger states, is ultimately "a problem of freedom."

The experience of Being is expunged wherever individuals or entire cultures, in their various rituals of dealing with reality, have gone rigid—theoretically, practically, morally—when they are "dazed" by their own concept and have lost the awareness of the relativity of this Being-relation, and with it the strength for transcending it. It is a relativity with regard to the "great hidden flow" of time (Heidegger) on which our truths and cultures are drifting like fragile rafts.

Being, therefore, is not something that redeems us; Being is, to put it without pathos, the limiting concept and quintessence of all practiced, all thinkable and also still unthinkable Being-relations. The history of Being is thus for Heidegger a historical sequence of fundamental Being-relations. In his ideology article Heidegger had given an outline of this sequence of Being-relations—one might also say cultural paradigms. The sequence itself does not realize any "higher meaning" lying beyond it. To Heidegger this is more like playing with the possibilities. In a later essay he says: "Being has no ground, it acts as an abyss . . . Thinking, by performing a leap, gets into the vastness of that game on which our human essence is staked."

To Heidegger the thinking of Being is that "playful" movement of holding open for the infinite horizon of possible Being-relations. That is why one must not ask him about what Being is, for that would be asking for a definition of something that is itself the horizon of all possible definitions. And because the question about Being is this opening up of the horizon, its meaning cannot be in being answered. One of Heidegger's formulas for evading the insistent request for an answer to the question about Being reads, in the Nietzsche lectures, "Being has nothing about it." In other words, Being is nothing that one can hold on to. It is, compared with the solid and security-offering ideologies, that which simply dissolves. The question about Being is meant to prevent the world from becoming a world picture. When Heidegger discovered that this "Being" *(Sein)* might itself become a world picture, he spelled it *Seyn,* with a *y,* or else he used the device of spelling out *Sein* and then crossing it out. To Heidegger, Nietzsche was still a world-picture philosopher.

In actual fact, this thinking operates with particular picturelike plasticity in the doctrine of the eternal return of the same. This idea does away with the dimension of time by rounding it into a circle, despite the fact that Nietzsche, taking up Heraclitus's "becoming," really intended to push thinking out into time. Here probably lies the crux of the contrast between Nietzsche and Heidegger—Nietzsche thinks of time in the dynamic of the will to power and rounds it back into Being in his thesis of the eternal return. Heidegger tries to hold on to the thought that the meaning of Being is time. Nietzsche makes time a Being; Heidegger makes Being into time.

The Japanese philosopher Nishida has described religions, meaning creations, and cultures as fragile rafts that men build on the open sea and on which they drift through the ages. Nietzsche, in Heidegger's view, intoxicated by his inventive work and by his triumph over completing his raft, has failed to consider the tides and the open sea. That is oblivion-of-Being *(Seinsvergessenheit).* Heidegger, for his part, wants to gaze out on the sea, and that is why he is reminded, by the question about Being, of the swaying of things.

However—as Karl Löwith pointed out in a critique of Heidegger's Nietzsche lectures—it must remain questionable which of the two, Heidegger or Nietzsche, was more radical in pushing his thinking out into the open and which of them eventually sought support in something transcendent. To

Nietzsche, at any rate, the all-transcending Dionysian life was not a load-bearing base but an abyss, dangerous to our Apollonian attempts at self-consolidation. Perhaps Nietzsche would have accused Heidegger of a lack of radicalism in overcoming the need for security. Perhaps he would have regarded Heidegger's Being merely as a Platonic behind-world offered to us for protection and safety.

In discussing the theory of the eternal return, Heidegger suggests that Nietzsche may have withheld his best insights because, for some of his ideas, there had not yet come a "place for unfolding" (N I, 264). He quotes a sentence by Nietzsche: "One no longer loves one's insight sufficiently once one has communicated it" (N I, 265).

Heidegger's comment on Nietzsche's silence is so understanding that one instantly realizes that Heidegger is here also pleading his own case. "If our knowledge were confined to what Nietzsche himself published, we would never discover what Nietzsche already knew or was getting ready or consistently thinking through, but kept to himself. Only study of the handwritten papers provides a clear picture" (N I, 266).

At the time Heidegger made this remark, he was himself working on a manuscript that he "withheld," on ideas for which he evidently did not think the time to publish had yet come—his *Beiträge zur Philosophie* (Contributions to Philosophy), with the subtitle *Vom Ereignis* (On Happening).

18

THE PHILOSOPHICAL DIARY AND PHILOSOPHICAL ROSARY

In about 1938 the official version of Heidegger's ideas on Being was: "There is nothing to Being." Being withdraws when we attempt to get hold of it directly, because anything that we get hold of thereby becomes something that is—an object that we transfer to the order of our knowledge or our values, that we categorize or dissect, that we can establish as a yardstick or pass on appellatively. None of this is Being, but all of this exists because we stand in a relationship to Being. It is the open horizon in which the existent encounters us. And the question about Being does not look for some supreme being that at one time used to be called God; instead the question is designed to create the distance that permits us to experience this relation. However, this experience transforms us. Man discovers that in relation to the world he is "free," a "free region" has opened up within him.

In one of the Nietzsche lectures there is a dark hint that leads us onto the track of a different version of Heidegger's question about Being. "As soon as man lets himself be bound by Being in his view upon it, he is cast beyond himself, so that he is stretched, as it were, between himself and Being and is outside himself. Such elevation beyond himself and such being drawn toward Being itself is erōs" (N I, 226).[1]

His *Beiträge zur Philosophie* (Contributions to Philosophy), written between 1936 and 1938 and not originally intended for publication, forms a single document of this philosophical Eros. Heidegger wishes to be "transported" beyond himself. By what? By the exercises of his own thinking. Where to? Hard to say if one wants to exclude the ideas about the God of the Christian Occident. And yet the *Contributions* continually refer to God, albeit to a God unknown to tradition in this form. He springs from the thinking about Being. God who is believed to have created Being out of Nothingness is, in Heidegger, himself created out of Nothingness. He is produced by ecstatic thought.

In his *Contributions* we see Heidegger transporting himself into that "other state" with a delirium of concepts and a litany of sentences. The *Contributions* are a laboratory for the invention of a new way of speaking about God. They are a diary in which Heidegger records his experiments to discover whether it is possible to create a religion without a positive doctrine.

Initially Heidegger proceeds along the classical model of founding a religion—the invention of a new God begins with the staging of a twilight of the idols. The false gods must yield, the space must be swept clear. To this end Heidegger develops his by now familiar critique of modern thought. This critique results in the finding that God, too, has become a disposable object of reason or imagination. As the ideas of God were fading in the modern age, they were being replaced by substitute ideas about the highest value, the *prima causa,* or the meaning of history. All that would have to disappear, for it belonged to the register of the existent, but the existent must "collapse and fall" before Being *(das Seyn)* can emerge.

These exercises in thinking about Being thus proceed from a discovery. In just the way Meister Eckhart and Jakob Böhme had wanted to experience their God, Heidegger was to fill the empty heart with his reality.

What God, then, arrives in Heidegger's emptied thinking? Carefully he reveals his secret. "Let us have the courage for the direct word," he writes. "Being is the trembling of Godding" *(Das Seyn ist die Erzitterung des Götterns)* (GA 65, 239).

Words, newly invented words. Can Heidegger mean anything by them? He tries to establish meaning, in several hundred pages. A God or a Being, whether spelled *Sein* or *Seyn,* will find it difficult to reveal itself if it is not allowed to reveal itself as "something." Visualizing thought surely begins with "what something is," but this is just what is supposed to be forbidden in thinking about Being. Even in the Jewish religion, with its prohibition of images, God at least is something that says "I" to itself: "I am that which I am." Heidegger's Being, however, is not a transcendental "I-ness." It is not anything confronting *Dasein* but something that proceeds in it. To avoid the idea of a substantial God, Heidegger speaks of "Godding" in the sense of a happening that causes us to "tremble"—hence not God or gods, but "Godding." When Godding happens to us, we not only tremble but also experience a whole range of moods—"fright, restrainedness, mildness, jubilation, awe." From this "ore of fundamental moods" the "essential thinking" extracts its thoughts and sentences. "If the fundamental mood fails to arise, all is forced chatter of concepts and verbal husks" (GA 65, 21).

Heidegger fills page upon page with his thinking about Being, but since these fundamental moods, as Heidegger himself emphasizes, are rare and momentary, his sentences all too often do not spring from the mood but instead endeavor to create the mood. This is the essence of the litany with which Heidegger, the Catholic backslider, is all too familiar. The *Contributions* are his rosary. Hence the repetitive formulas, the monotonous mantras, which seem monotonous only to he who is not touched or "transformed" by them. What matters is the transforming power, and here the barrel organ of sentences plays a vital part. What else are these continually recited sentences than sentences that no longer state anything, in which, therefore, silence can spread. Heidegger calls this "attainment of silence" *(Erschweigung)* the "logic of philosophy," provided that philosophy wants to get close to Being (GA 65, 78). One should therefore not be surprised when in one of his Nietzsche lectures Heidegger demonstrates, with the example of Zarathustra, how, for the person not gripped, the "doctrine" must turn into "a mere ditty, into empty talk" (N I, 310).[2] Here no doubt he is pleading his own case. The "mere ditty" is a method of eloquent "attainment of silence."

In his introductory notes to the *Contributions* Heidegger states: "Here there is no describing and no explicating; here stating is not confronting that which is to be stated, but it is this itself as the essence of Being [*die Wesung des Seyns*]" (GA 65, 4). In Heidegger the *Seyn* speaks just as the world spirit did in Hegel—a bold claim, and stated so openly only in these secret notes.

But how does the *Seyn* speak? This devotional litany of stating, this mumbling about the "fugue of the truth of *Seyn*," the "trembling of its essence," and the "relaxed mildness of the intimacy of that Godding of the God of gods" (GA 65, 4), this whole metaphysical dadaism, is, in terms of semantic content, Nothing. This, of course, may not be a bad statement about a God who withdraws and whom thought tries to follow in that very withdrawal. Heidegger's *Contributions,* insofar as they directly address Being, are the reflection of a kind of thinking that suffers from withdrawal symptoms. (The Heidegger school, incidentally, no longer has this problem. It is, as a rule, dried out.)

So long as Heidegger is deconstructing the philosophical tradition, his ideas, even in the *Contributions,* are precise and poignant—which, of course, they can be because they address a real object. But the emptiness that follows, and is designed to follow, such deconstruction remains empty. There is no new fulfillment.

This would not matter so much if Heidegger were able to fall back on faith. But he tries to produce the fulfilling event out of thinking. He no longer holds the position of his 1927 Marburg lecture, "Phenomenology and Theology." Then, in good Lutheran manner, he had strictly separated thinking and faith. Faith, then, was the undisposable event of God penetrating into man's life. Thinking could do no more than determine the point of penetration. The event of God itself was not a matter for thinking.

Yet in his *Contributions* Heidegger dedicates himself to just that ambitious project of experiencing the presence of the divine through thinking. However, since the divine will not assume any clear shape in thinking, Heidegger has to content himself with the brief statement: "Proximity to the last God is concealment by silence [*Verschweigung*]" (GA 65, 12). And, like John the Baptist, he points to a coming God and describes himself as a "precursor," or a "provisional" *(ein Vorläufiger).* Waiting for Godot began in Heidegger's *Contributions.*

Vom Ereignis (On Happening) is the subtitle of *Beiträge zur Philosophie.* Strictly speaking, it deals with two "happenings." The first is the happening of the modern age, the age of ideologies, technology, organizations, "manipulation"—in short, "the age of consummate meaninglessness." It is the fateful connection of oblivion of Being, whose prerequisites go back as far as Plato. The second happening—the end of the modern age, the turning point—is taking shape in Heidegger's thinking on Being. The first happening is the one he speaks about, because he believes that he has, at least in part, wriggled out of it. The other happening is one out of which he speaks; it prepares a new epoch, but in the meantime it is the happening of a solitary person, which is why Heidegger attempts an alliterative chain of words, some of them of his own invention, beginning with happening *(Ereignis)* and ending with solitude *(Einsamkeit)*—"Happening always means Happening [*Er-eignis*] as appropriation [*Er-eignung*], decision [*Ent-scheidung*], riposte [*Ent-gegnung*], deposition [*Ent-setzung*], withdrawal [*Ent-zug*], simplicity [*Einfachheit*], uniqueness [*Einzigkeit*], solitude [*Einsamkeit*]" (GA 65, 471). With his solitary thinking on Being, Heidegger has set out to catch a god. "The happening [*Er-eignis*] and its jointing [*Erfügung*] into the abyss of time-space is the net in which the last God hangs himself [or catches himself—*hängt* or *fängt*—both readings are possible from the handwritten text], in order to tear it up and let it end in its uniqueness, divine and odd and the most strange in all that is" (GA 65, 263).

Heidegger, of course, was aware of the strangeness, indeed the nonsense, of his language. Carl Friedrich von Weizsäcker once told him the Jewish anecdote about a man who perpetually sits in a tavern. When asked why he does so, he answers: "Well, it's my wife." "What about your wife?" "Oh, she talks and talks and talks . . ." "What does she talk about?" "That she doesn't say." When Heidegger heard the story he said, "Yes, that's how it is."[3]

That is how it is with the *Contributions*. They are, as a whole, strictly structured, even though in detail they contain some aphoristic and fragmentary passages. For "structuring" Heidegger uses "interlocking" *(fügen)*. The whole thing is to be a "fugue." A fugue with two principal voices; these are the two "happenings" that sound harmonically and contrapuntally and eventually end in the unison of the cleared *(gelichtet)* Being. The sequence of the sections is to suggest the road of approach. The "forward gaze" covers the entire stretch of the road through the thicket to the clearing. The "accord" substantivizes the Being at the stage of oblivion-of-Being—that is, the present. The "pass" tells the story of how, time and again in Western metaphysics, there have been echoes and surmises of Being. The "leap" contains reflections on how matters of self-evidence and accustomed thought have to be jettisoned before the crucial step can be taken, which is not a step but a risky leap. In the "foundation," Heidegger concerns himself mainly with his analysis of *Dasein* from *Being and Time*, a self-interpretation that assigns the work to the moment when the leap has been made and one tries once more to get a foothold. In the sections "The Future Ones" ("Die Zu-Künftigen") and "The Last God" ("Der letzte Gott") a kind of ascension takes place. In the final section, "Being"

("Das Seyn"), the whole is once more viewed from above, to ascertain how far one has got and how high one has climbed. "What summits do we have to scale to get a free overview of man in his essential distress [*Wesensnot*]?" (GA 65, 491).

Heidegger had meanwhile come to realize that National Socialism had been unable to change anything about this "essential distress." Quite the opposite—it was part of the "manipulation" and the total mobilization of the modern age. What it offered was "most shallow sentimentality" and "a drunkenness with experience" *(Erlebnistrunkenholdigkeit)* (GA 65, 67). However, this critique applies to the whole period. The intellectual and practical tendencies opposing National Socialism are similarly rejected from the perspective of thinking about Being. The whole is the untrue. No matter whether the different ideologies support the "I" or the "We," the proletariat or the people, whether they aim at preserving the humanism of enlightenment or traditional Christianity as a value, whether they pose as nationalist, internationalist, revolutionary, or conservative—all these distinctions are null and void, because in all cases what matters is that "the subject (man)" props himself up into "the center of the existent" (GA 65, 443). The self-legislation by man is called by Heidegger "liberalism," and ethnic biologism and racism can thus be called by him "biological liberalism." In this night of thinking about Being, all cats, viewed politically, are gray. The clearing exists only around Heidegger. Heidegger against the rest of the world—this is how he sees himself in the dialogue of the *Contributions.*

It is interesting that Heidegger philosophizes not only "out of" the happening of thinking about Being, but—perhaps even more often—"about" himself, as though about a Being-historical fact. Upon his imaginary stage he sees himself acting the role of the "seeker, preserver, custodian" (GA 65, 17). He regards himself as belonging to the circle of those "who summon the supreme courage to solitude, in order to think the nobility of the *Seyn*" (GA 65, 11).

He indulges in fantasies of how thinking about Being might gradually penetrate the body of society through the establishment of a league. This would consist—in the innermost circles—of "those few individuals who preestablish the place and the moments for the realms of the existent." A wider circle would be represented by "those more numerous league members" who allow themselves to be gripped by the charisma of the great "individual" and who place themselves in the service of the "re-creation of the existent." Finally, there are "those numerous directed toward each other," those who, united by common historical origin, willingly allow themselves to be fitted into the new order of things. This "transformation" should take place in complete silence, away from the "noise of the 'world-historical' upheavals," which to Heidegger are no upheavals (GA 65, 96). Heidegger paints for himself an "authentic" history that unrolls in concealment and whose witness and author he is, at one and the same time.

One would be looking in vain for a specific vision of the new order in his *Contributions.* Heidegger escapes into metaphor. "The great philosophies," he says, which provide the people with a spiritual place of abiding, are like the "towering mountains. They grant a country that which is highest and they indicate its primal rock. They stand as the point of orientation and invariably establish the range of vision" (GA 65, 187).

If it is Heidegger's dream to stand, with his philosophy, "as a mountain among mountains," if he hopes to "achieve something essential" in order that the people in the plains should be able to orient themselves by the "towering" of his philosophy, then this shows that, even though Heidegger's political intoxication with power may have evaporated, his philosophy is still infected with ideas of power. Hence his images of petrifaction. In the 1920s he had used a very different pattern of metaphors; then he had intended to "liquefy" the petrified edifice of thought. Now he lets it tower. Now he sends his own philosophy up into the "mountains of *Seyn.*"

Strictly speaking, this runs counter to the idea of philosophy evolved by Heidegger prior to 1933. Then he was concerned with the free—albeit finite—mobility of a way of thinking that rises from the fact of Being-in-the-world in order to illumine *Dasein* for a while and then to disappear with it again—thinking as an event, as equally contingent as *Dasein* itself. Now his mountain metaphors clearly indicate that Heidegger wishes to inscribe himself and his philosophy on an enduring world, that he wishes to participate in something that towers above his accidental existence and the historical situation. This tendency toward the towering contradicts his philosophy of finitude. The process of the clearing becomes an event of epiphany that involves a sphere that used to be labeled "the eternal" or "the transcendental." The solitary philosopher, who works on his writings day after day, does not wish to be alone with his ideas. He seeks contact—now no longer with a political movement but with the ominous spirit of a history of Being or a destiny of Being. In the imaginary arena of Being, great and enduring things are happening, and Heidegger is in the midst of them.

While he is thus gazing out toward the great and the whole, reflecting himself in it, no philosophical attention remains for his personal life or his real actions. He does not submit to self-examination, once a philosophical discipline of high repute—or at least not in his *Contributions.* He considers the wholesale mischief of "oblivion of Being," but he disregards his own contingency without even noticing it. He remains in his own blind spot. He hopes to bring light into the condition of the world with his question about Being, but his own self-relation remains obscured.

Heidegger had always avoided applying the question about Being to his own *Dasein.* Even though in a letter to Jaspers of July 1, 1935, he admitted that he had "two stakes," and very troublesome ones, sticking in his flesh—"the conflict with the faith of his origin and the failure of his rectorship"—the *Contributions* reveal his skill in avoiding himself as the leading actor in his own historical drama. Habermas has called this method "abstraction by essentialization"—an accurate definition. The loss of the faith of his origin is reinterpreted and upgraded into an epochal destiny, and the failure of his rectorship becomes an honorable defeat in the struggle against the frenzy of the modern age.

Is it that the thinker on the stage of the history of Being regards a moral self-examination as being beneath him? Perhaps this is still a legacy of his Catholic origins, the fact that Protestant pangs of conscience are unknown to him. Certainly, to be able to hold on to the concept of the whole and to his thinking, he separates it from the purely personal. Thus he is able, with a strange indifference, to watch how the movement that once filled him with such enthusiasm is leading, even in his immediate surroundings, to consequences that to him are no longer acceptable. One only has to remember the fate of Hannah Arendt, Elisabeth Blochmann, or Edmund Husserl.

After the end of World War II in 1945, Hannah Arendt and Karl Jaspers agreed in their correspondence that Heidegger was evidently a person whose moral sensibility was not up to the passion of his thinking. Jaspers wrote: "Can one, as an impure soul—that is, as a soul that is unaware of its impurity and not permanently trying to escape from it, but thoughtlessly continuing to live in the dirt—can one see the most pure in insincerity? . . . It is strange that he knows about something that people today hardly notice" (September 9, 1949, BwAJ, 177). Hannah Arendt replied: "What you call impurity, I would call lack of character, but in the sense that he literally has none, certainly not a particularly bad one. And yet he lives in a profundity and with a passion that one cannot easily forget" (September 29, 1949, BwAJ, 178).

Lack of moral reflection, however, is not just an aspect of character but also a philosophical problem, because what is lacking in thinking is the composure that takes Heidegger's often invoked "finitude" seriously. Part of it is the fact that one can make oneself guilty and that one accepts such contingent guilt as a challenge to *Dasein*. There is no room in the *Contributions* for the venerable philosophical discipline of self-reflection and self-examination. As a result, the ideal of "authentic existence" is missed—the transparency of *Dasein* for itself. Heidegger's famous silence is also an inner concealment, almost a kind of obduracy against himself—and also a contribution to oblivion of Being.

In an ambiguous manner, the power of Heidegger's thought passes over him. For one thing, it disregards the entirely commonplace person of the thinker, and for another it overcomes the thinker.

Heidegger, according to Georg Picht's recollection, was "filled with the awareness of being, as it were, struck with the mission of thinking." He had at times felt "threatened by what he had to think himself."[4] Another contemporary witness, Hans A. Fischer-Barnicol, who made Heidegger's acquaintance after the war, recalls: "It seemed to me as if the thinking of this old man took possession of him as of a medium. It spoke out of him."[5] Hermann Heidegger, his son, confirms this impression. His father, he reports, would sometimes say to him: "It thinks in me. I cannot resist it."

Heidegger used similar terms in his letters to Elisabeth Blochmann. On April 12, 1938, he described to her his loneliness. He did not complain about it but accepted it as the outward consequence of the fact that he was marked by the "fate of thinking" and thereby also singled out. "Solitude does not arise from or consist of the nonarrival of someone who belongs, but in the arrival of a different truth, in the assault of the plenitude of the only-surprising and unique" (BwHB, 91).

This is what he writes at a time when he jots down the following ideas in his *Contributions:* "The *Seyn* is God's peril in which alone he finds himself. But why God? Whence the peril? Because the abyss is hidden? Because he is a surpassing, and the surpassed therefore are, in a sense, the higher ones. Whence the surpassing, the abyss, the ground, the Being? In what does the godhead of the gods consist? Why the *Seyn?* Because of the gods? Why the gods? Because of the *Seyn?*" (GA 65, 508).

He gets over the "strangeness" of his own sentences by following Nietzsche's example in approaching the undiscovered strangeness of the great thinkers. "Altogether I am only now, in the most strange of all great thinkers, learning to experience their true proximity. This helps toward seeing the strange in oneself and bringing it into play, because it evidently is the origin of all the essential that succeeds—if it succeeds" (letter to Elisabeth Blochmann, April 14, 1937, BwHB, 90).

In another letter to Blochmann he describes his alternation between his official teaching activities, where he had to make concessions to comprehensibility and thus got onto an alien "track," and his "backswing into what is [his] own and the authentic" (December 20, 1935, BwHB, 87). The *Contributions* certainly belong to the innermost sphere of this "own." However, as will have become clear by now, this was not a thinker's encounter with himself but something entirely different—this was not a thinking about Being but a thinking by Being. The Being takes control of him and thinks through him. His is a quasi-medium existence.

Heidegger torments himself, but there is also happiness. It is significant that in his *Contributions,* more often than in his other writings, there is mention of "jubilation." Being encounters us also in "jubilation." Anxiety, boredom, and jubilation—this, in the *Contributions,* is the holy trinity of the experience of Being. In jubilation *Dasein* becomes that heaven whither the world and the things will go when they reveal themselves in their astonishment-causing "That."

To preserve this "open place" of *Dasein,* thinking must withdraw and ensure that this openness is not obstructed by all kinds of imaginings. To think is to settle down and become "still." But Heidegger does not find his way out of the paradox of verbose silence. Moreover, there is the tradition of the great thinkers. A whole mountain range towers into the clearing. Would it not first have to be worn down? In this work he sees that a mass of unmined treasure awaits him here. This is what happens to him with all the "great ones." After two decades of intensive occupation with Plato, he said to Georg Picht at the end of the 1930s: "I have to confess one thing to you; the structure of Platonic thought is totally obscure to me."

In a letter to Blochmann of June 27, 1936, he describes his dilemma: "It seems that the struggle for the preservation of tradition is wearing us down; to create something of one's own and to preserve the great—to do both is beyond human strength. And yet that preservation is not strong enough unless it springs from new acquisition. There is no way out of this circle, and so it happens that one's own work seems important at one time and soon afterwards entirely indifferent and bungling" (BwHB, 89).

In his letters to Jaspers he emphasizes this feeling of bungling. On May 16, 1936, in his last letter before he broke off the relationship for a decade, he wrote that, face to face with the great philosophers, one's "own wriggling [became] very unimportant and served merely as a makeshift" (BwHJ, 161).

In his letters to Blochmann, and more especially in his *Contributions,* Heidegger displays another mood—a sense, at times even euphoric, of great achievement and of the great significance of his work. At those moments he believes that "the advent of another truth" has taken place in him.

19

HEIDEGGER UNDER SURVEILLANCE

"The pressure of external matters is abating," Heidegger wrote to Elisabeth Blochmann on April 14, 1937 (BwHB, 90). What were these external matters? The Göttingen chair that had been held by Georg Misch, the compulsorily retired son-in-law of Dilthey, was to be filled. In July 1935 the philosophy faculty put Heidegger's name in first place on the proposal list. With Heidegger, the assessment signed by the dean stated, "we would have the privilege of welcoming at the same time one of the first figures in contemporary German philosophy . . . and a thinker ready to work in the direction of the National Socialist concept of the world."[1]

Meanwhile, however, the Ministry of Education had become aware that Heidegger, while continuing to support National Socialism in important political respects (foreign policy, economy, labor service, the führer principle), by no means supported the National Socialist concept of the world. For this reason the ministry notified the faculty that it proposed to nominate Professor Heyse from Königsberg to succeed Misch. The faculty thereupon hurriedly modified its original proposal in favor of Heyse. Even though Heidegger had not been interested in a move to Göttingen, he felt slighted. In terms of philosophy Heyse was an epigone of Heidegger and, at the same time, a stout and politically skillful Nazi. He was the president of the Kant Society, imposed from above on the famous worldwide association of philosophers, and he would be the leader of the German delegation to the international philosophy congress in Paris in 1937.

The affront he suffered in Göttingen confirmed Heidegger in the belief that he was no longer in favor among the political circles that mattered. But he still—and right up to the end—had his supporters in the political power apparatus; there can be no other explanation for the fact that, before the year was out, the ministry in Berlin intended to appoint him dean of the philosophy faculty in Freiburg. This did not in fact happen, however, as the rector then in office opposed the move. According to Victor Farías, "During his rectorate, Heidegger lost the confidence of his colleagues. The administration of the region of Baden also had troubles with him."[2]

The political authorities wanted to make use of Heidegger's international prestige, despite their increasing reservations about his philosophy. In October 1935 he was requested to join a committee charged with the preparation of a new edition of Nietzsche. Heidegger received numerous invitations for lectures abroad and was not prevented from accepting them. At the beginning of 1936 he spoke in Zurich, and he spoke later that year in Rome; in the early 1940s he was due to give lectures in Spain, Portugal, and Italy. He had declared himself ready and had even announced his subjects, but the dates kept being postponed until, in the final stage of the war, they were no longer realizable.

At the beginning of April 1936 Heidegger accepted an invitation from the Istituto italiano di studi germanici in Rome. The plan originally envisaged his giving several lectures in Rome, Padua, and Milan. However, Heidegger confined himself to Rome, where he remained for ten days, speaking to a large audience on "Hölderlin and the Nature of Poetry." On this occasion he met with Karl Löwith, who, although he was an émigré from Germany, had also been invited by the Italians to give a lecture.

In his memoirs Löwith describes his encounter with his former teacher. After his lecture Heidegger and his wife accompanied the Löwiths to their small apartment and "showed himself visibly taken aback by our scanty furnishings."[3] On the following morning the two couples made a joint excursion to Frascati and Tusculum. It was a brilliant day, but with a lot of awkwardness.

Elfride, in particular, seemed to be embarrassed by the Löwiths' company. Heidegger was wearing his Nazi Party badge, clearly unaware that the swastika was out of place when he was spending a day with Löwith. Heidegger's behavior, however, was amicable, though he avoided any reference to conditions in Germany. Löwith, on the other hand, who had been driven into exile by these very conditions, deliberately touched on them. He turned the conversation to the controversy in the Swiss press that had followed Heidegger's lecture in Zurich.

Heinrich Barth, the brother of the great theologian, had introduced his report on Heidegger's lecture, "The Work of Art," in *Neue Zürcher Zeitung* with the words:

> Obviously we should regard it as an honor that Heidegger delivers a lecture in a democratic state, seeing that—at least for a time—he was regarded as the philosophical spokesman of the new Germany. Many people, however, still remember that Heidegger dedicated his *Being and Time* in "admiration and friendship" to the Jew Edmund Husserl and that he forever linked his Kant interpretation with the memory of the half-Jew Max Scheler. The former in 1927, the latter in 1929. Most people are not heroes—not even philosophers, though there are exceptions. One cannot therefore expect a person to swim against the tide; yet a certain obligation toward one's past enhances the respect for philosophy, which, after all, is not only knowledge but at one time was also wisdom.[4]

Emil Staiger, then still a *Privatdozent,* had reacted angrily. Barth, he claimed, being unable to make anything of Heidegger, had issued a "political warrant" in order to denounce his philosophy. But Heidegger, he wrote, stood "alongside Hegel, alongside Kant, Aristotle and Heraclitus. And once this is recognized, there may perhaps still be regret that Heidegger ever accepted that occasion, just as it is always tragic when the spheres are confused—yet one will not be deflected from one's admiration, any more than one would be deflected from one's respect for the 'phenomenology of the spirit' by the thought of the Prussian reactionary."[5] To which Heinrich Barth retorted that it was impermissible "to separate the philosophical and the human, thinking and Being, by abysses."[6]

In his conversation with Heidegger, Löwith declared that he could not agree either with Barth's political attack or with Staiger's defense; he himself "believed that Heidegger's partisanship for National Socialism lay in the essence of his philosophy." Heidegger agreed "without reservation"[7] and pointed out that his concept of "historicity" was the basis of his political engagement.

"Historicity," in Heidegger's sense, opens up a limited horizon of options within which philosophy, if it hopes to "control its time," then moves. Heidegger had regarded the revolution of 1933 as an opportunity to break out of the fatal context of modern "machinations." And even though he had by then begun to see things differently, he still maintained to Löwith that the opportunity of a new beginning had not been finally lost: "one simply had to hold out long enough." Even so, he admitted to some disappointment with political developments, though he immediately blamed the "educated" and their hesitant attitude for the fact that the new beginning had not come up to its early promise. "If these gentlemen had not been too refined to get involved, then everything would be different; but, instead, I am entirely alone now."[8]

Heidegger's fascination with Hitler, however, was as strong as ever. As so many other Germans, for anything that was bad he was very ready with the excuse: "This would never happen if the Führer knew." Karl Löwith was disappointed, but at the same time he regarded Heidegger's reaction as typical: "Nothing is easier for Germans than to be radical when it comes to ideas and to be indifferent to facts. They manage to ignore all individual facts in order to cling all the more decisively to their concept of the whole, and to separate 'matters of fact' from 'persons.'"[9]

Heidegger's concept of the whole, however, had, in parallel with his increasing aloofness from day-to-day politics, detached itself even further from concrete history. This can be seen in his Rome lecture, which presents Hölderlin as a person who, between the "beckoning of the gods" and the "voice of the people" is an "outcast—cast out into that in-between world between the gods and man" (EH, 47). It is the "night of the gods"; they have escaped and have not yet returned. It is a "needy time," which demands—and this is the conclusion of Heidegger's lecture—that one stay with Hölderlin in the "nothingness of this night, 'for not always a frail, a delicate vessel can hold them, / Only at times can our kind bear the full impact of gods. / Ever after our life is dream about them.'"[10]

Heidegger's letter to Karl Jaspers after his stay in Rome conveys something of the atmosphere of those days, especially of how Heidegger as a philosopher felt in Hölderlin's proximity as a "poet in a needy time: In fact we ought to consider it a wonderful state of affairs that 'philosophy' is without esteem, because now our job is to fight for philosophy in a quiet, unobtrusive way" (May 16, 1936, BwHJ, 162).[11]

German reactions to the Hölderlin lecture, to which the Roman audience had listened so devoutly, made Heidegger realize that he was no longer in favor with those in power. A Dr. Könitzer observed in the Hitler Youth periodical *Wille und Macht* (Will and Power) that "our youth are more likely to understand Hölderlin than Professor Heidegger."[12] For someone attuning himself to Hölderlin's "night of the gods," Heidegger reacted with marked irritation: "The claim of the famous gentleman at *Wille und Macht,* that according to him my attitude on Hölderlin is quite foreign for our youth, shows clearly that we must not expect much from such Germans. A former SS leader who knows Marburg society informs me that Dr. K. was still a Social Democrat in 1933. Now, however, he is a big fish at *Völkischer Beobachter.*"[13]

Not so harmless as the criticism in a Hitler Youth journal was another process that began after Heidegger's return from Rome. On May 14 the National Socialist University Teachers' Union in Munich received an inquiry from Alfred Rosenberg's office on "what view is taken of the character of Professor Martin Heidegger, of Freiburg."[14]

Hugo Ott has researched the background of this process. Evidently, mistrust had sprung up in Rosenberg's office; no doubt the opinions of Jaensch and Krieck had been effective. Trouble was also being caused by the rumor that Heidegger was giving regular lectures at the Beuron monastery. There was a suspicion that Heidegger might be engaged in Jesuitical subversion. The inquiry from Rosenberg's office stated that "his philosophy is closely tied to scholasticism, so that it is something of a mystery why Heidegger is able to exercise such an influence at times even on National Socialists."[15]

This suspicion of secret clericalism came at just the moment when Heidegger, in a series of doctoral and habilitation proceedings (for Max Müller, for example), had officially in his assessments expressed his conviction that a "Christian" philosophy was ultimately "a wooden iron and a misunderstanding."

Be that as it may, the information provided by the University Teachers' Union on Heidegger was such that Rosenberg's office on May 29, 1936, decided to pass its Heidegger dossier on to the Reich Central Security Department, Office for Science, with the result that instructions were issued to place Heidegger under surveillance. In *Tatsachen und Gedanken* (Facts and Thoughts) Heidegger reports that in the summer semester of 1937 a Dr.

Hanke from Berlin appeared in his seminar, a "very gifted and interested" person. After working in the seminar for some time he had requested a personal interview with Heidegger. There, Heidegger records, "he confessed to me that he could no longer conceal from me the fact that he was working on orders from Dr. Scheel, who was then head of the south-west regional section of the secret service" (R, 41).[16]

If one bears in mind that Heidegger was aware of being under surveillance, his critique of biologism and racism in his Nietzsche lectures was therefore clearly an act of some personal courage. This was also felt by the students attending these lectures at the time. They were all the more surprised to see Heidegger, more emphatically than other professors, sticking to the Hitler salute.

Important party authorities, Heidegger writes in *Facts and Thoughts,* had endeavored to impede and "eliminate" his philosophical work ever since the mid-1930s. Thus some government departments tried to exclude him from participation in the International Descartes Congress in Paris in 1937. The French organizers of the congress, however, intervened and only then was he invited at the last moment to be a member of the German delegation. "The whole business was done in a manner that made it impossible for me to go to Paris with the German delegation" (R, 43).

Victor Farías, however, discovered papers in the Berlin Document Center and in the Potsdam archives from which it emerges that Heidegger was in Paris as early as the summer of 1935 to prepare for the German participation in the congress. Heidegger attached particular importance to this event; after all, Descartes was the founder of a modern movement in philosophy to which his own philosophy was opposed. The Paris congress was therefore bound to be attractive to him as an arena for a major contest of strength. He was only too ready to face this challenge. He intended to develop those ideas that, on June 9, 1939, he presented under the title "The Foundation of the Modern Picture of the World through Metaphysics," which were published as *Zeit des Weltbildes* (The Age of the World Picture).

Heidegger was therefore anxious to go to Paris and was waiting—at first in vain—to be sent there officially by the German authorities. But the German invitation came too late, too late for Heidegger. Farías discovered a letter written by Heidegger to the rector of Freiburg University on July 14, 1937, in which he explained why he was no longer willing to join the German delegation at such short notice:

> The invitation was sent me about one year and a half ago by the president of the Conference. I sent it to the Ministry of Education, indicating that this Conference centered on the anniversary of Descartes was a conscious attack coming from the dominant liberal-democratic concept of science and that therefore we had to prepare a strong and effective German delegation . . . Since my proposition received no answer, I did not send the Ministry the subsequent invitations from Paris. It is not the desires of the French leaders on this subject that are important to me, but only the initial will of the German authorities to have me there or not as part of the German delegation.[17]

Heidegger evidently felt offended that the German authorities had not immediately got in touch with him about the strategic preparations for the congress and the composition of a delegation. He had probably expected to be sent to Paris as the leader of the delegation. However, in mid-1936 the government and party quarters appointed Heyse to lead the German delegation. In a memorandum of August 1936 Heyse characterized the intention of the congress. He said it seemed that Descartes' rationalism was to be identified with the concept of philosophy altogether. In consequence, "the present German philosophical will" would be bracketed out and presented as a "complete denial of the great European traditions, as an expression of a naturalistic particularism, a denial of rational thought." The strategic aim of the event was the "intellectual isolation of Germany and the role of France as the spiritual guide for Europe."[18] This would have to be opposed by something highly effective. The delegation would have to be able to do more than "champion the National Socialist German spiritual will and win recognition for it"; what was needed was not only a strong defense; one had to be able to go over to the attack. What mattered, according to Heyse, was "the attempt at a German intellectual thrust into the European space." Unfortunately, however, there were very few philosophers in the new Germany capable of even joining in the struggle for the "international standing" of German philosophy. Heyse's proposed list included Heidegger, Carl Schmitt, and Alfred Baeumler.

The proposals were accepted, and Heyse, in the spring of 1937, approached Heidegger, who, however, now declined to participate. At least he was saved some embarrassment, as the delegation had been chosen not only on ideological but also on racial grounds. Husserl, earmarked by the congress management for a keynote speech, was not, as a "non-Aryan," allowed to accept the invitation. The German authorities assumed, quite correctly, that Husserl's participation would completely overshadow the official delegation; there were fears of exceptional ovations for Husserl as a demonstration against the German delegation.

In Paris the delegation displayed martial behavior—some of the professors even wore the party uniform. A French newspaper expressed surprise that, compared with international philosophical congresses in the past, there were evidently no "individuals" on the German side but only representatives of a collective spirit. The fact that "the land of poets and thinkers" was now sending its philosophers forward in closed formation was regarded as rather alarming.

Heidegger stayed at home and worked on his own contribution to German-French understanding. "Roads to Discussion" was the title of his essay on the argument between the German and French spirit, published in a collection entitled *Alemannenland.* This volume, published by Franz Kerber, the *Oberbürgermeister* of Freiburg and former editor-in-chief of the Nazi journal *Der Alemanne,* appeared at a time when, following his march into the Rhineland, Hitler was propagating an understanding with France. Heidegger's essay, however, was not intended for such ephemeral propaganda purposes. According to Heinrich Petzet, he was fond of reading this text, "which seemed very important to him,"[19] to his circle of friends, and it was later also included in his *Denkerfahrungen* (Thought Experiences).

The essay's subject is understanding between the French and German nations. Heidegger does not concern himself with geopolitical, economic, or military conflicts and controversies. The "present hour of the world" has charged the "history-creating Western nations" with a far greater task—the "salvation of the Occident." This salvation cannot be achieved by the compromise of assimilating or intermingling different modes of thought or cultures between nations, but only by each nation remembering what is particular to it and, on this basis, making its contribution to the salvation of the Western identity. In France, Cartesianism was dominant, the vision of rational disposition over the *res extensa.* In Germany, by contrast, historical thinking had evolved more powerfully. The significant aspect of this juxtaposition, which, taken by itself, was not particularly original, resided in the fact that Heidegger regarded it as the ultimate differentiation of trends that, in the Greek protoscene of the Occident, were not yet separate or decided. Plato's Being and Heraclitus's Becoming, in other words: rationalism and historicity, then still cooperated polemically in the common space of the polis, thereby achieving a spiritual identity that was capable of standing up to the "Asiatic" that beat upon Greece as an ocean beats against an island.

What, then, is the "Asiatic" at the "present hour of the world"? Heidegger does not spell it out explicitly, but this is what emerges from the logic of his presentation: the Asiatic of the present day is nothing "barbaric," but the modern spirit in its unfettered form in North America and Russia. However, as French Cartesianism is the more recent origin of this modern spirit, any Franco-German cooperation for the salvation of the Occident will be marked by a characteristic asymmetry. French rationalism will have to attend the school of German historicity, more particularly the school of Heidegger's thinking on Being. Only from the perspective of such thinking can rationalism overcome its delusion of objectivity and open out to the riches of the history of Being. Consequently, the German spirit does not need the French spirit in the same measure as the other way around. Heidegger's friendly observations thus refer to the fact that the French spirit has evidently in the meantime realized what it lacks—a Hegel, a Schelling, a Hölderlin. But there is help at hand.

There is no indication that Heidegger had read the philosophical pamphlet of Julien Benda, the French Kantian, *La trahison des clercs* (The Treason of the Intellectuals). This tract, which caused a sensation in France immediately upon publication in 1927, can be read as an anticipated reply from France to Heidegger's offer of talks. For Benda the treason of the intellectuals begins at the very moment when they surrender themselves to the drifting sands of history, when they surrender the universal spiritual values of truth, justice, and freedom to the irrational powers of the instinct, of the "spirit of the people," of institutions, and so on. It was the task of the *clercs,* the philosophical and literary intellectuals, here defined as secular clerics, to preserve these universal values against the encroachments of the political zeitgeist of the day. Who else was to do it, seeing that the "laymen" were necessarily involved in secular conflicts and passions? A rigorous humanist rationalism here resists the siren song of the romantic "people's spirits." There is nothing, according to Benda, to be learned from the German spirit since the death of Kant—one can only warn against it. Benda quotes a sentence of Renan that sounds like a retort to Heidegger: "Man belongs neither to his language, nor to his race; he belongs only to himself, for he is a free, that is, a moral, being."[20]

Julien Benda is convinced that anyone who banishes the human spirit from its universal home, making it the object of dispute between nations, will soon find himself among those who are calling for a "war of cultures." This certainly is not what Heidegger wants. He hopes to explore, in his own way, the possibility of fruitful neighborliness. This would involve "the persistent will to listen to one another and the quiet courage for one's own mission" (D, 21). This, however, changes nothing about the fact that the "roads to discussion" must lead to the point where a decision is possible on which relationship of Being is more in accord with the openness of Being—the Cartesian-rational or the historical. "Evasion of the most difficult task—provision of an area of decidability" (D, 20) is not an option. It is clear that Heidegger sees his thinking as appropriate to this task. For a German-French understanding in matters of philosophy, one would have to meet not somewhere halfway but on the heights of Todtnauberg.

Three years later, the war that Hitler started is in full swing. In the summer of 1940 France is defeated. And in the summer semester of that year Heidegger, in his Nietzsche lecture on European nihilism, refers to the French capitulation and in doing so arrives at an astonishing conclusion:

> We today are witness to a mysterious law of history which states that one day a people no longer measures up to the metaphysics that arose from its own history; that day arrives precisely when such metaphysics has been transformed into the absolute . . . It is not enough that one possess tanks, airplanes, and communication apparatus; nor is it enough that one has at one's disposal men who can service such things . . . What is needed is a mankind that is from top to bottom equal to the unique fundamental essence of *modern* technology and its metaphysical truth; that is to say, one that lets itself be entirely dominated by the essence of technology precisely in order to steer and deploy individual technological processes and possibilities. In the sense of Nietzsche's metaphysics only the Over-man is appropriate to an absolute "machine economy," and vice versa he needs for it the institution of absolute dominion over the earth. (N II, 165–166)[21]

This implies that Germany has proved herself more Cartesian than the Cartesian nation of France. Germany has been more successful than France in realizing Descartes's dream of domination over the *res extensa;* that is, the technological control of nature. Only Germany accomplished the "total mobilization" (N II, 21), the technological and organizational adjustment of the entire society and the individual. Here all conclusions have been drawn from modern metaphysics, according to which "Being" is only "Being presented" and ultimately "Being provided." Germany was victorious because she—"in a superhuman way"—materialized the mischief of the modern age. The French are the sorcerer's apprentices. They triggered a process that was no longer "within their strength." Only in Hitler's totalitarian Germany has that "human material" formed that is "up to" modern technology. There the people themselves have evidently become missiles. Subsequently Heidegger would, with a mixture of horror and fascination, report how one of his Japanese students had volunteered for a kamikaze mission as a pilot.

As recently as 1935, in his metaphysics lecture, Russia and America were still the vanguard powers of the "hopeless raving of unleashed technology" (EM, 28); now Heidegger regards Germany as being in the lead. A tone of quiet satisfaction about this state of affairs cannot be missed. This is reminiscent of Heinrich Mann's *Der Untertan* (The Man of Straw), in which Diederich Hessling, painfully offended by a tough lieutenant, remarks with satisfaction: "Nowhere else could you find a man like him!" Germany is victorious, Heidegger declares, because she surrenders herself more effectively than the others to the "mischief" of technology—and yet, this steel-like consequence of oblivion of Being cannot be found anywhere else.

Heidegger's sons, Jörg and Hermann, had been called up and, from 1940, were on the front. Lecture and seminar rooms were filled with young war wounded, soldiers on convalescent leave, and older men. The percentage of women students was growing. Reports of men killed in action or missing in the operational zones were increasing.

On September 26, 1941, Heidegger wrote to the mother of a former student of his who was killed in action: "For us who are left behind it is a difficult step to the knowledge that every one of the many young Germans who are today sacrificing their lives with a still genuine spirit and reverential heart may be experiencing the most beautiful fate."[22]

What "most beautiful fate," then, are those killed experiencing? Is it being remembered by Heidegger? Most of the dead were known only to a few friends, but preserved in the philosopher's memory, Heidegger claims, they will "reawaken the German's innermost mission for the spirit and the loyalty of the heart." Does the war thereby acquire a meaning? Did not Heidegger in his Nietzsche lectures describe the war as the expression of the "will to power," oblivious of Being?

This is what is repeated by Heidegger in his lectures time and again. And he claims, moreover, that philosophy at the present historical moment, "the cynical utilization of 'human resources' in service to the absolute empowering of will to power" (N II, 333),[23] threatens to become entirely superfluous. As a "structure of culture" it disappears from the public machinery, since it is nothing but a "being-addressed by Being itself" (GA 54, 179). However, there is no time now for any such being-addressed. One consequence of the war is that in Germany the belief in "belonging to a nation of poets and thinkers" is thought to have been "overcome and put behind" (GA 54, 179). How then can the sacrifice for such a war still be meaningful?

To this there are two answers, from Heidegger's point of view. The first is the well-known response that the authenticity of a life performance depends not on the moral character of the overall situation but solely on the "attitude" one adopts. In this sense Heidegger, in his letter to the mother of his killed student, commends the "inner fire" and the "reverence for the essential"—whatever that may mean in the specific instance. Heidegger himself does not know this, since he is unaware of the actual circumstances of the young man's death.

The second answer is that the sacrifice is meaningful to the extent that the war itself is meaningful. On this point, however, Heidegger's judgment vacillates. On the one hand he comprehends the war as an expression of the epochal will to power—without anywhere conceding Hitlerite Germany's sole responsibility—and thus altogether as a meaningless total mobilization of the modern age. From this point of view, any sacrifice would be bound to be meaningless. With America's entry into the war, however, the situation changes for him. In his Hölderlin lecture of the summer of 1942 he states: "Today we know that the Anglo-Saxon world of Americanism is determined to destroy Europe, and thus our homeland, and thus the origin of the Occidental" (GA 53, 68).

But where does this "Occidental" still exist? Official Germany can no longer be its location, for there, as Heidegger keeps reiterating, the "machine economy" and man's degradation into mere material have been victorious.

But surely there remains the "unofficial," the imaginary, Germany in which Hölderlin had believed. The Germany whose language preserves the philosophical spirit as only ancient Greece had. In his Heraclitus lecture of 1943 Martin Heidegger says: "The planet is in flames. The essence of man is out of joint. Only from the Germans, provided they discover and preserve 'the German,' can world-historical consciousness come" (GA 55, 123). This authentic Occidental Germany that is being betrayed all round—does it not ultimately live only in Heidegger's philosophy?

This is the case even if Heidegger does not wish to have anything to do with the "rebellious awareness of mission" (GA 54, 114). During the final months of the war his philosophy turns entirely to the "memory" of the great founders—Hölderlin, Parmenides, Heraclitus. The gap between Heidegger's thinking and external events is growing ever wider. While events are drifting toward their disastrous conclusion and the crimes of the Hitler regime are reaching a horrible peak with the murder of the Jews, Heidegger immerses himself ever more deeply into the "beginnings. The hidden spirit of the beginnings in the Occident will not have even a glance of contempt left for this process of self-devastation of the beginningless, but will, with the composure of the calm of the beginnings, await its great moment" (GA 53, 68).

Unlike in 1933, however, Heidegger no longer expects these beginnings from a great social-political event. The "great moment" is one of solitary poetry and thought. This does not, for the moment, find or even seek "support" from any political or societal movement. "The essential thinking observes the slow signs of the unpredictable," Heidegger wrote in 1943 in a new postscript to *What Is Metaphysics?* (WM, 51). This kind of thinking does not produce any "success." There remains only the hope that, possibly, here and there, a similar thinking may be "lit," as a result of which a secret brotherhood will arise of those who are getting out of the present world game. "World game" *(Weltspiel)* is the expression first used by Heidegger in a lecture in 1941 to characterize the great wretchedness. The contemporary world game knows only "workers and soldiers." There are two ways of escaping from this "normalcy." One is described by Heidegger—in allusion to Ernst Jünger—as adventurousness: "Who can be surprised that at a time when the former world is entirely coming apart, the thought arises that now only pleasure in danger, 'adventure,' is the manner in which man makes sure of reality?" (GA 51, 36). The adventurer endows oblivion of Being with garish colors and élan vital. He plunges into the machinery of the modern age, even if it is out to crush him. He raises his stakes to get more excitement out of the game.

The other manner of resisting the world game as a connection of destiny is the "urgency" of contemplative thinking. In the past this used to be called meditation, the *vita contemplativa*—terms that Heidegger rejects for his own program. Heidegger moves this "urgency" close to the simple life. Deprive modern man, he says in his Heraclitus lecture, of everything that entertains and holds him, "the cinema, the radio, the newspaper, the theater, concerts, boxing bouts, travel" (GA 55, 84), and he would die of emptiness, since "simple things" no longer appeal to him. In contemplative thinking, however, emptiness becomes an opportunity for "remembering Being" (GA 55, 84). At the climax of the war—"the planet is in flames"—Heidegger reattunes himself to the great theme of his postwar philosophy, composure.

Finding such composure in the middle of the war was due to his skill in turning away from oppressive reality. In the above-quoted postscript to the fourth edition of *What Is Metaphysics?* (1943) Heidegger writes the obscure sentence: "Being probably exists [*west*] without the existent" (WM, 46). In the year of the incipient inferno, Heidegger thought far beyond the existent *(das Seiende),* so far that Being now became for him something that it was not before—a reference parameter independent of the existent. In the 1949 edition of the text he would take this extravagance back again; "probably" would become "never," so that the sentence, stripped of its dizziness, would read: "Being never exists [*west*] without the existent."

The manner in which Being is present at this unhappy time is formulated by Heidegger in a Hölderlin essay as the "chaos of the gaping-open" (GA 4, 62). The abyss has gaped open, the earth is shaking.

By way of contrast Heidegger, at the same time, proceeding from Hölderlin, shapes his own hymn to his Swabian homeland: "Suevia, the mother, lives close to 'the hearth of the house.' The hearth guards the ever-saved glow of the fire which, when it flares, opens up air and light into the Serene . . . That is why a man, when obliged to, finds it difficult to leave the place of nearness" (GA 4, 23).

20

HEIDEGGER FACES THE DENAZIFICATION COMMITTEE: BARRED FROM UNIVERSITY TEACHING

On the night of November 27, 1944, British and American bomber squadrons devastated the city of Freiburg. Shortly before, Martin Heidegger had left for Breisach with a Volkssturm (People's Militia) detachment. The intention was to prevent the French Army from reaching the eastern bank of the Rhine, but it was too late for that. The Volkssturm men, including Heidegger, returned.

Heidegger had been enlisted on the basis of Hitler's decree of October 18, 1944, which ordered the call-up of all men between sixteen and sixty, with no exception for reserve occupations. The only criterion was fitness for work. And since Heidegger was fit for work, he was also fit for military service. Yet not all Heidegger's colleagues were called up; recruitment was in the hands of the local party authorities. There was a great deal of confusion. The members of the philosophy faculty therefore tried to get Heidegger released. On their behalf a letter was sent to the leader of the University Teachers' Union, Kurt Scheel, by Eugen Fischer, formerly a notorious director of the Kaiser Wilhelm Institute for Eugenics in Berlin and at the time an emeritus professor in Freiburg. Fischer requested that Heidegger be released from the Volkssturm, concluding with the words: "If, at this gravest hour, faced with the fact that the enemy in German Alsace is barely fifty kilometers from our city, we make this request, we hereby demonstrate our confidence in the future of German science." By the time Scheel replied, three weeks later—"Because of the confused situation I was unable to do anything for Heidegger"—the matter had settled itself. Back from the Volkssturm, Heidegger was granted leave from the university to enable him to sort out his manuscripts and take them to safety near Messkirch. Before leaving Freiburg, wrecked by bombs and awaiting the entry of the Allies, he visited the philosopher Georg Picht and his wife, the subsequently famous pianist Edith Picht-Axenfeld. Heidegger wanted to hear her play once more. Frau Picht played Schubert's posthumous Sonata in B-flat Major. Heidegger looked at Picht and said: "This we can't do with philosophy."[1] On that December night in 1944 Heidegger wrote in Picht's guest book: "Going down is different from ending. Every going down is sheltered in a rising."

What is "ending" or "going down" all around him? Heidegger's entry in the guest book leaves this question open. But six months later, in a letter to Rudolf Stadelmann, his "squire" from the days of the science camp and by then dean in Tübingen, Heidegger would answer it: "Everyone now thinks of doom and downfall. But we Germans cannot go under because we have not yet arisen and must persevere still through the night."[2]

During those six months, between his flight from Freiburg and his return to the city—meanwhile occupied by the French—Heidegger lived in a pastoral idyll. Together with his brother, Fritz, he spent the winter in Messkirch tidying his manuscripts. And when spring came, the whole of the philosophy faculty, or what was left of it, arrived. It had been decided in Freiburg that sections of the university would be moved out of the city, and Wildenstein Castle above Beuron, in the vicinity of Messkirch, had been chosen as a safe retreat. Some on foot, some on bicycles and heavily laden with books, ten professors and thirty students, most of them women, arrived in March 1945, having made their way through the Black Forest and the Upper Danube, to find accommodation in the castle—a property of the Fürstenberg family—and in nearby Leibertingen. The hike from Messkirch to Wildenstein Castle was one frequently made by Heidegger in his youth, and he made it now to hold a little seminar in the castle tavern, while in the valley below French troops were advancing toward Sigmaringen, where the remnants of the collaborationist Vichy government had fled. At the end of May, hay making began. Professors and students lent a hand and were paid for it in foodstuffs. Only scant news trickled through from Freiburg. All one knew was that the city was occupied. Luckily there had been no battle for Freiburg. Down in the valley, at the Beuron monastery, a military hospital had been set up; wounded were arriving every day. And up there on the rock, where a family of robber barons once resided, Kant's *Critique of Pure Reason,* medieval history, and Hölderlin were being studied—above all, Hölderlin. In his "Ister" hymn Hölderlin had sung the praises of the Upper Danube:

> But this one is called the Ister.
> Beautiful is his abode. On its columns the foliage is burning
> and stirring . . .

Heidegger had interpreted this poem many times before, and he now did so again. Hölderlin had, in the meantime, become part of his personal genealogy. To his "Ister" lecture in 1942 he had, as already observed, added the observation (not contained in the edited volume): "It was perhaps inevitable that the poet Hölderlin should become the determining influence on the critical thought of one whose grandfather was born at the very time when the 'Ister' hymn . . . [was] written—born, according to the records, 'in ovili' (that is to say, in a sheepfold on a farm), which lies near the bank of the river in the valley of the Upper Danube, beneath the lofty crags. Nothing is chance in the unseen history of poetic discourse. All is destiny."[3]

From Wildenstein Castle one can see the ancient house by the Danube to which the sheepfold belonged, where Heidegger's grandfather was born.

This unusual summer semester was concluded on June 24 with a party at the castle. The people of the neighborhood were invited, and they came with food. In the castle courtyard there was theater and dancing. Three days later, in the nearby hunting lodge of Prince Bernhard of Saxony-Meiningen, Heidegger had another major performance—the last for a number of years. A short piano recital introduced the event. Heidegger spoke on a statement by Hölderlin: "All our thoughts are concentrated on the things of the mind. We have become poor, that we might become rich."[4]

In occupied Freiburg the first measures were being taken for the requisitioning of living quarters by the French military government. "Heidegger is regarded in the city as a Nazi (his rectorship)";[5] this short note in the files of the acting *Oberbürgermeister* was enough for Heidegger's house at Rötebuck

47 to be placed on the "black list" as early as mid-May. At that stage it was not yet decided whether this meant merely the billeting of troops or that the Heideggers would have to leave their home. There was even a threat that his library might be confiscated. Elfride Heidegger, who during the first few weeks had to conduct the difficult negotiations with the authorities on her own, lodged a protest and asked for the decision to be postponed until her husband returned to the city.

Even before Heidegger's return she was notified by the acting *Oberbürgermeister* that, to solve the worst of the housing shortage, the military government had ruled that "the homes of former Party members are to be requisitioned first,"[6] and Heidegger had undeniably been a party member.

When Heidegger returned from Wildenstein at the beginning of July, his situation had dramatically changed. After being reverently listened to at the castle and the forester's hunting lodge, almost overnight he found himself in the role of the accused in Freiburg. The authorities suggested that he might well do without his library, as he would no longer be able to pursue his profession. On July 16 Heidegger drafted a letter to the *Oberbürgermeister*—a first draft of the self-justification that would be written during the years to come.

> I wish to protest in the strongest possible terms against this attack on my person and on my work. Why should I have been singled out for punishment and defamation before the eyes of the whole city—indeed before the eyes of the world—not only by having my home requisitioned in this manner, but also by being stripped of my employment? I never held office of any kind within the Party, and was never active in the Party or in any of its organizations. If there are those who regard my rectorship as politically compromising, then I must insist on being given an opportunity to defend myself against any charges or accusations, made by whomsoever—which means being told, first and foremost, what *specifically* has been alleged against me and my official activities.[7]

At first it was only a case of the house and the library. For the time being Heidegger was still in his post. However, the French military government had already started on its denazification measures. The university, anxious to reestablish itself as an independent body, tried to prove that it could muster the strength for self-purification. On May 8, 1945, the academic senate had decided on an intrauniversity questionnaire and a list of criteria for judging the political past of the members of the university. This was to cover only major activities. Three categories were envisaged—work for the Security Service (denunciations), work as a party functionary, and the holding of senior administrative and representative functions (rectors, deans). That Heidegger would be required to answer for himself was therefore a matter of course even for the university.

The French military government did not yet recognize the university as an independent body and therefore refused to leave the denazification procedure to the university. The French liaison officer set up a commission that represented the university vis-à-vis the military government and was responsible for operating the investigation. This denazification committee, as it was called, included the professors Constantin von Dietze, Gerhard Ritter, and Adolf Lampe. These three men had been involved in the July 20 conspiracy and had just been released from detention. Added to these were the theologian Artur Allgeier and the botanist Friedrich Oehlkers, a friend of Karl Jaspers and, like him, married to a Jewish woman—as a result of which he had lived in great fear for the past few years. It was before this committee that Heidegger first had to justify himself on July 23, 1945. The committee's attitude to Heidegger was, on the whole, friendly. Gerhard Ritter, for instance, testified that, from intimate acquaintance with Heidegger, he knew that Heidegger had been a secret opponent of National Socialism ever since the Röhm putsch. Adolf Lampe alone among the members of the committee resolutely opposed Heidegger's rehabilitation. Lampe, an economist, had suffered under Heidegger's rectorship when Heidegger opposed an extension of Lampe's temporary tenure on grounds of political unreliability.

From the first hearing on July 23 Heidegger realized it was mainly against Lampe that he would have to direct his defense. For this reason he requested a personal talk with him two days later. Of this conversation Lampe made a full record for the committee. According to this record, Lampe, to avoid an "embarrassing situation" and to clear himself of the suspicion of prejudice, stated right away that the events of 1934, insofar as they concerned him, played no part in his judgment. And then he repeated the charges of the committee: first, the rector's appeals to the student body, couched, as they were, entirely in the style of Nazi propaganda; second, Heidegger's also formally uncompromising application of the führer principle; and third, the rector's circulars to the members of the teaching staff, whose contents, according to Lampe, had to be assessed "as a painful restriction of the independence to be expected from and to be preserved for a university teacher."[8] Heidegger's international reputation merely magnified the weight of his mistakes and amounted to "substantial support for the then particularly dangerous development of National Socialism." In his response to Lampe, Heidegger rehearsed the line of defense to which he would adhere for the next few years, until the *Spiegel* interview. He had supported National Socialism because he had hoped it would bring about an equalization of social conflicts on the basis of a new sense of community. Moreover, a halt had to be called to the advance of communism. He had been "most reluctant" to let himself be elected to the rectorship and he had then remained in office for the first year to forestall "something worse" (such as the election of the party bigwig Aly). However, his colleagues had even then not understood his actions and had therefore failed to support him in a proper manner. Since the mid-thirties he had then publicly—especially in his Nietzsche lectures—voiced criticism of the power thinking of National Socialism, to which the party had suitably reacted by sending a spy to his lectures and causing him difficulties with the publication of his work.

Lampe was outraged at the absence of any sense of guilt in Heidegger and called for "personal responsibility." Someone who had championed the führer principle the way Heidegger had done could not now excuse himself by talking of "intrigues" or lack of support. So far as Heidegger's later criticism of the system was concerned, he, Lampe, could not regard it as "compensation"; this could only have been achieved through "open criticism in line with the resoluteness of his rectorship, at the risk of any personal danger resulting from it."[9]

Heidegger's self-defense was motivated by fear. Similarly incriminated colleagues, including the Freiburg professor of romance studies Hugo Friedrich, had already been arrested by the French. He was afraid the same fate might befall him. He was afraid for his house and for his library. He was gazing into the abyss—not that of his own political mistakes, but that of social degradation and the loss of his opportunity to work. He said to Lampe that a negative vote of the committee would make him "a proscribed person." In consequence he made an all-out effort to defend and justify himself.

Heidegger, therefore, showed no sense of guilt. But in fact neither did he feel any. The situation, as he saw it, was this: he had, for a short while, committed himself to the National Socialist revolution because he had regarded it as a metaphysical revolution. When it failed to live up to its promises—and what its promises to him had been he never accurately disclosed—he had withdrawn and pursued his philosophical work, unaffected by the party's approval or rejection. He had made no secret of his critical distance from the system but openly declared it in his lectures. To that extent he was less responsible for the system than the vast majority of scholars who had adapted, and none of whom was now being made to justify himself. What did he have to do with the crimes of the system? Heidegger was actually surprised to be required to justify himself at all. He experienced, as he later admitted to Jaspers on April 8, 1950, "shame" at having for a short time collaborated—that he admitted. But it was shame at having made a mistake, of having been "deluded." What he had himself hoped for—a new beginning, renewal—that, from his point of view, had little to do with what eventually happened in reality. The fact that, after his philosophically motivated political engagement, he had once more separated the spheres of politics and philosophy now seemed to him to be a recapturing of the purity of his philosophical points of view. He believed that the road of his own thinking, which he had professed in public, had rehabilitated him. Hence he felt no guilt, neither in a legal sense nor probably even in a moral one.

Against Lampe's vote, the denazification committee in August 1945 arrived at a very lenient judgment on Heidegger's political behavior. While at first he had placed himself in the service of the National Socialist revolution, the committee stated, thereby doing "a great deal to justify this revolution in the eyes of educated Germans and making it more difficult for German science and scholarship to maintain its independence amidst the political upheaval,"[10] he had not been a Nazi since 1934. The committee's recommendation was that Heidegger should be prematurely retired but not dismissed from office. He was to keep his teaching rights but was to be excluded from participation in university administration.

The university senate, however—and not yet the French military government—objected to this lenient recommendation by arguing that if Heidegger got off virtually untouched, there would be no case for proceeding against other incriminated members of the teaching body. The committee was therefore instructed to reexamine Heidegger's case.

Until then Heidegger's defense had aimed at full rehabilitation. He wanted to be a member of the teaching staff with all rights and duties. Now he observed that the university, to maintain its credibility vis-à-vis the military government, was evidently prepared to make an example of his case. The situation was getting worse for him. He therefore indicated his readiness to accept emeritus status. He wanted to keep only his right to teach and, needless to say, his pension. He proposed that Karl Jaspers be asked for an expert opinion; he expected that this would exonerate him. Karl Jaspers's opinion, however, drafted during the Christmas holidays of 1945 (and rediscovered by Hugo Ott), was to have the opposite effect.

Jaspers, at first, felt like refusing altogether; later, however, he regarded it as his duty, especially as, during that very winter semester, he had given a lecture on the need to reappraise guilt. If Heidegger had been aware of this lecture he would probably not have asked Jaspers for an expert opinion. Jaspers had evidently been thinking partly of Heidegger when he said:

> Many intellectuals who went along in 1933, hoping for a leading influence for themselves, and who publicly ideologically supported the new power—and who subsequently found themselves pushed aside and lost their enthusiasm . . . these now feel that they have suffered under the Nazis and were therefore called upon for what followed after them. They regard themselves as anti-Nazis. There was, all through those years, an ideology of these intellectual Nazis: in spiritual matters—they would claim—they had spoken the truth without inhibitions, they had preserved the tradition of the German spirit, they had prevented destruction, they had achieved positive things in detail . . . Anyone who, as a mature person, in 1933 had the inner conviction that was rooted not only in political error but in a life experience enhanced by National Socialism, cannot now become pure except through a remelting that would have to go deeper than any other.[11]

The ties between Jaspers and Heidegger had been severed in the summer of 1936. In his last letter of May 16, 1936—which Heidegger did not answer—Jaspers had acknowledged the receipt of a Heidegger essay on Hölderlin with the words: "You will understand and approve . . . my silence. My soul has fallen silent; for in this world I do not remain with a philosophy 'without respect,' as you write of yourself, yet I will . . . but words fail me" (BwHJ, 162).

Jaspers had been driven out of his post in 1937 and was prohibited from teaching and publishing. Heidegger had not reacted to this with as much as a single word. During the years that followed, Gertrud Jaspers, who was Jewish, had expected deportation at any moment. Against this eventuality the couple had always carried poison capsules with them.

During the early years of Nazi rule, Jaspers had blamed himself for not having been sufficiently open toward Heidegger and for failing to challenge him on his political development. In a letter to Heidegger of March 1, 1948, which he never posted, he explains why he had not done so. "I did not do so out of mistrust of everybody who in this terror state had not positively proved a real friend to me. I followed Spinoza's caution and Plato's advice: at such times to seek cover as in a rainstorm . . . I have . . . since 1933, suffered vis-à-vis yourself, until, as often happens in the course of events, this suffering almost disappeared in the 1930s under the weight of far more terrible things. There was left only a distant memory and an occasionally recurring astonishment" (BwHJ, 167).

The fact that Heidegger in his troubles at the end of 1945 was indirectly turning to him came as a disappointment to Jaspers; he had hoped for a word of explanation from Heidegger immediately after liberation. Nothing, however, arrived, not even when, in the autumn of 1945, he had sent Heidegger an issue of the periodical *Wandlung* (Transformation) of which he was coeditor.

In his (unsent) letter of 1948 Jaspers comments on his expert opinion of 1945: "In the cool detachment of these observations you cannot perceive what is in my heart. My letter was conceived in the intention to let the inevitable come into effect and to help achieve for you the best possible in a dangerous situation, to enable you to continue your work" (BwHJ, 167).

The "inevitable" that Jaspers wanted to come into effect was this: he reported how Heidegger had denounced Eduard Baumgarten, but, on the other hand, had enabled his Jewish assistant Dr. Brock to establish himself in England through good references and his personal support. As for Heidegger's anti-Semitism—the committee had expressly questioned Jaspers on this point—Jaspers concluded that since the 1920s Heidegger had not been anti-Semitic, though "in certain contexts," as the Baumgarten case proved, he had nevertheless allowed himself to be carried along.

For the senate's decision the most crucial passage in Jaspers's statement was this:

> In our present situation the education of the younger generation needs to be handled with the utmost responsibility and care. Total academic freedom should be our ultimate aim, but this cannot be achieved over-

> night. Heidegger's mode of thinking, which seems to me to be fundamentally unfree, dictatorial and uncommunicative, would have a very damaging effect on students at the present time. And the mode of thinking itself seems to me more important than the actual content of political judgements, whose aggressiveness can easily be channeled in other directions. Until such time as a genuine rebirth takes place within him, and is *seen* to be at work within him, I think it would be quite wrong to turn such a teacher loose on the young people of today, who are psychologically extremely vulnerable. First of all the young must be taught how to think for themselves.[12]

Jaspers's expert opinion wastes no time about assessing Heidegger's outward engagement for National Socialism, but judges his philosophical style of thinking to be harmful to the necessary political and moral reconstruction of Germany.

On the strength of this assessment, the senate on January 19, 1946, resolved to propose to the French military government that Heidegger be deprived of his teaching license and removed from his post with a reduced pension. At the end of 1946 the military government adopted this proposal and even increased its severity by ordering the discontinuation of Heidegger's pension as from 1947. This decision, however, was rescinded in May 1947.

This harsh treatment had, as mentioned earlier, been preceded by a change of mood at the university and among the French occupation authorities. As recently as in the early autumn, Heidegger could have expected a lenient conclusion to the proceedings. Even the French military government was then still more or less favorably disposed toward Heidegger, in spite of the approved requisitioning of his home. He had been classified as *"disponible,"* which meant not greatly incriminated, and could have shortly been reinstated in his post.

What most alarmed the opponents of Heidegger's rehabilitation, however, were reports and rumors of a veritable pilgrimage of French intellectuals to Freiburg and Todtnauberg. According to rumor, there had even been a meeting between Heidegger and Sartre in October 1945. Heidegger, it was said, had been officially asked to comment in French newspapers on the German situation. We shall presently see what the facts were behind these stories; at any rate, however, the rumors produced their effect. Heidegger's opponents, especially Adolf Lampe, succeeded in November with their demand for a continuation of the investigation and a more severe verdict. Lampe argued that if Heidegger supposed "that he of all people was now called to speak words of illumination and guidance," then he was either acting irresponsibly in denying the magnitude of his own guilt "when he drove our University by brute force down the road of National Socialism," or else he was "staggeringly blind to reality."[13] In view of all that, it was surely desirable finally to withdraw this philosopher from operation.

The situation therefore arose in which the university and the French military government were moving more drastically against Heidegger at the very moment when his second great career began on the French cultural scene.

Heidegger's influence in France had begun to take effect in the early 1930s in connection with an intellectual current that had been given the name of "existentialism" by Jean Wahl and Gabriel Marcel as early as the late 1920s. In 1929 a new Kierkegaard translation had appeared in France, and in this context Jean Wahl had defined the concept of existence as follows: "Existing means: choosing; being passionate; becoming; being solitary and subjective; being infinitely concerned about oneself; knowing oneself to be a sinner; standing before God."[14]

Two ideas, both of them conceived in sharp contrast to Cartesianism, were at the center of the "new thinking" in France in the 1930s. The first was the idea of existence understood as physical, finite, splintered, and totally uprooted Being. Neither Cartesian rationality nor Bergsonian intuition paves the way to great security. Reality has lost its compact, guaranteed meaning; man finds himself thrown amid possibilities between which he has to choose—for which reason he can also become guilty. The idea of existence therefore puts an end to the fantasies about the panlogism of the world.

The idea of existence was also linked to the idea of contingency. The individual experiences himself as the embodiment of chance—in the literal sense. To him a definite body was assigned, and with it a definite place in space and time. He does not have free decision over these, and hence he does not have it over most things. Matters always, beyond his disposition, began with him, even before he could begin anything with himself. Contingency means that what is might equally well not be. Man can no longer be certain of any higher intention, and if he nevertheless believes in one, he has to leap across a Kierkegaardian abyss.

The idea of contingent existence from the very beginning also implied the idea of a radically comprehended freedom. To the Christian understanding of existence, freedom means the option, innate in man, of deciding against God and the absolute, of cutting himself off from it. And for existence comprehended in a non-Christian sense, this freedom means being cast out into a void.

In the development of this French existentialism—which the above-quoted Julien Benda was opposing—where the mystique of Being, decisionism of grace, absurdism, and nihilism were meeting on a common anti-Cartesian ground, yet another intellectual force played a part: phenomenology. From the 1920s onward, Husserl and Scheler were being discovered in France.

If existentialism doubts that there is an a priori, guaranteed, meaningful coherence in human life and culture, then the phenomenological method offers itself for the development of a kind of blissful awareness of the disparate things of the world. In France, phenomenology becomes the art of deriving from attention itself a pleasure that compensates for the fact that a meaningful whole has broken up. Even in an absurd world phenomenology still allows for the happiness of cognition. Camus formulated this connection between the passion for phenomenology and the sufferings of an absurd world in his *Myth of Sisyphus.* What made Husserl's thinking attractive to him was his renunciation of an explanatory unifying principle and his description of the world in its irregular diversity. "Thinking is learning all over again how to see, directing one's consciousness, making of every image a privileged place."[15]

When Raymond Aron, who had studied in Germany and there made the acquaintance of phenomenology, reported on his phenomenological "experiences" to his friend Jean-Paul Sartre at the beginning of the 1930s, Sartre was positively electrified. So there is a philosophy that allows us to philosophize about everything, about this cup, this spoon that I am stirring with, the chair, the waiter taking my order? The rumor of phenomenology—it was no more than a rumor then—would induce Sartre to travel to Berlin in 1930 to study Husserl there, and to say about phenomenology: "For centuries we have not felt in philosophy so realistic a current. The phenomenologists have plunged man back into the world; they have given full measure to man's agonies and sufferings, and also to his rebellions."[16]

In this existentialist and phenomenologistic scene, Heidegger's philosophy began to be effective after the beginning of the 1930s. In 1931 Heidegger's lectures "The Essence of Reason" and "What Is Metaphysics?" appeared in French philosophical journals. These were the first translations. They were followed in 1938 by a selection containing two chapters from *Being and Time* (about Care and Death), a chapter from the Kant book, and the essay "Hölderlin and the Nature of Poetry." However, Heidegger owed his secret fame among the Paris intelligentsia not so much to these scanty translations as to the legendary Hegel lectures given by the Russian émigré Alexander Kojève between 1934 and 1938.

Roger Caillois has since referred to Kojève's "absolutely exceptional intellectual dominance over an entire generation." Bataille reported that each encounter with Kojève had "broken him, crushed him, killed him ten times in succession, and left him stifled and pressed to the ground." For Raymond Aron, Kojève belonged to the three genuinely superior minds (along with Sartre and Eric Weil) he had encountered in his life.

Aleksandr Vladimirovich Kozhevnikov—his original name—came from the Russian high aristocracy and, after the October Revolution, had fled to Germany in 1920. He lived by the sale of the remains of his family's jewelry, which he had smuggled out. He also possessed a few paintings by his uncle Vassily Kandinsky, on which it was easy to borrow money. He studied in Heidelberg under Jaspers, where he also got his doctorate, and during all those years he kept a philosophical diary on the subject of "the philosophy of the non-being." His friend Alexander Koyré, another Russian émigré, brought him to Paris in the early 1930s. Kojève had made his acquaintance when he started a love affair with Koyré's sister-in-law and eloped with her. Koyré was charged by the family with the task of retrieving the young woman from her seducer. But Koyré was so impressed by Kojève at their first meeting that he admitted: "The girl is quite right. Kojève is much better than my brother."[17]

Kojève was in financial difficulties. He had invested his money in shares of the cheese manufacturer La vache qui rit and lost it in the crash of the stock market. He therefore jumped at the offer of lecturing on Hegel at the Ecole pratique des Hautes Etudes.

Kojève, a kind of Nabokov of European philosophy, presented Hegel as he had never been known before—a Hegel almost indistinguishable from Heidegger. Everybody knew Hegel's thesis that "the real is reasonable." Hegel was regarded as a rationalist. And now Kojève was demonstrating that Hegel had done nothing other than reveal the unreasonable origin of reason—in its struggles for recognition. A Self demands of another to be recognized in its Being-thus. Kojève takes up Heidegger's "care" and, proceeding from Hegel, turns it into "care for recognition." The historical reality stemming from this care for recognition is man's fight to the death for sometimes ridiculous stakes—one risks one's life to correct a frontier, defend a flag, obtain satisfaction for an affront, and so forth. Hegel does not need to be put upside down; he already stands on his feet and strides through the mud of history. At the core of reason is contingency, and contingencies are what often clash so bloodily. That is history.

Proceeding from Hegel and, more explicitly, from Heidegger, Kojève asks: "What is the meaning of all Being?" His answer, with Heidegger: it is "Time." Time, however, is not real in the same sense as things are, which themselves age and have their time. Man alone experiences how something that, a little later, is no longer, and how something that is not yet enters into Being. Man is the open place in Being, the arena where Being turns into Nothingness and Nothingness into Being.

The most exciting passages in Kojève's lectures deal with death and nothingness. Kojève states that the totality of reality includes "human or speaking reality," which means that "without man Being would be mute; it would be there, but it would not be the True one."[18] This "discourse revealing the reality" (Kojève), however, presupposes that although man belongs in the compact context of Being, he is at the same time cut off, severed, from it. That alone is why he can err. Man—Kojève formulates it in the meaning of Hegel—is the "error which maintains itself in *Dasein,* which endures in reality."[19] He then interprets this statement in Heidegger's sense: "That is why one can say that the man who errs is a Nothing nihilating [*nichtend*] in Being." The basis and source of human reality, Kojève claims, is "the Nothing"; it manifests and reveals itself "as a negating or creative action that is free and aware of itself."[20]

In conclusion Kojève once more quotes Hegel: "Man is this night, the empty Nothingness that contains everything in its simplicity, a wealth of an infinite number of ideas . . . This is the night, the inside of nature that exists here—pure Self . . . This night is perceived when one looks man in the eyes—into a night that becomes terrible; the night of the world hangs before one."[21] These sentences formulate the transition from *Being and Time* to *Being and Nothingness.*

Sartre had not attended Kojève's lectures but obtained lecture notes. In the winter of 1933–34 he had been in Berlin, studying Husserl and Heidegger, and had so engrossed himself in their philosophy that he took hardly any notice of the Nazi regime.

What fascinated him about phenomenology was, first, its attention to the massive, seductive, but also frightening, presence of things; it led back again to the persistent enigma of their "Being-in-itself." Second, by contrast, it sensitized one for the inner riches of consciousness; it retrieved an entire world of the "for-itself." Third, it seemed, albeit vaguely, to contain the promise that it could somehow resolve the inner tension of this double ontology of "in-itself" and "for-itself."

The "in-themselves" of natural things, which in their overpowering meaning-rejecting presence offer themselves to the phenomenological attitude, had been impressively described by Sartre toward the end of the 1930s in his novel *Nausea.* This description was soon to become the classic example of contingency experience: "I was in the municipal park just now. The root of the chestnut tree plunged into the ground, just underneath my bench. I no longer remembered that it was a root. Words had disappeared, and with them the meaning of things, the method of using them, the feeble landmarks which men have traced onto their surface. I was sitting, slightly bent, head bowed, alone in the face of that black, knotty mass, which was utterly crude, and frightened me. And then I had this revelation."[22] What was that illumination? Roquentin, the narrator, sees things without context, and without the meaning given them by consciousness, they stand there naked. They are spreading out before him downright obscenely, making him "the confession of their existence." Existence here means pure being-present and contingency. "The essential thing is contingency . . . no necessary being can explain existence: contingency is not an illusion, an appearance which can be dissipated; it is absolute, and consequently perfect gratuitousness. Everything is gratuitous, this park, this city, and myself. When you realize that, it turns your stomach over."[23]

The experience in the park confronts a Being that breaks through reasoned discourse. The scene is a literary arrangement by which Kojève's statement, "without man Being would be mute; it would be there, but it would not be the True one," is tested visually. The narrator experiences himself as a thing among things, a heavy impenetrable Something, and this drives him back, fearful, into the world of consciousness, the world of the "for-itself," in order there to experience the lack of Being. "Man is the being through whom nothingness comes into the world," Sartre says in *Being and Nothingness,* developing formulations of Kojève and Heidegger.[24]

Sartre saw his great philosophical work, published in 1943, as a continuation of the fundamental ontology begun by Heidegger. What Heidegger calls *Dasein* is called by Sartre, in Hegel-Kojève terminology, the "for-itself." Man is the being that does not, unquestioning, rest in Being, but that must, in a precarious situation, always first establish, map out, choose, his relation with Being. Man is real, yet he must first realize himself. He has come into the world yet must ever anew bring himself into the world. Consciousness as conscious Being is always also a lack of Being, Sartre declares. Man will never be able to rest in himself like a god or like a stone. His characteristic is transcendence. This transcendence, needless to say, is understood by Sartre not in the sense of a realm of supersensory ideas; it is, instead, self-transcendence, that motion in which the Self continually eludes itself, is always ahead of itself, caring, reflecting, taking in the glances of the others. In these analyses Heidegger's teaching of the existentials thrownness, design, and care are readily recognized—except that Sartre commands an even more impressive skill in describing these phenomena. Sartre also follows Heidegger's theses on the temporality of *Dasein.* It is the privileged access to time, which does not permit human Being to remain with itself. Privileged access means man is not "in" time as a fish is in the water, but that he realizes time, he "timifies" it. This time of consciousness, Sartre states, is "nothingness slipping into a totality as a detotalizing ferment."[25]

This is in fact an ingenious continuation of the phenomenological analysis of *Dasein* in *Being and Time,* one which vigorously moves the area of Being-with—somewhat underexposed in Heidegger—into the center. Admittedly Sartre performs a change of terminology that would lead to serious misunderstandings and also some mock battles, and that would subsequently give Heidegger cause, after initial agreement with him, to distance himself from Sartre. The reason is that Sartre uses the term "existence" in the traditional Cartesian sense. Existence means the empirical presence of something, in contrast to its merely thought destinations. Sartre therefore uses the term in the sense of Heidegger's "being-at-hand." Man "exists" means that, initially, he is simply at hand and that it is part of his destiny to adopt an attitude to his own being at hand. He has to make something of it, map himself out, and so on. In that sense Sartre, in his 1946 lecture "Existentialism and Humanism," will say that existence precedes essence. However, Heidegger's concept of existence in

Being and Time does not mean this pure being-at-hand, this facticity, but describes the transitive meaning of existence, the self-relationship—that man does not simply live but has to "lead" his life. This self-relation of Heidegger's is, of course, what Sartre is concerned with, although he calls this phenomenon "for-itself." Like Heidegger, Sartre attempts to overcome the being-at-hand metaphysics with regard to man, except that he uses different terminology. Like Heidegger, Sartre points out that discourse about man always runs the risk of self-materialization *(Selbstverdinglichung).* Man is not trapped within the enclosed sphere of Being but is an ecstatic creature. That is why Sartre regards his philosophy as a phenomenology of freedom—just as Heidegger, too, sees man's capability of truth founded in his freedom. Truth, Heidegger said in his metaphysics lectures of 1935, is freedom. Nothing more.

Sartre's *Being and Nothingness* was written and published in Nazi-occupied France. Within a web of subtleties, it develops an entire philosophy of antitotalitarianism. To totalitarian thinking, man is a thing. A fascist, Sartre says in his *Anti-Semite and Jew,* is someone desiring to be "an implacable rock, a fierce torrent, a devastating stroke of lightning—anything except a human being." Sartre's philosophy tries to give man back his dignity by making him discover his freedom as an element in which all solid Being dissolves. In this sense the book is an apotheosis of Nothingness, with Nothingness, however, understood as the creative force of annihilation. What matters is to say no to whatever negates one.

In the autumn of 1945 Sartre's fame had traveled far beyond France, and Heidegger's fame was about to penetrate into France. Heidegger received visitors from France, including young Alain Resnais, who would later become a film producer, and Frédéric de Towarnicki.

Towarnicki, a young soldier of the Rhine Division and a cultural officer in the French Army, had read *What Is Metaphysics?* and decided to visit Heidegger in Freiburg. He conceived the bold plan of brokering a meeting between Heidegger and Sartre. Towarnicki spoke to people close to Heidegger and was assured by them that Heidegger had protected Jewish university teachers. He reported this to Sartre, who, as a result, abandoned his original resistance to such a meeting. Heidegger, for his part, requested Towarnicki to help him rebuild his connections with France. A letter to Emile Brehier, professor of philosophy at the Sorbonne, had remained unanswered. Heidegger admitted that, apart from having read a few articles about him, he did not know Sartre's work. Towarnicki therefore lent Heidegger a French copy of *Being and Nothingness*, which Heidegger started to read at once. Towarnicki reports that in conversation Heidegger showed himself impressed by Sartre's skill of presentation. He declared himself downright enchanted by those passages in which Sartre philosophized about skiing. To illustrate his argument that "techniques" fundamentally determined appropriation of the world, Sartre had pointed out that a Savoyard, skiing by the French method, would experience mountain slopes quite differently from a Norwegian: "In fact according to whether one will employ the Norwegian method, which is better for gentler slopes, or the French method which is better for steep slopes, the same slope will appear as steeper or more gentle."[26] To philosophize about skiing was something Heidegger had considered at one time, as Hermann Mörchen reports from his Marburg days, but in the end he had lacked the courage to do so in a published work.

Heidegger was interested in meeting Sartre. Naturally he hoped that this might also help his position with regard to his case, which was then being investigated by the denazification committee. Towarnicki thus had Heidegger's and Sartre's agreement to meet in Baden-Baden; he even tried to persuade Camus to join the project, but Camus declined because of Heidegger's rectorship.

In the end, the meeting did not come about. At first there were no travel passes, and then there was no room on the train. At least that is what Towarnicki reported when, in 1993, he published the French translation of a letter from Heidegger to Sartre, written on October 28, 1945, after the missed opportunity. A copy of this letter has recently been discovered by Hugo Ott.

About his reading of Sartre, Heidegger had this to say: "Here for the first time I encountered an independent thinker who, from the foundations up, has experienced the area out of which I think. Your work shows such an immediate comprehension of my philosophy as I have never before encountered."[27] Heidegger expressly accepts Sartre's "emphasis on the Being-for-one-another," as well as Sartre's critique of the "explication of death" in *Being and Time*. Sartre had objected that Heidegger's "projecting oneself toward death" covered up the scandal of death, its absurdity and absolute contingency. He had argued that death could not accomplish anything else but "deprive life of all meaning."[28] But these differences did not stop Heidegger—as he wrote to Sartre—in "the wish, together with you, of bringing thinking back to a point from which it can be experienced as a basic event of history, and bringing present-day man back into an original relation with Being." He had looked forward to the meeting in Baden-Baden and was sorry it had not materialized. But perhaps, he thought, the matter should be tackled altogether more intensively and thoroughly. "It would be great if you could come and see us in the course of the winter. We might jointly philosophize in our small ski hut and from there make ski tours in the Black Forest." Heidegger concludes his letter with a grandiloquent proposal, painting a picture of the Dioscuri of Being-thinking, one of whom attacks the matter from the side of nothingness and the other from that of Being. "The task now is to grasp the world's moment with supreme earnestness and to put it into words, beyond all mere party congresses, trends of fashion, academic strands, in order that, at long last, the crucial experience awakens of how abysmally deep in essential nothingness the wealth of Being is concealed."

That Heidegger is serious about his tribute to, indeed almost admiration for, Sartre, and that he therefore had high expectations of his meeting with him, emerges from a personal note, dated October 5, 1945, published in the appendix of his Kant book. The note, which has usually been disregarded, reads: "Effect on Sartre crucial; only from there *Being and Time* understood" (K, 251).

Sartre's visit to the ski hut did not come off. Not until 1952 would the two men meet in person, in Freiburg. In the intervening years, however, Heidegger will write his public critique of Sartre's existentialism, formulated in his *Über den Humanismus* (Letter on Humanism). More about this later.

This philosophical cross-frontier traffic between Germany and France did not initially help Heidegger's defense; on the contrary, the opponents of his premature rehabilitation were, if anything, alarmed by it.

Toward the end of 1945, when Heidegger realized that his case was going badly and hoped Jaspers's opinion would exonerate him, he also turned to another friend from his early days—Conrad Gröber, the archbishop of Freiburg and the spiritual mentor of his youth. At the beginning of Nazi rule, Gröber had been one of the most ardent supporters of the "national upsurge" and had played a vital part in the conclusion of the Concordat. Later, however, Gröber had changed course and, from a conservative clerical attitude, become an opponent of political and ideological adjustment to the system. As a result he was able to act with authority toward the French military government in 1945. Heidegger was hoping that Gröber might help him and therefore called on him at his official residence in December 1945. According to Max Müller, the following scene appears to have taken place in Gröber's anteroom. The archbishop's sister entered and said (in the broad Swabian dialect that Heidegger, too, had spoken in his youth): "Well now, Martin's come to see us again! For twelve years he didn't show himself." Heidegger replied with some embarrassment: "Marie, I've paid for it dearly. It's all over with me now."[29] At Christmastime Gröber composed a letter to the French military government. This document has not been found, but the fact that Gröber tried to use his influence to ensure Heidegger's return to the university emerges from a letter sent to the archbishop by an official of the military government, stating that "it will be difficult to get Heidegger reinstated at the University if the rector votes against it. However, I will do whatever I can, since you recommend the man."[30] Gröber's efforts did prove unavailing against the opposition of the university. Nevertheless, Heidegger's visit gave Gröber profound satisfaction. In a report on the local political situation, written on March 8, 1946, to a member of the staff of Pope Pius XII, he said:

> The philosopher Martin Heidegger, a fellow-countryman and former pupil of mine, has been given emeritus status and is not allowed to lecture. He is at present staying at the Haus Baden sanatorium in Badenweiler, and is becoming increasingly withdrawn, as I learned yesterday from Professor Gebsattel. It was a great consolation to me when he came to see me at the start of his misfortunes and conducted himself in a most edifying way. I told him the truth and he listened with tears in his eyes. I shall not break off relations with him, because I am hopeful of a spiritual change of heart within him.[31]

Heidegger in fact had a physical and mental breakdown in the spring of 1946 and underwent psychosomatic treatment by Victor Baron von Gebsattel, a physician and psychologist of the Biswanger school of *Dasein* analysis, a psychoanalytical method that had been inspired by Heidegger's philosophy, whose practitioners also included Heidegger's later friend Medard Boss.

Heidegger's own information on his breakdown and sanatorium stay is vague. To Petzet he said that he had broken down at the "inquisitional hearing" in December 1945—though more probably this was in February 1946.

Thereupon Kurt Beringer, the dean of the faculty of medicine, had come and taken him to Dr. Gebsattel. "And what did he do? He took me on a hike up through the forest in the snow. That was all. But he showed me human warmth and friendship. Three weeks later I came back a healthy man again."[32]

Heidegger was well again, but for a while he was to be lonely. Many who were anxious to appear politically uncompromised thought it wise to avoid him. Robert Heiss, a friend of Heidegger from the Freiburg faculty, wrote to Jaspers in July 1946 that it had become obvious that "Herr Heidegger is going into a kind of exile; it may be said that he is reaping what he has sown."[33]

What then did he reap? He had to answer for his commitment in 1933. Yet his philosophical harvest was once more to be plentiful.

21

WHAT DO WE DO WHEN WE THINK?

What are we actually doing when we are thinking? We think to prepare our action and, subsequently, to examine it. In this twofold sense we think about it. Both times, thinking relates to action, but it is, in itself, something else. Since, however, it relates to action, it has its meaning in action and fulfills itself in action—why else would one think?

But could we not imagine some thinking that has its purpose in thinking alone? That does not aim at any effect outside itself? Thinking that fulfills itself through itself? That sweeps one along in a somewhat eerie way, and when it is all over one rubs one's eyes in surprise and once more, relieved or perhaps a little reluctantly, returns to the ground of so-called facts. The German writer E. T. A. Hoffmann tells the story of a reality-minded pedant who, after listening to a symphony, asked his deeply moved neighbor: "And what, sir, does this prove to us?" Is there a kind of thinking with regard to which this question would seem foolish?

Heidegger is convinced that his thinking is of just that kind. "Thinking does not bring knowledge as do the sciences, . . . does not produce usable practical wisdom, . . . solves no cosmic riddles, . . . does not endow us directly with the power to act" (WHD, 161).[1] What is this inclination that uses our capacity for thinking for more than mere action?

In his 1946 essay *On Humanism* Heidegger relates an anecdote told by Aristotle about Heraclitus. Strangers were seeking out Heraclitus to discover how a thinker lived and what it looked like when he was thinking. But they found him warming himself at a baking oven. "They stopped short, surprised, mainly because, as they hesitated, he encouraged them to come in with the words, 'The gods are present here too'" (ÜH, 45).

Heidegger reads this anecdote as information on the question of thinking. In it we have the "bland situation" of a person being cold and warming himself by the oven. That the gods are present "here too" signifies that they are present not only in special areas or special activities but also in everyday situations—but only if the everyday situation is specially thought about. To think about something means to return its dignity to it. The gods are present in the bakery because and so long as Heraclitus brings them into discourse. Such bringing into discourse means, to Heidegger, thinking. Being is brought out of its seclusion, and in the opening space of discourse it becomes the "There-is." This is the first aspect of thinking. Heraclitus, warming himself by the oven, warms himself and the strangers in yet another way—through discourse. It opens up and invites the strangers in. The second aspect of thinking: it is communication, designed to use discourse to share the opened situation with others.

When Heidegger, in *On Humanism,* thinks about thinking, his personal situation is that of a person proscribed. No doubt the Heraclitus anecdote occurred to him because it reminded him of his own circumstances. He, too, was now leading a scant, impoverished life. He too would have been glad of a baking oven to keep warm. In Freiburg there was no fuel; the cabin at Todtnauberg, where wood could have been cut in the neighborhood, was in need of repair. It was no longer fit for winter occupation, and there was a shortage of materials to restore it. Nevertheless, Heidegger withdrew to it from spring to late autumn. Life at his Freiburg home was too confined by the people billeted there. Besides, food supplies were more plentiful in the Black Forest. The peasants of the neighborhood were helpful.

There was a lot to depress him: his disgraceful removal from the university; waiting for the return of his two sons, who were still in Russian captivity. Yet despite his gloomy circumstances Heidegger's philosophy maintained the strangely relaxed fundamental note of the final years of the war.

His reaction to the measures against him was very different from that of, for instance, Carl Schmitt. Schmitt, the "court lawyer of the Third Reich," far more deeply involved in the criminal system, had been hit much harder. He, too, had lost his post, his library had been confiscated, and he had been interned for a year (September 1945 to October 1946) and then taken into custody afresh for the Nuremberg war crime trials (April to May 1947). No formal indictment was ultimately drafted, and Schmitt was able to withdraw to his native Plettenberg. At his release from detention a memorable dialogue took place between him and Robert Kempner, who represented the prosecution. Kempner: "What will you do now?" Schmitt: "I shall enter the safety of silence." But this was no composed silence. As shown by Schmitt's *Glossarium: Aufzeichnungen der Jahre 1947–1951,* his notes from 1947 to 1951, he was ceaselessly working on his self-justification; with embarrassing tearfulness he lamented his fate as a "hunted animal." He saw himself as the prophet Jonah spewed out from the belly of the leviathan. He fulminated against the "accusers in Nuremberg" and sneered, "The crimes against humanity are committed by Germans. The crimes for humanity are committed against Germans. That is the whole difference." He had particular contempt for those who participated in the "spectacle of a brawl between repentance preachers." He refused to submit to the denazification procedure, arguing: "If anyone wants to confess, let him go to the priest!" For the public he chose the attitude of heroic silence, and in his notes he complained that his voice was being deprived of a space for resonance, so that "without a throat" he had to shout. But it was a lot better, he wrote, to belong to the tormented than to the "self-tormentors."

Heidegger was not one of the "self-tormentors" either. Instead he saw himself as the "wise man from the mountain," who in broad perspectives and panoramas described the mischief of the modern age, in which the crimes of National Socialism were included but not especially highlighted. In this respect Heidegger also behaved differently from Alfred Baeumler, who (in his memoirs) wrote that "to declare myself 'guilty' in public seems to me undignified and pointless," but who, in his inward arena, judged himself more critically. Baeumler diagnosed in himself a tendency to avoid the difficulties of a complex and contradictory history in favor of the "absolute" ideas of nation, leader, race, historical mission. Instead of seeking real *"closeness to the things, distant vistas*" had triumphed and done violence to reality.[2] This was a reflection of German "lagging behind the West (unworldliness),"[3] which Baeumler elsewhere called "abstraction into the indefinite."[4] In political matters the longing for the exalted should be resisted. He prescribed for himself a sobering-up treatment, which eventually led him to an appreciation of democracy. Democracy was the "antiexalted." It lacked the grand prospect of the future, and was "all present"; in it there was no certainty of historical missions but only life with "probabilities."[5] Under the impact of Germany's catastrophe, as well as his personal one, Baeumler embarked on the (for him) difficult lesson of thinking about politics without metaphysics.

Heidegger's thinking was neither as self-pitying and aggressively self-opinionated as Carl Schmitt's, nor as political and self-critical as Alfred Baeumler's. The first published document on his thinking after 1945 was the essay *Über den Humanismus* (On Humanism), written in 1946 as an open letter to Jean Beaufret, Heidegger's principal apostle on the postwar French philosophical scene. Beaufret, as he has himself reported, had his first experience of Heidegger on June 4, 1944, the day the Allies landed in Normandy; for the first time, he understood him. This to him was such a happy moment that it quite overshadowed any joy over the impending liberation of France. When the French entered Freiburg, Beaufret got an officer to convey to Heidegger an exuberant letter: "Yes, with you it is philosophy itself that resolutely frees itself of all platitude and maintains the essential of its dignity."[6] Heidegger thereupon invited Beaufret for a visit. This visit materialized in September 1946 and marked the beginning of an intense lifelong friendship between them. The first result of this new relationship was *On Humanism.* Beaufret had asked Heidegger: "In what way can the word 'humanism' have its meaning restored to it?"

Heidegger readily took up the question, the more so as it gave him an opportunity to reply to Sartre's essay—published a few months earlier and discussed everywhere, including Germany—*Existentialism and Humanism.* Even though a personal meeting between them had not materialized, Heidegger was anxious for discussion with Sartre. Following a lecture given by him on October 29, 1945, which was the basis of the essay, Sartre had overnight become a European cult figure. A huge crowd had filled the Salle des Centraux in the expectation that the existentialist encyclical would be proclaimed that evening. And that was what happened: "scrimmages, blows, broken chairs, fainting spells. Box office destroyed, no tickets could be sold."[7] It took Sartre fifteen minutes to push his way through to the dais. In this "overheated, overcrowded, overexcited room"[8] he then, with his hands lazily in his pockets, embarked on his explanations which, sentence by sentence, immediately conveyed the impression of final and valid formulations. Those in the tightly squashed, buffeted, half-stifled audience were entitled to think that they were hearing sentences that would be quoted forever thereafter. Scarcely a day passed after that lecture, and not only in France, when Sartre and existentialism were not mentioned or quoted. Only a few months earlier Sartre had said: "Existentialism? I don't know what that is. My philosophy is a philosophy of existence." But by December 1945 the first popular breviaries of existentialism were in circulation. Now the answer to "Existentialism—what's that?" was: "Commit yourself, sweep mankind along with you, re-create yourself time and again, solely through your actions."

Sartre's catchy formulation that "existence precedes essence" was bound, more so in a devastated Germany than elsewhere, to touch those who were finding each other again under the rubble of the catastrophe, in the realization that they had got away by the skin of their teeth. Anyone who had saved his existence could start afresh. It was in this sense that Sartre's philosophically subtle dictum gained currency in postwar Germany. When Erich Kästner, the novelist and poet, returned from captivity toward the end of 1946 to a destroyed Dresden, he realized, as he stated in a reportage, that most things had become unimportant. "In this dark Germany one feels that essence makes up existence."[9]

In his legendary lecture on October 29, 1945, Sartre answered the question about the fate of humanism in an epoch that had just witnessed excesses of barbarism. Sartre's answer was that humanist values that we can rely on because allegedly they are firmly installed in our civilization do not exist. They exist only if we, in the situation of decision, reinvent them anew and let them become real. Existentialism confronts man with this freedom and with the responsibility associated with it. Existentialism, therefore, is not a philosophy of escape from reality, of pessimism, quietism, selfishness, or despair. It is a philosophy of commitment. Sartre introduces striking formulations, which soon become known throughout Europe: "Existentialism defines man by his actions. It tells him that hope lies only in action, and that the only thing that allows man to live is action. Man commits himself to his life and thereby draws his image, beyond which there is nothing. We are alone without excuses. This is what I mean when I say that man is condemned to be free."[10]

In France, just as in Germany, the problem of humanism—the problem of its revival or renewal after years of barbarism and betrayal—had become topical again after 1945, which was why Sartre and, a little later, Heidegger felt induced to deal with it. Sartre had to defend himself against the accusation that, at a historical moment when the values of civilization—solidarity, truth, freedom—had revealed their fragility, he further weakened the ethical norms by leaving it to the individual to decide on their validity. Sartre argued that, with God eliminated, someone must invent those values. Matters had to be faced as they were. Enlightenment had long removed all naïveté: we have awakened from a dream, we find ourselves beneath an empty heaven, and we can no longer rely on the community. Thus there is no choice but to create the values and defend their validity by our actions and as individuals, with a blessing from above, without exuberant authorization from God or the spirit of the people, or from some universal idea of humanity. The fact that everyone must invent "humanity" for himself means that "there is no sense in life *a priori*."[11] It is up to each individual to give it sense by choosing certain values through his actions. It is on this existentialist choice of the individual that the possibility of a "human community"[12] is based. Any such action is a draft, an act of "transcending."[13] Sartre argues that man does not rest within himself as in a ready reality; he is driven out of himself and must, time and again, realize himself. And what he realizes is his transcendence—understood not as some Beyond but as the quintessence of the possibilities toward which man can transcend himself. Transcendence is not something to find rest in; it is the heart of the unrest that surrounds man. Existentialism is therefore a form of humanism "because we remind man that there is no legislator but himself; that he himself, thus abandoned, must decide for himself; also because we show that it is not by turning back upon himself, but always by seeking, beyond himself, an aim which is one of liberation or some particular realization, that man can realize himself as truly human."[14]

Against this view, Gabriel Marcel—a Christian humanist who had absorbed existential elements and become known in Germany along with Sartre—argued that Sartre's transcendence remained empty. Not only was this a philosophical problem, but it also meant surrendering man to social-political disasters. In an essay for the journal *Der Monat* entitled "What Is a Free Person?" (September 1950), he asked: "How was it possible for unfreedom to establish itself in the totalitarian systems of fascism and Stalinism?" This unfreedom, he states, was able to triumph because secularization had not left anything but the realization of inner-worldly purposes. In consequence man had been surrendered to the world totally and unreservedly, so that he was unable to do anything better with his exalting world-transcending intentions than to declare inner-worldly aims to be absolutes and turn them into his idols. The God who had left man free scope with regard to reality thus becomes an idol of man's own making, an idol that enslaves. Marcel speaks of "idolatry of race and idolatry of class."[15] Marcel's thesis that "man can be free, and remain free, only to the extent to which he remains linked to transcendence"[16] brings into play a transcendence that is experienced at moments of ecstatic alienation from the world. The "creative inventiveness," of which Marcel speaks with the same enthusiasm as Sartre produces not only human civilization; its élan carries further: it no longer wants just to live, it wants more than to live. Only if we remain citizens of two worlds can we preserve the human world in its humanity.

Gabriel Marcel in effect reminds us of a fundamental thesis of religion. Transcendence is the relation that relieves men of having to be everything for each other. They can therefore stop shuffling off their lack of Being onto one another and holding each other responsible when they feel like strangers in the world. They no longer have to fight so anxiously for their identity, because they are now allowed to believe that God truly knows them. This transcendence thus helps man come into the world by keeping alive, and even sanctifying, his sense of being a stranger. It prevents his out-and-out incorporation, reminding man that he is only a guest with a limited permit to stay. It therefore expects him to admit his own impotence, his finitude, his fallibility, and his capability of guilt. However, it makes this admission one man can live with, and in that respect it is the spiritual answer to the limit of feasibility.

For Marcel, Sartre cannot be right in his assertion that there is no other universe than that of the human ego. If that were so, then the world would be hell. It is not enough for man to transcend himself; he must and can transcend himself toward something that he himself is not and can never become. He must not try to realize himself; he must be helped to rediscover the dimension in which he can develop.

In Germany during those first few postwar years, the Christian humanism of Reinhold Schneider and Romano Guardini argued along similar lines to Marcel. Reinhold Schneider had been living in Freiburg since 1938. Toward the end of the Nazi regime he had been accused of high treason. He had arranged for his religious reflections, sonnets, and stories to circulate in private copies in their thousands, letting them reach even frontline troops. In these writings Schneider tried to arouse a religious conscience against barbarism. He clung to this basic aspect of his thinking even after 1945. Is it a fact—he asks in his essay *Das Unzerstörbare* (The Indestructible)—that no one is to be held responsible for collective crimes? He answers his question like this: neither must the political holders of power be permitted to escape their responsibility, nor, on the other hand, must all responsibility be attributed to them in order that the individual might be spared self-examination. Such self-examination would yield the comfortable knowledge that we are all sinners, and, if conducted seriously, it would reveal the extent to which we need the experience of sin. What, Schneider asks, becomes of guilt vis-à-vis men if the community of men pursues a criminal road? Then such guilt no longer exists. Once guilt disappears in the socialization of crime, all that remains is sin before God. Only the relation to God can save man from himself. This lesson is derived by Schneider from the catastrophe of National Socialism. But a relation to God is not something we can "produce." God is not our "design." Schneider cannot propose a therapy, he has no political concept handy, he is left only with a belief in a history that, possibly, will treat us mercifully. "History is God's bridge-building across immense abysses. We must cross that bridge. But each day it grows by perhaps only the length of one step . . . We walk into a different, an entirely unfamiliar world . . . History has no break, but its changes appear like downfalls."[17]

Like Reinhold Schneider, Romano Guardini also saw the light in the downfall. Guardini, who for a short time in 1946 had been considered as a successor to Heidegger's chair, in 1950 published a widely read book, *The End of the Modern Age,* which was based on his lectures in Tübingen in the winter of 1947–48.

The modern age, according to Guardini, unfolded from an understanding of nature as a protective power, from human subjectivity as an autonomous personality, and from culture as an intermediate sphere with its own laws. Everything, he claimed, had received its meaning from nature, culture, and subjectivity. With the end of the modern age, which his time was witnessing, these ideas fade away. Nature loses its protective force and becomes unfamiliar and dangerous. "Mass man" displaces the individual, and the old faith in culture dies in the malaise of culture. The totalitarian systems are both expressions of and responses to this crisis, which also opens up the chance of a new beginning. Man evidently must first lose his natural and cultural riches in order that, in such "poverty," he may rediscover himself as a "naked" person before God. Perhaps the "mists of secularization" will disperse and a new day of history will begin.

It can hardly be claimed that it was a modest or reticent humanism that came to the fore during the first few years after the collapse. Although there was a lot of confusion and dispute over details, especially on specific questions of political reconstruction, there was nevertheless a widespread tendency toward a grand Occidental whole that would ensure a new beginning. In his preface to the journal *Die Wandlung* (Transformation), Karl Jaspers wrote in November 1945:

> The mere fact that we are alive should have a meaning. Face to face with Nothing we are pulling ourselves together . . . We have by no means lost everything unless, in desperate fury, we squander away what could be beyond loss—the foundation of history, for us primarily the millennium of German history, next of Occidental history, and finally of human history altogether. Wide open to man, we may engross ourselves in these foundations, in our nearest and most distant memories.[18]

For many contemporaries these were even then rather grand words, a repetition of that German specialty of extravagant wretchedness, as diagnosed as early as 1935 in his Groningen exile by Helmuth Plessner in his essay *The Destiny of the German Spirit at the End of Its Bourgeois Era*, published in 1959 under the title *Die verspätete Nation* (The Belated Nation). But then, in a Germany that had followed its Führer to the very end, where politics had been replaced by loyal obedience, a country now divided into zones of occupation and governed by the Allies, a country happy to be excused from personal responsibility—where was political reasoning to come from, any reasoning that did not immediately escape into overly grand questions, a kind of thinking that might have provided a counterweight to a spirit that aimed either too high or too low, that started either from nothingness or from God, from downfall or ascent?

Dolf Sternberger, with Karl Jaspers a coeditor of *Die Wandlung*, very soon voiced his uneasiness at these "high" notes of "spirit-politics." He saw a danger that the old bad habit of the German spirit of regarding itself as too noble for politics might live on. It was a mistake, he claimed, to see culture and the spirit as a separate sphere, separate from politics, the economy, technology, everyday matters. Care should be taken to tackle all spheres of life with spirit and culture. Such cultivation and refinement of human affairs represented humanity. "I would gladly," he said in 1950 at the Congress for Cultural Freedom, "sacrifice some of the so-called culture in Germany if we acquired a little civilization in return. *Less* fog and smoke of a vague mass of ideals and superior values," and instead more appreciation of what was closer, of a civic spirit. "Let us not be led into the maze of culture. If we want to defend freedom, we must defend it in its unambiguousness, completeness, and indivisibility, as political, personal, and spiritual freedom. Let us cultivate freedom! In this way everything else will come to us."[19]

Sternberger realized, of course, that especially in Germany this issue of a culture of freedom was bound to provoke a clash of opinions and programs. Was it to be achieved on a liberal-democratic basis, on a socialist or capitalist basis, or by some third road? Was it to be based on Christian values or on radical pluralism? Time and again Sternberger had to point out what had by no means yet become a matter of course in Germany—that such argument was part of culture and not just interparty squabbling, and that it did not mean the decline of the West. The dispute was not the problem, but the fact that once again the "spirit" believed itself to be above these issues and that, once again, in its gnostic despair, its apocalyptic obsessions, and its fantasies about the twilight of mankind, it was surrendering to ideas of ascent or decline.

In point of fact, the situation in Germany was exceedingly difficult for any thinking that came down from the peaks of global reflection and exposed itself to the demands of the real situation. Could one, for instance, accept the judicial measures that the Allies were practicing with the Nuremberg Tribunal and the denazification procedures? Was this not an abandonment of responsibility for one's own history? But, then, who was to judge in Germany? Was not the experiment of moral politics doomed to failure, since the Soviet Union, an equally criminal totalitarian power, was participating in it? How, after the defeat of fascism, was one to behave toward the new threat of communism? The war was over, but already new threatening war clouds were gathering. Liberation and catastrophe—where did the one begin and the other end? How could there be democratic reconstruction in a nation that a moment earlier, in its overwhelming majority, had jubilantly cheered the Führer? The capitalist economic elites, the academic elites—they had all supported the system. Was there still any tradition of democratic civic sense? Could a revival of German educational idealism help? A return to Goethe, as proposed by Meinecke—was that a solution? Would it not be better to rely on the civilizing effect of a market economy? Would merchandise, once it was again more plentifully available, dispose of the problem of moral purification and living in truth? Why a process of grieving, if it kept people from working? Was the idea that a nation should go through a process of grieving not simply an unpolitical fantasy, an impermissible transfer of the attitudes of individuals to a collective subject?

The day-to-day politics of that period were not unduly troubled by this whirl of questions, but the Western zones confidently progressed along the road that proved, in practice, successful—monetary reform, amalgamation of the Western zones, establishment of the Federal Republic, and integration of the West in the face of the incipient cold war. In West Germany there arose an open society, domesticated by patriarchal authority. Thus, in a situation of general spiritual helplessness, began the success story of the Adenauer state.

Revealing in this context are Hannah Arendt's observations on her first postwar visit to Germany in 1950. She describes how people still moving among the ruins were already sending one another picture postcards of churches and market squares, public buildings and bridges that no longer existed. The mood fluctuated between apathy and fiendishly efficient hard work, with hustle and bustle in small things and indifference to the political fate of the community. "The reality of destruction that surrounds every German is resolved in a brooding, though not very deeply rooted, self-pity, which, however, vanishes rapidly when in some wide thoroughfares ugly little flat buildings, originating in some main street in America, are erected."[20] What, asks Arendt, had become of the Germans' love of their land? They were crawling out of their rubble, they were complaining about the wickedness of the world, and when they were starving and freezing they said: So this is the democracy you wish to bring us! Things were no better among the "intellectuals." Here, too, was a rejection of reality. "The intellectual atmosphere is permeated with vague commonplaces, with attitudes formed long before the present events, to which they are now supposed to apply; one feels crushed by a spreading political stupidity."[21] Part of this "stupidity," according to Arendt, was also a certain type of German profundity that sought the causes of the war, the destruction of Germany, and the murder of the Jews not in the actions of the Nazi regime but "in the events that led to the expulsion of Adam and Eve from Paradise."[22]

In the immediate postwar situation, Heidegger's letter *On Humanism* seems a document of helplessness. Certainly it, too, contains the "stupidity" from essentialization observed by Hannah Arendt. Admittedly Heidegger does not seek the beginning of the bad end in Adam and Eve, nor in Ulysses—as did Adorno and Horkheimer's simultaneously published *Dialectics of Enlightenment*—but he nevertheless seeks it in the gray mists of prehistory, in Plato and his successors.

Politically, this is a blunt text. But Heidegger no longer makes any claim to mapping a specific political road. That was something he had given up after the failure of his rectorship. Politically, Heidegger was just as lost as Thomas Mann, who, in an address in 1949, the Goethe Year (the two hundredth anniversary of his birth), expressly rejected the role of adviser with the disarming confession: "If it were not for the refuge of fantasy, if it were not for the games which, after each completion, lure one on to new adventures and exciting experiments, to intensified continuation, if it were not for the entertainment of invention, creation, art—I really would not know how to live, let alone give advice or preach to others."[23]

Just as Mann said, "I am only a poet," so Heidegger said, "I am only a philosopher." Strictly speaking, he does not wish to be even that—he wants to be "just" a thinker. He is attracted by the tempting adventures and exciting experiments of thinking; they, too, seduce to "intensified continuation." If he could not surrender himself to this business of thinking, he would have to say, like Mann, "I really would not know how to live, let alone give advice or preach to others."

The letter *On Humanism* is a document of such "intensified continuation" and, at the same time, a balance sheet in his own case. As an intervention in the political direction-finding attempts of his day, the letter must seem inept. But as an attempt to recapitulate his own thinking and to determine his present place, as an opening up of a horizon revealing certain problems of life in our civilization, the work is a magnificent and highly effective document along Heidegger's path of thinking. Besides, all of Heidegger's late philosophy is present in it already.

Heidegger's letter, therefore, is an indirect answer to Sartre, to the by then rampant existentialist fashion, and to the equally topical renaissance of humanism. To remind ourselves: Beaufret had asked, "In what way can the word 'humanism' be given a meaning?"

Sartre had declared his existentialism to be a new humanism of personal responsibility and commitment in a situation of metaphysical homelessness. And Heidegger now tries to explain why humanism is itself the problem to which it believes itself to be the solution, why thinking must go beyond humanism, and why thinking has quite enough to do when it commits itself to itself, to the business of thinking.

Heidegger starts his reflections at just this business of thinking, at commitment, in order from there to arrive at the question of humanism. What, then, is thinking? The answer that suggests itself is a concept of a disparateness and a consecutiveness of theory and practice. First reflection, the model, the hypothesis, the theoretical blueprint, and then its translation into practice. Practice thus understood is the real action; theory, by comparison, is at best a kind of trial action. In this pattern, any thinking not related to action as something external to it loses its dignity and worth; it becomes void. Such a linking of thinking and action implies the dominance of the useful. The demand that thinking should commit itself evidently means usefulness for the implementation of certain practical requirements in politics, the economy, and society. Evidence of practical use and laudable commitment thus also serves as proof of thinking's public entitlement to existence.

Heidegger brushes this idea aside. He calls it a "technical interpretation of thinking" (ÜH, 6), one that is age-old and has, since Plato's day, been the great temptation for thinking. It is the timid way, intimidated by life's practical expectations, of losing faith in oneself, as it views itself as a "procedure of reflection in the service of doing and acting" (ÜH, 6). This intimidation by the demand of practice had a disastrous effect on philosophy, Heidegger believes. In competition with the practically successful sciences, philosophy finds itself in the embarrassing position of having to prove its usefulness. Philosophy wished to be an equal of the sciences that had emancipated themselves from it. It wished to be "elevated to the rank of a science" (ÜH, 6), but it failed to notice that it would only lose itself in the sciences or crash into them. Not because it was something "superior" or exalted, but because it would have to start from something closer, from an experience that precedes any scientific attitude. By distancing itself from that experience, it suffers the fate of a fish out of water. "For a long time, for much too long, thinking has been out of its element," Heidegger says (ÜH, 7). But where, then, is this real location of thinking? What is that something that is close to thinking?

It was only natural that Heidegger should have sought to answer the question of proximity by looking back to *Being and Time.* There he had tried to discover what is the closest, the primal, for the *Dasein* that finds itself in the world. The bottom line of this investigation had been that initially we do not experience ourselves or our world in a quasi-scientific attitude. The world is not, in this sense, our "representation," because first of all we experience our Being-in-the-world. This Being-in is decisive and primary. The attuned Being-in is fearful, bored, worried, busy, dazed, devoted, ecstatic. Only against this background of the initial Being-in can it happen that we reflect ourselves outward, that we make certain ideas for ourselves, that we carve out "objects" from the continuum of our caring and relating. The fact that there is a "subject" that is confronted by "objects" is not a basic experience but is the result of a secondary, abstract performance. If original Being-in is the closest, if in that proximity the things of life can unfold in their whole profusion, then a paradoxical constellation arises. Since thinking causes us to lose immediacy, any thinking that strives for proximity is, in consequence, expected to think against its own distancing tendency. Thinking that is at home in mediation is expected to get close to the immediate. But, in doing so, will it not then be like the fish out of water? Would this not amount to making thinking undo the effects of thinking? A revival of Hegel's "mediated immediacy"? And is it at all possible to think back into that proximity? Heidegger's reply is laconic: thinking is doing its job only if it is "broken" by that job. "The philosophy about the foundering," Heidegger says, that philosophy now in fashion, is divided by a chasm from what is really needed, "from a foundered thinking" (ÜH, 34). This wrecked thinking is no misfortune, indeed it shows that one is on the right road. Where does the road lead? To proximity. But what is it looking for in that proximity of which we have meanwhile learned that it means the elementary and primary Being-in? Is this location so attractive only because science has "bypassed" it? Surely science is not so important that anything it misses must therefore be ennobled? Has not Heidegger, leading the life of an academic, become obsessed with an ideal competition with science? Is the ontological difference that he makes such a fuss about perhaps no more than an insistence on the narcissistic difference from the academic pursuit of philosophy?

We have, of course, long known that this "proximity" holds a great promise, a sacred promise, that in fact goes well beyond what can be found in the scientific sphere. It is the experience of Being. In *Being and Time,* Heidegger states, he had been on the way to this experience and its formulation, but had not "got through." His intention toward "science" and "research" (ÜH, 47) had impeded and "misled" him. Even then it had not been his intention to contribute to scientific anthropology; he had been concerned with questioning the most questionable, with man's *Dasein* as an open place that has opened in Being. *Dasein* understood as the location where that which is *(das Seiende)* is touched upon and thereby becomes Being, and this means it becomes bright, friendly, opening, even in its impenetrability and its "withdrawal."

In point of fact, Heidegger had performed his *Dasein* analysis with an eye to Being; *Dasein* to him was that *essent (Seiende)* that was concerned with its own "Being-able." In the end, however, he had allowed himself, against his earlier intention, to be drawn too far into *Dasein.* With so much *Dasein,* Being had been lost sight of. This can be shown by the concept of "existence." When in *Being and Time* Heidegger states: "The kind of Being towards which *Dasein* can comport itself in one way or another, and always does comport itself somehow, we call 'existence' [*Existenz*],"[24] then the concept of Being here had the specific meaning of an own Being to be realized. That is why Heidegger also speaks of "Being-to" in the sense of intention and planning. This is also the sense of the thesis of the "priority of *existentia* over *essentia,*"[25] to which Sartre can, with some justification, refer when he emphasizes the provisional character of *Dasein:* "Existence precedes essence."

But now that he wishes to lead his original intention out of the captivity of academic philosophy, Heidegger attaches a different meaning to the concept of existence. Now it signifies not only the Being-nature of a creature that is concerned about its own Being-able, but also existence, now spelled by Heidegger "*Ek-sistenz*": "The standing in the clearing of Being I call the *Ek-sistenz* of man. Man alone possesses this quality." This *Ek-sistenz* signifies endurance but also ecstasy. We are by now aware of Heidegger's fondness, ever since the 1930s, of quoting Hölderlin's letter in which he confides to his friend Böhlendorff how Apollo's thunderbolt had struck him.

"Existence" at best got as far as resolution; *Ek-sistenz,* on the other hand, means being open to ecstatic experiences of different kinds. Heidegger's famous *Kehre* (reversal, about-face), which triggered an avalanche of interpretations, should be understood as *simply* as intended by him. At his first attempt (up to *Being and Time*) he got stuck in *Dasein;* in his second attempt—or in his about-facing approach—he aims at a Being that is addressed by *Dasein* and claimed by it. This entails quite a string of reinterpretations, with the activist possibilities of relation, derived from individual *Dasein,* having their polarity reversed to a register of more passive, permissive, tolerant modes of behavior. The "thrownness" of *Dasein* now becomes its "destiny"; "caring for" one's own affairs becomes "guardianship" of something that has been imposed and entrusted to one. "Falling" into the world is replaced by the world's "crowding in." And in the "designs" *(Entwürfe),* it is Being itself that "throws" *(wirft)* itself through the world.

Being-thought, which seeks proximity, there finds something that in Nietzsche is still, rather naively and unguardedly, called "the moment of true sensation."

Does this then answer the question: What is the business of thinking if it is to be more than just a service for action? It does answer it. Thinking is inward action, it is a different state that is revealed in *Dasein* through, and during, thinking. Thinking is a transformed way of being in the world; in Heidegger's words: "This thinking is neither theoretical nor practical. It takes place before this differentiation. This thinking, insofar as it is, is the remembrance of Being and nothing else . . . Such thinking has no result. It has no effect. It satisfies its nature simply by being" (ÜH, 48). Then follows a sentence that should be memorized, because it contains the whole of Heidegger's late philosophy. This kind of thinking—what does it do? "It lets Being be" (ÜH, 48).

And what about humanism? Grandly disregarding the fact that National Socialism has only recently so disastrously "underbid" humanism, Heidegger now embarks on "overbidding" it. The humanist calling of man, he says, whether as a theonomous or autonomous humanism, "does not yet lead to the experience of man's real dignity" (ÜH, 21). His thinking is "against" humanism, not because he is pleading for "bestiality," but because humanism "does not value man's *humanitas* highly enough" (ÜH, 22). How highly should it be valued? As highly as God was valued in the past. Man as the "shepherd of Being" was a creature of which we should not make a graven image. As the "undetermined animal" (Nietzsche), as a creature that cannot be objectively fixed but which lives in the plentitude of its relations, man does indeed need moral ties, even though "they may hold together only as a makeshift and only for the present day" (ÜH, 43). These ties, therefore, are really no more than makeshifts; they are something penultimate of which we must not believe that they mark the end of thinking. Thinking advances further, until with its inspired élan it makes the genuine "experience of the durable. The truth of Being gives away the constraint for all comportment" (ÜH, 51).

At this point Heidegger is worlds away from Sartre, who states: "Man must first find himself again and convince himself that nothing can save him from himself, not even valid proof of the existence of God."[26]

Even though Heidegger declares that "'Being' is not God, nor a foundation for the world" (ÜH, 22), this alters nothing about the fact that experience of Being attunes man to a Being-relation that is devout, meditative, grateful, reverent, and relaxed. The entire circle of effects that God causes around himself is present, except that Heidegger places on this God a stricter prohibition of images than any of the established religions. Heidegger's God owns the "clearing." He is not yet experienced in the "essent" *(in dem Seienden)* that is encountered in the clearing. He is encountered only if this clearing is specifically experienced and gratefully accepted as the enablement of visibility.

Whichever way one tries to tackle the problem, it ultimately remains a restatement of Schelling's wonderful idea that nature opens its eyes in man and notices that it exists. Man as the place of the self-visibility of Being. "Without man Being would be mute; it would be there, but it would not be the True one."[27]

What follows from this? We already know—nothing follows. "In all this it seems as though nothing at all has occurred through thinking speech" (ÜH, 52). And yet, the entire relationship with the world has changed. There is a different state of mind; the world is being viewed differently. Heidegger would use the years remaining to him to test that view—against technology, against building and homemaking, against language, and, however delicately, against God. His thinking, which he no longer calls "philosophy," would endeavor to let be that which lets one be. "Because in this thinking there is something simple to think, it presents such difficulty to a visualization traditionally offered as philosophy. Yet the difficulty lies not in searching out some specially profound meaning or in creating involved concepts, it lies concealed in the step backward" (ÜH, 33).

22

MARTIN HEIDEGGER, HANNAH ARENDT, AND KARL JASPERS AFTER THE WAR

"The distortions are insufferable, and the mere fact that he now dresses up everything as if it were an interpretation of *Being and Time* suggests that everything will again come out distorted. I've read the letter against humanism, also very questionable and frequently ambiguous, but at any rate the first thing that's again on the old level" (BwAJ, 178). This was Hannah Arendt's judgment of Heidegger's first postwar publication, written in a letter to Karl Jaspers dated September 29, 1949. She had resumed contact with Jaspers in the late autumn of 1945, through the mediation of Melvin Lasky. Before that, Jaspers and Arendt had not heard anything from each other since 1938. He had scarcely hoped that she was still alive, Jaspers wrote in his first letter after the war. And Hannah answered: "Since I've known that both of you have come through this whole infernal spectacle safely, I've been feeling a little more at home again in this world" (BwAJ, 58). There was a feeling of having got away unscathed. Arendt wrote that she was still stateless and had not "become 'respectable' in any way"; she still believed "that an existence worthy of a human being is possible today only on the fringe of society" (BwAJ, 65).

She was underplaying a little, since she had meanwhile made a name for herself in America as a political journalist. But she was living in modest circumstances in New York—which, however, did not prevent her from sending Jaspers and his wife three parcels of provisions each month.

Karl Jaspers himself had suddenly become very "respectable" after the war. Having been ostracized during the Nazi period made him, almost overnight, the conscience of the nation—something which at first he regarded as an imposition and a hypocrisy. He mistrusted this sudden fame; it was to him like "living in a fiction" (BwAJ, 70), which he tried to escape when, in the summer of 1946, he accepted an invitation to the University of Basel in Switzerland.

Hannah Arendt immediately resumed contact with Jaspers, but it was not so with Heidegger. Just before her escape from Germany she had witnessed Heidegger the rector become a man of the Nazi system. And everything she subsequently heard about him in America suggested that he had remained one. Throughout her years of exile it was almost impossible for Arendt to hold on to the "indelible" that linked her to Heidegger. How could she stay loyal to Heidegger, whom, politically, she had to regard as belonging to those who had persecuted her, without abandoning her agreement with herself? She tried to tear herself free by squaring accounts with him—until, after their first meeting again, she could write with relief: "That evening and that [the next] morning are a confirmation of a whole life."[1]

But first, that squaring of accounts that preceded the meeting. At the beginning of 1946 Arendt published an essay in *Partisan Review* entitled "What Is Existential Philosophy?" That winter the existentialist method had spread to America. Sartre happened to be there just then, and Arendt met him. She was now to explain to the public the solid philosophical background of a spiritual attitude that had, until then, been known only from fashionable slogans. In his lectures in the United States, Sartre always emphasized the social commitment of existentialism. Arendt, by contrast, developed the thesis that in the German version of existentialism, from Schelling via Nietzsche to Heidegger, there had been an increasing tendency to confront the individual human Self as a place of truth with the untrue social whole. Only in Jaspers was this tendency overcome. Heidegger, on the other hand, in her presentation, figured as the peak of existential solipsism. In Heidegger the authentic Self had taken over the inheritance of God. Ordinary Being-in-the-world meant a loss of original purity. "What, consequently, appears as 'Fall' in Heidegger are all those modes of existence which rest on the fact that Man lives together in the world with his fellows."[2] Heidegger therefore was missing the *conditio humana.* Man could be all kinds of things but presumably never an "authentic Self." Anyone, Arendt argues, who rejects the ordinary world of the "They" abandons the ground of the human. What is left is a flirtation with one's own "nothingness," which, she suggests, had made Heidegger susceptible to barbarism. Had not the philosophical negation of the concept of humanity eventually resulted in the practical negation of humanity?

Hannah Arendt sent this essay to Karl Jaspers, still with the "old childish fear" (BwAJ, 73) of the severe judgment of her former philosophy teacher. However, Karl Jaspers, who found the manuscript in a parcel, wedged between tins of corned beef, evaporated milk, and bars of chocolate, was "delighted." He merely objected to the rumor, passed on by Arendt in a footnote, that Heidegger had forbidden Husserl access to the faculty: "What you report is, of course, true in substance, only the account of what actually took place may not be entirely accurate" (BwAJ, 79). Heidegger—Jaspers suspects—could only have signed the relevant official directive, as had other rectors. (This, however, as mentioned earlier, was not the case either. Heidegger was able to inform Husserl of the annulment of his "temporary suspension from office," as he did not come under the law on the Restoration of a Professional Civil Service.) Arendt sticks to her point; she regards Heidegger as a "potential murderer" (BwAJ, 84) because his behavior had broken Husserl's heart. Karl Jasper's comment on this was "I fully share your assessment of Heidegger" (BwAJ, 99).

Despite such remarks, Arendt and Jaspers were not yet through with Heidegger. Even though Arendt resists for another couple of years the project of her friend Dolf Sternberger to publish Heidegger's *On Humanism* in *Neue Rundschau,* when Jaspers informs her on September 1, 1949, that he is again exchanging occasional letters with Heidegger, she writes: "Since, as is well known, one is not consistent, at least I'm not, I was glad to hear it" (BwAJ, 178).

Karl Jaspers had started his renewed correspondence with Heidegger when he championed the revocation of the teaching ban imposed on Heidegger. At the beginning of 1949 he had written to Gerd Tellenbach, the rector of Freiburg University: "Professor Martin Heidegger is recognized throughout the world for his achievements as one of the most important philosophers of the present. There is no one in Germany to surpass him. His almost concealed philosophy, which is in touch with the most profound questions and which is only indirectly revealed in his writings, possibly makes him a unique figure today in a philosophically poor world" (quoted in BwHJ, 275). Steps should be taken, Jaspers said, to ensure that Heidegger could work in peace and, should he so desire, also teach.

When Heidegger's denazification procedure ended in March 1949 with the verdict "Fellow traveler. No punitive measures," consultations were resumed at the university about lifting the ban on his teaching. In May 1949 the academic senate, with a bare majority, proposed to the Ministry of Education that Heidegger be reinstated with the rights of an emeritus professor and that, in consequence, the ban on his teaching be lifted. Negotiations, however, dragged on for quite a while. Not until the winter semester of 1951–52 was Heidegger able to lecture again.

In his first letter to Heidegger, written February 6, 1949, Jaspers took cautious soundings on whether the state of affairs "that we are silent toward each other" might not be brought to an end. This would certainly be a difficult task. "The infinite sadness since 1933 and the present state of affairs, under which my German soul is suffering more and more, did not unite us, but silently separated us," he wrote. However, even though there was "darkness" between them, he thought an attempt might be made to discover if, in the private and philosophical sphere, "a word might not pass between us, from one to the other." Jaspers concluded his letter with the words: "I salute you as though from a distant past, across an abyss of time, holding firm to something that was and that cannot be just nothing" (BwHJ, 170).

Jaspers's letter at first did not reach Heidegger. But in June Heidegger learned from Robert Hess that Jaspers had written to him. Without having read the letter, Heidegger drafted a short note whose forced tone clearly betrayed his insecurity. "Through all straying and confusion and a temporary disattunement, my relation with you has remained unaffected." On what level was that "relation" to be continued, or how was it to be resumed? Heidegger initially opted for communion on an exalted level. "There are but few guardians of thinking in the growing distress of the world; yet they must stand up against dogmatism of every kind, without expecting effect. The international public and its organization are not the place where the fate of humanity is decided. One should not speak about loneliness. But it remains the only location where thinkers and poets, as far as humanly possible, stand by Being. From this location I greet you cordially" (BwHJ, 171).

Jaspers replied laconically and with ill-concealed mistrust: "What you call the revelation of Being has not so far been accessible to me. The 'location' from which you greet me—perhaps I have never yet entered it, but I am happy, with astonishment and suspense, to receive such a greeting" (July 10, 1949, BwHJ, 176).

To Hannah Arendt he commented on Heidegger's letter disdainfully: "He is entirely in his Being speculation, he writes *'Seyn.'* Two and a half decades ago he backed 'existence' and basically distorted matters. Now he backs more essentially . . . I hope he doesn't distort it again. But I doubt it. Can one, as an impure soul . . . can one see greatest purity in insincerity?" But he immediately takes back his harsh judgment and observes: "The strange thing is that he knows about something that hardly anyone notices today, and that his surmise is so impressive" (BwAJ, 177).

Arendt similarly fluctuates in her judgment. She is pleased that Jaspers has made contact again with Heidegger, and at the same time she endorses his negative opinions. "This living in Todtnauberg, ranting against civilization, and writing Sein with a 'y' is surely in reality just the bolt-hole into which he has withdrawn, because he rightly assumes that there he needs to see only those people who make a pilgrimage to him full of admiration; surely hardly anyone will climb 1200 meters just to make a scene" (BwAJ, 178).

In November 1949 Arendt visited Europe for four months, charged by the Commission for Jewish Cultural Reconstruction in Europe with inspecting and recording what remained of Jewish cultural treasures after looting by the Nazis. On this trip, in December 1949, she first visited Karl and Gertrud Jaspers in Basel. According to Elżbieta Ettinger, Jaspers, who had a fatherly fondness for Arendt, now learned for the first time of the love affair between her and Heidegger. "Ach, but this is very exciting," he said.[3] Hannah was relieved at his reaction. It had been entirely possible that Jaspers would react with moral criticism or even jealousy. The two of them talked at such length about Heidegger that Jaspers, scrupulous as he was, began to feel uncomfortable: "Poor Heidegger, we sit here now, the two best friends he has, and see right through him."[4]

When Arendt's friend Hilde Fränkel asked her before her trip if she was more pleased to be visiting Basel or Freiburg, Arendt replied: "Darling, to be 'pleased' over Freiburg would require a kind of animal boldness—but, then, I do not have such."[5] On January 3, 1950, a few days before traveling to Freiburg, she wrote to Heinrich Blücher: "Whether I'll see Heidegger, I don't know yet . . . I'm leaving it to chance."[6] Heidegger's most recent letters, which Jaspers had shown her, repelled her: "The same medley of genuineness and constant lying, or rather cowardice."[7]

What followed when Arendt arrived in Freiburg on February 7 has been reconstructed by Ettinger from Arendt and Heidegger's correspondence. From her hotel Hannah sent Heidegger a note, whereupon he immediately came to the hotel. There he handed over a letter at the reception desk. In it he invited her to his house for that same evening, slipping in the information that Elfride by then knew about their love affair. Evidently Heidegger, too, was ill at ease and initially wanted to delay a personal encounter. But having handed in his letter, he nevertheless asked a room waiter to announce him to Arendt. In a letter written to him two days later she said

> When the waiter announced your name . . . it was as though suddenly time had stopped. Then, in a flash I became aware—I have never before admitted it, not to myself and not to you and not to anyone else—that the force of my impulse . . . has mercifully saved me from committing the only truly unforgivable disloyalty, from mishandling my life. But you must know one thing (since we have not communicated much or very often) that had I done so, it would have been out of pride only—that is, out of pure, plain, crazy stupidity. Not for any reason.[8]

The "reason"—according to Ettinger—was probably Heidegger's Nazi past, which evidently would not have deterred her from meeting him. What she called "pride" was probably her fear of being once more bewitched by Heidegger. But as her letter of February 9, 1950, shows, this bewitching had begun anew. What to him she had called the "confirmation of a whole life" she described as a tragicomedy in a letter to Hilde Fränkel, once she had regained her distance: "He has absolutely no idea that all this lay 25 years in the past and that he had not seen me for more than 17 years." Heidegger had stood in her room "like a dog with his tail between his legs."[9]

Heidegger returned home and awaited Arendt's visit that same evening; the two of them were to spend the evening alone with each other. Arendt wrote about it to Blücher: "We really spoke to one another, it seemed to me, for the first time in our lives."[10] Arendt no longer felt herself to be Heidegger's pupil. She came from the big world, a woman with a lot of experience, a survivor of the catastrophe, a political philosopher who had just completed her book

Origins of Totalitarianism, soon to become a worldwide best-seller. But this was not what they talked about. According to Ettinger, Heidegger told her about his political entanglement, how the "devil" had then egged him on. He complained about having been made an outlaw. Arendt saw a man who was opinionated, remorseful, and embittered; to her he seemed in need of help. And she was ready to help him.

Arendt would negotiate for Heidegger with publishers in America, arrange contracts, supervise translations, and send food parcels, books, and phonograph records. And he would write her tender letters, occasionally enclosing a blade of quaking grass; he would tell her about his work, describe the view from his window, remind her of the green dress she used to wear in Marburg. And invariably there would be regards from Elfride.

At this first meeting, Heidegger wanted to establish a triple alliance. According to Ettinger, he explained to Arendt that it was Elfride who had encouraged him to resume his friendship with her. For the second day of her visit, Heidegger had arranged a meeting *à trois.* Two days later Hannah wrote to Heidegger: "I was and still am shaken by the honesty and forcefulness of [Elfride's] approach."[11] A "sudden feeling of solidarity" had gripped her. But to Blücher she described the situation in a different way:

> This morning an argument with his wife. For the last twenty-five years, or ever since she somehow squeezed the story out of him, she apparently never stopped making life for him hell on earth. And he, who of course lies notoriously always and at each opportunity, had also apparently, as this odd conversation among the three of us proved, never denied, during all the twenty-five years, that I was once the passion of his life. I'm afraid his wife is ready to drown all the Jews as long as I am alive. Alas, she is simply stupendously stupid.[12]

Heidegger—if one follows Ettinger's interpretation—experienced the situation differently. To him there was argument, but also reconciliation. He was touched when the women embraced on parting. He also wanted immediately to include Heinrich Blücher in their league of friends and asked Arendt to convey his best regards to him. She tried to moderate Heidegger's effusiveness and reminded him that she accepted Elfride only for his sake. She followed her old principle—"to make nothing more difficult than it already was. I left Marburg exclusively because of you."[13]

Two days after this triple-alliance scene, Arendt wrote her first and only letter to Elfride. She managed the trick of proceeding from their new intimacy and, at the same time, restoring the former distance: "You broke the ice," she admitted, "and for this I thank you with all my heart."[14] But, she said, she had no sense of guilt about the secrecy in the past. She had suffered enough as a consequence of her love affair: "You see, when I left Marburg, I was absolutely determined never to love a man again, and then I married, just someone, without loving him."[15] She had been punished enough, so she wanted no accusations from the past. As for the present, Hannah Arendt wrote as if the embrace of two days earlier had never taken place: "You have surely never made a secret of your sentiments, nor do you today, including how they relate to me. This sentiment brings matters to such a pass that a conversation is almost impossible, because whatever the other person might say is beforehand characterized and, pardon me, categorized—Jewish, German, Chinese."[16]

On Arendt's next visit, two years later, on May 19, 1952, the last remnants of the forced idyll of the triple alliance have vanished. Arendt writes to Blücher:

> The woman is jealous almost to the point of madness. After the years of apparently nursing the hope that he would simply forget me, her jealousy only intensified. In his absence she made a half-antisemitic scene with me. Anyway the political persuasion of the lady . . . her narrow-mindedness, her stupidity untouched by all experiences, reeking with ugly resentment, makes everything directed against him easily understandable . . . To cut a long story short I made him a regular scene, and afterwards the situation improved considerably.[17]

For Arendt it is a fact that Elfride is to blame for everything. What she and Karl Jaspers in their letters called Heidegger's "uncleanness" is for her nothing else than pollution through contact with that woman.

But Arendt was mistaken in seeing Elfride merely as the evil demon in Heidegger's life. In point of fact, Elfride was a good wife and faithful companion to him. She had married him before there was any hint of his subsequent fame. During the years when he was a *Privatdozent,* she had kept the family going by teaching school. She was an emancipated, self-assured woman, a rare instance of a female economics graduate. She stood by his side when he broke with the Catholic Church, when sudden fame descended on him, and after the war, when he was an outcast. She provided the domestic conditions that enabled him to work undisturbed. It was on her initiative that the cabin in Todtnauberg had been built. It is true that she became a Nazi before he did, but Heidegger had his own reasons for his "intoxication with power." For her the ideas of women's rights were of great importance, and it was in this sphere that she expected a lot from the National Socialist revolution. Unlike Heidegger, who did not go along with her on this issue, she also endorsed the racial and anti-Semitic ideology of the Nazi movement. She remained a Nazi longer than her husband. Some of her neighbors were actually afraid of her and in her presence avoided all critical remarks about the "system." Elfride was said to have earned the hatred of the local community in the autumn of 1944 because, as a party activist, she had been "brutally mistreating the women of Zähringen" and had no scruples in "sending sick and pregnant women to dig entrenchments," according to a report by Friedrich Oehlkers, a member of the denazification committee, to Karl Jaspers.[18] During the denazification proceedings Elfride was evidently regarded as an aggravating circumstance for Heidegger. Yet he himself used his wife as a barrier against what he saw as a hostile environment. Elfride readily accepted this role. She did not idealize her husband, but she understood his passion for the business of thinking and did everything in her power to enable him to follow that passion. Heidegger acknowledged this and remained grateful to her all his life. What impressed him especially was that she tolerated his need for solitude, while, simultaneously, making him feel at home. She bore the brunt of their daily worries and child rearing—a convenient division of labor for him. In earlier years he had frequently given her cause for jealousy, because he was a man women were ready to fall in love with. Little affairs were a regular occurrence. But he had never, not even during his relationship with Hannah Arendt, thought of leaving her. And now that Arendt had reentered his life, he was dreaming of a triple alliance that would enable him to hang on to Elfride while regaining Hannah—no longer, perhaps, as a lover but as a loved woman friend. However, such an arrangement was impossible; neither woman wanted it. Elfride's jealousy mobilized all her anti-Semitic prejudices. And to Arendt his marriage was quite simply the "alliance between the mob and the elite."

During the few hours that she spent alone with Heidegger on her visit in May 1952 Arendt—as Ettinger reports—was again fascinated by her philosopher, who discussed with her some passages from his lecture "What Is Called Thinking?" At such moments, as she wrote to Blücher, she had the "certitude of a fundamentally good nature . . . of a trust that never ceases to affect me deeply (I can hardly describe it differently); and there is a complete absence—as soon as we are alone together—of all these things that otherwise emerge so easily; and there is his genuine helplessness and defenselessness. As long as he can work there is no danger; the only thing I'm afraid of are his recurring periods of depression. I am trying to fortify him against the depression. Perhaps he will remember when I'm no longer here."[19]

Arendt sees herself in the role of guardian angel for the "better Heidegger." She wants to help him maintain his productivity, and Heinrich Blücher supports her in this, writing: "'What is called thinking?' is one of the most wonderful philosophical questions after God. So help him to ask it."[20]

Arendt not only helped Heidegger ask his questions but also replied to him philosophically. When *Vita activa,* the German edition of her principal philosophical work, *The Human Condition,* appeared in 1960, she sent Heidegger a copy, and according to Ettinger she enclosed a covering letter to the effect that "the book evolved directly from the first Marburg days and it owes you just about everything in every regard."[21] On a separate sheet of paper, which she did not send off and which Ettinger has discovered, she wrote:

> Re *Vita Activa*
> The dedication of this book is left out.
> How could I dedicate it to you,
> my trusted friend,
> to whom I remained faithful
> and unfaithful,
> and both in love.[22]

In what way did Arendt remain philosophically "faithful" to her teacher? She went along with Heidegger's revolutionary break with traditional philosophical thought. She therefore holds the view that man's relation with the world is not primarily a cognitive-theoretical one but a caring and active one, and that such action is, at the same time, an opening occurrence, an occurrence of truth. For Heidegger as for Arendt, openness, called "clearing" by Heidegger, is an inner *telos* of *Dasein.* But Heidegger, unlike Arendt, distinguishes such openness from "publicness." In *Being and Time* he had stated that "by publicness everything gets obscured, and what has thus been covered up gets passed off as something familiar and accessible to everyone" (SuZ,

127).[23] In publicness Being, as a rule, is dominated by the They. "Everyone is the other, and no one is himself" (SuZ, 128).[24] This publicness is confronted, in Heidegger, by "authenticity."

Like Heidegger, Hannah Arendt is guided by this idea of openness, but she is prepared to see this idea realized also in publicness. She expects openness not from the transformed relationship of the individual with himself—that is, not from Heidegger's "authenticity"—but from the consciousness of plurality, from the realization that our Being-in-the-world means sharing a world with "many" and being able to shape it. Openness exists only where the experience of human plurality is taken seriously. Any supposedly authentic thinking that discredits the many does not accept the challenge of plurality, which is an indispensable part of the human condition. Such thinking, which speaks of man not in the plural but in the singular, is to Arendt treason by philosophy to politics. Like Heidegger, she looks to ancient Greece for an original depiction of what she means. Heidegger has Plato's simile of the cave; Arendt has her image of Greek democracy as reported by Thucydides:

> In [their] forever newly beginning conversations, the Greeks discovered that the world common to us all is normally viewed from infinitely many different standpoints, to which the most varied points of view correspond . . . The Greeks learned to understand—not to understand one another as separate persons, but to view the same world from the other's standpoint, and to see the same under very different and often opposite aspects. The speeches in which Thucydides explains the standpoints and interests of contending parties are still living testimony to the high degree of objectivity of these explications.[25]

It might be said that Arendt rehabilitates the "cave chatter" (Heidegger) of the prisoners in Plato's cave. Plato's light of a perfect truth or Heidegger's ascent from the "essent" *(vom Seienden)* to the "more essent" *(dem Seienderen)* do not exist for her. For her there are only perspectives of a shared world and the varying ability to handle such multiplicity. Alluding to Heidegger's anathema against the "chatter" among the public, Arendt in her Lessing address of 1959 observed that the world would remain inhuman "unless there was continual talk in it by humans."[26] Not authenticity, but the "virtuosity of acting together with others,"[27] she argues, gives the world the openness that is also sought by Heidegger.

On the problem of truth, too, Arendt had learned from Heidegger and then gone a step further. Taking up his concept of truth as unconcealedness, she does not, like Heidegger, let the event of truth take place predominantly in the relationship of man with things, but finds it in those relationships between human beings. Only there, in the tragedies and comedies of humans living together, does the concept of truth as unconcealedness become plausible to her. The primal scenes of truth are, for her, played out in the social arena: "In acting and speaking, men show who they are, reveal actively their unique personal identities and thus make their appearance in the human world."[28]

Because human behavior has theatrical qualities, the whole phenomenological world can become a stage. Only because humans have their entrances and can show themselves do they gain the impression that things are no different for nature, and that nature, too, wants to "show" itself. Even Plato's ascent to the pure ideas remains tied to this social game of entrance and appearance, because these ideas want to be seen—on the inner stage of the philosopher's mind.

The "world" that Arendt speaks about is this stagelike, societal, opening space. The world opens among people; it should not, therefore, be understood as the sum total of all things, men, and events, but as the place where men encounter each other and things may appear to them, and where, ultimately, they produce something that is more than the sum of the activities of the individual. This "between" is what Arendt refers to in her letter to Heidegger in which she informs him that she is sending him her *Vita activa:* "Had the relations between us not been star-crossed—but I mean between, that is neither you nor me—I would have asked you whether I may have dedicated it to you."[29] Arendt, at any rate, felt that in this relationship the only options were surrender to Heidegger or self-assertion against him. In such a relationship, the world that lay in between was bound, in a sense, to be consumed by the flames. There was no room left for free movement; too much remained undone, unsaid, unnoticed.

In *The Human Condition* Arendt explores the question how this world preserves the In-between and how it can be destroyed, in the life of the individual and on a historical scale. She distinguishes between "working," "producing," and "action." Here, too, she proceeds from Heidegger by turning his Being-in-the-world into a stepladder of different activities by which men work their way out into the open, as it were, thereby creating the prerequisites of openness.

"Work," as Hannah Arendt understands the term, means only the biological sustenance of life. Here man organizes his metabolism with nature. Work and rest, work and consumption succeed one another rhythmically; they have, strictly speaking, neither beginning nor end. Like birth and death, they are included in the life cycle of the species. In work, man consumes nature, and in work he uses up his life. No enduring results are produced. Work, strictly speaking, is not "world-creating."

Things are different with producing. There, products are created, by craftsmen or artists, that go beyond what is necessary for life—articles that cannot be immediately consumed. Instruments, buildings, furniture, works of art, all of them designed to endure for generations. The more an object is designed to endure, the more "worldly" is the activity directed toward its production. The process of production is linear, aimed at an external objective. Something is being established, set up, produced, that will maintain its place in the world and become part of the firm framework that men create for themselves in order to find in it support, abidance, and a relation with their going along the road of life. The moving force here is not the bare necessity of living but a need to endow the temporal existence between birth and death with an element of endurance, of time transcendence.

Even more effective than producing, action lifts man out of the primal natural life cycles. Action—*praxis* in Greek—as Aristotle first defined it, differs from production—*poiesis*—by being the self-portrayal and form of expression of human freedom. "In acting and speaking, men show who they are, reveal actively their unique personal identities and thus make their appearance in the human world."[30]

In action, humans present themselves, they show who they are and what they wish to do and make of themselves. Action is everything that occurs between men unless it directly serves work or production. Action is the theater of the world, and that is why action takes place on the stage that signifies the world—the dramas of love, jealousy, politics, war, talk, education, friendship. Only because they are free can men act. And the multiplicity of intersecting and interweaving action produces the chaos of human reality. That is why there is such a thing as human history, which does not follow any logic. History is never "produced," nor is it a "work process," indeed it is no process at all but a discontinuous happening, caused by the controversial plurality of acting humans. Humans manufacture machines and operate them, but neither individual nor collective history is a machine, even though there has been no lack of attempts to turn it into one. That Heidegger, too, with his "history of Being," succumbed to the temptation to seek an authentic logic behind the confusion of the period is a suggestion that Arendt would make in the second volume of her posthumous work, *The Life of the Spirit.* In his effort Heidegger comes close to those "professional thinkers" who cannot reconcile themselves with freedom or with their "ineluctable randomness,"[31] who "are unwilling to pay the price of contingency for the questionable gift of spontaneity."[32] Arendt writes that from the "standpoint of nature . . . action seen from the viewpoint of the automatic processes which seem to determine the course of the world, looks like a miracle."[33] Action means being able to seize the initiative. *Initium* is the beginning.

Arendt, who had escaped the holocaust, in *The Human Condition* develops the grand outlines of a philosophy of being able to begin. And this philosophy in particular bears a trace of her love for Heidegger. When he used to climb up to her attic in Marburg, he was working on his philosophy of gaining authenticity through "anticipation of death." She, having escaped death, replies, in the complementary manner of lovers, with a philosophy of being able to begin. "The miracle that saves the world, the realm of human affairs, from its normal, 'natural' ruin is ultimately the fact of natality, in which the action is ontologically rooted. It is, in other words, the birth of new men and the new beginning, the action they are capable of by virtue of being born."[34]

This impressive reply to Heidegger's philosophy of mortality, this philosophy of natality, knows the mood of anxiety, yet it also knows the jubilation of arrival in the world. From the philosophy of being able to begin, Arendt develops her concept of democracy. Democracy ensures that in being together everyone retains the chance of staging his own beginning; it is the great task of learning to live with nonagreement. For if in a shared world we wish to come together or even to harmonize, we discover that we all come from a different beginning and will terminate at a totally different end. This is something that democracy recognizes by being prepared to let the discussion of questions of the common life begin anew each time. Such new beginnings, whether individual or collective, are possible only if two things are present—promise and forgiveness. By acting we trigger processes that we cannot be responsible for; what we put into the world always becomes something irrevocable and uncontrollable. "The possible redemption from irreversibility—for being unable to undo what one has though one did not, and could not, know what he was doing—is the faculty of forgiving. The remedy for unpredictability, for the chaotic uncertainty of the future—is contained in the faculty to make and keep promises."[35]

Hannah Arendt had promised herself to hold on to Martin Heidegger. This she was able to do only because she had the strength to forgive him. However, he made it difficult for her, again and again.

On her next visit to Germany, in 1955, she did not see him. "That I don't go [to see Heidegger] seems to me like a silent agreement between Heidegger and me," she wrote to Heinrich Blücher.[36] Arendt had been invited to present her book on totalitarianism, which had just been published in Germany. By then she was famous, and she realized that Heidegger would notice at once if, in that great hullabaloo, she were not able to give him her undivided attention. Her trip to Germany was a real triumphal progress. Here was a proud Jewish woman returning, with a balance sheet of the totalitarian temptations of the century and some harsh judgments on the German mandarins of her day.

> The self-willed immersion in the suprahuman forces of destruction seemed to be a salvation from the automatic identification with pre-established functions in society and their utter banality, and at the same time to help destroy the functioning itself. These people felt attracted to the pronounced activism of the totalitarian movements, to their curious and only seemingly contradictory insistence on both the primacy of sheer action and the overwhelming force of sheer necessity.[37]

Such sentences were bound to hurt Heidegger. He probably had only glanced at the book, but the passages on the "temporary alliance between the mob and the elite"[38] had aroused so much attention among the public that they could not have escaped Heidegger. As for the fundamental argument of the book—the thesis of the similarity and comparability of totalitarian systems—this, ever since the Nietzsche lectures, he was now ready to endorse. Nevertheless, he must have been embarrassed by the reminder that, in his justifications during the immediate postwar period, he had defended his championship of Nazism as an attempt to save the West from the danger of communism. It is possible, therefore, that one of the reasons Arendt did not visit Heidegger this time was that she expected from him an angry reaction to her book.

In the summer of 1951—she had just participated in the Eichmann trial, and the publication of her book about it would trigger a huge scandal in

America, because it described the collaboration of Jewish organizations in the deportation—Arendt visited Germany again. Meanwhile her principal philosophical work, *The Human Condition,* had been published in Germany. When she stopped off in Freiburg, she wrote to Jaspers, "I wrote to Heidegger that I was here, and that he could reach me at this or that time. He made no contact, which did not really surprise me since I didn't even know if he was in town" (BwAJ, 484). According to Ettinger, she was invited to a party by a Freiburg law professor named Kaiser and expressed her wish to see Eugen Fink, an acquaintance from her student days. Fink, however, "brusquely" rejected the invitation. From the whole occurrence she concluded that Heidegger was behind it—that he had induced Fink to reject the invitation.

Three months later she wrote to Jaspers:

> Heidegger—a most annoying business . . . My explanation . . . is that last winter I first had one of my books sent to him . . . I know that he can't bear to see my name appear in public, that I write books, etc. All my life I have, as it were, pretended to him, always acting as if all this didn't exist, that, in a manner of speaking, I couldn't count up to three, except of course in interpreting his own writings; in that respect he was always very pleased to find that I could count up to three and sometimes perhaps up to four. Now, suddenly, I got tired of this pretending, and so I've collected a bloody nose. For a moment I was rather furious, but no longer. Indeed, I tend to think that I asked for it somehow—both for having pretended and for suddenly stopping the game. (BwAJ, 494)

Five years passed before Heidegger again wrote to Hannah Arendt—wishing her all the best on her sixtieth birthday. Enclosed with this letter, according to Ettinger, was a picture postcard of Todtnauberg and a poem entitled "Herbst" (Autumn).

At the beginning of 1966 the publication of Alexander Schwan's book *Political Philosophy in Heidegger's Thinking* was the occasion for an article in *Der Spiegel* on Heidegger's National Socialism. This became the subject of an exchange of letters between Hannah Arendt and Karl Jaspers. Arendt suspected that the "Wiesengrund-Adorno people" were the "string-pullers behind it" (BwAJ, 670), and Karl Jaspers defended Heidegger against the suspicion uttered in *Spiegel* that Heidegger had stopped visiting him because of his Jewish wife. "The fact is that Gertrud and myself simply became increasingly uninteresting to him," Jaspers wrote to Arendt on March 9, 1966. "Heidegger did not plan to break off contact with us. It just happened. Myself, I did not, after 1945, decide never to see him again, it just came about that way, unintentionally. But it does seem that there is an analogy of unintentionality" (BwAJ, 665–666).

However, Jaspers had not yet done with Heidegger. After Karl Jaspers's death three years later, his notes would be found lying ready on his desk. But there had been no thought for a long time of a continuous correspondence, let alone a personal meeting, after the brief revival of their relations in 1949 and 1950.

It was Jaspers who had withdrawn again—more particularly after Heidegger's letter of March 7, 1950. That was shortly after Arendt's first visit. She had encouraged Heidegger to be frank vis-à-vis Jaspers, and Heidegger had thereupon written to him: "The reason why I did not visit your house after 1933 was not because a Jewish woman was living there, but because I was, quite simply, ashamed" (BwHJ, 196). In a brief reply, Jaspers had thanked him for his "unreserved statement," but after that he had remained silent for two years. When finally, on July 24, 1952, Jaspers wrote to him, it was clear that he mistrusted Heidegger's oracular tone. Heidegger had written that "the cause of evil" was not yet at an end and that in this "homelessness" an "advent" was about to emerge "whose furthest hints we may perhaps still experience in a soft murmur and that we must capture in order to save it for a future" (BwHJ, 202–203). Jaspers replied: "Does not a philosophy that surmises and poetizes in such phrases in your letter, a philosophy that aroused the vision of the monstrous, once more prepare the ground for the victory of totalitarianism by severing itself from reality?" On Heidegger's "advent" he observes: "This, as far as I can see, is pure dreaming, in a string of so many dreams that . . . have deluded us throughout this half-century" (BwHJ, 210).

After this letter Jaspers and Heidegger exchanged only more or less extensive birthday wishes. In 1956 Jaspers read the following sentences in an essay titled *Zur Seinsfrage,* Heidegger's birthday tribute to Ernst Jünger: "Anyone who today believes he can more clearly see through and follow the metaphysical questioning in the entirety of its character and history, should, while moving so happily and in superior manner through light spaces, ask himself one day from where he took the light to clearer vision" (W, 410). Jaspers jotted down: "From the linguistic phrases chosen there is, unfortunately, no doubt that he means me . . . Here begins a nastiness with which I will not be further involved."[39] When she visited Germany that year, Hannah Arendt was enlisted by Jaspers for a kind of "general discussion" on Heidegger. Jaspers, she informed Blücher, virtually "presented me with an ultimatum involving Heidegger." He demanded that she sever her ties with him. "I became furious and told him I will not accept any ultimatum."[40]

Heidegger left no notes on Jaspers. In the relationship between the two men, Heidegger was the one wooed. Jaspers had sensed a philosophical charisma in Heidegger that time and again fascinated him. There was no such reaction to Jaspers on Heidegger's part. And yet it was Heidegger who, in the early 1920s, had referred to a "comradeship in arms" in the sense of a revolt against academic philosophy in the name of existence. And it was Heidegger who had first spoken of friendship and even love. "Since September 1923 I have lived with you on the assumption that you are my friend. That is the all-bearing faith in love" (April 17, 1924, BwHJ, 46). Both sought this friendship, yet they scarcely read each other's writings. The only book by Jaspers that Heidegger had studied thoroughly for a review was the *Psychology of an Ideology.* But Jaspers had hardly reacted to the review. He was interested more in conversation with Heidegger than in his writings. Frequently, when reading him, he would add marginal glosses: "I don't understand him." In 1950 Jaspers made a note of a sentence by Löwith, expressing his agreement with it: "No one will in fact be able to assert that he has actually understood what that Being, that mystery, is of which Heidegger speaks."[41]

In his main work, *Philosophy,* published in 1932, Jaspers, like Heidegger, had presented "searching for Being" as the most important task of philosophy. But he was probably looking for a different Being, or rather he sought it by different means. For Jaspers, Being is the "embracing" that can be experienced only in the movement of freedom, in transcendence. It cannot be perceived through direct attack by philosophical thought.

In a note dated 1965 Jaspers contrasts his position with Heidegger's. This is the terse result of a lifelong debate: "H: Thought itself is Being—the talking around it and pointing to it without ever getting there. J: Thought has existential relevance—which, in the inner action of the meditating person, it demonstrates (provisionally, expresses) and in practical life brings to realization—without this being possible to happen in the philosophical work."[42] Heidegger, too, had noticed this difference and, in his Nietzsche lectures in the winter of 1936–37, had formulated it as follows (though these passages were not included in the printed edition of the lecture series published in Jaspers's lifetime). For Jaspers, he argued, philosophy was basically an "illusion for the purpose of the moral enlightenment of the human personality." Jaspers "no longer" took philosophical knowledge "seriously." Philosophy for him became a "moralizing psychology of human existence" (GA 43, 26).

Jaspers suspected that Heidegger's overestimation of thinking was linked with the fact that—despite his polemics against science—he had not really distanced himself from the idea of a "scientific philosophy." He was attaching too much importance to the stringency of concepts and to a purely invented and artificial architecture of thought structure. Jaspers had found *Being and Time* to be such an artificially constructed work. In Heidegger's late writings Jaspers noted a radical break with "scientificality," but instead observed the other extreme, an emancipation of language. It concerned itself with itself and thus became an artistic performance, or else it presented itself as a revelation of Being and thus turned into magic. Jaspers remained skeptical about Heidegger's language philosophy. To Jaspers, language was not the domicile of Being, because "Being," as the "all-embracing," did not fit into any shell, not even the spacious shell of language. In a letter to Heidegger, Jaspers had written: "Surely language, as communication, should be brought to conservation in reality itself, through action, presence, and love" (July 10, 1949, BwHJ, 179).

Jaspers, for whom philosophy reached its objective when it became the inner action of existence, observed in Heidegger a clear intention to make philosophy a "work." Every work emphasizes the dividing line from the rest of life. That his own philosophy did not, in this sense, enclose itself in a work was obvious to Jaspers, and he regarded this as a gain for philosophy. On Heidegger he noted in this context: "From the outset this is a specifically philosophical work, which preserves its linguistic act and theme, delimiting it as something specific and taking it out of the rest of life . . . My own way has something unlimited about it . . . In its way of thinking there is no separation from everyday thinking and philosophizing, between a podium lecture and live conversation."[43]

And yet, in spite of critique and distancing, Jaspers held on to the view that in a "philosophically poor world" Heidegger was a "unique figure." In his last note on Heidegger, Jaspers, by then an old man, wrote:

The philosophers of their day have always met high up in the mountains on a wide rocky plateau. From there one looks down on the snow-capped mountains and further down into the valleys inhabited by humans, and in all directions under the sky to the distant horizon. Sun and stars are brighter there than anywhere else. The air is so pure it consumes everything murky, so cool that it does not allow smoke to arise, so bright that thought soars up into infinite spaces. Access is not difficult. The climber on the many paths has only to be determined to leave his abode time and again for a while in order to experience at this altitude that which really is. There the philosophers engage in an astonishing merciless struggle. They are seized by powers that contend with one another through their thoughts, through human thoughts . . . It seems that today there is no one left there to be encountered. Yet to me it seemed as though, seeking in vain in the eternal speculations for men who might think them important, I encountered but one, and no one else. This one, however, was my polite enemy. For the powers we served were incompatible. Soon it seemed that we could not talk to each other at all. Joy turned into pain, into a strange hopeless pain, as though a chance that was within arm's reach had been missed. That is what happened to me with Heidegger.[44]

23

HEIDEGGER'S OTHER PUBLIC

When Heidegger's reinstatement as an ordinary emeritus professor at the University of Freiburg (with license to teach) was being discussed at the beginning of the 1950s, some people not only voiced political misgivings but also actually questioned whether Heidegger was not perhaps a "vogue philosopher" or indeed a charlatan. Was he, they asked, still respectable as a scholar? Did he still have about him the right academic aura? There had been stories of Heidegger giving lectures at the fashionable Bühlerhöhe sanatorium to an exclusive audience of ladies and gentlemen, or to ship brokers, merchants, and captains at the Club zu Bremen.

In point of fact, while still banned from the university, Heidegger had been looking for another public. There had been a connection with Bremen since the early 1930s, established by Heinrich Wiegand Petzet, the scion of a Bremen patrician family and a subsequent cultural historian. Petzet had been a student of Heidegger and remained a lifelong admirer. In that club, in a semiprivate framework, Heidegger then gave the lecture "On the Essence of Truth." A friendship had developed with the Petzet family. Heinrich Wiegand

Petzet's father was a wealthy ship broker, and Heidegger had repeatedly been a guest at the family's summer residence at Icking in Bavaria. At the beginning of the war he had stored some of his manuscripts there. In the late autumn of 1949 Heidegger received an invitation to Bremen. His first series of lectures, headed "Einblick in Das Was Ist" (Insight into That Which Is)—with the individual lectures entitled "Das Ding" (The Thing), "Das Gestell" (The Framework), "Die Gefahr" (The Danger), "Die Kehre" (The Turn)—was held on December 1 and 2, 1949, in the Fireplace Hall of the New City Hall. A reverent audience had assembled, and the proceedings were opened by the mayor. Heidegger began: "Nineteen years ago I gave a lecture here in which I then uttered things which are only now being slowly understood and beginning to be effective. I took a risk then—and I will take a risk again today!"[1]

The group of Hanseatic patricians that had invited Heidegger also felt imbued by the proud knowledge of having risked something. After all, officially Heidegger was still under a teaching ban. These people were therefore anxious to stand up to what they saw as injustice and discrimination and to grant him free speech in a free city. This cycle of lectures was the first in a series of eight further lectures given by Heidegger in Bremen in the 1950s. Gottfried Benn, the German poet, in 1953 asked his friend F. W. Oelze what it was that linked Heidegger so much to Bremen. Oelze, who as a member of the Bremen upper class must have known the reason, replied: "I explain his attachment to Bremen by the fact that here, and perhaps only here, he found himself face to face with a social class that does not exist in such a compact majority in university cities, in administrative centers, or on the Bühler Höhe—captains of industry, overseas specialists, directors of shipping companies and shipyards. all of them people for whom a famous thinker is a fabled beast or a demigod."[2]

Heidegger felt comfortable in that *haute-bourgeois* setting of liberal conservatism. The businessmen, with their solid middle-class education, mostly in the humanities, were untouched by academic doctrines. To them philosophy was a kind of worldly religiosity that they assumed was very necessary in the upheavals of the postwar period, even though one did not properly understand it in detail. Perhaps it was necessary just because of that. The venerable incomprehensible—had this not always been a mark of higher things? The invitation to Bremen came from people who wished to prove their position through excursions into an exotic philosophical world. That Heidegger was not being particularly well understood was confirmed even by Petzet, who was anxious to build bridges between his native environment and the philosopher he admired. Heidegger had chosen this forum, where he sensed "free air," for the pilot project of his late philosophy. It was in Bremen that he first presented his difficult and strange reflection on the *Gestell* (frame), on *Einblick* and *Einblitz* (insight and in-flash), and on the "mirror play of the fourfold of earth and heaven, the divine and the mortal." A report published by Egon Vietta a few days after the first lecture stated that the city could be proud that Heidegger had come to it in order to "venture here the boldest statement of his thinking so far."[3]

Heidegger found yet another forum—the Bühlerhöhe spa high above Baden-Baden, among the mountains of the northern Black Forest. The physician Gerhard Stroomann had founded this sanatorium in the early 1920s, in an art nouveau building that had originally housed a casino. Stroomann was a doctor of the type the character Behrens is modeled after in Thomas Mann's *Magic Mountain.* Dynamic, authoritarian, with the charisma of a spa doctor, he prescribed for his wealthy clientele from all over Europe a treatment based on the therapeutic effect of an encounter with the "creative mind." Most conveniently, the creative minds were found not only among the invited speakers but also among the patients. Ernst Toller, Heinrich Mann, and Karl Kerényi had undergone treatment there, and anybody who was anybody in the intellectual world of the 1920s and 1930s was invited. This tradition was revived by Stroomann after the war. In 1949 he established the so-called Wednesday evening lectures, which continued until 1957. Audiences grew and media interest increased as the "great spiritual problems" of the day were discussed. Scientists, artists, and politicians gave lectures and took part in discussions with those present, who regarded themselves as an elite. If there was a preeminent place in the 1950s for the "jargon of authenticity," it was the Bühlerhöhe. This emerges also from Stroomann's notes on Heidegger's performances: "Heidegger gave . . . four lectures at the Bühlerhöhe—and each time there arose that totally exceptional excitement that swept his lecture, his appearance at the rostrum, as with no one else . . . But who can close himself to the erupting power of his thinking and knowledge, reflected as it is creatively in every new word, showing that there are still undiscovered sources."[4] The events with Heidegger had been "like a celebration, an inner glow. Words fall silent. But when discussion starts, then this is supreme responsibility and also ultimate peril." The Bühlerhöhe audience that exposed itself to this supreme responsibility and ultimate peril consisted of the most prominent retired citizens of Baden-Baden, captains of industry, bankers, wives, senior civil servants, politicians, foreign dignitaries, and a handful of students who were conspicuous in their modest attire. So Bühlerhöhe was where Heidegger lectured and with the Afghan minister of culture discussed abstract art and the meaning of the verb *einräumen* (to concede). On another occasion the topic was poetry and rhythm. Heidegger explained that rhythm in life and poetry was the "interplay of the wherefrom and whereto." The audience was perplexed; an explanation was demanded. A rough voice intervened: "Why does everything always have to be explained?" Heidegger thereupon replied: "That is a mistake—we're not interested here in explaining, but in clearing!"[5] The discussion ebbed and flowed for a while, then it ran dry. Then a voice called: "To enliven things a little, wouldn't a lady say something?" After a moment's embarrassed silence Stroomann's secretary came to the rescue. She recalled there was an Indian proverb that said "he who understands the mystery of vibration understands everything." Another lady agreed: the poet could not himself summon the divine appearance, but he wove the veil behind which it might be surmised. Now the room came to life again, because the lady who had made that remark was rather attractive. "Can we exist without works of art at all?" someone asked. "I can exist very well without works of art," exclaimed someone else. A third said: "Attuning and fitting oneself into a rhythm"—as had just been suggested—surely was pure dadaism; one would only have to babble. A confusion of merriment and irritation followed. Then came the next performance. Gustaf Gründgens and Elisabeth Flickenschildt appeared on the platform to present a sketch called "The Spirit of the Modern Stage." Heidegger left the room without awaiting the end of the performance.[6]

In the late 1950s the Wednesday evenings were rounded off by a matinee on the following day. On one occasion Heidegger had already left, but his brother had stayed on. A lady who presumably thought Fritz was Martin wanted to know Heidegger's opinion of Mao Tse-tung. The cunning brother replied: "Mao Tse is the *Gestell* of Lao tse."

This exchange occurred at a time when Heidegger's term *Gestell*, as a designation for the technological world, was making the rounds in Germany. Heidegger had first used it in Bremen, but it owed its fame to his 1953 lecture to the Bavarian Academy of Fine Arts, "Die Frage nach der Technik" (The Question of Technology).

The Bavarian Academy had been inviting Heidegger for lectures since the early 1950s. Initially these invitations were rather controversial in Munich. There was a debate in the Bavarian Diet during which Minister Hundhammer criticized the academy for allowing Heidegger, that "former backer of the Nazi regime,"[7] to speak. While students were traveling to Munich from Vienna, Frankfurt, and Hamburg to hear Heidegger, the Kant Society, evidently fearing for its members' eternal salvation, announced a counterlecture for the same evening. Heidegger very nearly canceled that first Munich lecture in the summer of 1950. He had been asked by telegram for the title of his lecture. Through some writing slip "title of lecture" had become "style of lecture." Heidegger felt he was being treated like a child from whom an appropriate style was demanded. Outraged, he wrote to Petzet: "The cup is now almost full . . . Regardless of everything else about this business, they don't even trust me to have something very essential to say to that Academy. Nothing of this kind ever happened to me throughout the whole Hitler period."[8] When the misunderstanding was cleared up Heidegger agreed to come to Munich. But to Petzet he said: "This remains an ambiguous business and the indispensable tribute to the *Gestell*."[9] On the evening of the lecture the hall was stormed. The invited guests were squeezed by the uninvited, who crowded on dragged-up chairs, on the steps, on window shelves, in niches, and in the corridors. Heidegger spoke about "The Thing." Again there was talk of the "square" of the world, but when Heidegger started on the "mirror image of heaven and earth, of the divine and the mortal," this was too much for the present secretary of state, who left the hall in outrage, forcing his way through the crowd with difficulty. That was in the summer of 1950. Three years later came the lecture "The Question of Technology." That evening saw a gathering of the whole Munich intelligentsia of the 1950s; those present included Hans Carossa, Friedrich Georg Jünger, Werner Heisenberg, Ernst Jünger, José Ortega y Gasset. It was probably Heidegger's biggest success in postwar Germany. When Heidegger concluded with the now-famous sentence: "Questioning is the piety of thinking," there was no reverent silence but a standing ovation. Heidegger's performance was viewed as a philosophical bel canto aria, and those present applauded because he had hit the very high notes that people liked to hear in the 1950s.

With his thoughts on technology, Heidegger touched on what were by then no longer very secret anxieties of his day. He was not the only person to do so. During the period of the cold war, which suggested the idea that politics was man's real destiny, more and more voices were being heard criticizing the fixation on politics as self-delusion and arguing that technology had in effect become our destiny—a destiny, it was suggested, that we could no longer control by political means, or certainly not if we clung to the traditional concepts of politics, no matter whether of "planning" or "the market." The Germans' "inability to mourn" the universal complicity in the crimes of National Socialism, subsequently lamented by the Mitscherlichs, may have existed in the 1950s; the horrors of the past may have been suppressed; yet despite the economic miracle and the zeal for reconstruction, there was clearly an unease about the future of the technological world. There were countless conferences of Protestant academies, the malaise haunted the Sunday speeches of politicians, the journals discussed it at length. It found direct expression in the Fight Atomic Death movement. Important books had been published on the subject. The first reinterpretation of Kafka after the war saw his work as a metaphysical critique of technology and of the managed world. Günther Anders gained fame in 1951 through his essay *Kafka, Pro and Con,* which presented Kafka as an author who was horrified by the "superior power of the objectivized world" and who turned his horror into "holy" terror—a mystic in the age of technology. Aldous Huxley's *Brave New World* appeared in German in 1953 and became a best-seller of the 1950s. The novel offered an alarming vision of a world in which people were programmed for their happiness and profession in the test tube, a world destined to have no destiny any longer, a world fusing into a totalitarian system—entirely without politics, merely through technology. Alfred Weber's book *The Third or Fourth Man* appeared in the same year. This got a lot of attention because it described a horrific vision of a technical civilization of robots in the language of solid sociology and cultural philosophy. Moreover, it gave the reader the impression of being a contemporary witness to an epoch-making caesura, the third in human history. First came Neanderthal man, then primitive man of the horde and tribal society, and finally high-culture man who, in the Occident, had produced technology. But amid this technological civilization, mankind, according to Weber, is once more engaged in retrodeveloping itself emotionally and intellectually. What is happening to us is nothing less than the sociogenesis of a mutation. Ultimately there will be two types of man—the robotlike cerebral animals and the new primitives, who move about the artificial world as in a jungle, uninhibited, unsuspecting, yet fearful. Such visions gave readers a frisson while, at the same time, they had entertainment value.

That same year, 1953, also saw the publication of Friedrich Georg Jünger's

Die Perfektion der Technik (Perfection of Technology). Jünger had developed his theory during the 1930s as a reply to *Der Arbeiter* (The Worker), his brother Ernst Jünger's great essay of 1932. Ernst Jünger had there proposed the thesis that, so long as it appeared as an alien, external power, the technological world would not be achieved any more than the technologization of the inward man. Ernst Jünger dreamed of a "new mankind," realized in the "figure of the worker." This type of man moves, as a matter of course, in a landscape of the "icy geometry of light," of the "white glow of overheated metal."[10] He reacts quickly, cold-bloodedly, accurately, flexibly; he can adapt to the technological rhythms. Yet he remains master of the machine, because he possesses an inner "technicity." He can handle himself with technological ease, much as Nietzsche had envisaged it in his fantasy of the "free man" who handles his "virtues as tools," operates with them, detaches and reattaches them as he pleases and as it suits his purpose. Such men, according to Jünger, will no longer regard it as a loss if "the last remnants of coziness" have disappeared and one can traverse one's living space like "volcanic regions or depopulated lunar landscapes."[11] An adventurous heart that seeks the cold.

We shall perish in that cold, Friedrich Georg Jünger answers his brother, who, incidentally, is no longer among the apologists but among the dissidents of technology, the "forest walkers." Friedrich Georg Jünger's main thesis is that technology is no longer just a "means," an instrument that modern man can use for his purposes. Because, he argues, technology has already inwardly transformed men, the purposes he can set himself are already technologically determined. Production of needs is part of industrial production. Seeing, hearing, speaking, attitudes, and reactions, the experience of time and space, have all—due to the automobile, film, and radio—fundamentally changed. The dynamics of this process leaves no Beyond of technology. The main feature of technological civilization is not the exploitation of man by man but the gigantic exploitation of the earth. Industrialism tracks down the energy matter accumulated by natural history, consumes it, and thereby suffers the fate of entropy. "Technology in general and the universal working plan developed by it, aiming as it does at technical perfection, is linked to a universal machine and is therefore subject to the laws of thermodynamics just as any other machine."[12] By making everything available, by recognizing nothing as untouchable or sacred, technology destroys the planetary ground on which it rests. So far the ground still bears us, so far part of the world's population is still enjoying the advantages of civilizational comfort, and that is why the price paid for the "perfection of technology" still seems appropriate. But this is a delusion, Friedrich Georg Jünger says: "Not the beginning, but the end bears the load."[13]

These prophecies of doom from the critics of technology were ridiculed by others. "In the Cabinet of Horrors of Technology" was the headline of an article in *Der Monat*, which developed the argument that the "evil" was not in the technology but in man. Technology cannot be "evil," said the writer, only the purposes to which it is applied can. One should avoid demonizing technology and take a closer look at the "technique of demonization."[14] "The fear of technology today is a repetition, on a higher intellectual level and in a sublimated form, of the witch mania of the Middle Ages."[15] The critique of technology, the anticritics argued, failed to accept the challenge of the day and refused to develop an ethos appropriate to technology. If we had such an ethos, we would not have to be afraid of technology. The spokesman of these anticritics was Max Bense:

> We have given rise to a world, and an exceptionally long tradition confirms the origin of that world from the earliest efforts of our intelligence. Yet today we are unable to control that world theoretically, spiritually, intellectually, or rationally. Its theory is lacking, and with it the clarity of the technological ethos, in other words, the possibility of making appropriate ethical judgments within that world . . . We may still be perfecting that world, but we are unable to perfect the human being of this world. This is the depressing situation of our technological existence.[16]

This "discrepancy" between man and the technological world he has created, the discrepancy highlighted by Bense, would later be called "Promethean shame" by Günther Anders in his 1956 book *The Obsoleteness of Man.* Man is ashamed in the face of his products, which are more perfect and more effective than himself. In the case of the nuclear bomb, for instance, he can no longer visualize the effects of what he has produced. Central to reflection on technology is, therefore, the question: Should man—as Bense demands—adapt himself to technology, or should—as Friedrich Georg Jünger and Günther Anders urge—technology be cut back to a human scale?

It will be obvious by now that Heidegger's technology lecture in 1953 was no solitary foray in this field. He merely spoke up in a debate that was already in full swing. By distancing himself from the "instrumental" idea of technology and by understanding technology as the fundamental characteristic of a modern Being-in-the-world, he says nothing new compared with Friedrich Georg Jünger (and later Günther Anders). Both Jünger and Anders leave the origin of the process that transformed the human world into a technological universe deliberately in the dark. Heidegger wishes to bring light to this matter. His thesis was first formulated in his philosophy of the 1930s, especially in his essay *Zeit des Weltbildes* (The Age of the World Picture). The origin of technology, he says, lies in the way we face nature, whether we allow it to emerge on its own—as in the ancient Greek *aletheia* idea—or whether we challenge it to come out. Technology, Heidegger says, is a "manner of unprotecting" *(Entbergen)* (TK, 16). This uncovering that reigns throughout modern technology has "the character of standing up in the sense of challenge" (TK, 16). Around the central concept of "challenge" Heidegger groups the ways of technological empowerment. The opposite concept is "bringing forth" (TK, 17) in the sense of letting emerge. Michelangelo has said that the sculpture was already dormant in the stone; it merely had to be liberated. This, more or less, illustrates what Heidegger means by producing and letting emerge.

These two attitudinal modes toward nature—challenging it and letting it emerge—were impressively characterized in the lecture Heidegger had delivered a short time before, "Was heisst Denken?" (What Is Called Thinking?). One is facing a tree in bloom. Only at a scientifically unguarded and practically disinterested moment will its bloom be correctly experienced. From a scientific point of view one will let the experience of its blooming drop as something naive. However, says Heidegger, "the thing that matters first and foremost, and finally, is not to drop the tree in bloom, but for once let it stand where it stands. Why do we say 'finally'? Because to this day, thought has never let the tree stand where it stands" (WHD, 38).[17] We therefore do not let nature emerge but challenge it and tackle it in a way that "it appears in some quantifiable manner, remaining determinable as a system of information" (TK, 22).

After *Herausfordern* (challenging) the second central term is *Bestellen* (providing, ordering). What has been provided becomes available *Bestand* (inventory). A bridge links the two banks of a river, and with the gesture of arching over it respects the river. It leaves it be. A hydroelectric power plant, on the other hand, for the sake of which the river is diverted or straightened, turns the river into inventory. It is not the power plant that is built into the river but the river that is "built into the power plant" (TK, 15). To demonstrate the "enormity" of what is happening here, Heidegger points to the contrast between a Rhine built into a hydroelectric power plant and the Rhine of Hölderlin's eponymous hymn. But, it may be objected, the Rhine still remains a river in the landscape. Perhaps. But how does it remain? "Not otherwise than as a provided *(bestellbar)* object of inspection by a party of tourists sent *(bestellt)* there by a vacation industry" (TK, 16).

Technical intervention transforms nature into real or potential inventory *(Bestand).* And to prevent this from collapsing on our heads, the inventory must be safeguarded by calculation and planning. Technology calls for more technology. The consequences of technology can be only mastered by technological means. Nature has been challenged, and now it demands continuation—on pain of ruin. Thus the ring closes into a vicious circle of oblivion of Being. Challenge, inventory, securing of inventory—this entity is called by Heidegger *Gestell* (frame), his name for the epoch of technological civilization in which everything is connected to everything else in the manner of cybernetic positive feedback. "Industrial society exists on the basis of its occlusion in its own concoction" (TK, 19).

The *Gestell* is something man-made, but we have lost our freedom with regard to it. The *Gestell* has become our "destiny." What is so dangerous about this is that life in the *Gestell* threatens to become one-dimensional, lacking alternatives, and that the memory of a different kind of world encounter and world sojourn is expunged. The threat to mankind does not come only from potentially fatally acting machines and technological apparatus. The real threat has already affected man in his nature. The reign of the *Gestell* harbors the risk that man may be denied access to his original unprotecting and thus be deprived of the encouragement of a more original truth (TK, 28).

We are by now familiar with Heidegger's "more original truth." This is the truth of the free, letting-it-be glance at things. Letting the tree bloom or finding the way out of Plato's cave, so that under the sun, in the open clearing of Being, the "essent" should become "more essent." The panic midday hour of truth. It is the expectation that, if we asked it differently, nature might answer differently. In *On Humanism* Heidegger had said: "It could well be that nature conceals its essence on the very side that she turns toward man's technical power-seizing" (ÜH, 16).

However, Heidegger does not content himself with the view that "contemplative" thinking might, here and there, leave standing those trees in bloom, or that a different Being-in-the-world might occur in thought. He projects the change of attitude that occurs in his thinking into history. The turn in the mind of the philosopher becomes a surmise about a turn in history. For his festive lecture Heidegger therefore finds a suitable conclusion that dismisses the audience with the solemn feeling of having listened to something serious but also edifying. Heidegger quotes Hölderlin: "But where danger threatens / That which saves from it also grows."[18]

Needless to say, any thinking that thinks about the fateful connection of the *Gestell* is, by this mere fact, one step beyond; it opens up a free space in which it is then possible to see what is happening. In that sense there is a "turn" in thinking. It is the attitude of *Gelassenheit* (composure) that Heidegger, in a lecture in Messkirch in 1955, describes in these words: "We let the technical devices enter our daily life, and, at the same time, leave them outside, that is, let them alone, as things which are nothing absolute but remain dependent on something higher. I would call this comportment toward technology which expresses 'yes' and at the same time 'no' by an old word—releasement toward things" (G, 23).[19] Yet this "releasement toward things," understood as a turn in thinking, does not make the assumption of a turn in real history plausible.

Heidegger would dismiss this charge of lacking plausibility by pointing out that "plausibility" is a category of technologically calculating thought; anyone thinking in "plausibilities" remained in the *Gestell*—even while trying to escape from it. For Heidegger there simply is no "feasible" solution to the problem of technology. "No human calculation and action can, on its own and solely through itself, bring about a turn in the present state of the world; if only because human dealings are molded by this state of the world and at its mercy. How then can it ever hope to master it?" (December 24, 1963, BwHK, 59). The turn will come about as an event of history or it will not come about at all. This event, however, casts its shadow forward—into contemplative thinking. To the real "turn" applies what St. Paul said about the return of Christ—it comes like a thief in the night. "The turn of danger happens suddenly. In the turn, the clearing of the essence of Being clears abruptly. The sudden clearance is the flash" (TK, 43).

These are dreams of a future destiny. Matters are very different when Heidegger allows these dreams to affect his personal destiny and, at long last, sets out for where his dreams are located both in the ancient past and, still, in the present.

After much hesitation—Medard Boss, Erhart Kästner, and Jean Beaufret had been encouraging him for years—Martin Heidegger in 1962 undertakes a journey to Greece, along with his wife, who had made him a present of the trip. What he would seek there he had stated repeatedly, most recently in his technology lecture: "At the beginning of the Western destiny the arts in Greece rose to the greatest height of *Entbergen* vouchsafed to them. They brought the presence of the gods, they brought the dialogue between divine and human destiny to radiant brightness" (TK, 34).

A trip to Greece was first planned for 1955, along with Erhart Kästner, whose acquaintance Heidegger had made at the technology lecture in Munich and with whom he had since become friends. At the last moment, when the boat and railway tickets had already arrived, Heidegger canceled the plan. Five years later, he repeated the performance: maps had already been studied and a route decided on when Heidegger again pulled back. He wrote to Kästner: "It will probably remain like this—I will be allowed to think certain things about Greece without seeing the country. I must now make sure that what stands before my inner eye is retained in appropriate language. The necessary concentration is best found at home" (February 21, 1960, BwHK, 43). Two years later Heidegger was at last ready to cross the "dream threshold" (Erhart Kästner) and to set out on his journey. He dedicated his travel notes, entitled *Aufenthalte* (Sojourns) to his wife on her seventieth birthday.

On a cold rainy day in Venice, before boarding ship for Greece, he was again assailed by doubts about "whether what is attributed to the land of the fled gods is not perhaps something imagined and might prove one's path of thinking to have been a wrong road" (A, 3). Heidegger was aware that a lot was at stake. Would Greece receive him just as this Venice, now only a dead "object of history" and a "loot of the tourist industry"? After the second night on board, they sighted the island of Corfu, the ancient Kephallenia. This was supposed to be the land of the Phaeacians? On the upper deck Heidegger reread the sixth book of the *Odyssey* and found no agreement. The surmised did not appear. Everything was more like an Italian landscape. Ithaca, the home of Ulysses, similarly did not move him. Heidegger wondered whether the search for the "original Greek" was the right way of discovering Greece; did it not spoil the "immediate experience" (A, 5)? They dropped anchor off the coast, on a sunny spring morning, and traveled by bus to Olympia. It was an unprepossessing village; half-finished new American tourist hotels lined the road. Heidegger prepared himself for the worst. Would his own "arbitrariness of imagination" be all that remained of his Greece (A, 8)? But on the field of the ruins of Olympia the morning song of the nightingales, the "scythed and scattered drums of the columns" still retained their "supporting towering." Slowly this world penetrated into him after all. At midday they rested in the grass under trees, amid deep silence. He realized that the visit might yet be a success—"a faint surmise of the hour of Pan." The next stop was the neighborhood of Mycenae. It seemed like "a unique stadium inviting for festive games" (A, 12). On a hill stood three columns of what was once a temple of Zeus, "in the expanse of the landscape like three strings of a lyre on which, inaudibly to mortals, the winds are perhaps playing laments. Echoes of the flight of the gods" (A, 12).

Heidegger began to immerse himself in his element. Their ship approached the Greek islands off the coast of Asia Minor. There lay Rhodes, the rose island. Heidegger did not go ashore; "concentration into renewed reflection demands its tribute" (A, 16). The Greek element then had to struggle with the Asiatic; it was fully taken up by its contemporary conflicts. And we, today, are challenged by technology. To learn from the Greeks—did this not mean to stand up to our own challenges today? Was "memory" of the Greeks not an "unworldly occupation" that actually betrayed the Greek spirit with its openness to the present? "At least it seems so," he wrote (A, 16). With these words, Heidegger closed his reflection for the time being. Meanwhile the ship anchored off the island of Delos. The name of the island said it all—it meant "the manifest, the apparent" (A, 19). It was a brilliant day; along the beach women were offering colorful woven and embroidered things for sale—a "cheerful prospect." Otherwise the island was almost deserted, but strewn with the ruins of temples and ancient buildings. "The veiledness of a former beginning spoke from everything." Across overgrown bedrock, across chunks of masonry, they climbed in a stiff wind up to the ragged summit of Kynthos. Now comes the great moment. The mountains, the sky, the sea, the islands all around "are rising," showing themselves in the light. "What is it that appears in them? Where are they waving us to?" They wave us into a feast of visibility as "they cause that which is present in one way or another to emerge and become visible" (A, 21). On the hills of Delos, with their panorama of the open sea and scattered islands, Heidegger celebrates his arrival in the Promised Land. Why Delos in particular? From his accounts we can only surmise why this place is singled out. Is it perhaps only the magic of the name, or is Heidegger simply unable to offer another explanation? He speaks cautiously of the presence of the divine but at the same time holds himself back; he wished to avoid any "blurred pantheism." Heidegger reached back to his familiar formulas of the truth event, now not recapitulating earlier ideas but pointing to the locality to which these ideas are owed. He had no wish "to record what [he had] seen in a simple narrative account" (A, 5) but chose the following words to express his ecstatic sense of happiness: "The apparently only imagined came to fulfillment, filling itself with presence, with what, lightened, once granted Being-present *(Anwesen)* to the Greeks" (A, 21).

The journey continued to Athens, up to the Acropolis in the early morning before the tourist crowds arrived, and on to Delphi, whose sacred precinct was swarming with people who, instead of observing "a feast of thinking" (A, 32), were ceaselessly taking photographs. They had lost their memory, he wrote, their ability to "remember."

The experience of Delos remained the unforgettable highlight. Six months later Heidegger wrote to Erhart Kästner from Freiburg: "I 'am' often on the island. Yet there hardly exists an adequate word for it." What remained was the preservation in the memory of "the surprising moment of pure presence" (August 23, 1962, BwHK, 51).

That was Heidegger's first visit to the place of his dreams. Others would follow—in 1964, 1966, and 1967.

Around the same time Heidegger also discovered Provence, his second Greece. Following a conference at Cérisy-la-Salle in Normandy in 1955, Jean Beaufret introduced him to the French poet René Char. The acquaintance soon grew into friendship with a man famous not only as a poet but also as a Resistance leader. Char's poems, according to Heidegger, were a "tour de force into the ineffable," yet always in search of the poet's beloved native region, Provence. Char invited Heidegger to his house at Le Thor in the Vaucluse area. Beaufret arranged for Heidegger's visit to be linked with a small seminar for a few friends and the closest circle of Beaufret's students, among whom were Fédier and Vazin, later to become the French translators of *Being and Time.* These seminars, which took place in 1966, 1968, and 1969, developed into a rigid ritual. In the mornings participants would sit under the plane trees in front of the house, discussing, to the accompaniment of the cicadas, Heraclitus or Hegel's statement "A torn stocking is better than a darned one"; "not so self-consciousness"; the Greek concept of fate; or—in 1969—Marx's eleventh Feuerbach thesis: "The philosophers have merely differently interpreted the world. What matters is to change it." On that particular morning, under the dancing shadows of the trees, everybody concurred: one must so interpret the world that one can beautify it again. Records were kept, even though the mistral sometimes carried the sheets away. They were retrieved again and jointly edited. One of these records begins: "Here under the olive trees, which cling to the slope before us, all the way down into the plain where, in the distance and not yet visible, the Rhône flows, we start again with Fragment 2 [of Heraclitus]. Behind us lies the Delphic mountain massif. That is the landscape of the Rebanque. Whoever finds his way there, is the guest of the gods" (VS, 13).

In the afternoons, excursions would be made into the neighborhood, to Avignon, to the vineyards of the Vaucluse, and above all to Cézanne's Mont Sainte-Victoire. Heidegger loved that walk into the quarry of Bibemus to the point where, after a bend in the road, the whole mass of Mont Sainte-Victoire hove into sight. This was Cézanne's path, Heidegger said, and it was matched "in its own way, from start to finish by my own path of thinking."[20] Sitting on a boulder, facing the mountain, Heidegger would sit and gaze for a long time. A "moment of equilibrium of the world," Cézanne once said of this spot. Naturally, the friends were reminded of the story of Socrates remaining motionless, deep in thought, for hours on end. In the evenings they would again sit with René Char, of whom Heidegger claimed that in his speaking and behavior, and in his place, ancient Greece was once more revived. And Char was grateful to Heidegger for once more clearing people's eyes for the essence of poetry, which was nothing other than "the world at its best place." When Heidegger left, Char always gave him armfuls of plants to take with him—lavender and sage from his garden, thyme and the herbs of the land—as well as olive oil and honey.

"It is really impossible to reproduce the atmosphere of those radiant days," one of the friends wrote. "The restrained respect and veneration of the participants for Heidegger—all of them deeply pervaded by the historic importance of this revolutionary thinking; but equally the relaxed close contact with the teacher—in a word, the southern light, that is the composed serenity of those unforgettable days" (VS, 147).

The second half of the 1960s was also the most fertile and intensive period of Heidegger's seminars at Zollikon, at the home of Medard Boss. These were attended by physicians and psychotherapists, pupils and collaborators of Boss, who taught at the university's psychiatric clinic in Zurich, the Burghölzli, the place where Carl Jung had worked. During the war, Medard Boss had been a battalion medical officer with a mountain unit of the Swiss Army. He had had little to do then, and to deal with his boredom he had read *Being and Time.* Gradually he realized that this work formulated some "fundamentally new unheard-of insights into human existence and its world" (ZS, 8) that might be used in psychotherapy. In 1947 he wrote his first letter to Heidegger, who replied courteously and asked for a "small package of chocolate." In 1949 Medard Boss visited Todtnauberg for the first time. Their pen friendship soon ripened into real friendship. Martin Heidegger had great expectations of a link with a doctor who seemed to understand his thought. "He saw the possibility," Medard Boss reports, "that his philosophical insights might not remain stuck in the philosophers' studies, but might benefit many more people, and especially those in need of help" (ZS, 10).

The series of seminars began in 1959 and ended in 1969. At first the participants had the impression that "a Martian was for the first time meeting a group of Earth dwellers and trying to communicate with them" (ZS, 12). Patiently, again and again starting afresh, Heidegger elucidated his principle that *Dasein* meant being open to the world. At the first seminar he drew semicircles on the blackboard to represent that primary openness to the world. Heidegger tried for the first time to make psychic disorders comprehensible through the basic concepts of his *Dasein* analysis in *Being and Time.* Medical histories were discussed. The principal question was whether and to what degree the open relationship to the world was impaired in a psychiatric patient. An open relationship to the world meant "sustaining" the present without escaping into the future or the past. Heidegger criticizes Freudian psychoanalysis for rendering this relationship to the present more difficult with contrived theories. An open relationship to the world also meant preserving that space in which humans and things can appear. Manic depressives, for instance, do not know this free, open encounter; they cannot leave either the things or their fellow humans where, in space-time terms, they belong. They are either too far from them or too near; they either devour them or they are devoured by them—or they vanish in a great void, an inner one and an outer one. What speaks to the manic depressive from the world, he can no longer hear or retain. A distance-preserving nearness, either to things or to people, is no longer possible. What is lacking is the composure that lets itself, and one's fellow being, be. Time and again Heidegger restates his view that most mental diseases can be understood as a disturbance in "existing," in the most literal sense—a failure to "sustain" the open relationship to the world. For Heidegger there is no break between sickness and normality. One moment he would be speaking about a manic depressive or a melancholic, and a few sentences later he would be with Descartes and the general "darkening of the world" in the modern age. The behavior of the maniac, who sees the world as something that has to be grabbed, overcome, and devoured, was for Heidegger the normal contemporary will to power raised to a pathological degree. The two issues were always present in the Zollikon seminars—the mental illness of individuals and the pathology of modern civilization. In the disturbance of the individual Heidegger recognized the madness of the modern age.

Heidegger had found a friend in Medard Boss, but he did not use him as a therapist. Nevertheless he confided to him what he claimed was his only, though often recurring, dream. He dreamed that he had to take his school-graduation exam again, with the same teachers as in the past. "This stereotype dream came definitely to an end," Boss reports, "when he [Heidegger] in wakeful thinking was able to experience 'Being' in the light of 'emergence'" (ZS, 308).

24

ADORNO AND HEIDEGGER: FROM THE JARGON OF AUTHENTICITY TO THE AUTHENTIC JARGON OF THE 1960S

In 1965 a broadcast discussion, which has since become legendary, was held between two adversaries, one of whom assumed the part of Grand Inquisitor and the other that of the friend of mankind. The Grand Inquisitor was Arnold Gehlen; his opponent was Theodor Adorno.

> *Gehlen:* Mr. Adorno, you see the problem of emancipation here once again, of course. Do you really believe that the burden of fundamental problems, of extensive reflection, of errors in life that have profound and continuing effects, all of which we have gone through because we were trying to swim free of them—do you really believe one ought to expect everyone to go through this? I should be very interested to know your views on this.
>
> *Adorno:* I can give you a simple answer: Yes! I have a particular conception of objective happiness and objective despair, and I would say that, for as long as people have problems taken away from them, for as long as they are not expected to take full responsibility and full self-determination,

> their welfare and happiness in this world will merely be an illusion. And it will be an illusion that will one day burst. And when it bursts, it will have dreadful consequences.[1]

Gehlen rejoined that this was a nice thought, but unfortunately valid only in a utopian anthropology. Adorno replied that man's need for exoneration was not, as Gehlen claimed, an anthropological natural constant, but a reaction to the stresses that men, with their social institutions, placed upon themselves. To escape those stresses they sought refuge with the very power that was inflicting on them the injuries they suffered. This "identification with the attacker" had to be broken. Gehlen's reply, with which he concluded the debate, was: "Mr. Adorno, . . . Although I have the feeling that we are united in certain profound premisses, it's my impression that it is dangerous—and that you have the tendency—to make people dissatisfied with the little that still remains to them out of the whole catastrophic situation."[2]

The Whole is the Untrue—this position is held by both of them. And this is also Heidegger's position. The best thing, Gehlen says, is to help people pursue their business, immune to criticism and objections, and to spare them the effort of reflection that would merely confront them with the catastrophic state of the Whole. Not so, says Adorno; in the name of liberation we must encourage them to reflect, to make them realize how bad their situation is. Gehlen, not seeing any practicable alternative to the actual state of affairs, would wish to spare people from reflection, while Adorno believes they can stand up to it, even though he can only remind them of delicate promises of salvation of the kind preserved in childhood experiences, in poetry, in music, and in the *metaphysics of the moment of their fall.*

What is significant is that philosophers such as Gehlen, Adorno, and also Heidegger can agree that the situation, viewed as a whole, is catastrophic. Yet this catastrophe lacks an alarming aspect. One can live with it. For Adorno, one consequence of this is that people become doubly alienated—they are alienated and they have lost all awareness of their alienation. To Gehlen, civilization anyway is nothing other than catastrophe in a state of supportability. And for Heidegger the *Gestell* is a *destiny* that man cannot cope with. The fundamental problems of the technological world are not solvable by technology. *Only a God can save us,* Heidegger says.

The Cassandras up on the mountain peaks of bad prospects are calling to each other, exchanging their gloomy insights across the lowlands where efficiency and "Carry on as you are" hold sway. The 1950s and early 1960s have given rise to a disaster discourse that coexists peacefully with reconstruction zeal, with smug prosperity, with optimism in small things and in the short term. The critics of culture provide a gloomy minor-key accompaniment to the cheerful hustle of the prospering Federal Republic.

They all, each in a different way, take part in the mischief they criticize. Gehlen wishes to protect society from the intellectuals by technological means. Adorno paints a horror picture of capitalist alienation and, to regain respect for the Institute for Social Research, investigates the working climate in the Mannesmann company on behalf of its management. Heidegger uses edifying talk to reject edifying talk against technology.

Heidegger, the critic of his time, suffered a fate similar to Adorno's—he was being listened to like an artistic oracle. Not the academies of sciences but the academies of fine arts were wooing Heidegger, just as they would soon woo Adorno. Fundamental critique, which did not wish to become political and which was fighting shy of religiousness, was inevitably received on the aesthetic plane. When the Berlin Academy of Fine Arts in 1957 was discussing Heidegger's election, a great majority agreed with Gertrud von le Fort when she said that Heidegger's work had to be read as "great poetry" (quoted in BwHK, 32). This kind of resonance was not unwelcome to Heidegger, because thinking and poetry were for him moving ever closer together, and jointly they removed him from the quarrels of the day. "The shepherds live invisible and outside the wasteland of the devastated earth, which is to serve solely the securing of man's domination."

Even in the 1920s Heidegger's impact had not been confined to the universities; nor was it later, though a large number of professors, and those hoping to become professors, claimed him for their own in the 1950s. There was a lot of "Heideggering" going on in German university departments, his works were analyzed in minute detail, lame studies were published on throwing and thrownness, Heidegger's grandiose philosophy of boredom was turned into boring philosophy, and scholars argued about the categories of the existential. But none of this made Heidegger the master thinker of the 1950s and the early 1960s. In an article written for *Frankfurter Allgemeine Zeitung* by Jürgen Habermas on Heidegger's seventieth birthday, there was particular emphasis on the "circles of lay brothers" that sprang up throughout the country, "lay brothers" who worshiped Heidegger's words.[3] A few years later Adorno, in his *Jargon of Authenticity,* would reduce Heidegger's effect to the formula:

"Irrationality in the midst of the rational is the working atmosphere of authenticity."[4] Adorno, as a researcher of working atmospheres, should know.

> In Germany a jargon of authenticity is spoken—even more so written. Its language is the hallmark of societalized chosenness, noble and homey at once—sub-language and superior language. The jargon extends from philosophy and theology—not only of Protestant academies—to pedagogy, evening schools, and youth organizations, even to the elevated diction of the representatives of business and administration. While the jargon overflows with the pretense of deep human emotion, it is just as standardized as the world that it officially negates.[5]

In point of fact, the spare parts and terminological assemblies of Heidegger's philosophy made it possible to manage his discourse so that his academic reputation did not suffer. When talking about death, for instance, one could choose a middle road between existential seriousness and a philosophical erudition that showed that nothing human is alien to it. If it was embarrassing to speak about God, but one did not wish to dispense with anonymous spirituality, then one could always resort to Being, to *Sein* spelled in the traditional way or *Seyn.* What Camus and Sartre were to the younger generation, Heidegger was for the older, who often regarded the ponderous as the more serious and sound.

To Adorno's critical gaze, in the "German ideology" of the day, the jargon of authenticity and Martin Heidegger as its prompter were something far more dangerous—the reflection of the mentality of an educated class that was predisposed to fascism. Adorno proceeds from harmless-sounding words like "mission, appeal, encounter, genuine conversation, statement, request, link"—words with which, according to Adorno, the "ascension of the word"[6] can be staged in suitable contexts. He who hears the "appeal," chooses the "encounter," declares his "request," and does not flinch from "link," reveals himself as someone who is called for higher things because he aims at higher things. This is the—for the moment still gentle—superman, above the bustle of the managed world. The authentic person proves his ability to prevail with his heart; he plays the "Wurlitzer organ of the spirit."[7]

The *Jargon of Authenticity* deals with the spirit of an epoch that, by the time the book appeared in the mid-1960s, was no longer in existence. These were the years of Ludwig Erhard's chancellorship. An unctuous jargon had flourished in the patriarchal Adenauer period, but when Adorno's pamphlet was published a new matter-of-factness had gained ground. The "meeting house" gave way to the "multipurpose hall," pedestrian zones conquered the cities, bunker and prison construction triumphed in architecture. The charm of naked reality was being discovered, in philosophy as much as in the sex shops, and it was not long before unmasking, criticism, and relentless questioning governed the world of discourse.

One function of the jargon was that "it causes all its words to say more than each single one."[8] They sound like that in Adorno's text as well, except that he is setting the stage not for an ascent into heaven but a crash into hell. Adorno's preeminent intention is his suspicion of fascism, which endows some comical rather than dangerous facts with significance. Thus Adorno remarks on Heidegger's careful paragraph subdivision in his chapter on death in *Being and Time:* "Even death is handled by the book, in SS-orders and in existential philosophies; red tape ridden as Pegasus, in extremis ridden as an apocalyptic steed."[9] Elsewhere Adorno turns Heidegger into a philosopher of secondary virtues: "In the name of contemporary authenticity even a torturer could put in all sorts of claims for compensation, to the extent that he was simply a true torturer."[10] But these are merely the preliminaries of Adorno's critique. He is out to trace fascism inside Heidegger's fundamental ontology. Ontology, especially Heidegger's, is the systematized "readiness to sanction a heteronomous order, removed from justification by consciousness,"[11] Adorno says in his principal work, *Negative Dialectics,* to which the *Jargon of Authenticity* belongs conceptually.

In 1959 Adorno had declared: "I regard the survival of National Socialism in our democracy as potentially more dangerous than the survival of fascist tendencies *against* democracy." He was referring mainly to the fact that the anticommunism of the Cold War was providing a cloak for the fascist demon. All it had to do was to present itself as the defender of the West against the "red flood" to pick up the tradition of the anti-Bolshevism of the Nazis. This anticommunism of the Adenauer era certainly also exploited a racially tinged "Russophobia" and appealed to authoritarian, and at times chauvinist, leanings. To consolidate the front against the East, the rehabilitation and reintegration of the National Socialist elite had been hurriedly driven forward in the 1950s. Adenauer had repeatedly demanded that the differentiation between "two classes of people," between the politically impeccable and the not-so-impeccable, should disappear as soon as possible. In May 1951 a law had been enacted that once again allowed "compromised" persons to hold public office. Additionally, the Loyalty Law of 1952 ensured that members of the Association of Persons Persecuted under the Nazi Regime were removed from public posts on suspicion of communism. Anti-Semitism was also reviving. Adorno, who, along with Horkheimer, had returned from exile in France to the University of Frankfurt, was to experience it most particularly. In 1953 he was appointed to an extraordinary chair in philosophy and sociology, which was quite openly called a compensation chair—a convenient designation for defamation. Adorno's hopes of receiving an ordinary professorship solely on the grounds of his standing as a scholar remained unfulfilled for a long time. When eventually, in 1956, Adorno's appointment as a full professor, an *Ordinarius,* was under discussion, Hellmut Ritter, professor of Oriental Studies, immediately spoke of "rigging."[12] All a man needed in Frankfurt to make a career, he said, was to be a protégé of Horkheimer and to be a Jew. This was not the only remark of this kind. Matters reached such a pass that even Horkheimer, whose position as a former rector and dean was more consolidated, applied for early retirement in 1956 because of anti-Semitism. Adorno and Horkheimer again had to undergo the old Jewish experience: even though they had attained privileged positions, they still remained stigmatized and vulnerable. "As a minister he will be a Jewish minister, His Excellency and a pariah at the same time" was how Sartre had characterized this state of affairs in his *Anti-Semite and Jew.*[13] Adorno was "vulnerable" in the 1950s and early 1960s also because of his Marxist background. The weekly *Die Zeit* in 1955 described him as a "propagandist for the 'classless society.'"[14]

However, if Adorno searched Heidegger's philosophy for fascist continuity, then he was doing so not only because he hoped to strike at the spirit of *juste milieu* of the Adenauer era. What was at stake was also a dangerous philosophical affinity with the person he attacked. There was, moreover, in Adorno some irritation with a philosopher who was practicing his philosophy as if sociology and psychoanalysis, these two great opponents of the philosophical mind, had never come about. Such ignorance was bound to outrage Adorno who, for his own part, had been taken to task by these powers of disenchantment, with the result that his own philosophical Eros suffered damage. The fact that Heidegger totally ignored, or even condemned, this "scientific modernism" was to Adorno "provincialism" in Heidegger. However, though Adorno, as a historian of philosophy, had very clear ideas of what was "no longer possible," he failed to take a firm philosophical stand. All that was left to his philosophical passion was long-term virtuoso reflection and, of course, art. Indeed, this turning to art as a refuge for philosophy was another thing the two men had in common. Adorno hardly envied Heidegger his difficult road, but he may have envied him the fact that he was not ashamed of his undisguised metaphysical activity. Adorno wrote at one time: "Modesty resists the direct expression of metaphysical intentions; to venture such expression would be to expose oneself to gleeful misunderstanding."[15] When Herbert Marcuse tried to publish his *Eros and Civilization* in the mid-1950s as a special issue of the journal *Zeitschrift für Sozialforschung* (it would later be published by Suhrkamp under the alluring title *Urge Structure and Society*), Adorno wrote to him that he was "left uneasy with a certain directness and immediacy."[16] Adorno, who would generally get Horkheimer to help him eliminate any unwelcome competition, succeeded in preventing publication of the book as part of the institute's series. Marcuse's inexcusable error had been that he had too openly revealed a production secret of critical theory—the idea of a successful culture based on a sexuality liberated into eroticism. Adorno, at any rate, could pursue his "metaphysical intentions" only under the cover of considerable awkwardness of all kinds.

Regardless of all this, Adorno's authentic concern—this would have been the term in the "jargon of authenticity"—was really akin to Heidegger's. And he was aware of this. In 1949 Adorno had urged Horkheimer to write a review for *Der Monat* of Heidegger's just published book *Holzwege* (False Trails). He wrote to him that "for false trails" Heidegger was "in a way . . . not all that different from us."[17]

Adorno and Heidegger arrived at a similar diagnosis of the modern age. Heidegger speaks of a "rebellion of the subject" for whom the world becomes an object of "machinations," a process that reflects on the subject with the result that it can comprehend itself only as a thing among things. In Adorno and Horkheimer's *Dialectic of Enlightenment* we find the same fundamental idea—the violence that modern man does to nature turns against man's inner nature: "Every attempt to break the natural thralldom, because nature is broken, enters all the more deeply into that natural enslavement. Hence the course of European civilization."[18] The way Heidegger puts it is: the world becomes a disposable object, a picture, an idea for producing. Adorno and Horkheimer speak of "the awakening of the self [being] paid for by the acknowledgement of power as the principle of all relations,"[19] just as "men pay for the increase of their power with alienation from that over which they exercise their power."[20] For Adorno this power principle of the alienated bourgeois world leads, as its final consequence, to the horror of the production-line murder of the Jews: "Genocide is the absolute integration. It is on its way wherever men are being leveled off—polished off . . . until one exterminates them."[21] When Heidegger in his 1949 Bremen lecture stated that "agriculture is now motorized food industry, essentially the same as the manufacture of corpses and gas chambers," this remark, when it leaked out later, triggered great indignation, especially among people who had taken no offense to Adorno's similar thoughts. And yet Heidegger's remark was entirely in the sense of that categorical imperative formulated by Adorno: "It is necessary to arrange thoughts and actions, so that Auschwitz will not repeat itself, so that nothing similar will happen."[22] Heidegger understood his thinking on Being as an overcoming of the modern will to power that had led to disaster. This thinking on Being is not too far removed from what Adorno was seeking under the heading of "the thinking of nonidentity." This Adorno saw as a way of thinking that allows things and men to be themselves in their uniqueness, instead of doing them violence and regimenting them through "identification." Nonalienating, nonidentifying cognition "seeks to say what something is, while identitarian thinking says what something comes under, what it exemplifies or represents, and what, accordingly, it is not itself."[23]

What in Adorno is called "nonidentifying thinking" is to Heidegger an "opening thinking" in which that which is can show itself without having violence done to it. But Adorno mistrusts this kind of thinking on Being. He makes the old charge of irrationalism: "We cannot, by thinking, assume any position in which the separation of subject and object will directly vanish, for the separation is inherent in each thought, it is inherent in thinking itself. That is why Heidegger's moment of truth levels off into an irrationalist weltanschauung."[24] Adorno commends Heidegger's "moments of truth," by which he means his refusal to bow to positivistically dressed-up "facts" and surrender the ontological-metaphysical need. Adorno, too, approves "a longing that Kant's verdict on a knowledge of the Absolute should not be the end of the matter."[25] But where Heidegger transcends with solemn devotion, Adorno stages the play of negative dialectics, which remains faithful to metaphysics through the negation of its negation. That is why Adorno can also call this dialectic an "organon of transcendence of longing."[26] The two men differ in the way they progress but not in their direction. This closeness to Heidegger, however, irritates Adorno's narcissism of the small difference. He shies away from the solidarity of the secret and uncanny metaphysicians. The similarity of their direction is also confirmed by the fact that Adorno, too, invokes Hölderlin as a metaphysical witness, and that he looks to southern Germany—that is, Heidegger's region—as to a promised land. In his "Speech on Lyrical Poetry and Society" Adorno says, in connection with a Möricke interpretation: "Up surges the image of the promise of happiness which the small south German town still grants its guests on the right day, but not the slightest concession is made to pseudo-Gothic small-town idyll."[27]

Toward the end of his "Meditations on Metaphysics" (in *Negative Dialectics*), Adorno discusses where in the modern age the places still accessible to metaphysical experience are to be found. We no longer find them in totality, in the grand survey, and it has even escaped us in the passage of spirit through history, where Hegel still regards it as present. Now there is only horror there—no epiphany, no edifying world spirit, only the heart of darkness. Where, then, does metaphysics live? Where can one "solidarize" with it at the "moment of its fall"? Adorno answers: "What is a metaphysical experience? If we disdain projecting it upon allegedly primal religious experiences, we are most likely to visualize it, as Proust did, in the happiness, for instance, that is promised by village names like Applebachsville, Wind Gap, or Lords Valley. One thinks that going there would bring the fulfillment, as if there were such a thing."[28] Adorno presented his search for his lost-and-found-again metaphysics in his short sketch "Amorbach." It was in the little Odenwald village of that name that he had spent his childhood. There he finds many motifs assembled that subsequently sprouted for him. The lakeside garden of a monastery becomes the primal image of a beauty "for whose reason I ask in vain in the face of the whole."[29] He still hears the sound of an ancient ferry across the Main, the acoustic emblem of a departure for new shores—this is how one crosses from one world to the other. On a hill he experiences how, in the village down below, the recently electrified light abruptly, as at a single blow, flashes up at the fall of darkness—a cautious practice run for the later shocks of modernity in New York and elsewhere. "So well had my little town looked after me that it prepared me for the very opposite."[30] Adorno walks along the paths of Amorbach as Heidegger does his Feldweg; for both of them, these are real and simultaneously imaginary locations of metaphysical experience, nourished by memory and the incantatory power of speech. Heidegger: "Time and again thinking walks . . . along the path which the Feldweg draws through the lees . . . The expanse of all grown things which live around the

Feldweg grants world. It is only in the unuttered of their language, as the old reading and living master Eckehardt says, that God is God" (D, 39).

For Adorno, who draws his metaphysical lyricisms from the Odenwald forest, Heidegger's Feldweg is cheap "folklore art." Heidegger's statement that "to grow means to open up to the expanse of the heavens and, at the same time, strike root in the darkness of the ground" (D, 38) immediately earns itself Adorno's accusation of fascism and "*Blubo* [blood-and-soil] ideology."

One gains the impression that Heidegger's temporary entanglement in National Socialism rather suited Adorno; in this way he could aggressively philosophize with Heidegger and yet keep a distance—which, in philosophical matters, was not all that marked.

Adorno's attacks on Heidegger—the two men never met after 1945, and Heidegger never addressed a single word to Adorno in public—marked the victorious advance of the jargon of dialectics, which maintained its position well into the 1970s as the jargon of high pretensions. When in the mid-1960s Marcuse was asked by a newspaper what book he thought should be written at the time, he replied: "I suggest a very serious one, entitled 'We Can't Quite Manage without Dialectics: On the Pathology of the Spirit of Our Age.'"[31] Such dialectics arise in the attempt to outbid the complexity of reality in discourse. The will to outbid stems not only from a fear of banality but also from the effort, amid the general "delusional context" (Adorno) to discover the totally different, the trace of a succeeding life, without succumbing to the suggestion of the Hegelian or Marxist concept of progress. "Critical theory," Sloterdijk said, "was the attempt to come into the inheritance of dialectics without spinning victors' fantasies."[32] However, some victories were won with such dialectics, albeit only in the world of discourse. A high-falutin, arrogant attitude, adorning itself with unuttered mysteries, was spreading north and south of the Main. Ulrich Sonnemann, for example, wrote about the evil of banality, emphasizing that banality was "the Within of the True, but could not support being this Within, and therefore, out of the tension of a perverted conscience, both is what it is and, at the same time, cannot bear the certainty that this is nothing; and that in this nonbearing of itself, which in its world role simultaneously appears as a nonbearing of the True, its inability to bear emerges."[33] Améry, who picked up this sentence, so interprets it as the "evil banal" that "the person who contents himself with thought clichés instead of destroying them commits a sin of omission and thereby becomes an enemy of truth."[34]

In Adorno the language of dialectics was still a work of art of supreme subtlety: "The cognitive utopia would be to use concepts to unseal the nonconceptual with concepts without making them equal."[35] It was, as Jean Améry put it, an "unclearness acting up as superclearness."[36] Yet the jargon became more robust and distinct, especially when the negative dialectics became positive again and, around 1968, began, step by step, tendentially to discover—these were the formulas of the jargon—the universal scientific worker, an unrepressed Eros, a restrictive code, the potential of the marginalized, and finally the old working class as a subject for the reconstruction of the system-transcending social emancipation process. In this context Adorno's somewhat aesthetic dialectics was no longer in demand. The change of climate to "operationalization" and "practice relevance" led to collisions in Frankfurt, and indeed elsewhere. When the Institute of Sociology was occupied by students, Adorno called in the police. These events probably broke his heart, for a year later he died.

These were the years when Heidegger sought refuge for his philosophy in Provence, when many regarded him as a Swabian Taoist, and when he himself was convinced that for the public he was as good as dead. Hannah Arendt's loving essay on Heidegger's eightieth birthday has the ring of an obituary: "The gale that blows through Heidegger's thinking—like that which still, after thousands of years, blows to us from Plato's work—is not of our century. It comes from the primordial, and what it leaves behind is something perfect which, like everything perfect, falls back to the primordial."[37]

A few years earlier there had once more been great excitement. On February 7, 1966, an article had appeared in *Der Spiegel* in connection with Alexander Schwan's book *Political Philosophy in Heidegger's Thought.* The article bore the headline "Heidegger, Midnight of a World Night," and contained a number of inaccurate assertions, such as that Heidegger had forbidden Husserl to enter the university, and that he had stopped visiting Jaspers because of his Jewish wife. Jaspers had been irritated by the article and had written to Arendt: "At such moments *Der Spiegel* relapses into its old bad manners" (March 9, 1966, BwAJ, 655). Arendt had reacted with an outburst of fury against Adorno, who, however, had had absolutely nothing to do with the *Spiegel* article:

> Although I can't prove it, I am pretty much convinced that the real string-pullers here are the Wiesengrund-Adorno people in Frankfurt.

> And that is the more grotesque, as it has now been established (the students have discovered it) that Wiesengrund (half Jewish and one of the most repulsive people I know) tried to fall in line with the Nazis. For years he and Horkheimer have accused everyone who opposed them of anti-Semitism or threatened that they would do so. Truly an abominable crowd. (April 18, 1966, BwAJ, 670).

Heidegger was urged by his friends and acquaintances to defend himself against the critique in *Der Spiegel.* Erhart Kästner wrote him on March 4: "There is nothing I wish for more keenly . . . than that you would stop not defending yourself. You have no idea what pain you are causing your friends by, so far, obstinately disdaining to do so. It is one of the strongest arguments . . . that calumnies, unless one defends oneself against them audibly, become facts" (BwHK, 80).

Heidegger wrote a short letter to the editor of *Der Spiegel,* but Kästner did not think that was enough. He wanted to see a more extensive and vigorous refutation. He himself had shortly before resigned from the Berlin Academy of Fine Arts because he did not want to belong to it together with Günter Grass who, in an episode of his novel *Dog Years,* had attacked Heidegger: "Get this straight, dog: he was born in Messkirch. That's near Braunau on the Inn. He and the Other had their umbilical cords cut in the same stockingcap year. He and the Other Guy invented each other."[38] When Kästner found out that *Der Spiegel* was interested in an interview with Heidegger and tried to persuade him to give it, Heidegger at first declined: "If there were any real interest in *Der Spiegel* in my thinking, Herr Augstein could have visited me on the occasion of his lecture at this university during the past winter semester, just as, after his lecture here he visited Jaspers in Basel" (March 11, 1966, BwHK, 82).

Kästner persisted. On March 21 he wrote: "No one will love *Der Spiegel,* its tone, or overrate its standard. But I think one should not underrate the favorable wind that is blowing at the moment, when Herr Augstein is angry and contemptuous toward Grass. I hear reports . . . that dislike of the modern idolization of science and a deep skepticism are favorite ideas of Herr Augstein. I can really see no grounds for not wishing this visit" (BwHK, 85).

The interview finally came about because *Der Spiegel* accepted Heidegger's condition that it would not be published in his lifetime. It took place on September 23, 1966, at Heidegger's Freiburg home. In addition to Heidegger,

Augstein, Georg Wolf (an editor of *Der Spiegel*), and Digne Meller-Markovic (a photographer), Heinrich Wiegand Petzet was present as Heidegger's "silent second." Petzet reports that, prior to the interview, Augstein had confessed to him that he was "hellishly afraid" of the "famous thinker."[39] This had made Augstein, whom he had at first regarded as an "inquisitorial executioner," immediately likable to him. Heidegger was excited too. He awaited the participants by the door of his study. "I was a little alarmed," Petzet reports, "when I looked at him and saw the excessive tension he was under . . . The veins at his temples and forehead stood out massively, and his eyes protruded with excitement."[40]

Augstein's "hellish" fear was evident mainly at the beginning of the conversation. With extreme care, contortion, and delicacy, the "hot potato" was tackled: "Professor Heidegger, we have stated time and again that your philosophical work has been somewhat overshadowed by some events in your life which, while they did not last very long, have still never been cleared up, either because you were too proud or else did not think it appropriate to comment on them."[41]

Heidegger had expected that the talk would focus mainly on his involvement with National Socialism. He was surprised to find Augstein in a positive hurry to get that topic behind them in order to address Heidegger's philosophical interpretation of the modern age and, in particular, his philosophy on technology. Time and again Augstein and Georg Wolf apologized when passages from his rectorial address or from the Schlageter celebration speech had to be quoted or when Heidegger had to be confronted with rumors about his alleged participation in the book burning or his behavior toward Husserl. So delicate were the questioners' references to his engagement that Heidegger himself proposed a stronger version. Augstein and Wolf offered Heidegger the interpretation that, during his rectorship, he had been obliged to say certain things *ad usum Delphini.* But Heidegger objected that "the phrase *ad usum Delphini* says too little. I then believed that in the argument with National Socialism a new, and the only still possible, way might open up towards a renewal."[42] But even these words were not strong enough: not the "argument with National Socialism" but the National Socialist revolution—as he had then comprehended it—had meant to him "renewal." He did not mention that this renewal was understood by him as a history-making event, as a metaphysical revolution, as an "overthrow of the whole German *Dasein*" and indeed that of the entire Occident. He did not mention that he had been seized by an intoxication with power, that he had wanted to defend the purity of the revolution and for that reason had become an informer, that he had come into conflict with the Nazi authorities and with his colleagues and had been a failure as rector because he had wished to move the revolution forward. Instead he conveyed the impression that he had carried on in order to offer some kind of resistance. He emphasized his unpolitical attitude prior to 1933 and presented his acceptance of the rectorate as a sacrifice in order to prevent something worse—the seizure of power at the university by party functionaries. In short, Heidegger in this interview concealed the National Socialist revolutionary he had, for a certain period, been, and he kept silent about the philosophical motivations that had led him to that point.

While, on the one hand, he presented his role during the Nazi period as more harmless than it was, he was not, on the other hand, prepared to act the "purged democrat" as so many others were doing in Germany at the time. When the interview turned to the problem "that technology tears men loose from the earth and uproots them,"[43] Heidegger pointed out that National Socialism had originally intended to oppose such a development but had subsequently become its motor. Heidegger admitted that he was perplexed about the question: "How can a political system accommodate itself to the technological age, and which political system would this be? I have no answer to this question. I am not convinced that it is democracy."[44] It was at this point in the interview that Heidegger said: "Only a God can save us,"[45] which provided the heading for the *Spiegel* interview.

It had been thought that the interview would bring the argument about Heidegger's political engagement to an end, but instead it merely fanned it. Heidegger defended himself just as all other incriminated persons were then defending themselves—in a manner that Carl Schmitt sarcastically described in his *Glossarium* as being as though they had discovered fellow-traveling as a form of resistance. But what the multitude did was nevertheless bound to make an undignified impression when followed by an authenticity philosopher, one who had demanded that a "resolute *Dasein*" also show the courage of responsibility. Responsibility extends not only to the range of one's own intentions but also to the unintended consequences of one's actions. But was Heidegger to accept shared responsibility for the monstrous crimes of Nazism in which he had genuinely played no part—not even in terms of ideological prerequisites? Heidegger had never been a racist.

A lot has been said about Heidegger's silence. What had been expected of him? Herbert Marcuse, who had written to him on August 28, 1947, expected a "word" that would finally clear Heidegger of being identified with Nazism. He was hoping that he would "publicly acknowledge [his] change and transformation."[46] Heidegger in his reply pointed out that he had already publicly (in his lectures) performed this transformation, even during the Nazi era. Subsequently, in 1945, "it was impossible for me, because the Nazi partisans demonstrated their change of heart in a disgusting manner, and I have nothing in common with them."[47] That he should, on public demand, distance himself from the murder of millions of Jews—that Heidegger, rightly, regarded as monstrous. To do so would imply that the public considered him capable of complicity with the murder. His self-esteem demanded that he decline this unreasonable request.

The fact that Heidegger rejected the idea that he should defend himself as a potential accomplice to murder did not mean that he shied away from the challenge "to think Auschwitz." When Heidegger refers to the perversion of the modern will to power, for which nature and man have become mere "machinations," he always, explicitly or not, also means Auschwitz. To him, as to Adorno, Auschwitz is a typical crime of the modern age.

If, therefore, one understands Heidegger's critique of the modern age also as philosophizing about Auschwitz, then it becomes clear that the problem of his silence is not that he was silent on Auschwitz. In philosophical terms he was silent about something else: about himself, about the philosopher's seducibility by power. He too—as happened so often in the history of thought—failed to ask the one question: Who am I really when I am thinking? The thinker has thoughts, but sometimes it is the other way around—the thoughts have him. The "Who" of thinking transforms himself. He who thinks the great things can easily be tempted to regard himself as a great event; he is anxious to match up to Being and is concerned about how he will figure in history, not how he appears to himself. The contingency of one's own person disappears in the thinking Self and its great dimensions. The ontological long-distance view lets the ontically nearest become blurred. There is a lack of acquaintance with oneself, with one's own time-conditioned contradictions, biographical accidents, and idiosyncrasies. He who is acquainted with his contingent self is less likely to confuse himself with the heroes of his thinking self, or to let the little stories drown in great history. In short: knowledge of self protects against seduction by power.

Heidegger's silence was to play a part once more in his encounter with Paul

Celan. The poet Paul Celan, born in 1920 in Czernowitz, who by a mere chance escaped the death camps where his parents were murdered and had lived in Paris since 1948, found himself attracted especially by Heidegger's late philosophy. The philosopher Otto Pöggeler recalls that, in their conversation, Celan defended Heidegger's late, linguistically involved formulations, and that in 1957 he wanted to send Heidegger the poem "Schlieren," which subsequently appeared in the volume *Sprachgitter.* The poem speaks of an eye whose injury embraces the world and preserves its memory:

> Streak in the eye:
> to preserve
> a sign
> borne through dark.[48]

Perhaps this poem was itself intended as a sign of a desired relationship, one that would remember the "wound" that divided the two men, Celan and Heidegger. It is not certain that Celan really sent off the poem. Following their numerous extensive conversations about the philosopher, Pöggeler asked Celan if he might dedicate his book on Heidegger to him. Celan reluctantly declined. He had to insist, he said, that, prior to a meeting with Heidegger, his own name not be linked with that of the philosopher. Celan nevertheless thoroughly studied Heidegger's work. His copy of *Being and Time* contains extensive notes; he was familiar with Heidegger's interpretations of Hölderlin, Trakl, and Rilke. In his poem "Largo" he refers to the "*heidegängerisch Nahen*" [the close heath-walker, but clearly a play on Heidegger's name]. Martin Heidegger for his part had closely followed Paul Celan's work since the 1950s. When in the summer of 1967 the German scholar Gerhart Baumann was organizing a reading with Paul Celan in Freiburg and informed Heidegger of this by letter, Heidegger replied: "I have long wished to meet Paul Celan. He stands further forward than anyone else and keeps back more than anyone. I know everything he's written, I also know about the grave crisis from which he struggled free as far as a man can do that . . . It would be good and salutary to show Paul Celan the Black Forest."[49]

At his reading in Freiburg on July 24, 1967, in the university's biggest lecture hall, Paul Celan found himself faced with the biggest audience of his life. More than a thousand listeners had come, including Martin Heidegger, who sat in the front row. Before the reading Heidegger had visited the local bookstores and asked that Celan's volumes of poetry be given pride of place in their shop windows. This was done. On his first walk through the city, the poet saw his volumes in all the bookstores and happily reported this fact to a group of friends in the foyer of his hotel, an hour before the reading. Martin Heidegger, who was among them, did not disclose the role he had played in this.

At this first meeting between Heidegger and Celan, the following scene took place. After a lively conversation, someone wanted to take a photograph. Celan jumped to his feet and declared that he did not wish to be photographed with Heidegger. Heidegger remained composed, turned aside, and remarked to Gerhart Baumann: "He doesn't want—so we'll let it be."[50] Celan disappeared for a short time, and when he returned he let it be understood that he no longer had any objection to being photographed with Heidegger. But that first rejection lingered, and no one renewed the suggestion. Now it was Celan who showed himself unhappy about the effect of his behavior and tried to undo the injury. After the reading the group met again for a glass of wine. Heidegger proposed driving up into the Black Forest early in the morning and visit a mountain moor and his cabin at Todtnauberg. This was arranged. No sooner had Heidegger left than Celan, who had remained behind with Baumann, rose to his feet and again voiced doubts and misgivings about the proposal he had just agreed to. He found it difficult, he said, to be together with a man whose past he could not forget. "His misgivings rapidly grew into refusal," Baumann reports, having reminded Celan of his explicit wish. Celan made no attempt to resolve his conflicts. His reservations persisted, yet on the other hand he was impressed by Heidegger's work and personality. He felt himself attracted and, at the same time, blamed himself for it. He sought his presence, yet he forbade himself to seek it. The following day Celan made the excursion to Todtnauberg. He spent a morning with Heidegger at his cabin. What the two talked about is unknown. Celan's entry in the cabin's logbook read: "Into the cabin logbook, with a view toward the Brunnenstern, with hope of a coming word in the heart."[51]

The "coming word" could mean a variety of things. Had Celan expected a confession of guilt and was he disappointed that Heidegger did not make one? But Baumann, who met the two men a few hours later at an inn, reports that Celan did not seem at all disappointed: "I was pleasantly surprised to find the poet and the thinker in cheerful mood. They sketched out the events of the preceding hours, with special mention of the walk to the cabin. All heaviness had gone from Celan."[52] Celan left for Frankfurt the following day, in high spirits. Marie Luise Kaschnitz was surprised to find a totally transformed Paul Celan. To her friends she said: "What did they do to him in Freiburg, what happened to him there? He isn't the same person."[53] In this elated mood Celan on August 1, 1967, wrote the poem "Todtnauberg":

Arnica, eyebright, the
draft from the well with the
star-crowned die above it,

in the
hut,

the line
—whose name did the book
register before mine?—
the line inscribed in that book about
a hope, today,
of a thinking man's
coming (un-
tarryingly coming)
word
in the heart.[54]

The "coming word"—this line also responds to Heidegger's metaphysical adventism, to his "coming God," to his "On the Way to Language," which can bring about a "Turn." The "coming word," therefore, is not just a word of Heidegger's political absolution.

The "un-tarryingly coming) word" is what it says in the first version of the poem, which Celan sent Heidegger in 1968. In the volume *Lichtzwang,* published in 1970, Celan deleted the bracketed hope of the "untarryingly coming" word.

Meanwhile there were other meetings, letters were exchanged, the relationship became closer. In the summer of 1970 Heidegger wanted to guide Celan through the Hölderlin landscape of the Upper Danube. He had already made preparations for it when, in the spring of 1970, Celan took his own life in Paris.

Heidegger's attitude to Celan was wooing, attentive, at times caring. At their last meeting, on Maundy Thursday in 1970, there once more occurred a minor clash. Celan had recited poems; they had talked about them. Heidegger had followed the reading so attentively that he was able afterward to quote entire verses exactly. Nevertheless Celan, in the course of their conversation, accused him of inattentiveness. They parted in a dejected mood. Baumann accompanied Heidegger on his way home. As they parted at the garden gate, Heidegger said to Baumann "with emotion: Celan is sick—hopelessly."[55]

What had Celan expected of Heidegger? Probably he himself did not know. Heidegger's word *Lichtung* (clearing) was to him a promise for whose redemption he was waiting. Perhaps Celan's word *Lichtzwang* (light compulsion) contains his impatient answer.

25

SUNSET OF LIFE

Next to the bell push of Rötebuckweg 47 was a little card: "Visits after 5 P.M." There were a lot of visits, and Heidegger had to keep his working time free for himself. Petzet recalls an amusing incident when, on a Sunday afternoon, a large South American family requested admission, with the only, haltingly uttered wish "*Seulement voir Monsieur Heidegger*" (Just to see Mr. Heidegger).[1] Heidegger appeared, the family gazed in admiration at the fabulous beast, and, with a lot of bowing, they moved off without another word. Visitors who were admitted to Heidegger's study—a particular honor—had to climb a circular wooden staircase to the second floor, where the door into the study was next to an enormous family wardrobe. The study was darkened by bookshelves along all the walls, with light coming from a window surrounded by ivy. In front of the window was the writing desk; from it one had a view of the Zähringer Castle ruin. Next to the desk was a leather armchair in which generations of visitors had sat—Bultmann, Jaspers, Sartre, Augstein. The desktop was piled high with folders of manuscripts, mockingly referred to by his brother, Fritz, as "Martin's shunting depots."

It was in this room that, after a break of fifteen years, Hannah Arendt once again sat in 1967. Since her last visit, in 1952, there had been exchanges of letters. On her sixtieth birthday Heidegger had sent her his poem "Autumn." In it Arendt had heard the elegiac tone, the sunset mood of his life. Heidegger was then approaching eighty, and she wanted to see him once more; his birthday greetings had encouraged her. Thus, after the disagreements of the earlier years, another reconciliation. Hannah and Elfride decided to address each other by their first names. Two years later, in August 1969, shortly before Heidegger's eightieth birthday, Hannah Arendt brought her husband, Heinrich Blücher, along with her for another visit. The atmosphere was cordial and relaxed. If only Hannah did not smoke so much! It took Elfride days to air the apartment afterward. According to Elżbieta Ettinger, the gift of a book was inscribed by Heidegger: "For Hannah and Heinrich—Martin and Elfride."[2] A repetition of the meeting was planned for the following year, but Blücher died in October 1970. Arendt devoted the final years of her life to work on her great unfinished book, *The Life of the Mind: Thinking—Willing—Judging.* In the thoughts developed there, she is closer to Heidegger than anywhere else. Heidegger, she sums up, had regained for philosophy "a thinking that expresses gratitude that the 'naked That' had been given at all."[3] Thenceforward her link with Heidegger would no longer be broken. She visited him every year and vigorously promoted the publication and translation of his work in America. Heidegger gratefully acknowledged her help; no one, he confirmed, understood his thinking better than she did.

Ettinger also reports the following typical episode. As Heidegger was getting increasingly frail, he and Elfride decided to construct a small single-story house in the garden of their house, to provide a comfortable setting for his old age. To finance the building, Heidegger hoped to sell the manuscript of *Being and Time* to a foundation, a library, or a private collector. It was Elfride who, in April 1969, consulted Arendt on this matter. How much should one ask, and where would a better price be achieved, in America or in Germany? Arendt immediately started to make inquiries among experts. They believed that the best sale price could probably be obtained from the University of Texas and that a sum of around 100,000 deutsche marks could confidently be expected.

In the end, however, the manuscript of *Being and Time* did not go to Texas in the New World, but remained in the Old—the Schiller Literature Archive in Marburg declared its interest. That was where all of Heidegger's papers eventually ended up. The small house in the garden was built, and Arendt sent flowers when the couple moved in.

Heidegger was thus able to keep up his accustomed lifestyle—work in the morning, a siesta after lunch, followed by more work into the later afternoon. His walks often led him to the Jägerhäusle, a hillside inn with a view of the city. There he was fond of meeting with friends and acquaintances over a *Viertele* (about half a pint). In spring and autumn he would spend some time in Messkirch with his brother. On St. Martin's Day, November 11, Heidegger invariably sat in front in his old church, among the choir stalls, where he used to sit as a boy bell ringer. The natives of Messkirch appreciated his presence, even though some who had known him from childhood were a little embarrassed to find themselves face to face with the famous professor with the beret. On his round-number birthdays, there were festivities in the municipal banquet hall. A Swiss musician had composed a Heidegger march based on the notes H-E-D-E-G-G-E, which the Messkirch town band included in its repertoire on these festive occasions. The adage that the prophet is not honored in his own country was clearly not true of Messkirch; indeed in 1959 he was awarded honorary citizenship.

Heidegger by then was a venerable old gentleman, and his former brusqueness and severity had mellowed with the years. He would go to a neighbor's house to watch European Cup matches on television. During the legendary match between Hamburg and Barcelona, he knocked a teacup over in his excitement. The then director of the Freiburg theater met Heidegger on a train one day and tried to conduct a conversation with him on literature and the stage. He did not succeed, however, because Heidegger, still under the impact of an international soccer match, preferred to talk about Franz Beckenbauer. He was full of admiration for this player's delicate ball control—and actually tried to demonstrate some of Beckenbauer's finesses to his astonished interlocutor. He called Beckenbauer an "inspired player" and praised his "invulnerability" in duels on the field. Heidegger pronounced his expert opinion with assurance; while in Messkirch he had not only rung the bells but also been a useful left wing.

During the final years of his life, Heidegger's main concern was the preparation of his collected works. Originally he wanted to call them *Paths,* but they ended up as his *Collected Works.*

Near the end of his life, Arthur Schopenhauer once said: "Mankind has learned a few things from me that it will never forget." No such statement is known from Heidegger. He did not create any constructive philosophy in the sense of a world picture or a moral doctrine. There are no "results" of Heidegger's thinking, in the sense that there are "results" of the philosophy of Leibniz, Kant, or Schopenhauer. Heidegger's passion was for questioning, not answering. Questioning appeared to him as "piety of thinking," because it opened up new horizons—just as religion, while it was still alive, had extended horizons and sanctified what appeared in them. For Heidegger it was one question in particular that had this opening-up power, the question he had asked all through his life, the question about Being. The meaning of this question was none other than this keeping open, this moving forward into a clearing where the matter of course suddenly finds the miracle of its "Here" returned to it, where man experiences himself as a location where something gapes open, where nature opens its eyes and notices that it is there, where, therefore, amid the "essent" *(das Seiende)* there is an open spot, a clearing, and where, for all that exists, gratitude is possible. Hidden in the question about Being is readiness for jubilation. The question about Being, in Heidegger's sense, means to lighten things, the way one weighs anchor to sail out into the open sea. It is a sad irony of history that the question about Being has, in the reception of Heidegger's work, mostly lost this opening, lightening feature and that it has rather tended to intimidate, knot, and cramp all thought. With the question about Being, most people find themselves in the situation of the pupil in a Zen story. This pupil had long pondered over the problem how a fully grown goose could be brought out of a bottle's narrow neck without killing the animal or breaking the bottle. The pupil, having tortured his brain, went to the master and asked him to solve the problem for him. The master turned away for a moment, then vigorously clapped his hands and called the pupil's name. "Here I am, master," the pupil replied. "You see," said the master, "the goose is out!" So much for the meaning of the question about Being.

As for the meaning of Being, the meaning that the question of Being asks about, there exists another nice Zen dictum, entirely in Heidegger's spirit. It states that before concerning himself with Zen, a man sees mountains as mountains and waters as waters. Once he has attained a certain inner vision of the truth of Zen, he realizes that the mountains are no longer mountains and the waters no longer waters. But once he is illuminated, he again sees the mountains as mountains and the waters as waters.

In the 1920s Heidegger was fond of using the abstract-sounding term *formale Anzeige* (formal notification). His students, according to Gadamer, had problems with this expression, assuming its meaning to lie in some degrees of abstraction. Heidegger explained his term to them as meaning "savoring and fulfilling." A notification kept at the distance of showing, demanding that the other person, who is shown something, looks at it himself. He must, in good phenomenological manner, himself see that which is notified, or shown, to him, and by his own viewing "fulfill" it. And by fulfilling it he savors what there is to be seen. But the seeing must be done in person.

When on one occasion Heidegger in a letter to Jaspers described himself as a museum attendant who draws the curtains aside so that the great works of philosophy should be seen more clearly, he was thinking of the more modest version of his activity. He really hoped to let people look into life—and not only into philosophy—as if they were doing so for the first time. Enlightenment to Heidegger was the restoration of dawn's early light at the surprising and hence overwhelming arrival of *Dasein* in the world. That was the grand gesture of Heidegger's beginnings—to remove, and indeed to destroy, the concealing, the accustomed, the rigidified, that which has become abstract. And what would emerge then? Nothing other than that which surrounds us without confining us, this "There" *(Da)* of *Dasein.* That has to be savored and fulfilled. Heidegger's philosophy never desists from this exercise of letting see. It may be mountains or waters, as in the Zen story—but it can also be a bridge. About a bridge Heidegger once wrote a wonderful reflection (VA, 146).

We use a bridge without thinking much about it. A glance into the abyss under the bridge might frighten us; it arouses a sense of the riskiness of *Dasein,* it shows us the nothingness above which we are balanced. The bridge spans the abyss. With its ends it is firmly supported on the ground. It continues this support by the ground, on which we depend, into the gesture of bearing. Thus our own design, our own élan, safeguards our passage across. The bridge rises above the abyss into the openness of the sky. The bridge, therefore, resting on the ground, not only links two banks with each other but also holds us out into the open and there gives us support. Heidegger says that by the passage of the "mortals," the bridge links the earth with the sky. On ancient bridges, the venture of bridging, this perilous delight at standing and walking in the open between heaven and earth, is specifically represented and celebrated—in bridge sculptures, in the statues of saints on the bridges, which encourage confidence and reflect gratitude for the gift of life, for this sojourn in the open expanse between heaven and earth, for safe conduct during passage.

A poetic vision, a metaphor? No. Heidegger's analysis of *Dasein* is a continual attempt to show that we are creatures who build bridges because we can experience open expanses, distances, and, above all, abysses—above ourselves, around ourselves, and within ourselves—and who therefore know that life means bridging abysses and keeping in transit. Thus *Dasein* is a Being that looks across to itself and sends itself across—from one end of the bridge to the other. And the point is that the bridge grows under our feet only as we step on it.

The later Heidegger made quite a number of other playful, obscure, and arabesque-like reflections that might give food for thought but hardly for seeing. Such totally incomprehensible (and, of course, untranslatable) sentences like *"Die Vierung west als das ereignende Spiegel-Spiel der einfältig einander Zugetrauten,"* or *"Die Vierung west als das Welten von Welt. Das Spiegel-Spiel von Welt ist der Reigen des Ereignens"* (VA, 173) should not be mocked, but neither should one search for a profound meaning in them. These sentences are rather like the tattoos on the body of Queequeg, the harpooner in Melville's *Moby Dick.* This Queequeg, a religious savage from the South Seas, had once had a whole secret history of his tribe tattooed on his body, "a complete theory of the heaven and the earth, and a mystical treatise," and thenceforth he was himself part of the hieroglyphic mysteries that he could not decipher, "even though his own live heart beat against them."[4] Everyone, including Queequeg himself, knows that these messages will perish undeciphered with the skin on which they are written. When Queequeg felt his end approaching, he got the ship's carpenter to make a coffin and transferred to the wood the inscriptions he bore on his body. Much of what is enigmatic in Heidegger's vast collected writings probably has to be read like the lettering on the coffin of the savage from the South Seas.

On December 4, 1975, Hannah Arendt died. Heidegger, too, was preparing for death, calmly, composedly, relaxedly. When his childhood playmate Karl Fischer congratulated him on his eighty-sixth birthday, Heidegger replied: "Dear Karle . . . I often now think back to our young years and also to your parental home with the many animals on the terrace, among them an eagle owl."[5]

In the light of the evening, the memories of the morning emerge. It may be assumed that Heidegger again saw that eagle owl very clearly before him. The moment when that bird would take off on its flight had come. Maybe Heidegger also recalled on that occasion what Karl Fischer—with whom I had a chance to talk—recalled, that little Martin had a saber that was so long he had to drag it behind him. It was not of tin but of steel. "But then he was the captain," said Fischer, still full of admiration for his fellow urchin.

In the winter of 1975 Petzet visited Heidegger for the last time.

> As always, he made me tell him about everything; he asked with interest about people and things, experiences and work—with a clear and wide-ranging mind, as ever. When I was about to leave at an advanced hour and Frau Heidegger had already left the room, I turned once more at the door. The old man's eyes followed me, he raised his hand, and I heard him say softly: "Yes, Petzet, the end is now drawing near." For a last time his eyes greeted me.[6]

In January 1976 Heidegger requested that his Messkirch compatriot, the Freiburg professor of theology Bernhard Welte, visit him for a talk. He informed him that, when the time came, he would like to be buried in the Messkirch cemetery. He asked for a Church funeral and for Welte to speak at his graveside. This last conversation between the two men centered on the experience that proximity of death included within itself proximity to one's native soil. "Floating in the room," Welte reported, "was also Eckhart's idea that God equalled Nothingness."[7] On May 22, two days before his death, Heidegger again wrote to Welte—a greeting on the occasion of the awarding of Messkirch's honorary citizenship to the theologian. This greeting is Martin Heidegger's last utterance in his own hand: "Cordial greetings to the new honorary citizen of their common hometown Messkirch—Bernhard Welte—from an older one . . . May this feastday of homage be joyful and life-giving. May the contemplative spirit of all participants be unanimous. For there is need for contemplation whether and how, in the age of a uniform technological world civilization, there can still be such a thing as home" (D, 187).

On May 26, 1976, after awakening refreshed, Heidegger a little later fell asleep again and died.

The interment in Messkirch was on May 28. Did Heidegger return to the bosom of the Church? Max Müller reports that, on hikes, whenever they came to a church or a chapel, Heidegger always dipped his finger in the stoup and genuflected. On one occasion he had asked him if this was not inconsistent, since he had distanced himself from the dogma of the Church. Heidegger's answer had been: "One must think historically. And where there has been so much praying, there the divine is present in a very special way."[8]

How to finish? Most appropriately with the sentence with which Martin Heidegger prefaced a lecture in Marburg in 1928, after Max Scheler's death: "Yet once more a way of doing philosophy sinks into the darkness."[9]

NOTES

1. CHILDHOOD AND SCHOOL

1. M. Heidegger, *Being and Time,* trans. J. Macquarrie and E. Robinson, 437.
2. Quoted in H. Ott, *Martin Heidegger,* trans. A. Blunden, 14.
3. C. Gröber, *Der Altkatholizismus in Messkirch,* 158.
4. Quoted in A. Müller, *Der Scheinwerfer,* 11.
5. Quoted in L. Braun, "Da-da-dasein."
6. Quoted in A. Müller, *Der Scheinwerfer,* 9.
7. Ibid., 9.
8. Ibid., 11.
9. G. Dehn, *Die alte Zeit,* 37.
10. Ibid., 38.
11. Quoted in H. Ott, *Martin Heidegger,* 52.
12. G. Dehn, *Die alte Zeit,* 39.
13. Quoted in W. Kiefer, *Schwäbisches und allemannisches Land,* 324.
14. Quoted in H. Ott, *Martin Heidegger,* 56.
15. Ibid., 84.

2. IDEALISM AND MATERIALISM

1. H. Ott, *Martin Heidegger,* trans. A. Blunden, 84.
2. C. Braig, "Was soll der Gebildete von dem Modernismus wissen?" 37.
3. Ibid.
4. Quoted in V. Farías, *Heidegger and Nazism,* ed. J. Margolis and T. Rockmore, 41.
5. Ibid., 44.
6. Ibid., 43.
7. Ibid.
8. Ibid., 86.
9. Ibid.
10. M. Heidegger, *On Time and Being,* trans. J. Stambaugh, 75.
11. F. Nietzsche, *Sämtliche Werke,* vol. 1, 245 f.
12. Quoted in F. A. Lange, *The History of Materialism,* trans. E. C. Thomas, vol. 2, 290.
13. Ibid., vol. 3, 360.
14. W. James, "Der Wille zum Glauben," 146.
15. Quoted in A. Hermann, "Auf eine höhere Stufe des Daseins erheben," 812.
16. P. Natorp, *Philosophie und Pädagogik,* 235.
17. Ibid., 237.
18. H. Rickert, *Kulturwissenschaft und Naturwissenschaft,* 18.
19. G. Simmel, *The Philosophy of Money,* ed. D. Frisby, trans. T. Bottomore and D. Frisby, 291.
20. Ibid., 236–237.

3. CAREER PLANNING AND CAREER PROBLEMS

1. Quoted in H. Ott, *Martin Heidegger,* trans. A. Blunden, 68.
2. Ibid., 67.
3. Ibid., 71.
4. Ibid., 73.
5. Ibid.
6. Ibid., 78.
7. Ibid.
8. Ibid.
9. Ibid.
10. Ibid., 77.
11. Ibid., 78.
12. Ibid.
13. V. Farías, *Heidegger and Nazism,* ed. J. Margolis and T. Rockmore, 45.
14. H. Rickert, *Die Philosophie des Lebens,* 155.
15. W. Dilthey, *Der Aufbau der geschichtlichen Welt in den Geisteswissenschaften.*
16. M. Scheler, *Vom Umsturz der Werte,* 323.
17. Ibid.
18. Ibid.
19. Ibid., 339.

4. THE OUTBREAK OF WORLD WAR I

1. L. Marcuse, *Mein zwanzigstes Jahrhundert*, 30.
2. Ibid.
3. Quoted in V. Farías, *Heidegger and Nazism*, ed. J. Margolis and T. Rockmore, 51.
4. Quoted in W. Falk, *"Literatur vor dem ersten Weltkrieg,"* 247.
5. Quoted in C. von Krockow, *Die Deutschen in ihrem Jahrhundert*, 101.
6. Quoted in Fritz K. Ringer, *The Decline of the German Mandarins*, 183.
7. T. Mann, *Reflections of a Nonpolitical Man*. Trans. Walter D. Morris.
8. M. Scheler, *Der Genius des Krieges*, 136.
9. E. Troeltsch, *Deutscher Geist und Westeuropa*, 39.
10. Quoted in H. Glaser, *Sigmund Freuds Zwanzigstes Jahrhundert*, 187.
11. M. Scheler, *Der Genius des Krieges*, 144.
12. See M. Weber, "Der Beruf zur Politik."
13. See C. Schmitt, *Political Romanticism*, trans. G. Oakes.
14. Quoted in H. Ott, *Martin Heidegger*, trans. A. Blunden, 80.
15. Ibid., 86–87.
16. Ibid., 90.
17. Ibid., 106.
18. Ibid., 92.
19. Ibid., 94.
20. Ibid., 89.
21. Ibid., 99.
22. Ibid., 101.
23. Ibid., 118.

5. THE TRIUMPH OF PHENOMENOLOGY

1. Quoted in H. R. Sepp, ed., *Edmund Husserl und die Phänomenologische Bewegung*, 13.
2. Quoted in E. Endres, *Edith Stein*, 87.
3. H. von Hofmannsthal, *Gesammelte Werke*, vol. 7, 465.
4. Quoted in H. R. Sepp, ed., *Edmund Husserl und die Phänomenologische Bewegung*, 42.
5. Ibid., 61.
6. Ibid., 42.
7. S. Zweig, *The World of Yesterday*, trans. C. and E. Paull, 14.
8. Quoted in H. R. Sepp, ed., *Edmund Husserl und die Phänomenologische Bewegung*, 66.
9. R. Musil, *The Man without Qualities*, trans. E. Wilkins and E. Kaiser, 3.
10. E. Husserl, *Cartesian Meditations*, trans. D. Cairns, 157.
11. Quoted in H. Rombach, *Phänomenologie des gegenwärtigen Bewusstseins*, 48.
12. Quoted in H. R. Sepp, ed., *Edmund Husserl und die Phänomenologische Bewegung*, 63.
13. H.-G. Gadamer, quoted in ibid., 15.
14. E. Husserl, *Ideas Pertaining to a Pure Phenomenology*, trans. F. Kersten, vol. 1, 142.
15. Quoted in H. Rombach, *Phänomenologie des gegenwärtigen Bewusstseins*, 103.
16. Ibid., 71.

17. M. Haga, quoted in H. R. Sepp, ed., *Edmund Husserl und die Phänomenologische Bewegung,* 18.
18. M. Proust, *Remembrance of Things Past,* trans. C. K. Scott Moncrieff and T. Kilmartin, vol. 1, 4.
19. M. Heidegger, *History of the Concept of Time, Prolegomena,* trans. T. Kisiel, 29.
20. Ibid., 86.
21. Quoted in H. Ott, *Martin Heidegger,* trans. A. Blunden, 102.
22. Ibid., 104.
23. Ibid., 104–105.
24. E. Stein, *Briefe an Roman Ingarden,* 108.

6. REVOLUTION IN GERMANY AND THE QUESTION OF BEING

1. K. Löwith, *My Life in Germany before and after 1933,* trans. E. King, 17.
2. M. Weber, *Soziologie—Weltgeschichtliche Analysen—Politik,* 322.
3. Ibid., 338.
4. Quoted in F. K. Ringer, *The Decline of the German Mandarins,* 357.
5. See U. Linse, *Barfüssige Propheten,* 27.
6. Ibid.
7. Quoted in F. K. Ringer, *The Decline of the German Mandarins,* 365.
8. H. Ball, *Flight out of Time,* ed. J. Elderfield, trans. A. Raimes, 66.
9. E. Bloch, *Geist der Utopie,* 245.
10. Ibid., 19.
11. W. Heisenberg, *The Physicist's Conception of Nature,* trans. A. J. Pomerans, 12.
12. W. Wundt, *Sinnliche und übersinnliche Welt,* 147.
13. E. Bloch, *Spuren,* 284.

7. PARTING WITH CATHOLICISM

1. Quoted in H. Ott, *Martin Heidegger,* trans. A. Blunden, 106–107.
2. E. Husserl, *Cartesian Meditations,* trans. D. Cairns, 157.
3. K. Barth, *The Epistle to the Romans,* trans. E. C. Hoskyns, 330–331.
4. Ibid., 296.
5. K. Jaspers, *Philosophische Autobiographie,* 92.
6. Ibid., 34.
7. K. Löwith, *My Life in Germany Before and After 1933,* trans. E. King, 31.

8. MARBURG UNIVERSITY AND HANNAH ARENDT

1. H. Ott, *Martin Heidegger,* trans. A. Blunden, 154.
2. Ibid., 124.
3. V. Farías, *Heidegger and Nazism,* ed. J. Margolis and T. Rockmore, 57.
4. H. Ott, *Martin Heidegger,* 124.
5. Ibid.
6. Ibid.
7. H. Mörchen, "Aufzeichnungen."

8. H. G. Gadamer, *Philosophical Apprenticeships,* trans. R. R. Sullivan, 13.
9. Quoted in G. Neske, ed., *Erinnerung an Martin Heidegger,* 112.
10. Ibid.
11. T. Mann, *Doctor Faustus,* 120–121.
12. A. von Buggenhagen, *Philosophische Autobiographie,* 134.
13. Ibid., 11.
14. Ibid.
15. H. Mörchen, "Aufzeichnungen," 4.
16. H. G. Gadamer, "Martin Heidegger und die Marburger Theologie," 169.
17. H. Zahrnt, *The Question of God,* trans. R. A. Wilson, 223.
18. M. Heidegger, *The Concept of Time,* trans. W. McNeill, 11R–12E.
19. Ibid., 12E.
20. H. Arendt, "Martin Heidegger wird achtzig Jahre alt," 235–237.
21. B. von Wiese, *Ich erzähle mein Leben,* 88.
22. Quoted in E. Young-Bruehl, *Hannah Arendt,* 62.
23. E. Ettinger, *Hannah Arendt—Martin Heidegger,* 15.
24. Quoted in ibid., 16.
25. Ibid.
26. Ibid.
27. Ibid., 18.
28. Ibid., 20.
29. E. Young-Bruehl, *Hannah Arendt,* 53.
30. Ibid., 51.
31. Quoted in ibid., 53.
32. H. Arendt, *The Human Condition,* 1958, 242.
33. Ibid., 57.
34. Ibid., 97.
35. Quoted in E. Ettinger, *Hannah Arendt—Martin Heidegger,* 101.
36. Ibid., 26.
37. Ibid., 27.
38. Ibid., 28.
39. H. Arendt, *Rahel Varnhagen,* trans. R. and C. Winston, 37–38.
40. Quoted in E. Young-Bruehl, *Hannah Arendt,* 348.

9. *BEING AND TIME:* WHAT BEING? WHAT MEANING?

1. H. Mörchen, "Aufzeichnungen."
2. M. Heidegger, *Being and Time,* trans. J. Macquarrie and E. Robinson, 19.
3. Ibid.
4. Ibid.
5. Ibid., 36.
6. Ibid., 271.
7. Ibid., 32.
8. Ibid., 228.
9. Ibid., 230.
10. Ibid., 232.

11. C. Bry, *Verkappte Religionen*, 13.
12. S. Freud, *Civilization and Its Discontents*, trans. J. Riviere, 70.
13. M. Heidegger, *Being and Time*, 375.
14. M. Heidegger, *The Concept of Time*, trans. W. McNeill, 151.
15. Ibid., 152.
16. Ibid., 69.
17. Ibid., 242.
18. Ibid., 173.
19. Ibid., 175.
20. Ibid., 173.
21. Ibid., 174.
22. H. Plessner, *Die Stufen des Organischen und der Mensch*, 288.
23. Ibid., 292.
24. A. Gehlen, *Studien zur Anthropologie und Soziologie*, 245.
25. M. Heidegger, *Being and Time*, 165.
26. Ibid.
27. R. Musil, *The Man without Qualities*, trans. E. Wilkins and E. Kaiser, 257.
28. V. Baum, *Grand Hotel*, 38.
29. M. Heidegger, *Being and Time*, 165–166.
30. Ibid., 167.
31. Ibid., 297.
32. Ibid.
33. Ibid., 358.
34. Ibid., 318.
35. Ibid., 157.
36. Ibid., 159.
37. Ibid., 344.
38. F. Tönnies, *Community and Society*, trans. C. F. Loomis, 39.
39. M. Heidegger, *Being and Time*, 165.
40. Ibid., 455.
41. Ibid., 437.
42. Ibid., 233.
43. Ibid., 436.

10. THE MOOD OF THE TIME

1. M. Heidegger, *The Fundamental Concepts of Metaphysics*, trans. W. McNeill and N. Walker, 149.
2. Ibid.
3. H. Ball, *Flight out of Time*, trans. A. Raimes, 108.
4. W. Benjamin, *Das Passagen-Werk*, 1250.
5. O. Spengler, *Man and Technics*, trans. F. Atkinson, 30.
6. F. Nietzsche, *Human, All Too Human*, trans. R. J. Hollingdale, 7.
7. C. Schmitt, *Political Theology*, trans. G. Schwab, 15.
8. Ibid., 31–32.
9. P. Tillich, *The Socialist Decision*, trans. F. Sherman, 22.

10. C. Schmitt, *Political Theology,* 5.
11. M. Heidegger, *Fundamental Concepts of Metaphysics,* 164.
12. H. W. Petzet, *Auf einen Stern zugehen,* 18.
13. M. Heidegger, "What Is Metaphysics?" in D. F. Krell, ed., *Martin Heidegger: Basic Writings,* 105.
14. Ibid., 101.
15. Ibid.
16. Ibid., 106.
17. Ibid.
18. Ibid., 105.
19. Ibid., 103.
20. E. Ettinger, *Hannah Arendt—Martin Heidegger,* 34.
21. E. Jünger, *Der Arbeiter,* 42.
22. O. F. Bollnow, "Gespräche in Davos," 28.
23. Quoted in G. Schneeberger, *Nachlese zu Heidegger,* 4.
24. Ibid., 7.

11. A SECRET PRINCIPAL WORK: THE METAPHYSICS LECTURES

1. Quoted in V. Farías, *Heidegger and Nazism,* ed. J. Margolis and T. Rockmore, 69.
2. M. Heidegger, *The Fundamental Concepts of Metaphysics,* trans. W. McNeill and N. Walker, 9.
3. Ibid., 19.
4. Ibid., 7.
5. Ibid., 19.
6. Ibid., 29–30.
7. Ibid., 43.
8. M. Heidegger, *Being and Time,* trans. J. Macquarrie and E. Robinson, 437.
9. M. Heidegger, *Fundamental Concepts of Metaphysics,* 13.
10. Ibid., 80.
11. Ibid., 91.
12. Ibid., 75.
13. Ibid.
14. Ibid., 76.
15. Ibid., 142.
16. Ibid., 133.
17. Ibid., 149.
18. Ibid.
19. Ibid., 162–163.
20. Ibid., 163.
21. Ibid., 165.
22. Ibid., 163.
23. Ibid., 164.
24. Ibid., 172.
25. Ibid., 13.
26. Ibid., 173.

27. Ibid., 23.
28. Ibid., 255.
29. Ibid., 258.
30. Ibid., 364.
31. Ibid., 365–366.

12. BALANCE SHEETS AT THE END OF THE REPUBLIC

1. Quoted in K. Sontheimer, *Antidemokratisches Denken in der Weimarer Republik,* 53.
2. W. Rathenau, *Zur Kritik der Zeit,* 17.
3. R. Musil, *Bücher und Literatur.*
4. Quoted in K. Sontheimer, *Antidemokratisches Denken in der Weimarer Republik,* 41.
5. Ibid., 145.
6. N. Berdjajew [Berdyayev], *Das neue Mittelalter,* 107.
7. Quoted in K. Sontheimer, *Antidemokratisches Denken in der Weimarer Republik,* 41.
8. T. Mann, *Das essayistische Werk,* vol. 2, 192.
9. Quoted in S. Reinhardt, ed., *Lesebuch,* 173.
10. M. Scheler, *Man's Place in Nature,* trans. H. Meyerhoff, 92.
11. Ibid.
12. H. Plessner, "Macht und menschliche Natur," 286.
13. Ibid., 284.
14. M. Heidegger, *Being and Time,* trans. J. Macquarrie and E. Robinson, 446.
15. Ibid., 436.
16. Ibid., 437.
17. Ibid., 217.
18. Quoted in V. Farías, *Heidegger and Nazism,* ed. J. Margolis and T. Rockmore, 73.
19. Ibid., 75.
20. Ibid., 74.
21. V. Meja and N. Stehr, eds., *Knowledge and Politics,* 97.
22. V. Meja and N. Stehr, eds., *Der Streit um die Wissenssoziologie,* vol. 1, 403; passage not in the (selective) English translation.
23. V. Meja and N. Stehr, eds., *Knowledge and Politics,* 58.
24. V. Meja and N. Stehr, eds., *Der Streit um die Wissenssoziologie,* vol. 1, p. 345; passage not in the (selective) English translation.
25. Ibid., 356.
26. Ibid., 350.
27. Ibid., 369.
28. M. Heidegger, "On the Essence of Truth," in D. F. Krell, ed., *Martin Heidegger: Basic Writings,* 125.
29. Ibid., 127–128.
30. M. Heidegger, *The Fundamental Concepts of Metaphysics,* trans. W. McNeill and N. Walker, 13.
31. Plato, *The Republic,* trans. R. Waterfield, 496 c5–e2.

13. THE NATIONAL SOCIALIST REVOLUTION

1. H. Mörchen, "Aufzeichnungen."
2. M. Müller, "Martin Heidegger: Ein Philosoph und die Politik," 193.
3. Letter to Hans-Peter Hempel (unpublished).
4. M. Müller, "Martin Heidegger: Ein Philosoph und die Politik," 198.
5. Quoted in J. and R. Becker, eds., *Hitlers Machtergreifung,* 311.
6. Ibid.
7. S. Haffner, *The Ailing Empire,* trans. J. Steinberg, 185.
8. Quoted in J. and R. Becker, eds., *Hitlers Machtergreifung,* 307.
9. Ibid., 308.
10. Quoted in G. Picht, "Die Macht des Denkens," 199.
11. G. Benn, *Werke,* vol. 4, 246.
12. K. Jaspers, *Philosophische Autobiographie,* 101.
13. Ibid.
14. B. Martin, ed., *Martin Heidegger und das "Dritte Reich,"* 202.
15. Ibid.
16. H. Arendt, *The Origins of Totalitarianism,* 326 (1966 ed.).
17. Ibid., 329.
18. Quoted in J. C. Fest, *Hitler,* trans. R. and C. Winston, 381.
19. B. Martin, ed., *Martin Heidegger und das "Dritte Reich,"* 202.
20. J. Jaspers, *Philosophische Autobiographie,* 101.
21. B. Martin, ed., *Martin Heidegger und das "Dritte Reich,"* 177.
22. Ibid.
23. Ibid., 178.
24. Ibid.
25. E. Krieck, *Volk im Werden,* 328 ff.
26. Ibid.
27. Quoted in T. Laugstien, *Philosophieverhältnisse im deutschen Faschismus,* 45.
28. M. Heidegger, *Being and Time,* trans. J. Macquarrie and E. Robinson, 165.
29. Ibid., 41.
30. Ibid., 47.
31. H. Ott, *Martin Heidegger,* trans. A. Blunden, 144.
32. Ibid.
33. Ibid., 145.
34. H. Tietjen, "Verstrickung und Widerstand."
35. H. Ott, *Martin Heidegger,* 170.
36. Ibid., 170.
37. Quoted in B. Martin, ed., *Martin Heidegger und das "Dritte Reich,"* 166.
38. M. Heidegger, *Being and Time,* 294.
39. Quoted in V. Farías, *Heidegger and Nazism,* ed. J. Margolis and T. Rockmore, 72.
40. H. Ott, *Martin Heidegger,* 152–153.
41. M. Heidegger, "The Self-Assertion of the German University," in R. Wolin, ed., *The Heidegger Controversy,* 32.
42. Ibid., 38.

43. Ibid., 33.
44. F. Nietzsche, *Thus Spoke Zarathustra,* trans. W. Kaufmann, 17–18.
45. M. Heidegger, "The Self-Assertion of the German University," 35–36.
46. Ibid., 33.
47. Ibid., 34.
48. A. Schopenhauer, *Der Briefwechsel mit Goethe,* 15.
49. M. Heidegger, "The Self-Assertion of the German University," 33.
50. Ibid., 31.
51. Quoted in U. Hass, *Militante Pastorale,* 31.
52. M. Heidegger, *The Basic Problems of Phenomenology,* trans. A. Hofstadter, 285.

14. IS HEIDEGGER ANTI-SEMITIC?

1. Quoted in V. Farías, *Heidegger and Nazism,* ed. J. Margolis and T. Rockmore, 112.
2. Ibid., 109.
3. Ibid., 110.
4. Ibid.
5. Ibid.
6. Ibid., 139.
7. K. Jaspers, *Philosophische Autobiographie,* 101.
8. K. Jaspers, *Notizen zu Martin Heidegger,* 182.
9. BwHJ, notes, 260.
10. Documented in ibid., 159 ff.
11. Ibid., 260.
12. Quoted in H. Ott, *Martin Heidegger,* trans. A. Blunden, 155.
13. Ibid.
14. Ibid., 176.
15. Ibid.
16. Ibid., 177.
17. Ibid., 207.
18. Ibid., 108.
19. Ibid.
20. E. Ettinger, *Hannah Arendt—Martin Heidegger,* 35.
21. Ibid., 35–36.
22. Ibid., 36.
23. S. Haffner, *The Meaning of Hitler,* trans. E. Osers, 91.
24. In *Die Zeit,* no. 52 (December 22, 1989), published by Ulrich Sieg.
25. M. Müller, "Martin Heidegger: Ein Philosoph und die Politik," 204.
26. H. Ott, *Martin Heidegger,* 207.
27. BwHJ, 271. English translation in R. Wolin, ed., *The Heidegger Controversy,* 148.
28. See Farías, *Heidegger and Nazism,* 114–115.
29. M. Müller, "Martin Heidegger: Ein Philosoph und die Politik," 205.
30. Quoted in ibid.
31. M. Müller, "Erinnerungen an Husserl," 37.
32. Ibid., 38.

33. H. Ott, "Edmund Husserl und die Universität Freiburg," 102.
34. Quoted in H. Ott, *Martin Heidegger,* 170.
35. Quoted in V. Farías, *Heidegger and Nazism,* 217.
36. Ibid., 128.
37. Ibid.
38. Ibid.
39. Ibid., 129.
40. Ibid., 130.
41. Ibid.
42. Ibid.
43. Quoted in H. Ott, *Martin Heidegger,* 226.
44. Ibid., 229.
45. Ibid.
46. Ibid.
47. Ibid.
48. H. Buhr, "Die weltliche Theologie," 53; quoted in H. Ott, *Martin Heidegger,* 227.
49. Quoted in H. Ott, *Martin Heidegger,* 232.
50. Ibid., 233.
51. Ibid., 234.

15. HEIDEGGER'S STRUGGLE FOR THE PURITY OF THE MOVEMENT

1. Hannah Arendt, *Was ist Politik?* 9.
2. Victor Farías, *Heidegger and Nazism,* ed. J. Margolis and T. Rockmore, 163.
3. Quoted in ibid., 164.
4. Ibid., 167.
5. Ibid., 204.
6. Ibid.
7. Quoted in G. Schneeberger, *Nachlese zu Heidegger,* 225.
8. Ibid., 168.
9. Quoted in T. Laugstien, *Philosophieverhältnisse im deutschen Faschismus,* 49.
10. Quoted in H. Ott, *Martin Heidegger,* trans. A. Blunden, 239.
11. Ibid.
12. Ibid., 240; also quoted in A. Schwan, *Politische Philosophie im Denken Heideggers,* 219.
13. Quoted in A. Schwan, *Politische Philosophie im Denken Heideggers,* 219.
14. Quoted in B. Martin, ed., *Martin Heidegger und das "Dritte Reich,"* 179.
15. Quoted in V. Farías, *Heidegger and Nazism,* 178–179.
16. Ibid., 210.
17. K. Jaspers, *Notizen zu Martin Heidegger,* 15.
18. Quoted in H. Ott, *Martin Heidegger,* 213.
19. Ibid., 214–215.
20. Ibid., 217.

21. Ibid., 217.
22. Ibid., 221.

16. DEPARTURE FROM THE POLITICAL SCENE

1. H. Arendt, *The Life of the Mind,* 200.
2. F. Nietzsche, *The Will to Power,* trans. W. Kaufmann and R. J. Hollingdale, 225–226.
3. Quoted in V. Farías, *Heidegger and Nazism,* ed. J. Margolis and T. Rockmore, 201.
4. Ibid., 203.
5. See ibid., 205; the English translation, however, does not contain the text of the opinion.
6. Quoted in ibid., 206.
7. K. Löwith, *My Life in Germany,* here quoted in "My Last Meeting with Heidegger in Rome," in R. Wolin, ed., *The Heidegger Controversy,* 142.
8. M. Heidegger, *Schelling's Treatise on the Essence of Human Freedom,* trans. J. Stambaugh, 2.
9. F. Hölderlin, *Sämtliche Werke und Briefe,* vol. 2, 94.
10. M. Kommerell, *Der Dichter als Führer in der deutschen Klassik,* 5.
11. F. Hölderlin, *Sämtliche Werke und Briefe,* vol. 1, 738.
12. Quoted in *An Unofficial Rilke: Poems 1912–1926,* trans. M. Hamburger.
13. M. Heidegger, *An Introduction to Metaphysics,* trans. R. Manheim, 62.
14. See also F. Hölderlin, *Hyperion,* trans. W. Trusk.
15. F. Hölderlin, *Poems and Fragments,* trans. M. Hamburger, 249.
16. Ibid., 375–377.
17. M. Heidegger, *Introduction to Metaphysics,* 45.
18. Ibid., 47.
19. Ibid., 38.
20. Ibid., 57.
21. Ibid., 47.
22. Ibid., 37.

17. THE AGE OF IDEOLOGY AND TOTAL MOBILIZATION

1. Quoted in S. Haffner, *The Meaning of Hitler,* trans. E. Osers, 32–33.
2. Quoted in V. Farías, *Heidegger and Nazism,* ed. J. Margolis and T. Rockmore, 128.
3. K. Löwith, "My Last Meeting with Heidegger in Rome," in R. Wolin, ed., *The Heidegger Controversy,* 142.
4. M. Heidegger, *Nietzsche,* vol. 3, *The Will to Power as Knowledge and as Metaphysics,* trans. J. Stambaugh, D. F. Krell, and F. A. Capuzzi, 163.
5. M. Heidegger, *An Introduction to Metaphysics,* trans. R. Manheim, 26.
6. Ibid., 155.
7. Ibid., 62.
8. Quoted in W. Müller-Lauter, "Über den Umgang mit Nietzsche," 845.
9. Ibid.
10. M. Heidegger, *Nietzsche,* trans. J. Stambaugh, D. F. Krell, and F. A. Capuzzi, 4, 147–8.
11. Quoted in G. Schneeberger, *Nachlese zu Heidegger,* 225.

18. THE PHILOSOPHICAL DIARY AND PHILOSOPHICAL ROSARY

1. M. Heidegger, *Nietzsche*, trans. D. F. Krell, vol. 1, 194.
2. Ibid., 55.
3. C. F. von Weizsäcker, *Vier Jahrzehnte*, 244.
4. G. Picht, "Die Macht des Denkens," 181.
5. H. A. Fischer-Barnicol, *Spiegelungen—Vermittlungen*, 88.

19. HEIDEGGER UNDER SURVEILLANCE

1. V. Farías, *Heidegger and Nazism*, ed. J. Margolis and T. Rockmore, 213.
2. Ibid., 234–235.
3. K. Löwith, *My Life in Germany Before and After 1933*, trans. E. King, 59.
4. H. Barth, *Vom Ursprung des Kunstwerks*, 265.
5. E. Staiger, *Noch einmal Heidegger*, 269.
6. H. Barth, *Vom Ursprung des Kunstwerks*, 265.
7. K. Löwith, *My Life in Germany*, 60.
8. Ibid., 60.
9. Ibid., 61.
10. F. Hölderlin, *Poems and Fragments*, trans. M. Hamburger, 249.
11. Quoted in H. Ott, *Martin Heidegger*, trans. A. Blunden, 267.
12. Quoted in V. Farías, *Heidegger and Nazism*, 237.
13. Ibid.
14. Quoted in H. Ott, *Martin Heidegger*, 268.
15. Ibid.
16. Ibid., 269.
17. V. Farías, *Heidegger and Nazism*, 246–247.
18. Ibid., 247.
19. H. W. Petzet, *Auf einen Stern zugehen*, 47.
20. J. Benda, *The Treason of the Intellectuals*, trans. R. Aldington, 64.
21. M. Heidegger, *Nietzsche*, trans. D. F. Krell, vol. 4, 116–117.
22. Quoted in R. Mehring, *Heideggers Überlieferungsgeschick*, 91.
23. M. Heidegger, *Nietzsche*, vol. 3, 250.

20. HEIDEGGER FACES THE DENAZIFICATION COMMITTEE

1. G. Picht, "Die Macht des Denkens," 205.
2. Quoted in H. Ott, *Martin Heidegger*, trans. A. Blunden, 16.
3. Ibid., 14.
4. Ibid., 305.
5. Ibid., 313.
6. Ibid., 314.
7. Ibid., 315.
8. Quoted in B. Martin, ed., *Martin Heidegger und das "Dritte Reich,"* 187.
9. Ibid., 188.
10. Quoted in H. Ott, *Martin Heidegger*, 327.

11. K. Jaspers, *Die Schuldfrage,* 46.
12. Quoted in H. Ott, *Martin Heidegger,* 339.
13. Ibid., 331.
14. Quoted in B. Waldenfels, *Phänomenologie in Frankreich,* 14.
15. A. Camus, *The Myth of Sisyphus,* trans. J. O'Brien, 44.
16. J.-P. Sartre, *The Transcendence of the Ego,* trans. F. Williams and R. Kirkpatrick, 105.
17. Quoted by M. Lilla in "Das Ende der Philosophie," 19.
18. A. Kojève, *Hegel,* 152.
19. Ibid., 151.
20. Ibid., 267.
21. Ibid., 268.
22. J.-P. Sartre, *Nausea,* trans. R. Baldick, 182.
23. Ibid., 188.
24. J.-P. Sartre, *Being and Nothingness,* trans. H. E. Barnes, 24.
25. Ibid., 287.
26. Ibid., 513.
27. *Frankfurter Allgemeine Zeitung,* January 19, 1994, 27 (see also November 30, 1993).
28. J.-P. Sartre, *Being and Nothingness,* 544.
29. M. Müller, *Martin Heidegger,* 212.
30. Quoted in H. Ott, *Martin Heidegger,* 344.
31. Ibid., 347.
32. Ibid., 319.
33. Ibid., 343.

21. WHAT DO WE DO WHEN WE THINK?

1. M. Heidegger, *What Is Called Thinking?,* trans. F. D. Wieck and J. G. Gray, 159.
2. A. Baeumler, "Hitler und der Nationalsozialismus," 172.
3. Ibid.,160.
4. Ibid.
5. Ibid., 174.
6. Quoted in J. Altweg, ed., "Heidegger in Frankreich—und zurück?" 33.
7. A. Cohen-Solal, *Sartre: A Life,* 413.
8. Ibid.
9. Quoted in H. Glaser, *Kleine Kulturgeschichte der Bundesrepublik,* 19.
10. A. Cohen-Solal, *Sartre: A Life,* 251.
11. J.-P. Sartre, *Existentialism and Humanism,* trans. P. Mairet, 54.
12. Ibid.
13. Ibid., 55.
14. Ibid., 55–56.
15. *Der Monat,* no. 24 (1950): 502.
16. Ibid., 502.
17. R. Schneider, *Das Unzerstörbare,* 12.
18. Quoted in H. Glaser, ed., *Bundesrepublikanisches Lesebuch,* 166 f.
19. Ibid.
20. H. Arendt, "Besuch in Deutschland," in Arendt, *Zur Zeit: Politische Essays,* 46.

10. Ibid., 125.
11. T. W. Adorno, *Negative Dialectics*, trans. E. B. Ashton, 369 (1973 ed.).
12. R. Wiggershaus, *The Frankfurt School*, 467.
13. J.-P. Sartre, *Drei Essays*, 149.
14. R. Wiggershaus, *The Frankfurt School*, 510.
15. T. W. Adorno, *Notes to Literature*, ed. R. Tiedeman, trans. S. W. Nicholson, 1991–1992, vol. 1, 111.
16. R. Wiggershaus, *The Frankfurt School*, 498.
17. Ibid., 593.
18. T. W. Adorno and M. Horkheimer, *Dialectic of Enlightenment*, trans. J. Cumming, 13.
19. Ibid., 9.
20. Ibid., 13.
21. T. W. Adorno, *Negative Dialectics*, trans. E. B. Ashton, 362 (1990 ed.).
22. Ibid., 365.
23. Ibid., 149.
24. Ibid., 85.
25. Ibid., 61.
26. T. W. Adorno, *Kierkegaard: Konstruktion des Ästhetischen*, 251.
27. T. W. Adorno, *Notes to Literature*, vol. 1, 48.
28. T. W. Adorno, *Negative Dialectics*, 373.
29. T. W. Adorno, *Ohne Leitbild*, 20.
30. Ibid., 22.
31. Quoted in J. Améry, "Jargon der Dialektik," 598.
32. P. Sloterdijk, *Critique of Cynical Reason*, trans. M. Eldred, 375.
33. Quoted in J. Améry, "Jargon der Dialektik," 604.
34. Ibid., 605.
35. T. W. Adorno, *Negative Dialectics*, 10.
36. J. Améry, "Jargon der Dialektik," 600.
37. H. Arendt, "Martin Heidegger ist achtzig Jahre alt," in Arendt, *Menschen in finsteren Zeiten*, 184.
38. G. Grass, *Dog Years*, trans. R. Manheim, 392.
39. H. W. Petzet, *Auf einen Stern zugehen*, 103.
40. Ibid.
41. "Only a God Can Save Us," *Der Spiegel*'s interview with Martin Heidegger, trans. Maria P. Alter and John D. Caputo, in *Philosophy Today* 20 (April 4, 1976): 267–285, quoted in R. Wolin, ed., *The Heidegger Controversy.*
42. Ibid., 87.
43. Ibid., 105.
44. Ibid., 104.
45. Ibid., 107.
46. Quoted in V. Farías, *Heidegger and Nazism*, ed. J. Margolis and T. Rockmore, 284.
47. Ibid., 285.
48. P. Celan, *Speech-grille, and Selected Poems*, trans. J. Neugroschel, 99.
49. Quoted in G. Baumann, *Erinnerungen an Paul Celan*, 60.
50. Ibid., 62.
51. Quoted in O. Pöggeler, *Spur des Wortes*, 259.

52. G. Baumann, *Erinnerungen an Paul Celan,* 70.
53. Ibid., 72.
54. P. Celan, *Poems,* trans. M. Hamburger, 300–301.
55. G. Baumann, *Erinnerungen an Paul Celan,* 80.

25. SUNSET OF LIFE

1. H. W. Petzet, *Auf einen Stern zugehen,* 198.
2. Quoted in E. Ettinger, *Hannah Arendt—Martin Heidegger,* 123.
3. H. Arendt, *The Life of the Mind,* 1-vol. ed., 185.
4. H. Melville, *Moby Dick, or The Whale,* 691.
5. Quoted from *Der Zauberer von Messkirch* (The Magician of Messkirch), a film by Rüdiger Safranski and Ulrich Boehm, 1989.
6. H. W. Petzet, *Auf einen Stern zugehen,* 230.
7. B. Welte, "Erinnerung an ein spätes Gespräch," 251.
8. M. Müller, "Martin Heidegger: Ein Philosoph und die Politik," 213.
9. H.-G. Gadamer, *Philosophical Apprenticeships,* trans. R. R. Sullivan, 34.

WORKS CITED

Adorno, Theodor W. *Eingriffe, Neue kritische Modelle.* Frankfurt, 1963.

———. *Jargon of Authenticity.* Trans. Knut Tarnowski and Frederick Will. Evanston, Ill., 1986.

———. *Kierkegaard: Konstruktion des Ästhetischen.* Frankfurt, 1974. English ed.: *Kierkegaard: Construction of the Aesthetic.* Minneapolis, 1989.

———. *Negative Dialectics.* Trans. E. B. Ashton. London, 1973; London, 1990.

———. *Notes to Literature,* 2 vols. Ed. Rolf Tiedeman. Trans. Shierry Weber Nicholson. New York, 1991–1992.

———. *Ohne Leitbild: Parva Ästhetica.* Frankfurt, 1967.

——— and Max Horkheimer. *Dialectic of Enlightenment.* Trans. John Cumming. London, 1973.

Altweg, Jürg, ed. *Die Heidegger Kontroverse.* Frankfurt, 1988.

———. "Heidegger in Frankreich—und zurück?" In *Die Heidegger Kontroverse.* Frankfurt, 1988.

Améry, Jean. "Jargon der Dialektik." In H. Glaser, ed., *Bundesrepublikanisches Lesebuch: Drei Jahrzente geistiger Auseinandersetzung.* Munich, 1978.

Arendt, Hannah. *Eichmann in Jerusalem: Ein Bericht von der Banalität des Bösen.* Munich, 1986.

———. "Freiheit und Politik." In *Die neue Rundschau* 69 (1958).

———. *The Human Condition.* University of Chicago Press, 1958.

———. *The Life of the Mind: Thinking—Willing—Judging.* New York, 1978; 1-vol. ed., San Diego, 1981.

———. "Martin Heidegger ist achtzig Jahre alt." In G. Neske and E. Kettering, eds., *Antwort: Martin Heidegger im Gespräch.* Pfullingen, 1988.

———. *Menschen in finisteren Zeiten.* Munich, 1983. English ed.: *Men in Dark Times.* London, 1970.

———. *The Origins of Totalitarianism.* London, 1958; New York, 1966.

———. *Rahel Varnhagen: The Life of a Jewess.* London, 1957.

———. *Was ist Politik?* Munich, 1993.

———. "What Is Existential Philosophy?" *Partisan Review,* Winter 1946: 50.

———. *Zur Zeit: Politische Essays.* Berlin, 1986.

Baeumler, Alfred. "Hitler und der Nationalsozialismus: Aufzeichnungen von 1945–1947." In *Der Pfahl: Jahrbuch aus dem Niemandsland zwischen Kunst und Wirtschaft.* Munich, 1991.

———. *Nietzsche, der Philosoph und Denker.* Berlin, 1931.

Ball, Hugo. *Flight out of Time: A Dada Diary.* Ed. John Elderfield. Trans. Ann Raimes. New York, 1974.

Barash, Jeffrey Andrew. "Die Auslegung der 'Öffentlichen Welt' als politisches Problem." In D. Papenfuss and O. Pöggeler, eds., *Zur philosophischen Aktualität Heideggers,* vol. 2. Frankfurt, 1990f.

Barth, Karl. *The Epistle to the Romans.* Trans. Edwyn C. Hoskyns. London, 1950.

Baum, Vicky. *Grand Hotel.* Mattituck, N.Y., 1976.

Baumann, Gerhart. *Erinnerungen an Paul Celan.* Frankfurt, 1992.

Becker, Josef and Ruth, eds. *Hitlers Machtergreifung: Dokumente vom Machtantritt Hitlers.* Munich, 1983.

Benda, Julien. *The Treason of the Intellectuals.* Trans. Richard Aldington. New York, 1969.

Benjamin, Walter. *Das Passagen-Werk: Gesammelte Schriften,* vol. V.2, Frankfurt, 1982.

Benn, Gottfried. *Briefe an F. W. Oelze,* 2 vols. Frankfurt, 1982.

———. *Werke,* 4 vols. Wiesbaden, 1961.

Bense, Max. *Technische Existenz.* Stuttgart, 1950.

Berdjajew, Nikolaus [Nikolay Berdyayev]. *Das neue Mittelalter.* Darmstadt, 1927.

Bloch, Ernst. *Geist der Utopie.* Frankfurt, 1978.

———. *Spuren.* Frankfurt, 1964.

Bollnow, Otto Friedrich. "Gespräche in Davos." In G. Neske, ed., *Erinnerung an Martin Heidegger.* Pfullingen, 1977.

Braig, Carl. "Was soll der Gebildete von dem Modernismus wissen?" In D. Thoma, ed., *Die Zeit des Selbst und die Zeit danach: Zur Kritik der Textgeschichte Martin Heideggers.* Frankfurt, 1990.

Braun, Luzia. "Da-da-dasein. Fritz Heidegger: Holzwege zur Sprache." In *Die Zeit* 39, September 22, 1989.

Bry, Carl Christian. *Verkappte Religionen.* Nördlingen, 1988.

Buggenhagen, Arnold von. *Philosophische Autobiographie.* Meisenheim, 1975.

Buhr, Heinrich. "Der weltliche Theologie." In G. Neske, ed., *Erinnerung an Martin Heidegger.* Pfullingen, 1977.

Camus, Albert. *The Myth of Sisyphus.* Trans. Justin O'Brien. Harmondsworth, England, 1975.

Celan, Paul. *Poems.* Trans. Michael Hamburger. London. 1997.

———. *Speech-grille, and Selected Poems.* Trans. Joachim Neugroschel. New York, 1971.

Char, René. "Eindrücke von früher." In G. Neske, ed., *Erinnerung an Martin Heidegger.* Pfullingen, 1977.

Cohen-Solal, Anne. *Sartre: A Life.* London, 1991.

Dehn, Günther. *Die alte Zeit, die vorigen Jahre: Lebenserinnerungen.* Munich, 1962.

Dilthey, Wilhelm. *Der Aufbau der geschichtlichen Welt in den Geisteswissenschaften.* Frankfurt, 1981.

Endres, Elisabeth. *Edith Stein.* Munich, 1987.

Ettinger, Elżbieta. *Hannah Arendt—Martin Heidegger.* New Haven, Conn., 1995.

Falk, Walter. "Literatur vor dem ersten Weltkrieg." In A. Nitschke et al., eds. *Jahrhundertwende,* vol. 1. Reinbeck bei Hamburg, 1990.

Farías, Victor. *Heidegger and Nazism.* Ed. Joseph Margolis and Tom Rockmore. French material trans. Paul Burrell with Dominic Di Bernardi. German material trans. Gabriel R. Ricci. Philadelphia, 1989.

Fest, Joachim C. *Hitler.* Trans. Richard and Clara Winston. London, 1987.

Freud, Sigmund. *Civilization and Its Discontents.* Trans. Joan Riviere. New York, 1994.

———. "Martin Heidegger und die Marburger Theologie." In O. Pöggeler, ed. *Heidegger: Perspektiven zur Deutung seines Werkes.* Königstein, 1984.

———. *Philosophical Apprenticeships.* Trans. Robert R. Sullivan. Cambridge, Mass., 1985.

Gadamer, Hans-Georg. *Hegel—Husserl—Heidegger.* Tübingen, 1987.

Gehlen, Arnold. *Studien zur Anthropologie und Soziologie.* Neuwied, 1963.

Gethmann-Siefert, Annemarie, and Otto Pöggeler, eds. *Heidegger und die praktische Philosophie.* Frankfurt, 1988.

Glaser, Hermann, ed. *Bundesrepublikanisches Lesebuch: Drei Jahrzehnte geistiger Auseinandersetzung.* Munich, 1978.

———. *Kleine Kulturgeschichte der Bundesrepublik.* Munich, 1991.

———. *Sigmund Freuds Zwanzigstes Jahrhundert.* Munich, 1976.

Grass, Günter. *Dog Years.* New York, 1986.

Gröber, Conrad. *Der Altkatholizismus in Messkirch.* Freiburg, 1934.

Habermas, Jürgen. *Philosophical-Political Profiles.* Trans. Frederick G. Lawrence. Cambridge, Mass., 1983.

Haffner, Sebastian. *The Ailing Empire: Germany from Bismarck to Hitler.* Trans. Jean Steinberg. New York, 1989.

———. *The Meaning of Hitler.* Trans. Ewald Osers. London, 1979.

Hass, Ulrike. *Militante Pastorale: Zur Literatur der antimodernen Bewegung.* Munich, 1993.

Heisenberg, Werner. *The Physicist's Conception of Nature.* Trans. Arnold J. Pomerans. New York, 1958.

Hermann, Armin. "Auf eine höhere Stude des Daseins erheben: Naturwissenschaft und Technik." In A. Nitschke et al., eds. *Jahrhundertwende,* vol. 1. Reinbeck bei Hamburg, 1990.

Hofmannsthal, Hugo von. *Gesammelte Werke in zehn Bänden.* Frankfurt, 1979.

Hölderlin, Friedrich. *Hyperion.* Trans. Willard Trusk. New York, 1965.
———. *Poems and Fragments,* bilingual ed. Trans. Michael Hamburger. Cambridge, 1980.
———. *Sämtliche Werke und Briefe,* 2 vols. ed. G. Mieth. Munich, 1970.
Husserl, Edmund. *Cartesian Meditations: An Introduction to Phenomenology.* Trans. Dorion Cairns. The Hague, 1960.
———. *Ideas Pertaining to a Pure Phenomenology and to a Phenomenological Philosophy.* Trans. F. Kersten. The Hague, 1982.
———. *Die Konstitution der geistigen Welt.* Hamburg, 1984.
———. *Die Krisis der empirischen Wissenschaften und die transzendentale Phänomenologie.* Hamburg, 1977.
———. *Philosophie als strenge Wissenschaft.* Frankfurt, 1965.
James, William. "Der Wille zum Glauben." In Ekkehard Martens, ed., *Texte der Philosophie des Pragmatismus.* Stuttgart, 1975.
Jaspers, Karl. *Die Schuldfrage.* Munich, 1987.
———. *Notizen zu Martin Heidegger.* Munich, 1978.
———. *Philosophische Autobiographie.* Munich, 1984.
Jünger, Ernst. *Der Arbeiter.* Stuttgart, 1981.
Jünger, Friedrich Georg. *Die Perfektion der Technik.* Frankfurt, 1953. English ed.: *The Failure of Technology: Perfection without Purpose.* Trans. F. D. Wieck. Hinsdale, Ill., 1949.
Kiefer, Wilhelm. *Schwäbisches und allemannisches Land.* Weissenhorn, 1975.
Kojève, Alexander. *Hegel.* Frankfurt, 1988.
Kommerell, Max. *Der Dichter als Führer in der deutschen Klassik.* Frankfurt, 1942.
Krell, David Farrell, ed. *Martin Heidegger: Basic Writings,* rev. ed. San Francisco, 1993.
Krieck, Ernst. *Nationalpolitische Erziehung.* Berlin, 1933.
———. *Volk im Werden.* Berlin, 1933.
Krockow, Christian Count von. *Die Deutschen in ihrem Jahrhundert.* Reinbek bei Hamburg, 1990.
Lange, Friedrich Albert. *The History of Materialism.* Trans. Ernest Chester Thomas. New York, 1925.
Laugstien, Thomas. *Philosophieverhältnisse im deutschen Faschismus.* Hamburg, 1990.
Leithäuser, Joachim G. "Im Gruselkabinett der Technik," *Der Monat* 29 (1959).
Lilla, Mark. "Das Ende der Philosophie." In *Merkur* 514 (1992).
Linse, Ulrich. *Barfüssige Propheten: Erlöser der zwanziger Jahre.* Berlin, 1983.
Löwith, Karl. *My Life in Germany before and after 1933: A Report.* Trans. Elizabeth King. London, 1994.
Mann, Thomas. *Das essayistische Werk in acht Bänden.* Frankfurt, 1968.
———. *Doctor Faustus.* London, 1949.
———. *Reflections of a Nonpolitical Man.* New York, 1983.
Marcuse, Ludwig. *Mein zwanzigstes Jahrhundert.* Zurich, 1975.
Martin, Bernd, ed. *Martin Heidegger und das "Dritte Reich."* Darmstadt, 1989.
Mehring, Reinhard. *Heideggers Überlieferungsgeschick.* Würzburg, 1992.
Meja, Volker, and Nico Stehr, eds. *Der Streit um die Wissenssoziologie.* Frankfurt, 1982. English ed.: *Knowledge and Politics: The Sociology of Knowledge Dispute.* London, 1990.
Melville, Herman. *Moby Dick, or The Whale.* New York, 1930.
Mörchen, Hermann. "Aufzeichnungen." Unpublished manuscript.

Müller, Andreas. *Der Scheinwerfer: Anekdoten und Geschichten um Fritz Heidegger.* Messkirch, 1989.

Müller, Max. "Erinnerungen an Husserl." In H. R. Sepp, ed., *Edmund Husserl und die Phänomenologische Bewegung Zeugnisse in Text und Bild.* Freiburg, 1988.

———. "Martin Heidegger: Ein Philosoph und die Politik." In G. Neske and E. Kettering, eds. *Antwort: Martin Heidegger im Gespräch.* Pfullingen, 1988.

Müller-Lauter, Wolfgang. "Über den Umgang mit Nietzsche." In *Sinn und Form* 1995: 5.

Musil, Robert. *Bücher und Literatur: Essays.* Reinbek bei Hamburg, 1982.

———. *The Man without Qualities.* Trans. Eithne Wilkins and Ernest Kaiser. London, 1979.

Natorp, Paul. *Philosophie und Pädagogik.* Marburg, 1909.

Neske, Günther, ed. *Erinnerung an Martin Heidegger.* Pfullingen, 1977.

——— and Emil Kettering, eds. *Antwort: Martin Heidegger im Gespräch.* Pfullingen, 1988.

Nietzsche, Friedrich. *Human, All Too Human: A Book for Free Spirits.* Trans. R. J. Hollingdale. Cambridge, 1986.

———. *Sämtliche Werke: Kritische Studienausgabe.* 2 vols. Munich, 1980.

———. *Thus Spoke Zarathustra.* Trans. Walter Kaufmann. New York, 1978.

———. *The Will to Power.* Trans. Walter Kaufmann and R. J. Hollingdale. Ed. Walter Kaufmann. London, 1968.

Nitschke, August, et al., eds. *Jahrhundertwende: Der Aufbruch in die Moderne,* 2 vols. Reinbek bei Hamburg, 1990.

Noack, Paul. *Carl Schmitt: Eine Biographie.* Berlin, 1993.

Ott, Hugo. "Edmund Husserl und die Universität Freiburg." In H. R. Sepp, ed., *Edmund Husserl und die Phänomenologische Bewegung Zeugnisse in Text und Bild.* Freiburg, 1988.

———. *Martin Heidegger: A Political Life.* Trans. Allan Blunden. London, 1994.

Papenfuss, Dietrich, and Otto Pöggeler, eds. *Zur philosophischen Aktualität Heideggers,* 3 vols. Frankfurt, 1990 f.

Petzet, Heinrich Wiegand. *Auf einen Stern zugehen: Begegnungen mit Martin Heidegger.* Frankfurt, 1983.

Picht, Georg. "Die Macht des Denkens." In G. Neske, ed., *Erinnerung an Martin Heidegger.* Pfullingen, 1977.

Plato. *The Republic.* Trans. Robin Waterfield. Oxford, 1993.

Plessner, Helmuth. *Die Stufen des Organischen und der Mensch.* Berlin, 1975.

———. "Macht und menschliche Natur." In Plessner, *Zwischen Philosophie und Gesellschaft.* Frankfurt. 1979.

Pöggeler, Otto. *Heidegger: Perspektiven zur Deutung seines Werkes.* Königstein, 1984.

———. "Heidegger's Political Self-Understanding." In R. Wolin, ed., *The Heidegger Controversy: A Critical Reader.* New York, 1991.

———. *Martin Heidegger's Path of Thinking.* Atlantic Highlands, N.J., 1987.

———. *Spur des Wortes: Zur Lyrik Paul Celans.* Freiburg, 1986.

Poliakov, Léon, and Joseph Wulf, eds. *Das Dritte Reich und seine Denker.* Berlin, 1959.

Proust, Marcel. *Remembrance of Things Past.* Trans. C. K. Scott Moncrieff and Terence Kilmartin. London, 1976; New York, 1982.

Rathenau, Walter. *Zur Kritik der Zeit.* Berlin, 1912.
Reinhardt, Stefan, ed. *Lesebuch: Weimarer Republik.* Berlin, 1982.
Rickert, Heinrich. *Die Philosophie des Lebens.* Tübingen, 1922.
———. *Kulturwissenschaft und Naturwissenschaft.* Freiburg, 1926.
Rilke, Rainer Maria. *An Unofficial Rilke: Poems 1912–1926.* Selected and trans. Michael Hamburger. London, 1980.
Ringer, Fritz K. *The Decline of the German Mandarins: The German Academic Community, 1890–1933.* Cambridge, Mass., 1969.
Rombach, Heinrich. *Phänomenologie des gegenwärtigen Bewusstseins.* Freiburg, 1980.
Salin, Edgar. *Hölderlin im Georgekreis.* Godesberg, 1950.
Sartre, Jean-Paul. *Being and Nothingness: An Essay on Phenomenological Ontology.* Trans. Hazel E. Barnes. New York, 1956.
———. *Drei Essays.* Berlin, 1977.
———. *Existentialism and Humanism.* Trans. Philip Mairet. London, 1973.
———. *Nausea.* Trans. Robert Baldick. Harmondsworth, 1982.
———. *The Transcendence of the Ego.* Trans. Forrest Williams and Robert Kirkpatrick. New York, 1957.
Scheler, Max. *Der Genius des Krieges und der Deutsche Krieg.* Leipzig, 1915.
———. *Man's Place in Nature.* Trans. Hans Meyerhoff. New York, 1961.
———. *Vom Umsturz der Werte.* Berne, 1991.
Schmitt, Carl. *Political Romanticism.* Trans. Guy Oakes. Cambridge, Mass., 1986.
———. *Political Theology: Four Chapters on the Concept of Sovereignty.* Trans. George Schwab. Cambridge, Mass., 1985.
Schneeberger, Guido. *Nachlese zu Heidegger: Dokumente zu seinem Leben und Denken.* Berne, 1962.
Schneider, Reinhold. *Der Unzerstörbare.* Freiburg, 1945.
Schopenhauer, Arthur. *Der Briefwechsel mit Goethe.* Zurich, 1992.
Schwan, Alexander. *Politische Philosophie im Denken Heideggers.* Opladen, 1989.
Sepp, Hans Rainer, ed. *Edmund Husserl und die Phänomenologische Bewegung Zeugnisse in Text und Bild.* Freiburg, 1988.
Simmel, Georg. *The Philosophy of Money.* Ed. David Frisby. Trans. Tom Bottomore and David Frisby. 2nd enlarged ed. London, 1990.
Sloterdijk, Peter. *Critique of Cynical Reason.* Trans. Michael Eldred. London, 1988.
Sontheimer, Kurt. *Antidemokratisches Denken in der Weimarer Republik.* Munich, 1978.
Spengler, Oswald. *Der Mensch und die Technik: Beiträge zu einer Philosophie des Lebens.* Munich, 1931. English ed.: *Man and Technics.* Trans. F. Atkinson. London, 1992.
Stein, Edith. *Briefe an Roman Ingarden.* Freiburg, 1991.
Thomä, Dieter, ed. *Die Zeit des Selbst und die Zeit danach: Zur Kritik der Textgeschichte Martin Heideggers.* Frankfurt, 1990.
Tietjen, Hartmut. "Verstrickung und Widerstand." Unpublished manuscript, 1989.
Tillich, Paul. *The Socialist Decision.* Trans. Franklin Sherman. New York, 1977.
Tönnies, Ferdinand. *Community and Society.* Trans. Charles F. Loomis. New Brunswick, N.J., 1988.
Troeltsch, Ernst. *Deutscher Geist und Westeuropa.* Tübingen, 1925.
Waldenfels, Bernhard. *Phänomenologie in Frankreich.* Frankfurt, 1983.

Weber, Max. "Der Beruf zur Politik." In Weber, *Soziologie—Weltgeschichtliche Analysen—Politik.* Stuttgart, 1964.
Weizsäcker, Carl Friedrich von. *Vier Jahrzehnte.* Berlin, forthcoming.
Welte, Bernhard. "Erinnerung an ein spätes Gespräch." In G. Neske, ed. *Erinnerung an Martin Heidegger.* Pfullingen, 1977.
Wiese, Benno von. *Ich erzähle mein Leben.* Frankfurt, 1982.
Wiggershaus, Rolf. *The Frankfurt School: Its History, Theories, and Political Significance.* Trans. Michael Robertson. Cambridge, Mass., 1994.
Wolin, Richard, ed. *The Heidegger Controversy: A Critical Reader.* New York, 1991.
Wundt, Wilhelm. *Sinnliche und übersinnliche Welt.* Leipzig, 1914.
Young-Bruehl, Elisabeth. *Hannah Arendt: For Love of the World.* New Haven, Conn., 1982.
Zahrndt, Heinz. *The Question of God: Protestant Theology in the Twentieth Century.* Trans. R. A. Wilson. New York, 1969.
Zweig, Stefan. *The World of Yesterday: An Autobiography.* Trans. Cedar and Eden Paull. London, 1987.

FURTHER READING

Anders, Günther. *Ketzereien.* Munich, 1991.

———. *Kosmologische Humoresken.* Frankfurt, 1978.

Apel, Karl-Otto. *Towards a Transformation of Philosophy.* London, 1980. Trans. Glyn Adey and David Frisby.

Biemel, Walter. *Martin Heidegger: An Illustrated Study.* Trans. J. L. Mehta. New York, 1976.

Blumenberg, Hans. *Lebenszeit und Weltzeit.* Frankfurt, 1986.

Bollnow, Otto Friedrich. *Existenzphilosophie.* Stuttgart, 1955.

———. *Das Wesen der Stimmung.* Frankfurt, 1988.

Boss, Medard. *Psychoanalysis and Daseinsanalysis.* Trans. Ludwig B. Lefebre. New York, 1963.

Bourdieu, Pierre. *The Political Ontology of Martin Heidegger.* Trans. Peter Collier. Stanford, 1991.

Breuer, Stefan. *Die Gesellschaft des Verschwindens.* Von der Selbstzerstörung der technischen Zivilisation. Hamburg, 1992.

Bubner, Rüdiger, et al., eds. *Neue Hefte für Philosophie.* Wirkungen Heideggers, Issue no. 23. Göttingen, 1984.

Caputo, John D. *The Mystical Elements in Heidegger's Thought.* Athens, Ohio, 1978.

Derrida, Jacques. *Of Spirit: Heidegger and the Question.* Trans. Geoffrey Bennington and Rachel Bowlby. Chicago, 1989.

Düttmann, Alexander Garcia. *Das Gedächtnis des Denkens: Versuch über Heidegger und Adorno.* Frankfurt, 1991.
Ebeling, Hans. *Heidegger: Geschichte einer Täuschung.* Würzburg, 1990.
Elias, Norbert. *Time: An Essay.* Trans. in part by Edmund Jephcott. Oxford, 1992.
Ferry, Luc, and Alain Renaut. *French Philosophy of the Sixties: An Essay on Antihumanism.* Trans. Mary H. S. Cattani. Amherst, Mass., 1990.
Figal, Günter. *Heidegger zur Einführung.* Hamburg, 1992.
———. *Martin Heidegger: Phänomenologie der Freiheit.* Frankfurt, 1988.
Fischer, Kurt. *Abschied: Die Denkbewegung Martin Heideggers.* Würzburg, 1990.
Forum für Philosophie, Bad Homburg, ed. *Martin Heidegger: Innen- und Aussenansichten.* Frankfurt, 1989.
Frank, Manfred. *Zeitbewusstsein.* Pfullingen, 1990.
Franzen, Winfried. *Von der Existentialontologie zur Seinsgeschichte.* Meisenheim am Glan, 1975.
Gadamer, Hans-Georg. *Truth and Method.* Trans. Joel Weinsheimer and Donald G. Marshall. New York, 1993.
Gebser, Jean. *The Ever-Present Origin.* Trans. Noel Barstad and Algis Mickunas. Athens, Ohio, 1984.
Grof, Stanislav. *Beyond the Brain: Birth, Death, and Transcendence in Psychotherapy.* Albany, N.Y., 1985.
Gudopp, Wolf-Dieter. *Der junge Heidegger.* Frankfurt, 1983.
Haag, Karl Heinz. *Der Fortschritt in der Philosophie.* Frankfurt, 1985.
Habermas, Jürgen. *The Philosophical Discourse of Modernity: Twelve Lectures.* Trans. Frederick G. Lawrence. Cambridge, Mass., 1987.
———. *Postmetaphysical Thinking: Philosophical Essays.* Trans. William Mark Hohengarten. Cambridge, Mass., 1992.
Heinrich, Klaus. *Versuch über die Schwierigkeit nein zu sagen.* Frankfurt, 1964.
Hempel, Hans-Peter. *Heideggers Weg aus der Gefahr.* Messkirch, 1993.
———. *Heidegger und Zen.* Frankfurt, 1987.
———. *Natur und Geschichte: Der Jahrhundertdialog zwischen Heidegger und Heisenberg.* Frankfurt, 1990.
Hösle, Vittorio. *Die Krise der Gegenwart und die Verantwortung der Philosophie.* Munich, 1990.
Hühnerfeld, Paul. *In Sachen Heidegger.* Hamburg, 1959.
Jamme, Christoph, and Karsten Harries, eds. *Martin Heidegger: Politics, Art, and Technology.* New York, 1994.
Jonas, Hans. *The Gnostic Religion: The Message of the Alien God and the Beginnings of Christianity.* London, 1992.
Jung, Matthias. *Das Denken des Seins und der Glaube an Gott.* Würzburg, 1990.
Kemper, Peter, ed. *Martin Heidegger—Faszination und Erschrecken: Die politische Dimension einer Philosophie.* Frankfurt, 1990.
Kettering, Emil. *Das Denken Martin Heideggers.* Pfullingen, 1987.
Kolakowski, Leszek. *Modernity on Endless Trial.* Chicago, 1990.
Koslowski, Peter. *Der Mythos der Moderne.* Munich, 1991.
Kuschbert-Tölle, Helga. *Martin Heidegger: Der letzte Metaphysiker?* Königstein/Ts., 1979.

Lacoue-Labarthe, Philippe. *Heidegger, Art, and Politics: The Fiction of the Political.* Trans. Chris Turner. Oxford, 1990.

Leidlmair, Karl. *Künstliche Intelligenz und Heidegger: Über den Zwiespalt von Natur und Geist.* Munich, 1991.

Lessing, Theodor. *Geschichte als Sinngebung des Sinnlosen.* Munich, 1983.

Löwith, Karl. *Heidegger—Denker in dürftiger Zeit.* Stuttgart, 1984.

Lyotard, Jean-François. *Heidegger and "the Jews."* Trans. Andreas Michel and Mark S. Roberts. Minneapolis, 1990.

Macho, Thomas H. *Todesmetaphern.* Frankfurt, 1987.

Marcuse, Herbert. *Kultur und Gesellschaft.* Frankfurt, 1967.

———. *One-Dimensional Man: Studies in the Ideology of Advanced Industrial Society.* London, 1991.

Margreiter, Reinhar, and Karl Leidlmair, eds. *Heidegger: Technik—Ethik—Politik.* Würzburg, 1991.

Marten, Rainer. *Denkkunst, Kritik der Ontologie.* Munich, 1989.

———. *Heideggers Lesen.* Munich, 1991.

Marx, Werner. *Heidegger and the Tradition.* Trans. Theodore Kisiel and Murray Greene. Evanston, Ill., 1971.

———. *Is There a Measure on Earth? Foundations for a Nonmetaphysical Ethics.* Trans. Thomas J. Nenon and Reginald Lilly. Chicago, 1987.

Merker, Barbara. *Selbsttäuschung und Selbsterkenntnis: Zu Heideggers Transformation der Phänomenologie Husserls.* Frankfurt, 1988.

Mörchen, Hermann. *Adorno und Heidegger: Untersuchung einer philosophischen Kommunikationsverweigerung.* Stuttgart, 1981.

———. *Macht und Herrschaft im Denken von Heidegger und Adorno.* Stuttgart, 1980.

Nolte, Ernst. *Heideggers Politik und Geschichte im Leben und Denken.* Berlin, 1992.

Padrutt, Hanspeter. *Und sie bewegt sich doch nicht: Parmenides im epochalen Winter.* Zurich, 1991.

Picht, Georg. *Glauben und Wissen.* Stuttgart, 1988.

Pöggeler, Otto. *The Paths of Heidegger's Life and Thought.* Trans. John Bailiff. Atlantic Highlands, N.J., 1996.

———. *Philosophie und Politik bei Heidegger.* Freiburg, 1972.

Rentsch, Thomas. *Martin Heidegger: Das Sein und der Tod.* Munich, 1989.

Riedel, Manfred. *Für eine zweite Philosophie.* Frankfurt, 1988.

Ritter, Joachim. *Metaphysik und Politik.* Frankfurt, 1969.

Rorty, Richard. *Contingency, Irony and Solidarity.* Cambridge, 1989.

Safranski, Rüdiger. *Wieviel Wahrheit braucht der Mensch? Über das Denkbare und das Lebbare.* Munich, 1990.

Schaeffler, Richard. *Die Wechselbeziehung zwischen Philosophie und katholischer Theologie.* Darmstadt, 1980.

Schirmacher, Wolfgang. *Technik und Gelassenheit: Zeitkritik nach Heidegger.* Freiburg, 1983.

Schulz, Walter. *Philosophie in der veränderten Welt.* Pfullingen, 1984.

Seubold, Günter. *Heideggers Analyse der neuzeitlichen Technik.* Freiburg, 1986.

Sloterdijk, Peter. *Weltfremdheit.* Frankfurt, 1993.

Sommer, Manfred. *Lebenswelt und Zeitbewusstsein.* Frankfurt, 1990.

Stachowiak, Herbert, ed. *Pragmatik: Handbuch des Pragmatischen Denkens.* Hamburg, 1986.

Steiner, George. *Martin Heidegger.* Chicago, 1991.

Sternberger, Dolf. *Über den Tod.* Frankfurt, 1981.

Theunissen, Michael. *Negative Theologie der Zeit.* Frankfurt, 1991.

———. *The Other.* Trans. Christopher Macann. Cambridge, Mass., 1986.

Tugendhat, Ernst. *Philosophische Aufsätze.* Frankfurt, 1992.

Vietta, Silvio. *Heideggers Kritik am Nationalsozialismus und an der Technik.* Tübingen, 1989.

Weinmayr, Elmar. *Einstellung: Die Metaphysik im Denken Martin Heideggers.* Munich, 1991.

Wetz, Franz Josef. *Das nackte Dass: Zur Frage der Faktizität.* Pfullingen, 1990.

Wisser, Richard, ed. *Martin Heidegger—Unterwegs im Denken.* Freiburg, 1987.

INDEX